Ideals and Ideologies

Ideals and Ideologies

A READER

SIXTH EDITION

TERENCE BALL

RICHARD DAGGER

Arizona State University

New York San Francisco Boston
London Toronto Sydney Tokyo Singapore Madrid
Mexico City Munich Paris Cape Town Hong Kong Montreal

Executive Editor: Eric Stano
Senior Marketing Manager: Elizabeth Fogarty
Supplements Editor: Kristi Olsen
Production Manager: Denise Phillip
Project Coordination, Text Design, and Electronic Page Makeup: Electronic Publishing Services Inc., NYC
Cover Design Manager: Wendy Ann Fredericks
Cover Designer: Kay Petronio
Manufacturing Buyer: Lucy Hebard
Printer and Binder: R.R. Donnelley & Sons
Cover Printer: Phoenix Color Corporation
Cover Art: clockwise from top left: Joseph Sohm/Corbis; DC Productions/Photodisc Green/Getty Images, Inc.; Roger Ressmeyer/Corbis; Peter Macdiarmid/Getty Images, Inc.; and Wathiq Khuzaie/Gamma/Getty Images, Inc.

For permission to use copyrighted material, grateful acknowledgment is made to the copyright holders throughout the text and is hereby made part of this copyright page.

Library of Congress Cataloging-in-Publication Data

Ideals and ideologies : a reader / [edited by] Terence Ball, Richard Dagger.
— 6th ed.
p. cm.
ISBN 0-321-39653-7
1. Political science—History. 2. Ideology. 3. Right and left (Political science) I. Ball, Terence. II. Dagger, Richard.
JA81.I34 2005
320.5—dc22

2005033053

Copyright © 2006 by Pearson Education, Inc.

All rights reserved. No part of this publication may be reproduced, stored in a retrieval system, or transmitted, in any form or by any means, electronic, mechanical, photocopying, recording, or otherwise, without the prior written permission of the publisher. Printed in the United States.

Please visit us at www.ablongman.com

ISBN 0-321-39653-7

1 2 3 4 5 6 7 8 9 10—DOH—08 07 06 05

Contents

Preface to the Sixth Edition

It has been more than fifteen years since we first decided to collect readings from primary sources into an anthology for courses in political ideologies and modern political thought. We knew that our choices—what to put in, what to leave out—would not please everyone. Nevertheless, we believed that we could compile a set of readings that would be comprehensive and rigorous enough to meet instructors' standards while satisfying students' desires for a readable and reasonably accessible "reader." The fact that we are now issuing a sixth edition of this book suggests that our belief was not ill founded.

As in the previous editions, we have been guided by our sense that an ideal anthology for this subject would combine four features. First, it would present a wide range of alternative ideological visions, right, left, middle, and unorthodox. Second, it would include a generous sampling of key thinkers in the different ideological traditions, old and new alike. Third, an ideal anthology would, when necessary, modernize the prose of thinkers long dead. Fourth, and finally, it would supply the student with some sense of the intellectual and political context within which these thinkers thought and wrote.

In this sixth edition of *Ideals and Ideologies* we have tried once again to satisfy these four criteria. First, we have attempted to cover the broad canvas of contemporary political ideologies, from the standard categories of liberalism-conservatism-socialism to a broader range of newly emerging ideological alternatives. Among these are the "liberation" ideologies, including indigenous or native people's liberation, an ecological or "green" ideology, and the ideology of radical Islam. This last topic receives expanded coverage in this edition, as does globalization. Second, we have tried to supply a fairly generous and reasonably representative sample of alternative ideological views, including those not represented in any other anthology. Third, we have, wherever possible, simplified the prose of older thinkers—in several instances providing our own translations of works not written in English. And finally, we have provided brief introductions and added explanatory notes to place these selections and their authors in their political and historical contexts.

We have, in short, tried to supply the student with an accessible and readable book of original sources. Even so, the end result does not necessarily make for easy reading. But then, as we remind our students, the adage "No pain, no gain" applies to the building not only of muscles, but of minds as well. We have merely attempted to remove some of the unnecessary strain from a profitable, if sometimes taxing, exercise.

The present volume is paired with the new sixth edition of our *Political Ideologies and the Democratic Ideal,* also published by Longman. Although each book stands alone, each complements and can be used in combination with the other.

In preparing this new edition, we had the benefit of detailed and thoughtful reviews from the following scholars, whom we wish to thank here: William Buschert, University of Saskatchewan; Allen Meyer, Mesa Community College; and Marvin S. Soroos, North Carolina State University. We are also grateful to Professor Stephen Chilton of the University of Minnesota–Duluth and his students for their helpful comments on the previous edition. And special thanks are due to our "junior fellows," Macy Hanson and Michael Harrell, for their able and enthusiastic assistance.

We should note, finally, that many of the readings included here easily fall under more than one heading. There are many combinations, and many ways to use this book. But whatever the preferred combination may be, the aim is always the same: to convey to the student-citizen a vivid sense of the centrality and ongoing importance of ideas, ideals, and ideologies in modern politics.

Terence Ball

Richard Dagger

About the Editors

TERENCE BALL received his Ph.D. from the University of California at Berkeley and teaches political theory at Arizona State University. He taught previously at the University of Minnesota and has held visiting professorships at Oxford University, Cambridge University, and the University of California, San Diego. His books include *Reappraising Political Theory* (Oxford University Press, 1995) and a mystery novel, *Rousseau's Ghost* (SUNY Press, 1998). He has also edited *The Federalist* (Cambridge University Press, 2003) and co-edited *The Cambridge History of Twentieth-Century Political Thought* (Cambridge University Press, 2003).

RICHARD DAGGER earned his Ph.D. from the University of Minnesota and is now a professor of political science and philosophy at Arizona State University, where he directs the Philosophy, Politics, and Law Program of the Barrett Honors College. He has been a faculty fellow of the Center for Ethics and Public Affairs, Tulane University, and is the author of many publications in political and legal philosophy, including *Civic Virtues: Rights, Citizenship, and Republican Liberalism* (Oxford University Press, 1997).

Introduction

As the terrorist attacks of September 11, 2001, and the subsequent "war on terror" attest, the world in which we live continues to be shaped and scarred by political ideologies. Indeed, the truth of the old saying "ideas have consequences" must now be evident to everyone. For better or for worse, the twenty-first century, like the one that preceded it, is a century of ideas—and particularly of those clusters or systems of ideas called "ideologies." These ideologies have raised hopes, inspired fear, and drawn blood from millions of human beings. To study political ideologies, then, is not to undertake a merely academic study. It is to dissect and analyze the tissue of our times.

At this early point in the twenty-first century, some ideologies, such as the Marxist-Leninist version of socialism, are clearly in eclipse, while others—such as radical Islam and a newly emerging ecological or "green" ideology—appear to be gaining in influence and importance. Yet, despite their differences, these ideologies are similar in at least one respect: they all have their histories. All, that is, have emerged out of particular historical contexts and have changed in response to changing conditions and circumstances. And all have been formed from the ideas of thinkers old and new. As the economist John Maynard Keynes observed in the 1930s, when Benito Mussolini, Adolf Hitler, and Joseph Stalin all held power, "madmen in authority, who hear voices in the air, are distilling their frenzy from some academic scribbler of a few years back."

This book is about, and by, those "academic scribblers"—and a number of those "madmen in authority" as well. Their ideas have formed the ideologies and fueled the conflicts that shaped and reshaped the political landscape of the twentieth century—and now the twenty-first. We live in the shadow, and under the influence, of these scribblers and madmen. To be ignorant of their influence is not to escape it. By tracing modern ideologies back to their original sources, we can see more clearly how our own outlooks—and those of our enemies—have been shaped by earlier thinkers. To return to and read these authors is to gain some insight into the shaping of the modern political mind—or rather minds, plural, since ideological disagreement continues unabated.

Some modern commentators have claimed—wrongly, we believe—that ideological disagreements are at last coming to an end. The age of ideology, they say, is over. As evidence, they cite the end of the Cold War, the emancipation of Eastern Europe, the collapse of the Soviet Union, and the democratizing of former dictatorships. Important as they are, however, these events do not presage "the end of ideology." Rather, they suggest that ours is an age of important ideological realignments. Marxism-Leninism may be dead in Eastern Europe and the former Soviet Union, but other versions of it linger on in the politics of China, Vietnam, North Korea, and Cuba. Radical Islam is increasingly influential in the Middle East, Southeast Asia, and elsewhere. And, of course, ideological conflict persists as conservatives, liberals, and socialists continue to disagree with one another, animal liberationists fight for animal rights, gays for gay rights, and Greens campaign to protect the environment. Other movements, motivated by other ideologies, are no less active.

Like it or not, in short, ours is likely to remain an age of ideological diversity and disagreement. Anyone who hopes to understand this diversity and disagreement will benefit, we believe, from a careful reading of the selections that follow, which provide a generous sampling of some of the writings that have helped to form the ideologically varied political terrain of the small planet on which we dwell together, if not always in peace or harmony.

T. B.

R. D.

PART ONE

The Concept of Ideology

That ideologies and ideological conflict have persisted throughout modern history should come as no surprise. Ideologies are born of crisis and feed on conflict. People need help to comprehend and cope with turbulent times and confusing circumstances, and ideologies provide this help. An ideology does this by performing four important and perhaps indispensable functions for those who subscribe to it. First, it *explains* political phenomena that would otherwise remain mysterious or puzzling. Why are there wars and rumors of war? Why are there conflicts between nations, between classes, and between races? What causes depressions? The answer that one gives to these, and to many other, questions depends to some degree on one's ideology. A Marxian socialist will answer one way, a fascist another, and a feminist yet another.

Second, an ideology provides its adherents with criteria and standards of *evaluation*—of deciding what is right and wrong, good and bad. Are class differences and vast disparities of wealth good or bad things? Is interracial harmony possible, and, if so, is it desirable? Is censorship permissible, and, if so, under what conditions? Again, the answers one gives will depend on which ideology one accepts.

Third, an ideology *orients* its adherents, giving them a sense of who they are and where they belong—a social and cultural compass with which to define and affirm their individual and collective identity. Fascists, for example, will typically think of themselves as members of a superior nation or race. Communists will see themselves as people who defend the working class against capitalist oppression and exploitation. Animal liberationists will identify themselves as defenders of animals that are unable to protect themselves against human abuse and exploitation.

Fourth and finally, an ideology supplies its adherents with a rudimentary political *program*. This program provides an answer to the question posed by the Russian revolutionary Lenin, among many others: What is to be done? And, no less important: Who is to do it? With what means? A Marxist-Leninist, for instance, will answer these questions as follows: The working class must be emancipated from capitalist exploitation by means of a revolution led by a vanguard party. Fascists, feminists, Greens, liberals, conservatives, and others will, of course, propose other programs of political action.

To summarize, a political ideology is a more or less systematic set of ideas that performs four functions for those who hold it: the explanatory, the evaluative, the orientative, and the programmatic functions. By performing these functions, an ideology serves as a guide and compass through the thicket of political life.

There are, as we shall see, many different political ideologies in the modern world. But what of democracy? Is it an ideology? In our view democracy is not an ideology but an *ideal* that different ideologies interpret in different ways. For the ancient Greeks, who coined the word, democracy meant rule by, and in the interest of, the common people. In the modern world, some Marxists have insisted that a "people's democracy" in which the leaders of a revolutionary party rule in the name of the masses is the best way to serve the interests of the common people. For liberals, however, democracy means "liberal democracy"—that is, majority rule, but with ample provision for the protection of minority rights. For modern Greens, democracy means decentralized "participatory" or "grassroots" democracy. Other ideologies interpret the democratic ideal in other ways. Democracy, then, is an ideal that most ideologies claim to strive for, but it is an ideal whose meaning they vigorously contest.

As with "democracy," so too with "freedom." What "freedom" means for liberals is something quite different from what it means for fascists, for example. We can see this more clearly by thinking of freedom (or liberty) as a triadic or three-sided relation among an *agent,* a *goal,* and any *obstacle* standing between the agent and the goal that he, she, or they seek to achieve. We represent this relationship in the diagram below.

Every ideology identifies the three elements of the triad in its own way. A liberal will typically identify the agent as an individual, the goal as the satisfaction of an individual's own desires, and the obstacle as any unreasonable restraint or restriction on such "want satisfaction." A Marxist, by contrast, will characteristically identify the agent as an entire class—the working class or "proletariat"—that struggles to overcome capitalist exploitation in order to achieve a classless communist society. A fascist will conceive of the agent as a whole nation or race attempting to overcome so-called inferior nations or races in a collective search for racial or national supremacy and purity. And other ideologies conceive of freedom in still other ways. Understanding how they conceive of freedom is, in fact, one of the best ways to understand the differences that separate any political ideology from its ideological rivals.

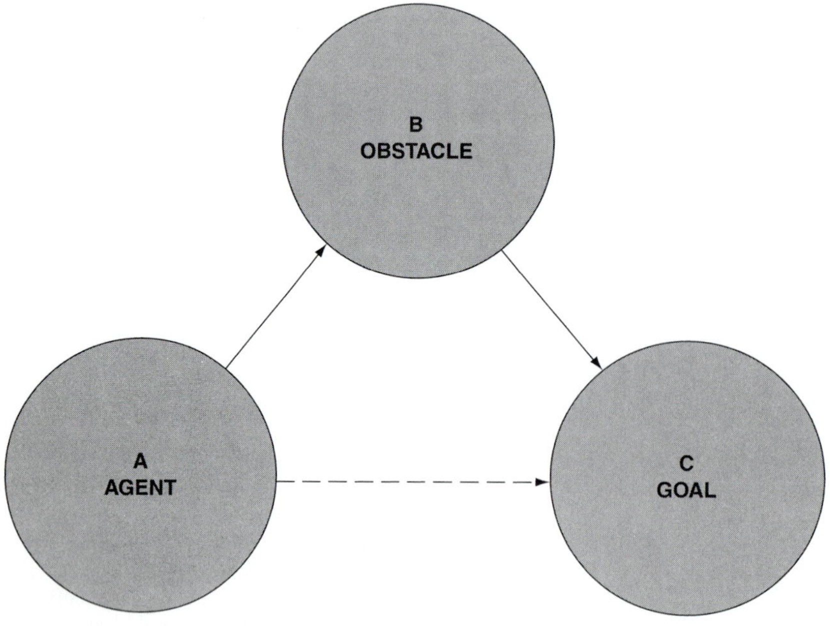

Triadic Model of Freedom

1

Ideology: The Career of a Concept

TERRELL CARVER

The concept of ideology has undergone dramatic changes in meaning since the term *ideologie* was first coined in eighteenth-century France. In the following essay, the Anglo-American political theorist Terrell Carver (1946–) traces these changes, concluding with a critical consideration of the ways in which the term "ideology" is used today.

Source: This essay was written expressly for *Ideals and Ideologies.*

As a coined word, the term "ideology" has a precise origin in the era of the French Revolution. The decisive shifts in its meaning, moreover, have been associated with some of the most colorful and influential figures in modern history—Napoleon Bonaparte (1769–1821), Karl Marx (1818–1883), Friedrich Engels (1820–1895), and V. I. Lenin (1870–1924). From its very inception, in fact, ideology has been associated with highly abstract philosophy and forceful, even brutal, political repression.

Behind the term "ideology" are the familiar features of politics—ideas and power. Philosophers have not been conspicuous for their participation in politics, but through the actions of others they have been influential at times. Improving the connection between philosopher and politician to extend this influence was one of the main concerns of Antoine Louis Claude Destutt, Comte de Tracy (1754– 1836), one of the Enlightenment *philosophes.* De Tracy coined the term "ideology" during the wild revolutionary decade in France when ideas inspired many thousands to test their powers in politics and to put their immediate material interests, even lives, at risk. Although the substance of de Tracy's thought drew on the specific philosophies of Étienne Bonnot de Condillac (1715–1780) and John Locke (1632–1704), among others, his work was explicitly directed toward political action. He assumed that criteria for the truth and falsity of ideas could be established and definitively employed, and that there was a point to doing so. That point was overtly political.

De Tracy and his colleagues aimed to promote progress in all areas of human endeavor, theoretical and practical, by reforming elite and middle-class opinion. Their Institut de France was established by the Convention in 1795 to disseminate higher learning as the *savants* of the revolution defined it. Their work began with three assumptions: that progress in social life is desirable; that progress comes only from correct ideas; and that incorrect ideas must be resisted, especially in the schools. In opposition to the traditions of the Catholic Church and to the personal authority of anointed monarchs, de Tracy and his colleagues in the Institut favored the ideals of the new science associated with Francis Bacon (1561–1626), Galileo Galilei (1564–1642), Réné Descartes (1596–1650), and other thinkers who espoused rational inquiry into the natural and social world. The rationalism of the Institut was especially hostile to religious thought if conceived mystically.

In 1796 a British commentator reported that de Tracy had read a paper at the Institut in which he proposed to call the philosophy of mind "ideology." Five years later, in his *Elements of Ideology* (1801; translated into English by Thomas Jefferson for an edition of 1817), de Tracy summarized the results of his logic within a "plan of the elements of ideology…to give a complete knowledge of our intellectual faculties, and to deduce from that knowledge the first principles of all other branches of our knowledge." Without these first principles "our knowledge" could "never be founded on any other solid base."[1] With correct ideas would come a correct psychology or theory of human behavior, and with that the justification for such political prescriptions as intellectuals might devise and enlightened politicians might enforce.

De Tracy's system, while sweeping, was disarmingly simplistic, dismissive of skepticism, and surprisingly concise. Even at the time it must have raised some strong doubts among philosophers. Indeed, the association of ideology with intellectual shortcuts, oversimplification, and distortion seems inherent in de Tracy's original conception. That de Tracy also associated his ideology with a political program and authoritarian politics provides further clues to the way the concept has functioned since his day.

There are three important features of de Tracy's conception of ideology: (1) the explicit linkage between logic, psychology, and politics, set down in a "table" of simple propositions and backed up with more extensive observations; (2) the assumption that intellectuals discover the truth and that well-advised political authorities implement policies to match; and (3) the claim that logic, psychology, and politics, as linked, are coincident with science and history, properly understood.

In 1797 Napoleon Bonaparte, the leading general of the revolutionary army, became an honorary member of the Institut, and his fellow "ideologues" supported the *coup d'état* by which he seized power in 1799. With their boundless faith in reason, the "ideologues," de Tracy amongst them, expected to achieve the same success in psychology, morality, social and economic relations, and politics that the new "natural philosophers" had achieved in studying planetary and terrestrial motion, optics, and mathematics. Such was their certainty that they committed themselves to an administrative structure to promote their ideas and to discourage what they termed prejudices—and with that they necessarily engaged in politics. As their concept of truth presupposed the authority of the intellectual (validated by the "correct" assumptions and methods), so their politics created no great obstacles to authoritarian rule—provided, of course, that the authority had proper intellectual guidance. There was little in the doctrines of the "ideologues" to favor the unenlightened intellect or to afford it any great role in decisionmaking. Because politics was supposed to be subject to the new science, democracy with its popular decisionmaking would have little to recommend itself to the Enlightenment intellectual unless it were properly guided. Tutoring rulers was obviously the easier and more immediately efficacious task. With Napoleon a member of the Institut, furthermore, the "ideologues" could expect enlightenment and progress to spread all the more quickly throughout France and beyond its borders. The forces of reaction were to be swept away by the enlightened use of political power as the resources of the state were made available to the intellectual elite.

The crucial event in the development of the concept of ideology came when Napoleon turned against the "ideologues" and decisively reversed their interpretation of the proper relationship between intellectuals and rulers, philosophers and politicians. Around 1812 he dismissed de Tracy's work and the work of the Institut de France as "ideology, that sinister metaphysics." This hostility to the "ideologues" apparently reflected a shift in Napoleon's political tactics—from alliance with the rationalists of the Institut against religion and the Church, to the reverse. Eradicating what the "ideologues" saw as prejudice was politically costly, and Napoleon sought to increase his personal power by making peace with the Church and allying himself with other conservative forces.[2]

About thirty years later the German Communist Karl Marx seized on "ideology" as a term of abuse. He criticized German intellectuals whose philosophy and politics displeased him by dismissing them as "ideologists," proponents of "the German ideology." He and Friedrich Engels coauthored a manuscript of that name which remained unpublished as a whole until 1932, though sections of the large work appeared in excerpts from 1903 onward.[3] In other published works that circulated during his lifetime and in his private correspondence, Marx used the term "ideology" in ways that drew on the more extensive airing he had given the concept in *The German Ideology*.

Ideologies and ideologists arise in class-divided societies, according to Marx. In particular, "the class which has the means of material production at its disposal consequently also controls the means of mental production." Thinkers are "producers of ideas," in other words, while ruling classes regulate "the production and distribution of the ideas of their age." Thus "the ideas of the ruling class are in every epoch the ruling ideas: i.e., the class which is the ruling *material* force of society is at the same time its ruling *intellectual* force." Within the ruling class the division of labor divides mental from material tasks, so that:

> Inside this class one part appears as the thinkers of the class (its active, conceptualizing ideologists, who make the formation of the illusions of the class about itself their chief source of livelihood), while the other's attitude to these ideas and illusions is more passive and receptive, because they are in reality the active members of this class and have less time to make up illusions and ideas about themselves.[4]

The German ideology was to be explained, Marx argued, "from its connection with the illusion of ideologists in general, e.g., the illusions of the jurists, politicians (including practical statesmen), from the dogmatic dreamings and distortions of these fellows." All those illusions and distortions were "explained perfectly easily from their practical position in life, their job, and the division of labour."[5] In this realm of jobs and economic activity Marx introduced a notion of material interest which made illusions demonstrably functional for some individuals and classes in societies as they pursued economic advantages for themselves at others' expense. Some of these useful illusions were dressed up as claims about nature or God—for example, "some people are slaves by nature," "God made woman to serve man"—and some were more elaborately cloaked in a universalism that Marx dismissed as spurious. He argued, for example, that the "rights of man and the citizen" proclaimed in the French Revolution ultimately worked for the benefit of owners of private property at the expense of workers, who had no property to sell but their own labor. Thus in Marx's analysis an ideology came to mean not just a body of ideas that conformed to certain formal characteristics, such as those of de Tracy's system, but any ideas, however unsophisticated, that gave apparent validity and assumed authority to the claims that members of different classes might make when they pursued their various interests. Those who characteristically made such claims were deemed "ideologists"; others merely repeated in their speech or reflected in their behavior an "ideology."

In Marx's view ideologies could be reactionary, conservative, reformist, or revolutionary, depending on the way that material interests (typically the use and control of resources, goods, and services) were pursued by individuals and then protected socially and politically. In keeping with his depiction of history as the history of class struggles—now hidden, now open—Marx defined ideologies as the "legal, political, religious, aesthetic or philosophic—in short, ideological—forms" in which people become conscious of class conflict "and fight it out."[6] In that way, "the existence of revolutionary ideas in a particular period," he wrote, "presupposes the existence of a revolutionary class."[7]

Marx thus extended de Tracy's term "ideology" to cover ideas that reflected, and were somehow useful in pursuing, the material interests of classes. But his own work was supposed to identify, explain, and promote working-class interests in current political struggles. It might seem, therefore, to be ideological itself. Marx did not refer to his work in those terms, however, or to the pursuit of working-class politics as requiring an ideology. He identified the working class as a revolutionary class, but one distinguished from previous revolutionary classes in that it was becoming a majority and already expressed "the dissolution of all classes, nationalities etc., within present society."[8] A revolutionary class was to overthrow a ruling class, as had already happened many times, but with the *proletarian* revolution would come the abolition of class society altogether. This could happen, Marx said, because the interest of the proletariat coincides with the interests of all individuals "as individuals."[9]

Marx's arguments for the proletariat's abolition of class-divided society are sketchy and unconvincing, but they are quite distinct from the views he described as ideological. His communism, and the theory behind it, were not ideologies on his definition, because the formal properties and political reference were profoundly different. Instead, Marx considered his work to be scientific, taking due regard for the historical character of the social phenomena under investigation. It was also supposed to have political significance in the struggle for socialism. But it was not formally identical to the pattern for an "ideology" established by de Tracy because there was no Marxian logic and psychology from which his politics were deduced. Rather he worked from a less comprehensive conception, that of economic activity ("so-called material interests"), towards prescriptions that could be useful, so he argued, in proletarian politics.[10] The role of the theoretically informed individual or group was said, in the *Communist Manifesto* and elsewhere, to be advisory, not authoritative. Marx contemptuously dismissed sects and other ways in which ideals were supposed to be imposed on people so that reality could be created, in a sense, by ideas. Communism, he claimed, was a "real movement" already in existence, to which his science was intended to contribute.[11]

Friedrich Engels was the architect of a Marxism that fitted the formal requirements of an ideology, though he himself dismissed ideology all too simplistically as mere "false consciousness," a phrase not used by Marx.[12] While he did not term Marx's work an ideology, but a science—namely, "scientific socialism"—Engels elaborated a view that Marx's science had specified fundamental laws of dialectics in the realm of "thought" (presumably a proto-psychology), in the development of human behavior in history, and in the matter-in-motion of the universe itself. Engels's widely circulated *Anti-Dühring* (1878) advertised those pretensions, producing extended discussions of historical and contemporary economic development that were supposed to substantiate his claims for a materialistic dialectic in logic. These were repeated in his later *Ludwig Feuerbach and the End of Classical German Philosophy* (1888) and the posthumously published *Dialectics of Nature* (1925), edited from notebooks largely contemporary with *Anti-Dühring*.

Whether Marx shared Engels's views is a matter of controversy.[13] There is no explicit endorsement of them in his works. Indeed, as I am arguing here, the way that Marx identified such logico-deductive constructions as "ideological" suggests that he could not have agreed with Engels's views without major inconsistency.

Thus Marx's followers did their best to make his ideas fit the formal and political definitions of ideology that Marx himself had applied to other systems of ideas. In doing so his followers seemed to undermine the pejorative connotations of the term. This introduced an obvious contradiction between Marx's own consistently pejorative usage with respect to German ideologists and other apologists for the ruling classes, on the one hand, and his followers' use of the term in an approving sense, on the other, to identify his work as a comprehensive system that promoted the interests of one particular class in society—the working class. This working-class or proletarian "ideology" was a science, Marx's followers said, precisely because it was a body of thought reflecting proletarian interests. As a result we have Marxism identified by Soviet philosophers and many others as a "scientific ideology"—a contradiction in terms from Marx's own point of view.

The Russian revolutionary Lenin (pseudonym for Vladimir Ilyich Ulyanov) followed Engels in identifying Marxism as a comprehensive science derived from an abstract logic, thus accepting it formally as an ideology. While this identification was merely tacit in Engels's case, Lenin made it specific and went one stage further in his highly influential *What Is to Be Done?* (1902). Citing Engels on the necessity for political, economic, and theoretical struggle in pursuing working-class interests, Lenin concluded very generally and with particular reference to Russia that "without revolutionary theory there can be no revolutionary practice." "Modern socialist consciousness," he wrote, "can only arise on the basis of profound scientific knowledge."[14]

Lenin identified this science as "socialist ideology" and claimed that the only political choice available in his time was between the bourgeois ideology and the socialist one. He thus defined ideologies as doctrines reflecting class interests that were in some sense products of theoretical thinking, not the common-place consciousness of class members themselves. For the working class this was crucial in Lenin's eyes, because he viewed them as likely victims of bourgeois ideology (or unwitting servants of it via "trade union consciousness"), unless socialist intellectuals and party workers, using the "socialist ideology," awakened the workers to the "irreconcilable antagonism of their interests to the whole of the modern political and social system."[15] On this view it was a matter of fact that science served proletarian interests because it revealed the true character of class antagonism in capitalist society, the very truth that bourgeois ideology had veiled in illusions, such as "self-help," "parliamentary democracy," "market forces," etc.

Presumably Lenin's use of "ideology" to include science, as well as the interest-serving mystifications Marx had loosely identified as ideologies, was a kind of shorthand. Lenin conceived of a "scientific ideology" opposed to unscientific ones, all serving different class interests. In that political sense—ideology as ideas serving class interests—Lenin made Marxism ideological. By the early twentieth century, then, ideology had wandered in meaning from a science of ideas, to a sinister metaphysics, to class-serving illusions, to false consciousness as opposed to scientific socialism, to scientific socialism as one ideology competing with others.

The "science" within the socialism of Engels and Lenin was very vulnerable to criticism, as the first principles of their dialectical materialism were incomplete and unconvincing. But the insight, derived ultimately from Marx, that ideas serve the interests of individuals, groups, and classes, and that individuals, groups, and classes often generate and defend the ideas that do this, has made a systematic sociology of consciousness possible. This project was set out by the German sociologist Karl Mannheim (1893–1947), who explained that the principal thesis of his "sociology of knowledge" is that there are modes of thought which cannot be adequately understood as long as their social origins are obscured. In his view the study of these "ideologies" involves unmasking the more or less conscious deceptions and disguises of interest groups, particularly those of political parties.[16] For Mannheim "ideology" was a name for two related conceptions which he distinguished as "particular" and "total":

> The particular conception of ideology is implied when the term denotes that we are skeptical of the ideas and representations advanced by our opponent. They are regarded as more or less conscious disguises of the real nature of a situation, the true recognition of which would not be in accord with his interests.

"This conception of ideology," wrote Mannheim, "has only gradually become differentiated from the commonsense notion of the lie." It was "particular" by comparison with the more inclusive "total" conception of ideology: "Here we refer to the ideology of an age or of a concrete historico-social group, e.g., of a class, when we are concerned with the characteristics and composition of the total structure of the mind of this epoch or of this group."[17]

Mannheim argued that this total conception of ideology raised the problem of "false consciousness" as "the totally distorted mind which falsified everything." The possibility that our whole conception of reality might be systematically distorted and continuously distorting had "a special significance and relevance for the understanding of our social life." From the awareness of this possibility arose a "profound disquietude" which Mannheim felt very deeply.[18]

De Tracy confidently described his ideology, a general grammar and logic, as a science, about whose methods, truth, and timelessness he had no doubts. Since the time of the *philosophes* confidence has given way to skepticism, and the term ideology has reflected this exactly. When there was certainty about truth and science, a new word, "ideology," was coined. This fell victim to a vengeful politics when Napoleon dismissed it as "sinister metaphysics," and the term came to stand for illusion as opposed to science. Because of Marx's attacks on the elitism of the philosopher-politicians and his pithy theorizing on the origins of ideas in class-divided societies, the concept has almost become synonymous with ax-grinding. Engels's "scientific socialism" and Lenin's "proletarian ideology" reincarnate de Tracy's confidence, but to less than universal satisfaction, as modern skepticism about truth admits no conclusive grounds for the judgments that those doctrines claim to justify. Ideology has thus been moved from denoting the elements of a comprehensive, programmatic politics to functioning as an element in a supremely doubtful academic taxonomy. It is confused to the point of babel, as it variously signifies unambiguous truth, myth or illusion, false consciousness, scientific socialism, and ideas that distort and conceal a dynamically changing social reality.

This has not stopped contemporary writers from trying to extract order from chaos. Recently Malcolm B. Hamilton has formulated no fewer than 27 "definitional elements" of the concept from no less than 85 sources. His own selective synthesis is as follows: "An ideology is a system of collectively held normative and reputedly factual ideas and beliefs and attitudes advocating a particular pattern of social relationships and arrangements, and/or aimed at justifying a particular pattern of conduct, which its proponents seek to promote, realize, pursue or maintain."[19]

Hamilton recommends this definition for purposes of "empirical application and research," and so excludes some of the "definitional elements" that have historically been important to participants in and theorists of political action.

Hence the association of ideology with class interest that has been so important to Marxist politics is rejected, as is the whole question of the relationship between ideology and science. Indeed, a number of other issues that have been famously explored in discussions about what ideology is and what are examples of it are rather flippantly discarded, as if specialists in epistemology or philosophy of science were the only ones competent to "settle" such questions. These include the way that ideas are determined in society, the distinction between descriptive and explanatory claims, the relationship between political advocacy and social science, and the way in which ideas are or are not "functional." In justifying his exclusions Hamilton appeals to a realm of "reason, logic or...evidence" that he believes is independent of the interests of the human beings who use such concepts.[20] One can argue, however, that this claim is not only impossible to sustain, but that it lays the author open to the very kind of scrutiny in which the term ideology has figured. What exactly are the interests of social scientists? Are these not reflected in their concept of an "empirical fact"? Can they escape their own social and political context so easily by modeling themselves on what they take to be the natural sciences? Can they appeal so conveniently to what philosophers term reason and logic?

Ideology, in sum, is not a concept that denotes some particular phenomenon in the world. It is not a template against which something is or is not an ideology; nor is it a recipe stating how to make an ideology correctly. Rather it is an agenda of things to discuss, questions to ask, hypotheses to make. We should be able to use it when considering the interaction between ideas and politics, especially systems of ideas that make claims, whether justificatory or hortatory. Cutting the concept off from its history, even if historically it has been used in contradictory ways, is no service. Political theory is not an exercise in grave-digging, so that inconvenient problems can "disappear." Instead, it provides a wealth of critical perspective, if only we are prepared to use it.

NOTES

1. Count Destutt de Tracy, *A Treatise on Political Economy; to Which Is Prefixed a Supplement to a Preceding Work on the Understanding, or Elements of Ideology; with an Analytical Table, and an Introduction on the Faculty of the Will,* translated by Thomas Jefferson, in John M. Dorsey, *Psychology of Political Science* (Detroit: Center for Health Education, 1973), "Advertisement," p. ix.
2. George Lichtheim, *The Concept of Ideology and Other Essays* (New York: Random House, 1967), pp. 4–5.
3. Karl Marx and Friedrich Engels, *Collected Works,* vol. 5 (London: Lawrence and Wishart, 1976), pp. 586–587.
4. Ibid., pp. 59–60.
5. Ibid., p. 62.
6. Karl Marx and Friedrich Engels, *Selected Works in One Volume* (London: Lawrence and Wishart, 1984), p. 183.
7. Marx and Engels, *Collected Works,* vol. 5, p. 60.
8. Ibid., p. 52.
9. Ibid., p. 80.
10. Marx and Engels, *Selected Works in One Volume,* p. 181.
11. Marx and Engels, *Collected Works,* vol. 5, p. 49.
12. Terrell Carver, *Marx's Social Theory* (Oxford: Oxford University Press, 1982), p. 44.
13. See Terrell Carver, *Marx and Engels: The Intellectual Relationship* (Brighton: Wheatsheaf Books, 1983), *passim.*
14. V. I. Lenin, *Collected Works,* vol. 5, translated by Joe Fineberg and George Hanna, ed. Victor Jerome (Moscow: Progress Publishers, 1973), pp. 369, 370, 383–384.
15. Ibid., pp. 375, 383–384.
16. Karl Mannheim, *Ideology and Utopia,* translated by Louis Wirth and Edward Shils (London: Routledge and Kegan Paul, 1948), pp. 2, 238.
17. Ibid., pp. 49–50.
18. Ibid., p. 62.
19. Malcolm B. Hamilton, "The Elements of the Concept of Ideology," *Political Studies* 35 (1987), p. 38.
20. Ibid., p. 32.

PART TWO

The Democratic Ideal

Many politicians, scholars, and journalists speak of democracy as if it were an ideology, distinct from and in opposition to other ideologies—especially communism and fascism. But this is mistaken. Democracy is not itself an ideology but an *ideal* that different ideologies define and pursue (or reject) in different ways and for different reasons. Everyone agrees that "democracy" means "rule by the people," of course, but what *is* rule by the people? Who are *the people,* and *how* are they to rule? On these points there is little agreement because each ideology answers these questions in its own way. With the exception of fascism, Nazism, and radical Islam, however, all of the ideologies now agree that democracy is certainly the most desirable form of government—an ideal toward which all societies should strive.

The popularity of democracy in our time is extraordinary not only because so many people of such different views claim to be democrats but also because democracy was long regarded as a bad or corrupt form of government. The word "democracy" itself first came into use in ancient Greece, where a conflict developed between those who favored democracy—rule by the *demos* or the common people—and those who preferred aristocracy—literally, "rule by the best." In Athens in the fifth century B.C., the *demos,* or people, found a leader in Pericles, whose "Funeral Oration" was one of the first defenses of democracy as a way of life. The Athenian democracy was short lived, however, and philosophers such as Plato (c. 428–348 B.C.) and Aristotle (384–322 B.C.) concluded that democracy is inherently unstable. The common people, Plato argued, are simply too shortsighted and too unruly to govern wisely. Democracy will soon descend into anarchy, a lawless condition that will lead the people to call for a strong leader to restore law and order. But that strong leader will be a despot who subjects everyone else to slavery. From democracy, according to Plato, it is but a short step to despotism, the worst of all forms of government.

Like Plato, his pupil Aristotle regarded democracy as a selfish or corrupt form of government. Democracy is "rule by the many" in the selfish interest of the common people as a distinct class, he said, not rule in the interest of the community as a whole. But Aristotle also noted that democracy has some desirable features, and he went further to argue that rule by many in the interests of the whole community is not only possible but probably the best of all forms of government.

Aristotle called this best form of government a polity, but it later became better known by the Roman name of "republic," from the Latin *res publica* (meaning "public thing" or "public business"). The republican idea was that the forms of government must be mixed in such a way that some power is in the hands of the common people, some in the hands of the aristocratic few, and some in the hands of a single person. Because each element of society would have some power, but not enough to rule without the cooperation of the other two elements, a system of checks and balances would lead to a government that ruled in the common interest. It would then be a popular government because the people (*populus*) would have a significant voice, but it would not be a democracy. In a republic the power of the people would be tempered and guided by the wisdom of the few.

For centuries, the republic, and not democracy, was considered the ideal form of popular government. Its supporters included Niccolò Machiavelli (1469–1527) and John Adams (1735–1826), the second president of the United States. But in the late eighteenth and early nineteenth centuries sentiment began to shift in favor of democracy. Exactly why this happened is not clear. But with the growth of cities and industry came increasing literacy and improved means of communications, and the nineteenth century soon came to be known as the age of "the common man." In the United States this change was associated with Jacksonian democracy, as the period of Andrew Jackson's presidency (1829–1837) was called. Democracy was taken to be a means of expression or self-government for the common man, as well as a device by which he could protect his rights and interests. But "rule by the people" did not include women and members of other groups, such as slaves in the United States, who were not yet counted among "the people."

Some observers saw the rise of democracy as a mixed blessing. Alexis de Tocqueville (1805–1859), a French aristocrat who traveled throughout the United States in the 1830s, welcomed the increased opportunities that democracy brought to the common people. In his *Democracy in America,* Tocqueville particularly praised the opportunities for participation in local government that democracy made possible. But he also worried that democracy placed so much emphasis on equality that a new form of tyranny would emerge—the "tyranny of the majority." The emphasis on equality will lead to the pressure to conform, Tocqueville feared, so that people will be afraid to think and act for themselves. In England John Stuart Mill (1806–1873) reached much the same conclusion. The old days of tyrannical rule by kings and emperors were vanishing, he wrote in *On Liberty,* but now the individual's ability to think and live freely was subject to "the moral coercion of public opinion" (see the selection from *On Liberty* in Part Three). Like Tocqueville, Mill welcomed the increased opportunities for political participation that democracy opened, for he saw participation as a way of educating and improving men and women. But he also suggested that it might be prudent, at least temporarily, to give the wiser, better-informed, and more responsible members of society more votes than the common person.

Despite these concerns, democracy became more widespread throughout the nineteenth century. Voting rights were extended to almost all adult males in the industrialized countries of Europe and North America by the end of the century, and then extended to women in the early or middle years of the twentieth century. Fascism reacted against this democratic trend in the years following World War I, but the defeat of Germany, Italy, and Japan in World War II seems, for a time, to have crushed fascism as a significant antidemocratic force. Now, throughout the world, democracy is recognized rhetorically—if not always in practice—as the best of all forms of government.

But "democracy" means different things to different people. In particular, three conceptions of democracy competed with one another in the twentieth century. The most familiar in the English-speaking world is *liberal democracy.* For liberals like Mill, democracy is indeed government by the people, but the people must be willing to respect the rights and liberties of the individuals who compose society. In liberal democracy, then, the chief concern is to prevent majority rule from becoming majority tyranny. The advocates of *social democracy* accept the need to protect individual rights, but they argue that some of these rights—especially the right to own and dispose of property—may be used to frustrate true democracy. Like Michael Walzer, whose essay "Town Meetings and Workers' Control" is reprinted below, social democrats take the socialist point of view that property ought to be controlled directly for the public good, not for the private benefit of individuals. Property and wealth are forms of power, they say, and no society can be truly democratic when some people have considerably more power than others. Social democrats thus stress the importance of equality for democracy, with equality understood as a roughly equal chance to influence the decisions that govern one's society. A not-so-distant echo of this theme is often heard in debates over campaign financing, in which critics complain that the campaign contributions of wealthy citizens and special-interest groups buy them political influence that ordinary or poor citizens can never achieve.

The third conception of democracy that vied for acceptance in the twentieth century—but with little success in recent years—is *people's democracy.* This view is linked most closely with communism, or Marxism-Leninism. In this view, democracy is rule by, or *in the interests of,* the common people, which means that it is possible for a single group, such as the Communist party, to wield power democratically so long as it acts to promote the interests of the working class or proletariat. Democracy and dictatorship are compatible with each other, in other words, as the Chinese leader Mao Zedong (1893–1976) insisted in his essay "On the People's Democratic Dictatorship" (in Part Six).

In the first decade of the twenty-first century, the idea of "people's democracy" seems to have few adherents outside the ranks of the Chinese Communist party and Communist parties in Cuba, North Korea, and Vietnam. But democracy in general is more popular than ever, and the question we now face is whether liberals and socialists will continue to quarrel over the proper definition of democracy, or whether they will find enough common ground to satisfy—and perhaps unite—the two groups.

2

Democracy and Despotism

EURIPIDES

Greeks of fifth and fourth centuries B.C. Athens took pride in a form of government that they had invented—democracy (from *demos,* meaning "people" or "common people," and *kratein,* meaning "rule"). While other peoples chafed under the rule of despots, the Athenians ruled themselves. In his play *The Suppliants,* first performed in 422 B.C., Euripides (c. 485–407 B.C.) contrasts democratic and despotic government, celebrating the former while condemning the latter. The occasion is the arrival in Athens of an envoy from Thebes, which was then ruled by the tyrant Creon. The envoy cannot quite believe that the people are capable of ruling themselves.

Source: Euripides, *The Suppliants,* ll. 394–465; translated by Terence Ball.

THE SUPPLIANTS

Theban Messenger: Who is the tyrant who rules this land? To whom must I deliver my message from Creon, ruler of Thebes?

Theseus: Noble visitor, your speech proceeds from a false premise. No tyrant rules here, for this city is free. Here the people rule, each taking his turn without respect of wealth or poverty.

Theban Messenger: Surely you are playing games with me. The city from which I come is ruled not by the gullible multitude but by one man only. No one there uses high-sounding words to pander to the crowd, manipulating them for his own advantage while cloaking his crimes and failures in fair-sounding phrases. So I ask you: Since the people are such poor judges of everything, how can they possibly govern the city? They have neither the time nor the talent to understand the intricacies of politics. Even if he had been educated, a poor working stiff would have no time or energy left over from his labors to learn about political affairs. Besides, wiser and better people would recoil from a system in which such a man might, through his own way with words, fool the people and rise from being a nobody to occupy a position of political prominence.

Theseus: You yourself have a way with words and would, if you could, fool us with your kit of clever verbal tricks. But since you have chosen to play this game of words, permit me to take my turn while you listen. Nothing is worse for a city than a tyrant. Wherever he rules, the law does not. In his hands there is no law that rules over all alike. But where the laws rule, all—rich and poor, powerful and weak—are equal before them. There the poor are able to speak the same language as the strong—the language of law and justice. If his cause be just, the poor man can prevail against a wealthy adversary. The hallmark of freedom is this: Anyone having good advice to give to the city should be heard, and anyone with nothing to say may choose to remain silent. What greater equality can exist in a city? Where all the citizens rule, they take pride in their young people. But where a tyrant rules, he fears them, and, seeing the most talented among them as a threat to his own power, he puts them to the sword. How can the city survive and prosper, where its ruler stifles all initiative and uses his sword like a scythe, cutting down its youths like the flowers of spring? Why work and save for the sake of your children, only to have the tyrant take it all away? Why raise your daughters to be virtuous, when they can be ravished at whim by a lustful tyrant while their tearful parents are powerless to prevent it? I would rather die than have my children be subjected to such arbitrary power!

This thunderbolt I hurl in answer to your words.... If you weren't a messenger and therefore under the protection of the law, you would pay dearly for your outrageous remarks. It is the messenger's duty to deliver one message and to return with another. So take this reply back to Creon: Next time, send to our city a messenger who talks less foolishly than this one.

3

Funeral Oration

PERICLES

After defeating the numerically larger forces of the despotic Persian Empire in 480 B.C., democratic Athens assumed a preeminent position among the city-states of Greece. But other Greek city-states grew wary of Athens's power and angry at its arrogance. Led by Athens's chief rival, Sparta, they waged war—the Peloponnesian War—against Athens. In his famous Funeral Oration (430 B.C.), Pericles (c. 495–429 B.C.) commemorates the sacrifice of the Athenians who died in battle in the first years of the war and celebrates the ideals of Athenian democracy.

Source: Thucydides, *The Peloponnesian War,* 2nd ed., revised, vol. 1, translated by Benjamin Jowett (Oxford: Clarendon Press, 1900), pp. 126–135. The editors have altered the translation slightly for purposes of clarity.

FUNERAL ORATION

Most of those who have spoken here before me have commended the lawgiver who added this oration to our other funeral customs; it seemed to them a worthy thing that such an honour should be given at their burial to the dead who have fallen on the field of battle. But I should have preferred that, when men's deeds have been brave, they should be honoured in deed only, and with such an honour as this public funeral, which you are now witnessing. Then the reputation of many would not have been imperilled on the eloquence or want of eloquence of one, and their virtues believed or not as he spoke well or ill. For it is difficult to say neither too little nor too much; and even moderation is apt not to give the impression of truthfulness. The friend of the dead who knows the facts is likely to think that the words of the speaker fall short of his knowledge and of his wishes; another who is not so well informed, when he hears of anything which surpasses his own powers, will be envious and will suspect exaggeration. Mankind are tolerant of the praises of others so long as each hearer thinks that he can do as well or nearly as well himself, but, when the speaker rises above him, jealousy is aroused and he begins to be incredulous. However, since our ancestors have set the seal of their approval upon the practice, I must obey, and to the utmost of my power shall endeavour to satisfy the wishes and beliefs of all who hear me.

...But before I praise the dead, I should like to point out by what principles of action we rose to power, and under what institutions and through what manner of life our empire became great. For I conceive that such thoughts are not unsuited to the occasion, and that this numerous assembly of citizens and strangers may profitably listen to them.

Our form of government does not enter into rivalry with the institutions of others. We do not copy our neighbours, but are an example to them. It is true that we are called a democracy, for the administration is in the hands of the many and not of the few. But while the law secures equal justice to all alike in their private disputes, the claim of excellence is also recognised; and when a citizen is in any way distinguished, he is preferred to the public service, not as a matter of privilege, but as the reward of merit. Neither is poverty a bar, but a man may benefit his country whatever be the obscurity of his condition. There is no exclusiveness in our public life, and in our private intercourse we are not suspicious of one another, nor angry with our neighbour if he does what he likes; we do not put on sour looks at him which, though harmless, are not pleasant. While we are thus unconstrained in our private intercourse, a spirit of reverence pervades our public acts; we are prevented from doing wrong by respect for the authorities and for the laws, having an especial regard to those which are ordained for the protection of the injured as well as to those unwritten laws which bring upon the transgressor of them the reprobation of the general sentiment.

And we have not forgotten to provide for our weary spirits many relaxations from toil; we have regular games and sacrifices throughout the year; our homes are beautiful and elegant; and the delight which we daily feel in all these things helps to banish melancholy. Because of the greatness of our city the fruits of the whole earth flow in upon us; so that we enjoy the goods of other countries as freely as of our own.

Then, again, our military training is in many respects superior to that of our adversaries. Our city is thrown open to the world, and we never expel a foreigner or prevent him from seeing or learning anything of which the secret if revealed to an enemy might profit him. We rely not upon management or trickery, but upon our own hearts and hands. And in the matter of education, whereas they from early youth are always undergoing laborious exercises which are to make them brave, we live at ease, and yet are equally ready to face the perils which they face. And here is the proof. The Lacedaemonians [i.e., Spartans] come into Attica [i.e., Athenian territory] not by themselves, but with their whole confederacy following; we go alone into a neighbour's country; and although our opponents are fighting for their homes and we on a foreign soil, we have seldom any difficulty in overcoming them. Our enemies have never yet felt our united strength; the care of a navy divides our attention, and on land we are obliged to send our own citizens everywhere. But they, if they meet and defeat a part of our army, are as proud as if they had routed us all, and when defeated they pretend to have been vanquished by us all.

If then we prefer to meet danger with a light heart but without laborious training, and with a courage which is gained by habit and not enforced by law, are we not greatly the gainers?

...For we are lovers of the beautiful, yet simple in our tastes, and we cultivate the mind without loss of manliness. Wealth we employ, not for talk and ostentation, but when there is a real use for it. To avow poverty with us is no disgrace; the true disgrace is in doing nothing to avoid it. An Athenian citizen does not neglect the state because he takes care of his own household; and even those of us who are engaged in business have a very fair idea of politics. We alone regard a man who takes no interest in public affairs, not as a harmless, but as a useless character; and if few of us are originators, we are all sound judges of a policy. The great impediment to action is, in our opinion, not discussion, but the want of that knowledge which is gained by discussion preparatory to action. For we have a peculiar power of thinking before we act and of acting too, whereas other men are courageous from ignorance but hesitate upon reflection. And they are surely to be esteemed the bravest spirits who, having the clearest sense both of the pains and pleasures of life, do not on that account shrink from danger. In doing good, again, we are unlike others; we make our friends by conferring, not by receiving, favours. Now he who confers a favour is the firmer friend, because he would fain by kindness keep alive the memory of an obligation; but the recipient is colder in his feelings, because he knows that in requiting another's generosity he will not be winning gratitude but only paying a debt. We alone do good to our neighbours not upon a calculation of interest, but in the confidence of freedom and in a frank and fearless spirit. To sum up: I say that Athens is the school of Hellas [i.e., Greece], and that the individual Athenian in his own person seems to have the power of adapting himself to the most varied forms of action with the utmost versatility and grace. This is no passing and idle word, but truth and fact; and the assertion is verified by the position to which these qualities have raised the state. For in the hour of trial Athens alone among her contemporaries is superior to the report of her. No enemy who comes against her is indignant at the reverses which he sustains at the hands of such a city; no subject complains that his masters are unworthy of him. And we shall assuredly not be without witnesses; there are mighty monuments of our power which will make us the wonder of this and of succeeding ages; we shall not need the praises of Homer or of any other panegyrist whose poetry may please for the moment, although his representation of the facts will not bear the light of day. For we have compelled every land and every sea to open a path for our valour, and have everywhere planted eternal memorials of our friendship and of our enmity. Such is the city for whose sake these men nobly fought and died; they could not bear the thought that she might be taken from them; and every one of us who survive should gladly toil on her behalf.

I have dwelt upon the greatness of Athens because I want to show you that we are contending for a higher prize than those who enjoy none of these privileges, and to establish by manifest proof the merit of these men whom I am now commemorating. Their loftiest praise has been already spoken. For in magnifying the city I have magnified them, and men like them whose virtues made her glorious. And of how few Hellenes [i.e., Greeks] can it be said as of them, that their deeds when weighed in the balance have been found equal to their fame! I believe that a death such as theirs has been gives the true measure of a man's worth; it may be the first revelation of his virtues, but is at any rate their final seal. For even those who come short in other ways may justly plead the valour with which they have fought for their country; they have blotted out the evil with the good, and have benefited the state more by their public services than they have injured her by their private actions. None of these men were weakened by wealth or hesitated to forgo the pleasures of life; none of them put off the evil day in the hope, natural to poverty, that a man, though poor, may one day become rich. But, deeming that the punishment of their enemies was sweeter than any of these things, and that they could fall in no nobler cause, they determined at the hazard of their lives to be honourably avenged, and to leave the rest. They resigned to hope their unknown chance of happiness; but in the face of death they resolved to rely upon themselves alone. And when the moment came they were minded to resist and suffer, rather than to flee and save their lives; they ran away from the word of dishonour, but on the battle-field their feet stood fast, and in an instant, at the height of their fortune, they passed away from the scene, not of their fear, but of their glory.

Such was the end of these men; they were worthy of Athens, and the living need not desire to have a more heroic spirit, although they may pray for a less fatal result. The value of such a spirit is not to be expressed in words. Any one can talk to you forever about the advantages of a brave defence, which you know already. But instead of listening to him I would have you day by day fix your eyes upon the greatness of Athens, until you become filled with the love of her; and when you are impressed by the spectacle of her glory, reflect that this empire has been acquired by men who knew their duty and had the courage to do it, who in the hour of conflict had the fear of dishonour always present to them, and who, if ever they failed in an enterprise, would not allow their virtues to be lost to their country, but freely gave their lives to her as the fairest offering which they could present at her feast. The sacrifice which they collectively made was individually repaid to them; for they received again each one for himself a praise which grows not old, and the noblest of all sepulchres—I speak not of that in which their remains are laid, but of that in which their glory survives, and is proclaimed always and on every fitting occasion both in word and deed. For the whole earth is the sepulchre of famous men; not only are they commemorated by columns and inscriptions in their own country, but in foreign lands there dwells also an unwritten memorial of them, graven not on stone but in the hearts of men. Make them your examples, and, esteeming courage to be freedom and freedom to be happiness, do not weigh too nicely the perils of war. The unfortunate who has no hope of a change for the better has less reason to throw away his life than the prosperous who, if he survives, is always liable to a change for the worse, and to whom any accidental fall makes the most serious difference. To a man of spirit, cowardice and disaster coming together are far more bitter than death striking him unperceived at a time when he is full of courage and animated by the general hope.

Wherefore I do not now commiserate the parents of the dead who stand here; I would rather comfort them. You know that your life has been passed amid many great changes; and that they may be deemed fortunate who have gained most honour, whether an honourable death like theirs, or an honourable sorrow like yours, and whose days have been so ordered that the term of their happiness is likewise the term of their life. I know how hard it is to make you feel this, when the good fortune of others will too often remind you of the gladness which once lightened your hearts. And sorrow is felt at the want of those blessings, not which a man never knew, but which were a part of his life before they were taken from him. Some of you are of an age at which they may hope to have other children, and they ought to bear their sorrow better; not only will the children who may hereafter be born make them forget their own lost ones, but the city will be doubly a gainer. She will not be left desolate, and she will be safer. For a man's counsel cannot have equal weight or worth, when he alone has no children to risk in the general danger. To those of you who have passed their prime, I say: "Congratulate yourselves that you have been happy during the greater part of your days; remember that your life of sorrow will not last long, and be comforted by the glory of those who are gone. For the love of honour alone is ever young, and not riches, as some say, but honour is the delight of men when they are old and useless."

To you who are the sons and brothers of the departed, I see that the struggle to emulate them will be an arduous one. For all men praise the dead, and, however preeminent your virtue may be, hardly will you be thought, I do not say to equal, but even to approach them. The living have their rivals and detractors, but when a man is out of the way, the honour and good which he receives is unalloyed. And, if I am to speak of womanly virtues to those of you who will henceforth be widows, let me sum them up in one short admonition: To a woman not to show more weakness than is natural to her sex is a great glory, and not to be talked about for good or for evil among men.

I have paid the required tribute, in obedience to the law, making use of such fitting words as I had. The tribute of deeds has been paid in part; for the dead have been honourably buried, and it remains only that their children should be maintained at the public charge until they are grown up: This is the solid prize with which, as with a wreath, Athens crowns her sons living and dead, after a struggle like theirs. For where the rewards of virtue are greatest, there the noblest citizens are enlisted in the service of the state. And now, when you have duly lamented, every one his own dead, you may depart.

4

Democratic Judgment and the "Middling" Constitution

ARISTOTLE

Although critical of democracy as a form of government, the Greek philosopher Aristotle (384–322 B.C.) nevertheless recognized the democratic principle that "many heads are better than one." Just as a feast to which many people contribute is richer, more varied, and more nourishing than a meal prepared by one or a few, so a government that makes use of many talents and perspectives is wiser than one that does not. That is Aristotle's argument in Book III, Chapter 11, of his *Politics*. But the best form of government, as he goes on to say in Book IV, Chapter 11, is not democracy but "polity," that is, rule by the many in the interest of all. Aristotle thus anticipates the kind of popular self-rule that came to be called "republican." On the republican form of government, see selections 5 and 6.

Source: Aristotle, *The Politics*, translated by Benjamin Jowett (New York: Modern Library, 1943), pp. 145–149, 189–193. The editors have altered the translation slightly for the sake of clarity.

THE POLITICS: BOOK IIIThe New Communitarians

Chapter 11

...The principle that the multitude ought to be supreme rather than the few best is one that is maintained, and, though not free from difficulty, yet seems to contain an element of truth. For the many, of whom each individual is but an ordinary person, when they meet together may very likely be better than the few good, if regarded not individually but collectively, just as a feast to which many contribute is better than a dinner provided out of a single purse. For each individual among the many has a share of virtue and prudence, and when they meet together, they become in a manner of speaking one man, who has many feet, and hands, and senses.... Hence the many are better judges than a single man of music and poetry; for some understand one part, and some another, and among them they understand the whole. There is a similar combination of qualities in good men, who differ from any individual of the many, as the beautiful are said to differ from those who are not beautiful, and works of art from realities, because in them the scattered elements are combined, although, if taken separately, the eye of one person or some other feature in another person would be fairer than in the picture. Whether this principle can apply to every democracy, and to all bodies of men, is not clear. Or rather, by heaven, in some cases it is impossible of application; for the argument would equally hold about animals; and wherein, it will be asked, do some men differ from animals? But there may be bodies of men about whom our statement is nevertheless true. And if so, the difficulty which has been already raised, and also another which is akin to it—viz. what power should be assigned to the mass of freemen and citizens, who are not rich and have no personal merit—are both solved. There is still a danger in allowing them to share the great offices of state, for their folly will lead them into error, and their dishonesty into crime. But there is a danger also in not letting them share, for a state in which many poor men are excluded from office will necessarily be full of enemies. The only way of escape is to assign to them some deliberative and judicial functions. For this reason Solon and certain other legislators[1] give them the power of electing to offices, and of calling the magistrates to account, but they do not allow them to hold office singly. When they meet together their perceptions are quite good enough, and combined with the better class they are useful to the state (just as impure food when mixed with what is pure sometimes makes the entire mass more wholesome than a small quantity of the pure would be), but each individual, left to himself, forms an imperfect judgement. On the other hand, the popular form of government involves certain difficulties. In the first place, it might be objected that he who can judge of the healing of a sick man would be one who could himself heal his disease, and make him whole—that is, in other words, the physician; and so in all professions and arts. As, then, the physician ought to be called to account by physicians, so ought men in general to be called to account by their peers. But physicians are of three kinds: there is the ordinary practitioner, and there is the physician of the higher class, and thirdly the intelligent man who has studied the art: in all arts there is such a class; and we attribute the power of judging to them quite as much as to professors of the art. Secondly, does not the same principle apply to elections? For a right election can only be made by those who have knowledge; those who know geometry, for example, will choose a geometrician rightly, and those who know how to steer, a pilot; and, even if there be some occupations and arts in which private persons share in the ability to choose, they certainly cannot choose better than those who know. So that, according to this argument, neither the election of magistrates, nor the calling of them to account, should be entrusted to the many. Yet possibly these objections are to a great extent met by our old answer, that if the people are not utterly degraded, although individually they may be worse judges than those who have special knowledge: as a body they are as good or better. Moreover, there are some arts whose products are not judged of solely, or best, by the artists themselves, namely those arts whose products are recognized even by those who do not possess the art; for example, the knowledge of the house is not limited to the builder only; the user, or, in other words, the master, of the house will be even a better judge than the builder, just as the pilot will judge better of a rudder than the carpenter, and the guest will judge better of a feast than the cook.

This difficulty seems now to be sufficiently answered, but there is another akin to it. That inferior persons should have authority in greater matters than the good would appear to be a strange thing, yet the election and calling to account of the magistrates is the greatest of all. And these, as I was saying, are functions which in some states are assigned to the people, for the assembly is supreme in all such matters. Yet persons of any age, and having but a small property qualification, sit in the assembly and deliberate and judge, although for the great officers of state, such as treasurers and generals, a high qualification is required. This difficulty may be solved in the same manner as the preceding, and the present practice of democracies may be really defensible. For the power does not reside in the juror, or senator, or assemblyman, but in the court, and the senate, and the assembly, of which individual senators, or assemblymen or jurors, are only parts or members. And for this reason the many may claim to have a higher authority than the few; for the people, and the senate, and the courts consist of many persons, and their property collectively is greater than the property of one or of a few individuals holding great offices. But enough of this.

The discussion of the first question shows nothing so clearly as that laws, when good, should be supreme; and that the magistrate or magistrates should regulate those matters only on which the laws are unable to speak with precision owing to the difficulty of any general principle embracing all particulars. But what are good laws has not yet been clearly explained; the old difficulty remains. The goodness or badness, justice or injustice, of laws varies of necessity with the constitutions of states. This, however, is clear, that the laws must be adapted to the constitutions. But if so, true forms of government will of necessity have just laws, and perverted forms of government will have unjust laws.

Chapter 12

In all sciences and arts the end is a good, and the greatest good and in the highest degree a good is the most authoritative of all—this is the political science of which the good is justice, in other words, the common interest. All men think justice to be a sort of equality; and to a certain extent they agree in the philosophical distinctions which have been laid down by us about Ethics.[2] For they admit that justice is a thing and has a relation to persons, and that equals ought to have equality.

THE POLITICS: BOOK IV

Chapter 11

We have now to inquire what is the best constitution for most states, and the best life for most men, neither assuming a standard of virtue which is above ordinary persons, nor an education which is exceptionally favoured by nature and circumstances, nor yet an ideal state which is an aspiration only, but having regard to the life in which the majority are able to share, and to the form of government which states in general can attain. As to those aristocracies, as they are called, of which we were just now speaking, they either lie beyond the possibilities of the greater number of states, or they approximate to the so-called constitutional government [or polity], and therefore need no separate discussion. And in fact the conclusion at which we arrive respecting all these forms rests upon the same grounds. For if what was said in the *Ethics* is true, that the happy life is the life according to virtue lived without impediment, and that virtue is a mean, then the life which is in a mean, and in a mean attainable by every one, must be the best. And the same principles of virtue and vice are characteristic of cities and of constitutions; for the constitution is in a figure of speech the life of the city.

Now in all states there are three elements: one class is very rich, another very poor, and a third is a mean. It is admitted that moderation and the mean are best, and therefore it will clearly be best to possess the gifts of fortune in moderation; for in that condition of life men are most ready to follow rational principle. But he who greatly excels in beauty, strength, birth, or wealth, or on the other hand who is very poor, or very weak, or very much disgraced, finds it difficult to follow rational principle. Of these two the one sort grow into violent and great criminals, the others into rogues and petty rascals. And two sorts of offences correspond to them, the one committed from violence, the other from roguery. Again, the middle class is least likely to shrink from rule, or to be overambitious for it; both of which are injuries to the state. Again, those who have too much of the goods of fortune, strength, wealth, friends, and the like, are neither willing nor able to submit to authority. The evil begins at home; for when they are boys, by reason of the luxury in which they are brought up, they never learn, even at school, the habit of obedience. On the other hand, the very poor, who are in the opposite extreme, are too degraded. So that the one class cannot obey, and can only rule despotically; the other knows not how to command and must be ruled like slaves. Thus arises a city, not of freemen, but of masters and slaves, the one despising, the other envying; and nothing can be more fatal to friendship and good fellowship in states than this: for good fellowship springs from friendship; when men are at enmity with one another, they would rather not even share the same path. But a city ought to be composed, as far as possible, of equals and similars; and these are generally the middle classes. Wherefore the city which is composed of middle-class citizens is necessarily best constituted in respect of the elements of which we say the fabric of the state naturally consists. And this is the class of citizens which is most secure in a state, for they do not, like the poor, covet their neighbours' goods; nor do others covet theirs, as the poor covet the goods of the rich; and as they neither plot against others, nor are themselves plotted against, they pass through life safely. Wisely then did [the poet] Phocylides pray—"Many things are best in the mean; I desire to be of a middle condition in my city."

Thus it is manifest that the best political community is formed by citizens of the middle class, and that those states are likely to be well-administered, in which the middle class is large, and stronger if possible than both the other classes, or at any rate than either singly; for the addition of the middle class turns the scale, and prevents either of the extremes from being dominant. Great then is the good fortune of a state in which the citizens have a moderate and sufficient property; for where some possess much, and the others nothing, there may arise an extreme democracy, or a pure oligarchy; or a tyranny may grow out of either extreme—either out of the most rampant democracy, or out of an oligarchy; but it is not so likely to arise out of the middle constitutions and those akin to them. I will explain the reason of this hereafter, when I speak of the revolutions of states. The mean condition of states is clearly best, for no other is free from faction; and where the middle class is large, there are least likely to be factions and dissensions. For a similar reason large states are less liable to faction than small ones, because in them the middle class is large; whereas in small states it is easy to divide all the citizens into two classes who are either rich or poor, and to leave nothing in the middle. And democracies are safer and more permanent than oligarchies, because they have a middle class which is more numerous and has a greater share in the government; for when there is no middle class, and the poor greatly exceed in number, troubles arise, and the state soon comes to an end. A proof of the superiority of the middle class is that the best legislators have been of a middle condition; for example, Solon, as his own verses testify; and Lycurgus, for he was not a king; and Charondas, and almost all legislators.[3]

These considerations will help us to understand why most governments are either democratical or oligarchical. The reason is that the middle class is seldom numerous in them, and whichever party, whether the rich or the common people, transgresses the mean and predominates, draws the constitution its own way, and thus arises either oligarchy or democracy. There is another reason—the poor and the rich quarrel with one another, and whichever side gets the better, instead of establishing a just or popular government, regards political supremacy as the prize of victory, and the one party sets up a democracy and the other an oligarchy. Further, both the parties which had the supremacy in Hellas looked only to the interest of their own form of government, and established in states, the one, democracies, and the other, oligarchies; they thought of their own advantage, of the public not at all. For these reasons the middle form of government has rarely, if ever, existed, and among a very few only. One man alone of all who ever ruled in Hellas was induced to give this middle constitution to states. But it has now become a habit among the citizens of states, not even to care about equality; all men are seeking for dominion, or, if conquered, are willing to submit.

What then is the best form of government, and what makes it the best, is evident; and of other constitutions, since we say that there are many kinds of democracy and many of oligarchy, it is not difficult to see which has the first and which the second or any other place in the order of excellence, now that we have determined which is the best. For that which is nearest to the best must of necessity be better, and that which is furthest from it worse, if we are judging absolutely and not relatively to given conditions: I say "relatively to given conditions," since a particular government may be preferable, but another form may be better for some people.

NOTES

1. Solon (c. 638–559 B.C.) was the "legislator" or "lawgiver" who drafted the fundamental laws, or constitution, of Athens.—Eds.
2. Here Aristotle refers to his *Nicomachean Ethics* (especially Book V, Chapter 3).—Eds.
3. Like Solon in Athens, Lycurgus and Charondas were "legislators" who drafted the fundamental laws of their city-states: in Lycurgus's case, Sparta; in Charondas's, Catana, a Greek colony in what is now Sicily.—Eds.

5

What's Wrong with Princely Rule?

NICCOLÒ MACHIAVELLI

The Italian Renaissance of the fourteenth and fifteenth centuries saw the rebirth of many of the ideals of classical Greece and Rome, including the ideal of self-government. Among those who celebrated the rebirth of "republican" government was Niccolò Machiavelli (1469–1527). Machiavelli is best known as the author of *The Prince,* a short book in which he apparently advocates rule by a single person who should not hesitate to use cruelty and deceit to stay in power. In his longer book *The Discourses,* however, he takes a very different position. In the following excerpt from *The Discourses* Machiavelli criticizes the claim that the people, acting collectively, are less wise than a single king or prince.

Source: N. Machiavelli, *The Discourses,* translated by Christian Detmold (Boston: James R. Osgood and Co., 1882), chap. 58, pp. 214–219.

THE PEOPLE ARE WISER AND MORE CONSTANT THAN PRINCES

Titus Livius[1] as well as all other historians affirm that nothing is more uncertain and inconstant than the multitude; for it appears from what he relates of the actions of men, that in many instances the multitude, after having condemned a man to death, bitterly lamented it, and most earnestly wished him back. This was the case with the Roman people and Manlius Capitolinus, whom they had condemned to death and afterwards most earnestly desired him back, as our author [i.e., Livy] says in the following words: "No sooner had they found out that they had nothing to fear from him, than they began to regret and to wish him back." And elsewhere, when he relates the events that occurred in Syracuse after the death of Hieronymus, nephew of Hiero, he says: "It is the nature of the multitude either humbly to serve or insolently to dominate." I know not whether, in undertaking to defend a cause against the accusations of all writers, I do not assume a task so hard and so beset with difficulties as to oblige me to abandon it with shame, or to go on with it at the risk of being weighed down by it. Be that as it may, however, I think, and ever shall think, that it cannot be wrong to defend one's opinions with arguments founded upon reason, without employing force or authority.

I say, then, that individual men, and especially princes, may be charged with the same defects of which writers accuse the people; for whoever is not controlled by laws will commit the same errors as an unbridled multitude. This may easily be verified, for there have been and still are plenty of princes, and a few good and wise ones, such, I mean, as needed not the curb that controlled them. Amongst these, however, are not to be counted either the kings that lived in Egypt at that ancient period when that country was governed by laws, or those that arose in Sparta; neither such as are born in our day in France, for that country is more thoroughly regulated by laws than any other of which we have any knowledge in modern times. And those kings that arise under such constitutions are not to be classed amongst the number of those whose individual nature we have to consider, and see whether it resembles that of the people; but they should be compared with a people equally controlled by law as those kings were, and then we shall find in that multitude the same good qualities as in those kings, and we shall see that such a people neither obey with servility nor command with insolence. Such were the people of Rome, who, so long as that republic remained uncorrupted, neither obeyed basely nor ruled insolently, but rather held its rank honorably, supporting the laws and their magistrates....

Therefore, the character of the people is not to be blamed any more than that of princes, for both alike are liable to err when they are without any control. Besides the examples already given, I could adduce numerous others from amongst the Roman Emperors and other tyrants and princes, who have displayed as much inconstancy and recklessness as any populace ever did. Contrary to the general opinion, then, which maintains that the people, when they govern, are inconsistent, unstable, and ungrateful, I conclude and affirm that these defects are not more natural to the people than they are to princes. To charge the people and princes equally with them may be the truth, but to except princes from them would be a great mistake. For a people that governs and is well regulated by laws will be stable, prudent, and grateful, as much so, and even more, according to my opinion, than a prince, although he be esteemed wise; and, on the other hand, a prince, freed from the restraints of the law, will be more ungrateful, inconstant, and imprudent than a people similarly situated. The difference in their conduct is not due to any difference in their nature (for that is the same, and if there be any difference for good, it is on the side of the people); but to the greater or less respect they have for the laws under which they respectively live. And whoever studies the Roman people will see that for four hundred years they have been haters of royalty, and lovers of the glory and common good of their country; and he will find any number of examples that will prove both the one and the other.... But as regards prudence and stability, I say that the people are more prudent and stable, and have better judgment than a prince; and it is not without good reason that it is said, "The voice of the people is the voice of God"; for we see popular opinion prognosticate events in such a wonderful manner that it would almost seem as if the people had some occult virtue, which enables them to foresee the good and the evil. As to the people's capacity of judging of things, it is exceedingly rare that, when they hear two orators of equal talents advocate different measures, they do not decide in favor of the best of the two; which proves their ability to discern the truth of what they hear. And if occasionally they are misled in matters involving questions of courage or seeming utility (as has been said above), so is a prince also many times misled by his own passions, which are much greater than those of the people. We also see that in the election of their magistrates they make far better choices than princes; and no people will ever be persuaded to elect a man of infamous character and corrupt habits to any post of dignity, to which a prince is easily influenced in a thousand different ways. When we see a people take an aversion to anything, they persist in it for many centuries, which we never find to be the case with princes. Upon both these points the Roman people shall serve me as a proof, who in the many elections of Consuls and Tribunes had to regret only four times the choice they had made. The Roman people held the name of king in such detestation, as we have said, that no extent of services rendered by any of its citizens who attempted to usurp that title could save him from his merited punishment. We furthermore see the cities where the people are masters make the greatest progress in the least possible time, and much greater than such as have always been governed by princes; as was the case with Rome after the expulsion of the kings, and with Athens after they rid themselves of Pisistratus;[2] and this can be attributed to no other cause than that the governments of the people are better than those of princes.

It would be useless to object to my opinion by referring to what our historian [i.e., Livy] has said in the passages quoted above, and elsewhere; for if we compare the faults of a people with those of princes, as well as their respective good qualities, we shall find the people vastly superior in all that is good and glorious. And if princes show themselves superior in the making of laws, and in the forming of civil institutions and new statutes and ordinances, the people are superior in maintaining those institutions, laws, and ordinances, which certainly places them on a par with those who established them.

And finally to sum up this matter, I say that both governments of princes and of the people have lasted a long time, but both required to be regulated by laws. For a prince who knows no other control but his own will is like a madman, and a people that can do as it pleases will hardly be wise. If now we compare a prince who is controlled by laws, and a people that is restricted by them, we shall find more virtue in the people than in the prince; and if we compare them when both are freed from such control, we shall see that the people are guilty of fewer excesses than the prince, and that the errors of the people are of less importance, and therefore more easily remedied. For a licentious and mutinous people may easily be brought back to good conduct by the influence and persuasion of a good man, but an evil-minded prince is not amenable to such influences, and therefore there is no other remedy against him but cold steel. We may judge then from this of the relative defects of the one and the other; if words suffice to correct those of the people, whilst those of the prince can only be remedied by violence, no one can fail to see that where the greater remedy is required, there also the defects must be greater. The follies which a people commits at the moment of its greatest license are not what is most to be feared; it is not the immediate evil that may result from them that inspires apprehension, but the fact that such general confusion might afford the opportunity for a tyrant to seize the government. But with evil-disposed princes the contrary is the case; it is the immediate present that causes fear, and there is hope only in the future; for men will persuade themselves that the termination of his wicked life may give them a chance of liberty. Thus we see the difference between the one and the other to be, that the one touches the present and the other the future. The excesses of the people are directed against those whom they suspect of interfering with the public good; whilst those of princes are against apprehended interference with their individual interests. The general prejudice against the people results from the fact that everybody can freely and fearlessly speak ill of them in mass, even whilst they are at the height of their power; but a prince can only be spoken of with the greatest circumspection and apprehension.

NOTES

1. Titus Livius (59 B.C.–A.D. 17), or Livy, was a Roman historian. Machiavelli's *Discourses* is, in part, a commentary on the first 10 books of Livy's *History of Rome*.—Eds.
2. Pisistratus (?–527 B.C.) was notorious for his long, tyrannical rule of Athens.—Eds.

6

What Is a Republic?

JOHN ADAMS

The ideal of republican self-rule played an important part in the political struggles and debates of eighteenth-century America. Thomas Paine and Thomas Jefferson used republican arguments during the American Revolution to justify independence from Great Britain, and the Founding Fathers drafted a republican constitution in 1787. In 1776, when he was a member of the Continental Congress, John Adams (1735–1826) wrote the following selection, *Thoughts on Government,* in which he expounds and defends the principles of republican government.

Source: The Works of John Adams, ed. C. F. Adams (Boston: Little, Brown, 1851), pp. 193–200.

THOUGHTS ON GOVERNMENT

My Dear Sir,—If I was equal to the task of forming a plan for the government of a colony, I should be flattered with your request, and very happy to comply with it; because, as the divine science of politics is the science of social happiness, and the blessings of society depend entirely on the constitutions of government, which are generally institutions that last for many generations, there can be no employment more agreeable to a benevolent mind than a research after the best.

Pope[1] flattered tyrants too much when he said,

> For forms of government let fools contest,
> That which is best administered is best.

Nothing can be more fallacious than this. But poets read history to collect flowers, not fruits; they attend to fanciful images, not the effects of social institutions. Nothing is more certain, from the history of nations and nature of man, than that some forms of government are better fitted for being well administered than others.

We ought to consider what is the end of government, before we determine which is the best form. Upon this point all speculative politicians will agree, that the happiness of society is the end of government, as all divines and moral philosophers will agree that the happiness of the individual is the end of man. From this principle it will follow, that the form of government which communicates ease, comfort, security, or, in one word, happiness, to the greatest number of persons, and in the greatest degree, is the best.

All sober inquirers after truth, ancient and modern, pagan and Christian, have declared that the happiness of man, as well as his dignity, consists in virtue. Confucius, Zoroaster, Socrates, Mahomet [i.e., Mohammed], not to mention authorities really sacred, have agreed in this.

If there is a form of government, then, whose principle and foundation is virtue, will not every sober man acknowledge it better calculated to promote the general happiness than any other form?

Fear is the foundation of most governments; but it is so sordid and brutal a passion, and renders men in whose breasts it predominates so stupid and miserable, that Americans will not be likely to approve of any political institution which is founded on it.

Honor is truly sacred, but holds a lower rank in the scale of moral excellence than virtue. Indeed, the former is but a part of the latter, and consequently has not equal pretensions to support a frame of government productive of human happiness.

The foundation of every government is some principle or passion in the minds of the people. The noblest principles and most generous affections in our nature, then, have the fairest chance to support the noblest and most generous models of government.

A man must be indifferent to the sneers of modern Englishmen, to mention in their company the names of Sidney, Harrington, Locke, Milton, Nedham, Neville, Burnet, and Hoadly.[2] No small fortitude is necessary to confess that one has read them. The wretched condition of this country, however, for ten or fifteen years past, has frequently reminded me of their principles and reasonings. They will convince any candid mind, that there is no good government but what is republican. That the only valuable part of the British constitution is so; because the very definition of a republic is "an empire of laws, and not of men." That, as a republic is the best of governments, so that particular arrangement of the powers of society, or, in other words, that form of government which is best contrived to secure an impartial and exact execution of the laws, is the best of republics.

Of republics there is an inexhaustible variety, because the possible combinations of the powers of society are capable of innumerable variations.

As good government is an empire of laws, how shall your laws be made? In a large society, inhabiting an extensive country, it is impossible that the whole should assemble to make laws. The first necessary step, then, is to depute power from the many to a few of the most wise and good. But by what rules shall you choose your representatives? Agree upon the number and qualifications of persons who shall have the benefit of choosing, or annex this privilege to the inhabitants of a certain extent of ground.

The principal difficulty lies, and the greatest care should be employed, in constituting this representative assembly. It should be in miniature an exact portrait of the people at large. It should think, feel, reason, and act like them. That it may be the interest of this assembly to do strict justice at all times, it should be an equal representation, or, in other words, equal interests among the people should have equal interests in it. Great care should be taken to effect this, and to prevent unfair, partial, and corrupt elections. Such regulations, however, may be better made in times of greater tranquillity than the present; and they will spring up themselves naturally, when all the powers of government come to be in the hands of the people's friends. At present, it will be safest to proceed in all established modes, to which the people have been familiarized by habit.

A representation of the people in one assembly being obtained, a question arises, whether all the powers of government, legislative, executive, and judicial, shall be left in this body? I think a people cannot be long free, nor ever happy, whose government is in one assembly. My reasons for this opinion are as follows:

1. A single assembly is liable to all the vices, follies, and frailties of an individual; subject to fits of humor, starts of passion, flights of enthusiasm, partialities, or prejudice, and consequently productive of hasty results and absurd judgments. And all these errors ought to be corrected and defects supplied by some controlling power.
2. A single assembly is apt to be avaricious, and in time will not scruple to exempt itself from burdens, which it will lay, without compunction, on its constituents.
3. A single assembly is apt to grow ambitious, and after a time will not hesitate to vote itself perpetual. This was one fault of the Long Parliament;[3] but more remarkably of Holland, whose assembly first voted themselves from annual to septennial, then for life, and after a course of years, that all vacancies happening by death or otherwise, should be filled by themselves, without any application to constituents at all.
4. A representative assembly, although extremely well qualified, and absolutely necessary, as a branch of the legislative, is unfit to exercise the executive power, for want of two essential properties, secrecy and despatch.
5. A representative assembly is still less qualified for the judicial power, because it is too numerous, too slow, and too little skilled in the laws.
6. Because a single assembly, possessed of all the powers of government, would make arbitrary laws for their own interest, execute all laws arbitrarily for their own interest, and adjudge all controversies in their own favor.

But shall the whole power of legislation rest in one assembly? Most of the foregoing reasons apply equally to prove that the legislative power ought to be more complex; to which we may add, that if the legislative power is wholly in one assembly, and the executive in another, or in a single person, these two powers will oppose and encroach upon each other, until the contest shall end in war, and the whole power, legislative and executive, be usurped by the strongest.

The judicial power, in such case, could not mediate, or hold the balance between the two contending powers, because the legislative would undermine it. And this shows the necessity, too, of giving the executive power a negative upon the legislative, otherwise this will be continually encroaching upon that.

To avoid these dangers, let a distinct assembly be constituted, as a mediator between the two extreme branches of the legislature, that which represents the people, and that which is vested with the executive power.

Let the representative assembly then elect by ballot, from among themselves or their constituents, or both, a distinct assembly, which, for the sake of perspicuity, we will call a council. It may consist of any number you please, say twenty or thirty, and should have a free and independent exercise of its judgment, and consequently a negative voice in the legislature.

These two bodies, thus constituted, and made integral parts of the legislature, let them unite, and by joint ballot choose a governor, who, after being stripped of most of those badges of domination, called prerogatives, should have a free and independent exercise of his judgment, and be made also an integral part of the legislature. This, I know, is liable to objections; and, if you please, you may make him only president of the council, as in Connecticut. But as the governor is to be invested with the executive power, with consent of council, I think he ought to have a negative upon the legislative. If he is annually elective, as he ought to be, he will always have so much reverence and affection for the people, their representatives and counsellors, that, although you give him an independent exercise of his judgment, he will seldom use it in opposition to the two houses, except in cases the public utility of which would be conspicuous; and some such cases would happen.

In the present exigency of American affairs, when, by an act of Parliament, we are put out of the royal protection, and consequently discharged from our allegiance, and it has become necessary to assume government for our immediate security, the governor, lieutenant-governor, secretary, treasurer, commissary, attorney-general, should be chosen by joint ballot of both houses. And these and all other elections, especially of representatives and counsellors, should be annual, there not being in the whole circle of the sciences a maxim more infallible than this, "where annual elections end, there slavery begins."

These great men, in this respect, should be, once a year,

> Like bubbles on the sea of matter borne,
> They rise, they break, and to that sea
> return.

This will teach them the great political virtues of humility, patience, and moderation, without which every man in power becomes a ravenous beast of prey.

This mode of constituting the great offices of state will answer very well for the present; but if by experiment it should be found inconvenient, the legislature may, at its leisure, devise other methods of creating them, by elections of the people at large, as in Connecticut, or it may enlarge the term for which they shall be chosen to seven years, or three years, or for life, or make any other alterations which the society shall find productive of its ease, its safety, its freedom, or, in one word, its happiness.

A rotation of all offices, as well as of representatives and counsellors, has many advocates, and is contended for with many plausible arguments. It would be attended, no doubt, with many advantages; and if the society has a sufficient number of suitable characters to supply the great number of vacancies which would be made by such a rotation, I can see no objection to it. These persons may be allowed to serve for three years, and then be excluded three years, or for any longer or shorter term.

Any seven or nine of the legislative council may be made a quorum, for doing business as a privy council, to advise the governor in the exercise of the executive branch of power, and in all acts of state.

The governor should have the command of the militia and of all your armies. The power of pardons should be with the governor and council.

Judges, justices, and all other officers, civil and military, should be nominated and appointed by the governor, with the advice and consent of council, unless you choose to have a government more popular; if you do, all officers, civil and military, may be chosen by joint ballot of both houses; or, in order to preserve the independence and importance of each house, by ballot of one house, concurred in by the other. Sheriffs should be chosen by the freeholders of counties; so should registers of deeds and clerks of counties.

All officers should have commissions, under the hand of the governor and seal of the colony.

The dignity and stability of government in all its branches, the morals of the people, and every blessing of society depend so much upon an upright and skillful administration of justice, that the judicial power ought to be distinct from both the legislative and executive, and independent upon both, that so it may be a check upon both, as both should be checks upon that. The judges, therefore, should be always men of learning and experience in the laws, of exemplary morals, great patience, calmness, coolness and attention. Their minds should not be distracted with jarring interests; they should not be dependent upon any man, or body of men. To these ends, they should hold estate for life in their offices; or, in other words, their commission should be during good behavior, and their salaries ascertained and established by law. For misbehavior, the grand inquest of the colony, the house of representatives, should impeach them before the governor and council, where they should have time and opportunity to make their defence; but, if convicted, shall be removed from their offices, and subjected to such other punishment as shall be thought proper.

A militia law, requiring all men, or with very few exceptions besides cases of conscience, to be provided with arms and ammunition, to be trained at certain seasons; and requiring counties, towns, or other small districts, to be provided with public stocks of ammunition and intrenching utensils, and with some settled plans for transporting provisions after the militia, when marched to defend their country against sudden invasions; and requiring certain districts to be provided with field-pieces, companies of matrosses [i.e., gunners], and perhaps some regiments of light-horse, is always a wise institution, and, in the present circumstances of our country, indispensable.

Laws for the liberal education of youth, especially of the lower class of people, are so extremely wise and useful, that, to a humane and generous mind, no expense for this purpose would be thought extravagant.

The very mention of sumptuary laws [i.e., taxes on or prohibitions of luxury goods] will excite a smile. Whether our countrymen have wisdom and virtue enough to submit to them, I know not; but the happiness of the people might be greatly promoted by them, and a revenue saved sufficient to carry on this war [i.e., the Revolutionary War] forever. Frugality is a great revenue, besides curing us of vanities, levities, and fopperies, which are real antidotes to all great, manly, and war-like virtues.

But must not all commissions run in the name of a king? No. Why may they not as well run thus, "The colony of...to A. B. greeting," and be tested by the governor?

Why may not writs, instead of running in the name of the king, run thus, "The colony of...to the sheriff," etc., and be tested by the chief justice?

Why may not indictments conclude, "against the peace of the colony of...and the dignity of the same?"

A constitution founded on these principles introduces knowledge among the people, and inspires them with a conscious dignity becoming freemen; a general emulation takes place, which causes good humor, sociability, good manners, and good morals to be general. That elevation of sentiment inspired by such a government, makes the common people brave and enterprising. That ambition which is inspired by it makes them sober, industrious, and frugal. You will find among them some elegance, perhaps, but more solidity; a little pleasure, but a great deal of business; some politeness, but more civility. If you compare such a country with the regions of domination, whether monarchical or aristocratical, you will fancy yourself in Arcadia or Elysium.[4]

If the colonies should assume governments separately, they should be left entirely to their own choice of the forms; and if a continental constitution should be formed, it should be a congress, containing a fair and adequate representation of the colonies, and its authority should sacredly be confined to these cases, namely, war, trade, disputes between colony and colony, the post-office, and the unappropriated lands of the crown, as they used to be called.

These colonies, under such forms of government, and in such a union, would be unconquerable by all the monarchies of Europe.

You and I, my dear friend, have been sent into life at a time when the greatest lawgivers of antiquity would have wished to live. How few of the human race have ever enjoyed an opportunity of making an election of government, more than of air, soil, or climate, for themselves or their children! When, before the present epoch, had three millions of people full power and a fair opportunity to form and establish the wisest and happiest government that human wisdom can contrive? I hope you will avail yourself and your country of that extensive learning and indefatigable industry which you possess, to assist her in the formation of the happiest governments and the best character of a great people. For myself, I must beg you to keep my name out of sight; for this feeble attempt, if it should be known to be mine, would oblige me to apply to myself those lines of the immortal John Milton, in one of his sonnets:—

> I did but prompt the age to quit their clogs
> By the known rules of ancient liberty,
> When straight a barbarous noise environs me
> Of owls and cuckoos, asses, apes, and dogs.

NOTES

1. Alexander Pope (1688–1744), English poet and author of *An Essay on Man* (1734), from which Adams quotes here and below.—Eds.
2. Algernon Sidney, James Harrington, John Locke, John Milton, Marchamont Nedham, Henry Neville, Gilbert Burnet, and Benjamin Hoadley were English republican or "commonwealth" writers of the seventeenth and early eighteenth centuries.—Eds.
3. So called because the members of the British House of Commons who convened in 1640 enacted a law that denied the king the power to dissolve Parliament.—Eds.
4. Arcadia was a region of ancient Greece renowned for its simple, rural pleasures; in Greek mythology, Elysium was where the blessed dwelled after death.—Eds.

7

Bill of Rights of the United States

One of the central tensions within the democratic tradition concerns the conflict between majority rule and minority rights. How can the one be reconciled with the other? The men who drafted the U.S. Constitution thought that the separation of governmental powers and the system of checks and balances incorporated into the Constitution would protect the rights and interests of individuals from the power of the majority, but many others believed that a list of specific limits on government authority was needed to guarantee individual rights. When the first Congress met, it moved to add the following ten amendments to the Constitution. These amendments, known as the Bill of Rights, took effect November 3, 1791.

Articles in addition to, and Amendment of the Constitution of the United States of America, proposed by Congress, and ratified by the Legislatures of the several States, pursuant to the fifth Article of the original Constitution.

Art. I

Congress shall make no law respecting an establishment of religion, or prohibiting the free exercise thereof; or abridging the freedom of speech, or of the press; or the right of the people peaceably to assemble, and to petition the government for a redress of grievances.

Art. II

A well regulated Militia, being necessary to the security of a free State, the right of the people to keep and bear Arms, shall not be infringed.

Art. III

No Soldier shall, in time of peace be quartered in any house, without the consent of the Owner, nor in time of war, but in a manner to be prescribed by law.

Art. IV

The right of the people to be secure in their persons, houses, papers, and effects, against unreasonable searches and seizures, shall not be violated, and no Warrants shall issue, but upon probable cause, supported by Oath or affirmation, and particularly describing the place to be searched, and the persons or things to be seized.

Art. V

No person shall be held to answer for a capital, or otherwise infamous crime, unless on a presentment or indictment of a Grand Jury, except in cases arising in the land or naval forces, or in the Militia, when in actual service in time of War or public danger; nor shall any person be subject for the same offence to be twice put in jeopardy of life or limb; nor shall be compelled in any criminal case to be a witness against himself, nor be deprived of life, liberty, or property, without due process of law; nor shall private property be taken for public use, without just compensation.

Art. VI

In all criminal prosecutions, the accused shall enjoy the right to a speedy and public trial, by an impartial jury of the State and district wherein the crime shall have been committed, which district shall have been previously ascertained by law, and to be informed of the nature and cause of the accusation; to be confronted with the witnesses against him; to have compulsory process for obtaining witnesses in his favor, and to have the Assistance of Counsel for his defence.

Art. VII

In Suits at common law, where the value in controversy shall exceed twenty dollars, the right of trial by jury shall be preserved, and no fact tried by a jury, shall be otherwise re-examined in any Court of the United States, than according to the rules of the common law.

Art. VIII

Excessive bail shall not be required, nor excessive fines imposed, nor cruel and unusual punishments inflicted.

Art. IX

The enumeration in the Constitution, of certain rights, shall not be construed to deny or disparage others retained by the people.

Art. X

The powers not delegated to the United States by the Constitution, nor prohibited by it to the States, are reserved to the States respectively, or to the people.

8

Democracy and Equality

ALEXIS DE TOCQUEVILLE

One of the key features of democracy is its emphasis on equality. Among the first to trace the implications of this theme was the French writer and statesman Alexis de Tocqueville (1805–1859). After visiting the United States in 1831–1832, Tocqueville wrote *Democracy in America,* one of the first—and, some say, still the greatest—explorations of the American democratic experience. When Tocqueville analyzed American democracy, moreover, he did so with an eye to the implications of democracy for Europe as well.

Source: Alexis de Tocqueville, *Democracy in America,* vol. 1, translated by Henry Reeve (New York: Henry G. Langley, 1845), pp. 1–13.

DEMOCRACY IN AMERICA: INTRODUCTION

Among the novel objects that attracted my attention during my stay in the United States, nothing struck me more forcibly than the general equality of conditions. I readily discovered the prodigious influence which this primary fact exercises on the whole course of society, by giving a certain direction to public opinion, and a certain tenor to the laws; by imparting new maxims to the governing powers, and peculiar habits to the governed.

I speedily perceived that the influence of this fact extends far beyond the political character and the laws of the country, and that it has no less empire over civil society than over the government; it creates opinions, engenders sentiments, suggests the ordinary practices of life, and modifies whatever it does not produce.

The more I advanced in the study of American society, the more I perceived that the equality of conditions is the fundamental fact from which all others seem to be derived, and the central point at which all my observations constantly terminated.

I then turned my thoughts to our own hemisphere, where I imagined that I discerned something analogous to the spectacle which the New World presented to me. I observed that the equality of conditions is daily advancing toward those extreme limits which it seems to have reached in the United States; and that the democracy which governs the American communities, appears to be rapidly rising into power in Europe.

I hence conceived the idea of the book which is now before the reader.

It is evident to all alike that a great democratic revolution is going on among us; but there are two opinions as to its nature and consequences. To some it appears to be a novel accident, which as such may still be checked; to others it seems irresistible, because it is the most uniform, the most ancient, and the most permanent tendency which is to be found in history.

Let us recollect the situation of France seven hundred years ago, when the territory was divided among a small number of families, who were the owners of the soil and the rulers of the inhabitants; the right of governing descended with the family inheritance from generation to generation; force was the only means by which man could act on man; and landed property was the sole source of power.

Soon, however, the political power of the clergy was founded, and began to exert itself; the clergy opened its ranks to all classes, to the poor and the rich, the villain and the lord; equality penetrated into the government through the church, and the being who, as a serf, must have vegetated in perpetual bondage, took his place as a priest in the midst of nobles, and not unfrequently above the heads of kings.

The different relations of men became more complicated and more numerous, as society gradually became more stable and more civilized. Thence the want of civil laws was felt; and the order of legal functionaries soon rose from the obscurity of the tribunals and their dusty chambers, to appear at the court of the monarch, by the side of the feudal barons in their ermine and their mail.

While the kings were ruining themselves by their great enterprises, and the nobles exhausting their resources by private wars, the lower orders were enriching themselves by commerce. The influence of money began to be perceptible in state affairs. The transactions of business opened a new road to power, and the financier rose to a station of political influence in which he was at once flattered and despised.

Gradually the spread of mental acquirements, and the increasing taste for literature and art, opened chances of success to talent; science became the means of government, intelligence led to social power, and the man of letters took a part in the affairs of the state.

The value attached to the privileges of birth, decreased in the exact proportion in which new paths were struck out to advancement. In the eleventh century nobility was beyond all price; in the thirteenth it might be purchased; it was conferred for the first time in 1270; and equality was thus introduced into the government by the aristocracy itself.

In the course of these seven hundred years, it sometimes happened that, in order to resist the authority of the crown or to diminish the power of their rivals, the nobles granted a certain share of political rights to the people. Or, more frequently, the king permitted the lower orders to enjoy a degree of power, with the intention of repressing the aristocracy.

In France the kings have always been the most active and the most constant of levellers. When they were strong and ambitious, they spared no pains to raise the people to the level of the nobles; when they were temperate or weak, they allowed the people to rise above themselves. Some assisted the democracy by their talents, others by their vices. Louis XI and Louis XIV reduced every rank beneath the throne to the same subjection; Louis XV descended, himself and all his court, into the dust.

As soon as land was held on any other than a feudal tenure, and personal property began in its turn to confer influence and power, every improvement which was introduced in commerce or manufacture, was a fresh element of the equality of conditions. Henceforward every new discovery, every new want which it engendered, and every new desire which craved satisfaction, was a step toward the universal level. The taste for luxury, the love of war, the sway of fashion, the most superficial, as well as the deepest passions of the human heart, co-operated to enrich the poor and to impoverish the rich.

From the time when the exercise of the intellect became the source of strength and of wealth, it is impossible not to consider every addition to science, every fresh truth, and every new idea, as a germ of power placed within the reach of the people. Poetry, eloquence, and memory, the grace of wit, the glow of imagination, the depth of thought, and all the gifts which are bestowed by Providence with an equal hand, turned to the advantage of the democracy; and even when they were in the possession of its adversaries, they still served its cause by throwing into relief the natural greatness of man; its conquests spread, therefore, with those of civilization and knowledge; and literature became an arsenal, where the poorest and weakest could always find weapons to their hand.

In perusing the pages of our history, we shall scarcely meet with a single great event, in the lapse of seven hundred years, which has not turned to the advantage of equality.

The crusades and the wars of the English decimated the nobles, and divided their possessions; the erection of communes introduced an element of democratic liberty into the bosom of feudal monarchy; the invention of firearms equalized the villain and the noble on the field of battle; printing opened the same resources to the minds of all classes; the post was organized so as to bring the same information to the door of the poor man's cottage and to the gate of the palace; and protestantism proclaimed that all men are alike able to find the road to heaven. The discovery of America offered a thousand new paths to fortune, and placed riches and power within the reach of the adventurous and the obscure.

If we examine what has happened in France at intervals of fifty years, beginning with the eleventh century, we shall invariably perceive that a twofold revolution has taken place in the state of society. The noble has gone down on the social ladder, and the commoner has gone up; the one descends as the other rises. Every half-century brings them nearer to each other, and they will very shortly meet.

Nor is this phenomenon at all peculiar to France. Whithersoever we turn our eyes, we shall discover the same continual revolution throughout the whole of Christendom.

The various occurrences of national existence have everywhere turned to the advantage of democracy; all men have aided it by their exertions: those who have intentionally laboured in its cause, and those who have served it unwittingly—those who have fought for it, and those who have declared themselves its opponents—have all been driven along in the same track, have all laboured to one end, some ignorantly, and some unwillingly; all have been blind instruments in the hands of God.

The gradual development of the equality of conditions is, therefore, a providential fact, and it possesses all the characteristics of a divine decree: it is universal, it is durable, it constantly eludes all human interference, and all events as well as all men contribute to its progress.

Would it, then, be wise to imagine that a social impulse which dates from so far back, can be checked by the efforts of a generation? Is it credible that the democracy which has annihilated the feudal system, and vanquished kings, will respect the citizen and the capitalist? Will it stop now that it has grown so strong and its adversaries so weak?

None can say which way we are going, for all terms of comparison are wanting: the equality of conditions is more complete in the Christian countries of the present day, than it has been at any time, or in any part of the world; so that the extent of what already exists prevents us from foreseeing what may be yet to come.

The whole book which is here offered to the public, has been written under the impression of a kind of religious dread, produced in the author's mind by the contemplation of so irresistible a revolution, which has advanced for centuries in spite of such amazing obstacles, and which is still proceeding in the midst of the ruins it has made.

It is not necessary that God himself should speak in order to disclose to us the unquestionable signs of his will; we can discern them in the habitual course of nature, and in the invariable tendency of events; I know, without a special revelation, that the planets move in the orbits traced by the Creator's finger.

If the men of our time were led by attentive observation and by sincere reflection, to acknowledge that the gradual and progressive development of social equality is at once the past and future of their history, this solitary truth would confer the sacred character of a divine decree upon the change. To attempt to check democracy would be in that case to resist the will of God; and the nations would then be constrained to make the best of the social lot awarded to them by Providence.

The Christian nations of our age seem to me to present a most alarming spectacle; the impulse which is bearing them along is so strong that it cannot be stopped, but it is not yet so rapid that it cannot be guided: their fate is in their hands; yet a little while and it may be so no longer.

The first duty which is at this time imposed upon those who direct our affairs is to educate the democracy; to warm its faith, if that be possible; to purify its morals; to direct its energies; to substitute a knowledge of business for its inexperience, and an acquaintance with its true interests for its blind propensities; to adapt its government to time and place, and to modify it in compliance with the occurrences and the actors of the age.

A new science of politics is needed for a new world.

This, however, is what we think of least; launched in the middle of a rapid stream, we obstinately fix our eyes on the ruins which may still be descried upon the shore we have left, while the current sweeps us along, and drives us backward toward the gulf.

In no country in Europe has the great social revolution which I have been describing, made such rapid progress as in France; but it has always been borne on by chance. The heads of the state have never had any forethought for its exigencies, and its victories have been obtained without their consent or without their knowledge. The most powerful, the most intelligent, and the most moral classes of the nation have never attempted to connect themselves with it in order to guide it. The people have consequently been abandoned to its wild propensities, and it has grown up like those outcasts who receive their education in the public streets, and who are unacquainted with aught but the vices and wretchedness of society. The existence of a democracy was seemingly unknown, when, on a sudden, it took possession of the supreme power. Everything was then submitted to its caprices; it was worshipped as the idol of strength; until, when it was enfeebled by its own excesses, the legislator conceived the rash project of annihilating its power, instead of instructing it and correcting its vices; no attempt was made to fit it to govern, but all were bent on excluding it from the government.

The consequence of this has been that the democratic revolution has been effected only in the material parts of society, without that concomitant change in laws, ideas, customs, and manners, which was necessary to render such a revolution beneficial. We have gotten a democracy, but without the conditions which lessen its vices, and render its natural advantages more prominent; and although we already perceive the evils it brings, we are ignorant of the benefits it may confer.

While the power of the crown, supported by the aristocracy, peaceably governed the nations of Europe, society possessed, in the midst of its wretchedness, several different advantages which can now scarcely be appreciated or conceived.

The power of a part of his subjects was an insurmountable barrier to the tyranny of the prince; and the monarch who felt the almost divine character which he enjoyed in the eyes of the multitude, derived a motive for the just use of his power from the respect which he inspired.

High as they were placed above the people, the nobles could not but take that calm and benevolent interest in its fate which the shepherd feels toward his flock; and without acknowledging the poor as their equals, they watched over the destiny of those whose welfare Providence had entrusted to their care.

The people, never having conceived the idea of a social condition different from its own, and entertaining no expectation of ever ranking with its chiefs, received benefits from them without discussing their rights. It grew attached to them when they were clement and just, but it submitted without resistance or servility to their exactions, as to the inevitable visitations of the arm of God. Custom, and the manners of the time, had moreover created a species of law in the midst of violence, and established certain limits to oppression.

As the noble never suspected that any one would attempt to deprive him of the privileges which he believed to be legitimate, and as the serf looked upon his own inferiority as a consequence of the immutable order of nature, it is easy to imagine that a mutual exchange of good-will took place between two classes so differently gifted by fate. Inequality and wretchedness were then to be found in society; but the souls of neither rank of men were degraded.

Men are not corrupted by the exercise of power or debased by the habit of obedience; but by the exercise of power which they believe to be illegal, and by obedience to a rule which they consider to be usurped and oppressive.

On one side were wealth, strength, and leisure, accompanied by the refinement of luxury, the elegance of taste, the pleasures of wit, and the religion of art. On the other were labor, and a rude ignorance; but in the midst of this coarse and ignorant multitude, it was not uncommon to meet with energetic passions, generous sentiments, profound religious convictions, and independent virtues.

The body of a state thus organized, might boast of its stability, its power, and above all, of its glory.

But the scene is now changed, and gradually the two ranks mingle; the divisions which once severed mankind, are lowered; property is divided, power is held in common, the light of intelligence spreads, and the capacities of all classes are equally cultivated; the state becomes democratic, and the empire of democracy is slowly and peaceably introduced into the institutions and manners of the nation.

I can conceive a society in which all men would profess an equal attachment and respect for the laws of which they are the common authors; in which the authority of the state would be respected as necessary, though not as divine; and the loyalty of the subject to the chief magistrate would not be a passion, but a quiet and rational persuasion. Every individual being in the possession of rights which he is sure to retain, a kind of manly reliance and reciprocal courtesy would arise between all classes, alike removed from pride and meanness.

The people, well acquainted with its true interests, would allow, that in order to profit by the advantages of society, it is necessary to satisfy its demands. In this state of things, the voluntary association of the citizens might supply the individual exertions of the nobles, and the community would be alike protected from anarchy and from oppression.

I admit that in a democratic state thus constituted, society will not be stationary; but the impulses of the social body may be regulated and directed forward; if there be less splendour than in the halls of an aristocracy, the contrast of misery will be less frequent also; the pleasures of enjoyment may be less excessive, but those of comfort will be more general; the sciences may be less perfectly cultivated, but ignorance will be less common; the impetuosity of the feelings will be repressed, and the habits of the nation softened; there will be more vices and fewer crimes.

In the absence of enthusiasm and of an ardent faith, great sacrifices may be obtained from the members of a commonwealth by an appeal to their understandings and their experience: each individual will feel the same necessity for uniting with his fellow-citizens to protect his own weakness; and as he knows that if they are to assist he must co-operate, he will readily perceive that his personal interest is identified with the interest of the community.

The nation, taken as a whole, will be less brilliant, less glorious, and perhaps less strong; but the majority of the citizens will enjoy a greater degree of prosperity, and the people will remain quiet, not because it despairs of melioration, but because it is conscious of the advantages of its condition.

If all the consequences of this state of things were not good or useful, society would at least have appropriated all such as were useful and good; and having once and for ever renounced the social advantages of aristocracy, mankind would enter into possession of all the benefits which democracy can afford.

But here it may be asked what we have adopted in the place of those institutions, those ideas, and those customs of our forefathers which we have abandoned.

The spell of royalty is broken, but it has not been succeeded by the majesty of the laws; the people have learned to despise all authority. But fear now extorts a larger tribute of obedience than that which was formerly paid by reverence and by love.

I perceive that we have destroyed those independent beings which were able to cope with tyranny single-handed; but it is the government that has inherited the privileges of which families, corporations, and individuals, have been deprived; the weakness of the whole community has, therefore, succeeded to that influence of a small body of citizens, which, if it was sometimes oppressive, was often conservative.

The division of property has lessened the distance which separated the rich from the poor; but it would seem that the nearer they draw to each other, the greater is their mutual hatred, and the more vehement the envy and the dread with which they resist each other's claims to power; the notion of right is alike insensible to both classes, and force affords to both the only argument for the present, and the only guarantee for the future.

The poor man retains the prejudices of his forefathers without their faith, and their ignorance without their virtues; he has adopted the doctrine of self-interest as the rule of his actions, without understanding the science which controls it, and his egotism is no less blind than his devotedness was formerly.

If society is tranquil, it is not because it relies upon its strength and its well-being, but because it knows its weakness and its infirmities: a single effort may cost it its life; everybody feels the evil, but no one has courage or energy enough to seek the cure; the desires, the regret, the sorrows, and the joys of the time, produce nothing that is visible or permanent, like the passions of old men which terminate in impotence.

We have, then, abandoned whatever advantages the old state of things afforded, without receiving any compensation from our present condition; having destroyed an aristocracy, we seem inclined to survey its ruins with complacency, and to fix our abode in the midst of them.

The phenomena which the intellectual world presents are not less deplorable. The democracy of France, checked in its course or abandoned to its lawless passions, has overthrown whatever crossed its path, and has shaken all that it has not destroyed. Its control over society has not been gradually introduced, or peaceably established, but it has constantly advanced in the midst of disorder, and the agitation of a conflict. In the heat of the struggle each partisan is hurried beyond the limits of his opinions by the opinions and the excesses of his opponents, until he loses sight of the end of his exertions, and holds a language which disguises his real sentiments or secret instincts. Hence arises the strange confusion which we are beholding.

I cannot recall to my mind a passage in history more worthy of sorrow and of pity than the scenes which are happening under our eyes; it is as if the natural bond which unites the opinions of man to his tastes, and his actions to his principles, was now broken; the sympathy which has always been acknowledged between the feelings and the ideas of mankind, appears to be dissolved, and all the laws of moral analogy to be abolished.

Zealous Christians may be found among us, whose minds are nurtured in the love and knowledge of a future life, and who readily espouse the cause of human liberty, as the source of all moral greatness. Christianity, which has declared that all men are equal in the sight of God, will not refuse to acknowledge that all citizens are equal in the eye of the law. But, by a singular concourse of events, religion is entangled in those institutions which democracy assails, and it is not infrequently brought to reject the equality it loves, and to curse that cause of liberty as a foe, which it might hallow by its alliance.

By the side of these religious men I discern others whose looks are turned to the earth more than to heaven; they are the partisans of liberty, not only as the source of the noblest virtues, but more especially as the root of all solid advantages; and they sincerely desire to extend its sway, and to impart its blessings to mankind. It is natural that they should hasten to invoke the assistance of religion, for they must know that liberty cannot be established without morality, nor morality without faith; but they have seen religion in the ranks of their adversaries, and they inquire no farther; some of them attack it openly, and the remainder are afraid to defend it.

In former ages slavery has been advocated by the venal and slavish-minded, while the independent and the warm-hearted were struggling without hope to save the liberties of mankind. But men of high and generous characters are now to be met with, whose opinions are at variance with their inclinations, and who praise that servility which they have themselves never known. Others, on the contrary, speak in the name of liberty as if they were able to feel its sanctity and its majesty, and loudly claim for humanity those rights which they have always disowned.

There are virtuous and peaceful individuals whose pure morality, quiet habits, affluence, and talents, fit them to be the leaders of the surrounding population; their love of their country is sincere, and they are prepared to make the greatest sacrifices to its welfare, but they confound the abuses of civilization with its benefits, and the idea of evil is inseparable in their minds from that of novelty.

Not far from this class is another party, whose object is to materalise mankind, to hit upon what is expedient without heeding what is just; to acquire knowledge without faith, and prosperity apart from virtue; assuming the title of the champions of modern civilization, and placing themselves in a station which they usurp with insolence, and from which they are driven by their own unworthiness.

Where are we then?

The religionists are the enemies of liberty, and the friends of liberty attack religion; the high-minded and the noble advocate subjection, and the meanest and most servile minds preach independence; honest and enlightened citizens are opposed to all progress, while men without patriotism and without principles, are the apostles of civilization and of intelligence.

Has such been the fate of the centuries which have preceded our own? And has man always inhabited a world, like the present, where nothing is linked together, where virtue is without genius, and genius without honour; where the love of order is confounded with a taste for oppression, and the holy rites of freedom with a contempt of law; where the light thrown by conscience on human actions is dim, and where nothing seems to be any longer forbidden or allowed, honorable or shameful, false or true?

I cannot, however, believe that the Creator made man to leave him in an endless struggle with the intellectual miseries which surround us: God destines a calmer and a more certain future to the communities of Europe; I am unacquainted with his designs, but I shall not cease to believe in them because I cannot fathom them, and I had rather mistrust my own capacity than his justice.

There is a country in the world where the great revolution which I am speaking of seems nearly to have reached its natural limits; it has been effected with ease and simplicity, say rather that this country has attained the consequences of the democratic revolution which we are undergoing, without having experienced the revolution itself.

The emigrants who fixed themselves on the shores of America in the beginning of the seventeenth century, severed the democratic principle from all the principles which repressed it in the old communities of Europe, and transplanted it unalloyed to the New World. It has there been allowed to spread in perfect freedom, and to put forth its consequences in the laws by influencing the manners of the country.

It appears to me beyond a doubt, that sooner or later we shall arrive, like the Americans, at an almost complete equality of conditions. But I do not conclude from this, that we shall ever be necessarily led to draw the same political consequences which the Americans have derived from a similar social organization. I am far from supposing that they have chosen the only form of government which a democracy may adopt; but the identity of the efficient cause of laws and manners in the two countries is sufficient to account for the immense interest we have in becoming acquainted with its effects in each of them.

It is not, then, merely to satisfy a legitimate curiosity that I have examined America; my wish has been to find instruction by which we may ourselves profit. Whoever should imagine that I have intended to write a panegyric would be strangely mistaken, and on reading this book, he will perceive that such was not my design: nor has it been my object to advocate any form of government in particular, for I am of [the] opinion that absolute excellence is rarely to be found in any legislation; I have not even affected to discuss whether the social revolution, which I believe to be irresistible, is advantageous or prejudicial to mankind; I have acknowledged this revolution as a fact already accomplished or on the eve of its accomplishment; and I have selected the nation, from among those which have undergone it, in which its development has been the most peaceful and the most complete, in order to discern its natural consequences, and, if it be possible, to distinguish the means by which it may be rendered profitable. I confess that in America I saw more than America; I sought the image of democracy itself, with its inclinations, its character, its prejudices, and its passions, in order to learn what we have to fear or to hope from its progress.

9

Democratic Participation and Political Education

JOHN STUART MILL

As the English philosopher John Stuart Mill (1806–1873) noted, there are several reasons for preferring democracy to other forms of government. One is that it enables individuals to speak up for—and thus protect—their own interests. But, in addition to this "protectionist" argument, there is a second and perhaps more important educative argument to be made in favor of democracy: that it educates and improves citizens by providing them with "hands on" experience of self-rule.

Source: John Stuart Mill, *Considerations on Representative Government,* in *Liberty, Utilitarianism, and Representative Government,* ed. A. D. Lindsay (New York: E. P. Dutton and Co., 1910), chap. 3, pp. 202–205, 207–208, 211–218.

THAT THE IDEALLY BEST FORM OF GOVERNMENT IS REPRESENTATIVE GOVERNMENT

(From *Considerations on Representative Government*)

It has long (perhaps throughout the entire duration of British freedom) been a common saying, that if a good despot could be ensured, despotic monarchy would be the best form of government. I look upon this as a radical and most pernicious misconception of what good government is; which, until it can be got rid of, will fatally vitiate all our speculations on government.

The supposition is, that absolute power, in the hands of an eminent individual, would ensure a virtuous and intelligent performance of all the duties of government. Good laws would be established and enforced, bad laws would be reformed; the best men would be placed in all situations of trust; justice would be as well administered, the public burthens would be as light and as judiciously imposed, every branch of administration would be as purely and as intelligently conducted, as the circumstances of the country and its degree of intellectual and moral cultivation would admit. I am willing, for the sake of the argument, to concede all this: but I must point out how great the concession is; how much more is needed to produce even an approximation to these results, than is conveyed in the simple expression, a good despot. Their realization would in fact imply, not merely a good monarch, but an all-seeing one. He must be at all times informed correctly, in considerable detail, of the conduct and working of every branch of administration, in every district of the country, and must be able, in the twenty-four hours per day which are all that is granted to a king as to the humblest labourer, to give an effective share of attention and superintendence to all parts of this vast field; or he must at least be capable of discerning and choosing out, from among the mass of his subjects, not only a large abundance of honest and able men, fit to conduct every branch of public administration under supervision and control, but also the small number of men of eminent virtues and talents who can be trusted not only to do without that supervision, but to exercise it themselves over others. So extraordinary are the faculties and energies required for performing this task in any supportable manner, that the good despot whom we are supposing can hardly be imagined as consenting to undertake it, unless as a refuge from intolerable evils, and a transitional preparation for something beyond. But the argument can do without even this immense item in the account. Suppose the difficulty vanquished. What should we then have? One man of superhuman mental activity managing the entire affairs of a mentally passive people. Their passivity is implied in the very idea of absolute power. The nation as a whole, and every individual composing it, are without any potential voice in their own destiny. They exercise no will in respect to their collective interests. All is decided for them by a will not their own, which it is legally a crime for them to disobey. What sort of human beings can be formed under such a regimen? What development can either their thinking or their active faculties attain under it? On matters of pure theory they might perhaps be allowed to speculate, so long as their speculations either did not approach politics, or had not the remotest connexion with its practice. On practical affairs they could at most be only suffered to suggest; and even under the most moderate of despots, none but persons of already admitted or reputed superiority could hope that their suggestions would be known to, much less regarded by, those who had the management of affairs. A person must have a very unusual taste for intellectual exercise in and for itself, who will put himself to the trouble of thought when it is to have no outward effect, or qualify himself for functions which he has no chance of being allowed to exercise. The only sufficient incitement to mental exertion, in any but a few minds in a generation, is the prospect of some practical use to be made of its results. It does not follow that the nation will be wholly destitute of intellectual power. The common business of life, which must necessarily be performed by each individual or family for themselves, will call forth some amount of intelligence and practical ability, within a certain narrow range of ideas. There may be a select class of *savants* [i.e., wise people], who cultivate science with a view to its physical uses, or for the pleasure of the pursuit. There will be a bureaucracy, and persons in training for the bureaucracy, who will be taught at least some empirical maxims of government and public administration. There may be, and often has been, a systematic organization of the best mental power in the country in some special direction (commonly military) to promote the grandeur of the despot. But the public at large remain without information and without interest on all the greater matters of practice; or, if they have any knowledge of them, it is but a *dilettante* knowledge, like that which people have of the mechanical arts who have never handled a tool. Nor is it only in their intelligence that they suffer. Their moral capacities are equally stunted. Wherever the sphere of action of human beings is artificially circumscribed, their sentiments are narrowed and dwarfed in the same proportion. The food of feeling is action: even domestic affection lives upon voluntary good offices. Let a person have nothing to do for his country, and he will not care for it. It has been said of old, that in a despotism there is at most but one patriot, the despot himself; and the saying rests on a just appreciation of the effects of absolute subjection, even to a good and wise master. Religion remains: and here at least, it may be thought, is an agency that may be relied on for lifting men's eyes and minds above the dust at their feet. But religion, even supposing it to escape perversion for the purposes of despotism, ceases in these circumstances to be a social concern, and narrows into a personal affair between an individual and his Maker, in which the issue at stake is but his private salvation. Religion in this shape is quite consistent with the most selfish and contracted egoism, and identifies the votary as little in feeling with the rest of his kind as sensuality itself.

A good despotism means a government in which, so far as depends on the despot, there is no positive oppression by officers of state, but in which all the collective interests of the people are managed for them, all the thinking that has relation to collective interests done for them, and in which their minds are formed by, and consenting to, this abdication of their own energies. Leaving things to the Government, like leaving them to Providence, is synonymous with caring nothing about them, and accepting their results, when disagreeable, as visitations of Nature. With the exception, therefore, of a few studious men who take an intellectual interest in speculation for its own sake, the intelligence and sentiments of the whole people are given up to the material interests, and when these are provided for, to the amusement and ornamentation, of private life. But to say this is to say, if the whole testimony of history is worth anything, that the era of national decline has arrived: that is, if the nation had ever attained anything to decline from. If it has never risen above the condition of an Oriental people, in that condition it continues to stagnate. But if, like Greece or Rome, it had realized anything higher, through the energy, patriotism, and enlargement of mind, which as national qualities are the fruits solely of freedom, it relapses in a few generations into the Oriental state. And that state does not mean stupid tranquility, with security against change for the worse; it often means being overrun, conquered, and reduced to domestic slavery, either by a stronger despot, or by the nearest barbarous people who retain along with their savage rudeness the energies of freedom....

There is no difficulty in showing that the ideally best form of government is that in which the sovereignty, or supreme controlling power in the last resort, is vested in the entire aggregate of the community; every citizen not only having a voice in the exercise of that ultimate sovereignty, but being, at least occasionally, called on to take an actual part in the government, by the personal discharge of some public function, local or general.

To test this proposition, it has to be examined in reference to the two branches into which. . .the inquiry into the goodness of a government conveniently divides itself, namely, how far it promotes the good management of the affairs of society by means of the existing faculties, moral, intellectual, and active, of its various members, and what is its effect in improving or deteriorating those faculties.

The ideally best form of government, it is scarcely necessary to say, does not mean one which is practicable or eligible in all states of civilization, but the one which, in the circumstances in which it is practicable and eligible, is attended with the greatest amount of beneficial consequences, immediate and prospective. A completely popular government is the only polity which can make out any claim to this character. It is pre-eminent in both the departments between which the excellence of a political constitution is divided. It is both more favourable to present good government, and promotes a better and higher form of national character, than any other polity whatsoever.

Its superiority in reference to present well-being rests upon two principles, of as universal truth and applicability as any general propositions which can be laid down respecting human affairs. The first is, that the rights and interests of every or any person are only secure from being disregarded, when the person interested is himself able, and habitually disposed, to stand up for them. The second is, that the general prosperity attains a greater height, and is more widely diffused, in proportion to the amount and variety of the personal energies enlisted in promoting it.

Putting these two propositions into a shape more special to their present application; human beings are only secure from evil at the hands of others, in proportion as they have the power of being, and are, self-*protecting;* and they only achieve a high degree of success in their struggle with Nature, in proportion as they are self-*dependent,* relying on what they themselves can do, either separately or in concert, rather than on what others do for them....

If we now pass to the influence of the form of government upon character, we shall find the superiority of popular government over every other to be, if possible, still more decided and indisputable.

This question really depends upon a still more fundamental one—viz., which of two common types of character, for the general good of humanity, it is most desirable should predominate—the active, or the passive type; that which struggles against evils, or that which endures them; that which bends to circumstances, or that which endeavours to make circumstances bend to itself.

The commonplaces of moralists, and the general sympathies of mankind, are in favour of the passive type. Energetic characters may be admired, but the acquiescent and submissive are those which most men personally prefer. The passiveness of our neighbours increases our sense of security, and plays into the hands of our wilfulness. Passive characters, if we do not happen to need their activity, seem an obstruction the less in our own path. A contented character is not a dangerous rival. Yet nothing is more certain, than that improvement in human affairs is wholly the work of the uncontented characters; and, moreover, that it is much easier for an active mind to acquire the virtues of patience, than for a passive one to assume those of energy.

Of the three varieties of mental excellence, intellectual, practical, and moral, there never could be any doubt in regard to the first two, which side had the advantage. All intellectual superiority is the fruit of active effort. Enterprise, the desire to keep moving, to be trying and accomplishing new things for our own benefit or that of others, is the parent even of speculative, and much more of practical, talent. The intellectual culture compatible with the other type is of that feeble and vague description, which belongs to a mind that stops at amusement, or at simple contemplation. The test of real and vigorous thinking, the thinking which ascertains truths instead of dreaming dreams, is successful application to practice. Where that purpose does not exist, to give definiteness, precision, and an intelligible meaning to thought, it generates nothing better than the mystical metaphysics of the Pythagoreans or the Vedas.[1]

With respect to practical improvement, the case is still more evident. The character which improves human life is that which struggles with natural powers and tendencies, not that which gives way to them. The self-benefiting qualities are all on the side of the active and energetic character: and the habits and conduct which promote the advantage of each individual member of the community, must be at least a part of those which conduce most in the end to the advancement of the community as a whole.

But on the point of moral preferability, there seems at first sight to be room for doubt. I am not referring to the religious feeling which has so generally existed in favour of the inactive character, as being more in harmony with the submission due to the divine will. Christianity as well as other religions has fostered this sentiment; but it is the prerogative of Christianity, as regards this and many other perversions, that it is able to throw them off. Abstractedly from religious considerations, a passive character, which yields to obstacles instead of striving to overcome them, may not indeed be very useful to others, no more than to itself, but it might be expected to be at least inoffensive. Contentment is always counted among the moral virtues. But it is a complete error to suppose that contentment is necessarily or naturally attendant on passivity of character; and unless it is, the moral consequences are mischievous. Where there exists a desire for advantages not possessed, the mind which does not potentially possess them by means of its own energies, is apt to look with hatred and malice on those who do. The person bestirring himself with hopeful prospects to improve his circumstances, is the one who feels goodwill towards others engaged in, or who have succeeded in, the same pursuit. And where the majority are so engaged, those who do not attain the object have had the tone given to their feelings by the general habit of the country, and ascribe their failure to want of effort or opportunity, or to their personal ill luck. But those who, while desiring what others possess, put no energy into striving for it, are either incessantly grumbling that fortune does not do for them what they do not attempt to do for themselves, or overflowing with envy and ill-will towards those who possess what they would like to have....

There are, no doubt, in all countries, really contented characters, who not merely do not seek, but do not desire, what they do not already possess, and these naturally bear no ill-will towards such as have apparently a more favoured lot. But the great mass of seeming contentment is real discontent, combined with indolence or self-indulgence, which, while taking no legitimate means of raising itself, delights in bringing others down to its own level. And if we look narrowly even at the cases of innocent contentment, we perceive that they only win our admiration, when the indifference is solely to improvement in outward circumstances, and there is a striving for perpetual advancement in spiritual worth, or at least a disinterested zeal to benefit others. The contented man, or the contented family, who have no ambition to make any one else happier, to promote the good of their country or their neighbourhood, or to improve themselves in moral excellence, excite in us neither admiration nor approval. We rightly ascribe this sort of contentment to mere unmanliness and want of spirit. The content which we approve, is an ability to do cheerfully without what cannot be had, a just appreciation of the comparative value of different objects of desire, and a willing renunciation of the less when incompatible with the greater. These, however, are excellences more natural to the character, in proportion as it is actively engaged in the attempt to improve its own or some other lot. He who is continually measuring his energy against difficulties, learns what are the difficulties insuperable to him, and what are those which though he might overcome, the success is not worth the cost. He whose thoughts and activities are all needed for, and habitually employed in, practicable and useful enterprises, is the person of all others least likely to let his mind dwell with brooding discontent upon things either not worth attaining, or which are not so to him. Thus the active, self-helping character is not only intrinsically the best, but is the likeliest to acquire all that is really excellent or desirable in the opposite type....

Now there can be no kind of doubt that the passive type of character is favoured by the government of one or a few, and the active self-helping type by that of the many. Irresponsible rulers need the quiescence of the ruled, more than they need any activity but that which they can compel. Submissiveness to the prescriptions of men as necessities of nature, is the lesson inculcated by all governments upon those who are wholly without participation in them. The will of superiors, and the law as the will of superiors, must be passively yielded to. But no men are mere instruments or materials in the hands of their rulers, who have will or spirit or a spring of internal activity in the rest of their proceedings: and any manifestation of these qualities, instead of receiving encouragement from despots, has to get itself forgiven by them. Even when irresponsible rulers are not sufficiently conscious of danger from the mental activity of their subjects to be desirous of repressing it, the position itself is a repression. Endeavour is even more effectually restrained by the certainty of its impotence, than by any positive discouragement. Between subjection to the will of others, and the virtues of self-help and self-government, there is a natural incompatibility. This is more or less complete, according as the bondage is strained or relaxed. Rulers differ very much in the length to which they carry the control of the free agency of their subjects, or the supersession of it by managing their business for them. But the difference is in degree, not in principle; and the best despots often go the greatest lengths in chaining up the free agency of their subjects. A bad despot, when his own personal indulgences have been provided for, may sometimes be willing to let the people alone; but a good despot insists on doing them good, by making them do their own business in a better way than they themselves know of. The regulations which restricted to fixed processes all the leading branches of French manufacturers, were the work of the great Colbert.[2]

Very different is the state of the human faculties where a human being feels himself under no other external restraint than the necessities of nature, or mandates of society which he has his share in imposing, and which it is open to him, if he thinks them wrong, publicly to dissent from, and exert himself actively to get altered. No doubt, under a government partially popular, this freedom may be exercised even by those who are not partakers in the full privileges of citizenship. But it is a great additional stimulus to any one's self-help and self-reliance when he starts from even ground, and has not to feel that his success depends on the impression he can make upon the sentiments and dispositions of a body of whom he is not one. It is a great discouragement to an individual, and a still greater one to a class, to be left out of the constitution; to be reduced to plead from outside the door to the arbiters of their destiny, not taken into consultation within. The maximum of the invigorating effect of freedom upon the character is only obtained, when the person acted on either is, or is looking forward to becoming, a citizen as fully privileged as any other. What is still more important than even this matter of feeling, is the practical discipline which the character obtains, from the occasional demand made upon the citizens to exercise, for a time and in their turn, some social function. It is not sufficiently considered how little there is in most men's ordinary life to give any largeness either to their conceptions or to their sentiments. Their work is a routine; not a labour of love, but of self-interest in the most elementary form, the satisfaction of daily wants; neither the thing done, nor the process of doing it, introduces the mind to thoughts or feelings extending beyond individuals; if instructive books are within their reach, there is no stimulus to read them; and in most cases the individual has no access to any person of cultivation much superior to his own. Giving him something to do for the public, supplies, in a measure, all these deficiencies. If circumstances allow the amount of public duty assigned him to be considerable, it makes him an educated man. Notwithstanding the defects of the social system and moral ideas of antiquity, the practice of the dicastery [i.e., jury system] and the ecclesia [i.e., assembly] raised the intellectual standard of an average Athenian citizen far beyond anything of which there is yet an example in any other mass of men, ancient or modern. The proofs of this are apparent in every page of our great historian of Greece; but we need scarcely look further than to the high quality of the addresses which their great orators deemed best calculated to act with effect on their understanding and will. A benefit of the same kind, though far less in degree, is produced on Englishmen of the lower middle class by their liability to be placed on juries and to serve parish offices; which, though it does not occur to so many, nor is so continuous, nor introduces them to so great a variety of elevated considerations, as to admit of comparison with the public education which every citizen of Athens obtained from her democratic institutions, must make them nevertheless very different beings, in range of ideas and development of faculties, from those who have done nothing in their lives but drive a quill, or sell goods over a counter. Still more salutary is the moral part of the instruction afforded by the participation of the private citizen, if even rarely, in public functions. He is called upon, while so engaged, to weigh interests not his own; to be guided, in case of conflicting claims, by another rule than his private partialities; to apply, at every turn, principles and maxims which have for their reason of existence the common good: and he usually finds associated with him in the same work minds more familiarized than his own with these ideas and operations, whose study it will be to supply reasons to his understanding, and stimulation to his feeling for the general interest. He is made to feel himself one of the public, and whatever is for their benefit to be for his benefit. Where this school of public spirit does not exist, scarcely any sense is entertained that private persons, in no eminent social situation, owe any duties to society, except to obey the laws and submit to the government. There is no unselfish sentiment of identification with the public. Every thought or feeling, either of interest or of duty, is absorbed in the individual and in the family. The man never thinks of any collective interest, of any objects to be pursued jointly with others, but only in competition with them, and in some measure at their expense. A neighbour, not being an ally or an associate, since he is never engaged in any common undertaking for joint benefit, is therefore only a rival. Thus even private morality suffers, while public is actually extinct. Were this the universal and only possible state of things, the utmost aspirations of the law-giver or the moralist could only stretch to making the bulk of the community a flock of sheep innocently nibbling the grass side by side.

From these accumulated considerations it is evident, that the only government which can fully satisfy all the exigencies of the social state, is one in which the whole people participate; that any participation, even in the smallest public function, is useful; that the participation should everywhere be as great as the general degree of improvement of the community will allow; and that nothing less can be ultimately desirable, than the admission of all to a share in the sovereign power of the state. But since all cannot, in a community exceeding a single small town, participate personally in any but some very minor portions of the public business, it follows that the ideal type of a perfect government must be representative.

NOTES

1. Pythagoreans, or followers of the Greek philosopher and mathematician Pythagoras (d. 497 B.C.?), believed in, among other things, the mystical significance of numbers; the Vedas are the earliest Hindu sacred writings.—Eds.
2. Jean Baptiste Colbert (1619–1683), French minister of finance who oversaw improvements in industry and economic infrastructure.—Eds.

10

Town Meetings and Workers' Control

MICHAEL WALZER

To have a say in determining the direction of one's country or community is part of the idea of democracy. But how far should this principle extend? An American political philosopher and self-described "radical democrat," Michael Walzer (1935–) maintains that "what touches all should be decided by all." As he suggests in his fable of "J-town," this principle requires that much of what is considered "private" life in liberal societies ought to be subject to public control. Only socialism is consistent with democracy—or at least with *social democracy.*

Source: Michael Walzer, "Town Meetings and Workers' Control," from *Dissent,* Summer 1978, pp. 325–333.
Copyright © 1978 Dissent. Reprinted by permission of Michael Walzer and *Dissent.*

TOWN MEETINGS AND WORKERS' CONTROL: A STORY FOR SOCIALISTS

Introduction to the Story

There are thirteen arguments for socialism; they have to do with distributive justice, equality, the need for planning, self-respect, fraternity, and so on. But the one that seems to me the easiest and best is a political argument, an extension of the defense of democracy. It has been put forward often over the last one hundred years, but it has never, in this country at least, commanded general acceptance. I suppose no doctrine commands general acceptance that is, as [Thomas] Hobbes wrote, "contrary to any man's right of dominion or to the interest of men that have dominion."[1] And yet there is some sense in which we are all democrats, so I shall start from there, assuming that we have good reasons, and see how far I can go.

The central commitment of socialist politics has often been put in a phrase that must be intuitively appealing to democrats: *the abolition of the power of man over man.* Neither democrats nor socialists begin with an assertion of popular sovereignty. Since they everywhere encounter established sovereigns, authorities, hierarchies, conventional claims to rule, they begin with denials and rejections. They are abolitionists. They aim at abolishing two kinds of authority relations, those in which men and women are directly, and those in which they are indirectly, subject to the arbitrary will of another. I will consider these two separately. Direct subjection suggests the immediacy of bondage; it describes the slave, the serf, the servant, all those who bow before some powerful person, defer to him, obey his every command. Direct subjection is pervasive in the old regime, and it is not missing in the new. One recognizes it in those forms of speech, those bodily postures and motions that connote weakness, inferiority, humility, a certain zeal for service, which we are disinclined to accept as spontaneous or voluntary.

Indirect subjection is not so easy to recognize, for it has to do not with relationships but with systems of relationships, and the systems are invisible. What is at issue here is the right of a single person, acting on his own, for reasons of his own, to make decisions seriously affecting the welfare of his fellowmen, without the agreement of those whom his decisions affect. Now we all make decisions all the time that seriously affect others: when I decide to accept a job, for example, my decision has an immediate impact on the life of the next candidate, who would have received an offer had I declined. But it would be odd to think of him as my subject, and I am certainly not required to seek his agreement before making up my own mind. In every society, however, there are positions of recognized power, offices within some organizational structure, from which decisions of a different sort are made. The best way to characterize these is to say that they are authoritative decisions, for that invites us to inquire as to the source of the authority. And what is crucial in systems of indirect subjection is that the subjects are not the source. Men and women ruled by an absolute monarch are directly subject in that they must obey his commands and indirectly subject in that they must live with the consequences of his political, economic, and military decisions. Clearly, democratic argument must challenge and does challenge both these forms of subjection.

The principle of the second challenge is nicely expressed in an old maxim, a rule of law, I believe, in medieval times, honored regularly in the breach: *what touches all should be decided by all.* It's not every decision affecting others that must be democratically made, but only those affecting everyone. That does not mean everyone in the world; I think we should take it to mean everyone associated in some common enterprise the existence or success of which requires that decisions be made. Thus the medieval maxim was invoked in disputes about authority relations in guilds, churches, towns, and states. No doubt, there are problems with this (and every other) restriction on the reach of the maxim, for decisions made within some particular association are certain to affect not only members, but nonmembers as well—and may affect them seriously indeed, as the example of state decisions and international politics suggests. But since this is a general difficulty for democratic theory, and not a special difficulty for socialists, I am going to put it aside (I'll come back to it briefly later on). My own argument requires only this much: that for any authoritative decision seriously affecting others, there is some subset of those affected who ought to authorize the decision or to make it or approve it themselves. The subset includes, but is not necessarily limited to, those people whose association makes the decision possible or necessary—as the association of Frenchmen, for example, makes possible the French king's decision to go to war or requires him to oppose an armed invasion.

The argument also assumes that the king cannot decide to break up the association (or to cooperate with the invaders) rather than allow its members to join him in decision making. It is not the case that the authorities can seek support for their decisions just anywhere.

...The argument is not dependent upon an original contract; it works whatever stories about the origin and foundation of the common enterprise are accepted by the participants, including stories about great men, godlike acts, vanguard revolutions, and so on.

Now, it is the socialist claim that neither direct nor indirect subjection, neither the arbitrary power of persons nor that of positions has been abolished through the establishment of a democratic state. For the state is not our only common enterprise; nor do the laws of the state constitute the only disciplinary system to which we are subject. The capitalist economy proliferates what are plausibly called private governments. Within capitalist organizations a process of decision making can be marked out, dominated by officials, which has the crucial characteristics of a political regime. The process has outcomes that seriously affect thousands and hundreds of thousands of people, including men and women whose cooperative activity underlies the organization and who are in some sense its members. These outcomes take the form of decisions and rules that can be opposed or ignored by the members only at the risk of penalties. Here are participants who are subjects, officials who act with authority. What is the source of that authority? It clearly does not derive from the participants, else it would not be called private. It derives instead, or it is said to derive, from the ownership of the organization by particular persons. Their claim to govern, to make decisions affecting others, rests on the legal and, what is more important, the moral implications of private property. Socialists argue that this is not a tenable claim, and it is at this point that many democrats part company with them, insisting that economic enterprises are unlike political associations precisely because the former are subject to ownership and the latter are not.

It should be said, however, that in their time democrats also challenged the implications of ownership—as these were understood within the feudal economy. Feudalism, like capitalism, rested on a certain view of property rights, specifically on the view that the ownership of land entitled the owner to exercise direct disciplinary (judicial and police) powers over the men and women who lived on the land and also to make decisions (to go to war with some neighboring landowner, for example) seriously affecting their lives. In the course of many years of political conflict and revolutionary activity, the formal structure of feudal rights was abolished and the disciplinary powers of the feudal lords were socialized. Taxation, law enforcement, conscription: all these ceased to be property rights. In Marxist terms, the state was emancipated from civil society, that is, from the property system. The implications of ownership were redefined so as to exclude certain sorts of decision making that, it was thought, could only be authorized by the political community as a whole. This redefinition establishes the central division along which social life is organized today. On the one side are activities called political; on the other, activities called economic. On both sides, men and women make authoritative decisions affecting others, but the maxim *what touches all should be decided by all* applies only in the realm of politics. Hence socialism has commonly been described as the extension of democratic decision making from the political to the economic realm.

But this description may be misleading, for the two realms do not seem to me at all distinct.... Indeed, the political argument for socialism is strongest insofar as it suggests the radical similarity of decision making in the two realms. What justifies the contemporary version of property rights, we are commonly told, is the entrepreneurial zeal, the risk taking, the inventiveness, the capital investment, through which economic enterprises are founded, sustained, and expanded. Whereas feudal property was founded on armed force and sustained and expanded through the power of the sword (even though it was also traded and inherited), capitalist property rests upon forms of activity that are intrinsically noncoercive. The factory is distinguished from the manor, the disciplinary system of the first is upheld and that of the second condemned, because men and women come willingly to work in the factory, drawn by the wages, working conditions, prospects for the future that the owner offers, which are made possible by his energy and enterprise, while the workers on the manor are serfs, prisoners of their noble lords. All this may well be true; in any case, I will not question it now; it helps us understand why feudalism was not an ideal political or economic arrangement. But it does not draw the line between democratic politics and the capitalist economy, nor does it justify the present authority of owners. For political communities are also created by entrepreneurial energy and enterprise, and it's not implausible to say of cities and towns, if not always of states, that they recruit and hold their citizens by offering them an attractive place to live. Yet ownership is not an acceptable source of governmental authority in cities and towns. If we consider deeply why this is so, we will have to conclude, I think, that it should not be acceptable in companies or factories either. What is necessary is to imagine a man who claims to own a town, to tell a story—it must be a success story—about the life of a political entrepreneur.

The Story

Long ago, when the frontier was still somewhere east of the Great Plains, a young man named J. J. set out to make his fortune. He was bold, adventurous, energetic, and very smart, and he left Boston and New York, even Pittsburgh and Cincinnati behind him. After hardships and excitements not worth mentioning, he staked out a claim to a large and rich piece of land at the bend of a river, one of the smaller western tributaries of the Mississippi. But J. J. was not a farmer. He hated domestic animals, and while he could plow as straight a furrow as anyone in the West, the accomplishment gave him no joy. Soon, he acquired land on the other side of the river and built a ferry, which he ran himself. It was a well-built and well-run ferry. J. J. was a gregarious man, and he entertained his passengers as he took them across; he was warm and funny and full of stories. The enterprise was a success, and after a year or so a few men settled nearby, a storekeeper, a blacksmith, even a preacher, renting the land from J. J. He provided a small lot for a small church and happily watched the settlement grow. When word came of a threatened Indian attack, he organized its defense, bringing in (and paying for) vital supplies from the East. There was an attack of sorts, though only by a small raiding party, and J. J. was in the forefront of the defenders—twelve or fifteen people now, mostly heads of families, who recognized and accepted him as their leader. He would have been the newest of new men in Boston or New York, but in this little settlement, he was the oldest, the richest, the most well-established of the inhabitants.

About this time, J. J. went East to borrow some money. He now had visions of a city, for the river bend was a good location, the ferry was busy, there were new farms on both sides of the river, and the farmers needed supplies, schools, sermons, and company. He got the money from a young banker who was bold, adventurous, energetic, and very smart. Back home, he bought more land, laid out a square, set aside lots for a school and a town hall. Though no one had yet died in the settlement, he provided a cemetery too, sure that people would die and not unhappy about that. Dead bodies lend dignity to the place where they lie; a town with a cemetery has staying power. He incorporated the town in accordance with territorial law and gave it the name he had always had in mind: J-town. The law did not specify any particular form of government, but J. J. again had something in mind. When the town hall was built (at his own expense), he moved in. The settlers were not surprised; nor was there any opposition. J. J. was still a gregarious man; he knew them all, talked to them all, always consulted with them about matters of common interest. As at the time of the Indian raid, his leadership was recognized and accepted. Anyway, they all paid him rent, and it did not seem strange to pay him taxes too—a per-capita levy for the salary of the schoolteacher, the maintenance of public buildings, and other minor expenses. J. J. himself took no salary. His ferry was doing well, and he had begun to transport goods up and down the river. His enterprises expanded as the town grew and, to a considerable extent, the town grew because his enterprises expanded.

Years went by. J. J. prospered, paid off the loan, delighting himself and the Eastern banker. J-town prospered; new settlers arrived every year; there was money in the treasury. The town lines were redrawn. Now there were tax-payers who did not pay rent to J. J., though he still owned most of the town and continued to serve as mayor. When it became necessary to appoint other town officers, he talked to his friends and neighbors and always picked the right person. He had a knack for making decisions, not only decisions that paid off, but ones that pleased people. And if anyone wasn't pleased, he could always move on; J. J. would pat him on the back and talk about the wide Western spaces. He treated criminals the same way. He didn't like locking people up, and he thought it enough of a punishment to have to leave J-town.

J. J. was a natural leader, a man of substance, a man of power. He proved himself again when the flood came, risking his boats on the rapidly rising river in order to evacuate the settlers and their movable possessions, contributing freely to the relief fund. Later on, he went East for a second time to raise money, signing the papers in his own name and bringing home the capital that made it possible to rebuild J-town. The townspeople could hardly imagine another mayor. Nor could J. J.

Life was placid in J-town; time passed quickly. Revivalist preachers came and went; a labor organizer arrived one day and departed the next; the Republican party sent someone to talk to J. J., and the visitor did not find it necessary to talk to anyone else. The dissidence of dissent was absent. Or so it was until J. J., aging now, appointed his son chief of police. Perhaps there had been murmurings before that, but they were scarcely audible. Many of the new settlers did not remember J. J.'s earlier days, did not really believe the stories of his heroic exploits, or—what was worse—did not think the stories mattered. But the town was well run, and they were content not to worry about it; they didn't think of politics as something that was missing from their lives; to all appearances they didn't think about it at all.

Still, the appointment of his son was a political mistake—J. J.'s first. His son wasn't particularly bold, adventurous, energetic, or smart, and everyone in town knew it. A few of the newer inhabitants called a meeting at the Odd Fellow's Lodge (the town hall had no assembly room). Only a small number of people came, but they shouted a lot, worked one another up, formed a citizen's committee, and called another meeting. This time more people came; the speeches were exciting, and the participants went home feeling differently about J-town than they had ever felt before. There was a third meeting, and on the following afternoon a delegation of citizens called on J. J.

No one took notes that afternoon, but what was said was repeated all over town. The citizens told the mayor that he could appoint his son to any position he liked in J's River Haulage, Inc., but the town, they said, was not one of his businesses. Town government was the *public* business, and henceforth the public would have to be brought into it in some regularized manner. What touches all should be decided by all, they said. They demanded that elections be held, and they intimated that they had a candidate for mayor in mind whom they preferred to J. J.

J. J.'s reply was a passionate defense of entrepreneurial rights. What do you mean? he said. *This is my town.* I found this place; I built my ferry here, and other people came because of the ferry. I risked my life against the Indians. I risked my capital to buy this land and raise on it the buildings people needed. Your children are studying, right now, in schools I made possible; your dead are buried on land I gave. When the flood came, I did it all again, giving money, raising money, organizing reconstruction. This town wouldn't exist without me and, what's more, I still own most of it. All of you came here with your eyes open; you knew how this town was run; you knew who made the decisions around here. Don't talk to me about elections....

J. J. had never lacked for words. And everything he said was true. He did not have to make things up, for he was indeed a great man and had done great things. If it were possible to own a town, he certainly deserved to own this one. The citizens insisted, however, that it wasn't possible. J. J. was the founder, not the owner of J-town, they said, and they would happily put up a statue of him in Central Park. (On land I gave you, muttered J. J.) He was entitled to honor and glory, but not to obedience. He was entitled to rent, but they would tax themselves. They did not mean to sound ungrateful, they said; they weren't ungrateful, but political foundation and public service did not give a man the right to tyrannize over others.

How can I be a tyrant, shouted J. J., when it's my own town?

The next weeks were exciting, but the events are not worth mentioning here. The citizens' insurrection was successful. J. J. fell. His son never became chief of police. J. J. withdrew from public life, did not vote in the first town elections, never attended town meetings, turned away from his friends and neighbors. When he died, not long after, the town council commissioned a statue, as the insurgent citizens had promised. The new mayor made a fine speech when the statue was unveiled. J. J., he said, was a heroic figure, a man of the pioneering past, a founding father. The town owed him a profound debt, a spiritual debt, of which the statue could only be a lasting reminder. It was true, the mayor said, that J. J. had occasionally confused business and politics, but, after all, that was a confusion not uncommon in American life.

J. J.'s son had occasion to reflect upon that last remark when the town council, only a few years later, tried to take over the river haulage company. They would have paid him handsomely, had the state supreme court allowed the take-over, but money, they insisted, was all he was entitled to in return for his father's investment. Decisions about whether or not to expand the ferry service, buy new boats, and so on—those could not be made by one man, they said, considering only his private profit. The whole town was a transportation center; all its citizens depended on the haulage company; most of them worked for it. And what touches all, they said, should be decided by all....

Interpretation of the Story

I had originally planned to write about a company town, drawing upon actual historical accounts. The story would then have described how the owners of an economic enterprise created a political community, so to speak, on the side, as a place for their employees to live. Upon reflection, it seemed better to imagine a case where the major entrepreneurial activity was focused on the town itself, so that J. J. would stand in the great tradition of the political founder. He represents the liberal form of that tradition, which is to say, he has no deep convictions about the shape of the town or the moral character of its citizens. He merely wants them to live peaceably and to prosper. But he is clearly comparable, despite that, to the figures celebrated by Machiavelli and Rousseau—Lycurgus, Solon, Romulus[2]—who made or remade the political community. Now, in that tradition, founding or reforming the state generates no right of ownership and none of the subsidiary rights that ownership brings with it in feudal manors or in capitalist factories or companies. Most important, it does not give rise to any sort of disciplinary authority over those who join the new community. That authority belongs to the members, even if they were passive or entirely absent during the period of foundation.

Why are economic associations any different?

Not because of the entrepreneurial vision, energy, inventiveness, and so on, that go into the making of the company: the making of J-town required exactly the same qualities. There are certainly objects in the world that a man can acquire through enterprise and invention. Making them or mixing his labor with them, as John Locke argued, produces at least a presumption of ownership.[3] But it's not the case that *anything* can be acquired that way, and if towns cannot be, there is no reason to think that companies can. These two are much nearer to one another than either is to the land I cultivate, the wood I cut, the chair I build, the book I write—the examples that Locke had in mind. What brings them close together is that both of them involve other people, shared interests, cooperative activity.

Not because of the investment of capital: J. J. invested his own money in J-town without becoming an owner. Nor do men and women who buy municipal bonds come to own the municipality. They acquire no political rights at all. Unless they are already citizens, they cannot even participate in deciding how to spend their own money. They are entitled to a specified rate of interest, and that is their only entitlement. The members of the political community are conceived to have rights of a different sort, simply by virtue of their membership, whether they have invested money in the community or not. There seems no reason not to make the same distinction in economic associations, marking off investors from participants, a just return from authoritative decision making.

Not because men and women join a company voluntarily, with full knowledge of the established structure of authority: the settlers in J-town arrived freely, and the same knowledge was available to them, as J. J. told the citizens' delegation. If I settle in a state founded and ruled by a powerful despot, my knowledge of his despotism does not make the act of settlement into an act of consent. Nor is my prompt departure the only way I can express my opposition to despotic government. That may be the case with a man who joins a monastic order requiring strict and unquestioning obedience. Here the new member seems to be choosing a way of life, and his choice entails a particular disciplinary rule. We would not be paying him proper respect if we denied the efficacy of his choice; its purpose and its moral effect are precisely to authorize his superior; he can't withdraw that authority without himself withdrawing from the common life it makes possible.

But that is not true of a man who joins a company or who comes to work in a factory. In these associations, the common life does not require unquestioning obedience, and we respect the new member only if we assume that he does not seek subjection. Of course, he encounters supervisors, foremen, company police, as he knew he would, and it may be that the success of the economic enterprise requires his obedience, just as the success of the political association requires that citizens obey public officials. But in neither case do we want to say (what we might say to the novice monk): if you don't like these officials and the orders they give, you can always leave. It is important that there be options short of leaving, connected with the appointment of the officials and the making of the rules they enforce. We see this clearly in the case of towns and also, curiously, in the case of labor unions. In the United States today, the democratic rights of union members are legally protected. But the rights of company employees are only indirectly protected insofar as they are unionized (and insofar as their union has won some share in company decision making).[4]

Entrepreneurial vision, capital investment, the freedom to join or not to join: none of these satisfactorily distinguishes economic from political associations. None of them accounts for, let alone justifies, the privacy of a private government.

But there are two differences between towns and companies that I have not yet considered. First of all, a town is an association of residents; a company is an association of workers, who live somewhere else. Perhaps the maxim, *what touches all should be decided by all,* only applies to residential communities. Monasteries and unions are immediate counterexamples, monasteries because they are residential communities to which the maxim does not apply, unions because they are nonresidential communities to which it does apply. Nevertheless, it is true that ordinary democrats have generally tried to organize people where they live, socialists where they work (though not only there), and some distinction might be drawn along these lines. The self-government of residents, it might be said, is more obvious and important than that of workers. Men and women must collectively control the place where they live in order to be safe in their own homes.

There is certainly no other place where it is so important to be safe. Hence another ancient maxim: *a man's home is his castle.* I will assume that this maxim expresses a genuine moral imperative. What does it require? Not self-government, but rather the protection of a private sphere, a piece of nonpolitical space for withdrawal, rest, secrecy, and solitude. As a feudal baron retired to his castle to brood over public slights, so I retire to my home. But the political community is not a collection of brooding places, or not only that. It is a common enterprise, a public place where we are seen and heard by others, where we quarrel over the public interest, where we sometimes work together. That is why the meetings in J-town were so exciting. They represented the discovery or creation of a local republic, a public thing, which by its very nature had to be shared once it was known to exist. And in this sense, an economic enterprise seems to be very like a town, even though, or in part because, it is so unlike a home. It is not a place of withdrawal, but of cooperative activity. It is not a place that anyone needs to own in order to safeguard his independence and solitude. No one ever thought of saying, a man's factory is his castle. The moral independence of the men and women who work in a factory requires shared decision making and not the protection of a private sphere. Surely we grant that point whenever we require union democracy, and having done that, there seems no principled reason to stop short of company democracy.

But let's think about stopping short, exactly as we currently do. Imagine that the inhabitants of J-town, instead of calling for elections, had organized a citizens' union and bargained collectively with J. J. and his heirs. It is interesting to speculate on the ranges of issues they might have bargained about. Which matters would lie beyond their reach, once they had conceded the issue of ownership? Presumably, they would not have had much to say if J. J. had decided to relocate the town (since it was "his" town). But they could have bargained in detail about living conditions within it, about zoning laws, traffic control, sewage disposal, and so on. They could not have vetoed his choice for chief of police, but it is possible to imagine grievance machinery that would function somewhat like a civilian board of review. The picture is not entirely unattractive, but it is not what we mean by democracy or, at least, it is not all that we mean. Particular groups of city employees do form unions and negotiate with the mayor, but their members also vote for the mayor with whom they negotiate. Members of pressure groups participate in the same dual way, though the arrangements are less formal. They bargain and they vote, acting simultaneously as men and women with particular interests and as men and women with general interests. That seems the right arrangement for economic enterprises also, whose participants are concerned both with their immediate returns and with the well-being of the enterprise as a whole.

The second difference between towns and companies follows from the separation of residence and work. The citizens of a town are also the consumers of the goods and services the town provides—and they are, except for occasional visitors, the only consumers of those goods and services. But the "citizens" of a company are producers of goods and services; they are only sometimes consumers, and they are never the only consumers. Hence there are large numbers of other people, outside the company, who have a direct and material interest in what goes on inside. What should their role be in company decision making? The question is often raised in the literature on workers' control, and it is variously answered. Here I don't want to answer it again, only to insist that the sorts of arrangements required in a fully developed industrial democracy are not all that different from those required in a political democracy. For we don't, after all, grant absolute authority to town governments, even over the goods and services they produce for internal consumption. We enmesh our towns in a federal structure, and we regulate what they can and cannot do in areas like education, criminal justice, environmental use, and so on. No doubt, companies would be similarly enmeshed. In a developed economy, as in a developed polity, different decisions are made by different groups of people at different levels. The division of power in both these cases is only partly a matter of principle; it is also a matter of circumstance and expediency.

The case is similar with the particular constitutional arrangements necessary within companies and factories. There will, of course, be many difficulties in working these out; there will be false starts and failed experiments, as there have been in the previous history of political democracy. Nor should we expect a single resolution of all problems. Proportional representation, single member constituencies, mandated and independent representatives, bicameral and unicameral legislatures, city managers, regulatory commissions, public corporations—the common business is done and should continue to be done in many ways. What is important is that it be known to be common and that our participation in it be recognized as a matter of right.

Today, there are many men and women who preside over enterprises in which hundreds and thousands of their fellow citizens are involved, who make decisions that shape the lives of their fellows, and who defend and justify themselves exactly as J. J. did. I own this place, they say, I built this factory, I founded this company, I risked my capital, I make the decisions around here. It has been my purpose to argue that people who speak this way are wrong. They misunderstand the prerogatives of foundation and investment. They claim an authority to which they have no right. It has not been my purpose, however, to deny the significance of entrepreneurial activity. In both towns and companies one looks for energetic people, willing to innovate and take risks. It would be foolish to create a system that did not bring them forward. They are of no use to us if they just brood in their castles.

On the other hand, nothing they do or can do gives them a right to rule over others—unless they win the agreement of the others. This means that at a certain point in the development of an enterprise, it must pass out of entrepreneurial control. Its founders have created, or they have led other men and women in creating, a public thing, which must now be run in some public way. It is often said that economic entrepreneurs will not come forward if they cannot hope to own the companies they make. The best response is to point to the other side of that all-important but entirely conventional dividing line: we do not lack for political entrepreneurs, though they cannot hope to own the state. Possession is not the goal of public life, but that does not mean that there are not attractive and even compelling goals. For one thing, we can go on building statues of worthy men and women—the founders but not the owners of our common wealth.

NOTES

1. *Leviathan*, Part I, chap. 11.
2. Lycurgus and Solon were the legendary "legislators" who gave the Greek city-states Sparta and Athens, respectively, their fundamental laws; Romulus was the legendary founder, with his brother Remus, of Rome.—Eds.
3. The *Second Treatise of Government,* chap. 5, para. 27 [included in selection 13 of this volume.—Eds.]
4. There are other sorts of organizations that raise more difficult problems. What about bureaucracies, for example, or schools? Or consider an example that Marx used (in *Capital,* vol. 3) to illustrate the nature of authority in a Communist factory: cooperative labor requires, he wrote, "one commanding will," and he compared this will to that of an orchestra conductor. A strange comparison, for conductors have historically been tyrannical figures. Should their will be commanding? Perhaps it should, but I doubt that Marx's comparison is a good one, for orchestras must express a single interpretation of the music they play, while patterns of work in a factory are more readily negotiated. The political rights of individuals are relative to the character of the activities in which they voluntarily engage. But this general principle needs to be worked out in detail.

11

Democracy and the Power of Education

DANIELLE ALLEN

On September 20, 2001—just nine days after the terrorist attacks that damaged the Pentagon, destroyed the World Trade Center in New York, and killed nearly 3,000 people—Danielle Allen delivered the following lecture to the entering first-year class at the University of Chicago, where she is a professor of classical languages and literature, and political science. By connecting the political ideas of Thucydides, Plato, and other ancient thinkers to the challenges facing democracies in the aftermath of 9/11, Allen makes a case for "the power of education" as a vital force in the life of any democracy.

Source: Danielle Allen, "The Power of Education." Reprinted by permission of the author.

Last week for the first time in my life I discovered the full power of education. This sounds ridiculous coming from somebody who has herself never once in her life left school, but it's true. The aims of education therefore interest me less today than just this, the *power* of education. I present this discovery to you not modestly as a small side-effect of last week's events, nor as my own personal story of difficult times, but as a most vital discovery, equally significant for each of us individually and also for our larger democratic community. Education can ward off the paralysis of mind that is the worst danger for democratic citizens. Let me tell you what happened.

On Monday, September 10th, I had given a guest lecture about ancient Athenian democracy at the University of Wisconsin in Madison and I was scheduled to speak midday on Tuesday to my host's class on Thucydides, the ancient Greek historian who wrote *The History of the Peloponnesian War*—a book many of you will read before you leave Chicago. My fellow guest lecturer, who as it happens was also my own former undergraduate advisor, was to join me in this discussion. Tuesday was a beautiful early fall day in Madison—crisp, cool, commanding blue skies. This class was going to be a special pleasure because I would again enter conversations with my old teacher and now friend.

But by 10:12 A.M. I know pretty much what has happened in New York and Washington. From where I stand on the street, listening to a frustratingly insufficient, tinny radio, I turn back to my original path toward the Wisconsin Classics department. I go a few steps, then pause and return to the radio. A few moments more and I walk away again, only to go back to the radio. A few moments more and I repeat my departure and return. Turn and turn and turn about. I go nowhere. There is a Greek word for such behavior, this indecision, and for inaction arising from inefficiency of motion. It is *stasis*. Do you know it? Lately it has settled into my head like a swarm of bees.

The Oxford English Dictionary defines *stasis* as "a stagnation or stoppage of the circulation of any of the fluids of the body, esp. of the blood in some part of the blood-vessels." The word means paralysis and lack of motion. But the original Greek contains a secret that this OED entry does not tell. In Greek, *stasis* also carried the more common meaning of "civil war." *Stasis* meant not only paralysis but also total conflict, chaos, and confusion. How can the same word have such seemingly disjunctive definitions, meaning motionlessness on the one hand and an excess of motion on the other? Well, the Greeks knew that in a city-state when civil war was at its height, with two parties evenly matched, standing off against one another, the result is not that everything happens but that nothing happens; the very possibility of action is undone by extensive conflict.

Stasis comes to mean stagnation, inaction, and paralysis because it refers to the confusion and battling that undo the human ability to analyze, judge, and act. Plato was the philosopher who first applied this idea to the human *psyche*. In the *Republic* he argues that when our desires, our anger, and our reason are in conflict, we fall into such a state of confusion that action is impossible. He called this confusion "civil war" in the soul. Turning and returning and turning back again, my mind not working, I had fallen into *stasis*.

At least, I wasn't alone. You will remember, as I do, that in the first two days of the television, radio, and newspaper coverage of that Tuesday's events, countless people kept using the same limited vocabulary to describe their feelings: events were "unbelievable," "incredible," and "mind-numbing." One woman described herself as in a state of utter incomprehension. Everywhere people were saying that they found themselves unable to think. Minds were paralyzed, action brought to a standstill. Our inability to articulate anything beyond that was staggering. Over and over, the testimony was of *stasis* or paralysis.

As I walked away from the radio that morning to meet my Madison host and my former teacher, I believed I could not talk to the Thucydides class. A bright still pool had settled in my head; I had nothing to say. Sensibly, though, the University had decided to stay open to keep people from panicking, and my mentor, though visibly shaken, rose to the occasion. "If we really believe," he said, "that studying these old books is of any use, then now is surely the time to test that proposition. And if there is a book with which to test the proposition, it is surely Thucydides' *History of the Peloponnesian War*. After all, it's mostly about what happens to democracies in times of crisis." Thucydides' history is a dense, tangled, and difficult account of the war between ancient and democratic Athens and its highly militarized enemy Sparta. "And yes," I thought, "it is about what happens to democracy in times of crisis." I sat up.

The story of the Peloponnesian War may already be familiar to you. It begins with the early history of Athens itself. The transformation to democracy got underway in roughly 590 B.C.E. when the legislator Solon decreed that Athenians could no longer be sold into slavery to pay off their debts; that assured a free citizenry. Roughly eighty years, or three generations later, in 508 and 507 B.C.E., a quick and populist revolution finally democratized the city for good. Afterward the city was run almost entirely by citizens assigned to key offices through a lottery system; most citizens would have held office sometime or other.

Then democracy grew into empire. When the vast Persian Empire to the east attacked Greece, Athens together with Sparta fended off the threat and preserved Greek independence. Athens' pre-eminent role in this conflict set it at the forefront of Greek politics, giving it the opportunity to develop into an imperialist power. The Athenians seized the moment hungrily, developing the largest navy, greatest wealth, and farthest-reaching influence in the Greek world. As the navy grew, the city became more secure, then wealthier; as wealth increased, the navy grew stronger.

Round and round that cycle went: from security to wealth to strength to security. And as the city flourished, it also grew flashier, erecting great monuments and inviting the world to visit. One of the city's leading politicians, Pericles, would eventually describe Athens as the school of Hellas (or all Greece) and argue that "we throw our city open to all the world and we never by exclusion-acts debar anyone from learning or seeing anything which an enemy might profit by observing...; for we place our dependence not so much upon prearranged devices to deceive as upon the courage which springs from our own souls when we are called to action" (Book 2, ch. 39). Athens' very openness, he argued, had produced far greater human achievements than other regimes had seen. Its success grew from its willingness to trust that the strength of collective action could overcome any vulnerability deriving from the openness of its political debate and the latitude of its laws. The allegiance inspired by this openness would be the city's greatest strength. Indeed, all around the Greek world people had generally begun to think that there was something special about democracy that made it stronger and more successful than other political systems. After all, it did seem just to keep on growing.

But the fact of Athens' remarkable growth also made the rest of Greece nervous. Finally, in an atmosphere of general jitteriness, small conflicts among the allies of both Athens and Sparta pulled the two much larger cities into war with each other. That war lasted 27 years, from 431 to 404 B.C.E., attended by disease, famine, and massive casualties.

Worse, though, than all the physical disasters was what became of human relations during the war. In city after city, people took advantage of the confusions of wartime to prosecute old grudges and abuse one another; they abandoned traditional loyalties and became deceitful; they ignored the requirements and aspirations of legality; trust dissolved. In city after city, factional strife arose, and in two of the worst cases, Epidamnus and Corcyra, the cities eventually imploded in civil war. Thucydides' central theme is *stasis* of the worst kind: civil war, chaos, and confusion. As his account of the war progresses, and one sees one city after another caving beneath its pressures, one begins to wonder: what will happen to Athens, to the democracy, in the midst of all this mess? What will happen to the Athenians, who depend on collective and collaborative decision-making, and open public debate, when they are faced with such crises? When the world has become so uncertain, what will happen to the people who believe that a citizenry confident in its rights is always more loyal, and so stronger, than one subject to police scrutiny? Will Athenian resilience, tremendous in peace and prosperity, find ways to reckon with the stress of war? This resilience had always derived from citizens' willingness to trust their futures to one another's hands. What would happen to that trust now?

Thucydides was a critic of democracy and it is tempting to believe that his whole narrative is leading to the argument that democracy, too, would crack, descending into *stasis* and not finding a way out. Indeed, the Peloponnesian War as a whole does end with civil war in Athens. In 404–3 an oligarchic faction, with Spartan help, takes over the city. But Thucydides does not write about this civil war in Athens. Although he saw the war end, and early in his history (2.65) mentions its end and the *stasis* of 404, his text is incomplete, stopping short a few years before war's end. Why didn't he finish the story? Is it because the democrats did in fact recover from *stasis* despite Thucydides' hints that they wouldn't? Although the city broke down in 404, a year later the democrats were able to overthrow the oligarchs and re-establish democracy, democratic legality, and the system of citizenly rights on which they had previously depended. How did the democrats manage to maintain their expertise at being democratic citizens even when stressful events led too many people to abandon their democratic commitments?

For an hour, in that Wisconsin classroom, we wandered off to Greece, to the Peloponnese, where the dry heat of the summer fills the air with the scent of all the spices growing in the landscape, where temples, exposed to the elements on every promontory, provide the nervous traveler with reference points, where the life is tied to the land and the olives, not the sea and the fish. Today I am gone wandering again, this time with you. Are you with me? Can you imagine wooden ships hugging the shore or cutting out, daringly, straight across the sea, to the craggy volcanic masses of the island city-states? Are you beginning to wonder what happened to Athens when it was at war with Sparta? In Madison we wondered and we also began asking more general questions like these: What are the strains on collaborative, collective, democratic decision-making that are likely to arise in democracies in times of crisis? Why will democratic citizens, in crisis, come to see their freedoms as luxuries rather than as basic necessities and the true source of their strength? Of what does democratic resilience consist? Are you also entertaining these questions? For an hour in Madison we wandered away from ourselves, and yet we also, with our questions about Athens and Sparta, talked for the whole hour about what had just happened to us in the United States.

I had entered that classroom bereft of thought. But in the midst of my paralysis, I began to question again. In the midst of my confusion, I began to think. Despite my grief, my mind was not numb. For an hour, by discussing Thucydides, a small group of about sixteen of us escaped paralysis; in fact, I think, we put it behind us. We began to figure out what questions were relevant to understanding our present situation. Mind you, we did not once mention New York, Washington, hijackers, or incomprehensibility, for talking about Athens and Sparta, we found the problems of crisis in fact quite comprehensible. The distance to which the text took us was our salvation. If you now, this afternoon, have also followed me to Greece and into these questions about Athens, then the power of education is working on you. You are (I hope) being led out of yourself and into contemplation. This is something you should feel in your being as it happens, a sense of release, of slipping a trap, of anticipation; you should feel the glancing breezes of the future.

What good were ancient books on a day like Tuesday, September 11th? Thucydides, in years probably worse than our own, managed to ask questions. Holding events at arm's length, he thought and wrote. He thus made art, and it does us, its readers, good in giving us room to reflect. These days we often praise immediacy, the lived experience as the richest source of knowledge and authenticity, but by turning to a text from a distant time and place, those of us in that classroom were able to step outside ourselves, outside the immediacy of pain and confusion, outside the stagnation of our own minds. Applying our minds to problems that were not our own, we gently roused our minds to life. We spent an hour talking about the very subject that was most important to all of us but without disabling our minds by attending to the immediacy of grief.

Here was the power of education: it catapulted our minds outside of this particular place and moment, and its horrors, and thank god for that, because the flight gave us back our minds. No longer did we have to use the words "mind-numbing" or "incomprehensible" to describe the effect of events on us, for we could comprehend. Friendly conversation delivered us from *stasis*. Education restored our sense of agency.

I want to turn now to the political point of this account of education. I have throughout been suggesting that what we do in the classroom is like what we do in democracy. *Citizenship is the struggle, carried out through conversation, to achieve accounts of the world that accord with norms of friendship and provide grounds for action.* We have this conversation in the classroom; we have it in the world. I have also been suggesting that democracy, more than any other type of regime, needs its citizens to have strong, resilient habits of reflection. Let me explain why.

Plato, as I'm sure you know, argued in his book the *Republic* that the best government would be one in which philosopher-kings ruled everything and there were no democratic institutions. He, too, grew up in trying times. He was 16 when civil war first shook Athens, 23 when the oligarchs took over, and 28 when his favorite teacher Socrates was executed. Although he wrote the *Republic* in times far more settled and secure than those of his adolescence, he nonetheless believed that democracy could not in fact solve some of the basic problems of political life. The crucial argument of the *Republic* is that politics is the business of experts. Ordinary people, he maintained, should not pretend to have the intellectual resources necessary to weigh in on matters of state. By opposing the fundamental tenets of democracy, Plato also makes them clear: democracy is based on the idea that politics *is* the business of everybody, not of experts or, at any rate, not of experts alone. Against Plato, democratic citizens must argue that an expertise in collective decision-making can indeed be spread throughout the citizenry, that ordinary people can, by talking together, reason and judge well. Democratic life therefore fundamentally depends on citizens' ability to maintain their trust and confidence in their own status and that of their fellow citizens as reflective beings. Political crises are dangerous for democracy, as Thucydides suggests, precisely because they undermine that confidence.

In times of crisis, ordinary citizens, confused and disoriented, settling into paralysis, can come to believe that, as Plato had argued, they are not up to the job of making difficult decisions. In hard times, democratic citizens may become more willing to hand over the business of politics to experts and to abandon the institutional frameworks, the rights and liberties, that secure their position as participants in the political process. The danger of intellectual paralysis in the face of chaos is finally that it undermines the first premise of democracy: namely, that ordinary citizens will *always* be ready to think. To ward off the ill effects of confusion, then, democratic citizens must know in moments of crisis how to preserve their status as reflective beings. They must also know how to preserve their expertise in democratic conversation and decision-making. Finally, they must also be able to preserve their fellow citizens' commitment to democratic processes of judgment and action.

As we talked about Thucydides, we had restored to us our confidence in the status of democratic citizens, ordinary people, as reflective beings, and in the power of friendly collaborative conversation to enable intellectual progress. As we began to think again, we enacted the project of democracy, affirming that citizens, ordinary citizens, can maintain confidence in their own ability to judge even in the worst of times. *Stasis,* we realized—not plague, famine, and disaster, but chaos, confusion, and paralysis of thought—is the greatest threat to democracy. Democratic resilience consists of an ability to resist such intellectual *stasis,* just as we were doing with our conversation. Above all else, therefore, a democratic education must give citizens enduring habits of reflection and practices of collective conversation hardy enough to generate subtle thought even when individuals, trying to think on their own, feel overcome. That day, speaking together, questioning collaboratively, we could comprehend.

Let me conclude by reporting what we in that classroom comprehended. Although many around us were using the word "incomprehensible" to describe what happened, we realized that once we began to ask questions again, we could sort out what was and what wasn't comprehensible in the day's events. We could, actually, quite easily comprehend the physical processes by which the towers were destroyed, and also the loss of life—it was emotionally staggering, it deserves respectful silence—but we could grasp it. We also understood that what had been attacked was not random individuals or buildings but the well-springs of principle of our political system. These things we understood without difficulty. What we comprehended less well, however, was our vulnerability. That was the first point of incomprehension: how had we, given our strength, failed to secure ourselves? Second, we could not comprehend how that failure could be remedied. These two questions we plucked delicately, once we began to think again, out of the mass the media was calling incomprehension. And when the state of incomprehension is reduced to those two questions—how did we fail and how might we remedy the failure—it is less daunting.

But our conversation about Thucydides also rescued a third most vital question. Under pressure, democratic citizens are quick to believe that their own democratic procedures—their openness, their civil liberties, their commitment to educating anybody and everybody, in short, democratic magnanimity—are part of what have made them vulnerable. The third and fundamental question is how we can secure ourselves without undoing that which, though it does to some degree make us vulnerable, is also our greatest source of strength.

Why do these principles of freedom and equality, of trusting rather than policing fellow citizens, of educating anybody and everybody, make us strong? Let me answer with a fable. Imagine you are about to go on a journey through desert and jungle and over mountains and across grassy plains; there will be typhoons and droughts and earthquakes and plagues. And as you prepare to go you are presented with a choice: you may go with one of two parties preparing to make the journey. One party is known to be free and democratic, to let individuals speak about what the group should do, to be straightforward and frank about its intentions, and to develop norms of trust and openness. The other party is known to rely on deceit to carry out its plans. With which would you prefer to travel? In the final analysis, the party that commits itself to frank openness will always have vastly more friends than the other, and vastly more consent and freely given allegiance to support it. The deceitful party will eventually find itself alone, and so too weak to accomplish its aspirations. A democracy is not weak for opening itself to the world, nor for allowing its citizens great liberties. To the contrary, it is not merely that openness and rights make us who we are as democrats; they also make us strong, for they alone inspire the consent, allegiance, and commitment on which democratic power rests. Democratic authority rests on the state's securing a way of life that we are glad to share, and on nothing else.

As, in the coming days, we consider these issues of openness and frankness and their value, we should remember the first sentence of the Declaration of Independence: "When in the Course of human events, it becomes necessary for one people to dissolve the political bands, which have connected them with another, and to assume among the powers of the earth, the separate and equal station to which the Laws of Nature and of Nature's God entitle them, *a decent respect to the opinions of mankind requires that they should declare the causes which impel them to the separation.*" Those revolutionaries assigned themselves the task of proving their arguments by, in their words, letting "facts be submitted to a candid world." Their straightforward frankness was itself radical. The author of this document understood that a commitment to open argument, frank declarations of intent, and free discussion inspires powerful allegiance, loyalty, trust, and friendship. To destroy trust and friendship, and one's status as a worthy friend, by turning to deceit, guardedness, or the restriction of freedoms, is to undo the very sources of strength that are the most remarkable democratic invention.

In the university, too, we declare reasons. Accordingly, I now welcome you to a place where habits of reflection and argument are cultivated, where frankness in accord with friendship is the guiding norm. And I ask you to see your years here as not only an educational but also a democratic experience. As you speak with your fellow students, developing each of you a strong confidence in your own ability to think, talk, and judge as well as a confidence in the ability of others to do so with you, you practice citizenship. Understand that the intellectual progress you will make here is the product of freedom and a culture of openness. Come to feel the strength that exists in the friendships you will develop in this arena of openness. Understand that their rare strength, too, grows out of frankness and fairness. Finally, I charge you as you now undertake your own education, commit yourselves to warding off *stasis.* Commit yourselves to warding off the dangers that follow from intellectual paralysis among your fellow citizens. Develop methods of reasoning so that in moments of confusion you can, like my own teacher, lead yourself and others back into thinking. Do not let the current moment undermine your confidence in and commitment to democratic practices. No more allow confusion and disorientation to lead you to believe that democratic practices can be sacrificed without also sacrificing democracy. Restore your confidence in democratic forms of interaction—in openness and trust—by practicing them in the classroom. There restore your confidence in friendliness as a source of intelligence and strength.

PART THREE

Liberalism

Like "liberty," the word "liberal" is derived from the Latin *liber*, meaning "free." Liberals see themselves as champions of individual liberty who work to create or preserve an open and tolerant society—a society whose members are free to pursue their own ideas and interests with as little interference as possible. This has been their project since liberalism began as a reaction against two features of medieval society in Europe: religious conformity and ascribed status.

Religious conformity was taken for granted in a society in which the church and the state were supposed to be partners in the defense of "Christendom." Indeed, throughout the Middle Ages there was no clear distinction between church and state. The Christian Church saw its mission as saving souls for the kingdom of God, which could best be done by teaching and upholding orthodoxy, or "correct belief." Those who took an unorthodox view of Christianity—or rejected it altogether—thus threatened the church's attempts to do what it saw as the will of God. To counter this threat, the church called on the kings, princes, and other rulers of Christendom to use their power to enforce conformity to the church's doctrines.

The other feature of medieval society against which liberalism reacted was ascribed status—the view that a person's social standing rested not on achievement but on the status of his or her parents. One was simply born a nobleman, a free commoner, or a serf—and that, with few exceptions, was all there was to it. People may have been equal in the eyes of God, as the church taught, but men and women of different social ranks were not equals on God's earth or in man's state.

Against this society rooted in ascribed status and religious conformity, liberalism emerged as the first distinctive political ideology. Yet this liberal reaction did not take form until a series of social, economic, and cultural crises shook the medieval order to its foundations. Many of these changes were directly related to the outburst of creativity in the fourteenth and fifteenth centuries known as the Renaissance. Perhaps the most important impetus to the rise of liberalism was the Protestant Reformation of the sixteenth century. When Martin Luther (1483–1546) and other reformers taught that salvation comes through faith alone, they encouraged people to value individual conscience more than the preservation of unity and orthodoxy. Without intending to do so, they prepared the way for liberalism. The step from individual conscience to individual liberty was still radical for the time, but it was a step that liberals began to take in the seventeenth and eighteenth centuries.

The first book of philosophical significance to bear the distinctive stamp of liberalism was Thomas Hobbes's *Leviathan* (1651). All individuals are equal, Hobbes said. Everyone has a natural right to be free, and no one has the right to rule another without that person's consent. From these liberal premises, however, Hobbes reached the distinctly illiberal conclusion that people, for the sake of their security, must voluntarily grant absolute power over themselves to a sovereign ruler.

John Locke (1632–1704) and later writers used similar arguments to reach very different conclusions. Locke argued for a measure of religious liberty in his *Letter Concerning Toleration* (1689), and in the *Second Treatise of Government* he defended the right of the people to overthrow any government that does not protect their natural rights to life, liberty, and property. The arguments he advanced—the natural equality of men, natural rights, government founded on the consent of the governed—were invoked throughout the eighteenth century. They proved particularly attractive to revolutionaries in the American colonies and in France, where they found lasting expression in the American Declaration of Independence (1776) and the French Declaration of the Rights of Man and of Citizens (1789).

In their efforts to remove obstacles to individual liberty, many liberals argued that economic exchanges are a private matter between persons who ought to be free from government regulation. In France, a group of thinkers called the Physiocrats captured this view in the phrase *laissez faire, laissez passer*—"let it be, leave it alone." This is the core idea of capitalism, which found its most influential defense in Adam Smith's *Wealth of Nations* (1776). Smith argued that an economic policy that would allow individuals to compete freely in the marketplace would be not only the most efficient but also the fairest policy, because it gives everyone an equal opportunity to compete.

Throughout the eighteenth century, then, liberalism was a revolutionary doctrine that reshaped the religious, political, social, and economic relations of people in Europe and North America. In the nineteenth century, liberalism began to take new directions. In particular, the liberal attitude toward democracy and government shifted in the course of the 1800s. Whereas earlier liberals had spoken the language of equality, liberals in the nineteenth century went further and called for expansions of voting rights; and, whereas earlier liberals regarded government as, in Thomas Paine's words, "a necessary evil," some liberals in the nineteenth century came to see it as a necessary ally in the struggle to promote individual liberty. In both cases, John Stuart Mill (1806–1873) played a vital part.

An early supporter of women's rights, Mill argued that literate adults should have the right to vote. Yet he believed that it would be foolish to entrust the ignorant and uninformed with an equal voice in public decisions. Almost every person should have a vote, he concluded, but those with higher levels of education should have two, three, or more. This ambivalence toward democracy follows from Mill's fear of the "tyranny of the majority." Now that government is responsible to the people, he said in *On Liberty* (1859), the majority of voters could conceivably use the government to deny liberty to those whose views they find disagreeable or distasteful. More directly, the "moral coercion of public opinion" can and does stifle freedom of thought and action by making a social outcast of anyone who does not conform to social customs and beliefs. Mill's argument against this new tyranny rests on the claim that not only individuals but society as a whole will benefit if people are encouraged to act and think freely. Progress is possible only where there is open competition among different ideas, opinions, and beliefs—a marketplace of ideas.

With its distinction between private and public matters and its suggestion that individual liberty must be protected from interference by government and society, Mill's defense of liberty took a form familiar to earlier liberals. There was another dimension to Mill's view, however, that marked a shift in many liberals' attitude toward government. Freedom, as Mill conceived it, is largely a matter of being free to develop one's own individual potential. In some of Mill's later work, and especially in the writings of T. H. Green (1836–1882), this conception of freedom suggested that government could and should be something more than a night watchman protecting the life, liberty, and property of its citizens. Instead, government should promote the welfare of its people—and should do so in the name of individual liberty. Only in this way could people overcome some of the obstacles—for example, poverty, illness, ignorance, and prejudice—that prevented them from being truly free.

This way of thinking about government led to a split between those who clung to the older views—the neoclassical liberals—and those who followed Green along the path of "welfare" or "reform" liberalism. In the late 1800s, the most prominent version of neoclassical liberalism was the Social Darwinism of such writers as Herbert Spencer (1820–1903) and William Graham Sumner (1840–1910). As the franchise expanded to include the working class and the welfare state began to emerge, however, neoclassical liberalism began to fade. Welfare liberalism gradually came to be known simply as liberalism.

Yet neoclassical liberalism never entirely disappeared. After President Franklin Delano Roosevelt's New Deal (1933–1944) put welfare liberalism into practice in the United States, some economists (e.g., Friedrich Hayek [1899–1992] and Milton Friedman [1912–]) and at least one novelist, Ayn Rand (1905–1982), reasserted the case against active government and the welfare state in their writings. Their ideas and arguments helped to inspire the creation of the Libertarian party, which advocates what one libertarian—the Harvard philosopher Robert Nozick (1938–2002)—called "the minimal state." Some libertarians, such as Murray Rothbard (1926–1995), have even argued for anarchism on the grounds that government is an entirely *un*necessary evil.

So the debate within liberalism that began over one hundred years ago continues today. Both groups agree on the end they want to achieve—an open and tolerant society in which every person has an opportunity to live as freely as possible. But what are the best means to achieve this end? Is government the chief obstacle to individual liberty, as the neoclassical liberals claim, or an aid and an ally that is useful in removing other barriers to freedom, as the welfare liberals insist? On this point, welfare and neoclassical liberals continue to disagree, with no resolution in sight. Indeed, the debate has grown more complicated in recent years with the emergence of *communitarians*, who complain that welfare and neoclassical liberals both pay too little attention to what individuals owe to their communities. Liberals are right to stress the importance of individual liberty, according to Philip Selznick (1919–) and other communitarians, but they must also recognize that individuals have a duty to help preserve the communities that make individual liberty possible.

12

The State of Nature and the Basis of Obligation

THOMAS HOBBES

Thomas Hobbes (1588–1679) might best be described as a pre-liberal, or perhaps a proto-liberal, thinker. The main features of liberalism are to be found in his *Leviathan* (1651), particularly in the imaginary "state of nature," but his conclusions are seldom considered liberal. In the following excerpts from *Leviathan*, Hobbes invited his readers to imagine a world without laws, police, courts, and prisons—a world of "perfect" liberty and equality—and then went on to show "scientifically" that such a world would be nothing less than a "war of every man against every man." Thus, he concluded, rational, self-interested people would have every reason to enter into a "social contract" in which they put themselves under the unlimited authority of a sovereign ruler.

Source: The English Works of Thomas Hobbes of Malmesbury, vol. 3, ed. Sir William Molesworth (London: John Bohm, 1839), pp. 110–130. The editors have modernized the spelling of some words.

OF THE NATURAL CONDITION OF MANKIND AS CONCERNING THEIR FELICITY AND MISERY

(From *Leviathan,* Chapter 13)

Nature has made men so equal, in the faculties of the body, and mind; as that though there be found one man sometimes manifestly stronger in body, or of quicker mind than another; yet when all is reckoned together, the difference between man, and man, is not so considerable, as that one man can thereupon claim to himself any benefit, to which another may not pretend, as well as he. For as to the strength of body, the weakest has strength enough to kill the strongest, either by secret machination, or by confederacy with others, that are in the same danger with himself.

And as to the faculties of the mind, setting aside the arts grounded upon words, and especially that skill of proceeding upon general, and infallible rules, called science; which very few have, and but in few things; as being not a native faculty, born with us; nor attained, as prudence, while we look after somewhat else, I find yet a greater equality amongst men, than that of strength. For prudence, is but experience; which equal time, equally bestows on all men, in those things they equally apply themselves unto. That which may perhaps make such equality incredible, is but a vain conceit of one's own wisdom, which almost all men think they have in a greater degree, than the vulgar; that is, than all men but themselves, and a few others, whom by fame, or for concurring with themselves, they approve. For such is the nature of men, that howsoever they may acknowledge many others to be more witty, or more eloquent, or more learned; yet they will hardly believe there be many so wise as themselves; for they see their own wit at hand, and other men's at a distance. But this proves rather that men are in that point equal, than unequal. For there is not ordinarily a greater sign of the equal distribution of any thing, than that every man is contented with his share.

From this equality of ability, arises equality of hope in the attaining of our ends. And therefore if any two men desire the same thing, which nevertheless they cannot both enjoy, they become enemies; and in the way to their end, which is principally their own conservation, and sometimes their delectation only, endeavour to destroy, or subdue one another. And from hence it comes to pass, that where an invader has no more to fear, than another man's single power; if one plant, sow, build, or possess a convenient seat, others may probably be expected to come prepared with forces united, to dispossess, and deprive him, not only of the fruit of his labour, but also of his life, or liberty. And the invader again is in the like danger of another.

And from this diffidence of one another, there is no way for any man to secure himself, so reasonable, as anticipation; that is, by force, or wiles, to master the persons of all men he can, so long, till he see no other power great enough to endanger him: and this is no more than his own conservation requires, and is generally allowed. Also because there be some, that taking pleasure in contemplating their own power in the acts of conquest, which they pursue farther than their security requires; if others, that otherwise would be glad to be at ease within modest bounds, should not by invasion increase their power, they would not be able, long time, by standing only on their defence, to subsist. And by consequence, such augmentation of dominion over men being necessary to a man's conservation, it ought to be allowed him.

Again, men have no pleasure, but on the contrary a great deal of grief, in keeping company, where there is no power able to over-awe them all. For every man looks that his companion should value him, at the same rate he sets upon himself: and upon all signs of contempt, or undervaluing, naturally endeavours, as far as he dares, (which amongst them that have no common power to keep them in quiet, is far enough to make them destroy each other), to extort a greater value from his contemners, by damage; and from others, by the example.

So that in the nature of man, we find three principal causes of quarrel. First, competition; secondly, diffidence; thirdly, glory.

The first, makes men invade for gain; the second, for safety; and the third, for reputation. The first use violence, to make themselves masters of other men's persons, wives, children, and cattle; the second, to defend them; the third, for trifles, as a word, a smile, a different opinion, and any other sign of undervalue, either direct in their persons, or by reflection in their kindred, their friends, their nation, their profession, or their name.

Hereby it is manifest, that during the time men live without a common power to keep them all in awe, they are in that condition which is called war; and such a war, as is of every man, against every man. For WAR, consists not in battle only, or the act of fighting; but in a tract of time, wherein the will to contend by battle is sufficiently known: and therefore the notion of *time,* is to be considered in the nature of war; as it is in the nature of weather. For as the nature of foul weather, lies not in a shower or two of rain; but in an inclination thereto of many days together: so the nature of war, consists not in actual fighting; but in the known disposition thereto, during all the time there is no assurance to the contrary. All other time is PEACE.

Whatsoever therefore is consequent to a time of war, where every man is enemy to every man; the same is consequent to the time, wherein men live without other security, than what their own strength, and their own invention shall furnish them withal. In such condition, there is no place for industry; because the fruit thereof is uncertain: and consequently no culture of the earth; no navigation, nor use of the commodities that may be imported by sea; no commodious building; no instruments of moving, and removing, such things as require much force; no knowledge of the face of the earth; no account of time; no arts; no letters; no society; and which is worst of all, continual fear, and danger of violent death; and the life of man, solitary, poor, nasty, brutish, and short.

It may seem strange to some man, that has not well weighed these things; that nature should thus dissociate, and render men apt to invade, and destroy one another: and he may therefore, not trusting to this inference, made from the passions, desire perhaps to have the same confirmed by experience. Let him therefore consider with himself, when taking a journey, he arms himself, and seeks to go well accompanied; when going to sleep, he locks his doors; when even in his house he locks his chests; and this when he knows there be laws, and public officers, armed, to revenge all injuries shall be done him; what opinion he has of his fellow-subjects, when he rides armed; of his fellow citizens, when he locks his doors; and of his children, and servants, when he locks his chests. Does he not there as much accuse mankind by his actions, as I do by my words? But neither of us accuse man's nature in it. The desires, and other passions of man, are in themselves no sin. No more are the actions, that proceed from those passions, till they know a law that forbids them: which till laws be made they cannot know: nor can any law be made, till they have agreed upon the person that shall make it.

It may peradventure be thought, there was never such a time, nor condition of war as this; and I believe it was never generally so, over all the world: but there are many places, where they live so now. For the savage people in many places, of America, except the government of small families, the concord whereof depends on natural lust, have no government at all; and live at this day in that brutish manner, as I said before. Howsoever, it may be perceived what manner of life there would be, where there were no common power to fear, by the manner of life, which men that have formerly lived under a peaceful government, use to degenerate into, in a civil war.

But though there had never been any time, wherein particular men were in a condition of war one against another; yet in all times, kings, and persons of sovereign authority, because of their independency, are in continual jealousies, and in the state and posture of gladiators; having their weapons pointing, and their eyes fixed on one another; that is, their forts, garrisons, and guns upon the frontiers of their kingdoms; and continual spies upon their neighbours; which is a posture of war. But because they up-hold thereby, the industry of their subjects; there does not follow from it, that misery, which accompanies the liberty of particular men.

To this war of every man, against every man, this also is consequent; that nothing can be unjust. The notions of right and wrong, justice and injustice have there no place. Where there is no common power, there is no law: where no law, no injustice. Force, and fraud, are in war the two cardinal virtues. Justice, and injustice are none of the faculties neither of the body, nor mind. If they were, they might be in a man that were alone in the world, as well as his senses, and passions. They are qualities, that relate to men in society, not in solitude. It is consequent also to the same condition, that there be no propriety, no dominion, no *mine* and *thine* distinct; but only that to be every man's, that he can get: and for so long, as he can keep it. And thus much for the ill condition, which man by mere nature is actually placed in; though with a possibility to come out of it, consisting partly in the passions, partly in his reason.

The passions that incline men to peace, are fear of death; desire of such things as are necessary to commodious living; and a hope by their industry to obtain them. And reason suggests convenient articles of peace, upon which men may be drawn to agreement. These articles, are they, which otherwise are called the Laws of Nature: whereof I shall speak more particularly, in...following chapters.

OF THE FIRST AND SECOND NATURAL LAWS, AND OF CONTRACTS

(From *Leviathan*, Chapter 14)

The right of nature, which writers commonly call *jus naturale,* is the liberty each man has, to use his own power, as he will himself, for the preservation of his own nature; that is to say, of his own life; and consequently, of doing any thing, which in his own judgment, and reason, he shall conceive to be the aptest means thereunto.

By liberty, is understood, according to the proper signification of the word, the absence of external impediments: which impediments, may oft take away part of a man's power to do what he would; but cannot hinder him from using the power left him, according as his judgment, and reason shall dictate to him.

A law of nature, *lex naturalis,* is a precept or general rule, found out by reason, by which a man is forbidden to do that, which is destructive of his life, or takes away the means of preserving the same; and to omit that, by which he thinks it may be best preserved. For though they that speak of this subject, use to confound *jus,* and *lex, right* and *law:* yet they ought to be distinguished; because RIGHT, consists in liberty to do, or to forbear: whereas LAW, determines, and binds to one of them: so that law, and right, differ as much, as obligation, and liberty; which in one and the same matter are inconsistent.

And because the condition of man, as has been declared in the precedent chapter, is a condition of war of every one against every one; in which case every one is governed by his own reason; and there is nothing he can make use of, that may not be a help unto him, in preserving his life against his enemies; it follows, that in such a condition, every man has a right to every thing; even to one another's body. And therefore, as long as this natural right of every man to every thing endures, there can be no security to any man, how strong or wise soever he be, of living out the time, which nature ordinarily allows men to live. And consequently it is a precept, or general rule of reason, *that every man, ought to endeavour peace, as far as he has hope of obtaining it; and when he cannot obtain it, that he may seek, and use, all helps, and advantages of war.* The first branch of which rule, contains the first, and fundamental law of nature; which is, *to seek peace, and follow it.* The second, the sum of the right of nature; which is, *by all means we can, to defend ourselves.*

From this fundamental law of nature, by which men are commanded to endeavour peace, is derived this second law; *that a man be willing, when others are so too, as far-forth, as for peace, and defence of himself he shall think it necessary, to lay down this right to all things; and be contented with so much liberty against other men, as he would allow other men against himself.* For as long as every man holds this right, of doing any thing he likes; so long are all men in the condition of war. But if other men will not lay down their right, as well as he; then there is no reason for any one, to divest himself of his: for that were to expose himself to prey, which no man is bound to, rather than to dispose himself to peace. This is that law of the Gospel; *whatsoever you require that others should do to you, that do ye to them.* And that law of all men, *quod tibi fieri non vis, alteri ne feceris* [what you don't want done to you, don't do to others].

To *lay down* a man's *right* to any thing, is to *divest* himself of the *liberty*, of hindering another of the benefit of his own right to the same. For he that renounces, or passes away his right, gives not to any other man a right which he had not before; because there is nothing to which every man had not right by nature: but only stands out of his way, that he may enjoy his own original right, without hindrance from him; not without hindrance from another. So that the effect which redounds to one man, by another man's defect of right, is but so much diminution of impediments to the use of his own right original.

Right is laid aside, either by simply renouncing it; or by transferring it to another. By *simply* RENOUNCING; when he cares not to whom the benefit thereof redounds. By TRANSFERRING; when he intends the benefit thereof to some certain person, or persons. And when a man has in either manner abandoned, or granted away his right; then he is said to be OBLIGED, or BOUND, not to hinder those, to whom such right is granted, or abandoned, from the benefit of it: and that he *ought*, and it is his DUTY, not to make void that voluntary act of his own: and that such hindrance is INJUSTICE, and INJURY, as being *sine jure;* the right being before renounced, or transferred. So that *injury*, or *injustice*, in the controversies of the world, is somewhat like to that, which in the disputations of scholars is called *absurdity*. For as it is there called an absurdity, to contradict what one maintained in the beginning: so in the world, it is called injustice, and injury, voluntarily to undo that, which from the beginning he had voluntarily done. The way by which a man either simply renounces, or transfers his right, is a declaration, or signification, by some voluntary and sufficient sign, or signs, that he does so renounce, or transfer; or has so renounced, or transferred the same, to him that accepts it. And these signs are either words only, or actions only; or, as it happens most often, both words, and actions. And the same are the BONDS, by which men are bound, and obliged: bonds, that have their strength, not from their own nature, for nothing is more easily broken than a man's word, but from fear of some evil consequence upon the rupture.

Whensoever a man transfers his right, or renounces it; it is either in consideration of some right reciprocally transferred to himself; or for some other good he hopes for thereby. For it is a voluntary act: and of the voluntary acts of every man, the object is some *good to himself.* And therefore there be some rights, which no man can be understood by any words, or other signs, to have abandoned, or transferred. As first a man cannot lay down the right of resisting them, that assault him by force, to take away his life; because he cannot be understood to aim thereby, at any good to himself. The same may be said of wounds, and chains, and imprisonment; both because there is no benefit consequent to such patience; as there is to the patience of suffering another to be wounded, or imprisoned: as also because a man cannot tell, when he sees men proceed against him by violence, whether they intend his death or not. And lastly the motive, and end for which this renouncing, and transferring of right is introduced, is nothing else but the security of a man's person, in his life, and in the means of so preserving life, as not to be weary of it. And therefore if a man by words, or other signs, seem to despoil himself of the end, for which those signs were intended; he is not to be understood as if he meant it, or that it was his will; but that he was ignorant of how such words and actions were to be interpreted.

The mutual transferring of right, is that which men call CONTRACT.

There is a difference between transferring of right to the thing; and transferring, or tradition, that is delivery of the thing itself. For the thing may be delivered together with the translation of the right; as in buying and selling with ready-money; or exchange of goods, or lands: and it may be delivered some time after.

Again, one of the contractors, may deliver the thing contracted for on his part, and leave the other to perform his part at some determinate time after, and in the mean time be trusted; and then the contract on his part, is called PACT, or COVENANT: or both parts may contract now, to perform hereafter: in which cases, he that is to perform in time to come, being trusted, his performance is called *keeping of promise,* or faith; and the failing of performance, if it be voluntary, *violation of faith.*

When the transferring of right, is not mutual: but one of the parties transfers, in hope to gain thereby friendship, or service from another, or from his friends; or in hope to gain the reputation of charity, or magnanimity; or to deliver his mind from the pain of compassion; or in hope of reward in heaven; this is not contract, but GIFT, FREE-GIFT, GRACE: which words signify one and the same thing.

Signs of contract, are either *express,* or *by inference.* Express, are words spoken with understanding of what they signify: and such words are either of the time *present,* or *past;* as, *I give, I grant, I have given, I have granted, I will that this be yours:* or of the future; as, *I will give, I will grant:* which words of the future are called PROMISE.

Signs by inference, are sometimes the consequence of words; sometimes the consequence of silence; sometimes the consequence of actions; sometimes the consequence of forbearing an action: and generally a sign of inference, of any contract, is whatsoever sufficiently argues the will of the contractor....

In contracts, the right passes, not only where the words are of the time present, or past, but also where they are of the future: because all contract is mutual translation, or change of right; and therefore he that promises only, because he has already received the benefit for which he promises, is to be understood as if he intended the right should pass: for unless he had been content to have his words so understood, the other would not have performed his part first. And for that cause, in buying, and selling, and other acts of contract, a promise is equivalent to a covenant; and therefore obligatory....

If a covenant be made, wherein neither of the parties perform presently, but trust one another; in the condition of mere nature, which is a condition of war of every man against every man, upon any reasonable suspicion, it is void: but if there be a common power set over them both, with right and force sufficient to compel performance, it is not void. For he that performs first, has no assurance the other will perform after; because the bonds of words are too weak to bridle men's ambition, avarice, anger, and other passions, without the fear of some coercive power; which in the condition of mere nature, where all men are equal, and judges of the justness of their own fears, cannot possibly be supposed. And therefore he which performeth first, does but betray himself to his enemy; contrary to the right, he can never abandon, of defending his life, and means of living.

But in a civil estate, where there is a power set up to constrain those that would otherwise violate their faith, that fear is no more reasonable; and for that cause, he which by the covenant is to perform first, is obliged so to do....

Covenants entered into by fear, in the condition of mere nature, are obligatory. For example, if I covenant to pay a ransom, or service for my life, to an enemy; I am bound by it: for it is a contract, wherein one receives the benefit of life; the other is to receive money, or service for it; and consequently, where no other law, as in the condition of mere nature, forbids the performance, the covenant is valid. Therefore prisoners of war, if trusted with the payment of their ransom, are obliged to pay it: and if a weaker prince, make a disadvantageous peace with a stronger, for fear; he is bound to keep it; unless, as hath been said before, there arises some new, and just cause of fear, to renew the war. And even in commonwealths, if I be forced to redeem myself from a thief by promising him money, I am bound to pay it, till the civil law discharge me. For whatsoever I may lawfully do without obligation, the same I may lawfully covenant to do through fear: and what I lawfully covenant, I cannot lawfully break.

A former covenant, makes void a later. For a man that has passed away his right to one man today, has it not to pass tomorrow to another: and therefore the later promise passes no right, but is null.

A covenant not to defend myself from force, by force, is always void. For, as I have showed before, no man can transfer, or lay down his right to save himself from death, wounds, and imprisonment, the avoiding whereof is the only end of laying down any right; and therefore the promise of not resisting force, in no covenant transfers any right; nor is obliging. For though a man may covenant thus, *unless I do so, or so, kill me;* he cannot covenant thus, *unless I do so, or so, I will not resist you, when you come to kill me.* For man by nature chooses the lesser evil, which is danger of death in resisting; rather than the greater, which is certain and present death in not resisting. And this is granted to be true by all men, in that they lead criminals to execution, and prison, with armed men, notwithstanding that such criminals have consented to the law, by which they are condemned.

A covenant to accuse oneself, without assurance of pardon, is likewise invalid. For in the condition of nature, where every man is judge, there is no place for accusation: and in the civil state, the accusation is followed with punishment; which being force, a man is not obliged not to resist.

13

Toleration and Government

JOHN LOCKE

Although the word "liberal" was not used to describe a political position until the early 1800s, John Locke (1632–1704) usually is considered the first philosopher to take a clearly liberal perspective on political matters. The power of a political society or "commonwealth," Locke claimed, is limited to the protection of its members' "civil interests." These include life, liberty, and property, but not the private sphere of religious belief—as he argued in *A Letter Concerning Toleration* (1689). In his *Second Treatise of Government*—published in 1690 after the Glorious Revolution of 1688, but written earlier—Locke began from premises quite similar to those of Thomas Hobbes, but arrived at conclusions more recognizably liberal. Everyone has a natural right to life, liberty, and property, Locke said, and no one has authority over us without our consent. Any government that violates our rights releases us from any obligation to obey it and may, indeed, entitle us to overthrow it and establish a new government.

Sources: The Works of John Locke, 10 vols. (London: Thomas Tegg; W. Sharpe and Son; G. Offor; G. and J. Robinson; J. Evans and Co., 1823), pp. 9–21 (vol. 6) and 339–347, 352–367, 469–472 (vol. 5).

A LETTER CONCERNING TOLERATION

The commonwealth seems to me to be a society of men constituted only for the procuring, preserving, and advancing their own civil interests.

Civil interest I call life, liberty, health, and indolency of body; and the possession of outward things, such as money, lands, houses, furniture, and the like.

It is the duty of the civil magistrate, by the impartial execution of equal laws, to secure unto all the people in general, and to every one of his subjects in particular, the just possession of these things belonging to this life. If any one presume to violate the laws of public justice and equity, established for the preservation of these things, his presumption is to be checked by the fear of punishment, consisting in the deprivation or diminution of those civil interests, or goods, which otherwise he might and ought to enjoy. But seeing no man does willingly suffer himself to be punished by the deprivation of any part of his goods, and much less of his liberty or life, therefore is the magistrate armed with the force and strength of all his subjects, in order to the punishment of those that violate any other man's rights.

Now that the whole jurisdiction of the magistrate reaches only to these civil concernments; and that all civil power, right, and dominion, is bounded and confined to the only care of promoting these things; and that it neither can nor ought in any manner to be extended to the salvation of souls, these following considerations seem unto me abundantly to demonstrate.

First, Because the care of souls is not committed to the civil magistrate, any more than to other men. It is not committed unto him, I say, by God; because it appears not that God has ever given any such authority to one man over another, as to compel any one to his religion. Nor can any such power be vested in the magistrate by the consent of the people; because no man can so far abandon the care of his own salvation as blindly to leave it to the choice of any other, whether prince or subject, to prescribe to him what faith or worship he shall embrace. For no man can, if he would, conform his faith to the dictates of another. All the life and power of true religion consists in the inward and full persuasion of the mind; and faith is not faith without believing. Whatever profession we make, to whatever outward worship we conform, if we are not fully satisfied in our own mind that the one is true, and the other well-pleasing unto God, such profession and such practice, far from being any furtherance, are indeed great obstacles to our salvation. For in this manner, instead of expiating other sins by the exercise of religion, I say in offering thus unto God Almighty such a worship as we esteem to be displeasing unto him, we add unto the number of our other sins, those also of hypocrisy, and contempt of his Divine Majesty.

In the second place, The care of souls cannot belong to the civil magistrate, because his power consists only in outward force: but true and saving religion consists in the inward persuasion of the mind, without which nothing can be acceptable to God. And such is the nature of the understanding, that it cannot be compelled to the belief of any thing by outward force. Confiscation of estate, imprisonment, torments, nothing of that nature can have any such efficacy as to make men change the inward judgment that they have framed of things.

It may indeed be alleged that the magistrate may make use of arguments, and thereby draw the heterodox into the way of truth, and procure their salvation. I grant it; but this is common to him with other men. In teaching, instructing, and redressing the erroneous by reason, he may certainly do what becomes any good man to do. Magistracy does not oblige him to put off either humanity or Christianity. But it is one thing to persuade, another to command; one thing to press with arguments, another with penalties. This the civil power alone has a right to do; to the other, good-will is authority enough. Every man has commission to admonish, exhort, convince another of error, and by reasoning to draw him into truth: but to give laws, receive obedience, and compel with the sword, belongs to none but the magistrate. And upon this ground

I affirm, that the magistrate's power extends not to the establishing of any articles of faith, or forms of worship, by the force of his laws. For laws are of no force at all without penalties, and penalties in this case are absolutely impertinent; because they are not proper to convince the mind. Neither the profession of any articles of faith, nor the conformity to any outward form of worship, as has been already said, can be available to the salvation of souls, unless the truth of the one, and the acceptableness of the other unto God, be thoroughly believed by those that so profess and practise. But penalties are no ways capable to produce such belief. It is only light and evidence that can work a change in men's opinions; and that light can in no manner proceed from corporal sufferings, or any other outward penalties.

In the third place, The care of the salvation of men's souls cannot belong to the magistrate; because, though the rigour of laws and the force of penalties were capable to convince and change men's minds, yet would not that help at all to the salvation of their souls. For, there being but one truth, one way to heaven; what hopes is there that more men would be led into it, if they had no other rule to follow but the religion of the court, and were put under a necessity to quit the light of their own reason, to oppose the dictates of their own consciences, and blindly to resign up themselves to the will of their governors, and to the religion, which either ignorance, ambition, or superstition had chanced to establish in the countries where they were born? In the variety and contradiction of opinions in religion, wherein the princes of the world are as much divided as in their secular interests, the narrow way would be much straitened; one country alone would be in the right, and all the rest of the world put under an obligation of following their princes in the ways that lead to destruction: and that which heightens the absurdity, and very ill suits the notion of a Deity, men would owe their eternal happiness or misery to the places of their nativity.

These considerations, to omit many others that might have been urged to the same purpose, seem unto me sufficient to conclude, that all the power of civil government relates only to men's civil interests, is confined to the care of the things of this world, and hath nothing to do with the world to come.

Let us now consider what a church is. A church then I take to be a voluntary society of men, joining themselves together of their own accord, in order to the public worshipping of God, in such a manner as they judge acceptable to him, and effectual to the salvation of their souls.

I say, it is a free and voluntary society. Nobody is born a member of any church; otherwise the religion of parents would descend unto children, by the same right of inheritance as their temporal estates, and every one would hold his faith by the same tenure he does his lands; than which nothing can be imagined more absurd. Thus therefore that matter stands. No man by nature is bound unto any particular church or sect, but every one joins himself voluntarily to that society in which he believes he has found that profession and worship which is truly acceptable to God. The hopes of salvation, as it was the only cause of his entrance into that communion, so it can be the only reason of his stay there. For if afterwards he discover any thing either erroneous in the doctrine, or incongruous in the worship of that society to which he has joined himself, why should it not be as free for him to go out as it was to enter? No member of a religious society can be tied with any other bonds but what proceed from the certain expectation of eternal life. A church then is a society of members voluntarily uniting to this end.

It follows now that we consider what is the power of this church, and unto what laws it is subject.

Forasmuch as no society, how free soever, or upon whatsoever slight occasion instituted, (whether of philosophers for learning, of merchants for commerce, or of men of leisure for mutual conversation and discourse) no church or company, I say, can in the least subsist and hold together, but will presently dissolve and break to pieces, unless it be regulated by some laws, and the members all consent to observe some order. Place and time of meeting must be agreed on;

rules for admitting and excluding members must be established; distinction of officers, and putting things into a regular course, and such like, cannot be omitted. But since the joining together of several members into this church-society, as has already been demonstrated, is absolutely free and spontaneous, it necessarily follows, that the right of making its laws can belong to none but the society itself, or at least, which is the same thing, to those whom the society by common consent has authorized thereunto.

Some perhaps may object, that no such society can be said to be a true church, unless it have in it a bishop, or presbyter, with ruling authority derived from the very apostles, and continued down unto the present time by an uninterrupted succession.

To these I answer: In the first place, Let them show me the edict by which Christ has imposed that law upon his church. And let not any man think me impertinent, if, in a thing of this consequence, I require that the terms of that edict be very express and positive. For the promise he has made us, that "wheresoever two or three are gathered together in his name, he will be in the midst of them," Matth, xviii, 20, seems to imply the contrary. Whether such an assembly want any thing necessary to a true church, pray do you consider. Certain I am, that nothing can be there wanting unto the salvation of souls, which is sufficient for our purpose.

Next, pray observe how great have always been the divisions amongst even those who lay so much stress upon the divine institution, and continued succession of a certain order of rulers in the church. Now their very dissension unavoidably puts us upon a necessity of deliberating, and consequently allows a liberty of choosing that, which upon consideration, we prefer.

And, in the last place, I consent that these men have a ruler of their church, established by such a long series of succession as they judge necessary, provided I may have liberty at the same time to join myself to that society, in which I am persuaded those things are to be found which are necessary to the salvation of my soul. In this manner ecclesiastical liberty will be preserved on all sides, and no man will have a legislator imposed upon him, but whom himself has chosen.

But since men are so solicitous about the true church, I would only ask them here by the way, if it be not more agreeable to the church of Christ to make the conditions of her communion consist in such things, and such things only, as the Holy Spirit has in the holy Scriptures declared, in express words, to be necessary to salvation? I ask, I say, whether this be not more agreeable to the church of Christ, than for men to impose their own inventions and interpretations upon others, as if they were of divine authority; and to establish by ecclesiastical laws, as absolutely necessary to the profession of Christianity such things as the holy Scriptures do either not mention, or at least not expressly command? Whosoever requires those things in order to ecclesiastical communion, which Christ does not require in order to life eternal, he may perhaps indeed constitute a society accommodated to his own opinion, and his own advantage; but how that can be called the church of Christ, which is established upon laws that are not his, and which excludes such persons from its communion as he will one day receive into the kingdom of heaven, I understand not. But this being not a proper place to enquire into the marks of the true church, I will only mind those that contend so earnestly for the decrees of their own society, and that cry out continually the Church, the Church, with as much noise, and perhaps upon the same principle, as the Ephesian silversmiths did for their [goddess] Diana; this, I say, I desire to mind them of, that the Gospel frequently declares, that the true disciples of Christ must suffer persecution; but that the church of Christ should persecute others, and force others by fire and sword to embrace her faith and doctrine, I could never yet find in any of the books of the New Testament.

The end of a religious society, as has already been said, is the public worship of God, and by means thereof the acquisition of eternal life. All discipline ought therefore to tend to that end, and all ecclesiastical laws to be thereunto confined. Nothing ought, nor can be transacted in this society, relating to the possession of civil and worldly goods. No force is here to be made use of, upon any occasion whatsoever: for force belongs wholly to the civil magistrate, and the possession of all outward goods is subject to his jurisdiction.

But it may be asked, by what means then shall ecclesiastical laws be established, if they must be thus destitute of all compulsive power? I answer they must be established by means suitable to the nature of such things, where of the external profession and observation, if not proceeding from a thorough conviction and approbation of the mind, is altogether useless and unprofitable. The arms by which the members of this society are to be kept within their duty, are exhortations, admonitions, and advice. If by these means the offenders will not be reclaimed, and the erroneous convinced, there remains nothing farther to be done, but that such stubborn and obstinate persons, who give no ground to hope for their reformation, should be cast out and separated from the society. This is the last and utmost force of ecclesiastical authority: no other punishment can thereby be inflicted, than that the relation ceasing between the body and the member which is cut off, the person so condemned ceases to be a part of that church.

These things being thus determined, let us inquire, in the next place, how far the duty of toleration extends, and what is required from every one by it.

And first, I hold, that no church is bound by the duty of toleration to retain any such person in her bosom, as after admonition, continues obstinately to offend against the laws of the society. For these being the condition of communion, and the bond of society, if the breach of them were permitted without any animadversion, the society would immediately be thereby dissolved. But nevertheless, in all such cases care is to be taken that the sentence of excommunication, and the execution thereof, carry with it no rough usage, of word or action, whereby the ejected person may any ways be damnified [i.e., injured] in body or estate. For all force, as has often been said, belongs only to the magistrate, nor ought any private persons, at any time, to use force; unless it be in self-defence against unjust violence. Excommunication neither does nor can deprive the excommunicated person of any of those civil goods that he formerly possessed. All those things belong to the civil government, and are under the magistrate's protection. The whole force of excommunication consists only in this, that the resolution of the society in that respect being declared, the union that was between the body and some member, comes thereby to be dissolved; and that relation ceasing, the participation of some certain things, which the society communicated to its members, and unto which no man has any civil right, comes also to cease. For there is no civil injury done unto the excommunicated person, by the church-minister's refusing him that bread and wine, in the celebration of the Lord's supper, which was not bought with his, but other men's money.

Secondly, No private person has any right in any manner to prejudice another person in his civil enjoyments, because he is of another church or religion. All the rights and franchises that belong to him as a man, or as a denizen, are inviolably to be preserved to him. These are not the business of religion. No violence nor injury is to be offered him, whether he be Christian or pagan. Nay, we must not content ourselves with the narrow measures of bare justice: charity, bounty, and liberality must be added to it. This the Gospel enjoins, this reason directs, and this that natural fellowship we are born into requires of us. If any man err from the right way, it is his own misfortune, no injury to thee: nor therefore art thou to punish him in the things of this life, because thou supposest he will be miserable in that which is to come.

What I say concerning the mutual toleration of private persons differing from one another in religion, I understand also of particular churches; which stand as it were in the same relation to each other as private persons among themselves; nor has any one of them any manner of jurisdiction over any other, no, not even when the civil magistrate, as it sometimes happens, comes to be of this or the other communion. For the civil government can give no new right to the church, nor the church to the civil government. So that whether the magistrate join himself to any church, or separate from it, the church remains always as it was before, a free and voluntary society. It neither acquires the power of the sword by the magistrate's coming to it, nor does it lose the right of instruction and excommunication by his going from it. This is the fundamental and immutable right of a spontaneous society, that it has to remove any of its members who transgress the rules of its institution: but it cannot, by the accession of any new members, acquire any right of jurisdiction over those that are not joined with it. And therefore peace, equity, and friendship, are always mutually to be observed by particular churches, in the same manner as by private persons, without any pretence of superiority or jurisdiction over one another....

Nobody therefore, in fine, neither single persons, nor churches, nay, nor even commonwealths, have any just title to invade the civil rights and worldly goods of each other, upon pretence of religion. Those that are of another opinion, would do well to consider with themselves how pernicious a seed of discord and war, how powerful a provocation to endless hatreds, rapines, and slaughters, they thereby furnish unto mankind. No peace and security, no, not so much as common friendship, can ever be established or preserved amongst men, so long as this opinion prevails, "that dominion is founded in grace, and that religion is to be propagated by force of arms."

In the third place, Let us see what the duty of toleration requires from those who are distinguished from the rest of mankind, from the laity, as they please to call us, by some ecclesiastical character and office; whether they be bishops, priests, presbyters, ministers, or however else dignified or distinguished. It is not my business to inquire here into the origins of the power or dignity of the clergy. This only I say, that whencesoever their authority be sprung, since it is ecclesiastical, it ought to be confined within the bounds of the church, nor can it in any manner be extended to civil affairs; because the church itself is a thing absolutely separate and distinct from the commonwealth. The boundaries on both sides are fixed and immoveable. He jumbles heaven and earth together, the things most remote and opposite, who mixes these societies, which are, in their origins, end, business, and in every thing, perfectly distinct, and infinitely different from each other. No man therefore, with whatsoever ecclesiastical office he be dignified, can deprive another man, that is not of his church and faith, either of liberty, or of any part of his worldly goods, upon the account of that difference which is between them in religion. For whatsoever is not lawful to the whole church cannot, by any ecclesiastical right, become lawful to any of its members.

SECOND TREATISE OF GOVERNMENT

Of the State of Nature

4. To understand political power right, and derive it from its origins, we must consider what state all men are naturally in, and that is, a state of perfect freedom to order their actions and dispose of their possessions and persons, as they think fit, within the bounds of the law of nature; without asking leave, or depending upon the will of any other man.

A state also of equality, wherein all the power and jurisdiction is reciprocal, no one having more than another; there being nothing more evident than that creatures of the same species and rank, promiscuously born to all the same advantages of nature, and the use of the same faculties, should also be equal one amongst another without subordination or subjection; unless the Lord and Master of them all should, by any manifest declaration of his will, set one above another, and confer on him, by an evident and clear appointment, an undoubted right to dominion and sovereignty....

6. But though this be a state of liberty, yet it is not a state of licence: though man in that state have an uncontrollable liberty to dispose of his person or possessions, yet he has not liberty to destroy himself, or so much as any creature in his possession, but where some nobler use than its bare preservation calls for it. The state of nature has a law of nature to govern it, which obliges every one: and reason, which is that law, teaches all mankind, who will but consult it, that being all equal and independent, no one ought to harm another in his life, health, liberty, or possessions: for men being all the workmanship of one omnipotent and infinitely wise Maker; all the servants of one sovereign Master, sent into the world by his order, and about his business; they are his property, whose workmanship they are, made to last during his, not another's pleasure: and being furnished with like faculties, sharing all in one community of nature, there cannot be supposed any such subordination among us that may authorize us to destroy another, as if we were made for one another's uses, as the inferior ranks of creatures are for ours. Every one, as he is bound to preserve himself, and not to quit his station willfully, so by the like reason, when his own preservation comes not in competition, ought he, as much as he can, to preserve the rest of mankind, and may not, unless it be to do justice to an offender, take away or impair the life, or what tends to the preservation of life, the liberty, health, limb, or goods of another.

7. And that all men may be restrained from invading others' rights, and from doing hurt to one another, and the law of nature be observed, which willeth the peace and preservation of all mankind, the execution of the law of nature is, in that state, put into every man's hands, whereby every one has a right to punish the transgressors of that law to such a degree as may hinder its violation: for the law of nature would, as all other laws that concern men in this world, be in vain, if there were nobody that in the state of nature had a power to execute that law, and thereby preserve the innocent, and restrain offenders. And if any one in the state of nature may punish another for any evil he has done, every one may do so: for in that state of perfect equality, where naturally there is no superiority or jurisdiction of one over another, what any may do in prosecution of that law every one must needs have a right to do.

8. And thus, in the state of nature, one man comes by a power over another, but yet no absolute or arbitrary power to use a criminal, when he has got him in his hands, according to the passionate heats or boundless extravagancy of his own will; but only to retribute to him, so far as calm reason and conscience dictate, what is proportionate to his transgression; which is so much as may serve for reparation and restraint: for these two are the only reasons why one man may lawfully do harm to another, which is that we call punishment. In transgressing the law of nature, the offender declares himself to live by another rule than that of reason and common equity, which is that measure God has set to the actions of men for their mutual security; and so he becomes dangerous to mankind, the tie, which is to secure them from injury and violence, being slighted and broken by him: which being a trespass against the whole species, and the peace and safety of it, provided for by the law of nature; every man upon this score, by the right he hath to preserve mankind in general, may restrain, or, where it is necessary, destroy things noxious to them, and so may bring such evil on any one, who hath transgressed that law, as may make him repent the doing of it, and thereby deter him, and by his example others, from doing the like mischief. And in this case, and upon this ground, every man hath a right to punish the offender, and be executioner of the law of nature.

9. I doubt not but this will seem a very strange doctrine to some men: but, before they condemn it, I desire them to resolve me by what right any prince or state can put to death or punish an alien for any crime he commits in their country? It is certain their laws, by virtue of any sanction they receive from the promulgated will of the legislative, reach not a stranger: they speak not to him, nor, if they did, is he bound to hearken to them. The legislative authority, by which they are in force over the subjects of that commonwealth, hath no power over him. Those who have the

supreme power of making laws in England, France, or Holland, are to an Indian but like the rest of the world, men without authority: and therefore, if by the law of nature every man hath not a power to punish offences against it, as he soberly judges the case to require, I see not how the magistrates of any community can punish an alien of another country; since, in reference to him, they can have no more power than what every man naturally may have over another.

10. Besides the crime which consists in violating the law, and varying from the right rule of reason, whereby a man so far becomes degenerate, and declares himself to quit the principles of human nature, and to be a noxious creature, there is commonly injury done to some person or other, and some other man receives damage by his transgression: in which case he who hath received any damage, has, besides the right of punishment common to him with other men, a particular right to seek reparation from him that has done it: and any other person, who finds it just, may also join with him that is injured, and assist him in recovering from the offender so much as may make satisfaction for the harm he has suffered.

11. From these two distinct rights, the one of punishing the crime for restraint, and preventing the like offence, which right of punishing is in every body; the other of taking reparation, which belongs only to the injured party; comes it to pass that the magistrate, who by being magistrate hath the common right of punishing put into his hands, can often, where the public good demands not the execution of the law, remit the punishment of criminal offences by his own authority, but yet cannot remit the satisfaction due to any private man for the damage he has received. That he who has suffered the damage has a right to demand in his own name, and he alone can remit; the damnified [i.e., injured] person has this power of appropriating to himself the goods or service of the offender, by right of self-preservation, as every man has a power to punish the crime, to prevent its being committed again, by the right he has of preserving all mankind, and doing all reasonable things he can in order to that end: and thus it is that every man, in the state of nature, has a power to kill a murderer, both to deter others from doing the like injury, which no reparation can compensate, by the example of the punishment that attends it from every body; and also to secure men from the attempts of a criminal, who having renounced reason, the common rule and measure God hath given to mankind, hath, by the unjust violence and slaughter he hath committed upon one, declared war against all mankind; and therefore may be destroyed as a lion or a tiger, one of those wild savage beasts with whom men can have no society nor security: and upon this is grounded that great law of nature, "Whoso sheddeth man's blood, by man shall his blood be shed." And Cain was so fully convinced that every one had a right to destroy such a criminal, that, after the murder of his brother, he cries out, "Every one that findeth me shall slay me," so plain was it writ in the hearts of all mankind.

12. By the same reason may a man in the state of nature punish the lesser breaches of that law. It will perhaps be demanded, with death? I answer, each transgression may be punished to that degree, and with so much severity, as will suffice to make it an ill bargain to the offender, give him cause to repent, and terrify others from doing the like. Every offence that can be committed in the state of nature, may in the state of nature be also punished equally, and as far forth, as it may in a commonwealth: for though it would be beside my present purpose to enter here into the particulars of the law of nature, or its measures of punishment, yet it is certain there is such a law, and that too as intelligible and plain to a rational creature, and a studier of that law, as the positive laws of commonwealths; nay, possibly plainer, as much as reason is easier to be understood than the fancies and intricate contrivances of men, following contrary and hidden interests put into words; for so truly are a great part of the municipal laws of countries, which are only so far right, as they are founded on the law of nature, by which they are to be regulated and interpreted.

13. To this strange doctrine, viz. that in the state of nature every one has the executive power

of the law of nature, I doubt not but it will be objected, that it is unreasonable for men to be judges in their own cases, that self-love will make men partial to themselves and their friends: and, on the other side, that ill-nature, passion, and revenge will carry them too far in punishing others; and hence nothing but confusion and disorder will follow: and that therefore God hath certainly appointed government to restrain the partiality and violence of men. I easily grant, that civil government is the proper remedy for the inconveniencies of the state of nature, which must certainly be great, where men may be judges in their own case; since it is easy to be imagined, that he who was so unjust as to do his brother an injury, will scarce be so just as to condemn himself for it: but I shall desire those who make this objection to remember, that absolute monarchs are but men; and if government is to be the remedy of those evils, which necessarily follow from men's being judges in their own cases, and the state of nature is therefore not to be endured; I desire to know what kind of government that is, and how much better it is than the state of nature, where one man, commanding a multitude, has the liberty to be judge in his own case, and may do to all his subjects whatever he pleases, without the least liberty to any one to question or control those who execute his pleasure? and in whatsoever he doth, whether led by reason, mistake, or passion, must be submitted to? Much better it is in the state of nature, wherein men are not bound to submit to the unjust will of another: and if he that judges, judges amiss in his own, or any other case, he is answerable for it to the rest of mankind.

14. It is often asked, as a mighty objection, "where are or ever were there any men in such a state of nature?" To which it may suffice as an answer at present, that since all princes and rulers of independent governments, all through the world, are in a state of nature, it is plain the world never was, nor never will be, without numbers of men in that state. I have named all governors of independent communities, whether they are, or are not, in league with others: for it is not every compact that puts an end to the state of nature between men, but only this one of agreeing together mutually to enter into one community, and make one body politic; other promises and compacts men may make one with another, and yet still be in the state of nature. The promises and bargains for truck, etc., between the two men in the desert island, mentioned by Garcilasso de la Vega, in his history of Peru; or between a Swiss and an Indian, in the woods of America; are binding to them, though they are perfectly in a state of nature, in reference to one another: for truth and keeping of faith belongs to men as men, and not as members of society.

15. To those that say, there were never any men in the state of nature, I…affirm, that all men are naturally in that state, and remain so, till by their own consents they make themselves members of some politic society; and I doubt not in the sequel of this discourse to make it very clear….

Of Property

26. God, who hath given the world to men in common, hath also given them reason to make use of it to the best advantage of life and convenience. The earth, and all that is therein, is given to men for the support and comfort of their being. And though all the fruits it naturally produces, and beasts it feeds, belong to mankind in common, as they are produced by the spontaneous hand of nature; and nobody has originally a private dominion, exclusive of the rest of mankind, in any of them, as they are thus in their natural state: yet being given for the use of men, there must of necessity be a means to appropriate them some way or other before they can be of any use, or at all beneficial to any particular man. The fruit, or venison, which nourishes the wild Indian, who knows no enclosure, and is still a tenant in common, must be his, and so his, *i.e.*, a part of him, that another can no longer have any right to it, before it can do him any good for the support of his life.

27. Though the earth, and all inferior creatures, be common to all men, yet every man has a property in his own person: this nobody has

any right to but himself. The labour of his body, and the work of his hands, we may say, are properly his. Whatsoever then, he removes out of the state that nature hath provided, and left it in, he hath mixed his labour with, and joined to it something that is his own, and thereby makes it his property. It being by him removed from the common state nature hath placed it in, it hath by this labour something annexed to it that excludes the common right of other men. For this labour being the unquestionable property of the labourer, no man but he can have a right to what that is once joined to, at least where there is enough, and as good, left in common for others.

28. He that is nourished by the acorns he picked up under an oak, or the apples he gathered from the trees in the wood, has certainly appropriated them to himself. Nobody can deny but the nourishment is his. I ask then, when did they begin to be his? when he digested? or when he ate? or when he boiled? or when he brought them home? or when he picked them up? and it is plain, if the first gathering made them not his, nothing else could. That labour put a distinction between them and common: that added something to them more than nature, the common mother of all, had done; and so they became his private right. And will any one say, he had no right to those acorns or apples he thus appropriated, because he had not the consent of all mankind to make them his? Was it a robbery thus to assume to himself what belonged to all in common? If such a consent as that was necessary, man had starved, notwithstanding the plenty God had given him. We see in commons, which remain so by compact, that it is the taking any part of what is common, and removing it out of the state nature leaves it in, which begins the property; without which the common is of no use. And the taking of this or that part does not depend on the express consent of all the commoners. Thus the grass my horse has bit; the turfs my servant has cut; and the ore I have digged in any place, where I have a right to them in common with others; become my property, without the assignation or consent of any body. The labour that was mine, removing them out of that common state they were in, hath fixed my property in them.

29. By making an explicit consent of every commoner necessary to any one's appropriating to himself any part of what is given in common, children or servants could not cut the meat, which their father or master had provided for them in common, without assigning to every one his peculiar part. Though the water running in the fountain be every one's, yet who can doubt but that in the pitcher is his only who drew it out? His labour hath taken it out of the hands of nature, where it was common, and belonged equally to all her children, and hath thereby appropriated it to himself.

30. Thus this law of reason makes the deer that Indian's who hath killed it; it is allowed to be his goods who hath bestowed his labour upon it, though before it was the common right of every one. And amongst those who are counted the civilized part of mankind, who have made and multiplied positive laws to determine property, this original law of nature, for the beginning of property, in what was before common, still takes place; and by virtue thereof, what fish any one catches in the ocean, that great and still remaining common of mankind; or what ambergris any one takes up here, is by the labour that removes it out of that common state nature left it in made his property who takes that pains about it. And even amongst us, the hare that any one is hunting is thought his who pursues her during the chase: for being a beast that is still looked upon as common, and no man's private possession; whoever has employed so much labour about any of that kind, as to find and pursue her, has thereby removed her from the state of nature, wherein she was common, and hath begun a property.

31. It will perhaps be objected to this, that "if gathering the acorns, or other fruits of the earth, etc., makes a right to them, then any one may engross as much as he will." To which I answer, Not so. The same law of nature, that does by this means give us property, does also bound that property too. "God has given us all things richly," 1 Tim. vi 17, is the voice of rea-

son confirmed by inspiration. But how far has he given it us? To enjoy. As much as any one can make use of to any advantage of life before it spoils, so much he may by his labour fix a property in: whatever is beyond this, is more than his share, and belongs to others. Nothing was made by God for man to spoil or destroy. And thus, considering the plenty of natural provisions there was a long time in the world, and the few spenders; and to how small a part of that provision the industry of one man could extend itself, and engross it to the prejudice of others; especially keeping within the bounds, set by reason, of what might serve for his use; there could be then little room for quarrels or contentions about property so established.

32. But the chief matter of property being now not the fruits of the earth, and the beasts that subsist on it, but the earth itself; as that which takes in, and carries with it all the rest; I think it is plain, that property in that too is acquired as the former. As much land as a man tills, plants, improves, cultivates, and can use the product of, so much is his property. He by his labour does, as it were, enclose it from the common. Nor will it invalidate his right, to say every body else has an equal title to it, and therefore he cannot appropriate, he cannot enclose, without the consent of all his fellow-commoners, all mankind. God, when he gave the world in common to all mankind, commanded man also to labour, and the penury of his condition required it of him. God and his reason commanded him to subdue the earth, *i.e.,* improve it for the benefit of life, and therein lay out something upon it that was his own, his labour. He that, in obedience to this command of God, subdued, tilled, and sowed any part of it, thereby annexed to it something that was his property, which another had no title to, nor could without injury take from him.

33. Nor was this appropriation of any parcel of land, by improving it, any prejudice to any other man, since there was still enough, and as good left; and more than the yet unprovided could use. So that, in effect, there was never the less left for others because of his enclosure for himself: for he that leaves as much as another can make use of, does as good as take nothing at all. Nobody could think himself injured by the drinking of another man, though he took a good draught, who had a whole river of the same water left him to quench his thirst; and the case of land and water, where there is enough of both, is perfectly the same.

34. God gave the world to men in common; but since he gave it to them for their benefit, and the greatest conveniencies of life they were capable to draw from it, it cannot be supposed he meant it should always remain common and uncultivated. He gave it to the use of the industrious and rational (and labour was to be his title to it), not to the fancy or covetousness of the quarrelsome and contentious. He that had as good left for his improvement as was already taken up, needed not complain, ought not to meddle with what was already improved by another's labour: if he did, it is plain he desired the benefit of another's pains, which he had no right to, and not the ground which God had given him in common with others to labour on, and whereof there was as good left as that already possessed, and more than he knew what to do with, or his industry could reach to.

35. It is true, in land that is common in England, or any other country, where there are plenty of people under government, who have money and commerce, no one can enclose or appropriate any part without the consent of all his fellow-commoners; because this is left common by compact, *i.e.,* by the law of the land, which is not to be violated. And though it be common, in respect of some men, it is not so to all mankind, but is the joint property of this county, or this parish. Besides, the remainder, after such enclosure, would not be as good to the rest of the commoners as the whole was when they could all make use of the whole; whereas in the beginning and first peopling of the great common of the world it was quite otherwise. The law man was under was rather for appropriating. God commanded, and his wants forced him to labour. That was his property which could not be taken from him wherever he had fixed it.

And hence subduing or cultivating the earth, and having dominion, we see are joined together. The one gave title to the other. So that God, by commanding to subdue, gave authority so far to appropriate: and the condition of human life, which requires labour and materials to work on, necessarily introduces private possessions.

36. The measure of property nature has well set by the extent of men's labour and the conveniencies of life: no man's labour could subdue, or appropriate all; nor could his enjoyment consume more than a small part; so that it was impossible for any man, this way, to entrench upon the right of another, or acquire to himself a property, to the prejudice of his neighbour, who would still have room for as good and as large a possession (after the other had taken out his) as before it was appropriated. This measure did confine every man's possession to a very moderate proportion, and such as he might appropriate to himself, without injury to any body, in the first ages of the world, when men were more in danger to be lost, by wandering from their company, in the then vast wilderness of the earth, than to be straitened for want of room to plant in....

40. It is labour indeed that put the difference of value on every thing; and let any one consider what the difference is between an acre of land planted with tobacco or sugar, sown with wheat or barley, and an acre of the same land lying in common, without any husbandry upon it, and he will find, that the improvement of labour makes the far greater part of the value. I think it will be but a very modest computation to say, that of the products of the earth useful to the life of man, nine-tenths are the effects of labour: nay, if we will rightly estimate things as they come to our use, and cast up the several expenses about them, what in them is purely owing to nature, and what to labour, we shall find, that in most of them ninety-nine hundredths are wholly to be put on the account of labour.

41. There cannot be a clearer demonstration of any thing, than several nations of the Americans are of this, who are rich in land, and poor in all the comforts of life; whom nature having furnished as liberally as any other people with the materials of plenty, *i.e.*, a fruitful soil, apt to produce in abundance; yet, for want of improving it by labour, have not one-hundredth part of the conveniencies we enjoy: and a king of a large and fruitful territory there feeds, lodges, and is clad worse than a day-labourer in England.

42. To make this a little clearer, let us but trace some of the ordinary provisions of life, through their several progresses, before they come to our use, and see how much of their value they receive from human industry. Bread, wine, and cloth, are things of daily use, and great plenty; yet notwithstanding, acorns, water, and leaves, or skins, must be our bread, drink, and clothing, did not labour furnish us with these more useful commodities: for whatever bread is more worth than acorns, wine than water, and cloth or silk than leaves, skins, or moss, that is wholly owing to labour and industry; the one of these being the food and raiment which unassisted nature furnishes us with; the other, provisions which our industry and pains prepare for us; which, how much they exceed the other in value, when any one hath computed, he will then see how much labour makes the far greatest part of the value of things we enjoy in this world: and the ground which produces the materials is scarce to be reckoned in as any, or, at most, but a very small part of it; so little, that even amongst us, land that is left wholly to nature, that hath no improvement of pasturage, tillage, or planting, is called, as indeed it is, waste; and we shall find the benefit of it amount to little more than nothing.

This shows how much numbers of men are to be preferred to largeness of dominions; and that the increase of lands, and the right of employing of them, is the great art of government: and that prince, who shall be so wise and godlike, as by established laws of liberty to secure protection and encouragement to the honest industry of mankind, against the oppression of power and narrowness of party, will quickly be too hard for his neighbours: but this by the by. To return to the argument in hand.

43. An acre of land, that bears here twenty bushels of wheat, and another in America, which, with the same husbandry, would do the like, are, without doubt, of the same natural intrinsic value:

but yet the benefit mankind receives from the one in a year is worth 5£. and from the other possibly not worth a penny, if all the profit an Indian received from it were to be valued, and sold here; at least, I may truly say, not one thousandth. It is labour, then, which puts the greatest part of value upon land, without which it would scarcely be worth any thing: it is to that we owe the greatest part of all its useful products; for all that the straw, bran, bread, of that acre of wheat, is more worth than the product of an acre of as good land, which lies waste, is all the effect of labour: for it is not barely the ploughman's pains, the reaper's and thresher's toil, and the baker's sweat, is to be counted into the bread we eat; the labour of those who broke the oxen, who digged and wrought the iron and stones, who felled and framed the timber employed about the plough, mill, oven, or any other utensils, which are a vast number, requisite to this corn, from its being seed to be sown to its being made bread, must all be charged on the account of labour, and received as an effect of that: nature and the earth furnished only the almost worthless materials, as in themselves. It would be a strange catalogue of things, that industry provided and made use of, about every loaf of bread, before it came to our use, if we could trace them; iron, wood, leather, bark, timber, stone, bricks, coals, lime, cloth, dyeing, drugs, pitch, tar, masts, ropes, and all the materials made use of in the ship, that brought any of the commodities used by any of the workmen, to any part of the work, all which it would be almost impossible, at least too long, to reckon up.

44. From all which it is evident, that though the things of nature are given in common, yet man, by being master of himself, and proprietor of his own person, and the actions or labour of it, had still in himself the great foundation of property; and that which made up the greater part of what he applied to the support or comfort of his being, when invention and arts had improved the conveniencies of life, was perfectly his own, and did not belong in common to others.

45. Thus labour, in the beginning, gave a right of property, wherever any one was pleased to employ it, upon what was common, which remained a long while the far greater part, and is yet more than mankind makes use of. Men, at first, for the most part, contented themselves with what unassisted nature offered to their necessities: and though afterwards, in some parts of the world, (where the increase of people and stock, with the use of money, had made land scarce, and so of some value) the several communities settled the bounds of their distinct territories, and by laws within themselves regulated the properties of the private men of their society, and so, by compact and agreement, settled the property which labour and industry began: and the leagues that have been made between several states and kingdoms, either expressly or tacitly disowning all claim and right to the land in the other's possession, have, by common consent, given up their pretences to their natural common right, which originally they had to those countries, and so have, by positive agreement, settled a property amongst themselves, in distinct parts and parcels of the earth; yet there are still great tracts of ground to be found, which (the inhabitants thereof not having joined with the rest of mankind in the consent of the use of their common money) lie waste, and are more than the people who dwell on it do or can make use of, and so still lie in common; though this can scarce happen amongst that part of mankind that have consented to the use of money.

46. The greatest part of things really useful to the life of man, and such as the necessity of subsisting made the first commoners of the world look after, as it doth the Americans now, are generally things of short duration; such as, if they are not consumed by use, will decay and perish of themselves: gold, silver, and diamonds, are things that fancy or agreement hath put the value on, more than real use, and the necessary support of life. Now of those good things which nature hath provided in common, every one had a right (as hath been said) to as much as he could use, and had property in all that he could effect with his labour; all that his industry could extend to, to alter from the state nature had put it in, was his. He that gathered a hundred bushels of acorns or apples, had thereby a property in them; they were

his goods as soon as gathered. He was only to look that he used them before they spoiled, else he took more than his share, and robbed others. And indeed it was a foolish thing, as well as dishonest, to hoard up more than he could make use of. If he gave away a part to any body else, so that it perished not uselessly in his possession, these he also made use of. And if he also bartered away plums, that would have rotted in a week, for nuts that would last good for his eating a whole year, he did no injury; he wasted not the common stock; destroyed no part of the portion of goods that belonged to others, so long as nothing perished uselessly in his hands. Again, if he would give his nuts for a piece of metal, pleased with its colour; or exchange his sheep for shells, or wool for a sparkling pebble or a diamond, and keep those by him all his life, he invaded not the right of others; he might heap as much of these durable things as he pleased; the exceeding of the bounds of his just property not lying in the largeness of his possession, but the perishing of any thing uselessly in it.

47. And thus came in the use of money, some lasting thing that men might keep without spoiling, and that by mutual consent men would take in exchange for the truly useful, but perishable supports of life.

48. And as different degrees of industry were apt to give men possessions in different proportions, so this invention of money gave them the opportunity to continue and enlarge them....

51. And thus, I think, it is very easy to conceive, how labour could at first begin a title of property in the common things of nature, and how the spending it upon our uses bounded it.... This left no room for controversy about the title, nor for encroachment on the right of others; what portion a man carved to himself was easily seen: and it was useless, as well as dishonest, to carve himself too much, or take more than he needed....

Of the Dissolution of Government

222. The reason why men enter into society is the preservation of their property; and the end why they choose and authorize a legislative is, that there may be laws made, and rules set, as guards and fences to the properties of all the members of the society: to limit the power, and moderate the dominion, of every part and member of the society: for since it can never be supposed to be the will of the society that the legislative should have a power to destroy that which every one designs to secure by entering into society, and for which the people submitted themselves to legislators of their own making; whenever the legislators endeavour to take away and destroy the property of the people, or to reduce them to slavery under arbitrary power, they put themselves into a state of war with the people, who are thereupon absolved from any farther obedience, and are left to the common refuge, which God hath provided for all men, against force and violence. Whensoever therefore the legislative shall transgress this fundamental rule of society; and either by ambition, fear, folly, or corruption, endeavour to grasp themselves, or put into the hands of any other, an absolute power over the lives, liberties, and estates of the people; by this breach of trust they forfeit the power the people had put into their hands for quite contrary ends, and it devolves to the people, who have a right to resume their original liberty, and, by the establishment of a new legislative, (such as they shall think fit), provide for their own safety and security, which is the end for which they are in society. What I have said here, concerning the legislative in general, holds true also concerning the supreme executor, who having a double trust put in him, both to have a part in the legislative, and the supreme execution of the law, acts against both, when he goes about to set up his own arbitrary will as the law of the society. He acts also contrary to his trust, when he either employs the force, treasure, and offices of the society to corrupt the representatives, and gain them to his purposes; or openly pre-engages the electors, and prescribes to their choice, such, whom he has, by solicitations, threats, promises, or otherwise, won to his designs; and employs them to bring in such, who have promised beforehand what to vote, and what to enact. Thus to regulate candidates and electors, and new-model the ways of election, what is it but to cut

up the government by the roots, and poison the very fountain of public security? For the people having reserved to themselves the choice of their representatives, as the fence to their properties, could do it for no other end, but that they might always be freely chosen, and so chosen, freely act, and advise, as the necessity of the commonwealth and the public good should, upon examination and mature debate, be judged to require. This, those who give their votes before they hear the debate, and have weighed the reasons on all sides, are not capable of doing. To prepare such an assembly as this, and endeavour to set up the declared abettors of his own will, for the true representatives of the people, and the lawmakers of the society, is certainly as great a breach of trust, and as perfect a declaration of a design to subvert the government, as is possible to be met with. To which if one shall add rewards and punishments visibly employed to the same end, and all the arts of perverted law made use of, to take off and destroy all that stand in the way of such a design, and will not comply and consent to betray the liberties of their country, it will be past doubt what is doing. What power they ought to have in the society, who thus employ it contrary to the trust that went along with it in its first institution, is easy to determine; and one cannot but see, that he, who has once attempted any such thing as this, cannot any longer be trusted....

224. The people generally ill-treated, and contrary to right, will be ready upon any occasion to ease themselves of a burden that sits heavy upon them. They will wish, and seek for the opportunity, which in the change, weakness, and accidents of human affairs, seldom delays long to offer itself. He must have lived but a little while in the world, who has not seen examples of this in his time; and he must have read very little, who cannot produce examples of it in all sorts of governments in the world.

225. Such revolutions happen...not upon every little mismanagement in public affairs. Great mistakes in the ruling part, many wrong and inconvenient laws, and all the slips of human frailty, will be borne by the people without mutiny or murmur. But if a long train of abuses, prevarications, and artifices, all tending the same way, make the design visible to the people, and they cannot but feel what they lie under, and see whither they are going; it is not to be wondered, that they should then rouse themselves, and endeavour to put the rule into such hands which may secure to them the ends for which government was at first erected, and without which, ancient names, and specious forms, are so far from being better, that they are much worse, than the state of nature, or pure anarchy; the inconveniencies, being all as great and as near, but the remedy farther off and more difficult.

14

Government, Rights, and the Bonds Between Generations

THOMAS PAINE

Although he spent his first thirty-eight years in England, Thomas Paine (1737–1809) is most often associated with the American and French revolutions. Paine moved to Pennsylvania in 1775, and in February of the following year he published a pamphlet, *Common Sense,* that urged the colonists to declare themselves independent of Britain. The beginning of *Common Sense* appears below as the first selection from Paine's writings. He later moved to France, where he actively supported the French Revolution. The second selection is from *The Rights of Man* (1791, 1792), which Paine wrote to defend the revolution against Edmund Burke's *Reflections on the Revolution in France* (see selection 25 in this volume).

Sources: Common Sense, from *The Life and Writings of Thomas Paine,* vol. 2, ed. Daniel Edwin Wheeler (New York: Vincent Parke and Co., 1915), pp. 1–7; and *The Rights of Man: Being an Answer to Mr. Burke's Attack on the French Revolution* (Dublin: G. Burnet, R. Cross, P. Wogan et al., 1791), pp. 8–9.

COMMON SENSE

Some writers have so confounded society with government, as to leave little or no distinction between them; whereas they are not only different, but have different origins. Society is produced by our wants, and government by our wickedness; the former promotes our happiness *positively* by uniting our affections, the latter *negatively* by restraining our vices. The one encourages intercourse, the other creates distinctions. The first is a patron, the last a punisher.

Society in every state is a blessing, but government even in its best state is but a necessary evil; in its worst state an intolerable one; for when we suffer, or are exposed to the same miseries *by a government,* which we might expect in a country *without government,* our calamities are heightened by reflecting that we furnish the means by which we suffer. Government, like dress, is the badge of lost innocence; the palaces of kings are built on the ruins of the bowers of paradise. For were the impulses of conscience clear, uniform, and irresistibly obeyed, man would need no other lawgiver; but that not being the case, he finds it necessary to surrender up a part of his property to furnish means for the protection of the rest; and this he is induced to do by the same prudence which in every other case advises him out of two evils to choose the least. *Wherefore,* security being the true design and end of government, it unanswerably follows that whatever *form* thereof appears most likely to ensure it to us, with the least expense and greatest benefit, is preferable to all others.

In order to gain a clear and just idea of the design and end of government, let us suppose a small number of persons settled in some sequestered part of the earth, unconnected with the rest, they will then represent the first peopling of any country, or of the world. In this state of natural liberty, society will be their first thought. A thousand motives will excite them thereto, the strength of one man is so unequal to his wants, and his mind so unfitted for perpetual solitude, that he is soon obliged to seek assistance and relief of another, who in his turn requires the same. Four or five united would be able to raise a tolerable dwelling in the midst of a wilderness, but *one* man might labour out the common period of life without accomplishing any thing; when he had felled his timber he could not remove it, nor erect it after it was removed; hunger in the mean time would urge him from his work, and every different want call him a different way. Disease, nay even misfortune, would be death, for though neither might be mortal, yet either would disable him from living, and reduce him to a state in which he might rather be said to perish than to die.

Thus necessity, like a gravitating power, would soon form our newly arrived emigrants into society, the reciprocal blessings of which would supersede and render the obligations of law and government unnecessary while they remained perfectly just to each other; but as nothing but heaven is impregnable to vice, it will unavoidably happen, that in proportion as they surmount the first difficulties of emigration, which bound them together in a common cause, they will begin to relax in their duty and attachment to each other; and this remissness, will point out the necessity, of establishing some form of government to supply the defect of moral virtue.

Some convenient tree will afford them a State-House, under the branches of which, the whole colony may assemble to deliberate on public matters. It is more than probable that their first laws will have the title only of REGULATIONS, and be enforced by no other penalty than public disesteem. In this first parliament every man, by natural right will have a seat.

But as the colony increases, the public concerns will increase likewise, and the distance at which the members may be separated, will render it too inconvenient for all of them to meet on every occasion as at first, when their number was small, their habitations near, and the public concerns few and trifling. This will point out the convenience of their consenting to leave the legislative part to be managed by a select number chosen from the whole body, who are supposed to have the same concerns at stake which those have who appointed them, and who will act in the same manner as the whole body would act were they present. If the colony continue increasing, it will become necessary to augment the number of the representatives, and that the interest of every part of the colony may be attended to, it will be found best to divide the whole into convenient parts, each part sending its proper number; and that the *elected* might never form to themselves an interest separate from the *electors,* prudence will point out the propriety of having elections often; because as the *elected* might by that means return and mix again with the general body of the *electors* in a few months, their fidelity to the public will be secured by the prudent reflection of not making a rod for themselves. And as this frequent interchange will establish a common interest with every part of the community, they will mutually and naturally support each other, and on this (not on the unmeaning name of king) depends the *strength of government, and the happiness of the governed.*

Here then is the origin and rise of government; namely, a mode rendered necessary by the inability of moral virtue to govern the world; here too is the design and end of government, viz. freedom and security. And however our eyes may be dazzled with snow, or our ears deceived by sound; however prejudice may warp our wills, or interest darken our understanding, the simple voice of nature and of reason will say, it is right.

I draw my idea of the form of government from a principle in nature, which no art can overturn, viz. that the more simple any thing is, the less liable it is to be disordered, and the easier repaired when disordered; and with this maxim in view, I offer a few remarks on the so much boasted constitution of England. That it was noble for the dark and slavish times in which it was erected is granted. When the world was overrun with tyranny the least remove therefrom was a glorious rescue. But that it is imperfect, subject to convulsions, and incapable of producing what it seems to promise, is easily demonstrated.

Absolute governments (tho' the disgrace of human nature) have this advantage with them, that they are simple; if the people suffer, they know the head from which their suffering springs, know likewise the remedy, and are not bewildered by a variety of causes and cures....

There is something exceedingly ridiculous in the composition of monarchy; it first excludes a man from the means of information, yet empowers him to act in cases where the highest judgement is required. The state of a king shuts him from the world, yet the business of a king requires him to know it thoroughly; wherefore the different parts, unnaturally opposing and destroying each other, prove the whole character to be absurd and useless.

THE RIGHTS OF MAN

Every age and generation must be as free to act for itself, *in all cases,* as the ages and generation which preceded it. The vanity and presumption of governing beyond the grave, is the most ridiculous and insolent of all tyrannies.

Man has no property in man; neither has any generation a property in the generations which are to follow. The Parliament or the people of 1688, or of any other period, had no more right to dispose of the people of the present day, or to bind or to control them *in any shape whatever,* than the Parliament or the people of the present day have to dispose of, bind, or control those who are to live a hundred or a thousand years hence.

Every generation is, and must be, competent to all the purposes which its occasions require. It is the living, and not the dead, that are to be accommodated. When man ceases to be, his power and his wants cease with him; and having no longer any participation in the concerns of this world, he has no longer any authority in directing who shall be its governors, or how its government shall be organized, or how administered.

I am not contending for nor against any form of government, nor for nor against any party here or elsewhere. That which a whole nation chooses to do, it has a right to do. Mr. [Edmund] Burke says, No. Where then *does* the right exist? I am contending for the rights of the *living*, and against their being willed away, and controlled and contracted for, by the manuscript assumed authority of the dead; and Mr. Burke is contending for the authority of the dead over the rights and freedom of the living.

There was a time when kings disposed of their crowns by will upon their death-beds, and consigned the people, like beasts of the field, to whatever successor they appointed. This is now so exploded as scarcely to be remembered, and so monstrous as hardly to be believed. But the parliamentary clauses upon which Mr. Burke builds his political church, are of the same nature.

The laws of every country must be analogous to some common principle. In England, no parent or master, nor all the authority of Parliament, omnipotent as it has called itself, can bind or control the personal freedom even of an individual beyond the age of twenty-one years. On what ground of right, then, could the Parliament of 1688, or any other parliament, bind all posterity for ever?

Those who have quitted the world [i.e., died], and those who are not yet arrived in it, are as remote from each other, as the utmost stretch of moral imagination can conceive. What possible obligation, then, can exist between them; what rule or principle can be laid down, that two nonentities, the one out of existence, and the other not in, and who never can meet in this world, that the one should control the other to the end of time?

15

Declaration of Independence of the United States

On June 7, 1776, Richard Henry Lee, a representative to the Continental Congress from Virginia, introduced a resolution proclaiming that "these United Colonies are, and of right ought to be, free and independent States." Three days later Congress appointed a committee to prepare a declaration of independence. One member of the committee, Thomas Jefferson (1743–1826), wrote the initial draft, which the other members of the committee and then the Congress as a whole modified. Jefferson later characterized the Declaration in this way: "Neither aiming at originality of principle or sentiment, nor yet copied from any particular and previous writing, it was intended to be an expression of the American mind."

THE UNANIMOUS DECLARATION OF THE THIRTEEN UNITED STATES OF AMERICA

When in the Course of human events, it becomes necessary for one people to dissolve the political bands which have connected them with another, and to assume among the Powers of the earth, the separate and equal station to which the Laws of Nature and of Nature's God entitle them, a decent respect to the opinions of mankind requires that they should declare the causes which impel them to the separation.

We hold these truths to be self-evident, that all men are created equal, that they are endowed by their Creator with certain unalienable Rights, that among these are Life, Liberty and the pursuit of Happiness. That to secure these rights, Governments are instituted among Men, deriving their just powers from the consent of the governed. That whenever any Form of Government becomes destructive of these ends, it is the Right of the People to alter or to abolish it, and to institute new Government, laying its foundation on such principles and organizing its powers in such form, as to them shall seem most likely to effect their Safety and Happiness. Prudence, indeed, will dictate that Governments long established should not be changed for light and transient causes; and accordingly all experience hath shown, that mankind are more disposed to suffer, while evils are sufferable, than to right themselves by abolishing the forms to which they are accustomed. But when a long train of abuses and usurpations, pursuing invariably the same Object evinces a design to reduce them under absolute Despotism, it is their right, it is their duty, to throw off such Government, and to provide new Guards for their future security—Such has been the patient sufferance of these Colonies; and such is now the necessity which constrains them to alter their former Systems of Government. The history of the present King of Great Britain is a history of repeated injuries and usurpations, all having in direct object the establishment of an absolute Tyranny over these States. To prove this, let Facts be submitted to a candid world.

He has refused his Assent to Laws, the most wholesome and necessary for the public good.

He has forbidden his Governors to pass Laws of immediate and pressing importance, unless suspended in their operation till his Assent should be obtained; and when so suspended, he has utterly neglected to attend to them.

He has refused to pass other Laws for the accommodation of large districts of people, unless those people would relinquish the right of Representation in the Legislature, a right inestimable to them and formidable to tyrants only.

He has called together legislative bodies at places unusual, uncomfortable, and distant from the depository of their Public Records, for the sole purpose of fatiguing them into compliance with his measures.

He has dissolved Representative Houses repeatedly, for opposing with manly firmness his invasions on the rights of the people.

He has refused for a long time, after such dissolutions, to cause others to be elected; whereby the Legislative Powers, incapable of Annihilation, have returned to the People at large for their exercise; the State remaining in the mean time exposed to all the dangers of invasion from without, and convulsions within.

He has endeavoured to prevent the population of these States; for that purpose obstructing the Laws of Naturalization of Foreigners; refusing to pass others to encourage their migration hither; and raising the conditions of new Appropriations of Lands.

He has obstructed the Administration of Justice, by refusing his Assent to Laws for establishing Judiciary Powers.

He has made Judges dependent on his Will alone, for the tenure of their offices, and the amount and payment of their salaries.

He has erected a multitude of New Offices, and sent hither swarms of Officers to harass our People, and eat out their substance.

He has kept among us, in times of peace, Standing Armies without the Consent of our legislatures.

He has affected to render the Military independent of and superior to the Civil Power.

He has combined with others to subject us to a jurisdiction foreign to our constitution, and unacknowledged by our laws; giving his Assent to their acts of pretended legislation:

For quartering large bodies of armed troops among us:

For protecting them, by a mock Trial, from Punishment for any Murders which they should commit on the Inhabitants of these States:

For cutting off our Trade with all parts of the world:

For imposing taxes on us without our Consent:

For depriving us in many cases, of the benefits of Trial by Jury:

For transporting us beyond Seas to be tried for pretended offences:

For abolishing the free System of English Laws in a neighbouring Province, establishing therein an Arbitrary government, and enlarging its Boundaries so as to render it at once an example and fit instrument for introducing the same absolute rule into these Colonies:

For taking away our Charters, abolishing our most valuable Laws, and altering fundamentally the Forms of our Governments:

For suspending our own Legislatures, and declaring themselves invested with Power to legislate for us in all cases whatsoever.

He has abdicated Government here, by declaring us out of his Protection and waging War against us.

He has plundered our seas, ravaged our Coasts, burnt our towns, and destroyed the lives of our people.

He is at this time transporting large armies of foreign mercenaries to compleat the works of death, desolation and tyranny, already begun with circumstances of Cruelty & perfidy scarcely paralleled in the most barbarous ages, and totally unworthy the Head of a civilized nation.

He has constrained our fellow Citizens taken Captive on the high Seas to bear Arms against their Country, to become the executioners of their friends and Brethren, or to fall themselves by their Hands.

He has excited domestic insurrections amongst us, and has endeavoured to bring on the inhabitants of our frontiers, the merciless Indian Savages, whose known rule of warfare, is an undistinguished destruction of all ages, sexes and conditions.

In every stage of these Oppressions We have Petitioned for Redress in the most humble terms: Our repeated Petitions have been answered only by repeated injury. A Prince, whose character is thus marked by every act which may define a Tyrant, is unfit to be the ruler of a free People.

Nor have We been wanting in attention to our British brethren. We have warned them from time to time of attempts by their legislature to extend an unwarrantable jurisdiction over us. We have reminded them of the circumstances of our emigration and settlement here. We have appealed to their native justice and magnanimity, and we have conjured them by the ties of our common kindred to disavow these usurpations, which, would inevitably interrupt our connections and correspondence. They too have been deaf to the voice of justice and of consanguinity. We must, therefore, acquiesce in the necessity, which denounces our Separation, and hold them, as we hold the rest of mankind, Enemies in War, in Peace Friends.

We, therefore, the Representatives of the United States of America, in General Congress, Assembled, appealing to the Supreme Judge of the world for the rectitude of our intentions, do, in the Name, and by Authority of the good People of these Colonies, solemnly publish and declare, That these United Colonies are, and of Right ought to be Free and Independent States; that they are Absolved from all Allegiance to the British Crown, and that all political connection between them and the State of Great Britain, is and ought to be totally dissolved; and that as Free and Independent States, they have full Power to levy War, conclude Peace, contract Alliances, establish Commerce, and to do all other Acts and Things which Independent States may of right do. And for the support of this Declaration, with a firm reliance on the Protection of Divine Providence, we mutually pledge to each other our Lives, our Fortunes and our sacred Honor.

16

Declaration of the Rights of Man and of Citizens

In 1788, faced with a financial crisis, King Louis XVI of France called the Estates-General into session for the first time in over 170 years. The traditional representative body of France, the Estates-General consisted of representatives of the church, the nobility, and the people. When the Estates-General convened in 1789, the representatives of the Third Estate (the people) defied the king and declared themselves the National Assembly of France. As one of its first acts, the Assembly approved a declaration of rights that was to serve as the basis of a constitution. The Declaration appears here in Thomas Paine's translation, included in his book *The Rights of Man* (see selection 14).

DECLARATION OF THE RIGHTS OF MAN AND OF CITIZENS

By the National Assembly of France

The representatives of the people of FRANCE, *formed into a* NATIONAL ASSEMBLY, considering that ignorance, neglect, or contempt of human rights, are the sole causes of public misfortunes and corruptions of government, have resolved to set forth in a solemn declaration, these natural, imprescriptible, and unalienable rights: that this declaration, being constantly present to the minds of the members of the body social, they may be ever kept attentive to their rights and their duties: that the acts of the legislative and executive powers of government, being capable of being every moment compared with the end of political institutions, may be more respected: and also, that the future claims of the citizens, being directed by simple and incontestible principles, may always tend to the maintenance of the Constitution, and the general happiness.

For these reasons the NATIONAL ASSEMBLY doth recognize and declare, in the presence of the Supreme Being, and with the hope of His blessing and favor, the following *sacred* rights of men and of citizens:

1. Men are born, and always continue, free, and equal in respect of their rights. Civil distinctions, therefore, can be founded only on public utility.

2. The end of all political associations, is, the preservation of the natural and imprescriptible rights of man; and these rights are liberty, property, security, and resistance of oppression.

3. The nation is essentially the source of all sovereignty; nor can any INDIVIDUAL, or ANY BODY OF MEN, be entitled to any authority which is not expressly derived from it.

4. Political liberty consists in the power of doing whatever does not injure another. The exercise of the natural rights of every man has no other limits than those which are necessary to secure to every *other* man the free exercise of the same rights; and these limits are determinable only by the law.

5. The law ought to prohibit only actions hurtful to society. What is not prohibited by the law, should not be hindered; nor should any one be compelled to that which the law does not require.

6. The law is an expression of the will of the community. All citizens have a right to concur, either personally, or by their representatives, in its formation. It should be the same to all, whether it protects or punishes; and all being equal in its sight, are equally eligible to all honors, places, and employments, according to their different abilities, without any other distinction than that created by their virtues and talents.

7. No man should be accused, arrested, or held in confinement, except in cases determined by the law, and according to the forms which it has prescribed. All who promote, solicit, execute, or cause to be executed, arbitrary orders, ought to be punished; and every citizen called upon or apprehended by virtue of the law, ought immediately to obey, and renders himself culpable by resistance.

8. The law ought to impose no other penalties but such as are absolutely and evidently necessary: and no one ought to be punished, but in virtue of a law promulgated before the offense, and legally applied.

9. Every man being presumed innocent till he has been convicted, whenever his detention becomes indispensable, all rigor to him, more than is necessary to secure his person, ought to be provided against by the law.

10. No man ought to be molested on account of his opinions, not even on account of his *religious* opinions, provided his avowal of them does not disturb the public order established by the law.

11. The unrestrained communication of thoughts and opinions being one of the most precious rights of man, every citizen may speak, write, and publish freely, provided he is responsible for the abuse of this liberty in cases determined by the law.

12. A public force being necessary to give security to the rights of men and of citizens, that force is instituted for the benefit of the community, and not for the particular benefit of the persons with whom it is entrusted.

13. A common contribution being necessary for the support of the public force, and for defraying the other expenses of government, it ought to be divided equally among the members of the community, according to their abilities.

14. Every citizen has a right, either by himself or his representative, to a free voice in determining the necessity of public contributions, the appropriation of them, and their amount, mode of assessment, and duration.

15. Every community has a right to demand of all its agents, an account of their conduct.

16. Every community in which a separation of powers and a security of rights is not provided for, wants a constitution.

17. The rights to property being inviolable and sacred, no one ought to be deprived of it, except in cases of evident public necessity, legally ascertained, and on condition of a previous just indemnity.

17

Private Profit, Public Good

ADAM SMITH

Although he was one of the major philosophers of the Scottish Enlightenment, Adam Smith (1723–1790) is today best known for his work in political economy, notably his *An Inquiry into the Nature and Causes of the Wealth of Nations* (1776). Other writers had developed the laissez-faire theory that government should leave people alone in the economic marketplace, but Smith provided the most thorough and influential defense of this doctrine.

Source: Adam Smith, *An Inquiry into the Nature and Causes of the Wealth of Nations*, vol. 1 (London: T. Cadell and W. Davies, 1805), pp. 20–27.

OF THE PRINCIPLE WHICH GIVES OCCASION TO THE DIVISION OF LABOR

(From *The Wealth of Nations,* Book I, Chapter 2)

This division of labor, from which so many advantages are derived, is not originally the effect of any human wisdom which foresees and intends that general opulence to which it gives occasion. It is the necessary, though very slow and gradual, consequence of a certain propensity in human nature which has in view no such extensive utility: the propensity to truck, barter, and exchange one thing for another.

Whether this propensity be one of those original principles in human nature, of which no further account can be given; or whether, as seems more probable, it be the necessary consequence of the faculties of reason and speech, it belongs not to our present subject to enquire. It is common to all men, and to be found in no other race of animals, which seem to know neither this nor any other species of contracts. Two greyhounds, in running down the same hare, have sometimes the appearance of acting in some sort of concert. Each turns her toward his companion, or endeavors to intercept her when his companion turns her toward himself. This, however, is not the effect of any contract, but of the accidental concurrence of their passions in the same object at that particular time. Nobody ever saw a dog make a fair and deliberate exchange of one bone for another with another dog. Nobody ever saw one animal by its gestures and natural cries signify to another, this is mine, that yours; I am willing to give this for that. When an animal wants to obtain something either of a man or of another animal, it has no other means of persuasion but to gain the favor of those whose service it requires. A puppy fawns upon its dam, and a spaniel endeavors by a thousand attractions to engage the attention of its master who is at dinner, when it wants to be fed by him. Man sometimes uses the same arts with his brethren, and when he has no other means of engaging them to act according to his inclinations, endeavors by every servile and fawning attention to obtain their good will. He has not time, however, to do this upon every occasion. In civilized society he stands at all times in need of the co-operation and assistance of great multitudes, while his whole life is scarce sufficient to gain the friendship of a few persons. In almost every other race of animals each individual, when it is grown up to maturity, is entirely independent, and in its natural state has occasion for the assistance of no other living creature. But man has almost constant occasion for the help of his brethren, and it is in vain for him to expect it from their benevolence only. He will be more likely to prevail if he can interest their self-love in his favor, and show them that it is for their own advantage to do for him what he requires of them. Whoever offers to another a bargain of any kind, proposes to do this. Give me that which I want, and you shall have this which you want, is the meaning of every such offer; and it is in this manner that we obtain from one another the far greater part of those good offices which we stand in need of. It is not from the benevolence of the butcher, the brewer, or the baker, that we expect our dinner, but from their regard to their own interest. We address ourselves, not to their humanity but to their self-love, and never talk to them of our own necessities but of their advantages. Nobody but a beggar chooses to depend chiefly upon the benevolence of his fellow citizens. Even a beggar does not depend upon it entirely. The charity of well-disposed people, indeed, supplies him with the whole fund of his subsistence. But though this principle ultimately provides him with all the necessaries of life which he has occasion for, it neither does nor can provide him with them as he has occasion for them. The greater part of his occasional wants are supplied in the same manner as those of other people, by treaty, by barter, and by purchase. With the money which one man gives him he purchases food. The old clothes which another bestows upon him he exchanges for other old clothes which suit him better, or for lodging, or for food, or for money, with which he can buy either food, clothes, or lodging, as he has occasion.

As it is by treaty, by barter, and by purchase that we obtain from one another the greater part of those mutual good offices which we stand in need of, so it is this same trucking disposition which originally gives occasion to the division of labor. In a tribe of hunters or shepherds a particular person makes bows and arrows, for example, with more readiness and dexterity than any other. He frequently exchanges them for cattle or for venison with his companions; and he finds at last that he can in this manner get more cattle and venison than if he himself went to the field to catch them. From a regard to his own interest, therefore, the making of bows and arrows grows to be his chief business, and he becomes a sort of armorer. Another excels in making the frames and covers of their little huts or movable houses. He is accustomed to be of use in this way to his neighbors, who reward him in the same manner with cattle and with venison till at last he finds it his interest to dedicate himself entirely to this employment, and to become a sort of house carpenter. In the same manner a third becomes a smith or a brazier; a fourth a tanner or dresser of hides or skins, the principal part of the clothing of savages. And thus the certainty of being able to exchange all that surplus part of the produce of his own labor, which is over and above his own consumption, for such parts of the produce of other men's labor as he may have occasion for, encourages every man to apply himself to a particular occupation, and to cultivate and bring to perfection whatever talent or genius he may possess for that particular species of business.

The difference of natural talents in different men is, in reality, much less than we are aware of; and the very different genius which appears to distinguish men of different professions, when grown up to maturity, is not upon many occasions so much the cause as the effect of the division of labor. The difference between the most dissimilar characters, between a philosopher and a common street porter, for example, seems to arise not so much from nature as from habit, custom, and education. When they came into the world, and for the first six or eight years of their existence, they were, perhaps, very much alike, and neither their parents nor playfellows could perceive any remarkable difference. About that age, or soon after, they come to be employed in very different occupations. The difference of talents comes then to be taken notice of, and widens by degrees, till at last the vanity of the philosopher is willing to acknowledge scarce any resemblance. But without the disposition to truck, barter, and exchange, every man must have procured to himself every necessary and conveniency of life which he wanted. All must have had the same duties to perform, and the same work to do, and there could have been no such difference of employment as could alone give occasion to any great difference of talents.

As it is this disposition which forms that difference of talents so remarkable among men of different professions, so it is this same disposition which renders that difference useful. Many tribes of animals acknowledged to be all of the same species derive from nature a much more remarkable distinction of genius than what, antecedent to custom and education, appears to take place among men. By nature a philosopher is not in genius and disposition half so different from a street porter as a mastiff is from a greyhound, or a greyhound from a spaniel, or this last from a shepherd's dog. Those different tribes of animals, however, though all of the same species, are of scarce any use to one another. The strength of the mastiff is not in the least supported either by the swiftness of the greyhound, or by the sagacity of the spaniel, or by the docility of the shepherd's dog. The effects of those different geniuses and talents, for want of the power or disposition to barter and exchange, cannot be brought into a common stock, and do not in the least contribute to the better accommodation and conveniency of the species. Each animal is still obliged to support and defend itself separately and independently, and derives no sort of advantage from that variety of talents with which nature has distinguished its fellows.

18

Freedom and Enlightenment

IMMANUEL KANT

Immanuel Kant (1724–1804), the eminent German philosopher, wrote several influential books, including *The Critique of Pure Reason* (1781) and the *Groundwork of the Metaphysics of Morals* (1785). Kant held that autonomy, or self-rule, is the mark of a fully mature and moral person, and he believed that the eighteenth-century intellectual movement known as the Enlightenment embodied that ideal. He wrote the following essay, "What Is Enlightenment?" as a newspaper article in 1784 to describe and defend the ideals of the Enlightenment against some of its critics.

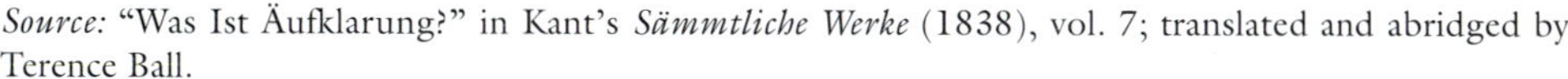

Source: "Was Ist Äufklarung?" in Kant's *Sämmtliche Werke* (1838), vol. 7; translated and abridged by Terence Ball.

WHAT IS ENLIGHTENMENT?

Enlightenment is mankind's leaving behind its self-imposed immaturity. Immaturity is the inability to employ one's own intelligence without being directed by someone else. This immaturity is self-imposed if it results not from lack of intellect but from a lack of willingness and courage to use it without another's guidance. *Sapere Aude!*—"Have the courage to think for yourself!"—that is the motto of the Enlightenment.

Because of laziness and cowardice, many supposedly grown men remain happily immature throughout their lives, readily allowing others to serve as their guardians. After all, it is so easy to remain immature! If I have a book which does my thinking for me, a priest or pastor who serves as my conscience, and a doctor who tells me what to eat, then I need not take the trouble to think for myself. If I have the money to pay them, others will perform that troublesome task for me. The guardians who have so kindly agreed to supervise me will warn me and others like me—including the entire "fair sex"—that any move toward adult maturity is not merely difficult but downright dangerous. Having already made their domestic animals dumb by seeing that these placid creatures remain on a short leash, our guardians likewise warn us of the danger of attempting to stand and walk on our own two feet. In fact, however, the danger is not all that great, since after falling a few times, one finally learns to walk by oneself. Even so, most people are so frightened by the warning that they dare not venture out on their own.

It is no easy task for a lone individual to outgrow the immaturity which has become second nature for him. He has grown fond of his infantile dependency, and is for the moment unable to employ his reason, since no one has previously permitted him to try. Rules and regulations—those mechanical tools of the use, or rather misuse, of his natural talents—are the chains which keep him bound to an endless childhood. Whoever broke these chains would have great difficulty in jumping over the smallest ditch, because he would be unused to moving freely. Thus only a handful of human beings have heretofore succeeded in freeing themselves from their childish dependency on others by cultivating their own minds at their own steady pace.

But it is even more possible that the public can enlighten itself. In fact, such enlightenment is virtually assured under conditions of freedom.... The only thing needed for such enlightenment is freedom, and particularly...the freedom to make public use of one's reason in every case. And yet I hear people shout from all sides: "Don't argue!" The military commander says: "Don't argue, drill!" The tax collector: "Don't argue, pay!" The priest or pastor: "Don't argue, believe!".... Everywhere there are restrictions on freedom.

Which of these restrictions hinders enlightenment, and which does not? I answer: The public use of one's reason must always be free, and this by itself can bring about enlightenment among human beings. By contrast, the private use of one's reason may be rather tightly restricted without necessarily impeding the progress of enlightenment. By the public use of one's reason I mean, for example, the way in which a scholar uses reason before the reading public. The private use of reason is the use which one may make of reason in a civil position or office with which he is entrusted. In the latter case, the public interest is served by the officeholder's neutrality and obedience—not by his argument and disagreement, which would be divisive and disruptive. Civil servants should not argue but obey.... A soldier, for example, should not argue with a superior officer who gives him a command.... Nor should a citizen refuse to pay his taxes.... Nor may a priest publicly disagree with the teachings of his church, offering instead his own personal interpretation of the gospel. But in their capacity as scholars, those same people would have the freedom and indeed the duty to criticize the military, the system of taxation, and the teachings of the church.... The scholar, speaking to the world through his writings, has an unrestricted freedom to use his own reason and to speak in his own voice. To insist that the people's spiritual guardians should themselves remain immature children would only perpetuate present-day ignorance.

But should an organization of clergymen be permitted to pledge itself to teach a particular unchanging doctrine, now and forevermore, in order to perpetuate its dominion over its members and their congregations? I say no. Any such agreement which aims to prevent the enlightenment of mankind is null and void. One generation cannot enter into a contract to stifle the intellectual and moral development of a later generation by making it impossible for the latter to expand its knowledge, to expose and eliminate error, and thereby to become ever more enlightened. To do so would be to commit a crime against human nature, whose destiny is to grow and progress. Later generations are utterly justified in ignoring or overturning such an agreement as unjust and illegal.... An individual may for a time hesitate to enlighten himself. But to opt out of such enlightenment entirely, either for oneself or one's descendants, is to ride roughshod over the sacred rights of mankind.... We can now pose the question: Is ours an enlightened age? I answer no: Ours is not an enlightened age, but it *is* an age of enlightenment. Many things continue to prevent people from using their own minds in matters of religion. But there is every indication that even this area is being opened up to critical scrutiny, thereby permitting people to escape from self-imposed immaturity....

I have stressed the primary point of enlightenment—i.e., of man's release from his self-imposed immaturity—mainly in matters of religion...because immaturity in this area is the most unfortunate and reprehensible kind. The ruler of a free state recognizes that there is no danger in legislation allowing his people to make public use of their own reason in publicly discussing and criticizing existing or proposed legislation.... A very large degree of civic freedom appears to be beneficial for the freedom of the spirit of a people.... Thus nature has nurtured, inside its tough shell, the embryo of the interest in and need for free thought. This free thought acts slowly but surely upon the mind of the people, permitting them to become ever more able to act freely. Eventually even the government will be influenced by this free thought, and will begin to treat men not as automata but as autonomous and responsible human beings.

19

Liberty and Individuality

JOHN STUART MILL

Like Alexis de Tocqueville (see selection 8), whose work he admired, John Stuart Mill (1806–1873) feared that the advent of democracy was bringing with it a stifling pressure to conform to the conventional or popular opinion. In Mill's view no one could live a fully human life unless he—or she, as he made clear in *The Subjection of Women* (1869)—was free to think and act for him- or herself. In the following excerpt from *On Liberty* (1859), Mill proposes "one very simple principle" for deciding just when society or government may rightfully regulate the individual's conduct and when the individual should be free to do as he or she sees fit.

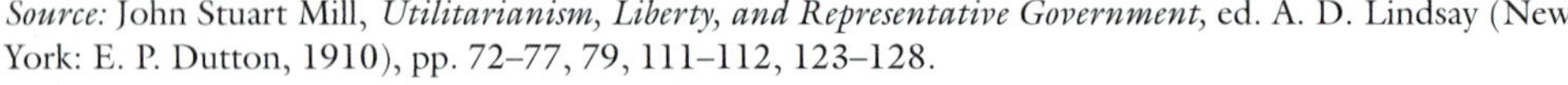
Source: John Stuart Mill, *Utilitarianism, Liberty, and Representative Government,* ed. A. D. Lindsay (New York: E. P. Dutton, 1910), pp. 72–77, 79, 111–112, 123–128.

ON LIBERTY: INTRODUCTORY

The object of this Essay is to assert one very simple principle, as entitled to govern absolutely the dealings of society with the individual in the way of compulsion and control, whether the means used be physical force in the form of legal penalties, or the moral coercion of public opinion. That principle is, that the sole end for which mankind are warranted, individually or collectively, in interfering with the liberty of action of any of their number, is self-protection. That the only purpose for which power can be rightfully exercised over any member of a civilized community, against his will, is to prevent harm to others. His own good, either physical or moral, is not a sufficient warrant. He cannot rightfully be compelled to do or forbear because it will be better for him to do so, because it will make him happier, because, in the opinions of others, to do so would be wise, or even right. These are good reasons for remonstrating with him, or reasoning with him, or persuading him, or entreating him, but not for compelling him, or visiting him with any evil in case he do otherwise. To justify that, the conduct from which it is desired to deter him, must be calculated to produce evil to some one else. The only part of the conduct of any one, for which he is amenable to society, is that which concerns others. In the part which merely concerns himself, his independence is, of right, absolute. Over himself, over his own body and mind, the individual is sovereign.

It is, perhaps, hardly necessary to say that this doctrine is meant to apply only to human beings in the maturity of their faculties. We are not speaking of children, or of young persons below the age which the law may fix as that of manhood or womanhood. Those who are still in a state to require being taken care of by others, must be protected against their own actions as well as against external injury. For the same reason, we may leave out of consideration those backward states of society in which the race itself may be considered as in its nonage. The early difficulties in the way of spontaneous progress are so great, that there is seldom any choice of means for overcoming them; and a ruler full of the spirit of improvement is warranted in the use of any expedients that will attain an end, perhaps otherwise unattainable. Despotism is a legitimate mode of government in dealing with barbarians, provided the end be their improvement, and the means justified by actually effecting that end. Liberty, as a principle, has no application to any state of things anterior to the time when mankind have become capable of being improved by free and equal discussion. Until then, there is nothing for them but implicit obedience to an Akbar or a Charlemagne, if they are so fortunate as to find one.[1] But as soon as mankind have attained the capacity of being guided to their own improvement by conviction or persuasion (a period long since reached in all nations with whom we need here concern ourselves), compulsion, either in the direct form or in that of pains and penalties for non-compliance, is no longer admissible as a means to their own good, and justifiable only for the security of others.

It is proper to state that I forgo any advantage which could be derived to my argument from the idea of abstract right, as a thing independent of utility.[2] I regard utility as the ultimate appeal on all ethical questions; but it must be utility in the largest sense, grounded on the permanent interests of man as a progressive being. Those interests, I contend, authorize the subjection of individual spontaneity to external control, only in respect to those actions of each, which concern the interest of other people. If any one does an act hurtful to others, there is a prima facie case for punishing him, by law, or, where legal penalties are not safely applicable, by general disapprobation. There are also many positive acts for the benefit of others, which he may rightfully be compelled to perform; such as, to give evidence in a court of justice; to bear his fair share in the common defence, or in any other joint work necessary to the interest of the society of which he enjoys the protection; and to perform certain acts of individual beneficence, such as saving a fellow creature's life, or interposing to protect the defenceless against ill-usage, things which whenever it is obviously a man's duty to do, he may rightfully be made responsible to society for not doing. A person may cause evil to others not only by his actions but by his inaction, and in either case he is justly accountable to them for the injury. The latter case, it is true, requires a much more cautious exercise of compulsion than the former. To make any one answerable for doing evil to others, is the rule; to make him answerable for not preventing evil, is, comparatively speaking, the exception. Yet there are many cases clear enough and grave enough to justify that exception. In all things which regard the external relations of the individual, he is *de jure* amenable to those whose interests are concerned, and if need be, to society as their protector. There are often good reasons for not holding him to the responsibility; but these reasons must arise from the special expediencies of the case: either because it is a kind of case in which he is on the whole likely to act better, when left to his own discretion, than when controlled in any way in which society have it in their power to control him; or because the attempt to exercise control would produce other evils, greater than those which it would prevent. When such reasons as these preclude the enforcement of responsibility, the conscience of the agent himself should step into the vacant judgement-seat, and protect those interests of others which have no external protection; judging himself all the more rigidly, because the case does not admit of his being made accountable to the judgement of his fellow creatures.

But there is a sphere of action in which society, as distinguished from the individual, has, if any, only an indirect interest; comprehending all that portion of a person's life and conduct which affects only himself, or if it also affects others, only with their free, voluntary, and undeceived consent and participation. When I say only himself, I mean directly, and in the first instance: for whatever affects himself, may affect others through himself; and the objection which may be grounded on this contingency will receive consideration in the sequel. This, then, is the appropriate region of human liberty. It comprises, first, the inward domain of consciousness; demanding liberty of conscience, in the most comprehensive sense; liberty of thought and feeling; absolute freedom of opinion and sentiment on all subjects, practical or speculative, scientific, moral, or theological. The liberty of expressing and publishing opinions may seem to fall under a different principle, since it belongs to that part of the conduct of an individual which concerns other people; but, being almost of as much importance as the liberty of thought itself, and resting in great part on the same reasons, is practically inseparable from it. Secondly, the principle requires liberty of tastes and pursuits; of framing the plan of our life to suit our own character; of doing as we like, subject to such consequences as may follow: without impediment from our fellow creatures, so long as what we do does not harm them, even though they should think our conduct foolish, perverse, or wrong. Thirdly, from this liberty of each individual, follows the liberty, within the same limits, of combination among individuals; freedom to unite, for any purpose not involving harm to others: the persons combining being supposed to be of full age, and not forced or deceived.

No society in which these liberties are not, on the whole, respected, is free, whatever may be its form of government; and none is completely free in which they do not exist absolute and unqualified. The only freedom which deserves the name, is that of pursuing our own good in our own way, so long as we do not attempt to deprive others of theirs, or impede their efforts to obtain it. Each is the proper guardian of his own health, whether bodily, or mental and spiritual. Mankind are greater gainers by suffering each other to live as seems good to themselves, than by compelling each to live as seems good to the rest....

Apart from the peculiar tenets of individual thinkers, there is also in the world at large an increasing inclination to stretch unduly the powers of society over the individual, both by the force of opinion and even by that of legislation: and as the tendency of all the changes taking place in the world is to strengthen society, and diminish the power of the individual, this encroachment is not one of the evils which tend spontaneously to disappear, but, on the contrary, to grow more and more formidable. The disposition of mankind, whether as rulers or as fellow citizens, to impose their own opinions and inclinations as a rule of conduct on others, is so energetically supported by some of the best and by some of the worst feelings incident to human nature, that it is hardly ever kept under restraint by anything but want of power; and as the power is not declining, but growing, unless a strong barrier of moral conviction can be raised against the mischief, we must expect, in the present circumstances of the world, to see it increase.

OF THE LIBERTY OF THOUGHT AND DISCUSSION

(From *On Liberty*, Chapter 2)

If all mankind minus one, were of one opinion, and only one person were of the contrary opinion, mankind would be no more justified in silencing that one person, than he, if he had the power, would be justified in silencing mankind. Were an opinion a personal possession of no value except to the owner; if to be obstructed in the enjoyment of it were simply a private injury, it would make some difference whether the injury was inflicted only on a few persons or on many. But the peculiar evil of silencing the expression of an opinion is, that it is robbing the human race; posterity as well as the existing generation; those who dissent from the opinion, still more than those who hold it. If the opinion is right, they are deprived of the opportunity of exchanging error for truth: if wrong, they lose, what is almost as great a benefit, the clearer perception and livelier impression of truth, produced by its collision with error.

It is necessary to consider separately these two hypotheses, each of which has a distinct branch of the argument corresponding to it. We can never be sure that the opinion we are endeavouring to stifle is a false opinion; and if we were sure, stifling it would be an evil still....

We have now recognized the necessity to the mental well-being of mankind (on which all their other well-being depends) of freedom of opinion, and freedom of the expression of opinion, on four distinct grounds; which we will now briefly recapitulate.

First, if any opinion is compelled to silence, that opinion may, for aught we can certainly know, be true. To deny this is to assume our own infallibility.

Secondly, though the silenced opinion be an error, it may, and very commonly does, contain a portion of truth; and since the general or prevailing opinion on any subject is rarely or never the whole truth, it is only by the collision of adverse opinions that the remainder of the truth has any chance of being supplied.

Thirdly, even if the received opinion be not only true, but the whole truth; unless it is suffered to be, and actually is, vigorously and earnestly contested, it will, by most of those who receive it, be held in the manner of a prejudice, with little comprehension or feeling of its rational grounds. And not only this, but, fourthly, the meaning of the doctrine itself will be in danger of being lost, or enfeebled, and deprived of its vital effect on the character and conduct: the dogma becoming a mere formal profession, inefficacious for good, but cumbering the ground, and preventing the growth of any real and heartfelt conviction, from reason or personal experience....

Persons of genius, it is true, are, and are always likely to be, a small minority; but in order to have them, it is necessary to preserve the soil in which they grow. Genius can only breathe freely in an *atmosphere* of freedom. Persons of genius are, *ex vi termini* [from the force of the term], *more* individual than any other people—less capable, consequently, of fitting themselves, without hurtful compression, into any of the small number of moulds which society provides in order to save its members the trouble of forming their own character. If from timidity they consent to be forced into one of these moulds, and to let all that part of themselves which cannot expand under the pressure remain unexpanded, society will be little the better for their genius. If they are of a strong character, and break their fetters, they become a mark for the society which has not succeeded in reducing them to commonplace, to point at with solemn warning as "wild," "erratic," and the like; much as if one should complain of the Niagara river for not flowing smoothly between its banks like a Dutch canal.

I insist thus emphatically on the importance of genius, and the necessity of allowing it to unfold itself freely both in thought and in practice, being well aware that no one will deny the position in theory, but knowing also that almost every one, in reality, is totally indifferent to it. People think genius a fine thing if it enables a man to write an exciting poem, or paint a picture. But in its true sense, that of originality in thought and action, though no one says that it is not a thing to be admired, nearly all, at heart, think that they can do very well without it. Unhappily this is too natural to be wondered at. Originality is the one thing which unoriginal minds cannot feel the use of. They cannot see what it is to do for them: how should they? If they could see what it would do for them, it would not be originality. The first service which originality has to render them, is that of opening their eyes: which being once fully done, they would have a chance of being themselves original. Meanwhile, recollecting that nothing was ever yet done which some one was not the first to do, and that all good things which exist are the fruits of originality, let them be modest enough to believe that there is something still left for it to accomplish, and assure themselves that they are more in need of originality, the less they are conscious of the want.

In sober truth, whatever homage may be professed, or even paid, to real or supposed mental superiority, the general tendency of things throughout the world is to render mediocrity the ascendant power among mankind. In ancient history, in the middle ages, and in a diminishing degree through the long transition from feudality to the present time, the individual was a power in himself; and if he had either great talents or a high social position, he was a considerable power. At present individuals are lost in the crowd. In politics it is almost a triviality to say that public opinion now rules the world. The only power deserving the name is that of masses, and of governments while they make themselves the organ of the tendencies and instincts of masses. This is as true in the moral and social relations of private life as in public transactions. Those whose opinions go by the name of public opinion, are not always the same sort of public: in America they are the whole white population; in England, chiefly the middle class. But they are always a mass, that is to say, collective mediocrity. And what is a still greater novelty, the mass do not now take their opinions from dignitaries in Church or State, from ostensible leaders, or from books. Their thinking is done for them by men much like themselves, addressing them or speaking in their name, on the spur of the moment, through the newspapers. I am not complaining of all this. I do not assert that anything better is compatible, as a general rule, with the present low state of the human mind. But that does not hinder the government of mediocrity from being mediocre government. No government by a democracy or a numerous aristocracy, either in its political acts or in the opinions, qualities, and tone of mind which it fosters, ever did or could rise above mediocrity, except in so far as the sovereign Many have let themselves be guided (which in their best times they always have done) by the counsels and influence of a more highly gifted and instructed One or Few. The initiation of all wise or noble things, comes and must come from individuals; generally at first from some one individual. The honour and glory of the average man is that he is capable of following that initiative; that he can respond internally to wise and noble things, and be led to them with his eyes open. I am not countenancing the sort of "hero-worship" which applauds the strong man of genius for forcibly seizing on the government of the world and making it do his bidding in spite of itself.[3] All he can claim is, freedom to point out the way. The power of compelling others into it, is not only inconsistent with the freedom and development of all the rest, but corrupting to the strong man himself. It does seem, however, that when the opinions of masses of merely average men are everywhere become or becoming the dominant power, the counterpoise and corrective to that tendency would be, the more and more pronounced individuality of those who stand on the higher eminences of thought. It is in these circumstances most especially, that exceptional individuals, instead of being deterred, should be encouraged in acting differently from the mass. In other times there was no advantage in their doing so, unless they acted not only differently, but better. In this age, the mere example of nonconformity, the mere refusal to bend the knee to custom, is itself a service. Precisely because the tyranny of opinion is such as to make eccentricity a reproach, it is desirable, in order to break through that tyranny, that people should be eccentric. Eccentricity has always abounded when and where strength of character has abounded; and the amount of eccentricity in a society has generally been proportional to the amount of genius, mental vigour, and moral courage which it contained. That so few now dare to be eccentric, marks the chief danger of the time....

...[N]or is it only persons of decided mental superiority who have a just claim to carry on their lives in their own way. There is no reason that all human existence should be constructed on some one or some small number of patterns. If a person possesses any tolerable amount of common sense and experience, his own mode of laying out his existence is the best, not because it is the best in itself, but because it is his own mode. Human beings are not like sheep; and even sheep are not undistinguishably alike. A man cannot get a coat or a pair of boots to fit him, unless they are either made to his measure, or he has a whole warehouseful to choose from: and is it easier to fit him with a life than with a coat, or are human beings more like one another in their whole physical and spiritual conformation than in the shape of their feet? If it were only that people have diversities of taste, that is reason enough for not attempting to shape them all after one model. But different persons also require different conditions for their spiritual development; and can no more exist healthily in the same moral, than all the variety of plants can in the same physical, atmosphere and climate. The same things which are helps to one person towards the cultivation of his higher nature, are hindrances to another. The same mode of life is a healthy excitement to one, keeping all his faculties of action and enjoyment in their best order, while to another it is a distracting burden, which suspends or crushes all internal life. Such are the differences among human beings in their sources of pleasure, their susceptibilities of pain, and the operation on them of different physical and moral agencies, that unless there is a corresponding diversity in their modes of life, they neither obtain their fair share of happiness, nor grow up to the mental, moral, and aesthetic stature of which their nature is capable....

There is one characteristic of the present direction of public opinion, peculiarly calculated to make it intolerant of any marked demonstration of individuality. The general average of mankind are not only moderate in intellect, but also moderate in inclinations: they have no tastes or wishes strong enough to incline them to do anything unusual, and they consequently do not understand those who have, and class all such with the wild and intemperate whom they are accustomed to look down upon. Now, in addition to this fact which is general, we have only to suppose that a strong movement has set in towards the improvement of morals, and it is evident what we have to expect. In these days such a movement has set in; much has actually been effected in the way of increased regularity of conduct, and discouragement of excesses; and there is a philanthropic spirit abroad, for the exercise of which there is no more inviting field than the moral and prudential improvement of our fellow creatures. These tendencies of the times cause the public to be more disposed than at most former periods to prescribe general rules of conduct, and endeavour to make every one conform to the approved standard. And that standard, express or tacit, is to desire nothing strongly. Its ideal of character is to be without any marked character; to maim by compression, like a Chinese lady's foot, every part of human nature which stands out prominently, and tends to make the person markedly dissimilar in outline to commonplace humanity....

The despotism of custom is everywhere the standing hindrance to human advancement, being in unceasing antagonism to that disposition to aim at something better than customary, which is called...the spirit of liberty....

The combination of all these causes forms so great a mass of influences hostile to Individuality, that it is not easy to see how it can stand its ground. It will do so with increasing difficulty, unless the intelligent part of the public can be made to feel its value—to see that it is good there should be differences, even though not for the better, even though, as it may appear to them, some should be for the worse. If the claims of Individuality are ever to be asserted, the time is now, while much is still wanting to complete the enforced assimilation. It is only in the earlier stages that any stand can be successfully made against the encroachment. The demand that all other people shall resemble ourselves, grows by what it feeds on. If resistance waits till life is reduced *nearly* to one uniform type, all deviations from that type will come to be considered impious, immoral, even monstrous and contrary to nature. Mankind speedily become unable to conceive diversity, when they have been for some time unaccustomed to seeing it.

NOTES

1. Akbar (1542–1605) was a Mughal (or Mogul) emperor of India; Charlemagne (742–814) was the first emperor of the Holy Roman Empire.—Eds.
2. By "utility" Mill means the principle that all actions, laws, or policies are to be judged according to whether they promote the greatest happiness of the greatest number, or not.—Eds.
3. Here Mill refers to Thomas Carlyle's *On Heroes and Hero-Worship* (1841), which attributes all social progress to the actions of heroic leaders such as Caesar and Napoleon.—Eds.

20

According to the Fitness of Things

WILLIAM GRAHAM SUMNER

Like his English contemporary Herbert Spencer, the American sociologist William Graham Sumner (1840–1910) vigorously developed and defended the theory of Social Darwinism. According to this theory, individual humans are locked in a competition for survival—a competition that the strong will win if nature is allowed to take its course. Spencer's and Sumner's adaptations of Darwin's theory of evolution to human society thus provided some of the first important statements of neoclassical liberalism. As the following excerpts from Sumner's *What Social Classes Owe to Each Other* indicate, the Social Darwinists believed that individuals should be left alone to succeed or to fail in life with no expectation of help from government or society.

Source: William Graham Sumner, *What Social Classes Owe to Each Other* (New York: Harper and Brothers, 1883), pp. 112–133.

ON THE VALUE, AS A SOCIOLOGICAL PRINCIPLE, OF THE RULE TO MIND ONE'S OWN BUSINESS

(From *What Social Classes Owe to Each Other*, Chapter 8)

The passion for dealing with social questions is one of the marks of our time. Every man gets some experience of, and makes some observations on social affairs. Except matters of health, probably none have such general interest as matters of society. Except matters of health, none are so much afflicted by dogmatism and crude speculation as those which appertain to society. The amateurs in social science always ask: What shall we do? What shall we do with Neighbor A? What shall we do for Neighbor B? What shall we make Neighbor A do for Neighbor B? It is a fine thing to be planning and discussing broad and general theories of wide application. The amateurs always plan to use the individual for some constructive and inferential social purpose, or to use the society for some constructive and inferential individual purpose. For A to sit down and think, What shall I do? is commonplace; but to think what B ought to do is interesting, romantic, moral, self-flattering, and public-spirited all at once. It satisfies a great number of human weaknesses at once. To go on and plan what a whole class of people ought to do is to feel one's self a power on earth, to win a public position, to clothe one's self in dignity. Hence we have an unlimited supply of reformers, philanthropists, humanitarians, and would-be managers-in-general of society.

Every man and woman in society has one big duty. That is, to take care of his or her own self. This is a social duty. For, fortunately, the matter stands so that the duty of making the best of one's self individually is not a separate thing from the duty of filling one's place in society, but the two are one, and the latter is accomplished when the former is done. The common notion, however, seems to be that one has a duty to society, as a special and separate thing, and that this duty consists in considering and deciding what other people ought to do. Now, the man who can do anything for or about anybody else than himself is fit to be head of a family; and when he becomes head of a family he has duties to his wife and his children, in addition to the former big duty. Then again, any man who can take care of himself and his family is in a very exceptional position, if he does not find in his immediate surroundings people who need his care and have some sort of a personal claim upon him. If, now, he is able to fulfill all this, and to take care of anybody outside his family and his dependents, he must have a surplus of energy, wisdom, and moral virtue beyond what he needs for his own business. No man has this; for a family is a charge which is capable of infinite development, and no man could suffice to the full measure of duty for which a family may draw upon him. Neither can a man give to society so advantageous an employment of his services, whatever they are, in any other way as by spending them on his family. Upon this, however, I will not insist. I recur to the observation that a man who proposes to take care of other people must have himself and his family taken care of, after some sort of a fashion, and must have an as yet unexhausted store of energy.

The danger of minding other people's business is twofold. First, there is the danger that a man may leave his own business unattended to; and, second, there is the danger of an impertinent interference with another's affairs. The "friends of humanity" almost always run into both dangers. I am one of humanity, and I do not want any volunteer friends. I regard friendship as mutual, and I want to have my say about it. I suppose that other components of humanity feel in the same way about it. If so, they must regard any one who assumes the *rôle* of a friend of humanity as impertinent. The reference to the friend of humanity back to his own business is obviously the next step.

Yet we are constantly annoyed, and the legislatures are kept constantly busy, by the people who have made up their minds that it is wise and conducive to happiness to live in a certain way, and who want to compel everybody else to live in their way. Some people have decided to spend Sunday in a certain way, and they want laws passed to make other people spend Sunday in the same way. Some people have resolved to be teetotalers, and they want a law passed to make everybody else a teetotaler. Some people have resolved to eschew luxury, and they want taxes laid to make others eschew luxury. The taxing power is especially something after which the reformer's finger always itches. Sometimes there is an element of self-interest in the proposed reformation, as when a publisher wanted a duty imposed on books, to keep Americans from reading books which would unsettle their Americanisms; and when artists wanted a tax laid on pictures, to save Americans from buying bad paintings....

The amateur social doctors are like the amateur physicians—they always begin with the question of *remedies,* and they go at this without any diagnosis or any knowledge of the anatomy or physiology of society. They never have any doubt of the efficacy of their remedies. They never take account of any ulterior effects which may be apprehended from the remedy itself. It generally troubles them not a whit that their remedy implies a complete reconstruction of society, or even a reconstitution of human nature. Against all such social quackery the obvious injunction to the quacks is, to mind their own business....

ON THE CASE OF A CERTAIN MAN WHO IS NEVER THOUGHT OF

(From *What Social Classes Owe to Each Other,* Chapter 9)

The type and formula of most schemes of philanthropy or humanitarianism is this: A and B put their heads together to decide what C shall be made to do for D. The radical vice of all these schemes, from a sociological point of view, is that C is not allowed a voice in the matter, and his position, character, and interests, as well as the ultimate effects on society through C's interests, are entirely overlooked. I call C the Forgotten Man. For once let us look him up and consider his case, for the characteristic of all social doctors is, that they fix their minds on some man or group of men whose case appeals to the sympathies and the imagination, and they plan remedies addressed to the particular trouble; they do not understand that all the parts of society hold together, and that forces which are set in action act and react throughout the whole organism, until an equilibrium is produced by a readjustment of all interests and rights. They therefore ignore entirely the source from which they must draw all the energy which they employ in their remedies, and they ignore all the effects on other members of society than the ones they have in view. They are always under the dominion of the superstition of government, and, forgetting that a government produces nothing at all, they leave out of sight the first fact to be remembered in all social discussion—that the State cannot get a cent for any man without taking it from some other man, and this latter must be a man who has produced and saved it. This latter is the Forgotten Man.

The friends of humanity start out with certain benevolent feelings toward "the poor," "the weak," "the laborers," and others of whom they make pets. They generalize these classes, and render them impersonal, and so constitute the classes into social pets. They turn to other classes and appeal to sympathy and generosity, and to all the other noble sentiments of the human heart. Action in the line proposed consists in a transfer of capital from the better off to the worse off. Capital, however, as we have seen, is the force by which civilization is maintained and carried on. The same piece of capital cannot be used in two ways. Every bit of capital, therefore, which is given to a shiftless and inefficient member of society, who makes no return for it, is diverted from a reproductive use; but if it was put to reproductive use, it would have to be granted in wages to an efficient and productive laborer. Hence the real sufferer by that kind of benevolence which consists in an expenditure of capital to protect the good-for-nothing is the industrious laborer. The latter, however, is never thought of in this connection. It is assumed that he is provided for and out of the account. Such a notion only shows how little true notions of political economy have as yet become popularized. There is an almost invincible prejudice that a man who gives a dollar to a beggar is generous and kind-hearted, but that a man who refuses the beggar and puts the dollar in a savings-bank is stingy and mean. The former is putting capital where it is very sure to be wasted, and where it will be a kind of seed for a long succession of future dollars, which must be wasted to ward off a greater strain on the sympathies than would have been occasioned by a refusal in the first place. Inasmuch as the dollar might have been turned into capital and given to a laborer who, while earning it, would have reproduced it, it must be regarded as taken from the latter. When a millionaire gives a dollar to a beggar the gain of utility to the beggar is enormous, and the loss of utility to the millionaire is insignificant. Generally the discussion is allowed to rest there. But if the millionaire makes capital of the dollar, it must go upon the labor market, as a demand for productive services. Hence there is another party in interest—the person who supplies productive services. There always are two parties. The second one is always the Forgotten Man, and any one who wants to truly understand the matter in question must go and search for the Forgotten Man. He will be found to be worthy, industrious, independent, and self-supporting. He is not, technically, "poor" or "weak"; he minds his own business, and makes no complaint. Consequently the philanthropists never think of him, and trample on him....

Society...maintains police, sheriffs, and various institutions, the object of which is to protect people against themselves—that is, against their own vices. Almost all legislative effort to prevent vice is really protective of vice, because all such legislation saves the vicious man from the penalty of his vice. Nature's remedies against vice are terrible. She removes the victims without pity. A drunkard in the gutter is just where he ought to be, according to the fitness and tendency of things. Nature has set up on him the process of decline and dissolution by which she removes things which have survived their usefulness. Gambling and other less mentionable vices carry their own penalties with them.

Now, we never can annihilate a penalty. We can only divert it from the head of the man who has incurred it to the heads of others who have not incurred it. A vast amount of "social reform" consists in just this operation. The consequence is that those who have gone astray, being relieved from Nature's fierce discipline, go on to worse, and that there is a constantly heavier burden for the others to bear. Who are the others? When we see a drunkard in the gutter we pity him. If a policeman picks him up, we say that society has interfered to save him from perishing. "Society" is a fine word, and it saves us the trouble of thinking. The industrious and sober workman, who is mulcted [i.e., robbed] of a percentage of his day's wages to pay the policeman, is the one who bears the penalty. But he is the Forgotten Man. He passes by and is never noticed, because he has behaved himself, fulfilled his contracts, and asked for nothing.

The fallacy of all prohibitory, sumptuary, and moral legislation is the same. A and B determine to be teetotalers, which is often a wise determination, and sometimes a necessary one. If A and B are moved by considerations which seem to them good, that is enough. But A and B put their heads together to get a law passed which shall force C to be a teetotaler for the sake of D, who is in danger of drinking too much. There is no pressure on A and B. They are having their own way, and they like it. There is rarely any pressure on D. He does not like it, and evades it. The pressure all comes on C. The question then arises, Who is C? He is the man who wants alcoholic liquors for any honest purpose whatsoever, who would use his liberty without abusing it, who would occasion no public question, and trouble nobody at all. He is the Forgotten Man again, and as soon as he is drawn from his obscurity we see that he is just what each one of us ought to be.

21

Liberalism and Positive Freedom

T. H. GREEN

Contrary to the Social Darwinists and other neoclassical liberals, the English philosopher Thomas Hill Green (1836–1882) insisted that liberalism requires an active government to ensure and promote individual liberty. In this excerpt from his speech "Liberal Legislation and Freedom of Contract" (1880), Green draws a distinction between two kinds of freedom, negative and positive. He then uses this distinction as the basis for his claim that government has a duty to promote the welfare of the people so that they can become free. In this and his other essays and books, Green thus helped to lay the philosophical foundations for welfare liberalism.

Source: The Works of Thomas Hill Green, ed. R. L. Nettleship, vol. 3 (London: Longmans, Green and Co., 1888), pp. 370–376.

(From *Liberal Legislation and the Freedom of Contract*)

We shall probably all agree that freedom, rightly understood, is the greatest of blessings; that its attainment is the true end of all our efforts as citizens. But when we thus speak of freedom, we should consider carefully what we mean by it. We do not mean merely freedom from restraint or compulsion. We do not mean merely freedom to do as we like irrespectively of what it is that we like. We do not mean a freedom that can be enjoyed by one man or one set of men at the cost of a loss of freedom to others. When we speak of freedom as something to be so highly prized, we mean a positive power or capacity of doing or enjoying something that we do or enjoy in common with others. We mean by it a power which each man exercises through the help or security given him by his fellow-men, and which he in turn helps to secure for them. When we measure the progress of a society by its growth in freedom, we measure it by the increasing development and exercise on the whole of those powers of contributing to social good with which we believe the members of the society to be endowed; in short, by the greater power on the part of the citizens as a body to make the most and best of themselves. Thus, though of course there can be no freedom among men who act not willingly but under compulsion, yet on the other hand the mere removal of compulsion, the mere enabling a man to do as he likes, is in itself no contribution to true freedom. In one sense no man is so well able to do as he likes as the wandering savage. He has no master. There is no one to say him nay. Yet we do not count him really free, because the freedom of savagery is not strength, but weakness. The actual powers of the noblest savage do not admit of comparison with those of the humblest citizen of a law-abiding state. He is not the slave of man, but he is the slave of nature. Of compulsion by natural necessity he has plenty of experience, though of restraint by society none at all. Nor can he deliver himself from that compulsion except by submitting to this restraint. So to submit is the first step in true freedom, because the first step towards the full exercise of the faculties with which man is endowed. But we rightly refuse to recognize the highest development on the part of an exceptional individual or exceptional class, as an advance towards the true freedom of man, if it is founded on a refusal of the same opportunity to other men. The powers of the human mind have probably never attained such force and keenness, the proof of what society can do for the individual has never been so strikingly exhibited, as among the small groups of men who possessed civil privileges in the small republics of antiquity. The whole framework of our political ideas, to say nothing of our philosophy, is derived from them. But in them this extraordinary efflorescence of the privileged class was accompanied by the slavery of the multitude. That slavery was the condition on which it depended, and for that reason it was doomed to decay. There is no clearer ordinance of that supreme reason, often dark to us, which governs the course of men's affairs, than that no body of men should in the long run be able to strengthen itself at the cost of others' weakness. The civilization and freedom of the ancient world were short-lived because they were partial and exceptional. If the ideal of true freedom is the maximum of power for all members of human society alike to make the best of themselves, we are right in refusing to ascribe the glory of freedom to a state in which the apparent elevation of the few is founded on the degradation of the many, and in ranking modern society, founded as it is on free industry, with all its confusion and ignorant licence and waste of effort, above the most splendid of ancient republics.

If I have given a true account of that freedom which forms the goal of social effort, we shall see that freedom of contract, freedom of all the forms of doing what one will with one's own, is valuable only as a means to an end. That end is what I call freedom in the positive sense: in other words, like liberation of the powers of all men equally for contributions to a common good. No one has a right to do what he will with his own in such a way as to contravene this end. It is only through the guarantee which society gives him that he has property at all, or, strictly speaking, any right to his possessions. This guarantee is founded on a sense of common interest. Every one has an interest in securing to every one else the free use and enjoyment and disposal of his possessions, so long as that freedom on the part of one does not interfere with a like freedom on the part of others, because such freedom contributes to that equal development of the faculties of all which is the highest good for all. This is the true and the only justification of rights of property. Rights of property, however, have been and are claimed which cannot thus be justified. We are all now agreed that men cannot rightly be the property of men. The institution of property being only justifiable as a means to the free exercise of the social capabilities of all, there can be no true right to property of a kind which debars one class of men from such free exercise altogether. We condemn slavery no less when it arises out of a voluntary agreement on the part of the enslaved person. A contract by which anyone agreed for a certain consideration to become the slave of another we should reckon a void contract. Here, then, is a limitation upon freedom of contract which we all recognize as rightful. No contract is valid in which human persons, willingly or unwillingly, are dealt with as commodities, because such contracts of necessity defeat the end for which alone society enforces contracts at all.

Are there no other contracts which, less obviously perhaps but really, are open to the same objection? In the first place, let us consider contracts affecting labor. Labor, the economist tells us, is a commodity exchangeable like other commodities. This is in a certain sense true, but it is a commodity which attaches in a peculiar manner to the person of man. Hence restrictions may need to be placed on the sale of this commodity which would be unnecessary in other cases, in order to prevent labor from being sold under conditions which make it impossible for the person selling it ever to become a free contributor to social good in any form. This is most plainly the case when a man bargains to work under conditions fatal to health, in an unventilated factory. Every injury to the health of the individual is, so far as it goes, a public injury. It is an impediment to the general freedom; so much deduction from our power, as members of society, to make the best of ourselves. Society is, therefore, plainly within its right when it limits freedom of contract for the sale of labor, so far as is done by our laws for the sanitary regulations of factories, workshops, and mines. It is equally within its right in prohibiting the labor of women and young persons beyond certain hours. If they work beyond those hours, the result is demonstrably physical deterioration; which, as demonstrably, carries with it a lowering of the moral forces of society. For the sake of that general freedom of its members to make the best of themselves, which it is the object of civil society to secure, a prohibition should be put by law, which is the deliberate voice of society, on all such contracts of service as in a general way yield such a result. The purchase or hire of unwholesome dwellings is properly forbidden on the same principle. Its application to compulsory education may not be quite so obvious, but it will appear on a little reflection. Without a command of certain elementary arts and knowledge, the individual in modern society is as effectually crippled as by the loss of a limb or a broken constitution. He is not free to develop his faculties. With a view to securing such freedom among its members it is as certainly within the province of the state to prevent children from growing up in that kind of ignorance which practically excludes them from a free career in life, as it is within its province to require the sort of building and drainage necessary for public health.

Our modern legislation then with reference to labor, and education, and health, involving as it does manifold interference with freedom of contract, is justified on the ground that it is the business of the state, not indeed directly to promote moral goodness, for that, from the very nature of moral goodness, it cannot do, but to maintain the conditions without which a free exercise of the human faculties is impossible....

Now, we shall probably all agree that a society in which the public health was duly protected, and necessary education duly provided for, by the spontaneous action of individuals, was in a higher condition than one in which the compulsion of law was needed to secure those ends. But we must take men as we find them. Until such a condition of society is reached, it is the business of the state to make the best security it can for the young citizens' growing up in such health and with so much knowledge as is necessary for their real freedom. In so doing it need not at all interfere with the independence and self-reliance of those whom it requires to do what they would otherwise do for themselves. The man who, of his own right feeling, saves his wife from overwork and sends his children to school, suffers no moral degradation from a law which, if he did not do this for himself, would seek to make him do it. Such a man does not feel the law as constraint at all. To him it is simply a powerful friend. It gives him security for that being done efficiently which, with the best wishes, he might have much trouble in getting done efficiently if left to himself. No doubt it relieves him from some of the responsibility which would otherwise fall to him as head of a family, but, if he is what we are supposing him to be, in proportion as he is relieved of responsibilities in one direction he will assume them in another. The security which the state gives him for the safe housing and sufficient schooling of his family will only make him the more careful for their well-being in other respects, which he is left to look after for himself. We need have no fear, then, of such legislation having an ill-effect on those who, without the law, would have seen to that being done, though probably less efficiently, which the law requires to be done. But it was not their case that the laws we are considering were especially meant to meet. It was the overworked women, the ill-housed and untaught families, for whose benefit they were intended. And the question is whether without these laws the suffering classes could have been delivered quickly or slowly from the condition they were in. Could the enlightened self-interest or benevolence of individuals, working under a system of unlimited freedom of contract, have ever brought them into a state compatible with the free development of the human faculties? No one considering the facts can have any doubt as to the answer to this question. Left to itself, or to the operation of casual benevolence, a degraded population perpetuates and increases itself. Read any of the authorized accounts, given before royal or parliamentary commissions, of the state of the laborers, especially of the women and children, as they were in our great industries before the law was first brought to bear on them, and before freedom of contract was first interfered with in them. Ask yourself what chance there was of a generation, born and bred under such conditions, ever contracting itself out of them. Given a certain standard of moral and material well-being, people may be trusted not to sell their labor, or the labor of their children, on terms which would not allow that standard to be maintained. But with large masses of our population, until the laws we have been considering took effect, there was no such standard. There was nothing on their part, in the way either of self-respect or established demand for comforts, to prevent them from working and living, or from putting their children to work and live, in a way in which no one who is to be a healthy and free citizen can work and live. No doubt there were many high-minded employers who did their best for their work-people before the days of state-interference, but they could not prevent less scrupulous hirers of labor from hiring it on the cheapest terms.

22

Paternalism vs. Democracy: A Libertarian View

DONALD ALLEN

In the last thirty years or so, neoclassical liberalism has enjoyed a revival in the form of the libertarian movement. In the United States the Libertarian party regularly nominates and supports candidates for public office, including president, and libertarian scholars are also quite active in academe. In the following essay, the libertarian writer Donald Allen (1944–) argues that democracy can survive only when individuals are free from government interference to control their own lives.

Source: This essay was written expressly for *Ideals and Ideologies.*

Paternalism—the doctrine that the state knows better than its citizens what is good for them—is especially insidious in a democracy. As the most morally and intellectually demanding form of government, democracy requires the free flow of information about alternatives and choices. Inasmuch as paternalists propose to dam and channel that flow as they see fit, they are inherently antidemocratic.

Censorship has always been the paternalist's weapon of choice. And it is easy to see why. The paternalist wishes not only to deliver us from evil but to prevent us from even being led into temptation in the first place. By blocking information about attractive but "unacceptable" alternatives, censorship precludes the possibility that some citizens will make the "wrong" choices about what to read, see, say, or smoke.

Now it might be objected that paternalists are good people who have the best of intentions and the interests of others at heart. And so they may be. But in matters moral and political, consequences count for more than intentions. And the consequences of paternalism, whether intended or not, are dangerous to the health of a democratic body politic and the individual citizens who comprise it. If you doubt it, consider the case of Prohibition.

Led by well-intentioned zealots like Carry A. Nation (1846–1911)—who, incidentally, believed that God had given her her name so that she might "carry a nation"—the Prohibitionists singled out for special censure not the consumers who abused alcohol but those who distilled and sold it. The Prohibitionists sincerely believed that their aim was noble and their cause a righteous one, and many Americans apparently agreed. After all, there were drunkards who were killing themselves with Demon Drink. To save such people from themselves the Constitution was amended to outlaw the production, sale, and distribution of intoxicating liquors (18th Amendment, 1920). Like many a well-intentioned scheme, this one went badly awry. The free market in alcohol was replaced by a black market in bootleg whiskey and bathtub gin. The supply of alcohol kept pace with the undiminished demand, even as the quality of the alcohol decreased and the price consumers paid for it (in dollars and in damaged livers) increased. And—not least—politicians and policemen were corrupted and organized crime gained a foothold in America that it has never lost. The harm caused by America's paternalistic experiment with Prohibition is with us even today.

One might think that Americans would have learned by now that paternalism will not and cannot work in a society supposedly blessed with free institutions and free markets. Apparently not, alas. Despite our many virtues, we Americans have, as Alexis de Tocqueville noted in *Democracy in America* more than a century and a half ago, two particularly nasty vices. The first is that we know next to nothing about history. And knowing so little about the past, we are in no position to learn from it, although we are all too apt to repeat its mistakes. We are therefore unable to follow the German Chancellor Bismarck's dictum that "The truly wise man does not learn from his mistakes; he learns from other people's mistakes." Ignorant even of our own recent history, we muddle on, naively trusting a new generation of elected or self-appointed Prohibitionists to tell us which products, ideas, and information we may or may not be exposed to.

Our second vice is one to which democracies may be peculiarly prone. Tocqueville, along with James Madison and John Stuart Mill, observed that in democracies without strong constitutional safeguards, a tyrannical majority can very easily ride roughshod over the rights of unpopular minorities. That is why a Bill of Rights was added to the U.S. Constitution and why the First Amendment comes first in that list of liberties. And that is why the whole of Mill's magnificent *On Liberty* (1859) is devoted to defending the right of free expression for all citizens, however obnoxious or distasteful others may think their views to be. Mill's essay is also a defense of diversity and a thoroughgoing critique of paternalism. "The only purpose for which power can be rightfully exercised over any member of a civilized community, against his will," wrote Mill, "is to prevent harm to others. His own good, either physical or moral, is not a sufficient warrant. He cannot rightfully be compelled to do or forbear because it will be better for him to do so, because it will make him happier, because, in the opinions of others, to do so would be wise or even right.... Over himself, over his own body and mind, the individual is sovereign." It is just this individual sovereignty that the New Prohibitionists find so intolerable.

The New Prohibitionists have in recent years turned their attention not to alcohol but toward drugs, tobacco, and pornography, in particular. To stop the flow of drugs into the United States they propose more laws, stiffer penalties, more police—in short, more state power devoted to preventing people from doing what they like with, and to, their own bodies. It has not worked, and will not work. Exactly the same things that happened during Prohibition are happening all over again. People who want to drink—or take drugs or view pornography or to have sex with another consenting adult—will do so. And if there is no free market in any product or service that is in demand, whether it be drugs or pornography or prostitution, there will inevitably be a black market in that product or service. Because black market goods and services are much more expensive than those sold on the free market, some consumers will pay for them by turning to other illegal, but profitable activities, including prostitution, theft, and the selling of drugs. This of course is exactly what has happened. The result is that our jails and prisons are overflowing, our police officers overworked or corrupted, and our taxes raised in a Canute-like effort to turn back the tide. Once again, well-meaning paternalists, in attempting to solve one "problem," have not only failed to solve it but have created many additional problems as well.

Not content to restrict or outlaw certain kinds of purely private conduct by or between consenting adults, the New Prohibitionists have recently turned their attention to public speech. Their most recent efforts include proposing legislation to restrict or outlaw the production, sale, and distribution of pornography and a ban on tobacco advertising. The first comes from paternalists on the religious Right, the second from the liberal Left. No matter what their motives, however, their message is essentially the same. Their claim is that certain words and pictures ought to be prohibited by law, lest people be tempted to think, and perchance to act, in ways that the state deems socially unacceptable. And the aim in both cases is to de-diversify a pluralistic society whose strength has traditionally resided in its citizens' diverse and often opposing outlooks, opinions, and tastes. This is, of course, a tall order. It requires nothing less than an assault on our fundamental freedoms, as articulated in the Bill of Rights, and the First Amendment in particular.

Since a full frontal assault on these freedoms would never be tolerated, the New Prohibitionists have turned to other tactics. Scare tactics, for example: some kinds of speech or expression are said to pose too great a danger to our morals or our health to be tolerated or otherwise countenanced. They must therefore be silenced. But, we are assured, this silencing isn't "really" censorship because "free speech" isn't involved. In the case of sexually explicit materials, they say, it isn't words—that is, speech—but morally objectionable pictures that the state should outlaw. The outlawing of tobacco ads is also said not to be censorship, but something else. Casting about for some less loaded euphemism, our Washington wordsmiths have coined the phrase, "ban on advertising." This ban, or whatever it is, is supposed to be highly selective. It is to be aimed only at a small minority whose activities are said to be injurious to the health or morals of the vast majority.

Who in good conscience could object to these or any other measure claiming to promote health or moral decency or any similarly admirable goal?

Answer: I can. And I think that any liberty-loving democrat can, too.

Let me be blunt: I have no particular affection for drug dealers (or users), or for pornographers and their customers, or for tobacco companies or smokers. Nor do I use any of their products. But the fact that they make such tempting targets for the New Prohibitionists should give us pause. It is precisely because there is so little love lost on drug dealers, pornographers, and tobacco producers that those who love liberty had better beware. As Mill warned—and as the history of the twentieth century shows with alarming clarity—scapegoating is always selective at first. Although the members of a particular unpopular minority are always the first to lose their liberty, they are never the last to lose it.

The modern movement toward the all-powerful paternal state has proceeded in a piecemeal way. It is a revolution wrought not by the single great bite but by a long series of small, highly selective nibbles around the unguarded edges of our liberties. For this reason the movement's most fitting symbol would not be the biblical whale Leviathan, as Thomas Hobbes suggested in the seventeenth century, but the humble piranha. The bite of a single piranha, I am told—though I have no wish to test this myself—is neither fatal nor even particularly painful. But the cumulative effect of a series of nibbles by a school of these tiny creatures is dreadful to behold.

So it is with censorship. A tiny bite here, a little nibble there, and we are very soon stripped of our liberties and the life and health of our greater public body—the body politic—is gravely imperiled. However small, however "selective" its target, however carefully it is aimed, the paternalist's favorite weapon must eventually destroy the liberties, and perchance even the lives, of those whose interests it initially purported to protect.

Like it or not, any government restriction on any form of speech—including advertising—amounts to an abridgement of the free speech and expression protected by the First Amendment. If it is to survive and flourish, democracy requires an intelligent and informed citizenry, just as the free market requires intelligent and informed consumers. Because the free society and the free market are alike in requiring the free flow of information in all its forms, a ban on the advertising of any product makes a mockery of both. Censorship—for that is what such restrictions amount to—is nothing less than the constricting of choice through the withholding of ideas and information about alternative ways of thinking and acting and living one's life as one sees fit.

The New Prohibitionists are right in at least one respect. They are correct in casting their crusade against free choice and free speech as a public health issue. The kind of legislation they wish to enact does raise profound questions about health, all right—the health of our democratic body politic. The real issue, in the final analysis, is not whether alcohol, drugs, tobacco, or any other product is bad for one's health but whether a democratic polity can survive the ministrations of well-meaning paternalists bent on protecting us from ourselves.

Every well-intentioned proposal to outlaw or restrict any sort of self-regarding or private action and speech in all its forms should be required to carry a label reading "Warning: Paternalism Is Dangerous to the Health of the Body Politic."

Paternalism promises illusory cures for imaginary ailments. In a free society paternalism can never be the remedy for anything. Paternalism is, instead, the disease for which the libertarian philosophy is the cure.

Postscript, 2005

In the late 1980s, when I wrote this essay, I thought that the main threat to liberty in the United States came from the liberal Left. I now believe that the primary threat comes from the conservative Right. The Republican Party, which now controls all three branches of the federal government, is no longer the quasi-libertarian party of Barry Goldwater and Ronald Reagan. That now-defunct party favored fiscal responsibility and small government. The administration of George W. Bush, however, seems bent on bankrupting the country by running record deficits and cutting taxes while fighting an ill-considered and enormously expensive war abroad. Moreover, the government is now using the very real threat of terrorism as a pretext for depriving a gullible American public of their liberties—not by small bites or nibbles but in huge gulps and gobbles by Patriot Acts I and II. These misnamed acts give the government *carte blanche* to snoop and spy on Americans in almost every aspect of their lives, from the books they check out of their local library to telephone conversations with family and friends. To make matters even worse, the Religious Right promotes legislation to make women's wombs into state property and to persecute gay men and lesbians for exercising their liberty to love whom and how they please. These and other assaults on personal privacy and individual liberty are the baleful result not of small-government conservatism but of large-government activism of the most intrusive, coercive, and paternalistic kind. For all the Bush administration's talk about promoting liberty and democracy abroad, it seems intent on depriving Americans of both at home. Be afraid. Be very afraid.

23

Libertarian Anarchism

MURRAY ROTHBARD

One of the best-known libertarian or neoclassical liberal writers, Murray Rothbard (1926–1995) was an American economist who taught at New York Polytechnic Institute and at the University of Nevada, Las Vegas. Rothbard believed not that government should be kept small but that it should be abolished altogether. Rothbard is thus a libertarian anarchist who contends, in the following excerpt from his *For a New Liberty*, that government is an entirely *un*necessary evil.

Source: Murray Rothbard, *For a New Liberty* (Macmillan, 1973), pp. 8–12, 18–19, 34–35, 40. Reprinted by permission of the Ludwig Von Mises Institute.

FOR A NEW LIBERTY

Throughout the numerous factions and splinters of the movement,...there is agreement on the central core of the libertarian creed. The crucial axiom of that creed is: no man or group of men have the right to aggress against the person or property of anyone else. This might be called the "nonaggression" axiom. "Aggression" is defined as the initiation of the use or threat of physical violence against the person or property of someone else. Aggression is therefore synonymous with "invasion." How this axiom may be arrived at will be discussed below, and the paths toward attaining the axiom vary among different groups of libertarians. But all libertarians agree on nonaggression as the central axiom of their doctrine.

If no man may aggress against—invade—the person or property of another, this means that every man is free to do whatever he wishes, except commit such aggression. The great nineteenth-century libertarian theorist Herbert Spencer formulated a similar axiom: "Law of Equal Liberty." "Freedom" or "liberty" is therefore rigorously defined in such a credo as: the absence of invasion. A man is free when he is not being aggressed against; and all men, or "society," are free when no aggression or invasion is being committed.

If no man may aggress against another; if, in short, everyone has the absolute right to be "free" from aggression, then this at once implies that the libertarian stands foursquare for what are generally known as "civil liberties": the freedom to speak, publish, assemble, and to engage in such "victimless crimes" as pornography, sexual deviation, and prostitution (which the libertarian does not regard as "crimes" at all, since he defines a "crime" as violent invasion of someone else's person or property). Furthermore, he regards conscription as slavery on a massive scale. And since war, especially modern war, entails the mass slaughter of civilians, the libertarian regards such conflicts as mass murder and therefore totally illegitimate.

All of these positions are now considered "leftist" on the contemporary ideological scale. On the other hand, since the libertarian also opposes invasion of the rights of private property, this also means that he just as emphatically opposes government interference with property rights or with the free market economy through controls, regulations, subsidies, or prohibitions. For if every individual has the right to his own property without having to suffer aggressive depredation, then he also has the right to give away his property (bequest and inheritance) and to exchange it for the property of others (free contract and the free market economy) without interference. The libertarian favors the right to unrestricted private property and free-exchange; hence, a system of "laissez-faire capitalism."

In current terminology again, the libertarian position on property and economics would be called "extreme right wing." But the libertarian sees no inconsistency in being "leftist" on some issues and "rightist" on others. On the contrary, he sees his own position as virtually the *only* consistent one, consistent on behalf of the liberty of every individual. For how can the leftist be opposed to the violence of war and conscription while at the same time supporting the violence of taxation and government control? And how can the rightist trumpet his devotion to private property and free enterprise while at the same time favoring war, conscription, and the outlawing of noninvasive activities and practices that he deems immoral? And how can the rightist favor a free market while seeing nothing amiss in the vast subsidies, distortions, and unproductive inefficiencies involved in the military-industrial complex?

While opposing any and all private or group aggression against the rights of person and property, the libertarian sees that throughout history and into the present day, there has been one central, dominant, and overriding aggressor upon all of these rights: the State. In contrast to all other thinkers, left, right, or in-between, the libertarian refuses to give the State the moral sanction to commit actions that almost everyone agrees would be immoral, illegal, and criminal if committed by any person or group in society. The libertarian, in short, insists on applying the general moral law to everyone, and makes no special exemptions for any person or group. But if we look at the State naked, as it were, we see that it is universally allowed, and even encouraged, to commit all the acts which even nonlibertarians concede are reprehensible crimes. The State habitually commits mass murder, which it calls "war," or sometimes "suppression of subversion"; the State engages in enslavement into its military forces, which it calls "conscription"; and it lives and has its being in the practice of forcible theft, which it calls "taxation." The libertarian insists that whether or not such practices are supported by the majority of the population is not germane to their nature: that, regardless of popular sanction, War is Mass Murder, Conscription is Slavery, and Taxation is Robbery. The libertarian, in short, is almost completely the child in the fable, pointing out insistently that the emperor has no clothes.

Throughout the ages, the emperor has had a series of pseudo-clothes provided for him by the nation's intellectual caste. In past centuries, the intellectuals informed the public that the State or its rulers were divine, or at least clothed in divine authority, and therefore what might *look* to the naïve and untutored eye as despotism, mass murder, and theft on a grand scale was only the divine working its benign and mysterious ways in the body politic. In recent decades, as the divine sanction has worn a bit threadbare, the emperor's "court intellectuals" have spun ever more sophisticated apologia: informing the public that what the government does is for the "common good" and the "public welfare," that the process of taxation-and-spending works through the mysterious process of the "multiplier" to keep the economy on an even keel, and that, in any case, a wide variety of governmental "services" could not possibly be performed by citizens acting voluntarily on the market or in society. All of this the libertarian denies: he sees the various apologia as fraudulent means of obtaining public support for the State's rule, and he insists that whatever services the government actually performs could be supplied far more efficiently and far more morally by private and cooperative enterprise.

The libertarian therefore considers one of his prime educational tasks is to spread the demystification and desanctification of the State among its hapless subjects. His task is to demonstrate repeatedly and in depth that not only the emperor but even the "democratic" state has no clothes; that all governments subsist by exploitive rule over the public; and that such rule is the reverse of objective necessity. He strives to show that the very existence of taxation and the State necessarily sets up a class division between the exploiting rulers and the exploited ruled. He seeks to show that the task of the court intellectuals who have always supported the State has ever been to weave mystification in order to induce the public to accept State rule, and that these intellectuals obtain, in return, a share in the power and pelf extracted by the rulers from their deluded subjects.

Take, for example, the institution of taxation, which statists have claimed is in some sense really "voluntary." Anyone who truly believes in the "voluntary" nature of taxation is invited to refuse to pay taxes and to see what then happens to him. If we analyze taxation, we find that, among all the persons and institutions in society, only the government acquires its revenues through coercive violence. Everyone else in society acquires income *either* through voluntary gift (lodge, charitable society, chess club) *or* through the sale of goods or services voluntarily purchased by consumers. If anyone *but* the government proceeded to "tax," this would clearly be considered coercion and thinly disguised banditry. Yet the mystical trappings of "sovereignty" have so veiled the process that only libertarians are prepared to call taxation what it is: legalized and organized theft on a grand scale....

Further, if taxation is robbery, then it becomes clear that a tax or monopoly-coercing government is a robber band, and deserves not reverence but abolition—or, if abolition cannot be achieved, at the least there should be a relentless whittling down of governmental power and activity. Civil disobedience to unjust laws and decrees—including not only the draft but taxation itself—becomes morally legitimate if not always strategically or tactically prudent.

Superpatriotism is at the least very difficult for any anarchist, so the great bulk of anarcho-capitalists have abandoned their former rightist devotion to the Cold War and to American foreign policy. Generally, they have adopted an "ultra-isolationist" foreign policy as the external corollary to their opposition to domestic statism....

If...land is nature- or God-given then so are the people's talents, health, and beauty. And just as all these attributes are given to specific individuals and not to "society," so then are land and natural resources. All of these resources are given to individuals and not to "society," which is an abstraction that does not actually exist. There is no existing entity called "society": there are only interacting individuals. To say that "society" should own land or any other property in common, then, must mean that a group of oligarchs—in practice, government bureaucrats—should own the property, and at the expense of expropriating the creator or the homesteader who had originally brought this product into existence.

Moreover, no one can produce *anything* without the cooperation of original land, if only as standing room. No man can produce or create anything by his labor alone; he must have the cooperation of land and other natural raw materials.

Man comes into the world with just himself and the world around him—the land and natural resources given him by nature. He takes these resources and transforms them by his labor and mind and energy into goods more useful to man.

Therefore, if an individual cannot own original land, neither can he in the full sense own any of the fruits of his labor. The farmer cannot own his wheat crop if he cannot own the land on which the wheat grows. Now that his labor has been inextricably mixed with the land, he cannot be deprived of one without being deprived of the other.

Moreover, if a producer is *not* entitled to the fruits of his labor, who is?... Land in its original state is unused and unowned. Georgists[1] and other land communalists may claim that the whole world population *really* "owns" it, but if no one has yet used it, it is in the real sense owned and controlled by no one. The pioneer, the homesteader, the first user and transformer of this land, is the man who first brings this simple valueless thing into production and social use. It is difficult to see the morality of depriving him of ownership in favor of people who have never gotten within a thousand miles of the land, and who may not even know of the existence of the property over which they are supposed to have a claim.

The moral, natural rights issue involved here is even clearer if we consider the case of animals. Animals are "economic land," since they are original nature-given resources. Yet will anyone deny full title to a horse to the man who finds and domesticates it—is this any different from the acorns and berries that are generally conceded to the gatherer? Yet in land, too, some homesteader takes the previously "wild," undomesticated land, and "tames" it by putting it to productive use.

The central core of the libertarian creed, then, is to establish the absolute right to private property of every man; first, in his own body, and second, in the previously unused natural resources which he first transforms by his labor. These two axioms, the right of self-ownership and the right to "homestead," establish the complete set of principles of the libertarian system. The entire libertarian doctrine then becomes the spinning out and the application of all the implications of this central doctrine.

NOTE

1. Followers of Henry George (1839–1897), an American economist, whose *Progress and Poverty* (1879) advocated a land-based redistribution of wealth.—Eds.

24

The Communitarian Persuasion

PHILIP SELZNICK

Welfare and neoclassical liberalism remain the principal forms of liberalism in the twenty-first century, but both have been challenged in recent years by a growing group of political thinkers and activists known as *communitarians.* In some cases these communitarians have regarded themselves as antiliberals challenging liberalism from the outside. For the most part, though, communitarians seem to see themselves as good liberals who are trying to correct the individualistic excesses of both welfare and neoclassical liberalism. Philip Selznick (1919—), an American sociologist and legal scholar, takes the latter position in the following essay, in which he advocates a "sturdy hybrid" of welfare liberalism and communitarian principles that he calls "communitarian liberalism."

Source: Philip Selznick, *The Communitarian Persuasion* (Washington, D.C.: Woodrow Wilson Center Press, 2002), pp. 3–11, 14–15. © 2002, the Woodrow Wilson International Center for Scholars. Reprinted with permission of the Johns Hopkins University Press.

THE COMMUNITARIAN PERSUASION

Americans have long embraced and mostly enjoyed the undeniable benefits of modern technology, free enterprise, and liberal democracy. We have been blessed by unprecedented prosperity, less burdensome work, ever widening opportunity, stable government based on the rule of law, and respect for popular will. We have welcomed the waning of male domination and of virulent racism. Real as they are, these achievements are far from complete. Inequality abounds, poverty and prejudice persist, social justice remains a moral imperative.

More is at stake than an unfulfilled dream. Negative forces are at work. A market mentality invades much of social life, undercutting values that need special protection. The pace of change, and widening demands for free choice and expression, erode the authority of parents, and of received tradition. In our liberal democracy it is hard to sustain the difference between liberty and license. Separation of sex and reproduction, sex and marriage, undermines personal responsibility. A remorseless logic of corporate power shifts major decisions to remote places, where accountability is limited or evaded. Modern government is experienced by many as opaque, distant, and oppressive. These and other social trends have generated widespread anxiety and discontent. Everyday life seems out of joint.

Of course, life goes on. Young people connect, love one another, and raise children; the economy hums, more or less vibrantly, many traditions are respected: taxes are collected. However, all is under stress: confidence is shaken even as we require, more than ever, high levels of collective will, energy, discipline, and intelligence.

This diagnosis does not deny the reality of progress. Progressive or not, many modern trends tend to loosen attachments and threaten stability. Under these conditions community—based on interdependence, commitment, and reconciliation—is bound to need healing and restoration. This necessity does not lessen the worth of modern ideals and institutions. But we must think more clearly about them. We cannot protect ideals we do not understand.

The New Communitarians

In response to modern and postmodern anxieties, a new voice has emerged, searching for clarity and struggling to be heard. This is the communitarian voice I wish to explain, interpret, and defend.

The label *communitarian* can be applied to any doctrine that prizes collective goods or ideals and limits claims to individual independence and self-realization. The main religious traditions are strongly communitarian in that they demand conformity to divine law, sometimes in excruciating detail. The communist and Nazi movements, and more moderate doctrines of socialism, social democracy, and Christian social thought, may also be called communitarian. Indeed, the quest for a communitarian morality is hardly new. A long list of thinkers—Hegel, Marx, Dewey, and many others, including several popes—have sought alternatives to what seemed to them an impoverished morality and an inadequate understanding of human society. There have been communitarians of left and right: anarchist, socialist, liberal, and conservative. Some of these doctrines and the regimes they created have given the idea of community a very bad name. We would surely want to reject any doctrine that demands supine obedience to tradition or unduly hampers freedom of choice in marriage, work, education, religion, and politics.

The claims of community can indeed go too far. However, all values are threatened when a society falls apart—that is, when it cannot provide its members adequate nurture, support, and coherence. Without *effective* opportunities, the pursuit of happiness is futile and liberty is self-defeating.

In the United States a new communitarian movement emerged in the early 1980s. This was a response to three important developments. It began as a controversy among philosophers, initiated by Alasdair MacIntyre's *After Virtue* and Michael Sandel's *Liberalism and the Limits of Justice* (both published in 1982). These and other philosophical writings criticized the premises of liberalism, especially political and economic individualism and the notion that people can readily and desirably free themselves from unchosen attachments and obligations. These critics were called "communitarian," and the so-called communitarian-liberal debate quickly became a staple of academic social and moral philosophy. This excitement among professors was doubtless driven in part by the wish to enliven college teaching and by the appeal of polemical exchanges. Nevertheless, something important was going on—the quest for a public philosophy that could take account of what liberalism failed to appreciate as well as what it could clearly see and rightly teach.

A second source of the new communitarianism, more closely tied to political issues, was a response to the Reagan/Thatcher era in the United States and Britain during the 1980s. Those leaders gave full rein to unbridled capitalism, encouraging distrust of government, resistance to taxation, and a strong preference for market solutions to all problems. This mentality, which ignored what Amitai Etzioni called "the moral dimension,"[1] sounded a full retreat from social responsibility.

Third was a growing uneasiness about the welfare state among those who had been its loyal supporters. This disaffection had already been expressed by Robert F. Kennedy when he campaigned for the presidency in 1968. As Michael Sandel recounts:

> RFK's political outlook was in some ways more conservative and in some ways more radical than the mainstream of his party. He worried about the remoteness of big government, favored decentralized power, criticized welfare as "our greatest domestic failure," challenged the faith in economic growth as a panacea for social ills, and took a hard line on crime.... Kennedy's clearest difference with mainstream liberal opinion was over welfare. Unlike conservatives, who opposed federal spending for the poor, Kennedy criticized welfare on the grounds that it made millions of Americans dependent on handouts and thus unable to play a role in the democracy. "Fellowship, community, shared patriotism—these essential values of our civilization do not come from just buying and consuming goods together. They come from a shared sense of interdependence and personal effort."[2]

With these words, Robert Kennedy gave early expression to what would become major themes in contemporary communitarian thought.

In 1996 a leading German Social Democrat offered this confession:

> We Social Democrats created an overly regulated, overly bureaucratic and overly professionalized welfare state. We believed, for example, that if the state bore the responsibility for the outcome of a process, it must regulate this process itself. This was a conceptual error. We did not believe in people's capacity for spontaneously helping and caring for others in the neighborhoods, we did not dare to hope that parents of schoolchildren would take care of the upkeep of classrooms; we did not believe that we could leave the running of a kindergarten to the parents.... To a certain extent, we succumbed to a blind faith in science and experts.[3]

This was another effort to rethink the moral and political premises of the welfare state.

The new communitarians are well aware that community has dangers and deficits as well as benefits. They have tried to think anew, conscious of the need to vindicate freedom as well as solidarity, rights as well as responsibilities.[4] A central theme is the enhancement of personal and social responsibility. The communitarian ethos is not mainly about sympathy, benevolence, or compassion. It is about meeting our obligations as responsible parents, children, employees, employers, officials, and citizens. These obligations are *eased* by love and *supported* by love. But they arise and persist even when love is absent or hard to sustain.

Communitarian Liberalism

Are the new communitarians antiliberal? It might seem so, since they have often criticized liberal theory and policy. But they have by no means rejected liberal institutions and the liberal tradition. Rather, the new communitarians have argued that liberal premises are overly individualistic, insufficiently sensitive to the social sources of selfhood and obligation, too much concerned with rights and too little with duty, too ready to accept an anemic conception of the common good. The operative words are *overly, insufficiently, too much, too ready.* Thus the main target of communitarian criticism is intellectual and practical excess. Good ideas are put forward without proper regard for limiting conditions, competing principles, and informing contexts.

The new communitarians accept and support the main liberal achievements. For their part, many contemporary liberals have adopted communitarian perspectives, especially with respect to economic policy, environmental protection, and social justice. Western ideals of freedom, equality, tolerance, and rationality owe much to the work of liberal thinkers and political leaders. However, some of the most important of these ideas are not unique to liberalism. They belong to the heritage of Western civilization, including ideas we associate with Greek, Roman, and Judeo-Christian experience.

Liberalism is a many-stranded tradition, not a well-defined ideology or tight system of premises and conclusions. Even a glance at the history of liberalism shows important differences among, for example, Locke, Rousseau, Mill, and Dewey. Most revealing is the transition from "classical" or "market" liberalism to "welfare" liberalism. The great liberal thinkers of the seventeenth and eighteenth centuries, such as John Locke and Adam Smith, sought freedom from ignorance, dogma, despotism, and privilege; they helped break the hold of a feudal, clerical, and mercantilist past. In doing so they laid foundations for democracy, the rule of law, and free enterprise. These great achievements were marred, however, by a basic flaw. Their chief targets were (and in the historical context had to be) arbitrary government and class privilege. They wanted justice, but this meant mainly *formal* justice. As Anatole France put it, in a memorable passage, "the law, in its majestic equality, forbids the rich as well as the poor to sleep under bridges, beg in the streets, and steal bread."[5]

This crippling condition was widely recognized in the nineteenth century. As the social costs of the Industrial Revolution were made plain, new demands were heard for a fuller measure of freedom, equality, and justice. Many liberals came to see that people cannot enjoy freedom if they are poor and ignorant; cannot receive justice if their circumstances are ignored; cannot be rational if they believe they must submit to unquestioned authority; cannot be citizens of a democracy if they are barred from joining with others to pursue their interests and claim their rights.

Even John Stuart Mill, in many ways the quintessential nineteenth-century liberal, came to reject economic individualism in favor of a more cooperative, more caring, more just society.[6] Other English "new liberals" supported active interventions by government to expand opportunity and regulate markets. Since Franklin D. Roosevelt's New Deal, American liberals have embraced welfare liberalism, leaving market liberalism to become the intellectual property of American conservatism. For welfare liberals, democratic government is not an enemy of freedom. So long as constitutional safeguards are in place, government can and should have a major role in defining and achieving the common good.

Welfare liberals share many communitarian ideas. They have criticized economic individualism, especially the view that the free play of private interests will necessarily serve the general welfare. Welfare liberalism's concern for the poor, and for disadvantaged minorities, is an expression of fraternity. These are communitarian sensibilities. However, important differences separate the new communitarians from welfare liberals. The latter have been overly complacent with respect to major social problems, such as widespread dependency on public assistance, premature pregnancies and fatherless children; unsafe neighborhoods, schools, parks, and other public spaces; erosion of support for traditional conceptions of good conduct and personal responsibility.

The new communitarians reject welfare-state programs that are overly bureaucratic or based on misconceptions about what people in poverty are like. They want to remedy past failures through policies that encourage personal responsibility on the part of clients, in health care and other social services, and more effective participation by local governments, concerned citizens, and private institutions.

The new communitarians also believe that American liberalism has gone too far in pressing demands for political liberty and personal autonomy. In the nineteenth and early twentieth centuries, liberals could speak comfortably about "ordered liberty," but that phrase has been retired. A fateful step was the distinction drawn by welfare liberals, beginning in the 1930s, between economic and political liberty. The New Deal introduced many restraints on business, rejected "freedom of contract" as a constitutional bar to laws protecting factory workers, and created a wide array of regulatory agencies to police finance, industry, and agriculture. At the same time, American liberals ardently supported civil rights and civil liberties. For them, First Amendment rights have special primacy. Rights of free speech and expression are sacred, to be vigorously defended against encroachment or erosion. This defense of freedom deserves the gratitude of all Americans. Yet the community is disarmed by liberal ideas that rationalize or excuse irresponsible conduct. A new balance is required, based on a better understanding of ordered liberty.

Too many contemporary American liberals have accepted a radical relativism whose message is that all values are subjective and of equal worth. Such ideas have undercut confidence in moral judgment and democratic decision. Closely related is the doctrine of liberal neutralism, the idea that government should not presume to say what sort of lives we ought to live and should not try to mold our preferences. According to this liberal view, moral judgments are properly made by individuals and not by communities, not even by democratic communities. An underlying assumption is that differences about values run deep and cannot be reconciled. Hence government should leave them alone. As we shall see, this is very different from the communitarian understanding of democracy.

American welfare liberalism has had a split personality. It has rejected the individualist assumptions of neoclassical economics about property and choice. Welfare liberals accept many government policies that limit free choice in matters of health, safety, education, and conservation. American liberals are not consistently libertarian. Although they are fervent defenders of civil liberties and civil rights, they do not shrink from asking people to give up riding bicycles without helmets or purchasing handguns without restrictions. They mostly favor public education, public television, government support for the arts, and regulation of spending in political campaigns. The troubled ethos of welfare liberalism badly needs a forthright acceptance of communitarian principles. This will produce a sturdy hybrid, which we may call communitarian liberalism.

The communitarian critique of liberalism has this main complaint: the liberal tradition as we have come to know it in the West lacks an ethic of responsibility. The focus has been on liberty and rights, without much concern for obligation and duty. This failing is easy to understand and even forgive. Modern liberalism emerged as an appeal for liberation from the shackles of a precapitalist and predemocratic age. Liberals fought for an end to class privilege, fixed status, suffocating tradition, and outmoded institutions. The guiding lights would be autonomy and choice. The sobering virtues of responsibility were given little weight, or were taken for granted.

The communitarian challenge seeks to amend liberalism, not to reject it. There is no question of idealizing, still less of returning to, a world of protected privilege; no question of giving up the chief economic, political, and social liberties championed by the architects of liberal government. Nevertheless, the communitarian amendments are not minor, and they claim coherence. The message is one of solidarity repaired, and of liberty protected by well-ordered institutions and norms of civility. In prospect is an alternative vision of human persons as free in vital respects but limited by duties that make those freedoms effective and secure.

Without Vision, the People Perish

The communitarian persuasion is a public philosophy, not a hardened ideology. This is an important distinction to maintain when we consider the role of ideas in public affairs. We cannot do without comprehensive doctrines. They are indispensable as guides to social policy and as foundations of our institutions. They express the sense we make of social reality and the grasp we have of moral truth. For communitarians the compelling reality is human interdependence. The important truth is a pervasive need for personal and social responsibility.

Without a coherent public philosophy we are vulnerable to drift, opportunism, and self-deception. A moral compass is lost or broken. This insight is captured by the biblical aphorism, "where there is no vision, the people perish" (Prov. 29:18).

Americans are rightly distrustful of ideology. The "-isms" of our time, and of earlier times as well, have too often demanded conformity, enforced exclusions, justified murder. Sectarian passions have poisoned Christianity, Marxism, and many other religious and secular movements. Prizing purity of doctrine and unconditional belief, these ideologies have often imposed stringent tests of adherence and loyalty. They have expected their beliefs to provide ready answers to all problems. Ideological thinking, it has been said, moves from thought to action "as the crow flies," unimpeded by the rough terrain of competing interests and contradictory values.[7]

Of course, a public philosophy must have some bite, promoting its own perspectives, as when Republicans in the United States seek to curb the role of government in economic and social life. It degenerates into a hardened ideology when adherents become participants in partisan combat rather than deliberative inquiry and when ideological preferences are given free rein, unchecked by concern for other interests or social reality. A true public philosophy is problem-centered: it deals with issues on their merits, in the light of relevant facts and genuine needs. Its principles are tested by their usefulness in promoting good policy. A public philosophy cannot be true to itself and also be a device for escaping the complexities and burdens of choice. When President Lincoln spoke of "firmness in the right as God gives us to see the right," he was not seeking a license for arrogance, still less for complacency or partisan judgment.[8] He was defending principled judgment, tempered by humility, disciplined by self-correction.

NOTES

1. See Amitai Etzioni, *The Moral Dimension: Toward a New Economics* (New York: Free Press, 1988).
2. Michael Sandel, "My RFK," *New Republic,* July 6, 1998, 11. See also Sandel, *Democracy's Discontent* (Cambridge, Mass.: Harvard University Press, 1996), pp. 299–304. Sandel notes: "Drawing on the voluntarist conception of freedom, many liberals of the day argued that the solution to poverty was welfare, ideally in the form of a guaranteed minimum income that imposed no conditions and made no judgments about the lives recipients led. Respecting persons as free and independent selves, capable of choosing their own ends, means providing each person as a matter of right a certain measure of economic security. Kennedy disagreed" (p. 302).
3. Rudolf Scharping, "Freedom, Solidarity, Individual Responsibility: Reflections on the Relationship between Politics, Money and Morality," comments prepared for a communitarian conference held in Geneva, Switzerland, August 1996. Scharping became Germany's minister of defense after the Social Democrats won the election in 1998.
4. *The Responsive Community,* edited by Amitai Etzioni, journal of the new communitarians, carries the subtitle "Rights and Responsibilities." The editorial board includes, among others, Benjamin R. Barber, Robert N. Bellah, Jean Bethke Elshtain, William Galston, Nathan Glazer, Mary Ann Glendon, and Charles Taylor.

5. The quotation is more famous than its source: Anatole France, *The Red Lily,* trans. Winfred Stephens (London: John Lane, 1914), p. 95.
6. See *Autobiography of John Stuart Mill* (1873; reprint, New York: Columbia University Press, 1924), p. 162.
7. Michael Oakeshott, *Rationalism in Politics* (New York: Basic Books, 1962), p. 69.
8. Lincoln's words are from his Second Inaugural Address.—Eds.

PART FOUR

Conservatism

As the name "conservatism" suggests, conservatives share a desire to *conserve* something—usually the traditions or customary way of life in their societies. Thus, conservatives generally resist change and prefer to cling to the "tried and true" or "time-tested" ways. But different conservatives have different ideas about what is valuable and worth preserving. Besides that, traditions and customs vary widely from one society to another, so a conservative in one society may want to preserve traditions that are at odds with the traditions of another society. Conservatives may all want to conserve something, in other words, but they do not all want to conserve the same things—and that is what makes their ideology so difficult to define.

For Edmund Burke (1729–1797), widely regarded as the father of conservatism, the desire to conserve a traditional way of life is quite clear. The most famous writings of Burke—an Irishman who served for many years as a member of the British Parliament—were directed against the French Revolution, which he saw as a misguided attempt to create an entirely new kind of society based on abstract theory and human reason. The revolutionaries, he charged in *Reflections on the Revolution in France* (1790), are attacking all the institutions—the king, the aristocracy, the church—that give order and stability to their country. If they succeed, Burke said, they will find themselves and their society adrift in a storm-tossed sea, all sail and no anchor.

Burke, like later conservatives, recognized that change is an inevitable part of life. But he believed that change can occur in either a healthy or a dangerous way. If it is the result of gradual or piecemeal reform, it will promote the health of society. But rapid change and radical innovation are likely to prove disastrous. Revolutionaries who want to transform whole societies overnight are like people who tear down their old house, only to find themselves freezing to death before they can build a new one.

Burke wrote his *Reflections* less out of concern for the future of France than out of fear that the revolution would inspire similar upheaval in England. He did not argue, in any case, that France could and should go back to the way things were before the revolution. But a more extreme group of conservatives reacted in just this way. These "reactionaries," such as Joseph de Maistre (1753–1821), hoped to turn back the clock, returning to a prerevolutionary France guided by "throne and altar," or king and church. Since then, the term "reactionary" has referred to anyone who wants to restore or return to an earlier way of life.

During the first half of the nineteenth century, conservatives generally opposed liberalism and democracy, which they blamed for upsetting the established social order. Liberalism, with its emphasis on the rights and interests of the individual, threatened to tear the delicate fabric of society. A person is not merely an individual, the conservatives maintained, but a part of a larger whole who has a duty to other members of the society. When all people are joined together, the society, like the criss-crossing threads of a fabric, is strong and beautiful. When each goes his or her own way, however, the social fabric frays and begins to unravel. Life then becomes dull and drab, especially as capitalism turns the individual's attention to commerce—to "getting and spending" that "lay waste our powers," as the English poet William Wordsworth (1770–1850) put it. Nature, literature, and religion are all reduced in the age of commerce to the lowest common denominator—money.

Many conservatives also regarded democracy as a threat to social order. Like Burke, they believed that human beings are ruled more by their passions than by their reason. If the people govern, who will govern the people? Who or what will keep the common people from destroying their society? At the worst, according to conservatives, democracy will lead to chaos and anarchy because the common people will be too shortsighted to take measures that will restrain their passions and desires. At best, democracy will "level" society by reducing everyone to the same condition. Either way, conservatives warned of the dangers of "mass society"—a warning also sounded in the twentieth century by José Ortega y Gasset (1883–1955) and other writers.

Throughout the twentieth century, an uneasy alliance prevailed between "Burkean" or "classical" conservatives, such as Michael Oakeshott (1901–1990) and Garry Wills (1934–), and modern conservatives, such as British Prime Minister Margaret Thatcher (1925–) and U.S. President Ronald Reagan (1911–2004), who declared that government should not "interfere" with individuals competing in the marketplace. The alliance has held together in large part because conservatives of both sorts share a respect for private property, an acceptance (sometimes grudging) of democracy, and a now-fading fear of communism. Now that the communist threat has receded, this conservative alliance is coming under increasing strain.

Whether terrorism will replace communism as a threat that binds conservatives of various kinds together remains to be seen. What is clear, however, is that conservatism now comes in several varieties, including the conservatism of the evangelical Protestants who compose the Religious Right in the United States and the conservatism of the increasingly prominent, and controversial, "neoconservatives." As we noted earlier, all conservatives wish to conserve something. But what they wish to conserve, and how they propose to do it, remain matters of difference and dispute.

25

Society, Reverence, and the "True Natural Aristocracy"

EDMUND BURKE

When the French Revolution began in 1789, many in England greeted it with enthusiasm. But Edmund Burke (1729–1797), an Irishman who moved to England and served for many years in Parliament, saw the revolution as a threat to order and liberty. In his *Reflections on the Revolution in France* (1790), Burke not only criticized the revolutionaries but virtually predicted that the revolution would end in chaos. This and his other speeches and writings—such as the *Appeal from the New to the Old Whigs* (1791), from which the second selection is drawn—have won for Burke the title of father of conservatism.

Source: The Works of Edmund Burke (London: George Bell and Sons, 1901), vol. 2, pp. 332–335, 359, 364–369, and vol. 3, pp. 85–87.

REFLECTIONS ON THE REVOLUTION IN FRANCE

Government is not made in virtue of natural rights, which may and do exist in total independence of it; and exist in much greater clearness, and in a much greater degree of abstract perfection: but their abstract perfection is their practical defect. By having a right to every thing they want every thing. Government is a contrivance of human wisdom to provide for human *wants.*[1] Men have a right that these wants should be provided for by this wisdom. Among these wants is to be reckoned the want, out of civil society, of a sufficient restraint upon their passions. Society requires not only that the passions of individuals should be subjected, but that even in the mass and body as well as in the individuals, the inclinations of men should frequently be thwarted, their will controlled, and their passions brought into subjection. This can only be done *by a power out of themselves;* and not, in the exercise of its function, subject to that will and to those passions which it is its office to bridle and subdue. In this sense the restraints on men, as well as their liberties, are to be reckoned among their rights. But as the liberties and the restrictions vary with times and circumstances, and admit of infinite modifications, they cannot be settled upon any abstract rule; and nothing is so foolish as to discuss them upon that principle.

The moment you abate any thing from the full rights of men, each to govern himself, and suffer any artificial positive limitation upon those rights, from that moment the whole organization of government becomes a consideration of convenience. This it is which makes the constitution of a state, and the due distribution of its powers, a matter of the most delicate and complicated skill. It requires a deep knowledge of human nature and human necessities, and of the things which facilitate or obstruct the various ends which are to be pursued by the mechanism of civil institutions. The state is to have recruits to its strength, and remedies to its distempers. What is the use of discussing a man's abstract right to food or to medicine? The question is upon the method of procuring and administering them. In that deliberation I shall always advise to call in the aid of the farmer and the physician, rather than the professor of metaphysics.

The science of constructing a commonwealth, or renovating it, or reforming it, is, like every other experimental science, not to be taught *a priori.* Nor is it a short experience that can instruct us in that practical science; because the real effects of moral causes are not always immediate; but that which in the first instance is prejudicial may be excellent in its remoter operation; and its excellence may arise even...from the ill effects it produces in the beginning. The reverse also happens; and very plausible schemes, with very pleasing commencements, have often shameful and lamentable conclusions. In states there are often some obscure and almost latent causes, things which appear at first view of little moment, on which a very great part of its prosperity or adversity may most essentially depend. The science of government being therefore so practical in itself, and intended for such practical purposes, a matter which requires experience, and even more experience than any person can gain in his whole life, however sagacious and observing he may be, it is with infinite caution that any man ought to venture upon pulling down an edifice which has answered in any tolerable degree for ages the common purposes of society, or on building it up again, without having models and patterns of approved utility before his eyes.

These metaphysic rights entering into common life, like rays of light which pierce into a dense medium, are, by the laws of nature, refracted from their straight line. Indeed in the gross and complicated mass of human passions and concerns, the primitive rights of men undergo such a variety of refractions and reflections, that it becomes absurd to talk of them as if they continued in the simplicity of their original direction. The nature of man is intricate; the objects of society are of the greatest possible complexity; and therefore no simple disposition or direction of power can be suitable either to man's nature, or to the quality of his affairs. When I hear the simplicity of contrivance aimed at and boasted of in any new political constitutions, I am at no loss to decide that the artificers are grossly ignorant of their trade, or totally negligent of their duty. The simple governments are fundamentally defective, to say no worse of them. If you were to contemplate society in but one point of view, all these simple modes of polity are infinitely captivating. In effect each would answer its single end much more perfectly than the more complex is able to attain all its complex purposes. But it is better that the whole should be imperfectly and anomalously answered, than that, while some parts are provided for with great exactness, others might be totally neglected, or perhaps materially injured, by the over-care of a favourite member.

The pretended rights of these theorists are all extremes; and in proportion as they are metaphysically true, they are morally and politically false. The rights of men are in a sort of *middle,* incapable of definition, but not impossible to be discerned. The rights of men in governments are their advantages; and these are often in balances between differences of good; in compromises sometimes between good and evil, and sometimes, between evil and evil. Political reason is a computing principle; adding, subtracting, multiplying, and dividing, morally and not metaphysically or mathematically, true moral denominations.

By these theorists the right of the people is almost always sophistically confounded with their power. The body of the community, whenever it can come to act, can meet with no effectual resistance; but till power and right are the same, the whole body of them has no right inconsistent with virtue, and the first of all virtues, prudence. Men have no right to what is not reasonable, and to what is not for their benefit....

We preserve the whole of our feelings still native and entire, unsophisticated by pedantry and infidelity. We have real hearts of flesh and blood beating in our bosoms. We fear God; we look up with awe to kings; with affection to parliaments; with duty to magistrates; with reverence to priests; and with respect to nobility. Why? Because when such ideas are brought before our minds, it is *natural* to be so affected; because all other feelings are false and spurious, and tend to corrupt our minds, to vitiate our primary morals, to render us unfit for rational liberty; and by teaching us a servile, licentious, and abandoned insolence, to be our low sport for a few holidays to make us perfectly fit for, and justly deserving of slavery, through the whole course of our lives.

You see, Sir, that in this enlightened age I am bold enough to confess, that we are generally men of untaught feelings; that instead of casting away all our old prejudices, we cherish them to a very considerable degree, and, to take more shame to ourselves, we cherish them because they are prejudices;[2] and the longer they have lasted, and the more generally they have prevailed, the more we cherish them. We are afraid to put men to live and trade each on his own private stock of reason; because we suspect that this stock in each man is small, and that the individuals would do better to avail themselves of the general bank and capital of nations, and of ages. Many of our men of speculation, instead of exploding general prejudices, employ their sagacity to discover the latent wisdom which prevails in them. If they find what they seek, and they seldom fail, they think it more wise to continue the prejudice, with the reason involved, than to cast away the coat of prejudice, and to leave nothing but the naked reason; because prejudice, with its reason, has a motive to give action to that reason, and an affection which will give it permanence. Prejudice is of ready application in the emergency; it previously engages the mind in a steady course of wisdom and virtue, and does not leave the man hesitating in the moment of decision, sceptical, puzzled, and unresolved. Prejudice renders a man's virtue his habit; and not a series of unconnected acts. Through just prejudice, his duty becomes a part of his nature....

The consecration of the state, by a state religious establishment, is necessary also to operate with an wholesome awe upon free citizens; because, in order to secure their freedom, they must enjoy some determinate portion of power. To them therefore a religion connected with the state, and with their duty towards it, becomes even more necessary than in such societies, where the people by the terms of their subjection are confined to private sentiments, and the management of their own family concerns. All persons possessing any portion of power ought to be strongly and awefully impressed with an idea that they act in trust; and that they are to account for their conduct in that trust to the one great master, author and founder of society.

This principle ought even to be more strongly impressed upon the minds of those who compose the collective sovereignty than upon those of single princes. Without instruments, these princes can do nothing. Whoever uses instruments, in finding helps, finds also impediments. Their power is therefore by no means compleat; nor are they safe in extreme abuse. Such persons, however elated by flattery, arrogance, and self-opinion, must be sensible that, whether covered or not by positive law, in some way or other they are accountable even here for the abuse of their trust. If they are not cut off by a rebellion of their people, they may be strangled by the very Janissaries kept for their security against all other rebellion.[3] Thus we have seen the king of France sold by his soldiers for an encrease of pay. But where popular authority is absolute and unrestrained, the people have an infinitely greater, because a far better founded confidence in their own power. They are themselves, in a great measure, their own instruments. They are nearer to their objects. Besides, they are less under responsibility to one of the greatest controlling powers on earth, the sense of fame and estimation. The share of infamy that is likely to fall to the lot of each individual in public acts, is small indeed; the operation of opinion being in the inverse ratio to the number of those who abuse power. Their own approbation of their own acts has to them the appearance of a public judgment in their favour. A perfect democracy is therefore the most shameless thing in the world. As it is the most shameless, it is also the most fearless. No man apprehends in his person he can be made subject to punishment. Certainly the people at large never ought: for as all punishments are for example towards the conservation of the people at large, the people at large can never become the subject of punishment by any human hand. It is therefore of infinite importance that they should not be suffered to imagine that their will, any more than that of kings, is the standard of right and wrong. They ought to be persuaded that they are full as little entitled, and far less qualified, with safety to themselves, to use any arbitrary power whatsoever; that therefore they are not, under a false show of liberty, but, in truth, to exercise an unnatural inverted domination, tyrannically to exact, from those who officiate in the state, not an entire devotion to their interest, which is their right, but an abject submission to their occasional will; extinguishing thereby, in all those who serve them, all moral principle, all sense of dignity, all use of judgment, and all consistency of character, whilst by the very same process they give themselves up a proper, a suitable, but a more contemptible prey to the servile ambition of popular sycophants or courtly flatterers.

When the people have emptied themselves of all the lust of selfish will, which without religion it is utterly impossible they ever should, when they are conscious that they exercise, and exercise perhaps in an higher link of the order of delegation, the power, which to be legitimate must be according to that eternal immutable law, in which will and reason are the same, they will be more careful how they place power in base and incapable hands. In their nomination to office, they will not appoint to the exercise of authority, as to a pitiful job, but as to an holy function; not according to their sordid selfish interest, nor to their wanton caprice, nor to their arbitrary will; but they will confer that power (which any man may well tremble to give or to receive) on those only, in whom they may discern that predominant proportion of active virtue and wisdom, taken together and fitted to the charge, such, as in the great and inevitable mixed mass of human imperfections and infirmities, is to be found.

When they are habitually convinced that no evil can be acceptable, either in the act or the permission, to him whose essence is good, they will be better able to extirpate out of the minds of all magistrates, civil, ecclesiastical, or military, any thing that bears the least resemblance to a proud and lawless domination.

But one of the first and most leading principles on which the commonwealth and the laws are consecrated, is lest the temporary possessors and life-renters in it, unmindful of what they have received from their ancestors, or of what is due to their posterity, should act as if they were the entire masters; that they should not think it amongst their rights to cut off the entail, or commit waste on the inheritance, by destroying at their pleasure the whole original fabric of their society; hazarding to leave to those who come after them, a ruin instead of an habitation—and teaching these successors as little to respect their contrivances, as they had themselves respected the institutions of their forefathers. By this unprincipled facility of changing the state as often, and as much, and in as many ways as there are floating fancies or fashions, the whole chain and continuity of the commonwealth would be broken. No one generation could link with the other. Men would become little better than the flies of a summer.

And first of all the science of jurisprudence, the pride of the human intellect, which, with all its defects, redundancies, and errors, is the collected reason of ages, combining the principles of original justice with the infinite variety of human concerns, as a heap of old exploded errors, would be no longer studied. Personal self-sufficiency and arrogance (the certain attendants upon all those who have never experienced a wisdom greater than their own) would usurp the tribunal. Of course, no certain laws, establishing invariable grounds of hope and fear, would keep the actions of men in a certain course, or direct them to a certain end. Nothing stable in the modes of holding property, or exercising function, could form a solid ground on which any parent could speculate in the education of his offspring, or in a choice for their future establishment in the world. No principles would be early worked into the habits. As soon as the most able instructor had completed his laborious course of instruction, instead of sending forth his pupil, accomplished in a virtuous discipline, fitted to procure him attention and respect, in his place in society, he would find every thing altered; and that he had turned out a poor creature to the contempt and derision of the world, ignorant of the true grounds of estimation. Who would insure a tender and delicate sense of honour to beat almost with the first pulses of the heart, when no man could know what would be the test of honour in a nation, continually varying the standard of its coin? No part of life would retain its acquisitions. Barbarism with regard to science and literature, unskilfulness with regard to arts and manufactures, would infallibly succeed to the want of a steady education and settled principle; and thus the commonwealth itself would, in a few generations, crumble away, be disconnected into the dust and powder of individuality, and at length dispersed to all the winds of heaven.

To avoid therefore the evils of inconstancy and versatility, ten thousand times worse than those of obstinacy and the blindest prejudice, we have consecrated the state, that no man should approach to look into its defects or corruptions but with due caution; that he should never dream of beginning its reformation by its subversion; that he should approach to the faults of the state as to the wounds of a father, with pious awe and trembling solicitude. By this wise prejudice we are taught to look with horror on those children of their country who are prompt rashly to hack that aged parent in pieces, and put him into the kettle of magicians, in hopes that by their poisonous weeds, and wild incantations, they may regenerate the paternal constitution, and renovate their father's life.

Society is indeed a contract. Subordinate contracts for objects of mere occasional interest may be dissolved at pleasure—but the state ought not to be considered as nothing better than a partnership agreement in a trade of pepper and coffee, callico or tobacco, or some other such low concern, to be taken up for a little temporary interest, and to be dissolved by the fancy of the parties. It is to be looked on with other reverence; because it is not a partnership in things subservient only to the gross animal existence of a temporary and perishable nature. It is a partnership in all science; a partnership in all art; a partnership in every virtue, and in all perfection. As the ends of such a partnership cannot be obtained in many generations, it becomes a partnership not only between those who are living, but between those who are living, those who are dead, and those who are to be born. Each contract of each particular state is but a clause in the great primaeval contract of eternal society, linking the lower with the higher natures, connecting the visible and invisible world, according to a fixed compact sanctioned by the inviolable oath which holds all physical and all moral natures, each in their appointed place.

APPEAL FROM THE NEW TO THE OLD WHIGS

...To enable men to act with the weight and character of a people, and to answer the ends for which they are incorporated into that capacity, we must suppose them (by means immediate or consequential) to be in that state of habitual social discipline in which the wiser, the more expert, and the more opulent conduct, and by conducting enlighten and protect, the weaker, the less knowing, and the less provided with the goods of fortune. When the multitude are not under this discipline, they can scarcely be said to be in civil society....

A true natural aristocracy is not a separate interest in the state, or separable from it. It is an essential integrant part of any large body rightly constituted. It is formed out of a class of legitimate presumptions, which, taken as generalities, must be admitted for actual truths. To be bred in a place of estimation; to see nothing low and sordid from one's infancy; to be taught to respect one's self; to be habituated to the censorial inspection of the public eye; to look early to public opinion; to stand upon such elevated ground as to be enabled to take a large view of the widespread and infinitely diversified combinations of men and affairs in a large society; to have leisure to read, to reflect, to converse; to be enabled to draw the court and attention of the wise and learned, wherever they are to be found; to be habituated in armies to command and to obey; to be taught to despise danger in the pursuit of honor and duty; to be formed to the greatest degree of vigilance, foresight, and circumspection, in a state of things in which no fault is committed with impunity and the slightest mistakes draw on the most ruinous consequences; to be led to a guarded and regulated conduct, from a sense that you are considered as an instructor of your fellow-citizens in their highest concerns, and that you act as a reconciler between God and man; to be employed as an administrator of law and justice, and to be thereby amongst the first benefactors to mankind; to be a professor of high science, or of liberal and ingenuous art; to be amongst rich traders, who from their success are presumed to have sharp and vigorous understandings, and to possess the virtues of diligence, order, constancy, and regularity, and to have cultivated an habitual regard to commutative justice: these are the circumstances of men that form what I should call a *natural* aristocracy, without which there is no nation.

The state of civil society which necessarily generates this aristocracy is a state of Nature,—and much more truly so than a savage and incoherent mode of life. For man is by nature reasonable; and he is never perfectly in his natural state, but when he is placed where reason may be best cultivated and most predominates. Art is man's nature. We are as much, at least, in a state of Nature in formed manhood as in immature and helpless infancy. Men, qualified in the manner I have just described, form in Nature, as she operates in the common modification of society, the leading, guiding, and governing part. It is the soul to the body, without which the man does not exist. To give, therefore, no more importance, in the social order, to such descriptions of men than that of so many units is a horrible usurpation.

When great multitudes act together, under that discipline of Nature, I recognize the PEOPLE. I acknowledge something that perhaps equals, and ought always to guide, the sovereignty of convention. In all things the voice of this grand chorus of national harmony ought to have a mighty and decisive influence. But when you disturb this harmony,—when you break up this beautiful order, this array of truth and Nature, as well as of habit and prejudice,—when you separate the common sort of men from their proper chieftains, so as to form them into an adverse army,—I no longer know that venerable object called the people in such a disbanded race of deserters and vagabonds. For a while they may be terrible, indeed,—but in such a manner as wild beasts are terrible. The mind owes to them no sort of submission. They are, as they have always been reputed, rebels.

NOTES

1. By "wants" Burke does not mean wishes or desires but "defects" or "lacks," as when we might (at the risk of sounding old-fashioned) say that the bicycle cannot be ridden because it wants a wheel.—Eds.
2. As Burke uses the term, "prejudices" are habitual, traditional, and/or unreflective prejudgments or biases. Thus the term does not, for Burke, carry the negative connotations it carries today.—Eds.
3. Janissaries were members of an elite military guard in Turkey.—Eds.

26

Conservatism as Reaction

JOSEPH DE MAISTRE

On the European continent some of the aristocratic opponents of the French Revolution saw it as the logical, if terrible, outcome of the eighteenth century, with its glorification of human reason. Because they reacted against the revolution, these writers came to be known as the "reactionaries." Perhaps the most important writer who sought to restore the old order of European society—with the church, monarchy, and aristocracy firmly in control—was Joseph de Maistre (1753–1821). The following selections are from Maistre's *Considerations on France* (1796) and *Study on Sovereignty* (first published in 1884).

Source: Oeuvres Complètes de Joseph de Maistre (Lyon: Librairie Générale Catholique et Classique, 1891), vol. 1, pp. 74–75, 343–345, 347–348, 353–355, 376–378, 399–400, 424–426, 449–450. Translated from the French by Terence Ball.

CONSIDERATIONS ON FRANCE

The French constitution of 1795, like its predecessors, was made for *man*. Yet the world contains no such creature as *man*. In my lifetime I have seen Frenchmen, Italians, Russians, etc....: but I swear that I have never ever encountered *man;* if he exists, I have missed him.... A constitution which is made for all nations is made for none; it is a pure abstraction, an academic exercise for the mind, modelled after some imaginary hypothesis, and must therefore be addressed to *man*, in whatever imaginary place he dwells.

What is a constitution? Is it not a solution to the following problem? Taking as given *the population, customs and traditions, religion, geographical situation, political relations, wealth, the good and bad features of a particular nation, to find the laws that fit it?*

Yet, the problem is not raised at all in the constitution of 1795, which was written only with *man* in mind.

STUDY ON SOVEREIGNTY

The Founders and the Political Constitution

The government of a nation is no more its own creation than is its language. Just as in nature the seeds of countless plants are destined to perish unless some human hand puts them where they can sprout, so, analogously, are there in nations particular qualities and potentials which will remain powerless unless aided by circumstances or by some helping hand.

The founder of a nation [*l'instituteur d'un peuple*] is precisely this helping hand. Blessed with an extraordinary penetration—or, more probably, with an infallible instinct (since individual genius rarely realizes what it is achieving, which makes it different from mere intellect)—he detects those hidden potentials and qualities which form the character of a nation, the means of giving them birth, of putting them into action, and putting them to the best possible use. He is never to be seen writing or debating; his manner of proceeding comes from inspiration; and if he sometimes takes pen in hand, it is not to debate but to issue commands.

One of the great errors of our time is to believe that the political constitution of nations is a purely human creation—that a constitution can be created much as a watchmaker manufactures a watch. Nothing could be more false, except perhaps the claim that a constitution can be created by an assembly of men. God gives a government to a nation in only two ways. In most cases he himself makes it grow, so to speak, slowly and like a plant, through that combination of circumstances that we call fortuitous. But when He wants to establish the foundations of a political edifice in a hurry, He imparts His power to a few truly exceptional men. Appearing only rarely through the centuries, these men rise like towering monuments along time's road, becoming ever rarer as the centuries advance. In order to render their unusual service, God equips them with extraordinary powers, which generally go unrecognized by their contemporaries and perhaps even by themselves....

No important and genuinely constitutional reform ever establishes anything new; it merely declares and defends rights that already exist—which is why one can never know the constitution of a country simply by reading its written laws, since these laws are made in different epochs to declare rights that have been disputed or forgotten, and since many things are never written down....

The different forms and degrees of sovereignty have led some to think that peoples have modified sovereignty as they please; nothing could be more false. Each people has the government that is suited to it, and yet none has chosen what they have. Even more remarkable is that, whenever a people (or, more precisely, some portion of a people) tries to give itself a government, they make themselves more miserable than before. For in their deep confusion a people invariably mistake their true interests, pursuing what is not good for them while simultaneously rejecting what is good for them. And we all know how terrible are the mistakes made in this field....

Human power is not able to create, and everything depends on the primordial aptitude of peoples and individuals.... Men never respect what they themselves have created—which is why an elected ruler never possesses the moral force of an hereditary sovereign, since he is not as *noble,* i.e., does not display the kind of grandeur that is independent of men and that comes only through the work of time....

In short, the majority of people play no part in politics. Indeed, they respect government only because they had no part in creating it. This sentiment is engraved deeply on their hearts and in their habits. They submit to sovereignty because they sense that it is something sacred that they have neither the power to create nor to destroy. If, through corruption and perfidious influences, this preserving sentiment is erased, if they come to the unhappy conclusion that they are required *en masse* to reform the State, then all is lost. This is why, even in free states, it is infinitely important for the men who govern to be separated from the mass of people by that personal respect that results from birth and wealth. For if opinion does not erect a barrier between itself and authority, if power is not outside its grasp, if the governed multitude think themselves equal to the governing few, then there is government no more. Thus the aristocracy is, in essence, a sovereign or ruling class, and the French Revolution a massive violation of the eternal laws of nature.

The National Soul

All nations ever known have been happy and strong insofar as they have unerringly followed the national soul...i.e., [a people's] useful prejudices. If everyone relied upon his own reason in religion, you would see at once an emerging anarchy of multiple and conflicting beliefs and the destruction of religious sovereignty. Similarly, were each man to make himself the sole judge of the principles of government, you would soon see the rise of civic anarchy and the complete destruction of political sovereignty. Government, like true religion, has its dogmas, its mysteries, its priests. To subject it to individual analysis would destroy it. It has its life only through the national soul, or political faith, i.e., its creed. Man's main need is that his tendency toward [individual and independent] reason should be restricted in two respects: it should be stifled, and it should submerge itself in the national soul, so that it exchanges its individual existence for an alternative *communal* existence, in much the same way that a river flowing into the sea still exists in the larger body of water, but without being distinct from it.

What is patriotism? It is this national soul of which I speak. It is individual *self-denial.* Faith and patriotism are the two great wonders of the world. Both are divine. They work in miraculous ways. Do not speak in their presence of criticism, choice, or debate, for they will reply that you blaspheme. They know only two words, *surrender* and *belief;* with these two levers they lift the earth. Even their mistakes are sublime. These two children of heaven demonstrate their divine origin by making and maintaining; and if they come together, they jointly take possession of a nation, they raise its stature, render it divine, and multiply its power many times over....

But you, lowly man—can you ignite this sacred fire that inflames nations? Can you impart a shared soul to millions of men? Can you unite them under laws of your own making? Can you give them a common cause? Can you shape the thoughts of future generations? Can you make them obey you and create those conserving prejudices that father the laws and are more powerful than they? How absurd!

The Same Subject Continued

Without doubt reason is, in one sense, good for nothing. We possess the physical knowledge needed to maintain society. We have made great advances in mathematics and the natural sciences. But, once we get beyond our circle of needs, our knowledge becomes either useless or uncertain. The always-restless human mind produces one theory after another. Theories are born, live, wither, and drop like leaves from a tree....

In the wider moral and political world, what do we know, and what can we do? We *know* the morality bequeathed to us by our parents, as a set of useful prejudices or dogmas believed by the rational mind. But here we owe nothing to anyone's individual reason. On the contrary, whenever this reason has interfered, it has twisted and subverted morality.

We *know*, in political matters, that we must respect those powers ordained by providence. We *know* that when the passage of time produces abuses that can pervert the basic principle of a government, we then need to remove these abuses, although without affecting the principle itself, through a delicate surgical procedure called reform....

Monarchy

Men are born for monarchy. Of all forms of government, monarchy is the oldest and most universal.... Monarchical government comes so naturally to men that they unwittingly equate it with sovereignty itself. Men appear to agree that, if there is no king, then there is no real *sovereign*....

Critics who deny the divine origin of monarchy...[deny] that the authority of kings comes from God. We need to ask, not about *royalty* in particular, but about *sovereignty* in general. All sovereignty has its source in God. Whatever its form, sovereignty is never the work of man. Sovereignty is in its very nature indivisible, inviolable, and absolute....

Men must always know about history, which is the one and only teacher in politics. Anyone who says that man is born for liberty has taken leave of his senses. If some superior being tried to write the *natural history* of man, he would have to look at the factual record. When he found what man is and has always been, what he does now and has always done, he would...reject the foolish idea that man is not what he should be and that his condition contradicts the laws of creation. The mere statement of this proposition suffices to disprove it.

History is the story of political experiments. And just as, in the physical sciences, entire volumes of speculative theories are falsified by a single experiment, so in political science no theory is credible if it is not the highly probable corollary of verified facts. If we ask, "What government is most natural to man?," history will answer: *monarchy*....

Man is hungry for power, has infinite desires, and—forever unhappy with what he already has—loves only what he does not have. People decry the despotism of princes; they should instead decry the despotism of *man*. We are all born despots, whether we be an absolute Asian monarch or a child who smothers a bird in his hand for the pleasure of proving that other creatures are weaker than himself. There is no man who does not abuse power, and experience shows the worst despots...are those who rail against despotism. But God has established limits to the abuse of power. He has decreed that power destroy itself once it exceeds its natural limits. This law He has written everywhere. In the physical as well as the moral world, this law surrounds and speaks to us.

Consider a gun: Up to some point, the longer its barrel, the more effective it will be; but once you exceed its natural limit, the less effective it will be.... This is a crude picture of power. To perpetuate itself, power must restrict itself, always stopping short of that limit beyond which its most extreme expression leads to its own destruction.

To be sure, I do not admire *popular* assemblies; but French folly should not blind us to the truth and wisdom of the happy medium. If there is any undeniable maxim, it is this: In all rebellions and revolutions, *the people always begin by being in the right and always end by being in the wrong.*

27

The Poet as Conservative

WILLIAM WORDSWORTH

One of the greatest poets in English literature, William Wordsworth (1770–1850) welcomed the French Revolution as a young man—as he acknowledged wistfully in the first selection. But Wordsworth later turned against the revolution and other sweeping attempts to remake society. Like Edmund Burke, he became a defender of "ordered liberty," an idea at the center of his "Sonnets Dedicated to Liberty and Order" (1838).

Source: The Complete Poetical Works of William Wordsworth, ed. Andrew J. George (Boston and New York: Houghton, Mifflin and Co., 1904), pp. 340, 761, and 758, respectively.

FRENCH REVOLUTION AS IT APPEARED TO ENTHUSIASTS AT ITS COMMENCEMENT[1]

Oh! pleasant exercise of hope and joy!
For mighty were the auxiliars which then stood
Upon our side, we who were strong in love!
Bliss was it in that dawn to be alive,
But to be young was very heaven!—Oh! times,
In which the meagre, stale, forbidding ways
Of custom, law, and statute, took at once
The attraction of a country in romance!
When Reason seemed the most to assert her rights,
When most intent on making of herself
A prime Enchantress—to assist the work
Which then was going forward in her name!
Not favoured spots alone, but the whole earth,
The beauty wore of promise, that which sets
(As at some moment might not be unfelt
Among the bowers of paradise itself)
The budding rose above the rose full blown.
What temper at the prospect did not wake
To happiness unthought of? The inert
Were roused, and lively natures rapt away!
They who had fed their childhood upon dreams,
The playfellows of fancy, who had made
All powers of swiftness, subtilty, and strength
Their ministers,—who in lordly wise had stirred
Among the grandest objects of the sense,
And dealt with whatsoever they found there
As if they had within some lurking right
To wield it;—they, too, who, of gentle mood,
Had watched all gentle motions, and to these
Had fitted their own thoughts, schemers more mild,
And in the region of their peaceful selves;—
Now was it that both found, the meek and lofty
Did both find, helpers to their hearts desire,
And stuff at hand, plastic as they could wish;
Were called upon to exercise their skill,
Not in Utopia, subterranean fields,
Or some secreted island, Heaven knows where!
But in the very world, which is the world
Of all of us,—the place where in the end
We find our happiness, or not at all!

SONNETS DEDICATED TO LIBERTY AND ORDER[2]

IV

Blest Statesman He, whose Mind's unselfish will
Leaves him at ease among grand thoughts: whose eye
Sees that, apart from magnanimity,
Wisdom exists not; nor the humbler skill
Of Prudence, disentangling good and ill
With patient care, What tho' assaults run high,
They daunt not him who holds his ministry,
Resolute, at all hazards, to fulfil
Its duties;—prompt to move, but firm to wait,—
Knowing, things rashly sought are rarely found;
That, for the functions of an ancient State—
Strong by her charters, free because imbound,
Servant of Providence, not slave of Fate—
Perilous is sweeping change, all chance unsound.

AT BOLOGNA, IN REMEMBRANCE OF THE LATE INSURRECTIONS, 1837[3]

As leaves are to the tree whereon they grow
And wither, every human generation
Is to the Being of a mighty nation,
Locked in our world's embrace through weal and woe;
Thought that should teach the zealot to forego
Rash schemes, to abjure all selfish agitation,
And seek through noiseless pains and moderation
The unblemished good they only can bestow.
Alas! with most, who weigh futurity
Against time present, passion holds the scales:
Hence equal ignorance of both prevails,
And nations sink; or, struggling to be free,
Are doomed to flounder on, like wounded whales
Tossed on the bosom of a stormy sea.

NOTES

1. Composed 1804, published October 26, 1809, in *The Friend*.
2. Composed and published 1838.
3. Composed probably 1837, published 1842. Third of three sonnets.

28

Revolt of the Masses

JOSÉ ORTEGA Y GASSET

Alexis de Tocqueville and John Stuart Mill, with their warnings of the "tyranny of the majority," sounded a theme that became a favorite of conservative writers in the nineteenth and twentieth centuries. One of the most forceful criticisms of "mass society" came from the Spanish philosopher José Ortega y Gasset (1883–1955). Although Ortega, like Tocqueville, does not fit neatly into either the liberal or conservative category, his *Revolt of the Masses* (1930) issues a protest and a warning against many of the "progressive" and "levelling" features of a democratic age.

Source: From *The Revolt of the Masses* by José Ortega y Gasset. Copyright 1932 by W.W. Norton & Company, Inc., renewed ©1960 by Teresa Carey. Used by permission of W.W. Norton & Company, Inc.

THE GREATEST DANGER: THE STATE

In a right ordering of public affairs, the mass is that part which does not act of itself. Such is its mission. It has come into the world in order to be directed, influenced, represented, organised—even in order to cease being mass, or at least to aspire to this. But it has not come into the world to do all this by itself. It needs to submit its life to a higher court, formed of the superior minorities. The question as to who are these superior individuals may be discussed *ad libitum,* but that without them, whoever they be, humanity would cease to preserve its essentials is something about which there can be no possible doubt, though Europe spend a century with its head under its wing, ostrich-fashion, trying if she can to avoid seeing such a plain truth. For we are not dealing with an opinion based on facts more or less frequent and probable, but on a law of social "physics," much more immovable than the laws of Newton's physics. The day when a genuine philosophy[1] once more holds sway in Europe—it is the one thing that can save her—that day she will once again realise that man, whether he like it or no, is a being forced by his nature to seek some higher authority. If he succeeds in finding it of himself, he is a superior man; if not, he is a mass-man and must receive it from his superiors.

For the mass to claim the right to act of itself is then a rebellion against its own destiny, and because that is what it is doing at present, I speak of the rebellion of the masses. For, after all, the one thing that can substantially and truthfully be called rebellion is that which consists in not accepting one's own destiny, in rebelling against one's self. The rebellion of the archangel Lucifer would not have been less if, instead of striving to be God—which was not his destiny—he had striven to be the lowest of the angels—equally not his destiny. (If Lucifer had been a Russian, like [Leo] Tolstoi, he would perhaps have preferred this latter form of rebellion, none the less against God than the other more famous one.)

When the mass acts on its own, it does so only in one way, for it has no other: it lynches. It is not altogether by chance that lynch law comes from America, for America is, in a fashion, the paradise of the masses. And it will cause less surprise, nowadays, when the masses triumph, that violence should triumph and be made the one *ratio,* the one doctrine. It is now some time since I called attention to this advance of violence as a normal condition.[2] Today it has reached its full development, and this is a good symptom, because it means that automatically the descent is about to begin. Today violence is the rhetoric of the period, the empty rhetorician has made it his own. When a reality of human existence has completed its historic course, has been shipwrecked and lies dead, the waves throw it up on the shores of rhetoric, where the corpse remains for a long time. Rhetoric is the cemetery of human realities, or at any rate a Home for the Aged. The reality itself is survived by its name, which, though only a word, is after all at least a word and preserves something of its magic power.

But though it is not impossible that the prestige of violence as a cynically established rule has entered on its decline, we shall still continue under that rule, though in another form. I refer to the gravest danger now threatening European civilisation. Like all other dangers that threaten it, this one is born of civilisation itself. More than that, it constitutes one of its glories: it is the State as we know it today. We are confronted with a replica of what we said in the previous chapter about science: the fertility of its principles brings about a fabulous progress, but this inevitably imposes specialisation, and specialisation threatens to strangle science.

The same thing is happening with the State. Call to mind what the State was at the end of the eighteenth century in all European nations. Quite a small affair!...

In our days the State has come to be a formidable machine which works in marvellous fashion; of wonderful efficiency by reason of the quantity and precision of its means. Once it is set up in the midst of society, it is enough to touch a button for its enormous levers to start working and exercise their overwhelming power on any portion whatever of the social framework.

The contemporary State is the easiest seen and best-known product of civilisation. And it is an interesting revelation when one takes note of the attitude that mass-man adopts before it. He sees it, admires it, knows that *there it is,* safeguarding his existence; but he is not conscious of the fact that it is a human creation invented by certain men and upheld by certain virtues and fundamental qualities which the men of yesterday had and which may vanish into air tomorrow. Furthermore, the mass-man sees in the State an anonymous power, and feeling himself, like it, anonymous, he believes that the State is something of his own. Suppose that in the public life of a country some difficulty, conflict, or problem presents itself, the mass-man will tend to demand that the State intervene immediately and undertake a solution directly with its immense and unassailable resources.

This is the gravest danger that today threatens civilisation: State intervention; the absorption of all spontaneous social effort by the State, that is to say, of spontaneous historical action, which in the long run sustains, nourishes, and impels human destinies. When the mass suffers any ill-fortune or simply feels some strong appetite, its great temptation is that permanent, sure possibility of obtaining everything—without effort, struggle, doubt, or risk—merely by touching a button and setting the mighty machine in motion. The mass says to itself, *"L'état, c'est moi,"* which is a complete mistake.[3] The State is the mass only in the sense in which it can be said of two men that they are identical because neither of them is named John. The contemporary State and the mass coincide only in being anonymous. But the mass-man does in fact believe that he is the State, and he will tend more and more to set its machinery working on whatsoever pretext, to crush beneath it any creative minority which disturbs it—disturbs it in any order of things: in politics, in ideas, in industry.

The result of this tendency will be fatal. Spontaneous social action will be broken up over and over again by State intervention; no new seed will be able to fructify. Society will have to live *for* the State, man *for* the governmental machine. And as, after all, it is only a machine whose existence and maintenance depend on the vital supports around it, the State, after sucking out the very marrow of society, will be left bloodless, a skeleton, dead with that rusty death of machinery, more gruesome than the death of a living organism....

Is the paradoxical, tragic process of Statism now realised? Society, that it may live better, creates the State as an instrument. Then the State gets the upper hand and society has to begin to live for the State.... This is what State intervention leads to: the people are converted into fuel to feed the mere machine which is the State. The skeleton eats up the flesh around it. The scaffolding becomes the owner and tenant of the house.

When this is realised, it rather confounds one to hear [Benito] Mussolini heralding as an astounding discovery just made in Italy, the formula: "All for the State; nothing outside the State; nothing against the State."[4] This alone would suffice to reveal in Fascism a typical movement of mass-men. Mussolini found a State admirably built up—not by him, but precisely by the ideas and the forces he is combating: by liberal democracy. He confines himself to using it ruthlessly, and, without entering now into a detailed examination of his work, it is indisputable that the results obtained up to the present cannot be compared with those obtained in political and administrative working by the liberal State. If he has succeeded in anything, it is so minute, so little visible, so lacking in substance as with difficulty to compensate for the accumulation of the abnormal powers which enable him to make use of that machine to its full extent.

Statism is the higher form taken by violence and direct action when these are set up as standards. Through and by means of the State, the anonymous machine, the masses act for themselves. The nations of Europe have before them a period of great difficulties in their internal life, supremely arduous problems of law, economics, and public order. Can we help feeling that under the rule of the masses the State will endeavour to crush the independence of the individual and the group, and thus definitely spoil the harvest of the future?

A concrete example of this mechanism is found in one of the most alarming phenomena of the last thirty years: the enormous increase in the police force of all countries. The increase of population has inevitably rendered it necessary. However accustomed we may be to it, the terrible paradox should not escape our minds that the population of a great modern city, in order to move about peaceably and attend to its business, necessarily requires a police force to regulate the circulation. But it is foolishness for the party of "law and order" to imagine that these "forces of public authority" created to preserve order are always going to be content to preserve the order that that party desires. Inevitably they will end by themselves defining and deciding on the order they are going to impose—which, naturally, will be that which suits them best.

NOTES

1. For philosophy to rule, it is not necessary that philosophers be the rulers—as Plato at first wished—nor even for rulers to be philosophers—as was his later, more modest, wish. Both these things are, strictly speaking, most fatal. For philosophy to rule, it is sufficient for it to exist; that is to say, for the philosophers to be philosophers. For nearly a century past, philosophers have been everything but that—politicians, pedagogues, men of letters, and men of science.
2. Vide España Invertebrada, 1912.
3. "I am the State"—a remark supposedly made by King Louis XIV of France.—Eds.
4. This was one of the many slogans Mussolini's regime used in its attempt to turn Italy into what the fascists called a "totalitarian" state.—Eds.

29

On Being Conservative

MICHAEL OAKESHOTT

One of the leading representatives of "classical" conservatism in the twentieth century was the British philosopher Michael Oakeshott (1901–1990), who insisted that politics must be rooted in tradition and experience, not abstract reason or principles. As he says in his essay "Political Education," "In political activity...men sail a boundless and bottomless sea; there is neither harbour for shelter nor floor for anchorage, neither starting-place nor appointed destination. The enterprise is to keep afloat on an even keel; the sea is both friend and enemy; and the seamanship consists in using the resources of a traditional manner of behaviour in order to make a friend of every hostile occasion." Oakeshott develops this theme in the following selection from his essay "On Being Conservative."

Source: From *Rationalism in Politics and Other Essays* by Michael Oakeshott ©1962 by Michael Oakeshott. Reprinted by permission of Basic Books, a member of Perseus books, L.L.C.

ON BEING CONSERVATIVE

1

The common belief that it is impossible (or, if not impossible, then so unpromising as to be not worth while attempting) to elicit explanatory general principles from what is recognized to be conservative conduct is not one that I share. It may be true that conservative conduct does not readily provoke articulation in the idiom of general ideas, and that consequently there has been a certain reluctance to undertake this kind of elucidation; but it is not to be presumed that conservative conduct is less eligible than any other for this sort of interpretation, for what it is worth. Nevertheless, this is not the enterprise I propose to engage in here. My theme is not a creed or a doctrine, but a disposition. To be conservative is to be disposed to think and behave in certain manners; it is to prefer certain kinds of conduct and certain conditions of human circumstances to others; it is to be disposed to make certain kinds of choices. And my design here is to construe this disposition as it appears in contemporary character, rather than to transpose it into the idiom of general principles.

The general characteristics of this disposition are not difficult to discern, although they have often been mistaken. They centre upon a propensity to use and to enjoy what is available rather than to wish for or to look for something else; to delight in what is present rather than what was or what may be. Reflection may bring to light an appropriate gratefulness for what is available, and consequently the acknowledgment of a gift or an inheritance from the past; but there is no mere idolizing of what is past and gone. What is esteemed is the present; and it is esteemed not on account of its connections with a remote antiquity, nor because it is recognized to be more admirable than any possible alternative, but on account of its familiarity: not, *Verweile doch, du bist so schön,*[1] but, *Stay with me because I am attached to you.*

If the present is arid, offering little or nothing to be used or enjoyed, then this inclination will be weak or absent; if the present is remarkably unsettled, it will display itself in a search for a firmer foothold and consequently in a recourse to and an exploration of the past; but it asserts itself characteristically when there is much to be enjoyed, and it will be strongest when this is combined with evident risk of loss. In short, it is a disposition appropriate to a man who is acutely aware of having something to lose which he has learned to care for; a man in some degree rich in opportunities for enjoyment, but not so rich that he can afford to be indifferent to loss. It will appear more naturally in the old than in the young, not because the old are more sensitive to loss but because they are apt to be more fully aware of the resources of their world and therefore less likely to find them inadequate. In some people this disposition is weak merely because they are ignorant of what their world has to offer them: the present appears to them only as a residue of inopportunities.

To be conservative, then, is to prefer the familiar to the unknown, to prefer the tried to the untried, fact to mystery, the actual to the possible, the limited to the unbounded, the near to the distant, the sufficient to the superabundant, the convenient to the perfect, present laughter to utopian bliss. Familiar relationships and loyalties will be preferred to the allure of more profitable attachments; to acquire and to enlarge will be less important than to keep, to cultivate and to enjoy; the grief of loss will be more acute than the excitement of novelty or promise. It is to be equal to one's own fortune, to live at the level of one's own means, to be content with the want of greater perfection which belongs alike to oneself and one's circumstances. With some people this is itself a choice; in others it is a disposition which appears, frequently or less frequently, in their preferences and aversions, and is not itself chosen or specifically cultivated.

Now, all this is represented in a certain attitude towards change and innovation; change denoting alterations we have to suffer and innovation those we design and execute.

Changes are circumstances to which we have to accommodate ourselves, and the disposition to be conservative is both the emblem of our difficulty in doing so and our resort in the attempts we make to do so. Changes are without effect only upon those who notice nothing, who are ignorant of what they possess and apathetic to their circumstances; and they can be welcomed indiscriminately only by those who esteem nothing, whose attachments are fleeting and who are strangers to love and affection. The conservative disposition provokes neither of these conditions: the inclination to enjoy what is present and available is the opposite of ignorance and apathy and it breeds attachment and affection. Consequently, it is averse from change, which appears always, in the first place, as deprivation. A storm which sweeps away a copse and transforms a favourite view, the death of friends, the sleep of friendship, the desuetude of customs of behaviour, the retirement of a favourite clown, involuntary exile, reversals of fortune, the loss of abilities enjoyed and their replacement by others—these are changes, none perhaps without its compensations, which the man of conservative temperament unavoidably regrets. But he has difficulty in reconciling himself to them, not because what he has lost in them was intrinsically better than any alternative might have been or was incapable of improvement, nor because what takes its place is inherently incapable of being enjoyed, but because what he has lost was something he actually enjoyed and had learned how to enjoy and what takes its place is something to which he has acquired no attachment. Consequently, he will find small and slow changes more tolerable than large and sudden; and he will value highly every appearance of continuity. Some changes, indeed, will present no difficulty; but, again, this is not because they are manifest improvements but merely because they are easily assimilated: the changes of the seasons are mediated by their recurrence and the growing up of children by its continuousness. And, in general, he will accommodate himself more readily to changes which do not offend expectation than to the destruction of what seems to have no ground of dissolution within itself.

Moreover, to be conservative is not merely to be averse from change (which may be an idiosyncrasy); it is also a manner of accommodating ourselves to changes, an activity imposed upon all men. For, change is a threat to identity, and every change is an emblem of extinction. But a man's identity (or that of a community) is nothing more than an unbroken rehearsal of contingencies, each at the mercy of circumstance and each significant in proportion to its familiarity. It is not a fortress into which we may retire, and the only means we have of defending it (that is, ourselves) against the hostile forces of change is in the open field of our experience; by throwing our weight upon the foot which for the time being is most firmly placed, by cleaving to whatever familiarities are not immediately threatened and thus assimilating what is new without becoming unrecognizable to ourselves. The Masai, when they were moved from their old country to the present Masai reserve in Kenya, took with them the names of their hills and plains and rivers and gave them to the hills and plains and rivers of the new country. And it is by some such subterfuge of conservatism that every man or people compelled to suffer a notable change avoids the shame of extinction.

Changes, then, have to be suffered; and a man of conservative temperament (that is, one strongly disposed to preserve his identity) cannot be indifferent to them. In the main, he judges them by the disturbance they entail and, like everyone else, deploys his resources to meet them. The idea of innovation, on the other hand, is improvement. Nevertheless, a man of this temperament will not himself be an ardent innovator. In the first place, he is not inclined to think that nothing is happening unless great changes are afoot and therefore he is not worried by the absence of innovation: the use and enjoyment of things as they are occupies most of his attention. Further, he is aware that not all innovation is, in fact, improvement; and he will think that to innovate without improving is either designed or inadvertent folly. Moreover, even when an innovation commends itself as a convincing improvement, he will look twice at its claims before accepting them. From his point of view, because every improvement involves change, the disruption entailed has always to be set against the benefit anticipated. But when he has satisfied himself about this, there will be other considerations to be taken into the account. Innovating is always an equivocal enterprise, in which gain and loss (even excluding the loss of familiarity) are so closely interwoven that it is exceedingly difficult to forecast the final up-shot: there is no such thing as an unqualified improvement. For, innovating is an activity which generates not only the "improvement" sought, but a new and complex situation of which this is only one of the components. The total change is always more extensive than the change designed; and the whole of what is entailed can neither be foreseen nor circumscribed. Thus, whenever there is innovation there is the certainty that the change will be greater than was intended, that there will be loss as well as gain and that the loss and the gain will not be equally distributed among the people affected; there is the chance that the benefits derived will be greater than those which were designed; and there is the risk that they will be off-set by changes for the worse.

From all this the man of conservative temperament draws some appropriate conclusions. First, innovation entails certain loss and possible gain, therefore, the onus of proof, to show that the proposed change may be expected to be on the whole beneficial, rests with the would-be innovator. Secondly, he believes that the more closely an innovation resembles growth (that is, the more clearly it is intimated in and not merely imposed upon the situation) the less likely it is to result in a preponderance of loss. Thirdly, he thinks that an innovation which is a response to some specific defect, one designed to redress some specific disequilibrium, is more desirable than one which springs from a notion of a generally improved condition of human circumstances, and is far more desirable than one generated by a vision of perfection. Consequently, he prefers small and limited innovations to large and indefinite. Fourthly, he favours a slow rather than a rapid pace, and pauses to observe current consequences and make appropriate adjustments. And lastly, he believes the occasion to be important; and, other things being equal, he considers the most favourable occasion for innovation to be when the projected change is most likely to be limited to what is intended and least likely to be corrupted by undesired and unmanageable consequences.

The disposition to be conservative is, then, warm and positive in respect of enjoyment, and correspondingly cool and critical in respect of change and innovation: these two inclinations support and elucidate one another. The man of conservative temperament believes that a known good is not lightly to be surrendered for an unknown better. He is not in love with what is dangerous and difficult; he is unadventurous; he has no impulse to sail uncharted seas; for him there is no magic in being lost, bewildered or shipwrecked. If he is forced to navigate the unknown, he sees virtue in heaving the lead every inch of the way. What others plausibly identify as timidity, he recognizes in himself as rational prudence; what others interpret as inactivity, he recognizes as a disposition to enjoy rather than to exploit. He is cautious, and he is disposed to indicate his assent or dissent, not in absolute, but in graduated terms. He eyes the situation in terms of its propensity to disrupt the familiarity of the features of his world.

2

It is commonly believed that this conservative disposition is pretty deeply rooted in what is called "human nature." Change is tiring, innovation calls for effort, and human beings (it is said) are more apt to be lazy than energetic. If they have found a not unsatisfactory way of getting along in the world, they are not disposed to go looking for trouble. They are naturally apprehensive of the unknown and prefer safety to danger. They are reluctant innovators, and they accept change not because they like it but (as

Rochefoucauld says they accept death) because it is inescapable. Change generates sadness rather than exhilaration: heaven is the dream of a changeless no less than of a perfect world. Of course, those who read "human nature" in this way agree that this disposition does not stand alone; they merely contend that it is an exceedingly strong, perhaps the strongest, of human propensities. And, so far as it goes, there is something to be said for this belief: human circumstances would certainly be very different from what they are if there were not a large ingredient of conservatism in human preferences. Primitive peoples are said to cling to what is familiar and to be averse from change; ancient myth is full of warnings against innovation; our folklore and proverbial wisdom about the conduct of life abounds in conservative precepts; and how many tears are shed by children in their unwilling accommodation to change. Indeed, wherever a firm identity is felt to be precariously balanced, a conservative disposition is likely to prevail. On the other hand, the disposition of adolescence is often predominantly adventurous and experimental: when we are young, nothing seems more desirable than to take a chance; *pas de risque, pas de plaisir.*[2] And while some peoples, over long stretches of time, appear successfully to have avoided change, the history of others displays periods of intense and intrepid innovation. There is, indeed, not much profit to be had from general speculation about "human nature," which is no steadier than anything else in our acquaintance. What is more to the point is to consider current human nature, to consider ourselves.

With us, I think, the disposition to be conservative is far from being notably strong. Indeed, if he were to judge by our conduct during the last five centuries or so, an unprejudiced stranger might plausibly suppose us to be in love with change, to have an appetite only for innovation and to be either so out of sympathy with ourselves or so careless of our identity as not to be disposed to give it any consideration. In general, the fascination of what is new is felt far more keenly than the comfort of what is familiar. We are disposed to think that nothing important is happening unless great innovations are afoot, and that what is not being improved must be deteriorating. There is a positive prejudice in favour of the yet untried. We readily presume that all change is, somehow, for the better, and we are easily persuaded that all the consequences of our innovating activity are either themselves improvements or at least a reasonable price to pay for getting what we want. While the conservative, if he were forced to gamble, would bet on the field, we are disposed to back our individual fancies with little calculation and no apprehension of loss. We are acquisitive to the point of greed; ready to drop the bone we have for its reflection magnified in the mirror of the future. Nothing is made to outlast probable improvement in a world where everything is undergoing incessant improvement: the expectation of life of everything except human beings themselves continuously declines. Pieties are fleeting, loyalties evanescent, and the pace of change warns us against too deep attachments. We are willing to try anything once, regardless of the consequences. One activity vies with another in being "up-to-date": discarded motor-cars and television sets have their counterparts in discarded moral and religious beliefs: the eye is ever on the new model. To see is to imagine what might be in the place of what is; to touch is to transform. Whatever the shape or quality of the world, it is not for long as we want it. And those in the van of movement infect those behind with their energy and enterprise. *Omnes eodem cogemur:*[3] when we are no longer light-footed we find a place for ourselves in the band.[4]

Of course, our character has other ingredients besides this lust for change (we are not devoid of the impulse to cherish and preserve), but there can be little doubt about its pre-eminence. And, in these circumstances, it seems appropriate that a conservative disposition should appear, not as an intelligible (or even plausible) alternative to our mainly "progressive" habit of mind, but either as an unfortunate hindrance to the movement afoot, or as the custodian of the museum in which quaint examples of superseded achievement are preserved for children to gape at, and as the guardian of what from time to time is considered not yet ripe for destruction, which we call (ironically enough) the amenities of life.

Here our account of the disposition to be conservative and its current fortunes might be expected to end, with the man in whom this disposition is strong last seen swimming against the tide, disregarded not because what he has to say is necessarily false but because it has become irrelevant; outmanoeuvred, not on account of any intrinsic demerit but merely by the flow of circumstance; a faded, timid, nostalgic character, provoking pity as an outcast and contempt as a reactionary. Nevertheless, I think there is something more to be said. Even in these circumstances, when a conservative disposition in respect of things in general is unmistakably at a discount, there are occasions when this disposition remains not only appropriate, but supremely so; and there are connections in which we are unavoidably disposed in a conservative direction.

In the first place, there is a certain kind of activity (not yet extinct) which can be engaged in only in virtue of a disposition to be conservative, namely, activities where what is sought is present enjoyment and not a profit, a reward, a prize or a result in addition to the experience itself. And when these activities are recognized as the emblems of this disposition, to be conservative is disclosed, not as prejudiced hostility to a "progressive" attitude capable of embracing the whole range of human conduct, but as a disposition exclusively appropriate in a large and significant field of human activity. And the man in whom this disposition is pre-eminent appears as one who prefers to engage in activities where to be conservative is uniquely appropriate, and not as a man inclined to impose his conservatism indiscriminately upon all human activity. In short, if we find ourselves (as most of us do) inclined to reject conservatism as a disposition appropriate in respect of human conduct in general, there still remains a certain kind of human conduct for which this disposition is not merely appropriate but a necessary condition....

This is so of friendship. Here, attachment springs from an intimation of familiarity and subsists in a mutual sharing of personalities. To go on changing one's butcher until one gets the meat one likes, to go on educating one's agent until he does what is required of him, is conduct not inappropriate to the relationship concerned; but to discard friends because they do not behave as we expected and refuse to be educated to our requirements is the conduct of a man who has altogether mistaken the character of friendship. Friends are not concerned with what might be made of one another, but only with the enjoyment of one another; and the condition of this enjoyment is a ready acceptance of what is and the absence of any desire to change or to improve. A friend is not somebody one trusts to behave in a certain manner, who supplies certain wants, who has certain useful abilities, who possesses certain merely agreeable qualities, or who holds certain acceptable opinions; he is somebody who engages the imagination, who excites contemplation, who provokes interest, sympathy, delight and loyalty simply on account of the relationship entered into. One friend cannot replace another; there is all the difference in the world between the death of a friend and the retirement of one's tailor from business. The relationship of friend to friend is dramatic, not utilitarian; the tie is one of familiarity, not usefulness; the disposition engaged is conservative, not "progressive." And what is true of friendship is not less true of other experiences—of patriotism, for example, and of conversation—each of which demands a conservative disposition as a condition of its enjoyment.

But further, there are activities, not involving human relationships, that may be engaged in, not for a prize, but for the enjoyment they generate, and for which the only appropriate disposition is the disposition to be conservative. Consider fishing. If your project is merely to catch fish it would be foolish to be unduly conservative. You will seek out the best tackle, you will discard practices which prove unsuccessful, you will not be bound by unprofitable attachments to particular localities, pieties will be fleeting, loyalties evanescent; you may even be wise to try anything once in the hope of improvement. But fishing is an activity that may be engaged in, not for the profit of a catch, but for its own sake; and the fisherman may return home in the evening not less content for being empty-handed. Where this is so, the activity has become a ritual and a conservative disposition is appropriate. Why worry about the best gear if you do not care whether or not you make a catch? What matters is the enjoyment of exercising skill (or, perhaps, merely passing the time), and this is to be had with any tackle, so long as it is familiar and is not grotesquely inappropriate.

All activities, then, where what is sought is enjoyment springing, not from the success of the enterprise but from the familiarity of the engagement, are emblems of the disposition to be conservative....

3

How, then, are we to construe the disposition to be conservative in respect of politics?...[T]o state my view briefly before elaborating it, what makes a conservative disposition in politics intelligible is nothing to do with a natural law or a providential order, nothing to do with morals or religion; it is the observation of our current manner of living combined with the belief (which from our point of view need be regarded as no more than an hypothesis) that governing is a specific and limited activity, namely the provision and custody of general rules of conduct, which are understood, not as plans for imposing substantive activities, but as instruments enabling people to pursue the activities of their own choice with the minimum frustration, and therefore something which it is appropriate to be conservative about....

...[T]he office of government is not to impose other beliefs and activities upon its subjects, not to tutor or to educate them, not to make them better or happier in another way, not to direct them, to galvanize them into action, to lead them or to coordinate their activities so that no occasion of conflict shall occur; the office of government is merely to rule. This is a specific and limited activity, easily corrupted when it is combined with any other, and, in the circumstances, indispensable. The image of the ruler is the umpire whose business is to administer the rules of the game, or the chairman who governs the debate according to known rules but does not himself participate in it.

Now people of this disposition commonly defend their belief that the proper attitude of government towards the current condition of human circumstance is one of acceptance by appealing to certain general ideas. They contend that there is absolute value in the free play of human choice, that private property (the emblem of choice) is a natural right, that it is only in the enjoyment of diversity of opinion and activity that true belief and good conduct can be expected to disclose themselves. But I do not think that this disposition requires these or any similar beliefs in order to make it intelligible. Something much smaller and less pretentious will do: the observation that this condition of human circumstance is, in fact, current, and that we have learned to enjoy it and how to manage it; that we are not children *in statu pupillari*[5] but adults who do not consider themselves under any obligation to justify their preference for making their own choices; and that it is beyond human experience to suppose that those who rule are endowed with a superior wisdom which discloses to them a better range of beliefs and activities and which gives them authority to impose upon their subjects a quite different manner of life. In short, if the man of this disposition is asked: Why ought governments to accept the current diversity of opinion and activity in preference to imposing upon their subjects a dream of their own? it is enough for him to reply: Why not? Their dreams are no different from those of anyone else; and if it is boring to have to listen to dreams of others being recounted, it is insufferable to be forced to reenact them. We tolerate monomaniacs, it is our habit to do so; but why should we be *ruled* by them? Is it not (the man of conservative disposition asks) an intelligible task for a government to protect its subjects against the nuisance of those who spend their energy and their wealth in the service of some pet indignation, endeavouring to impose it upon everybody, not by suppressing their activities in favour of others of a similar kind, but by setting a limit to the amount of noise anyone may emit?

Nevertheless, if this acceptance is the spring of the conservative's disposition in respect of government, he does not suppose that the office of government is to do nothing. As he understands it, there is work to be done which can be done only in virtue of a genuine acceptance of current beliefs simply because they are current and current activities simply because they are afoot. And, briefly, the office he attributes to government is to resolve some of the collisions which this variety of beliefs and activities generates; to preserve peace, not by placing an interdict upon choice and upon the diversity that springs from the exercise of preference, not by imposing substantive uniformity, but by enforcing general rules of procedure upon all subjects alike.

Government, then, as the conservative in this matter understands it, does not begin with a vision of another, different and better world, but with the observation of the self-government practised even by men of passion in the conduct of their enterprises; it begins in the informal adjustments of interests to one another which are designed to release those who are apt to collide from the mutual frustration of a collision. Sometimes these adjustments are no more than agreements between two parties to keep out of each other's way; sometimes they are of wider application and more durable character, such as the International Rules for the prevention of collisions at sea. In short, the intimations of government are to be found in ritual, not in religion or philosophy; in the enjoyment of orderly and peaceable behaviour, not in the search for truth or perfection....

...Innovation, then, is called for if the rules are to remain appropriate to the activities they govern. But, as the conservative understands it, modification of the rules should always reflect, and never impose, a change in the activities and beliefs of those who are subject to them, and should never on any occasion be so great as to destroy the *ensemble*. Consequently, the conservative will have nothing to do with innovations designed to meet merely hypothetical situations; he will prefer to enforce a rule he has got rather than invent a new one; he will think it appropriate to delay a modification of the rules until it is clear that the change of circumstance it is designed to reflect has come to stay for a while; he will be suspicious of proposals for change in excess of what the situation calls for, of rulers who demand extra-ordinary powers in order to make great changes and whose utterances are tied to generalities like "the public good" or "social justice," and of Saviours of Society who buckle on armour and seek dragons to slay; he will think it proper to consider the occasion of the innovation with care; in short, he will be disposed to regard politics as an activity in which a valuable set of tools is renovated from time to time and kept in trim rather than as an opportunity for perpetual re-equipment....

To some people, "government" appears as a vast reservoir of power which inspires them to dream of what use might be made of it. They have favourite projects, of various dimensions, which they sincerely believe are for the benefit of mankind, and to capture this source of power, if necessary to increase it, and to use it for imposing their favourite projects upon their fellows is what they understand as the adventure of governing men. They are, thus, disposed to recognize government as an instrument of passion; the art of politics is to inflame and direct desire. In short, governing is understood to be just like any other activity—making and selling a brand of soap, exploiting the resources of a locality, or developing a housing estate—only the power here is (for the most part) already mobilized, and the enterprise is remarkable only because it aims at monopoly and because of its promise of success once the source of power has been captured. Of course a private enterprise politician of this sort would get nowhere in these days unless there were people with wants so vague that they can be prompted to ask for what he has to offer, or with wants so servile that they prefer the promise of a provided abundance to the opportunity of choice and activity on their own account. And it is not all as plain sailing as it might appear: often a politician of this sort misjudges the situation; and then, briefly, even in democratic politics, we become aware of what the camel thinks of the camel driver.

Now, the disposition to be conservative in respect of politics reflects a quite different view of the activity of governing. The man of this disposition understands it to be the business of a government not to inflame passion and give it new objects to feed upon, but to inject into the activities of already too passionate men an ingredient of moderation; to restrain, to deflate, to pacify and to reconcile; not to stoke the fires of desire, but to damp them down. And all this, not because passion is vice and moderation virtue, but because moderation is indispensable if passionate men are to escape being locked in an encounter of mutual frustration....

4

Nobody pretends that it is easy to acquire or to sustain the mood of indifference which this manner of politics calls for. To rein-in one's own beliefs and desires, to acknowledge the current shape of things, to feel the balance of things in one's hand, to tolerate what is abominable, to distinguish between crime and sin, to respect formality even when it appears to be leading to error, these are difficult achievements; and they are achievements not to be looked for in the young.

Everybody's young days are a dream, a delightful insanity, a sweet solipsism. Nothing in them has a fixed shape, nothing a fixed price; everything is a possibility, and we live happily on credit. There are no obligations to be observed; there are no accounts to be kept. Nothing is specified in advance; everything is what can be made of it. The world is a mirror in which we seek the reflection of our own desires. The allure of violent emotions is irresistible. When we are young we are not disposed to make concessions to the world; we never feel the balance of a thing in our hands—unless it be a cricket bat. We are not apt to distinguish between our liking and our esteem; urgency is our criterion of importance; and we do not easily understand that what is humdrum need not be despicable. We are impatient of restraint; and we readily believe, like [the poet Percy Bysshe] Shelley, that to have contracted a habit is to have failed. These, in my opinion, are among our virtues when we are young; but how remote they are from the disposition appropriate for participating in the style of government I have been describing. Since life is a dream, we argue (with plausible but erroneous logic) that politics must be an encounter of dreams, in which we hope to impose our own. Some unfortunate people, like Pitt (laughably called "the Younger"), are born old, and are eligible to engage in politics almost in their cradles;[6] others, perhaps more fortunate, belie the saying that one is young only once, they never grow up. But these are exceptions. For most there is what [the novelist Joseph] Conrad called the "shadow line" which, when we pass it, discloses a solid world of things, each with its fixed shape, each with its own point of balance, each with its price; a world of fact, not poetic image, in which what we have spent on one thing we cannot spend on another; a world inhabited by others besides ourselves who cannot be reduced to mere reflections of our own emotions. And coming to be at home in this commonplace world qualifies us (as no knowledge of "political science" can ever qualify us), if we are so inclined and have nothing better to think about, to engage in what the man of conservative disposition understands to be political activity.

NOTES

1. "Stay with me, you are so beautiful."—Eds.
2. "No risk, no pleasure."—Eds.
3. "We are all brought to the same point."—Eds.
4. "Which of us," asks a contemporary (not without some equivocation), "would not settle, at whatever cost in nervous anxiety, for a febrile and creative rather than a static society?"
5. "In the status of pupils."—Eds.
6. The British statesman William Pitt (1759–1806) became known as "the Younger" because his father was also a prominent political figure named William Pitt (1708–1778).—Eds.

30

Modern Liberalism and Cultural Decline

ROBERT H. BORK

"Every new generation constitutes a wave of savages who must be civilized by their families, schools, and churches," Robert Bork (1927–) writes in his book *Slouching Towards Gomorrah*. In the following selection from that book, Bork advances the neoconservative argument that since the 1960s society has done a poor job of civilizing new generations. Bork is the John M. Olin Scholar in Legal Studies at the American Enterprise Institute. Previously, he taught constitutional law at Yale Law School, served as solicitor general and as acting attorney general of the United States, and was a U.S. Court of Appeals judge. President Ronald Reagan nominated him for a seat on the Supreme Court, but the Senate, in a controversial decision, did not confirm his nomination.

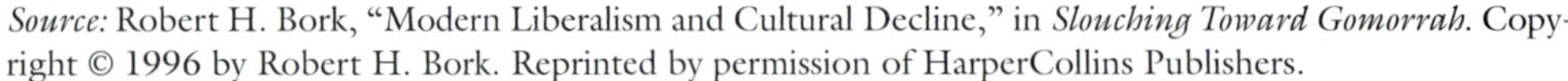

Source: Robert H. Bork, "Modern Liberalism and Cultural Decline," in *Slouching Toward Gomorrah*. Copyright © 1996 by Robert H. Bork. Reprinted by permission of HarperCollins Publishers.

MODERN LIBERALISM AND CULTURAL DECLINE

One morning on my way to teach a class at the Yale law school, I found on the sidewalk outside the building heaps of smoldering books that had been burned in the law library. They were a small symbol of what was happening on campuses across the nation: violence, destruction of property, mindless hatred of law, authority, and tradition. I stood there, uncomprehending, as a photograph in the next day's *New York Times* clearly showed. What did they want, these students? What conceivable goals led them to this and to the general havoc they were wreaking on the university? Living in the Sixties, my faculty colleagues and I had no understanding of what it was about, where it came from, or how long the misery would last. It was only much later that a degree of understanding came.

To understand our current plight, we must look back to the tumults of those years, which brought to a crescendo developments in the Fifties and before that most of us had overlooked or misunderstood. We noticed (who could help but notice?) Elvis Presley, rock music, James Dean, the radical sociologist C. Wright Mills, Jack Kerouac and the Beats. We did not understand, however, that far from being isolated curiosities, these were harbingers of a new culture that would shortly burst upon us and sweep us into a different country.

The Fifties were the years of Eisenhower's presidency. Our domestic world seemed normal and, for the most part, almost placid. The signs were misleading. Politics is a lagging indicator.

Culture eventually makes politics. The cultural seepages of the Fifties strengthened and became a torrent that swept through the nation in the Sixties, only to seem to die away in the Seventies. The election of Ronald Reagan in 1980 and the defeat of several of the most liberal senators seemed a reaffirmation of traditional values and proof that the Sixties were dead. They were not. The spirit of the Sixties revived in the Eighties and brought us at last to Bill and Hillary Clinton, the very personifications of the Sixties generation arrived at early middle age with its ideological baggage intact.

This is a book about American decline. Since American culture is a variant of the cultures of all Western industrialized democracies, it may even, inadvertently, be a book about Western decline. In the United States, at least, that decline and the mounting resistance to it have produced what we now call a culture war. It is impossible to say what the outcome will be, but for the moment our trajectory continues downward. This is not to deny that much in our culture remains healthy, that many families are intact and continue to raise children with strong moral values. American culture is complex and resilient. But it is also not to be denied that there are aspects of almost every branch of our culture that are worse than ever before and that the rot is spreading.

"Culture," as used here, refers to all human behavior and institutions, including popular entertainment, art, religion, education, scholarship, economic activity, science, technology, law, and morality. Of that list, only science, technology, and the economy may be said to be healthy today, and it is problematical how long that will last. Improbable as it may seem, science and technology themselves are increasingly under attack, and it seems highly unlikely that a vigorous economy can be sustained in an enfeebled, hedonistic culture, particularly when that culture distorts incentives by increasingly rejecting personal achievement as the criterion for the distribution of rewards.

With each new evidence of deterioration, we lament for a moment, and then become accustomed to it. We hear one day of the latest rap song calling for killing policemen or the sexual mutilation of women; the next, of coercive left-wing political indoctrination at a prestigious university; then of the latest homicide figures for New York City, Los Angeles, or the District of Columbia; of the collapse of the criminal justice system, which displays an inability to punish adequately and, often enough, an inability even to convict the clearly guilty; of the rising rate of illegitimate births; the uninhibited display of sexuality and the popularization of violence in our entertainment; worsening racial tensions; the angry activists of feminism, homosexuality, environmentalism, animal rights—the list could be extended almost indefinitely.

So unrelenting is the assault on our sensibilities that many of us grow numb, finding resignation to be the rational, adaptive response to an environment that is increasingly polluted and apparently beyond our control. That is what Senator Daniel Patrick Moynihan calls "defining deviancy down."[1] Moynihan cites the "Durkheim constant."[2] Emile Durkheim, a founder of sociology, posited that there is a limit to the amount of deviant behavior any community can "afford to recognize."[3] As behavior worsens, the community adjusts its standards so that conduct once thought reprehensible is no longer deemed so. As behavior improves, the deviancy boundary moves up to encompass conduct previously thought normal. Thus, a community of saints and a community of felons would display very different behavior but about the same amount of recognized deviancy.

But the Durkheim constant is now behaving in a very odd way. While defining deviancy down with respect to crime, illegitimacy, drug use, and the like, our cultural elites are growing intensely moralistic and disapproving about what had always been thought normal behavior, thus accomplishing what columnist Charles Krauthammer terms "defining deviancy up."[4] It is at least an apparent paradox that we are accomplishing both forms of redefining, both down and up, simultaneously. One would suppose that as once normal behavior became viewed as deviant, that would mean that there was less really bad conduct in the society. But that is hardly our case. Instead, we have redefined what we mean by such things as child abuse, rape, and racial or sexual discrimination so that behavior until recently thought quite normal, unremarkable, even benign, is now identified as blameworthy or even criminal. Middle-class life is portrayed as oppressive and shot through with pathologies. "As part of the vast social project of moral leveling," Krauthammer wrote, "it is not enough for the deviant to be normalized. The normal must be found to be deviant."[5] This situation is thoroughly perverse. Underclass values become increasingly acceptable to the middle class, especially their young, and middle-class values become increasingly contemptible to the cultural elites.

That is why there is currently a widespread sense that the distinctive virtues of American life, indeed the distinctive features of Western civilization, are in peril in ways not previously seen. This time the threat is not military—the Soviets and the Nazis are defunct. Nor is it external—the Tartar armies receded from Europe centuries ago. If we slide into a modern, high-tech version of the Dark Ages, we will have done it to ourselves without the assistance of the Germanic tribes that destroyed Roman civilization. This time we face, and seem to be succumbing to, an attack mounted by a force not only within Western civilization but one that is perhaps its legitimate child.

The enemy within is modern liberalism, a corrosive agent carrying a very different mood and agenda than that of classical or traditional liberalism. That the modern variety is intellectually bankrupt diminishes neither its vitality nor the danger it poses. A bankrupt philosophy can reign for centuries and, when its bankruptcy becomes apparent, may well be succeeded by an even less coherent outlook. That is what is happening to us now. Modernity, the child of the Enlightenment, failed when it became apparent that the good society cannot be achieved by unaided reason. The response of liberalism was not to turn to religion, which modernity had seemingly made irrelevant, but to abandon reason. Hence, there have appeared philosophies claiming that words can carry no definite meaning or that there is no reality other than one that is "socially constructed." A reality so constructed, it is thought, can be decisively altered by social or cultural edict, which is a prescription for coercion.

"Modern liberalism" may not be quite the correct name for what I have in mind. I use the phrase merely to mean the latest stage of the liberalism that has been growing in the West for at least two and a half centuries, and probably longer. Nor does this suggest that I think liberalism was always a bad idea. So long as it was tempered by opposing authorities and traditions, it was a splendid idea. It is the collapse of those tempering forces that has brought us to a triumphant modern liberalism with all the cultural and social degradation that follows in its wake. If you do not think "modern liberalism" an appropriate name, substitute "radical liberalism" or "sentimental liberalism" or even, save us, "postmodern liberalism." Whatever name is used, most readers will recognize the species.

The defining characteristics of modern liberalism are radical egalitarianism (the equality of outcomes rather than of opportunities) and radical individualism (the drastic reduction of limits to personal gratification). These may seem an odd pair, for individualism means liberty and liberty produces inequality, while equality of outcomes means coercion and coercion destroys liberty. If they are to operate simultaneously, radical egalitarianism and radical individualism, where they would compete, must be kept apart, must operate in different areas of life. That is precisely what we see in today's culture.

Radical egalitarianism reigns in areas of life and society where superior achievement is possible and would be rewarded but for coercion towards a state of equality. Quotas, affirmative action, and the more extreme versions of feminism are the most obvious examples but, as will be seen, radical egalitarianism is damaging much else in our culture. Radical individualism is demanded when there is no danger that achievement will produce inequality and people wish to be unhindered in the pursuit of pleasure. This finds expression especially in the areas of sexuality and the popular arts.

Sometimes the impulses of radical individualism and radical egalitarianism cooperate. Both, for example, are antagonistic to society's traditional morality—the individualist because his pleasures can be maximized only by freedom from authority, the egalitarian because he resents any distinction among people or forms of behavior that suggests superiority in one or the other. When egalitarianism reinforces individualism, denying the possibility that one culture or moral view can be superior to another, the result is cultural and moral chaos, both prominent and destructive features of our time.

Radical egalitarianism necessarily presses us towards collectivism because a powerful state is required to suppress the differences that freedom produces. That raises the sinister and seemingly paradoxical possibility that radical individualism is the handmaiden of collectivist tyranny. This individualism, it is quite apparent in our time, attacks the authority of family, church, and private association. The family is said to be oppressive, the fount of our miseries. It is denied that the church may legitimately insist upon what it regards as moral behavior in its members. Private associations are routinely denied the autonomy to define their membership for themselves. The upshot is that these institutions, which stand between the state and the individual, are progressively weakened and their functions increasingly dictated or taken over by the state. The individual becomes less of a member of powerful private institutions and more a member of an unstructured mass that is vulnerable to the collectivist coercion of the state. Thus does radical individualism prepare the way for its opposite.

Modern liberalism is very different in content from the liberalism of, say, the 1940s or 1950s, and certainly different from the liberalism of the last century. The sentiments and beliefs that drive it, however, are the same: the ideals of liberty and equality. These ideals produced the great political, social, and cultural achievements of Western civilization, but no ideal, however worthy, can be pressed forever without turning into something else, turning in fact into its opposite. That is what is happening now. Not a single American institution, from popular music to higher education to science, has remained untouched.

In one sense, decline is always with us. To hear each generation of Americans speak of the generation coming along behind it is to learn that our culture is not only deteriorating rapidly today but always has been. Regret for the golden days of the past is probably universal and as old as the human race. No doubt the elders of prehistoric tribes thought the younger generation's cave paintings were not up to the standard they had set. Given this straight-line degeneration for so many millennia, by now our culture should be not merely rubble but dust. Obviously it is not: until recently our artists did better than the cave painters.

Yet if the doomsayers are always with us, it is also true that sometimes they are right. Cultures do decline, and sometimes die. The agenda of liberalism has been and remains what historian Christopher Lasch called an "unremitting onslaught against bourgeois culture [that] was far more lasting in its effects, in the West at least and now probably in the East as well, than the attack on capitalism."[6] Making capitalism the explicit target became an unprofitable tactic when the case for the only alternative, socialism, collapsed in ruins. But capitalism cannot survive without a bourgeois culture; if that culture is brought down, so too will capitalism be replaced with one or another variety of statism presiding over a degenerate society.

Modern liberalism is powerful because it has enlisted our cultural elites, those who man the institutions that manufacture, manipulate, and disseminate ideas, attitudes, and symbols—universities, churches, Hollywood, the national press (print and electronic), foundation staffs, the "public interest" organizations, much of the congressional Democratic Party and some congressional Republicans as well, and large sections of the judiciary, including, all too often, a majority of the Supreme Court.

This, it must be stressed, is not a conspiracy but a syndrome. These are institutions controlled by people who view the world from a common perspective, a perspective not generally shared by the public at large. But so pervasive is the influence of those who occupy the commanding heights of our culture that it is important to understand what modern liberalism is and what its ascendancy means. That is what this book attempts to explain.

The wonder is that the culture of liberalism triumphed over conventional middle-class culture so rapidly. One would have expected rejection of radical individualism and radical egalitarianism by those whose interests would be damaged by them or whose idea of a good society was offended by them. Instead, resistance has been mild, disorganized, and ineffective. This suggests that the supposedly oppressive "Establishment," without realizing it themselves, had already been eaten hollow by the assumptions that flowered into modern liberalism. When the push came in the Sixties, an empty and guilt-ridden Establishment surrendered.

But why now? Liberalism has been with us for centuries; why should it become modern liberalism in the latter half of this century? The desire for self-gratification, which underlies individualism, has been around since the human species appeared; why should it become radical individualism in our time? The desire for equality, in large part rooted in self-pity and envy, is surely not a new emotion; why has it recently become the menace of radical egalitarianism?

The complete answer is surely not simple, but a large part of the answer surely is. Liberalism always had the tendency to become modern liberalism, just as individualism and equality always contained the seeds of their radical modern versions. The difference was that classical liberalism, the glory of the last century, was not simply a form of liberalism but an admixture of liberalism's drives and the forces that opposed those drives. As the opposing or constraining forces weakened and the drives of liberalism increasingly prevailed, we were brought to our present condition, and, it must be feared, will be taken still further, much further, in the same direction. Then a culture whose increasing degradation we observe will have attained ultimate degradation, unless, of course, we can rebuild the constraints that once made liberalism classical liberalism. A consideration of the nature of those constraints and what weakened them is not encouraging.

Men were kept from rootless hedonism, which is the end stage of unconfined individualism, by religion, morality, and law. These are commonly cited. To them I would add the necessity for hard work, usually physical work, and the fear of want. These constraints were progressively undermined by rising affluence. The rage for liberty surfaced violently in the 1960s, but it was ready to break out much earlier and was suppressed only by the accidents of history. It would be possible to make a case that conditions were ripe at the end of the nineteenth century and the beginning of the twentieth but that the trend was delayed by the Great War. The breaking down of restrictions resumed in the Roaring Twenties. But that decade was followed by the Great Depression, which produced a culture whose behavior was remarkably moral and law-abiding. The years of World War II created a sense of national unity far different from the cultural fragmentation of today. The generations that lived through those times of hardship and discipline were not susceptible to extreme hedonism, but they raised a generation that was.

Affluence reappeared in the late 1940s and in the decade of the 1950s and has remained with us since. Despite complaints, often politically motivated, about the economic hardships endured today by the American people, it is blindingly obvious that standards of living, even among the poorest, are far above any previous level in this or any other nation's history. Affluence brings with it boredom. Of itself, it offers little but the ability to consume, and a life centered on consumption will appear, and be, devoid of meaning. Persons so afflicted will seek sensation as a palliative, and that today's culture offers in abundance.

This brings us to the multiple roles rapidly improving technology plays in our culture. America was a nation of farmers, but the advance of technology required fewer and fewer farmers and more and more industrial workers. The continuing advance required fewer industrial workers and more white collar workers, and eventually still more sophisticated workers of a kind that made the term "white collar" seem denigrating. Hard physical work is inconsistent with hedonism; the new work is not. With the time and energy of so many individuals freed from the harder demands of work, the culture turned to consumerism and entertainment. Technology and its entrepreneurs supplied the demand with motion pictures, radio, television, and videocassettes, all increasingly featuring sex and violence. Sensations must be steadily intensified if boredom is to be kept at bay.

A culture obsessed with technology will come to value personal convenience above almost all else, and ours does. That has consequences we will explore. Among those consequences, however, is impatience with anything that interferes with personal convenience. Religion, morality, and law do that, which accounts for the tendency of modern religion to eschew proscriptions and commandments and turn to counseling and therapeutic sermons; of morality to be relativized; and of law, particularly criminal law, to become soft and uncertain. Religion tends to be strongest when life is hard, and the same may be said of morality and law. A person whose main difficulty is not crop failure but video breakdown has less need of the consolations and promises of religion.

The most frightening aspect of the march of technology, however, is the potential for reshaping human beings and their nature through genetic science. No one can predict what the full consequences of that technology will be, but horrifying prospects can easily be imagined. There seems no possibility that this technology can be halted—whatever scientists can do, they feel they must do—and little likelihood that the ability to reshape humans will not be used.

As will be seen, the possibilities of technology in all of these areas—from lightening work to providing ever more degenerate entertainments to reengineering humans—are far from exhausted. And it is impossible to imagine that the rapid advance of technology can be halted or even significantly slowed.

Radical egalitarianism also seems likely to continue to advance, although some of its manifestations are now being resisted politically for the first time in years. The simplistic notion that if social processes were fair, all races and ethnic groups and both sexes would be represented proportionately in all areas of endeavor dies hard. The absence of equality of results is taken to mean that equality of opportunity has been denied and must be remedied with coercive action to produce equality of results. Then, too, the spread and triumph of the democratic ideal leads, irrationally, to the belief that inequalities are unjust so that hierarchical institutions must be democratized. That leads to demands for corporate democracy, for student participation in running universities, and to criticism of the Roman Catholic Church because its doctrines do not conform to whatever it is that a large number of the laity prefer. The idea that democracy and equality are not suited to the virtues of all institutions is a hard sell today.

Demands for greater or complete equality seem to have other sources. Boredom plays a role here as well. It is impossible, for example, to observe radical feminists without thinking that their assertions of oppression and victimization, their never-ending search for fresh grievances, are ways of giving meaning to lives that would otherwise seem sterile to them. Self-pity and envy are also undoubtedly factors, as are the prestige and financial support to be had from pressing their claims, but I tend to think that the search for meaning plays a prominent and perhaps predominant role in many forms of radical egalitarianism.

A crucial factor in the creation of liberalism and its gradual transformation into modern liberalism has yet to be mentioned: the rise of intellectual and artistic classes independent of patrons toward the close of the eighteenth century and their subsequent growth in size and prestige.... [T]hese classes tend to be hostile to traditional culture and to the bourgeois state. They powerfully reinforce and mobilize the forces pressing towards radical individualism and radical egalitarianism.

The fact that resistance to modern liberalism is weakening suggests that we are on the road to cultural disaster because, in their final stages, radical egalitarianism becomes tyranny and radical individualism descends into hedonism. Those translate into a modern version of bread and circuses. Government grows larger and more intrusive in order to direct the distribution of goods and services in an ever more equal fashion while people are coarsened and diverted, led to believe that their freedoms are increasing, by a great variety of entertainments featuring violence and sex.

Having spoken of liberty and equality (in their modern, radical forms), it is time to complete the triad by mentioning fraternity. It is no mere rhetorical device to use the slogan of the French Revolution, for liberty, equality, and fraternity are enduring aspirations, and dilemmas, of humans in society. The desire for fraternity or community is inevitable in a social animal, but that desire is condemned to frustration, to be a wistful hope, anywhere modern liberalism holds sway. Radical individualism, radical egalitarianism, omnipresent and omni-incompetent government, the politicization of the culture, and the battle for advantages through politics shatter a society into fragments of isolated individuals and angry groups. Social peace and cohesion decline as loneliness and alienation rise. Life in such a culture can come close to seeming intolerable.

A fragmented society, one in which a sense of community has disappeared, is necessarily a society with low morale. It displays loss of nerve, which means that it cannot summon the will to suppress public obscenity, punish crime, reform welfare, attach stigma to the bearing of illegitimate children, resist the demands of self-proclaimed victim groups for preferential treatment, or maintain standards of reason and scholarship. That is precisely and increasingly our situation today.

Perversely, modern liberals seek to cure the disease of a politicized culture with the medicine of more politics. More politics means more clashes between interest groups, more anger and division, and more moral assaults upon opponents. The great danger, of course, is that eventually a collectivist solution will be adopted to control social turbulence. Turbulence is not limited to political and cultural warfare; it is increasingly a phenomenon of violence in streets and neighborhoods. If society should reach a chaotic condition of warring groups and individual alienation, a condition in which even personal security is problematic for a majority of its people, authoritarian government may be accepted. Worse, a movement with transcendental principles, not necessarily benign ones, may promise community and ultimately exact a fearful cost.

The encroachments of liberalism upon traditional ways of thinking and acting have created not just a battle here and a skirmish there but a conflict across the entire culture. This is different in kind from the usual piecemeal revisions we have seen in the past. "Now and then," according to literary scholar Lionel Trilling, "it is possible to observe the moral life in the process of revising itself, perhaps by reducing the emphasis it formerly placed upon one or another of its elements, perhaps by inventing and adding to itself a new element, some mode of conduct or of feeling which hitherto it had not regarded as essential to virtue."[7] A nation's moral life is, of course, the foundation of its culture. When Trilling's words were published in 1970, though he had seen the convulsions of the Sixties, he could not have imagined the scope and depth of the "revisions" yet to come. What we experience now is not the subtraction or addition of one or another of the elements of our moral life, but an assault that aims at, and largely accomplishes, sweeping changes across the entire cultural landscape. Large chunks of the moral life of the United States, major features of its culture, have disappeared altogether, and more are in the process of extinction. These are being, or have already been, replaced by new modes of conduct, ways of thought, and standards of morality that are unwelcome to many of us.

Trilling went on: "The news of such an event [a revision in moral life] is often received with a degree of irony or some other sign of resistance."[8] Given the comprehensive scope of the changes in our moral-cultural life, it is not surprising that signs of resistance, though late in appearing, are becoming equally widespread and vigorous. The addition or subtraction of a single virtue may provoke only a degree of irony, but when the changes are across the board, the thrust and the resistance add up to a major conflict. Irony there is in plentiful supply, but also anger, and even a continuing realignment of our political parties along cultural lines. In the future, our political contests will also be cultural struggles.

This book will examine the changes wrought by liberalism in a variety of seemingly disparate areas of life, from popular entertainment to religion to scholarship to constitutional law, from abortion to crime to feminism, and more. It will attempt to answer where modern liberalism came from and why its ideas are pressed so immoderately. Are cultural trends cyclical or is this trend inherent in Western civilization, or even, perhaps, in human nature itself? There is a case for one of the latter answers, and if that argument is correct, the future is probably bleak. No one can be certain of that, however. Cultures in decline have, unpredictably, turned themselves around before. Perhaps ours will too....

NOTES

1. Daniel Patrick Moynihan, "Defining Deviancy Down," *American Scholar*, Winter 1993, p. 17.
2. Ibid., pp. 17–20.
3. Ibid., p. 19.
4. Charles Krauthammer, "Defining Deviancy Up," *New Republic*, November 22, 1993, p. 20.
5. Ibid.
6. Christopher Lasch, *The Revolt of the Elites and the Betrayal of Democracy* (New York: W. W. Norton, 1995), pp. 233–234.
7. Lionel Trilling, *Sincerity and Authenticity: The Charles Eliot Norton Lectures, 1969–1970* (Cambridge, Mass.: Harvard University Press, 1974), p. 1.
8. Ibid.

31

The Neoconservative Persuasion

Irving Kristol (1920–), currently senior fellow at the American Enterprise Institute, is the author of many books, including *Neoconservatism: The Autobiography of an Idea* (1999). He has served as editor or co-editor of several journals, notably *Commentary* (1947–1952) and *Public Interest* (1965–2005). Kristol is one of the founders of the neoconservative movement—or, as he prefers to say, "persuasion." In the following essay he outlines the tenets of this persuasion and explains how it differs from other varieties of conservatism.

Source: Irving Kristol, "The Neoconservative Persuasion," *Weekly Standard*, August 25, 2003. Reprinted by permission of *The Weekly Standard*.

THE NEOCONSERVATIVE PERSUASION

What exactly is neoconservatism? Journalists, and now even presidential candidates, speak with an enviable confidence on who or what is "neoconservative," and seem to assume the meaning is fully revealed in the name. Those of us who are designated as "neocons" are amused, flattered, or dismissive, depending on the context. It is reasonable to wonder: Is there any "there" there?

Even I, frequently referred to as the "godfather" of all those neocons, have had my moments of wonderment. A few years ago I said (and, alas, wrote) that neoconservatism had had its own distinctive qualities in its early years, but by now had been absorbed into the mainstream of American conservatism. I was wrong, and the reason I was wrong is that, ever since its origin among disillusioned liberal intellectuals in the 1970s, what we call neoconservatism has been one of those intellectual undercurrents that surface only intermittently. It is not a "movement," as the conspiratorial critics would have it. Neoconservatism is what the late historian of Jacksonian America, Marvin Meyers, called a "persuasion," one that manifests itself over time, but erratically, and one whose meaning we clearly glimpse only in retrospect.

Viewed in this way, one can say that the historical task and political purpose of neoconservatism would seem to be this: to convert the Republican party, and American conservatism in general, against their respective wills, into a new kind of conservative politics suitable to governing a modern democracy. That this new conservative politics is distinctly American is beyond doubt. There is nothing like neoconservatism in Europe, and most European conservatives are highly skeptical of its legitimacy. The fact that conservatism in the United States is so much healthier than in Europe, so much more politically effective, surely has something to do with the existence of neoconservatism. But Europeans, who think it absurd to look to the United States for lessons in political innovation, resolutely refuse to consider this possibility.

Neoconservatism is the first variant of American conservatism in the past century that is in the "American grain." It is hopeful, not lugubrious; forward-looking, not nostalgic; and its general tone is cheerful, not grim or dyspeptic. Its 20th-century heroes tend to be TR [Theodore Roosevelt], FDR [Franklin Delano Roosevelt], and Ronald Reagan. Such Republican and conservative worthies as Calvin Coolidge, Herbert Hoover, Dwight Eisenhower, and Barry Goldwater are politely overlooked. Of course, those worthies are in no way overlooked by a large, probably the largest, segment of the Republican party, with the result that most Republican politicians know nothing and could not care less about neoconservatism. Nevertheless, they cannot be blind to the fact that neoconservative policies, reaching out beyond the traditional political and financial base, have helped make the very idea of political conservatism more acceptable to a majority of American voters. Nor has it passed official notice that it is the neoconservative public policies, not the traditional Republican ones, that result in popular Republican presidencies.

One of these policies, most visible and controversial, is cutting tax rates in order to stimulate steady economic growth. This policy was not invented by neocons, and it was not the particularities of tax cuts that interested them, but rather the steady focus on economic growth. Neocons are familiar with intellectual history and aware that it is only in the last two centuries that democracy has become a respectable option among political thinkers. In earlier times, democracy meant an inherently turbulent political regime, with the "have-nots" and the "haves" engaged in a perpetual and utterly destructive class struggle. It was only the prospect of economic growth in which everyone prospered, if not equally or simultaneously, that gave modern democracies their legitimacy and durability.

The cost of this emphasis on economic growth has been an attitude toward public finance that is far less risk averse than is the case among more traditional conservatives. Neocons would prefer not to have large budget deficits, but it is in the nature of democracy—because it seems to be in the nature of human nature—that political demagogy will frequently result in economic recklessness, so that one sometimes must shoulder budgetary deficits as the cost (temporary, one hopes) of pursuing economic growth. It is a basic assumption of neoconservatism that, as a consequence of the spread of affluence among all classes, a property-owning and tax-paying population will, in time, become less vulnerable to egalitarian illusions and demagogic appeals and more sensible about the fundamentals of economic reckoning.

This leads to the issue of the role of the state. Neocons do not like the concentration of services in the welfare state and are happy to study alternative ways of delivering these services. But they are impatient with the Hayekian notion that we are on "the road to serfdom."[1] Neocons do not feel that kind of alarm or anxiety about the growth of the state in the past century, seeing it as natural, indeed inevitable. Because they tend to be more interested in history than economics or sociology, they know that the 19th-century idea, so neatly propounded by Herbert Spencer in his "The Man Versus the State," was a historical eccentricity. People have always preferred strong government to weak government, although they certainly have no liking for anything that smacks of overly intrusive government. Neocons feel at home in today's America to a degree that more traditional conservatives do not. Though they find much to be critical about, they tend to seek intellectual guidance in the democratic wisdom of Tocqueville, rather than in the Tory nostalgia of, say, Russell Kirk.[2]

But it is only to a degree that neocons are comfortable in modern America. The steady decline in our democratic culture, sinking to new levels of vulgarity, does unite neocons with traditional conservatives—though not with those libertarian conservatives who are conservative in economics but unmindful of the culture. The upshot is a quite unexpected alliance between neocons, who include a fair proportion of secular intellectuals, and religious traditionalists. They are united on issues concerning the quality of education, the relations of church and state, the regulation of pornography, and the like, all of which they regard as proper candidates for the government's attention. And since the Republican party now has a substantial base among the religious, this gives neocons a certain influence and even power. Because religious conservatism is so feeble in Europe, the neoconservative potential there is correspondingly weak.

And then, of course, there is foreign policy, the area of American politics where neoconservatism has recently been the focus of media attention. This is surprising since there is no set of neoconservative beliefs concerning foreign policy, only a set of attitudes derived from historical experience. (The favorite neoconservative text on foreign affairs, thanks to professors Leo Strauss of Chicago and Donald Kagan of Yale, is Thucydides on the Peloponnesian War.) These attitudes can be summarized in the following "theses" (as a Marxist would say): First, patriotism is a natural and healthy sentiment and should be encouraged by both private and public institutions. Precisely because we are a nation of immigrants, this is a powerful American sentiment. Second, world government is a terrible idea since it can lead to world tyranny. International institutions that point to an ultimate world government should be regarded with the deepest suspicion. Third, statesmen should, above all, have the ability to distinguish friends from enemies. This is not as easy as it sounds, as the history of the Cold War revealed. The number of intelligent men who could not count the Soviet Union as an enemy, even though this was its own self-definition, was absolutely astonishing.

Finally, for a great power, the "national interest" is not a geographical term, except for fairly prosaic matters like trade and environmental regulation. A smaller nation might appropriately feel that its national interest begins and ends at its borders, so that its foreign policy is almost always in a defensive mode. A larger nation has more extensive interests. And large nations, whose identity is ideological, like the Soviet Union of yesteryear and the United States of today, inevitably have ideological interests in addition to more material concerns. Barring extraordinary events, the United

States will always feel obliged to defend, if possible, a democratic nation under attack from nondemocratic forces, external or internal. That is why it was in our national interest to come to the defense of France and Britain in World War II. That is why we feel it necessary to defend Israel today, when its survival is threatened. No complicated geopolitical calculations of national interest are necessary.

Behind all this is a fact: the incredible military superiority of the United States vis-à-vis the nations of the rest of the world, in any imaginable combination. This superiority was planned by no one, and even today there are many Americans who are in denial. To a large extent, it all happened as a result of our bad luck. During the 50 years after World War II, while Europe was at peace and the Soviet Union largely relied on surrogates to do its fighting, the United States was involved in a whole series of wars: the Korean War, the Vietnam War, the Gulf War, the Kosovo conflict, the Afghan War, and the Iraq War. The result was that our military spending expanded more or less in line with our economic growth, while Europe's democracies cut back their military spending in favor of social welfare programs. The Soviet Union spent profusely but wastefully, so that its military collapsed along with its economy.

Suddenly, after two decades during which "imperial decline" and "imperial overstretch" were the academic and journalistic watchwords, the United States emerged as uniquely powerful. The "magic" of compound interest over half a century had its effect on our military budget, as did the cumulative scientific and technological research of our armed forces. With power come responsibilities, whether sought or not, whether welcome or not. And it is a fact that if you have the kind of power we now have, either you will find opportunities to use it, or the world will discover them for you.

The older, traditional elements in the Republican party have difficulty coming to terms with this new reality in foreign affairs, just as they cannot reconcile economic conservatism with social and cultural conservatism. But by one of those accidents historians ponder, our current president and his administration turn out to be quite at home in this new political environment, although it is clear they did not anticipate this role any more than their party as a whole did. As a result, neoconservatism began enjoying a second life, at a time when its obituaries were still being published.

NOTES

1. Kristol refers here to Friedrich von Hayek, *The Road to Serfdom* (Chicago: University of Chicago Press, 1976).—Eds.
2. Russell Kirk (1918–1994) was an American conservative and author of many books, including the influential *The Conservative Mind* (New York: Avon Books, 1968).—Eds.

32

Standing Strong in a Confused Culture

JAMES DOBSON

James C. Dobson (1936–) is a licensed psychologist who has become one of the most prominent leaders of what is often called the Christian (or Religious) Right in the United States. After earning a Ph.D. in child development from the University of Southern California (1967), Dobson served as an associate clinical professor of pediatrics at the University of Southern California School of Medicine and established a national reputation as the author of *Dare to Discipline* and other books for parents and teachers. He subsequently founded Focus on the Family, a nonprofit organization that produces, among other things, his internationally syndicated radio programs, which are broadcast on nearly 3,500 radio facilities in the United States and more than 5,000 internationally. In the following essay from *Dr. Dobson's Newsletter,* Dobson takes issue with those—especially other Christian conservatives—who are wary of linking religious belief to political action.

Source: Dr. Dobson's Newsletter (May 2002). Reprinted by permission of the author.

STANDING STRONG IN A CONFUSED CULTURE

I want to say a few words about our culture's continued moral decline and, more importantly, the apparent hesitancy of some within the Christian community to try and stem the tide. Despite the relentless attacks by homosexual activists on the institution of marriage, and of "safe sex" ideology, pro-abortion sentiment, and other forms of immorality that are engulfing us, there are those within the church who remain convinced that it isn't our place to make our voices heard on these issues. In their estimation, controversy about sexuality, the sanctity of human life and the traditional family are "political" in nature and therefore unworthy of our attention. They believe that for Christians to involve themselves in cultural issues—even though they are profoundly moral in nature—is to dilute the gospel message. Some recent examples of this perspective are seen in the following quotes:

"God does not call the church to influence the culture by promoting legislation."

—*John MacArthur, Why Government Can't Save You, 2000*[1]

"I really believe, with all of my heart, one of the greatest mistakes in the religious world is the involvement in politics. I believe that I should not be on one side or the other. I believe I should be as neutral as possible and be able to teach the Word of God and not alienate anyone."

—*Jim Bakker, The San Diego Union-Tribune, 2000*[2]

Columnist Cal Thomas:

"There is no biblical mandate for reforming the world through government."[3] [...as if anybody has ever said our purpose is to reform the world through government. Jesus Christ is our lone source of redemption!]

"The time is ripe for conservative Christians to spend less time trying to influence Caesar, to consider what it means to render unto God, and to start rendering."[4]

And Thomas' favorite gag line:

"The kingdom of God is not going to arrive aboard Air Force One."[5]

Christianity Today published an editorial on April 1 titled "Enough Bullying." It severely criticized those of us who believe religious broadcasters should speak out on cultural issues. The statement read:

> "[Christian activists are] often seen as indignantly condemning the sins of the world more than proclaiming the good news of salvation from those sins."[6]

The editorial went on to decry "the politics of hysteria and outrage."

I do not doubt the sincerity of conviction or question the Christian commitment of my brothers and sisters who choose to remain silent in response to the moral free fall we are experiencing. But I do strongly disagree with them. I firmly believe that "engaging the culture" and "sharing the gospel message" are not two distinct things; rather, they are inexorably intertwined. I explained this perspective with some passion this past February [2002] when I presented the keynote address at the National Religious Broadcasters' annual convention in Nashville, Tennessee. I'd like to share the text of that speech with you, because I believe it explains, at least from my perspective, why we as Christians must use our influence to defend righteousness in this democratic system of government. The first half of my presentation dealt with the theme of my book *Bringing Up Boys*. In the second portion, however, I talked about one of the major reasons boys are in such trouble today and how it is related to the war against families. I will share only that second half in this letter because of space limitations.

Please note that because the following comments were originally part of an oral presentation, they have been edited to make them more readable. The spoken word is very imprecise when delivered. After you have read this speech, I would like to know how you see the issues raised.

What I want to say to you tonight comes from deep within my heart, although it is said with charity to those who disagree. My comments will not be directed at any individual. These thoughts are relevant to all of us in this time of moral decline.

The world into which today's children are born has become a very dangerous place. It has changed tremendously. Those of you who are 50 years of age or older know that when you were young, the culture reinforced positive values and attempted to help parents raise their kids properly.

But now, the culture is at war with parents. It is very difficult to get kids safely through the minefield of adolescence. We're seeing a relentless attack on childhood today. There are many people in the activist community who hate the Judeo-Christian system of values, and recognize that if they can gain control of children, they can change the entire culture in one generation. That's why there is a tsunami of propaganda flooding over our culture. Every day, it seems, some new effort to manipulate kids is becoming apparent.

With the limited time available to me tonight, I can't give you the history of this attack on children. Instead, let me simply go back to February 1 of this year and review what has occurred within that period of just two weeks and two days. Perhaps it will be apparent how rapidly the world of children is changing.

Exactly eight days ago, the National Education Association (NEA) announced its policy that is being disseminated to schools all over the country, urging every district to teach what amounts to homosexual propaganda to children of all ages.[7]

Because a child will typically spend 13 years in public schools, this indoctrination will begin in kindergarten and continue through high school. Perhaps you think this type of radical curriculum couldn't be implemented in public schools, but it has already become law in the state of California. The California Legislature passed a series of bills that the State Department of Education used as a framework to recommend that schools adopt a pro-homosexual curriculum.[8] Delaine Eastin, state superintendent of Public Instruction, sent out a vaguely crafted cover letter on April 5, 2001, which outlined the recommendations about how schools should implement the non-discrimination language from the bills into curricula. Eastin's letter left the impression that the recommendations were mandatory, although they weren't.[9] When children came back from their summer vacations in September of last year, this is what was waiting for millions of them. Sadly, the majority of parents either didn't notice or didn't seem to care, because the legislation passed with too little resistance. Where are the moms and dads who are supposed to be looking out for the welfare of their kids? Why was there not an avalanche of opposition in response? Perhaps it is because Christians have been told that public policy issues, even those that affect their children, are not their concern.

Imagine sending a little 5-year-old boy off to a school that has implemented what the National Education Association is promoting. He's wet behind the ears, or to use the vernacular, "He knows nothing about nothing." He doesn't have the information or the defenses to counter the lies he's being told. Can you imagine 15 or 20 of these children sitting in a circle around the kindergarten teacher who's describing for them adult perverse behavior? Again, I find it difficult to believe parents are holding still for this! What should be additionally shocking to us is not only what is being taught in this instance, but what is NOT being taught. Sixty-eight percent of fourth-graders cannot read at a proficient level, and yet, professional educators want to take precious class time to teach their students about homosexuality.[10] [Since this speech was given, a resolution has been introduced in the U.S. Congress calling for an annual day of silence in every public school, so that every student can contemplate the discrimination and oppression experienced by gay and lesbian children.[11] Though the resolution never made it out of committee, students at 1,430 high schools registered to participate in the April 10 event.[12]] And still, there are Christians who tell us that such concerns are "political" and that it is somehow ungodly to use their influence to oppose them.

[By the way, during a "Focus on the Family" interview with Pat Buchanan on March 28, I recommended something I have never said before. Because of the radical changes being made in California's schools, I indicated that I would not place my child in public schools in that state or any other that moves in this direction—if any other alternatives were available. Christian schools and home schools would be a far better option. I've heard the argument that we should not abandon the public schools and leave them to those with postmodern and politically correct views. I would agree, except for the fact that it is our vulnerable children who will be sacrificed if we keep them in a godless environment. Speaking personally, the welfare of my boy or girl would take priority over the need to influence the local public school. In the meantime, I would work tirelessly for the implementation of school choice.]

The radical proposal by the NEA occurred on February 8. What else has happened in the last couple of weeks? On February 4—12 days ago—the American Academy of Pediatrics announced its conclusion that gay and lesbian parents typically raise children as effectively as traditional families in which husbands and wives are committed to each other.[13] The committee that released this report had no convincing data to back its claim and, in fact, admitted that there wasn't enough information upon which to base valid findings.[14] And yet, almost every newspaper in the country reported the spurious "finding." The revolutionary concept was based not on science, but on politically correct propaganda.

On February 14—two days ago—United States Secretary of State Colin Powell went on MTV, broadcast internationally, and recommended that kids use condoms. Let me read a portion of his quote. Listen carefully to the words he used. "Forget about taboos." Guess whose taboos kids were being asked to forget about? "Forget about conservative ideas." Guess whose conservative ideas were to be forgotten? "It's lives of young people that are put at risk by unsafe sex, and therefore, protect yourself."[15]

What Secretary Powell didn't tell his young viewers is that the Centers for Disease Control and Prevention and the National Institutes of Health, the two primary departments of the federal government whose responsibility it is to protect the health of the nation, issued a report last year that the press barely disclosed to the public. It said there is no evidence that condoms protect against syphilis, gonorrhea, human papilloma virus, genital herpes and most of the other sexually transmitted diseases.[16] And yet, there was the secretary of state, not the secretary of health and human services, speaking to kids about something he knows little or nothing about.

And the beat goes on. A year ago, the Center for Reproductive Law and Policy filed a citizens' petition with the Food and Drug Administration recommending the distribution of the "morning-after pill" (medication that will kill tiny embryos if conception has occurred) to kids without parental knowledge or approval. And just three days ago, the group reiterated its position before the FDA in an effort to get the agency to immediately reclassify the pill from prescription to over-the-counter status.[17] [In a related development, three weeks after this speech, Washington Democratic Senator Patty Murray introduced the Emergency Contraception Education Act, calling for $10 million of taxpayer funds per year to develop an emergency contraception public-education campaign.[18]] So much for the concern about the sanctity of human life.

These developments that have occurred in the last 16 days are characteristic of what is happening month after month and year by year. You can take any two-week period and see the same unrelenting assault on morality and the well-being of children. Brick by brick, the wall is crumbling.

Now, what's going on here? What is behind this targeting of kids? Let me answer that question by relating it to the current debate on stem cell research. Do you know what a stem cell is? It is a cell that is not yet differentiated—not yet developed into a specific part of the body. In the beginning, it has the capacity to become any kind of bodily tissue or fluid, depending on the environment in which it grows. If it is located in the brain, it may become a nerve cell, or a neurotransmitter, or a hormone found in the brain. If it gravitates to the heart, it becomes heart tissue, or if it's in the eye, it becomes part of the visual apparatus. In other words, stem cells in their early stages of development will assume the characteristics of whatever surrounds them individually. In that way, they are the building blocks for the physical components of the body.

Likewise, children are the "stem cells" for the culture. The environment in which they are raised will influence what they grow up to be. Is the analogy clear? Those who control what children see and hear and believe are in a position to shape not only those individuals, but also the culture of tomorrow. Abraham Lincoln recognized this important nature of children. He said, "The philosophy of the classroom in one generation will be the philosophy of the government in the next."[19] Homosexual activists and other politically correct leaders obviously understand this phenomenon. That's why they place such emphasis on the indoctrination of children. By telling kids repeatedly what they want them to believe and think, they can change the culture, quite literally, in a single generation.

I saw a video clip on television the other day that featured a classroom in pre-war Afghanistan. These children were being taught how to slit the throats of Israelis. If you teach that kind of violence to 6-year-old boys, you will have violent men a few years later. The "stem cells" of babyhood will become like the environment in which they were raised.

This is what is behind the massive effort to install homosexuals and their influence into the Boy Scouts organization. The Girls Scouts have already been invaded, and now, according to one report, a third of Girl Scout leaders are lesbians.[20] Wherever you find large numbers of children, you will see this tug-of-war for their hearts and minds. So often, the activists take over the leadership of children's organizations without a fight. Why? One of the reasons is that Christians are standing around debating with each other about church and state issues and refusing to use their influence in the wider culture. It leaves boys and girls virtually defenseless.

Are you aware there is an international effort now to lower the age of sexual consent? In the U.K., it's 16. Here in the United States, it's as low as 16. In Canada, it's 14. In Portugal, it's 14. In Spain, it's 13. In the Netherlands, it's 12.[21] Is that shocking to you? It certainly is to me. We're beginning to witness a blatant campaign to demystify incest and the sexual abuse of children. You will hear more and more "experts" in the next few years telling us that boys and girls actually benefit from what they are calling "intergenerational sex."[22] They are dead wrong, of course, but the propaganda is already having an impact. Children are in the crosshairs, and there are many reasons to be concerned about them. And, of course, preborn and newborn human beings are at greatest risk.

There is an almost total disregard for the value of human life in some postmodern circles. Dr. Peter Singer is a tenured professor at Princeton University. Let me read you what he wrote. "Very often it is not wrong at all [to kill a child once it has left the womb]."[23] He said, and note the words he chose, "Simply killing an infant is never equivalent to killing a person."[24]

These are the words of a bioethicist, of all things! Do you know that it is a $25,000 fine to kill an eagle's egg, yet there is no federal law at all against killing a fully developed and healthy child after as much as 80 percent of his or her body has been delivered?[25]

Have you contemplated actually having to witness a partial-birth abortion? Can you imagine being invited into a women's clinic somewhere near your home (there is probably one located near you) where a 16-year-old girl who is eight months along in her pregnancy comes in to have her baby killed? You've been invited to witness the procedure. You watch in horror as the doctor delivers this little baby, but holds it in place when only the top of the head is in the birth canal. That infant is only a minute or two from final delivery. He is brimming with life, and his little hands and arms and legs are kicking. Then the doctor rolls him over and inserts a cannula (a steel tube) into the back of the head without an anesthetic and sucks the brains out of that infant. The head collapses and the doctor delivers a dead baby. It would buckle your knees to witness such a murder. Nevertheless, it is perfectly legal to do it—and we're letting it happen! But beware, you cannot kill an eagle's egg! To call that outrage "political" is itself an outrage! Have we gone absolutely crazy?

[I hope it will not be self-serving to tell you that at this point in my remarks, there was sustained applause from most of the 4,000 Christians in attendance, indicating their support for my emotional remarks. A few remained seated and silent, and in fact, I learned later that many of them were irate. I guess this is what *Christianity Today* referred to as "the politics of hysteria and outrage."]

Clearly, this issue burns in my heart. You may remember that Barbara Boxer, the senator from California, speaking on the floor of the Senate in a debate with Senator Rick Santorum about partial-birth abortion, said that a baby is not a baby until the child is taken home from the hospital.[26] In other words, you can kill that child with impunity as long as he or she remains in the hospital. This is where we are headed, taking us toward an even further disregard for the value of human life.

Let me argue with those of you who think the church has no responsibility to address such concerns, and that its only obligation is to preach the gospel. Suppose the year was 1858 and you were a pastor living in Raleigh, North Carolina; Richmond, Virginia; or somewhere else in the South. Would it have been satisfactory for you to say about slavery, "Well, I'm not called to deal with that contentious issue. To do so would make others angry and would limit my ministry. I'm called to minister to the people in my church. Slavery is not something I have to deal with"? All the while, you knew that black men and women in your community were being subjected to involuntary servitude, having been brought to this country under horrible conditions—circumstances that killed half of them on the ships that brought them here. Your entire congregation knew that slaves could be killed at the whim of their masters and that black family members were being separated, never to see each other again. You knew that children were sometimes taken away from their parents and sold like cattle or sheep. You and your people understood the brutality and the poverty of slavery, and yet you convinced yourself that this institution was not your concern—that it was a "political issue" and that the church should not discuss it. Could you take that position and feel justified in it? Thousands of pastors did exactly that, and their rationale was just as porous as the flimsy excuses today's Christians offer for ignoring the killing of babies and the manipulation of children.

Let me continue. The year is 1963, and Martin Luther King is sitting in a Birmingham jail for engaging in civil rights activities. When he is released, he goes to a church—yes, a church—from which he marches into the streets of Birmingham on behalf of oppressed minorities. Martin Luther King was a minister. Are you prepared to criticize him today for his violation of the separation of church and state? Should the church have been silent about the issues he raised?

What if today were 1943 and you were in Nazi Germany and knew that Hitler and his henchmen were killing Jews and Poles and Gypsies and homosexuals and the mentally handicapped, among other "undesirables"? You knew these helpless people were being gassed, and that little children were standing all day, on one occasion in a freezing rain, for their turn to die in the gas chambers. Would you have said if you were there, "We're not going to get political in my church! That's somebody else's problem. I'm not called to address controversial issues!" Would you try to make a case for silence in the church?

I thank God that Dietrich Bonhoeffer did not shrink in timidity when he saw unmitigated wickedness being perpetrated by the Nazis. He spoke out boldly, even though he had to know it would cost him his life. Bonhoeffer was hanged in 1945, naked and alone, because he called evil by its name.

John the Baptist said the same thing to Herod, a notoriously bloody tyrant. He said, "It is not lawful for you to have your brother's wife" (Mark 6:18, NIV). And his head was severed and placed on a platter. I suppose many Christians through the ages have been unwilling to address the moral issues when their lives were in danger. But what is new is this effort among some evangelical leaders to justify their silence in response to wickedness. In my view, theirs is an impossible case to make.

In 1983, I was invited to Washington, D.C., to attend a banquet that featured Dr. Francis Schaeffer. I am so grateful for the enduring influence of that man. He foresaw everything we're experiencing in the church today. He laid it all out in his final book, *The Great Evangelical Disaster*. He was the first to recognize the connection between abortion, infanticide and euthanasia, and warned about the coming unwillingness of Christians to oppose them. On the occasion of my visit to the nation's capital, Schaeffer was talking about the morality of a Christian's involvement in the military, especially when it involved war.

I had recently left my university position at the time and was just beginning to try to understand what was going on in the culture at large. Dr. Schaeffer said, "The morality of war comes down to this: Suppose you were walking down the right side of a street one night, and coming toward you on the other side was a cute little 6-year-old girl. She was skipping along alone. Just as you were parallel to her, a big, burly, six-foot man jumped out of the bushes and grabbed her. He began assaulting and abusing her. What would be your obligation to that child?" Dr. Schaeffer answered his own question this way: "I submit that you should cross that street and put your life in jeopardy, if necessary, to save that little girl. That would be your moral responsibility." And then he said, "That is what we were doing by our military involvement in World War II. We were trying to save the defenseless little girls—the Jews, the Gypsies, the Poles and the others who were being killed, and to rescue those who were living in tyranny."

I submit to you tonight that there are "little girls" in our culture today who are being abused by those who would kill or assault them. Who are these children whom we are called to defend? Some are yet to be born. Should we attempt to save them? Jesus said, "Inasmuch as you do it unto the least of these, my brethren, you do it unto Me" (Matthew 25:40, NIV). Would His words apply to those helpless little boys and girls who cannot speak on their own behalf? Can you ignore their plight, in good conscience, by saying, "Abortion is a political issue. I won't get involved. It's not my responsibility. Others are called to address it. I am not"?

How about the newborn? How about that "little girl" who's left to die on a porcelain table because she is developmentally disabled? What about the elementary school child who's being taught that homosexuality is just another lifestyle to be considered? What about the teenagers whom Colin Powell told to go ahead and have lots of really good sex as long as they do it the "safe" way? How about the unloved elderly person who is being subjected to "involuntary euthanasia" in Holland?[27] This practice may be right around the corner for us here in America. Will we have the courage to fight it when that day arrives? The state of Oregon is already engaging in a form of euthanasia called "physician-assisted suicide."[28] The next logical step is murder.

Do we have a responsibility to save each of those "little girls"? I submit that we most certainly do.

Finally, tonight, I want to share a personal story told by Dr. John Corts, who was formerly president of the Billy Graham organization. He said when he was 16 years of age, he and his younger cousins went to visit his grandfather's farm. They couldn't wait to get there and go out into the fields. They wanted to pitch hay and ride on the tractor. It sounded like so much fun.

But the grandfather was reluctant to let them go. They whined and begged until finally he said to John, "You are the eldest. You can take the kids to the field if you promise not to bring them back early. You must keep them out there until the end of the day."

John said, "I will do that, Grandfather." So they all got on the hay wagon and the tractor pulled them out to the field.

Very quickly, the kids got tired, and they started complaining. It was hot and sticky, and they were miserable. They began asking to go back to the house. But John said, "No, Grandfather told me to keep you out here."

At lunchtime, they were exhausted, and most of them were agitated. It was very hot; the hay was down their backs, and it itched, and they wanted to go back. But again John said, "No, Grandfather told me to keep you here."

At about 3:00 in the afternoon, a big black storm cloud came over, and the kids got scared. Some were crying. "Please!" they begged. "Let us go home." Still, the answer remained "no."

At about 5:00 John said, "All right, it's time to quit." He got them all on the hay wagon, and they went back to the house. After they had had their baths and been given something to eat, they rested for a while. Grandfather praised them warmly for the work they had done. Then, they became very proud of themselves.

That's when Grandfather told John why he wanted them to stay in the field. He said, "This farm has been successful through the years for one reason. We have stayed in the field when we felt like coming in. We did what needed to be done even when we wanted to quit. That is why I wanted the kids to have the satisfying experience of staying with something through the day."

John made his own application for his story, but let me tell you what it means to me. We're in a very difficult situation now. It's tough. It's hard moving against the tide of public opinion, the media, the entertainment industry, the Congress, the libraries, the professions and the other cultural forces that are making fun of us. Yes, what was said during our board meeting this morning is accurate. It is unpleasant to be called "the religious right" and "the far right" and "religious extremists" and "fundamentalist right-wing crazies." None of us likes that. But being ridiculed and marginalized is the price we must pay to defend what we believe. Jesus told us that it would be that way.

I can tell you that those of us at Focus on the Family have been subjected to some harsh treatment for the stands we have taken. We've had bloody animal parts brought to our front door. We've had our buildings spray-painted. We've had lies told about us in Denver and in Colorado Springs. We've been called "fanatics" and worse things. The easiest thing for us to have done would have been to quit.

But God has called us to stay in the field to the end of the day, and we will do that for as long as we have breath in our bodies. And I beg you to do the same. How can we remain silent when the next generation hangs in the balance? If we persevere to the end, we will hear those wonderful words of the Father, "Well done, thou good and faithful servant" (Matthew 25:21, NIV).

Late Breaking Developments: As I send this to the printer, the United States Supreme Court has just struck down a law banning "virtual" child pornography on the basis of it violating the First Amendment (*Ashcroft v. Free Speech Coalition*). Predictably, the ACLU applauded the decision—in essence, welcoming the further inevitable exploitation of children.[29] This is yet another example of the insidious moral deterioration that we're confronted with every day. This is a battle that we must fight—and a battle that we must win.

NOTES

1. John MacArthur, *Why Government Can't Save You* (Nashville: Word, 2000), p. 130.
2. Sandi Dolbee, "A House Divided: Christian Conservatives Debate Their Role As Political Activists," *The San Diego Union-Tribune,* 11 February 2000, p. E1.
3. Cal Thomas, "Christians Can't Change Country Through Politics," *The Wichita Eagle,* 12 December 2001, p. A11.
4. Ibid.
5. Marc Fisher, "The GOP, Facing A Dobson's Choice," *The Washington Post,* 2 July 1996, p. D1.
6. "Enough Bullying," *Christianity Today,* 1 April 2002, p. 37.

7. Greg Toppo, "NEA Approves Resolution to Protect Gay, Lesbian, Bisexual Students and Staff," *The Associated Press,* 8 February 2002.
8. CA State Legislature Bills: AB 499 (1988), AB 537 (1999), AB 1785 (2000), AB 1931 (2000), AB 1945 (2000), SB 257 (2001). See www.leginfo.ca.gov/bilinofo.html.
9. Letter From Delaine Eastin, state superintendent of Public Instruction, "School Safety and Violence Prevention Program Coordinators," California Department of Education, 5 April 2001.
10. National Center for Education Statistics, National Assessment for Education Progress (NAEP), 1992–2000 Reading Assessments, Reading Achievement Level Results for the Nation's Fourth-Graders, See nces:ed:gov/nationsreportcard/reading/results/achieve-pf.asp.
11. "National Day of Silence," House Congressional Resolution 346, 12 March 2002.
12. Steve Friess, "Students Observe Silence For Gays," *USA Today,* 10 April 2002, p. D7.
13. Ellen C. Perrin, M.D., and the Committee on Psychosocial Aspects of Child and Family Health, "Technical Report: Coparent or Second-Parent Adoption by Same-Sex Parents," American Academy of Pediatrics, *Pediatrics,* Vol. 109 No. 2, February 2002, p. 341.
14. Ibid. The study stated, "Accurate statistics regarding the number of parents who are gay or lesbian are impossible to obtain...hamper[ing] even basic epidemiologic research....The small and nonrepresentative samples studied and the relatively young age of most of the children suggest some reserve."
15. Ellen Sorokin, "Conservative Groups Scold Powell," *The Washington Times,* 16 February 2002.
16. "Sexually Transmitted Disease Surveillance, 2000," Centers for Disease Control and Prevention, Atlanta, GA, U.S. Department of Health and Human Services, September 2001. See www.cdc.gov/std/stats/TOC2000.htm.
17. Cheryl terHorst, "Emergencies Happen, And This Project Wants You To Be Prepared," *Chicago Tribune,* 20 March 2002, p. C3. Also, see www.fcs.gov/ohrms/dockets/dailys/02/feb02/0 21402/01p-0075_sup0002_vol10.pdf.
18. Cheryl Wetzstein "Emergency Contraception Topic On Hill," *The Washington Times,* 10 March 2002.
19. Jessica Garrison and Scott Martelle, "Wrapped in Red, White and Blue," *Los Angeles Times,* 11 October 2001, p. B1.
20. Kathryn Jean Lopez, "The Cookie Crumbles," *National Review,* 23 October 2000, p. 30.
21. See www.ageofconsent.com.
22. Mark O'Keefe, "University of Minnesota Press Book Challenges Anxiety About Pedophilia," Newhouse News Service, 26 March 2002.
23. Peter Singer, *Practical Ethics,* second ed. (Cambridge, UK: Cambridge University Press, 1993), p. 191.
24. Paul Zielbauer, "Princeton Bioethics Professor Debates Views on Disabilities and Euthanasia," *The New York Times,* 13 October 1999, p. B6.
25. Documents from the U.S. Fish and Wildlife Service, Division of Law Enforcement, Department of the Interior, "Endangered Species Act: Civil—$25,000."
26. Congressional Record, "Partial-Birth Abortion Ban Act of 1999," United States Senate, 20 October 1999, p. S12878.
27. Jeanne Malmgren, "Dutch Use Assisted Suicide Frequently," *St. Petersburg Times,* 10 January 1997, p. B1.
28. Dawn Gibeau, "Ethicists Alarmed At Oregon Law: Growth Of Assisted Suicide Efforts Feared," *National Catholic Reporter,* 2 December 1994, p. 5.
29. Robert S. Greenberger, "High Court Strikes Down Ban on 'Virtual' Child Pornography," *The Wall Street Journal,* 17 April 2002, p. A4.

PART FIVE

Socialism and Communism: More to Marx

Socialism and communism, though by no means identical, both belong to a common family of ideologies and spring from a common impulse. Both envision a society in which everyone contributes time, labor, and talent to a common pool and receives in return enough goods to satisfy his or her needs. Both condemn the exploitation of one individual or class by another that occurs, for example, when one profits from another's labor. And both believe that property should be so distributed as to benefit not the wealthy few but the public at large. Both, therefore, are critical of capitalism as an economic system and of liberalism (or liberal individualism) as an ideology.

But socialism and communism differ in important respects. One crucial difference concerns the means for attaining their ends. Socialists are more apt to favor peaceful and piecemeal reforms as a way of bringing about a socialist society, while communists—at least in the late nineteenth and the twentieth centuries—favored violent revolutionary transformations spearheaded by an elite "vanguard" party. Moreover, the kind of society that each hopes to create differs to some degree. Socialists envision a society in which the major means of production—mines, mills, factories, power plants, and so on—are either publicly owned or at least operated for the public benefit. Modern communists, by contrast, tend to favor public ownership and bureaucratic control of virtually all enterprises, large and small.

Perhaps the best way to understand these differences and the variety of forms socialism and communism have taken is to look back over the long history that socialists of all sorts have shared. As long ago as the fourth century B.C., for example, the Greek philosopher Plato envisioned in his *Republic* an ideal society in which one class, the Guardians, held everything in common, including spouses and children. Many early Christians were communists who shared all their worldly goods with one another—a practice that persists even today in some monasteries and nunneries. This early conception of communism is perhaps most memorably sketched in St. Thomas More's *Utopia* (1516). There More (1478–1535) imagines a society from which the forces of envy and greed have been banished. Private property and money have been abolished. The Utopians work not for personal profit but for the common good. Although the Utopians are pagans, More maintains that they put "Christian" Europe to shame by behaving selflessly and charitably toward each other.

Later idealistic or "utopian" socialists, such as Charles Fourier (1772–1837) and Robert Owen (1771–1858), provided more secular variations on More's theme. Fourier, for example, imagined an ideal society in which all would work for the common good, even if they did exactly as they pleased. The socialist principle of "harmonism" would harmonize diverse interests or "passions" and would make social cooperation not only possible but pleasant. Owen, a capitalist turned socialist, tried to put his plans for a perfect society into practice. Believing that human labor should be not only productive but morally uplifting, he designed and built factories and adjoining towns to promote these two ideals.

These and other schemes for socialist transformation were derided and condemned by those who thought of themselves as "scientific" socialists. Against the "utopianism" of earlier socialists, Karl Marx (1818–1883) and Friedrich Engels (1820–1895) argued that society is changed not through moral suasion but by understanding the hidden structures and process of material production. The key, they thought, was the "materialist conception of history." Unlike the "idealist" view of history advanced by G. W. F. Hegel (1770–1831), Marx and Engels's "materialist" view made material production and class struggle the primary determinants of social stability and change. All previously existing societies were divided along class lines. On the one side was the dominant or ruling class, the owners of the means of material production; on the other, a subservient class condemned to do the bidding of the ruling class. Who the rulers and the ruled are depends on the type of society or "social formation" one is talking about. In slave society, masters rule over slaves; in feudal society, lords rule over serfs; in capitalist society, the ruling capitalist class or *bourgeoisie* rules over the working class or *proletariat.* These "social relations of production" do not rest on force alone. If a class-divided society is to be stable and long lived, its members must view it as legitimate. The social order, with its inequalities of wealth and opportunity, must be seen as "normal," "natural," "necessary," or "inevitable." This is the function of ideology: to put the stamp of legitimacy on existing social arrangements. The "ruling ideas"—that is, the respectable or mainstream ideas—"are in every society the ideas of the ruling class." Only those ideas that serve the interest of the ruling class by helping it to perpetuate its rule will be disseminated from the pulpit, in the classroom, in the mass media, and elsewhere. All others will be regarded with suspicion or contempt.

Marx viewed his own theory as *critical,* that is, subversive of the orthodox opinions prevalent in capitalist society. The ideological prop and mainstay of such a society, he held, was political economy—the nineteenth-century term for the "science" of economics—with its laws of supply and demand and so on. Marx tried to show that political economy was really a smokescreen to obscure the system of exploitative social relations on which capitalism rested. By exposing the exploitative nature of the system, Marx hoped to enlighten or raise the consciousness of the proletariat, thereby paving the way for a revolution that would free it from the system that oppressed it. Only then, he thought, could the workers begin to bring about a classless communist society that operated according to the principle "From each according to his ability, to each according to his need."

33

Utopia

THOMAS MORE

Thomas More (1478–1535) was an important political and literary figure of the "Northern Renaissance" of the early sixteenth century. At one time a close adviser to Britain's King Henry VIII, More fell into disfavor when Henry broke with the Roman Catholic Church to establish the Church of England with himself as head. For refusing to approve Henry's action, More was beheaded. Four centuries later the Roman Catholic Church recognized him as a saint. Before his difficulties with Henry VIII began, More wrote *Utopia* (1516), a book in which he imagined a society from which the evils of envy and poverty had been banished. In the following selection More's main character, the fictitious explorer Raphael Hythloday, traces the evils of European society to the private ownership of property, which he contrasts to the virtues of the island commonwealth of Utopia, where private property and even money have been abolished.

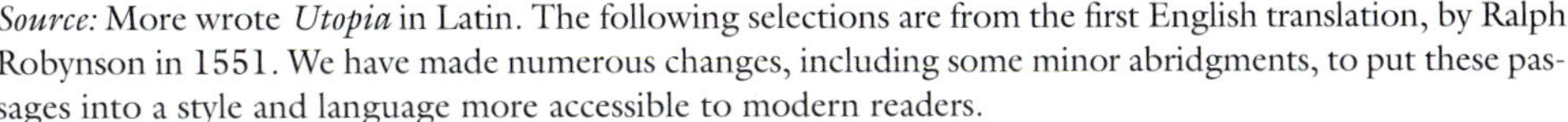

Source: More wrote *Utopia* in Latin. The following selections are from the first English translation, by Ralph Robynson in 1551. We have made numerous changes, including some minor abridgments, to put these passages into a style and language more accessible to modern readers.

UTOPIA[1]

From Book I

"I have no doubt, Master More," said Hythloday, "that wherever men have private property and money is the measure of everything, there it is hardly possible for the commonwealth to be justly governed or to flourish in prosperity. Unless, that is, you think that justice is done when all things are in the hands of evil men, or that prosperity and happiness are found when everything is divided among a few—and even those few do not really thrive—while all the rest live in misery and wretchedness.

"This is so different from the wise and godly ordinances of the Utopians, among whom a few laws are sufficient to keep everything well and happily ordered. In Utopia virtue is greatly esteemed, and even though all things are owned in common, everyone has everything in abundance. Now compare them with the many nations that are always making new, but unsatisfactory, laws. In these countries every man claims that he has his own property, or private goods; but the new laws they make every day are not enough to enable everyone to enjoy or defend those things that he calls his own. This much is made plain by the never-ending legal suits that constantly arise. When I consider these things, then, I have to agree with Plato, and I do not wonder that he made no laws for those who refused to share their wealth equally. For this wise man clearly foresaw that the only way to promote the well-being of the public as a whole is to establish equality of all goods.[2] Such equality can never be found where every man's goods are his private property. For there every man lays claims to as much as he can get. Then, no matter how great the abundance, a few divide all the riches among themselves, leaving the rest in poverty. And for the most part, the poor are more worthy to be happy and prosperous than the others. The rich are covetous, crafty, and really quite useless; the poor, on the other hand, are lowly, simple, and by their daily labor more beneficial to the common welfare than to themselves.

"Thus I am fully persuaded that no equitable and just distribution of goods can be made, and that there can be no true well-being in human affairs, unless private property is outlawed and banished. But as long as private property is the rule, the heavy and inevitable burden of poverty and wretchedness will weigh down the largest and best part of mankind. I grant that this burden may be eased, but it cannot be wholly removed while private property reigns. There might be a law that prohibits anyone from possessing more than a certain measure of land, perhaps, or more than a certain sum of money. Or there might be laws preventing the king from being too powerful, or the people from being too proud and unruly. Still other laws might proclaim that public offices must not be obtained by bribes and gifts, or that they cannot be bought or sold. Putting offices up for sale simply encourages the officials to regain the money they spent by defrauding and plundering the public; and if the offices go to those who offer bribes and gifts, the government will be in the hands of the rich, not the wise. By laws such as these, in short, the evils of which I have been speaking can be lightened and mitigated, just as people who are desperately ill and beyond cure can be kept alive with constant care. But these nations will never be completely cured and brought to a healthy condition while every man is master of his own property. You may cure one part, but in doing so you aggravate the illness of another. Helping one person harms another, for nothing can be given to anyone unless it is taken from someone else...."

From Book II (Hythloday's Account of Utopia)

Where money is the standard of everything, many vain and superfluous occupations must be pursued, although they serve only for wanton luxury and false pleasure. If the same multitude that now is occupied in work were divided into the few occupations that the truly necessary work requires, the abundance of goods that would ensue would be so great that the prices would doubtless be too low for the craftsmen to maintain their livelihood.

But if all these who are now busy in useless occupations, with the whole flock of those who live idly and slothfully, consuming and wasting every one of them more of those things that come from other men's labor than two of the workers themselves do—if all these, I say, were set to useful occupations, you can easily see how little would be enough, even too much, to supply us with everything we require for the sake of necessity or comfort. Yes, or even for pleasure, as long as the pleasure be true and natural.

This is made plain by the life of Utopia itself. There in each city, including the adjoining countryside, scarcely 500 persons of all those who are neither too old nor too weak to work are excused from labor. Among these are the Syphogrants,[3] who are exempted by law from labor. Yet they do not take advantage of the exemption because they want to set an example by their labor that will encourage others to work. There are also the scholars to whom the people, upon the recommendation of the priest and secret election by the Syphogrants, give an exemption from labor so that they may devote themselves to learning. But if any of the scholars fails to meet the expected standards, he is immediately plucked back to the company of workers. On the other hand, it often happens that a craftsman so earnestly devotes his free time to learning, and so profits by his diligence, that he is taken from his handicraft and promoted to the company of the learned.

From these scholars the ambassadors, priests, and Tranibors[4] are chosen, as is the prince himself, whom they in their old tongue called Barzanes, and now call Ademus.[5] The rest of the people are neither idle nor occupied with useless work, so it may easily be judged how much good work they may do in a few hours. They also have the advantage that in most of the necessary trades they need not work as much as other nations do. First of all, the building or repairing of houses takes everywhere else so many men's time because the careless heir allows the house his father built to fall into decay. So while he might have preserved it at little cost, his successor is now constrained to build it anew at great expense. Many times also one man has so refined and delicate a taste that he sets no value on a house that cost another man much money. As the house is neglected and shortly falls into ruin, the man of refined taste builds another one in another place at no less cost. But among the Utopians, where all things are in good order and the commonwealth is well-regulated, it very seldom happens that they choose a new plot to build a house upon. They not only find quick remedies for existing faults, but also prevent those that are likely to occur. In this way their houses last long with little labor and small repairs—so long that their carpenters and builders sometimes have almost nothing to do, in which case they hew timber at home, and square and trim stones, so that if any work needs to be done, it may be finished even more speedily.

Now note how few workers their clothing requires. First of all, while they are at work they are dressed in simple leather or skins that will last seven years. When they go out they put on a cloak which hides the other homely apparel. These cloaks throughout the island are all the same color, and that is the natural color of the wool. They therefore not only need much less wool than people in other countries, but the wool they do need costs them much less. Linen is made with less labor, so it is used more. But in linen only whiteness is valued, and in wool only cleanliness. As for the fineness of the thread, they don't care. Yet this is why in other places four or five cloth gowns of diverse colors, and as many silk coats, are not enough for one man. Yes, and if he is the fashionable sort, even ten are too few. But in Utopia one garment will serve a man very well for two years. Why should he desire more? If he had them, he would be neither better protected from the cold nor in any way appear better dressed.

Because they are all engaged in useful occupations, there is plenty of everything they need; and because a few workers are enough for each craft, they sometimes bring out great numbers of people to repair the highways, if any need repair. Many times, also, when they have no such work to do, an open proclamation is made that they should devote fewer hours to work. For the authorities do not force the citizens to labor unnecessarily. Why should they? The chief aim of the constitution and government is to spare people as much time as possible from necessary occupations so that they can leave the labor of the body and give time to the freedom and culture of the mind. For this, they suppose, is what makes for a truly happy life....

The Utopians use gold and silver in such a way as to prevent anyone from placing a greater value on these metals than they naturally deserve. Who does not see that these metals are less valuable than iron? Men can live no better without iron than without fire and water. But nature has given gold and silver no use that we could not do without. It is the folly of men that sets a higher value on them because they are rare. Nature, however, as a tender and loving mother, has placed the best and most necessary things in the open all about us, such as air, water, and the earth itself, and has hidden farthest from us vain and useless things....

The Utopians have devised, then, a plan that is as consistent with their laws and customs as it is contrary to ours, where gold is so cherished. The plan may even seem incredible, as a result, to those unfamiliar with it. They eat and drink from earthen and glass vessels, which are well and cleverly made, but which have little value. Of gold and silver, however, they make chamber pots and similar containers that serve for the most vile uses, not only in their common halls, but in everyone's private house.[6] Furthermore, they make great chains and fetters of these metals to bind their slaves.[7] Finally, those who commit crimes must wear gold rings on their ears and fingers, gold chains around their necks, and gold crowns around their heads. In this way the Utopians arrange to have gold and silver serve as marks of reproach and infamy. Other peoples grieve if they must do without these metals, as if gold and silver were their own lives. But if they should be taken all at once from the Utopians, no one there would think he had lost as much as a penny.

They gather pearls from the sea and diamonds and rubies from certain rocks. They do not search for them, but if they find them by chance they cut and polish them, then decorate their infants with them. In their early years the children are fond and proud of such ornaments. When they are a little older and wiser, though, they see that only children wear such trifles, and they put them away as shameful, without any bidding from their parents, just as our children cast away their marbles, rattles, and dolls when they grow older. How these laws and customs, so different from other nations, lead to different ideas and desires was made most clear to me by the arrival of the ambassadors of the Anemolians.[8]

These ambassadors came to Amaurot[9] while I was there. Because they came to negotiate great and weighty matters, three representatives from each Utopian city gathered before them. The ambassadors of other countries who had been there before knew the manners of the Utopians, so they knew that no honor was given to sumptuous and costly apparel—silks were condemned, gold considered disgraceful—and they came to Amaurot in plain and simple clothing. But the Anemolians, who lived far away and had little acquaintance with Utopia, decided upon hearing that Utopians all wore the same simple clothing that they must not have the things they did not wear. Being more proud than wise, the Anemolians determined to dress as gorgeously as the gods themselves, and thus to dazzle the eyes of the poor Utopians with their glistening clothes. So in came the three ambassadors with 100 servants dressed in many colors, most of them in silk. The ambassadors themselves, who were noblemen in their own country, wore clothes of gold, with great gold chains, gold hanging from their ears, gold rings on their fingers, brooches and strings of gold glistening with pearls and jewels upon their caps—trimmed and adorned, in short, with all those things which among the Utopians were either the punishment of slaves, the mark of disgrace upon wrong-doers, or trifles for young children's play. It would have done a man good, therefore, to have seen how proudly they displayed their peacock feathers, how much they made of their painted sheaths, and how loftily they advanced themselves when they compared their brilliant apparel with the poor garments of the Utopians, who swarmed into the streets. On the other hand, it was no less pleasant to see how much they were deceived and how far they missed their purpose. For to the eyes of the Utopians, except for the few who had been in other countries, all that gorgeous apparel seemed shameful. In fact, they saluted the lowest and most abject of the Anemolians, mistaking them for the nobles, while they ignored the ambassadors, whom they judged to be slaves because of their golden chains. You should have seen the children who had thrown away their pearls and jewels dig and push when they saw these items on the ambassadors' capes. "Look Mother," they said, "at that big ninny who still wears pearls and jewels like a little child." But the mother would earnestly say, "Hush, Son, I think he is one of the ambassador's fools." Others found fault with the golden chains because they were so small and weak that a slave could easily break them; or so large that he might slip them off and run away.

But when the ambassadors had been there a day or two and saw so much gold so little esteemed, and more gold in the chains of one fugitive slave than in all their costly ornaments, they put away shamefully all that gorgeous array of which they had been so proud. For their part, the Utopians marveled that anyone who may behold the stars or the sun could be so foolish as to delight in the sparkling of a trifling stone, or that any man is so mad as to count himself a better person for the fine quality of the wool he wears. No matter how fine, they say, the same wool was once worn by a sheep, which was nothing but a sheep the whole time she wore it.

They marvel also that gold, so useless in itself, is now valued so highly among all people that man himself is held in less esteem than gold. A lumpish blockhead, with no more wit than an ass, nevertheless shall have many wise and good men at his command simply because he has a great heap of gold. But if the gold should be taken from him and given to the lowest servant in his household either by fortune or by some subtle trick of the law (which no less than fortune raises up the low and pulls down the high), then he as well as his money shall shortly go into the service of his servant....

I have described to you as truly as I could the form and order of that commonwealth which in my judgment is not only the best, but the only one that can rightly claim the name of a commonwealth or republic. In other places they speak of the common good, but every man procures his private good. Here, where nothing is private, the common affairs are their real concern. In both cases they have good reason to act as they do. For in other countries, no matter how prosperous the country may be, who knows that he will not starve if he makes no special provision for himself? Therefore he is compelled to look out for himself rather than the people—that is, for others. Where all things are owned in common, on the contrary, no one shall lack anything necessary for his private use, so long as the common storehouses and barns are sufficiently stocked. There nothing is distributed in a niggardly way, nor is anyone poor. And though no one owns anything, yet everyone is rich. For what can be richer than to live joyfully, free from worries about making a living? No man is vexed by his wife's importunate complaints, nor dreads poverty for his sons, nor sorrows because he cannot provide a dowry for his daughter. Instead, the Utopians do not worry at all about the livelihood and prosperity of themselves and their kin: their wives, their children, their nephews, their children's children, and all that shall follow in their posterity. Besides this, they provide as much for those who were once laborers, but are now too weak to work, as for those who are still working.

Now I would like to see if anyone is so bold as to compare this with the so-called justice of other nations—among whom, upon my soul, I can find no sign of equity and justice. Is it justice when a rich goldsmith or moneylender, or anyone who either does nothing at all or nothing necessary to the common good, has a pleasant and prosperous life, while poor laborers, carters, ironsmiths, carpenters, and plowmen by great and continual toil are barely able to stay alive? Their work is so necessary that no commonwealth could last a year without it; yet their lives are so wretched and miserable that the condition of the beasts of burden may seem better.... Not only are these wretched workers tormented with hard and unprofitable labor, but they must also suffer the prospect of a penniless old age. For their daily wage is so little that it will not suffice for that day, much less yield any surplus that may be saved for the relief of old age.

Is this not an unjust country?[10] It gives great rewards to so-called gentlemen, goldsmiths, and other idlers and flatterers, or to those who devise useless pleasures, on the one hand; then, on the other, it fails to provide for poor plowmen, coal miners, laborers, carters, ironsmiths, and carpenters, without whom no commonwealth can survive. After it has abused the labors of their lusty and flowering years, it abandons them to a miserable death. Besides this, the rich men every day snatch away from the poor some part of their livelihood, either by private fraud or public law. So to their despicable treatment of the workers whose pains promote the public good, the rich now give the name of justice under law.

Therefore when I consider all these commonwealths which nowadays flourish everywhere, God help me but I perceive nothing but a conspiracy of the rich, who serve their own interests under the name of the common good. They invent all sorts of ways to keep what they have unjustly acquired, as well as ways to employ the labor of the poor for as little money as possible. These devices, the rich declare, must be kept and observed for the sake of the common good—that is, for the welfare also of the poor people—and so they are made laws. But when these most wicked and vicious men have by their insatiable covetousness divided among themselves all those things that would suffice for *all* men, they are still far from enjoying the happiness of the Utopian commonwealth. In Utopia, where the desire for money is banished along with its use, how great a heap of cares is cut away! How great an occasion for wickedness and mischief is pulled up by the roots! Who does not know that fraud, theft, plunder, brawling, quarreling, faction, strife, chiding, contention, murder, treason, and poisoning, which are revenged but not prevented by punishment, die out when money dies? Or that fear, grief, care, toils, and anxiety perish the same moment that money perishes? Yes, poverty itself, which only seemed to be the lack of money, would vanish if money were gone.

That you may perceive this more plainly, consider some barren and unfruitful year in which many thousands of people have starved. I dare to say that at the end of that desperate time enough grain might have been found in the rich men's barns to feed everyone whom famine and pestilence killed. So easily might men make their living if that worthy princess, Lady Money, did not stand in the way. I am sure that the rich understand this. Even they must know that it is better to lack nothing one really needs than to have many unnecessary things—better to be rid of innumerable cares and troubles than to be besieged with great riches. I do not doubt that every man's respect for his private interest, or the authority of our savior Christ (who knew and counselled what is best), would have brought all the world long ago into the ways of the public welfare if it were not for that one beast, the princess and mother of all wrongdoing—pride. Pride measures happiness and prosperity not by her own advantages, but by the miseries and disadvantages of others. She would not be content if there were no wretches to mock and scorn, no one whose misery might bring out her happiness, no one whose poverty she might torment and increase by gorgeously displaying her riches. This hellhound creeps into men's hearts and keeps them from entering the right path of life. Pride is so deeply rooted in men's breasts that she cannot easily be plucked out.

Although I would gladly wish the form of a true commonwealth for all nations, I am glad that it has chanced to fall to the Utopians. They have laid such foundations of their commonwealth as shall endure forever, as far as one can foresee. Because the chief causes of ambition and factions and the other vices have been pulled up by the roots, the Utopians are in no jeopardy of the domestic dissension that has brought to ruin the well fortified and strongly defended wealth and riches of many cities. And as long as perfect concord remains and wholesome laws are enforced at home, the envy of foreign princes will not be able to conquer or shake Utopia, for they have tried many times and always been driven back.

NOTES

1. More coined the word "utopia" as a pun from the Greek *eu-topos,* meaning either (or both) "happy place" or "no place."—Eds.
2. In the just society Plato envisions in his *Republic,* the rulers, or Guardians, share everything in common, although most of the people are allowed to own private property.—Eds.
3. Hythloday had earlier explained that Utopian cities are divided into groups of thirty households, with each group electing an official called a Syphogrant.—Eds.
4. A Tranibor is an official, elected annually, with authority over ten Syphogrants and the 300 families they represent.—Eds.
5. In classical Greek, *Barzanes* means "Son of Zeus"; *Ademus,* "without people."—Eds.
6. Strictly speaking, houses are not privately owned in Utopia. According to Hythloday's account, moreover, all houses are alike and every ten years they are redistributed by lottery.—Eds.
7. Most slaves in Utopia are either prisoners of war or people guilty of heinous offenses. There is also a group of what we now would call servants, comprising foreigners who prefer slavery in Utopia to life in their native land.—Eds.
8. *Anemolian* is Greek for "windy people."—Eds.
9. Amaurot is the capital city of Utopia.—Eds.
10. That is, England, and other European countries, and not Utopia.—Eds.

34

Address to the Inhabitants of New Lanark

ROBERT OWEN

In 1800, Robert Owen (1771–1858) took control of a cotton mill in New Lanark, Scotland. Unlike other mill owners, Owen took great interest in the living conditions of his workers, providing them with decent housing and schools for their children. New Lanark became a great success, as Owen indicates in this excerpt from his address to his workers, and this success encouraged Owen to engage in other social experiments on a broader scale. One of these was the socialist community of New Harmony, Indiana, which Owen launched in 1824, only to see it collapse at great personal expense within four years.

Source: Robert Owen, *A New View of Society and Other Writings*, ed. G. D. H. Cole (London: J. M. Dent, 1927).

ADDRESS TO THE INHABITANTS OF NEW LANARK

Every society which exists at present, as well as every society which history records, has been formed and governed on a belief in the following notions, assumed as *first principles:*

First,—That it is in the power of every individual to form his own character.

Hence the various systems called by the name of religion, codes of law, and punishments. Hence also the angry passions entertained by individuals and nations towards each other.

Second,—That the affections are at the command of the individual.

Hence insincerity and degradation of character. Hence the miseries of domestic life, and more than one-half of all the crimes of mankind.

Third,—That it is necessary that a large portion of mankind should exist in ignorance and poverty, in order to secure to the remaining part such a degree of happiness as they now enjoy.

Hence a system of counteraction in the pursuits of men, a general opposition among individuals to the interests of each other, and the necessary effects of such a system,—ignorance, poverty, and vice.

Facts prove, however—

First,—That character is universally formed *for*, and not *by*, the individual.

Second,—That *any* habits and sentiments may be given to mankind.

Third,—That the affections are *not* under the control of the individual.

Fourth,—That every individual may be trained to produce far more than he can consume, while there is a sufficiency of soil left for him to cultivate.

Fifth,—That nature has provided means by which population may be at all times maintained in the proper state to give the greatest happiness to every individual, without one check of vice or misery.

Sixth,—That any community may be arranged, on a due combination of the foregoing principles, in such a manner, as not only to withdraw vice, poverty, and, in a great degree, misery, from the world, but also to place *every* individual under circumstances in which he shall enjoy more permanent happiness than can be given to *any* individual under the principles which have hitherto regulated society.

Seventh,—That all the assumed fundamental principles on which society has hitherto been founded are erroneous, and may be demonstrated to be contrary to fact. And—

Eighth,—That the change which would follow the abandonment of those erroneous maxims which bring misery into the world, and the adoption of principles of truth, unfolding a system which shall remove and for ever exclude that misery, may be effected without the slightest injury to any human being.

Here is the groundwork,—these are the data, on which society shall ere long be re-arranged; and for this simple reason, that it will be rendered evident that it will be for the immediate and future interest of every one to lend his most active assistance gradually to reform society on this basis. I say *gradually*, for in that word the most important considerations are involved. Any sudden and coercive attempt which may be made to remove even misery from men will prove injurious rather than beneficial. Their minds must be gradually prepared by an essential alteration of the circumstances which surround them, for any great and important change and amelioration in their condition. They must be first convinced of their blindness: this cannot be effected, even among the least unreasonable, or those termed the best part of mankind, in their present state, without creating some degree of irritation. This irritation must then be tranquillized before another step ought to be attempted; and a general conviction must be established of the truth of the principles on which the projected change is to be founded. Their introduction into practice will then become easy,—difficulties will vanish as we approach them,—and, afterwards, the desire to see the whole system carried immediately into effect will exceed the means of putting it into execution.

The principles on which this practical system is founded are not new; separately, or partially united, they have been often recommended by the sages of antiquity, and by modern writers. But it is not known to me that they have ever been thus combined. Yet it can be demonstrated that it is only by their being *all brought into practice together* that they are to be rendered beneficial to mankind; and sure I am that this is the earliest period in the history of man when they could be successfully introduced into practice.

I do not intend to hide from you that the change will be great. "Old things shall pass away, and all shall become new."

But this change will bear no resemblance to any of the revolutions which have hitherto occurred. These have been alone calculated to generate and call forth all the evil passions of hatred and revenge: but that system which is now contemplated will effectually eradicate every feeling of irritation and ill will which exists among mankind. The whole proceedings of those who govern and instruct the world will be reversed. Instead of spending ages in telling mankind what they ought to think and how they ought to act, the instructors and governors of the world will acquire a knowledge that will enable them, in one generation, to apply the means which shall cheerfully induce each of those whom they control and influence, not only to think, but to act in such a manner as shall be best for himself and best for every human being. And yet this extraordinary result will take place without punishment or apparent force.

Under this system, before commands are issued it shall be known whether they can or cannot be obeyed. Men shall not be called upon to assent to doctrines and to dogmas which do not carry conviction to their minds. They shall not be taught that merit can exist in doing, or that demerit can arise from not doing that over which they have no control. They shall not be told, as at present, that they must love that which, by the constitution of their nature, they are compelled to dislike. They shall not be trained in wild imaginary notions, that inevitably make them despise and hate all mankind out of the little narrow circle in which they exist, and then be told that they must heartily and sincerely love all their fellow-men. No, my friends, that system which shall make its way into the heart of every man, is founded upon principles which have not the slightest resemblance to any of those I have alluded to. On the contrary, it is directly opposed to them; and the effects it will produce in practice will differ as much from the practice which history records, and from that which we see around us, as hypocrisy, hatred, envy, revenge, wars, poverty, injustice, oppression, and all their consequent misery, differ from that genuine charity and sincere kindness of which we perpetually hear, but which we have never seen, and which, under the existing systems, we never can see.

That charity and that kindness admit of no exception. They extend to every child of man, however he may have been taught, however he may have been trained. They consider not what country gave him birth, what may be his complexion, what his habits or his sentiments. Genuine charity and true kindness instruct, that whatever these may be, should they prove the very reverse of what we have been taught to think right and best, our conduct towards him, our sentiments with respect to him, should undergo no change; for, when we shall see things as they really are, we shall know that this our fellow-man has undergone the same kind of process and training from infancy which we have experienced; that he has been as effectually taught to deem his sentiments and actions right, as we have been to imagine ours right and his wrong; when perhaps the only difference is, that we were born in one country, and he in another. If this be not true, then indeed are all our prospects hopeless; then fierce contentions, poverty, and vice, must continue for ever. Fortunately, however, there is now a superabundance of facts to remove all doubt from every mind; and the principles may now be fully developed, which will easily explain the source of all the opinions which now perplex and divide the world; and their source being discovered, mankind may withdraw all those which are false and injurious, and prevent any evil from arising in consequence of the varieties of sentiments, or rather of feelings, which may afterwards remain.

In short, my friends, the New System is founded on principles which will enable mankind to *prevent,* in the rising generation, almost all, if not all of the evils and miseries which we and our forefathers have experienced. A correct knowledge of human nature will be acquired; ignorance will be removed; the angry passions will be prevented from gaining any strength; charity and kindness will universally prevail; poverty will not be known; the interest of each individual will be in strict unison with the interest of every individual in the world. There will not be any counteraction of wishes and desires among men. Temperance and simplicity of manners will be the characteristics of every part of society. The natural defects of the few will be amply compensated by the increased attention and kindness towards them of the many. None will have cause to complain; for each will possess, without injury to another, all that can tend to his comfort, his well-being, and his happiness.... Such will be the certain consequences of the introduction into practice of that system for which I have been silently preparing the way for upwards of five-and-twenty years.

35

The Communist Manifesto

KARL MARX AND FRIEDRICH ENGELS

Originally written at the request of a small group of radicals known as the Communist League, the *Manifesto of the Communist Party* (1848) has become the most famous, and perhaps the most influential, statement of Karl Marx's views. In other writings Marx (1818–1883) delves more deeply into philosophical, economic, and social issues, but none of these is as comprehensive or clear as the *Manifesto*. The clarity may be due largely to Friedrich Engels (1820–1895), Marx's longtime friend and collaborator, but the ideas were chiefly Marx's—as Engels himself acknowledged. Beginning with the statement "The history of all hitherto existing society is the history of class struggles," the *Manifesto* sets out Marx's materialist conception of history in bold terms, then draws on this analysis of history and economics to offer a program for radical change. If some of Marx's and Engels's proposals no longer seem radical—a "heavy progressive or graduated income tax," for example, or "free education for all children in public schools"—this is a sign of the changes since 1848. But even by today's standards, some of their proposals—for example, "abolition of property in land" and "equal liability of all to labour"—may seem very radical indeed.

Source: The following is an abridged version of the English edition of 1888, translated by Samuel Moore.

MANIFESTO OF THE COMMUNIST PARTY

A spectre is haunting Europe—the spectre of Communism. All the powers of old Europe have entered into a holy alliance to exorcise this spectre: Pope and Czar, Metternich and Guizot, French Radicals and German police-spies.[1]

Where is the party in opposition that has not been decried as Communistic by its opponents in power? Where the Opposition that has not hurled back the branding reproach of Communism, against the more advanced opposition parties, as well as against its reactionary adversaries?

Two things result from this fact.

1. Communism is already acknowledged by all European Powers to be itself a Power.
2. It is high time that Communists should openly, in the face of the whole world, publish their views, their aims, their tendencies, and meet this nursery tale of the Spectre of Communism with a Manifesto of the party itself.

To this end, Communists of various nationalities have assembled in London, and sketched the following Manifesto, to be published in the English, French, German, Italian, Flemish and Danish languages.

I Bourgeois and Proletarians

The history of all hitherto existing society is the history of class struggles.

Freeman and slave, patrician and plebeian, lord and serf, guild-master and journeyman, in a word, oppressor and oppressed, stood in constant opposition to one another, carried on an uninterrupted, now hidden, now open fight, a fight that each time ended, either in a revolutionary re-constitution of society at large, or in the common ruin of the contending classes.

In the earlier epochs of history, we find almost everywhere a complicated arrangement of society into various orders, a manifold gradation of social rank. In ancient Rome we have patricians, knights, plebeians, slaves; in the Middle Ages, feudal lords, vassals, guild-masters, journeymen, apprentices, serfs; in almost all of these classes, again, subordinate gradations.

The modern bourgeois society that has sprouted from the ruins of feudal society has not done away with class antagonisms. It has but established new classes, new conditions of oppression, new forms of struggle in place of the old ones.

Our epoch, the epoch of the bourgeoisie, possesses, however, this distinctive feature: it has simplified the class antagonisms: Society as a whole is more and more splitting up into two great hostile camps, into two great classes directly facing each other: Bourgeoisie and Proletariat.

From the serfs of the Middle Ages sprang the chartered burghers of the earliest towns. From these burgesses the first elements of the bourgeoisie were developed.

The discovery of America, the rounding of the Cape, opened up fresh ground for the rising bourgeoisie. The East-Indian and Chinese markets, the colonisation of America, trade with the colonies, the increase in the means of exchange and in commodities generally, gave to commerce, to navigation, to industry, an impulse never before known, and thereby, to the revolutionary element in the tottering feudal society, a rapid development.

The feudal system of industry, under which industrial production was monopolised by closed guilds, now no longer sufficed for the growing wants of the new markets. The manufacturing system took its place. The guild-masters were pushed on one side by the manufacturing middle class; division of labour between the different corporate guilds vanished in the face of division of labour in each single workshop.

Meantime the markets kept ever growing, the demand ever rising. Even manufacture no longer sufficed. Thereupon, steam and machinery revolutionised industrial production. The place of manufacture was taken by the giant, Modern Industry, the place of the industrial middle class, by industrial millionaires, the leaders of whole industrial armies, the modern bourgeois.

Modern industry has established the world market, for which the discovery of America paved the way. This market has given an immense development to commerce, to navigation, to communication by land. This development has, in its turn, reacted on the extension of industry; and in proportion as industry, commerce, navigation, railways extended, in the same proportion the bourgeoisie developed, increased its capital, and pushed into the background every class handed down from the Middle Ages.

We see, therefore, how the modern bourgeoisie is itself the product of a long course of development, of a series of revolutions in the modes of production and of exchange.

Each step in the development of the bourgeoisie was accompanied by a corresponding political advance of that class. An oppressed class under the sway of the feudal nobility, an armed and self-governing association in the mediaeval commune; here independent urban republic (as in Italy and Germany), there taxable "third estate" of the monarchy (as in France), afterwards, in the period of manufacture proper, serving either the semi-feudal or the absolute monarchy as a counterpoise against the nobility, and, in fact, cornerstone of the great monarchies in general, the bourgeoisie has at last, since the establishment of Modern Industry and of the world-market, conquered for itself, in the modern representative State, exclusive political sway. The executive of the modern State is but a committee for managing the common affairs of the whole bourgeoisie.

The bourgeoisie, historically, has played a most revolutionary part.

The bourgeoisie, wherever it has got the upper hand, has put an end to all feudal, patriarchal, idyllic relations. It has pitilessly torn asunder the motley feudal ties that bound man to his "natural superiors," and has left remaining no other nexus between man and man than naked self-interest, than callous "cash payment." It has drowned the most heavenly ecstasies of religious fervour, of chivalrous enthusiasm, of philistine sentimentalism, in the icy water of egotistical calculation. It has resolved personal worth into exchange value, and in place of the numberless indefeasible chartered freedoms, has set up that single, unconscionable freedom—Free Trade. In one word, for exploitation, veiled by religious and political illusions, it has substituted naked, shameless, direct, brutal exploitation.

The bourgeoisie has stripped of its halo every occupation hitherto honoured and looked up to with reverent awe. It has converted the physician, the lawyer, the priest, the poet, the man of science, into its paid wage-labourers.

The bourgeoisie has torn away from the family its sentimental veil, and has reduced the family relation to a mere money relation.

The bourgeoisie has disclosed how it came to pass that the brutal display of vigour in the Middle Ages, which Reactionists so much admire, found its fitting complement in the most slothful indolence. It has been the first to show what man's activity can bring about. It has accomplished wonders far surpassing Egyptian pyramids, Roman aqueducts, and Gothic cathedrals; it has conducted expeditions that put in the shade all former Exoduses of nations and crusades.

The bourgeoisie cannot exist without constantly revolutionising the instruments of production, and thereby the relations of production, and with them the whole relations of society. Conservation of the old modes of production in unaltered form was, on the contrary, the first condition of existence for all earlier industrial classes. Constant revolutionising of production, uninterrupted disturbance of all social conditions, everlasting uncertainty and agitation distinguish the bourgeois epoch from all earlier ones. All fixed, fast-frozen relations, with their train of ancient and venerable prejudices and opinions, are swept away, all new-formed ones become antiquated before they can ossify. All that is solid melts into air, all that is holy is profaned, and man is at last compelled to face with sober senses, his real conditions of life, and his relations with his kind.

The need of a constantly expanding market for its products chases the bourgeoisie over the whole surface of the globe. It must nestle everywhere, settle everywhere, establish connexions everywhere.

The bourgeoisie has through its exploitation of the world-market given a cosmopolitan character to production and consumption in every country. To the great chagrin of Reactionists [i.e., reactionaries], it has drawn from under the feet of industry the national ground on which it stood. All old-established national industries have been destroyed or are daily being destroyed. They are dislodged by new industries, whose introduction becomes a life and death question for all civilised nations, by industries that no longer work up indigenous raw material, but raw material drawn from the remotest zones; industries whose products are consumed, not only at home, but in every quarter of the globe. In place of the old wants, satisfied by the productions of the country, we find new wants, requiring for their satisfaction the products of distant lands and climes. In place of the old local and national seclusion and self-sufficiency, we have intercourse in every direction, universal interdependence of nations. And as in material, so also in intellectual production. The intellectual creations of individual nations become common property. National one-sidedness and narrow-mindedness become more and more impossible, and from the numerous national and local literatures, there arises a world literature.

The bourgeoisie, by the rapid improvement of all instruments of production, by the immensely facilitated means of communication, draws all, even the most barbarian, nations into civilisation. The cheap prices of its commodities are the heavy artillery with which it batters down all Chinese walls, with which it forces the barbarians' intensely obstinate hatred of foreigners to capitulate. It compels all nations, on pain of extinction, to adopt the bourgeois mode of production; it compels them to introduce what it calls civilisation into their midst, *i.e.*, to become bourgeois themselves. In one word, it creates a world after its own image.

The bourgeoisie has subjected the country to the rule of the towns. It has created enormous cities, has greatly increased the urban population as compared with the rural, and has thus rescued a considerable part of the population from the idiocy of rural life. Just as it has made the country dependent on the towns, so it has made barbarian and semi-barbarian countries dependent on the civilised ones, nations of peasants on nations of bourgeois, the East on the West.

The bourgeoisie keeps more and more doing away with the scattered state of the population, of the means of production, and of property. It has agglomerated population, centralised means of production, and has concentrated property in a few hands. The necessary consequence of this was political centralisation. Independent, or but loosely connected provinces, with separate interests, laws, governments and systems of taxation, became lumped together into one nation, with one government, one code of laws, one national class-interest, one frontier and one customs-tariff.

The bourgeoisie, during its rule of scarce one hundred years, has created more massive and more colossal productive forces than have all preceding generations together. Subjection of Nature's forces to man, machinery, application of chemistry to industry and agriculture, steam-navigation, railways, electric telegraphs, clearing of whole continents for cultivation, canalisation of rivers, whole populations conjured out of the ground—what earlier century had even a presentiment that such productive forces slumbered in the lap of social labour?

We see then: the means of production and of exchange, on whose foundation the bourgeoisie built itself up, were generated in feudal society. At a certain stage in the development of these means of production and of exchange, the conditions under which feudal society produced and exchanged, the feudal organisation of agriculture and manufacturing industry, in one word, the feudal relations of property became no longer compatible with the already developed productive forces; they became so many fetters. They had to be burst asunder; they were burst asunder.

Into their place stepped free competition, accompanied by a social and political constitution adapted to it, and by the economical and political sway of the bourgeois class.

A similar movement is going on before our own eyes. Modern bourgeois society with its relations of production, of exchange and of property, a society that has conjured up such gigantic means of production and of exchange, is like the sorcerer, who is no longer able to control the powers of the nether world whom he has called up by his spells. For many a decade past the history of industry and commerce is but the history of the revolt of modern productive forces against modern conditions of production, against the property relations that are the conditions for the existence of the bourgeoisie and of its rule. It is enough to mention the commercial crises that by their periodical return put on its trial, each time more threateningly, the existence of the entire bourgeois society. In these crises a great part not only of the existing products, but also of the previously created productive forces, are periodically destroyed. In these crises there breaks out an epidemic that, in all earlier epochs, would have seemed an absurdity—the epidemic of over-production. Society suddenly finds itself put back into a state of momentary barbarism; it appears as if a famine, a universal war of devastation had cut off the supply of every means of subsistence; industry and commerce seem to be destroyed; and why? Because there is too much civilisation, too much means of subsistence, too much industry, too much commerce. The productive forces at the disposal of society no longer tend to further the development of the conditions of bourgeois property; on the contrary, they have become too powerful for these conditions, by which they are fettered, and so soon as they overcome these fetters, they bring disorder into the whole of bourgeois society, endanger the existence of bourgeois property. The conditions of bourgeois society are too narrow to comprise the wealth created by them. And how does the bourgeoisie get over these crises? On the one hand by enforced destruction of a mass of productive forces; on the other, by the conquest of new markets, and by the more thorough exploitation of the old ones. That is to say, by paving the way for more extensive and more destructive crises, and by diminishing the means whereby crises are prevented.

The weapons with which the bourgeoisie felled feudalism to the ground are now turned against the bourgeoisie itself.

But not only has the bourgeoisie forged the weapons that bring death to itself; it has also called into existence the men who are to wield those weapons—the modern working class—the proletarians.

In proportion as the bourgeoisie, *i.e.*, capital, is developed, in the same proportion is the proletariat, the modern working class, developed—a class of labourers, who live only so long as they find work, and who find work only so long as their labour increases capital. These labourers, who must sell themselves piecemeal, are a commodity, like every other article of commerce, and are consequently exposed to all the vicissitudes of competition, to all the fluctuations of the market.

Owing to the extensive use of machinery and to division of labour, the work of the proletarians has lost all individual character, and consequently, all charm for the workman. He becomes an appendage of the machine, and it is only the most simple, most monotonous, and most easily acquired knack, that is required of him. Hence, the cost of production of a workman is restricted, almost entirely, to the means of subsistence that he requires for his maintenance, and for the propagation of his race. But the price of a commodity, and therefore also of labour, is equal to its cost of production. In proportion, therefore, as the repulsiveness of the work increases, the wage decreases. Nay more, in proportion as the use of machinery and division of labour increases, in the same proportion the burden of toil also increases, whether by prolongation of the working hours, by increase of the work exacted in a given time or by increased speed of the machinery, etc.

Modern industry has converted the little workshop of the patriarchal master into the great factory of the industrial capitalist. Masses of labourers, crowded into the factory, are organized like soldiers. As privates of the industrial army they are placed under the command of a perfect hierarchy of officers and sergeants. Not only are they slaves of the bourgeois class, and of the bourgeois State; they are daily and hourly enslaved by the machine, by the overlooker, and, above all, by the individual bourgeois manufacturer himself. The more openly this despotism proclaims gain to be its end and aim, the more petty, the more hateful and the more embittering it is.

The less the skill and exertion of strength implied in manual labour, in other words, the more modern industry becomes developed, the more is the labour of men superseded by that of women. Differences of age and sex have no longer any distinctive social validity for the working class. All are instruments of labour, more or less expensive to use, according to their age and sex.

No sooner is the exploitation of the labourer by the manufacturer, so far, at an end, that he receives his wages in cash, than he is set upon by the other portions of the bourgeoisie, the landlord, the shopkeeper, the pawnbroker, etc.

The lower strata of the middle class—the small tradespeople, shopkeepers, and retired tradesmen generally, the handicraftsmen and peasants—all these sink gradually into the proletariat, partly because their diminutive capital does not suffice for the scale on which Modern Industry is carried on, and is swamped in the competition with the large capitalists, partly because their specialised skill is rendered worthless by new methods of production. Thus the proletariat is recruited from all classes of the population.

The proletariat goes through various stages of development. With its birth begins its struggle with the bourgeoisie. At first the contest is carried on by individual labourers, then by the workpeople of a factory, then by the operatives of one trade, in one locality, against the individual bourgeois who directly exploits them. They direct their attacks not against the bourgeois conditions of production, but against the instruments of production themselves; they destroy imported wares that compete with their labour, they smash to pieces machinery, they set factories ablaze, they seek to restore by force the vanished status of the workman of the Middle Ages.

At this stage the labourers still form an incoherent mass scattered over the whole country, and broken up by their mutual competition. If anywhere they unite to form more compact bodies, this is not yet the consequence of their own active union, but of the union of the bourgeoisie, which class, in order to attain its own political ends, is compelled to set the whole proletariat in motion, and is moreover yet, for a time, able to do so. At this stage, therefore, the proletarians do not fight their enemies, but the enemies of their enemies, the remnants of absolute monarchy, the landowners, the nonindustrial bourgeois, the petty bourgeoisie. Thus the whole historical movement is concentrated in the hands of the bourgeoisie; every victory so obtained is a victory for the bourgeoisie.

But with the development of industry the proletariat not only increases in number; it becomes concentrated in greater masses, its strength grows, and it feels that strength more. The various interests and conditions of life within the ranks of the proletariat are more and more equalised, in proportion as machinery obliterates all distinctions of labour, and nearly everywhere reduces wages to the same low level. The growing competition among the bourgeois, and the resulting commercial crises, make the wages of the workers ever more fluctuating. The unceasing improvement of machinery, ever more rapidly developing, makes their livelihood more and more precarious; the collisions between individual workmen and individual bourgeois take more and more the character of collisions between two classes. Thereupon the workers begin to form combinations (Trade Unions) against the bourgeois; they club together in order to keep up the rate of wages; they found permanent associations in order to make provision beforehand for these occasional revolts. Here and there the contest breaks out into riots.

Now and then the workers are victorious, but only for a time. The real fruit of their battles lies, not in the immediate result, but in the ever-expanding union of the workers. This union is helped on by the improved means of communication that are created by modern industry and that place the workers of different localities in contact with one another. It was just this contact that was needed to centralise the numerous local struggles, all of the same character, into one national struggle between classes. But every class struggle is a political struggle. And that union, to attain which the burghers of the Middle Ages, with their miserable highways, required centuries, the modern proletarians, thanks to railways, achieve in a few years.

This organisation of the proletarians into a class, and consequently into a political party, is continually being upset again by the competition between the workers themselves. But it ever rises up again, stronger, firmer, mightier. It compels legislative recognition of particular interests of the workers, by taking advantage of the divisions among the bourgeoisie itself. Thus the ten-hours' bill [to limit working hours] in England was carried.

Altogether collisions between the classes of the old society further, in many ways, the course of development of the proletariat. The bourgeoisie finds itself involved in a constant battle. At first with the aristocracy; later on, with those portions of the bourgeoisie itself, whose interests have become antagonistic to the progress of industry; at all times, with the bourgeoisie of foreign countries. In all these battles it sees itself compelled to appeal to the proletariat, to ask for its help, and thus, to drag it into the political arena. The bourgeoisie itself, therefore, supplies the proletariat with its own elements of political and general education, in other words, it furnishes the proletariat with weapons for fighting the bourgeoisie.

Further, as we have already seen, entire sections of the ruling classes are, by the advance of industry, precipitated into the proletariat, or are at least threatened in their conditions of existence. These also supply the proletariat with fresh elements of enlightenment and progress.

Finally, in times when the class struggle nears the decisive hour, the process of dissolution going on within the ruling class, in fact within the whole range of society, assumes such a violent, glaring character, that a small section of the ruling class cuts itself adrift, and joins the revolutionary class, the class that holds the future in its hands. Just as, therefore, at an earlier period, a section of the nobility went over to the bourgeoisie, so now a portion of the bourgeoisie goes over to the proletariat, and in particular, a portion of the bourgeois ideologists, who have raised themselves to the level of comprehending theoretically the historical movement as a whole.

Of all the classes that stand face to face with the bourgeoisie today, the proletariat alone is a really revolutionary class. The other classes decay and finally disappear in the face of Modern Industry; the proletariat is its special and essential product.

The lower middle class, the small manufacturer, the shopkeeper, the artisan, the peasant, all these fight against the bourgeoisie, to save from extinction their existence as fractions of the middle class. They are therefore not revolutionary, but conservative. Nay more, they are reactionary, for they try to roll back the wheel of history. If by chance they are revolutionary, they are so only in view of their impending transfer into the proletariat, they thus defend not their present, but their future interests, they desert their own standpoint to place themselves at that of the proletariat.

The "dangerous class," the social scum, that passively rotting mass thrown off by the lowest layers of old society, may, here and there, be swept into the movement by a proletarian revolution; its conditions of life, however, prepare it far more for the part of a bribed tool of reactionary intrigue.

In the conditions of the proletariat, those of old society at large are already virtually swamped. The proletarian is without property; his relation to his wife and children has no longer anything in common with the bourgeois family-relations; modern industrial labour, modern subjection to capital, the same in England as in France, in America as in Germany, has stripped him of every trace of national character. Law, morality, religion, are to him so many bourgeois prejudices, behind which lurk in ambush just as many bourgeois interests.

All the preceding classes that got the upper hand, sought to fortify their already acquired status by subjecting society at large to their conditions of appropriation. The proletarians cannot become masters of the productive forces of society, except by abolishing their own previous mode of appropriation, and thereby also every other previous mode of appropriation. They have nothing of their own to secure and to fortify; their mission is to destroy all previous securities for, and insurances of, individual property.

All previous historical movements were movements of minorities, or in the interests of minorities. The proletarian movement is the self-conscious, independent movement of the immense majority, in the interests of the immense majority. The proletariat, the lowest stratum of our present society, cannot stir, cannot raise itself up, without the whole superincumbent strata of official society being sprung into the air.

Though not in substance, yet in form, the struggle of the proletariat with the bourgeoisie is at first a national struggle. The proletariat of each country must, of course, first of all settle matters with its own bourgeoisie.

In depicting the most general phases of the development of the proletariat, we traced the more or less veiled civil war, raging within existing society, up to the point where that war breaks out into open revolution, and where the violent overthrow of the bourgeoisie lays the foundation for the sway of the proletariat.

Hitherto, every form of society has been based, as we have already seen, on the antagonism of oppressing and oppressed classes. But in order to oppress a class, certain conditions must be assured to it under which it can, at least, continue its slavish existence. The serf, in the period of serfdom, raised himself to membership in the commune, just as the petty bourgeois, under the yoke of feudal absolutism, managed to develop into a bourgeois. The modern labourer, on the contrary, instead of rising with the progress of industry, sinks deeper and deeper below the conditions of existence of his own class. He becomes a pauper, and pauperism develops more rapidly than population and wealth. And here it becomes evident, that the bourgeoisie is unfit any longer to be the ruling class in society, and to impose its conditions of existence upon society as an over-riding law. It is unfit to rule because it is incompetent to assure an existence to its slave within his slavery, because it cannot help letting him sink into such a state, that it has to feed him, instead of being fed by him. Society can no longer live under this bourgeoisie, in other words, its existence is no longer compatible with society.

The essential condition for the existence, and for the sway of the bourgeois class, is the formation and augmentation of capital; the condition for capital is wage-labour. Wage-labour rests exclusively on competition between the labourers. The advance of industry, whose involuntary promoter is the bourgeoisie, replaces the isolation of the labourers, due to competition, by their revolutionary combination, due to association. The development of Modern Industry, therefore, cuts from under its feet the very foundation on which the bourgeoisie produces and appropriates products. What the bourgeoisie, therefore, produces, above all, is its own grave-diggers. Its fall and the victory of the proletariat are equally inevitable.

II Proletarians and Communists

In what relation do the Communists stand to the proletarians as a whole?

The Communists do not form a separate party opposed to other working-class parties.

They have no interests separate and apart from those of the proletariat as a whole.

They do not set up any sectarian principles of their own, by which to shape and mould the proletarian movement.

The Communists are distinguished from the other working-class parties by this only: (1) In the national struggles of the proletarians of the different countries, they point out and bring to the front the common interests of the entire proletariat, independently of all nationality. (2) In the various stages of development which the struggle of the working class against the bourgeoisie has to pass through, they always and everywhere represent the interests of the movement as a whole.

The Communists, therefore, are on the one hand, practically, the most advanced and resolute section of the working-class parties of every country, that section which pushes forward all others; on the other hand, theoretically, they have over the great mass of the proletariat the advantage of clearly understanding the line of march, the conditions, and the ultimate general results of the proletarian movement.

The immediate aim of the Communists is the same as that of all the other proletarian parties: formation of the proletariat into a class, overthrow of the bourgeois supremacy, conquest of political power by the proletariat.

The theoretical conclusions of the Communists are in no way based on ideas or principles that have been invented, or discovered, by this or that would-be universal reformer.

They merely express, in general terms, actual relations springing from an existing class struggle, from a historical movement going on under our very eyes. The abolition of existing property relations is not at all a distinctive feature of Communism.

All property relations in the past have continually been subject to historical change consequent upon the change in historical conditions.

The French Revolution, for example, abolished feudal property in favour of bourgeois property.

The distinguishing feature of Communism is not the abolition of property generally, but the abolition of bourgeois property. But modern bourgeois private property is the final and most complete expression of the system of producing and appropriating products, that is based on class antagonisms, on the exploitation of the many by the few.

In this sense, the theory of the Communists may be summed up in the single sentence: Abolition of private property.

We Communists have been reproached with the desire of abolishing the right of personally acquiring property as the fruit of a man's own labour, which property is alleged to be the groundwork of all personal freedom, activity and independence.

Hard-won, self-acquired, self-earned property! Do you mean the property of the petty artisan and of the small peasant, a form of property that preceded the bourgeois form? There is no need to abolish that; the development of industry has to a great extent already destroyed it, and is still destroying it daily.

Or do you mean modern bourgeois private property?

But does wage-labour create any property for the labourer? Not a bit. It creates capital, *i.e.*, that kind of property which exploits wage-labour, and which cannot increase except upon condition of begetting a new supply of wage-labour for fresh exploitation. Property, in its present form, is based on the antagonism of capital and wage-labour. Let us examine both sides of this antagonism.

To be a capitalist, is to have not only a purely personal, but a social *status* in production. Capital is a collective product, and only by the united action of many members, nay, in the last resort, only by the united action of all members of society, can it be set in motion.

Capital is, therefore, not a personal, it is a social power.

When, therefore, capital is converted into common property, into the property of all members of society, personal property is not thereby transformed into social property. It is only the social character of the property that is changed. It loses its class-character. Let us now take wage-labour.

The average price of wage-labour is the minimum wage, *i.e.*, that quantum of the means of subsistence, which is absolutely requisite to keep the labourer in bare existence as a labourer. What, therefore, the wage-labourer appropriates by means of his labour, merely suffices to prolong and reproduce a bare existence. We by no means intend to abolish this personal appropriation of the products of labour, an appropriation that is made for the maintenance and reproduction of human life, and that leaves no surplus wherewith to command the labour of others. All that we want to do away with, is the miserable character of this appropriation, under which the labourer lives merely to increase capital, and is allowed to live only in so far as the interest of the ruling class requires it.

In bourgeois society, living labour is but a means to increase accumulated labour. In Communist society, accumulated labour is but a means to widen, to enrich, to promote the existence of the labourer. In bourgeois society, therefore, the past dominates the present; in Communist society, the present dominates the past. In bourgeois society capital is independent and has individuality, while the living person is dependent and has no individuality.

And the abolition of this state of things is called by the bourgeois, abolition of individuality and freedom! And rightly so. The abolition of bourgeois individuality, bourgeois independence, and bourgeois freedom is undoubtedly aimed at.

By freedom is meant, under the present bourgeois conditions of production, free trade, free selling and buying.

But if selling and buying disappears, free selling and buying disappears also. This talk about free selling and buying, and all the other "brave words" of our bourgeoisie about freedom in general, have a meaning, if any, only in contrast with restricted selling and buying, with the fettered traders of the Middle Ages, but have no meaning when opposed to the Communistic abolition of buying and selling, of the bourgeois conditions of production, and of the bourgeoisie itself.

You are horrified at our intending to do away with private property. But in your existing society, private property is already done away with for nine-tenths of the population; its existence for the few is solely due to its non-existence in the hands of those nine-tenths. You reproach us, therefore, with intending to do away with a form of property, the necessary condition for whose existence is the non-existence of any property for the immense majority of society.

In one word, you reproach us with intending to do away with your property. Precisely so; that is just what we intend.

From the moment when labour can no longer be converted into capital, money, or rent, into a social power capable of being monopolised, *i.e.*, from the moment when individual property can no longer be transformed into bourgeois property, into capital, from that moment, you say, individuality vanishes.

You must, therefore, confess that by "individual" you mean no other person than the bourgeois, than the middle-class owner of property. This person must, indeed, be swept out of the way, and made impossible.

Communism deprives no man of the power to appropriate the products of society; all that it does is to deprive him of the power to subjugate the labour of others by means of such appropriation.

It has been objected that upon the abolition of private property all work will cease, and universal laziness will overtake us.

According to this, bourgeois society ought long ago to have gone to the dogs through sheer idleness; for those of its members who work, acquire nothing, and those who acquire anything, do not work. The whole of this objection is but another expression of the tautology: that there can no longer be any wage-labour when there is no longer any capital.

All objections urged against the Communistic mode of producing and appropriating material products, have, in the same way, been urged against the Communistic modes of producing and appropriating intellectual products. Just as, to the bourgeois, the disappearance of class property is the disappearance of production itself, so the disappearance of class culture is to him identical with the disappearance of all culture.

That culture, the loss of which he laments, is, for the enormous majority, a mere training to act as a machine.

But don't wrangle with us so long as you apply, to our intended abolition of bourgeois property, the standard of your bourgeois notions of freedom, culture, law, etc. Your very ideas are but the out-growth of the conditions of your bourgeois production and bourgeois property, just as your jurisprudence is but the will of your class made into a law for all, a will, whose essential character and direction are determined by the economical conditions of existence of your class.

The selfish misconception that induces you to transform into eternal laws of nature and of reason, the social forms springing from your present mode of production and form of property—historical relations that rise and disappear in the progress of production—this misconception you share with every ruling class that has preceded you. What you see clearly in the case of ancient property, what you admit in the case of feudal property, you are of course forbidden to admit in the case of your own bourgeois form of property.

Abolition of the family! Even the most radical flare up at this infamous proposal of the Communists.

On what foundation is the present family, the bourgeois family, based? On capital, on private gain. In its completely developed form this family exists only among the bourgeoisie. But this state of things finds its complement in the practical absence of the family among the proletarians, and in public prostitution.

The bourgeois family will vanish as a matter of course when its complement vanishes, and both will vanish with the vanishing of capital.

Do you charge us with wanting to stop the exploitation of children by their parents? To this crime we plead guilty.

But, you will say, we destroy the most hallowed of relations, when we replace home education by social.

And your education! Is not that also social, and determined by the social conditions under which you educate, by the intervention, direct or indirect, of society, by means of schools, etc.? The Communists have not invented the intervention of society in education; they do but seek to alter the character of that intervention, and to rescue education from the influence of the ruling class.

The bourgeois clap-trap about the family and education, about the hallowed co-relation of parent and child, becomes all the more disgusting, the more, by the action of Modern Industry, all family ties among the proletarians are torn asunder, and their children transformed into simple articles of commerce and instruments of labour.

But you Communists would introduce community of women, screams the whole bourgeoisie in chorus.

The bourgeois sees in his wife a mere instrument of production. He hears that the instruments of production are to be exploited in common, and, naturally, can come to no other conclusion than that the lot of being common to all will likewise fall to the women.

He has not even a suspicion that the real point aimed at is to do away with the status of women as mere instruments of production.

For the rest, nothing is more ridiculous than the virtuous indignation of our bourgeois at the community of women which, they pretend, is to be openly and officially established by the Communists. The Communists have no need to introduce community of women; it has existed almost from time immemorial.

Our bourgeois, not content with having the wives and daughters of their proletarians at their disposal, not to speak of common prostitutes, take the greatest pleasure in seducing each other's wives.

Bourgeois marriage is in reality a system of wives in common and thus, at the most, what the Communists might possibly be reproached with, is that they desire to introduce, in substitution for a hypocritically concealed, an openly legalised community of women. For the rest, it is self-evident that the abolition of the present system of production must bring with it the abolition of the community of women springing from that system, *i.e.*, of prostitution both public and private.

The Communists are further reproached with desiring to abolish countries and nationality.

The working men have no country. We cannot take from them what they have not got. Since the proletariat must first of all acquire political supremacy, must rise to be the leading class of the nation, must constitute itself *the* nation, it is, so far, itself national, though not in the bourgeois sense of the word.

National differences and antagonisms between peoples are daily more and more vanishing, owing to the development of the bourgeoisie, to freedom of commerce, to the world-market, to uniformity in the mode of production and in the conditions of life corresponding thereto.

The supremacy of the proletariat will cause them to vanish still faster. United action, of the leading civilised countries at least, is one of the first conditions for the emancipation of the proletariat.

In proportion as the exploitation of one individual by another is put an end to, the exploitation of one nation by another will also be put an end to. In proportion as the antagonism between classes within the nation vanishes, the hostility of one nation to another will come to an end.

The charges against Communism made from a religious, a philosophical, and, generally, from an ideological standpoint, are not deserving of serious examination.

Does it require deep intuition to comprehend that man's ideas, views and conceptions, in one word, man's consciousness, changes with every change in the conditions of his material existence, in his social relations and in his social life?

What else does the history of ideas prove, than that intellectual production changes its character in proportion as material production is changed? The ruling ideas of each age have ever been the ideas of its ruling class.

When people speak of ideas that revolutionise society, they do but express the fact, that within the old society, the elements of a new one have been created, and that the dissolution of the old ideas keeps even pace with the dissolution of the old conditions of existence.

When the ancient world was in its last throes, the ancient religions were overcome by Christianity. When Christian ideas succumbed in the 18th century to rationalist ideas, feudal society fought its death battle with the then revolutionary bourgeoisie. The ideas of religious liberty and freedom of conscience merely gave expression to the sway of free competition within the domain of knowledge.

"Undoubtedly," it will be said, "religious, moral, philosophical and juridical ideas have been modified in the course of historical development. But religion, morality, philosophy, political science, and law, constantly survived this change."

"There are, besides, eternal truths, such as Freedom, Justice, etc., that are common to all states of society. But Communism abolishes eternal truths, it abolishes all religion, and all morality, instead of constituting them on a new basis; it therefore acts in contradiction to all past historical experience."

What does this accusation reduce itself to? The history of all past society has consisted in the development of class antagonisms, antagonisms that assumed different forms at different epochs.

But whatever form they may have taken, one fact is common to all past ages, *viz.*, the exploitation of one part of society by the other. No wonder, then, that the social consciousness of past ages, despite all the multiplicity and variety it displays, moves within certain common forms, or general ideas, which cannot completely vanish except with the total disappearance of class antagonisms.

The Communist revolution is the most radical rupture with traditional property relations; no wonder that its development involves the most radical rupture with traditional ideas.

But let us have done with the bourgeois objections to Communism.

We have seen above, that the first step in the revolution by the working class, is to raise the proletariat to the position of ruling class, to win the battle of democracy.

The proletariat will use its political supremacy to wrest, by degrees, all capital from the bourgeoisie, to centralise all instruments of production in the hands of the State, *i.e.*, of the proletariat organised as the ruling class; and to increase the total of productive forces as rapidly as possible.

Of course, in the beginning, this cannot be effected except by means of despotic inroads on the rights of property, and on the conditions of bourgeois production; by means of measures, therefore, which appear economically insufficient and untenable, but which, in the course of the movement, outstrip themselves, necessitate further inroads upon the old social order, and are unavoidable as a means of entirely revolutionising the mode of production.

These measures will of course be different in different countries.

Nevertheless in the most advanced countries, the following will be pretty generally applicable.

1. Abolition of property in land and application of all rents of land to public purposes.
2. A heavy progressive or graduated income tax.
3. Abolition of all right of inheritance.
4. Confiscation of the property of all emigrants and rebels.
5. Centralisation of credit in the hands of the State, by means of a national bank with State capital and an exclusive monopoly.
6. Centralisation of the means of communication and transport in the hands of the State.
7. Extension of factories and instruments of production owned by the State; the bringing into cultivation of waste-lands, and the improvement of the soil generally in accordance with a common plan.
8. Equal liability of all to labour. Establishment of industrial armies, especially for agriculture.
9. Combination of agriculture with manufacturing industries; gradual abolition of the distinction between town and country, by a more equable distribution of the population over the country.
10. Free education for all children in public schools. Abolition of children's factory labour in its present form. Combination of education with industrial production, etc., etc.

When, in the course of development, class distinctions have disappeared, and all production has been concentrated in the hands of a vast association of the whole nation, the public power will lose its political character. Political power, properly so called, is merely the organised power of one class for oppressing another. If the proletariat during its contest with the bourgeoisie is compelled, by the force of circumstances, to organise itself as a class, if, by means of a revolution, it makes itself the ruling class, and, as such, sweeps away by force the old conditions of production, then it will, along with these conditions, have swept away the conditions for the existence of class antagonisms and of classes generally, and will thereby have abolished its own supremacy as a class.

In place of the old bourgeois society, with its classes and class antagonisms, we shall have an association, in which the free development of each is the condition for the free development of all....

In short, the Communists everywhere support every revolutionary movement against the existing social and political order of things.

In all these movements they bring to the front, as the leading question in each, the property question, no matter what its degree of development at the time.

Finally, they labour everywhere for the union and agreement of the democratic parties of all countries.

The Communists disdain to conceal their views and aims. They openly declare that their ends can be attained only by the forcible overthrow of all existing social conditions. Let the ruling classes tremble at a Communistic revolution. The proletarians have nothing to lose but their chains. They have a world to win.

WORKING MEN OF ALL COUNTRIES, UNITE!

NOTE

1. Clemens von Metternich (1773–1859) was foreign minister of the Hapsburg (or Austrian) Empire; Francois P. G. Guizot (1787–1874) was a French statesman.—Eds.

36

On the Materialist Conception of History

KARL MARX

The following excerpt from Marx's Preface to his *A Contribution to the Critique of Political Economy* (1859) provides a particularly clear and succinct account of what Marx meant by "the materialist conception [or interpretation] of history," which he called "a guiding thread for my studies." Following this historical-materialist thread led Marx to conclude that capitalism is a transitory historical stage that will be superseded and replaced by a less competitive, more cooperative, and truly humane economic and social system.

Source: Karl Marx and Friedrich Engels, *Selected Works in One Volume* (New York: International Publishers, 1968), pp. 181–185. Reprinted by permission.

ON THE MATERIALIST CONCEPTION OF HISTORY

In the year 1842–43, as editor of the *Rheinische Zeitung*, I experienced for the first time the embarrassment of having to take part in discussions on so-called material interests.... [A]t that time when the good will "to go further" greatly outweighed knowledge of the subject, a philosophically weakly tinged echo of French socialism and communism made itself audible in the *Rheinische Zeitung*. I declared myself against this amateurism, but frankly confessed at the same time...that my previous studies did not permit me even to venture any judgment on the content of the French tendencies....

The first work which I undertook for a solution of the doubts which assailed me was a critical review of the Hegelian philosophy of right.... My investigation led to the result that legal relations as well as forms of state are to be grasped neither from themselves nor from the so-called general development of the human mind, but rather have their roots in the material conditions of life.... The general result at which I arrived and which, once won, served as a guiding thread for my studies, can be briefly formulated as follows: In the social production of their life, men enter into definite relations that are indispensable and independent of their will, relations of production which correspond to a definite stage of development of their material productive forces. The sum total of these relations of production constitutes the economic structure of society, the real foundation, on which rises a legal and political superstructure and to which correspond definite forms of social consciousness. The mode of production of material life conditions [i.e., shapes or influences] the social, political and intellectual life process in general. It is not the consciousness of men that determines their being, but, on the contrary, their social being that determines their consciousness. At a certain stage of their development, the material–productive forces of society come in conflict with the existing relations of production, or—what is but a legal expression for the same thing—with the property relations within which they have been at work hitherto.

From forms of development of the productive forces these relations turn into their fetters. Then begins an epoch of social revolution. With the change of the economic foundation the entire immense superstructure is more or less rapidly transformed. In considering such transformations a distinction should always be made between the material transformation of the economic conditions of production, which can be determined with the precision of natural science, and the legal, political, religious, aesthetic or philosophic—in short, ideological—forms in which men become conscious of this conflict and fight it out. Just as our opinion of an individual is not based on what he thinks of himself, so can we not judge of such a period of transformation by its own consciousness; on the contrary, this consciousness must be explained rather from the contradictions of material life, from the existing conflict between the social productive forces and the relations of production. No social order ever perishes before all the productive forces for which there is room in it have developed; and new, higher relations of production never appear before the material conditions of their existence have matured in the womb of the old society itself. Therefore mankind always sets itself only such tasks as it can solve; since, looking at the matter more closely, it will always be found that the task itself arises only when the material conditions for its solution already exist or are at least in the process of formation. In broad outlines Asiatic, ancient, feudal, and modern bourgeois modes of production can be designated as progressive epochs in the economic formation of society. The bourgeois relations of production are the last antagonistic form of the social process of production—antagonistic not in the sense of individual antagonism, but of one arising from the social conditions of life of the individuals; at the same time the productive forces developing in the womb of bourgeois society create the material conditions for the solution of that antagonism. This social formation brings, therefore, the prehistory of human society to a close.

PART SIX

Socialism and Communism After Marx

Karl Marx, the most influential of all socialist thinkers, died in 1883, but socialism as an ideology did not die with him. On the contrary, socialism in the late nineteenth and early twentieth centuries was bursting with life—and with lively quarrels about the direction that socialism ought to take. Marx's followers, as we shall see, quarreled among themselves about how best to understand and implement Marx's writings. They also quarreled with the many other socialists—anarchists, Fabians, Christian socialists, and more—who did not look to Marx's theory for inspiration and guidance. Out of these quarrels two broad tendencies emerged. On one side were those Marxists who held that only the revolutionary overthrow of capitalism could make socialism possible; on the other were those, Marxists and non-Marxists, who insisted that socialism could and should be achieved gradually by peaceful political means. The revolutionary Marxism of the first group eventually came to be known as *communism*, while the members of the second group called their position *socialism* or, occasionally, *democratic socialism*.

It was not long after Marx's death that various sects calling themselves "Marxist" sprang up in Europe and elsewhere. Each claimed to be the only "true" or "real" Marxists. Each was critical of the others, and all were adamantly opposed to non-Marxian socialists of various stripes. The one thing on which they could all agree was that capitalism was doomed.

One group of Marxists, the "revisionists," held that Marx's theory, in the best scientific spirit, must be subjected to criticism and revision in the light of new factual evidence. This was the argument advanced by Eduard Bernstein (1850–1932) in his book *Evolutionary Socialism* (1899). Contrary to Marx's prediction about the ever-increasing "immiseration of the proletariat," the working classes in Europe and North America had actually become better off: Real wages had risen, working conditions had improved, and so had the average worker's standard of living. This was not, Bernstein hastened to add, because the capitalists had become benign or kindly employers but because the working class had developed its political muscles. Laborers had organized trade unions and called strikes to raise their wages and improve their working conditions. And they had organized and supported working-class parties to elect representatives pledged to promote their interests. By these means the proletariat had forced concessions from a reluctant ruling class that was beginning to lose its legitimacy and authority. Thus Bernstein believed that violent revolution was no longer necessary (if indeed it ever had been). Capitalist society was slowly but surely "evolving" into a more egalitarian, just, and humane socialist society. Instead of focusing on a distant utopian end—the creation of a communist society—Marxists and other socialists should devote their energies to day-to-day trade union activities and parliamentary politics.

Bernstein's "revisionist" views were harshly criticized by other Marxists. Rosa Luxemburg (1871–1919), Karl Kautsky (1854–1938), and other prominent German Marxists were highly critical of Bernstein's nonrevolutionary version of Marxism. But the harshest criticisms came from the East. Marxists in Russia—including Georgi Plekhanov (1856–1918) and Vladimir Ilyich Ulyanov (1870–1924), better known as Lenin—condemned Bernstein as a "bourgeois" traitor to Marxism.

The only Marxism worthy of the name, Lenin argued, was radical in its aims and revolutionary in its strategy. The aim was nothing less than the creation of a classless communist society. And this aim, he argued, could be accomplished only with the assistance of a revolutionary "vanguard party" whose leadership was composed of radicalized bourgeois intellectuals like himself. After all, as Lenin often noted, Marx and Engels were not workers but members of the intelligentsia. Left to themselves, the workers would behave just as Bernstein had said they would: that is, workers would organize themselves into trade unions and form working-class political parties in hopes of reforming the capitalist system from within. To cooperate with the capitalist system, said Lenin, was to be corrupted by it. Better to bury it once and for all. Hence the need for a relatively small, tightly knit, highly organized conspiratorial party to raise class consciousness, educate the workers about where their "real" interests lay, and prepare the way for a revolution made in the name of, but not directly by, the proletariat.

Yet Russia in the early twentieth century seemed an odd place for a proletarian revolution, if only because the vast majority of Russian workers were neither factory workers nor wage-laborers but poor and illiterate peasants who tilled the soil. Set in their ways, suspicious of outsiders, and often superstitious, such people seemed the very embodiment of what Marx had called the "idiocy of rural life." They appeared singularly ill suited to be the agents of radical revolutionary transformation, as Lenin readily acknowledged. But the peasants were discontented and they were numerous. They could therefore be the clay fit for molding by an elite vanguard party.

Lenin's reinterpretation of Marxism had two novel aspects, neither of which Marx had anticipated: the idea that revolutionary political consciousness had to be brought to the proletariat and the peasantry from outside and the idea that the source of such consciousness was to be an elite vanguard party. It is indeed this version of Marxism—Marxism-Leninism—that proved to be the single most influential and important variant of Marxism throughout the twentieth century. In the Soviet Union, China, Cuba, Vietnam, Eastern Europe, and elsewhere, the Marxist-Leninist model, as modified by Joseph Stalin (1879–1953), Mao Zedong (1893–1976), and others, served as an ideology to legitimize an all-powerful party ruling over a highly centralized government and a planned economy managed by government bureaucrats. It is this ideology, and the system it spawned and justified, that in the 1980s and early 1990s came under withering attack from within those countries and even from factions within their respective Communist Parties. Communism, as we once knew it, is now nearly extinct.

For more than a century—from Marx's death in 1883 until the collapse of the Soviet Union in 1991—communism was the dominant form of socialism. But it was never the only form. In fact, non-Marxian socialism has been no less varied than its communist counterparts. Anarchists such as Mikhail Bakunin (1814–1876) criticized Marx and the Marxists for the dictatorial implications of their theory and political program. Fabian socialists in England advocated a gradualist, parliamentary path to socialism, as did the American Edward Bellamy (1850–1898) in his utopian novel *Looking Backward*. Christian socialists—including Bellamy's cousin, the American Baptist minister Francis Bellamy (1855–1931), author of the Pledge of Allegiance—looked to Jesus's teachings for inspiration. In the course of the twentieth century, moreover, many socialists advocated a mixture of worker-owned businesses and free-market competition that they called *market socialism*. Whether these and other variants of socialism will flourish as communism falters remains an open question. If socialism does have a future, however, it seems clear that it will be in some form other than communism.

37

Evolutionary Socialism

EDUARD BERNSTEIN

Eduard Bernstein (1850–1932) believed that Marx's theory of social change was generally correct in outline but false or mistaken in several important details. He therefore favored revising Marx's theory to make it consistent with newly emerging facts—including the fact that the predicted "immiseration of the proletariat" had not occurred. Rather than becoming worse off, Bernstein noted, European and North American workers were increasingly prosperous. This had happened, he claimed, because the capitalist system was "evolving" into socialism as it was transformed by trade unions and working-class or socialist political parties. Bernstein's book *Evolutionary Socialism* (originally published in 1899) provided the classic statement of "revisionist" Marxism.

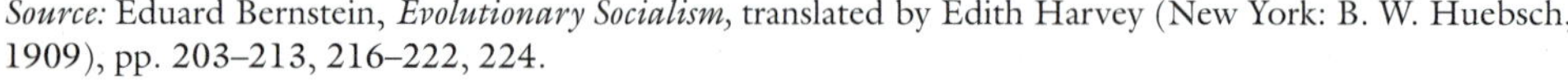
Source: Eduard Bernstein, *Evolutionary Socialism,* translated by Edith Harvey (New York: B. W. Huebsch, 1909), pp. 203–213, 216–222, 224.

EVOLUTIONARY SOCIALISM

...No socialist capable of thinking, dreams today in England of an imminent victory for socialism by means of a violent revolution—none dreams of a quick conquest of Parliament by a revolutionary proletariat. But they rely more and more on work in the municipalities and other self-governing bodies. The early contempt for the trade union movement has been given up; a closer sympathy has been won for it and, here and there also, for the co-operative movement.

And the ultimate aim? Well, that just remains an ultimate aim. "The working classes have no fixed and perfect Utopias to introduce by means of a vote of the nation. They know that in order to work out their own emancipation—and with it that higher form of life which the present form of society irresistibly makes for by its own economic development—they, the working classes, have to pass through long struggles, a whole series of historical processes, by means of which men and circumstances will be completely transformed. They have no ideals to realise, they have only to set at liberty the elements of the new society which have already been developed in the womb of the collapsing bourgeois society." So writes Marx in *Civil War in France.* I was thinking of this utterance, not in every point but in its fundamental thought in writing down the sentence about the ultimate aim. For after all what does it say but that the movement, the series of processes, is everything, whilst every aim fixed beforehand in its details is immaterial to it. I have declared already that I willingly abandon the form of the sentence about the ultimate aim as far as it admits the interpretation that every general aim of the working class movement formulated as a principle should be declared valueless. But the preconceived theories about the drift of the movement which go beyond such a generally expressed aim, which try to determine the direction of the movement and its character without an ever-vigilant eye upon facts and experience, must necessarily always pass into Utopianism, and at some time or other stand in the way, and hinder the real theoretical and practical progress of the movement.

Whoever knows even but a little of the history of German social democracy also knows that the party has become important by continued action in contravention of such theories and of infringing resolutions founded on them.... A theory or declaration of principle which does not allow attention being paid at every stage of development to the actual interests of the working classes, will always be set aside just as all forswearing of reforming detail work and of the support of neighbouring middle class parties has again and again been forgotten; and again and again at the congresses of the party will the complaint be heard that here and there in the electoral contest the ultimate aim of socialism has not been put sufficiently in the foreground.

[Some of my Marxist critics]...cart me over to the "opponents of scientific socialism."

Unfortunately for "scientific" socialism, the Marxist propositions on the hopelessness of the position of the worker have been upset in a book [by Marx himself] which bears the title, *Capital: A Critique of Political Economy.* There we read of the "physical and moral regeneration" of the textile workers in Lancashire through the [English] Factory Law of 1847, which "struck the feeblest eye." A bourgeois republic was not even necessary to bring about a certain improvement in the situation of a large section of workers! In the same book we read that the society of today is no firm crystal but an organism capable of change and constantly engaged in a process of change, that also in the treatment of economic questions on the part of the official representatives of this society an "improvement was unmistakable." Further that the author had devoted so large a space in his book to the results of the English Factory Laws in order to spur the Continent to imitate them and thus to work so that the process of transforming society may be accomplished in ever more humane forms. All of which signifies not hopelessness but capability of improvement in the condition of the worker. And, as since 1866, when this was written, the legislation depicted has not grown weaker but has been improved, made more general, and has been supplemented by laws and organisations working in the same direction, there can be no more doubt to-day than formerly of the hopefulness of the position of the worker. If to state such facts means following the "immortal Bastiat," then among the first ranks of these followers is—Karl Marx.[1]

Now, it can be asserted against me that Marx certainly recognised those improvements, but that the chapter on the historical tendency of capitalist accumulation at the end of the first volume of *Capital* shows how little these details influenced his fundamental mode of viewing things. To which I answer that as far as that is correct it speaks against that chapter and not against me.

One can interpret this chapter in very different kinds of ways. I believe I was the first to point out, and indeed repeatedly, that it was a summary characterisation of the tendency of a development which is found in capitalist accumulation, but which in practice is not carried out completely and which therefore need not be driven to the critical point of the antagonism there depicted. Engels has never expressed himself against this interpretation of mine, never, either verbally or in print, declared it to be wrong. Nor did he say a word against me when I wrote, in 1891: "It is clear that where legislation, this systematic and conscious action of society, interferes in an appropriate way, the working of the tendencies of economic development is thwarted, under some circumstances can even be annihilated. Marx and Engels have not only never denied this, but, on the contrary, have always emphasised it." If one reads the chapter mentioned with this idea, one will also, in a few sentences, silently place the word "tendency" and thus be spared the need of bringing this chapter into accord with reality by distorting arts of interpretation. But then the chapter itself would become of less value the more progress is made in actual evolution. For its theoretic importance does not lie in the argument of the general tendency to capitalistic centralisation and accumulation which had been affirmed long before Marx by bourgeois economists and socialists, but in the presentation, peculiar to Marx, of circumstances and forms under which it would work at a more advanced stage of evolution, and of the results to which it would lead. But in this respect actual evolution is really always bringing forth new arrangements, forces, facts, in face of which that presentation seems insufficient and loses to a corresponding extent the capability of serving as a sketch of the coming evolution. That is how I understand it.

One can, however, understand this chapter differently. One can conceive it in this way, that all the improvements mentioned there, and some possibly ensuing, only create temporary remedies against the oppressive tendencies of capitalism, that they signify unimportant modifications which cannot in the long run effect anything substantially against the critical point of antagonisms laid down by Marx, that this will finally appear—if not literally yet substantially—in the manner depicted, and will lead to catastrophic change by violence. This interpretation can be founded on the categoric wording of the last sentences of the chapter, and receives a certain confirmation because at the end reference is again made to the *Communist Manifesto*, whilst Hegel also appeared shortly before with his negation of the negation—the restoration on a new foundation of individual property negated by the capitalist manner of production.

According to my view, it is impossible simply to declare the one conception right and the other absolutely wrong. To me the chapter illustrates a dualism which runs through the whole monumental work of Marx, and which also finds expression in a less pregnant fashion in other passages—a dualism which consists in this, that the work aims at being a scientific inquiry and also at proving a theory laid down long before its drafting; a formula lies at the basis of it in which the result to which the exposition should lead is fixed beforehand. The return to the *Communist Manifesto* points here to a real residue of Utopianism in the Marxist system. Marx had accepted the solution of the Utopians in essentials, but had recognised their means and proofs as inadequate. He therefore undertook a revision of them, and this with the zeal, the critical acuteness, and love of truth of a scientific genius. He suppressed no important fact, he also forbore belittling artificially the importance of these facts as long as the object of the inquiry had no immediate reference to the final aim of the formula to be proved. To that point his work is free of every tendency necessarily interfering with the scientific method.

For the general sympathy with the strivings for emancipation of the working classes does not in itself stand in the way of the scientific method. But, as Marx approaches a point when that final aim enters seriously into the question, he becomes uncertain and unreliable. Such contradictions then appear as were shown in the book under consideration, for instance, in the section on the movement of incomes in modern society. It thus appears that this great scientific spirit was, in the end, a slave to a doctrine. To express it figuratively, he has raised a mighty building within the framework of a scaffolding he found existing, and in its erection he kept strictly to the laws of scientific architecture as long as they did not collide with the conditions which the construction of the scaffolding prescribed, but he neglected or evaded them when the scaffolding did not allow of their observance. Where the scaffolding put limits in the way of the building, instead of destroying the scaffolding, he changed the building itself at the cost of its right proportions and so made it all the more dependent on the scaffolding. Was it the consciousness of this irrational relation which caused him continually to pass from completing his work to amending special parts of it? However that may be, my conviction is that wherever that dualism shows itself the scaffolding must fall if the building is to grow in its right proportions. In the latter, and not in the former, is found what is worthy to live in Marx.

Nothing confirms me more in this conception than the anxiety with which some persons seek to maintain certain statements in *Capital*, which are falsified by facts. It is just some of the more deeply devoted followers of Marx who have not been able to separate themselves from the dialectical form of the work—that is the scaffolding alluded to—who do this. At least, that is only how I can explain the words of a man, otherwise so amenable to facts as Karl Kautsky, who, when I observed in Stuttgart that the number of wealthy people for many years had increased, not decreased, answered: "If that were true then the date of our victory would not only be very long postponed, but we should never attain our goal. If it be capitalists who increase and not those with no possessions, then we are going ever further from our goal the more evolution progresses, then capitalism grows stronger, not socialism."[2]

That the number of the wealthy increases and does not diminish is not an invention of bourgeois "harmony economists," but a fact established by the boards of assessment for taxes, often to the chagrin of those concerned, a fact which can no longer be disputed. But what is the significance of this fact as regards the victory of socialism? Why should the realisation of socialism depend on its refutation? Well, simply for this reason: because the dialectical scheme seems so to prescribe it; because a post threatens to fall out of the scaffolding if one admits that the social surplus product is appropriated by an increasing instead of a decreasing number of possessors. But it is only the speculative theory that is affected by this matter; it does not at all affect the actual movement. Neither the struggle of the workers for democracy in politics nor their struggle for democracy in industry is touched by it. The prospects of this struggle do not depend on the theory of concentration of capital in the hands of a diminishing number of magnates, nor on the whole dialectical scaffolding of which this is a plank, but on the growth of social wealth and of the social productive forces, in conjunction with general social progress, and, particularly, in conjunction with the intellectual and moral advance of the working classes themselves.

Suppose the victory of socialism depended on the constant shrinkage in the number of capitalist magnates, social democracy, if it wanted to act logically, either would have to support the heaping up of capital in ever fewer hands, or at least to give no support to anything that would stop this shrinkage. As a matter of fact it often enough does neither the one nor the other. These considerations, for instance, do not govern its votes on questions of taxation. From the standpoint of the catastrophic theory a great part of this practical activity of the working classes is an undoing of work that ought to be allowed to be done. It is not social democracy which is wrong in this respect. The fault lies in the doctrine which assumes that progress depends on the deterioration of social conditions....

[In earlier] circumstances a reference to politics could appear only to be a turning aside from more pressing duties. Today these conditions have been to some extent removed, and therefore no person capable of reflecting will think of criticising political action....

[L]aw, or the path of legislative reform, is the slower way, and revolutionary force the quicker and more radical. But that only is true in a restricted sense. Whether the legislative or the revolutionary method is the more promising depends entirely on the nature of the measures and on their relation to different classes and customs of the people.

In general, one may say here that the revolutionary way (always in the sense of revolution by violence) does quicker work as far as it deals with removal of obstacles which a privileged minority places in the path of social progress: that its strength lies on its negative side.

Constitutional legislation works more slowly in this respect as a rule. Its path is usually that of compromise, not the prohibition, but the buying out of acquired rights. But it is stronger than the revolution scheme where prejudice and the limited horizon of the great mass of the people appear as hindrances to social progress, and it offers greater advantages where it is a question of the creation of permanent economic arrangements capable of lasting; in other words, it is best adapted to positive social-political work.

In legislation, intellect dominates over emotion in quiet times; during a revolution emotion dominates over intellect. But if emotion is often an imperfect leader, the intellect is a slow motive force. Where a revolution sins by over haste, the every-day legislator sins by procrastination. Legislation works as a systematic force, revolution as an elementary force.

As soon as a nation has attained a position where the rights of the propertied minority have ceased to be a serious obstacle to social progress, where the negative tasks of political action are less pressing than the positive, then the appeal to a revolution by force becomes a meaningless phrase. One can overturn a government or a privileged minority, but not a nation. When the working classes do not possess very strong economic organisations of their own, and have not attained, by means of education on self-governing bodies, a high degree of mental independence, the dictatorship of the proletariat means the dictatorship of club orators and writers. I would not wish that those who see in the oppression and tricking of the working men's organisations and in the exclusion of working men from the legislature and government the highest point of the art of political policy should experience their error in practice. Just as little would I desire it for the working class movement itself.

One has not overcome Utopianism if one assumes that there is in the present, or ascribes to the present, what is to be in the future. We have to take working men as they are. And they are neither so universally pauperised as was set out in the *Communist Manifesto,* nor so free from prejudices and weaknesses as their courtiers wish to make us believe. They have the virtues and failings of the economic and social conditions under which they live. And neither these conditions nor their effects can be put on one side from one day to another.

Have we attained the required degree of development of the productive forces for the abolition of classes? In face of the fantastic figures which were formerly set up in proof of this and which rested on generalisations based on the development of particularly favoured industries, socialist writers in modern times have endeavoured to reach by carefully detailed calculations, appropriate estimates of the possibilities of production in a socialist society, and their results are very different from those figures. Of a general reduction of hours of labour to five, four, or even three or two hours, such as was formerly accepted, there can be no hope at any time within sight, unless the general standard of life is much reduced. Even under a collective organisation of work, labour must begin very young and only cease at a rather advanced age, if it is to be reduced considerably below an eight-hours' day. Those persons ought to understand this first of all who indulge in the most extreme exaggerations regarding the ratio of the number of the nonpropertied classes to that of the propertied. But he who thinks irrationally on one point does so usually on another....

[H]e who surveys the actual workers' movement will also find that the freedom from those qualities which appeared Philistine to a person born in the bourgeoisie, is very little valued by the workers, that they in no way support the morale of proletarianism, but, on the contrary, tend to make a Philistine out of a proletarian. With the roving proletarian without a family and home, no lasting, firm trade union movement would be possible. It is no bourgeois prejudice, but a conviction gained through decades of labour organisation, which has made so many of the English labour leaders—socialists and non-socialists—into zealous adherents of the temperance movement. The working class socialists know the faults of their class, and the most conscientious among them, far from glorifying these faults, seek to overcome them with all their power.

We cannot demand from a class, the great majority of whose members live under crowded conditions, are badly educated, and have an uncertain and insufficient income, the high intellectual and moral standard which the organisation and existence of a socialist community presupposes. We will, therefore, not ascribe it to them by way of fiction. Let us rejoice at the great stock of intelligence, renunciation, and energy which the modern working class movement has partly revealed, partly produced; but we must not assign, without discrimination to the masses, the millions, what holds good, say, of hundreds of thousands. I will not repeat the declarations which have been made to me on this point by working men [themselves].... [I]t is not every epoch that produces a Marx, and even for a man of equal genius the working class movement of to-day is too great to enable him to occupy the position which Marx fills in its history. Today it needs, in addition to the fighting spirit, the coordinating and constructive thinkers who are intellectually enough advanced to be able to separate the chaff from the wheat, who are great enough in their mode of thinking to recognise also the little plant that has grown on another soil than theirs, and who, perhaps, though not kings, are warm-hearted republicans in the domain of socialist thought.

NOTES

1. Claude-Frederic Bastiat (1801–1850) was a French economist and opponent of socialism.—Eds.
2. Karl Kautsky (1854–1938) was a Marxist theorist and a leader of the German Social Democratic Party.—Eds.

38

Revisionism, Imperialism, and Revolution

V. I. LENIN

Marxism-Leninism, as the ideology of the Soviet Union was officially called before the dramatic changes of the late 1980s, was largely the creation of one man. Vladimir Ilyich Ulyanov (1870–1924)—better known by his revolutionary pseudonym, Lenin—was, until his death, the preeminent Russian revolutionary and Marxian theorist. In "adapting" Marxism to Russian conditions, Lenin made several significant changes. For one, he held that a proletarian revolution could occur in Russia, despite the fact that Russia in the early twentieth century had a relatively small proletariat (the overwhelming majority of Russian workers were not wage-laborers but peasants who tilled the soil). For another, he claimed that only a small, highly organized, conspiratorial "vanguard" party could supply the political will (or "consciousness") and leadership required to radically transform such an economically and politically backward country. A fiercely combative critic of other interpretations of Marxism, Lenin claimed that his alone was the "true" interpretation; all others—including the "revisionist" view espoused by Bernstein—were deviations from or distortions of Marx's "scientific" outlook. If revolution had not come to the advanced capitalist countries, as Marx had predicted, that was because the workers in those countries were afflicted with "trade-union consciousness," that is, the mistaken view that they could organize themselves into unions and political parties to work for their interests. This strategy was successful, said Lenin, only because the capitalist countries were exploiting the workers of nonindustrial countries. Such exploitation would cease—and revolution would come to capitalist countries themselves—when workers in those underdeveloped countries made their own anti-colonial or anti-imperialist revolutions.

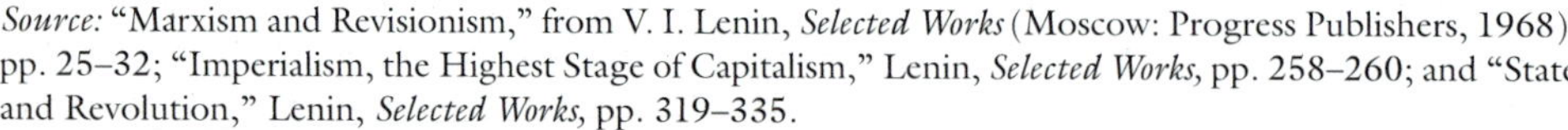
Source: "Marxism and Revisionism," from V. I. Lenin, *Selected Works* (Moscow: Progress Publishers, 1968), pp. 25–32; "Imperialism, the Highest Stage of Capitalism," Lenin, *Selected Works,* pp. 258–260; and "State and Revolution," Lenin, *Selected Works,* pp. 319–335.

MARXISM AND REVISIONISM

There is a well-known saying that if geometrical axioms affected human interests, attempts would certainly be made to refute them. Theories of natural history which conflicted with the old prejudices of theology provoked, and still provoke, the most rabid opposition. No wonder, therefore, that the Marxian doctrine, which directly serves to enlighten and organise the advanced class in modern society, indicates the tasks facing this class and demonstrates the inevitable replacement (by virtue of economic development) of the present system by a new order—no wonder that this doctrine has had to fight for every step forward in the course of its life.

Needless to say, this applies to bourgeois science and philosophy, officially taught by official professors in order to befuddle the rising generation of the propertied classes and to "coach" it against internal and foreign enemies. This science will not even hear of Marxism, declaring that it has been refuted and annihilated. Marx is attacked with equal zest by young scholars who are making a career by refuting socialism, and by decrepit elders who are preserving the tradition of all kinds of outworn "systems." The progress of Marxism, the fact that its ideas are spreading and taking firm hold among the working class, inevitably increases the frequency and intensity of these bourgeois attacks on Marxism, which becomes stronger, more hardened and more vigorous every time it is "annihilated" by official science.

But even among doctrines connected with the struggle of the working class, and current mainly among the proletariat, Marxism by no means consolidated its position all at once. In the first half-century of its existence (from the 1840s on) Marxism was engaged in combating theories fundamentally hostile to it.... And the second half-century of the existence of Marxism began (in the [1890s]) with the struggle of a trend hostile to Marxism within Marxism itself.

[Eduard] Bernstein, a one-time orthodox Marxist, gave his name to this trend, by coming forward with the most noise and with the most purposeful expression of amendments to Marx, revision of Marx, revisionism. Even in Russia where—owing to the economic backwardness of the country and the preponderance of a peasant population weighed down by the relics of serfdom—non-Marxist socialism has naturally held its ground longest of all, it is plainly passing into revisionism before our very eyes....

Pre-Marxist socialism has been defeated. It is continuing the struggle, no longer on its own independent ground, but on the general ground of Marxism, as revisionism. Let us, then, examine the ideological content of revisionism.

In the sphere of philosophy revisionism followed in the wake of bourgeois professional "science." The professors went "back to [Immanuel] Kant"—and revisionism dragged along after the neo-Kantians. The professors repeated the platitudes that priests have uttered a thousand times against philosophical materialism—and the revisionists, smiling indulgently, mumbled...that materialism had been "refuted" long ago. The professors treated [G. W. F.] Hegel as a "dead dog," and while themselves preaching idealism, only an idealism a thousand times more petty and banal than Hegel's, contemptuously shrugged their shoulders at dialectics—and the revisionists floundered after them into the swamp of philosophical vulgarisation of science, replacing "artful" (and revolutionary) dialectics by "simple" (and tranquil) "evolution." The professors earned their official salaries by adjusting both their idealist and their "critical" systems to the dominant medieval "philosophy" (i.e., to theology)—and the revisionists drew close to them, trying to make religion a "private affair," not in relation to the modern state, but in relation to the party of the advanced class.

What such "amendments" to Marx really meant in class terms need not be stated: it is self-evident....

Passing to political economy, it must be noted first of all that in this sphere the "amendments" of the revisionists were much more comprehensive and circumstantial; attempts were made to influence the public by "new data on economic development." It was said that concentration and the ousting of small-scale production by large-scale production do not occur in agriculture at all, while they proceed very slowly in commerce and industry. It was said that crises had now become rarer and weaker, and that cartels and trusts would probably enable capital to eliminate them altogether. It was said that the "theory of collapse" to which capitalism is heading was unsound, owing to the tendency of class antagonisms to become milder and less acute. It was said, finally, that it would not be amiss to correct Marx's theory of value, too....

The fight against the revisionists on these questions resulted in as fruitful a revival of the theoretical thought in international socialism as did Engels's controversy with Dühring twenty years earlier. The arguments of the revisionists were analysed with the help of facts and figures. It was proved that the revisionists were systematically painting a rose-coloured picture of modern small-scale production. The technical and commercial superiority of large-scale *production* over small-scale production not only in industry, but also in agriculture, is proved by irrefutable facts. But commodity production is far less developed in agriculture, and modern statisticians and economists are, as a rule, not very skilful in picking out the special branches (sometimes even the operations) in agriculture which indicate that agriculture is being progressively drawn into the process of *exchange* in world economy. Small-scale production maintains itself on the ruins of natural economy by constant worsening of diet, by chronic starvation, by lengthening of the working day, by deterioration in the quality and the care of cattle, in a word, by the very methods whereby handicraft production maintained itself against capitalist manufacture. Every advance in science and technology inevitably and relentlessly undermines the foundations of small-scale production in capitalist society; and it is the task of socialist political economy to investigate this process in all its forms, often complicated and intricate, and to demonstrate to the small producer the impossibility of his holding his own under capitalism, the hopelessness of peasant farming under capitalism, and the necessity for the peasant to adopt the standpoint of the proletarian. On this question the revisionists sinned, in the scientific sense, by superficial generalisations based on facts selected one-sidedly and without reference to the system of capitalism as a whole. From the political point of view, they sinned by the fact that they inevitably, whether they wanted to or not, invited or urged the peasant to adopt the attitude of a small proprietor (i.e., the attitude of the bourgeoisie) instead of urging him to adopt the point of view of the revolutionary proletarian.

The position of revisionism was even worse as regards the theory of crises and the theory of [capitalism's] collapse. Only for a very short time could people, and then only the most short-sighted, think of refashioning the foundations of Marx's theory under the influence of a few years of industrial boom and prosperity. Realities very soon made it clear to the revisionists that crises were not a thing of the past: prosperity was followed by a crisis. The forms, the sequence, the picture of particular crises changed, but crises remained an inevitable component of the capitalist system. While uniting production, the cartels and trusts at the same time, and in a way that was obvious to all, aggravated the anarchy of production, the insecurity of existence of the proletariat and the oppression of capital, thereby intensifying class antagonisms to an unprecedented degree. That capitalism is heading for a breakdown—in the sense both of individual political and economic crises and of the complete collapse of the entire capitalist system—has been made particularly clear, and on a particularly large scale, precisely by the new giant trusts. The recent financial crisis in America and the appalling increase of unemployment all over Europe, to say nothing of the impending industrial crisis to which many symptoms are pointing—all this has resulted in the recent "theories" of the revisionists having been forgotten by everybody, including, apparently, many of the revisionists themselves. But the lessons which this instability of the intellectuals had given the working class must not be forgotten.

As to the theory of value, it need only be said that...the revisionists have contributed absolutely nothing, and have therefore left no traces whatever on the development of scientific thought.

In the sphere of politics, revisionism did really try to revise the foundation of Marxism, namely, the doctrine of the class struggle. Political freedom, democracy and universal suffrage remove the ground for the class struggle—we were told—and render untrue the old proposition of the *Communist Manifesto* that the working men have no country. For, they said, since the "will of the majority" prevails in a democracy, one must neither regard the state as an organ of class rule, nor reject alliances with the progressive, social-reform bourgeoisie against the reactionaries.

It cannot be disputed that these arguments of the revisionists amounted to a fairly well-balanced system of views, namely, the old and well-known liberal-bourgeois views. The liberals have always said that bourgeois parliamentarism destroys classes and class divisions, since the right to vote and the right to participate in the government of the country are shared by all citizens without distinction. The whole history of Europe in the second half of the nineteenth century, and the whole history of the Russian revolution in the early twentieth, clearly show how absurd such views are. Economic distinctions are not mitigated but aggravated and intensified under the freedom of "democratic" capitalism. Parliamentarism does not eliminate, but lays bare the innate character even of the most democratic bourgeois republics as organs of class oppression. By helping to enlighten and to organise immeasurably wider masses of the population than those which previously took an active part in political events, parliamentarism does not make for the elimination of crises and political revolutions, but for the maximum intensification of civil war during such revolutions. The events in Paris in the spring of 1871 and the events in Russia in the winter of 1905 showed as clearly as could be how inevitably this intensification comes about. The French bourgeoisie without a moment's hesitation made a deal with the enemy of the whole nation, with the foreign army which had ruined its country [in the Franco-Prussian War], in order to crush the proletarian movement. Whoever does not understand the inevitable inner dialectics of parliamentarism and bourgeois democracy—which leads to an even sharper decision of the argument by mass violence than formerly—will never be able on the basis of this parliamentarism to conduct propaganda and agitation consistent in principle, really preparing the working-class masses for victorious participation in such "arguments."...

A natural complement to the economic and political tendencies of revisionism was its attitude to the ultimate aim of the socialist movement. "The movement is everything, the ultimate aim is nothing"—this catch-phrase of Bernstein's expresses the substance of revisionism better than many long disquisitions. To determine its conduct from case to case, to adapt itself to the events of the day and to the chopping and changing of petty politics, to forget the primary interests of the proletariat and the basic features of the whole capitalist system, of all capitalist evolution, to sacrifice these primary interests for the real or assumed advantages of the moment—such is the policy of revisionism. And it patently follows from the very nature of this policy that it may assume an infinite variety of forms, and that every more or less "new" question, every more or less unexpected and unforeseen turn of events, even though it changes the basic line of development only to an insignificant degree and only for the briefest period, will always inevitably give rise to one variety of revisionism or another.

The inevitability of revisionism is determined by its class roots in modern society. Revisionism is an international phenomenon. No thinking socialist who is in the least informed can have the slightest doubt that the relation between the orthodox and the Bernsteinians in Germany [and elsewhere] is similar....

Wherein lies its inevitability in capitalist society? Why is it more profound than the differences of national peculiarities and of degrees of capitalist development? Because in every capitalist country, side by side with the proletariat, there are always broad strata of the petty bourgeoisie, small proprietors. Capitalism arose and is constantly arising out of small production. A number of new "middle strata" are inevitably brought into existence again and again by capitalism (appendages to the factory, work at home, small workshops scattered all over the country to meet the requirements of big industries, such as the bicycle and automobile industries, etc.). These new small producers are just as inevitably being cast again into the ranks of the proletariat. It is quite natural that the petty-bourgeois world outlook should again and again crop up in the ranks of the broad workers' parties. It is quite natural that this should be so and always will be so, right up to the changes of fortune that will take place in the proletarian revolution. For it would be a profound mistake to think that the "complete" proletarianisation of the majority of the population is essential for bringing about such a revolution. What we now frequently experience only in the domain of ideology, namely, disputes over theoretical amendments to Marx; what now crops up in practice only over individual partial issues of the labour movement, as tactical differences with the revisionists and splits on this basis—is bound to be experienced by the working class on an incomparably larger scale when the proletarian revolution will sharpen all disputed issues, will focus all differences on points which are of the most immediate importance in determining the conduct of the masses, and will make it necessary in the heat of the fight to distinguish enemies from friends, and to cast out bad allies in order to deal decisive blows at the enemy.

The ideological struggle waged by revolutionary Marxism against revisionism at the end of the nineteenth century is but the prelude to the great revolutionary battles of the proletariat, which is marching forward to the complete victory of its cause despite all the waverings and weaknesses of the petty bourgeoisie.

IMPERIALISM: THE HIGHEST STAGE OF CAPITALISM

...When nine-tenths of Africa had been seized (by 1900), when the whole world had been divided up, there was inevitably ushered in the era of monopoly possession of colonies and, consequently, of particularly intense struggle for the division and the redivision of the world.

The extent to which monopolist capital has intensified all the contradictions of capitalism is generally known. It is sufficient to mention the high cost of living and the tyranny of the cartels. This intensification of contradictions constitutes the most powerful driving force of the transitional period of history, which began from the time of the final victory of world finance capital.

Monopolies, oligarchy, the striving for domination and not for freedom, the exploitation of an increasing number of small or weak nations by a handful of the richest or most powerful nations—all these have given birth to those distinctive characteristics of imperialism which compel us to define it as parasitic or decaying capitalism. More and more prominently there emerges, as one of the tendencies of imperialism, the creation of the "rentier state," the usurer state, in which the bourgeoisie to an ever-increasing degree lives on the proceeds of capital exports and by "clipping coupons." It would be a mistake to believe that this tendency to decay precludes the rapid growth of capitalism. It does not. In the epoch of imperialism, certain branches of industry, certain strata of the bourgeoisie and certain countries betray, to a greater or lesser degree, now one and now another of these tendencies. On the whole, capitalism is growing far more rapidly than before; but this growth is not only becoming more and more uneven in general, its unevenness also manifests itself, in particular, in the decay of the countries which are richest in capital (Britain).

In regard to the rapidity of Germany's economic development, Riesser, the author of the book on the big German banks, states: "The progress of the preceding period (1848–1870), which had not been exactly slow, compares with the rapidity with which the whole of Germany's national economy, and with it German banking, progressed during this period (1870–1905) in about the same way as the speed of the mail coach in the good old days compares with the speed of the present-day automobile...which is whizzing past so fast that it endangers not only innocent pedestrians in its path, but also the occupants of the car." In its turn, this finance capital which has grown with such extraordinary rapidity is not unwilling, precisely because it has grown so quickly, to pass on to a more "tranquil" possession of colonies which have to be seized—and not only by peaceful methods—from richer nations. In the United States, economic development in the last decades has been even more rapid than in Germany, *and for this very reason,* the parasitic features of modern American capitalism have stood out with particular prominence. On the other hand, a comparison of, say, the republican American bourgeoisie with the monarchist Japanese or German bourgeoisie shows that the most pronounced political distinction diminishes to an extreme degree in the epoch of imperialism—not because it is unimportant in general, but because in all these cases we are talking about a bourgeoisie which has definite features of parasitism.

The receipt of high monopoly profits by the capitalists in one of the numerous branches of industry, in one of the numerous countries, etc., makes it economically possible for them to bribe certain sections of the workers, and for a time a fairly considerable minority of them, and win them to the side of the bourgeoisie of a given industry or given nation against all the others. The intensification of antagonisms between imperialist nations for the division of the world increases this urge....

STATE AND REVOLUTION

In the usual arguments about the state, the mistake is constantly made against which Engels warned and which we have in passing indicated above, namely, it is constantly forgotten that the abolition of the state means also the abolition of democracy: that the withering away of the state means the withering away of democracy.

At first sight this assertion seems exceedingly strange and incomprehensible; indeed, someone may even suspect us of expecting the advent of a system of society in which the principle of subordination of the minority to the majority will not be observed—for democracy means the recognition of this very principle.

No, democracy is *not* identical with the subordination of the minority to the majority. Democracy is a *state* which recognises the subordination of the minority to the majority, i.e., an organisation for the systematic use of *force* by one class against another, by one section of the population against another.

We set ourselves the ultimate aim of abolishing the state, i.e., all organised and systematic violence, all use of violence against people in general. We do not expect the advent of a system of society in which the principle of subordination of the minority to the majority will not be observed. In striving for socialism, however, we are convinced that it will develop into communism and, therefore, that the need for violence against people in general, for the *subordination* of one man to another, and of one section of the population to another, will vanish altogether since people will *become accustomed* to observing the elementary conditions of social life *without violence* and *without subordination.*

In order to emphasise this element of habit, Engels speaks of a new *generation,* "reared in new, free social conditions," which will "be able to discard the entire lumber of the state"—of any state, including the democratic-republican state.

In order to explain this, it is necessary to analyse the economic basis of the withering away of the state.

Marx explains this question most thoroughly in his *Critique of the Gotha Programme*.... The polemical part of this remarkable work...has, so to speak, overshadowed its positive part, namely, the analysis of the connection between the development of communism and the withering away of the state.

1 Presentation of the Question by Marx ...The whole theory of Marx is the application of the theory of development—in its most consistent, complete, considered and pithy form—to modern capitalism. Naturally, Marx was faced with the problem of applying this theory both to the forthcoming collapse of capitalism and to the future development of future communism.

On the basis of what *facts*, then, can the question of the future development of future communism be dealt with?

On the basis of the fact that it *has its origin* in capitalism, that it develops historically from capitalism, that it is the result of the action of a social force to which capitalism *gave birth*. There is no trace of an attempt on Marx's part to make up a utopia, to indulge in idle guesswork about what cannot be known. Marx treated the question of communism in the same way as a naturalist would treat the question of the development of, say, a new biological variety, once he knew that it had originated in such and such a way and was changing in such and such a definite direction.

...The first fact that has been established most accurately by the whole theory of development, by science as a whole—a fact that was ignored by the utopians, and is ignored by the present-day opportunists, who are afraid of the socialist revolution—is that, historically, there must undoubtedly be a special stage, or a special phase, of *transition* from capitalism to communism.

2 The Transition from Capitalism to Communism Marx continued [in his *Critique of the Gotha Programme*]:

> ...Between capitalist and communist society lies the period of the revolutionary transformation of the one into the other. Corresponding to this is also a political transition period in which the state can be nothing but the *revolutionary dictatorship of the proletariat.*

Marx bases this conclusion on an analysis of the role played by the proletariat in modern capitalist society, on the data concerning the development of this society, and on the irreconcilability of the antagonistic interests of the proletariat and the bourgeoisie.

Previously the question was put as follows: to achieve its emancipation, the proletariat must overthrow the bourgeoisie, win political power and establish its revolutionary dictatorship.

Now the question is put somewhat differently: the transition from capitalist society—which is developing towards communism—to communist society is impossible without a "political transition period," and the state in this period can only be the revolutionary dictatorship of the proletariat.

What, then, is the relation of this dictatorship to democracy?

We have seen that the *Communist Manifesto* simply places side by side the two concepts: "to raise the proletariat to the position of the ruling class" and "to win the battle of democracy." On the basis of all that has been said above, it is possible to determine more precisely how democracy changes in the transition from capitalism to communism.

In capitalist society, providing it develops under the most favorable conditions, we have a more or less complete democracy in the democratic republic. But this democracy is always hemmed in by the narrow limits set by capitalist exploitation, and consequently always remains, in effect, a democracy for the minority, only for the propertied classes, only for the rich. Freedom in capitalist society always remains about the same as it was in the ancient Greek republics: freedom for the slave-owners. Owing to the conditions of capitalist exploitation, the modern wage slaves are so crushed by want and poverty that "they cannot be bothered with democracy," "cannot be bothered with politics"; in the ordinary, peaceful course of events, the majority of the population is debarred from participation in public and political life.

...Democracy for an insignificant minority, democracy for the rich—that is the democracy of capitalist society. If we look more closely into the machinery of capitalist democracy, we see everywhere, in the "petty"—supposedly petty—details of the suffrage (residential qualification, exclusion of women, etc.), in the technique of the representative institutions, in the actual obstacles to the right of assembly (public buildings are not for "paupers"!), in the purely capitalist organisation of the daily press, etc., etc.—we see restriction after restriction upon democracy. These restrictions, exceptions, exclusions, obstacles for the poor seem slight, especially in the eyes of one who has never known want himself and has never been in close contact with the oppressed classes in their mass life (and nine out of ten, if not ninety-nine out of a hundred, bourgeois publicists and politicians come under this category); but in their sum total these restrictions exclude and squeeze out the poor from politics, from active participation in democracy.

...But from this capitalist democracy—that is inevitably narrow and stealthily pushes aside the poor, and is therefore hypocritical and false through and through—forward development does not proceed simply, directly and smoothly, towards "greater and greater democracy," as the liberal professors and petty-bourgeois opportunists would have us believe. No, forward development, i.e., development towards communism, proceeds through the dictatorship of the proletariat, and cannot do otherwise, for the *resistance* of the capitalist exploiters cannot be *broken* by anyone else or in any other way.

And the dictatorship of the proletariat, i.e., the organisation of the vanguard of the oppressed as the ruling class for the purpose of suppressing the oppressors, cannot result merely in an expansion of democracy. *Simultaneously* with an immense expansion of democracy, which *for the first time* becomes democracy for the poor, democracy for the people, and not democracy for the moneybags, the dictatorship of the proletariat imposes a series of restrictions on the freedom of the oppressors, the exploiters, the capitalists. We must suppress them in order to free humanity from wage slavery, their resistance must be crushed by force; it is clear that there is no freedom and no democracy where there is suppression and where there is violence.

...Democracy for the vast majority of the people, and suppression by force, i.e., exclusion from democracy, of the exploiters and oppressors of the people—this is the change democracy undergoes during the *transition* from capitalism to communism.

Only in communist society, when the resistance of the capitalists has been completely crushed, when the capitalists have disappeared, when there are no classes (i.e., when there is no distinction between the members of society as regards their relation to the social means of production), *only* then "the state...ceases to exist," and *"it becomes possible to speak of freedom."* Only then will a truly complete democracy become possible and be realised, a democracy without any exceptions whatever. And only then will democracy begin to *wither away*, owing to the simple fact that, freed from capitalist slavery, from the untold horrors, savagery, absurdities and infamies of capitalist exploitation, people will gradually *become accustomed* to observing the elementary rules of social intercourse that have been known for centuries and repeated for thousands of years in all copy-book maxims. They will become accustomed to observing them without force, without coercion, without subordination, *without the special apparatus* for coercion called the state.

The expression "the state *withers away*" is very well chosen, for it indicates both the gradual and the spontaneous nature of the process. Only habit can, and undoubtedly will, have such an effect; for we see around us on millions of occasions how readily people become accustomed to observing the necessary rules of social intercourse when there is no exploitation, when there is nothing that arouses indignation, evokes protest and revolt, and creates the need for *suppression*.

And so in capitalist society we have a democracy that is curtailed, wretched, false, a democracy only for the rich, for the minority. The dictatorship of the proletariat, the period of transition to communism, will for the first time create democracy for the people, for the majority, along with the necessary suppression of the exploiters, of the minority. Communism alone is capable of providing really complete democracy, and the more complete it is, the sooner it will become unnecessary and wither away of its own accord.

In other words, under capitalism we have the state in the proper sense of the word, that is, a special machine for the suppression of one class by another, and, what is more, of the majority by the minority. Naturally, to be successful, such an undertaking as the systematic suppression of the exploited majority by the exploiting minority calls for the utmost ferocity and savagery in the matter of suppressing, it calls for seas of blood, through which mankind is actually wading its way in slavery, serfdom and wage-labour.

Furthermore, during the *transition* from capitalism to communism suppression is *still* necessary, but it is now the suppression of the exploiting minority by the exploited majority. A special apparatus, a special machine for suppression, the "state," is *still* necessary, but this is now a transitional state. It is no longer a state in the proper sense of the word; for the suppression of the minority of exploiters by the majority of the wage slaves of *yesterday* is comparatively so easy, simple and natural a task that it will entail far less bloodshed than the suppression of the risings of slaves, serfs or wage-labourers, and it will cost mankind far less. And it is compatible with the extension of democracy to such an overwhelming majority of the population that the need for a *special machine* of suppression will begin to disappear. Naturally, the exploiters are unable to suppress the people without a highly complex machine for performing this task, but *the people* can suppress the exploiters even with a very simple "machine," almost without a "machine," without a special apparatus, by the simple *organisation of the armed people* (such as the Soviets [i.e., councils] of Workers' and Soldiers' Deputies, we would remark, running ahead).

Lastly, only communism makes the state absolutely unnecessary, for there is *nobody* to be suppressed—"nobody" in the sense of a *class,* of a systematic struggle against a definite section of the population. We are not utopians, and do not in the least deny the possibility and inevitability of excesses on the part of *individual persons,* or the need to stop *such* excesses. In the first place, however, no special machine, no special apparatus of suppression, is needed for this; this will be done by the armed people themselves, as simply and as readily as any crowd of civilised people, even in modern society, interferes to put a stop to a scuffle or to prevent a woman from being assaulted. And, secondly, we know that the fundamental social cause of excesses, which consist in the violation of the rules of social intercourse, is the exploitation of the people, their want and their poverty. With the removal of this chief cause, excesses will inevitably begin to *"wither away."* We do not know how quickly and in what succession, but we do know they will wither away. With their withering away the state will also *wither away.*

Without building utopias, Marx defined more fully what can be defined *now* regarding this future, namely, the difference between the lower and higher phases (levels, stages) of communist society.

3 The First Phase of Communist Society

...It is this communist society, which has just emerged into the light of day out of the womb of capitalism and which is in every respect stamped with the birthmarks of the old society, that Marx terms the "first," or lower, phase of communist society.

The means of production are no longer the private property of individuals. The means of production belong to the whole of society. Every member of society, performing a certain part of the socially necessary work, receives a certificate from society to the effect that he has done a certain amount of work. And with this certificate he receives from the public store of consumer goods a corresponding quantity of products. After a deduction is made of the amount of labour which goes to the public fund, every worker, therefore, receives from society as much as he has given to it.

"Equality" apparently reigns supreme.

...But people are not alike: one is strong, another is weak; one is married, another is not; one has more children, another has less, and so on. And the conclusion Marx draws is:

> ...With an equal performance of labour, and hence an equal share in the social consumption fund, one will in fact receive more than

> another, one will be richer than another, and so on. To avoid all these defects, right would have to be unequal rather than equal.

The first phase of communism, therefore, cannot yet provide justice and equality: differences, and unjust differences, in wealth will still persist, but the *exploitation* of man by man will have become impossible because it will be impossible to seize the *means of production*—the factories, machines, land, etc.—and make them private property.

...Marx not only most scrupulously takes account of the inevitable inequality of men, but he also takes into account the fact that the mere conversion of the means of production into the common property of the whole of society (commonly called "socialism") *does not remove* the defects of distribution and the inequality of "bourgeois right," which *continues to prevail* so long as products are divided "according to the amount of labour performed." Continuing, Marx says:

> ...But these defects are inevitable in the first phase of communist society as it is when it has just emerged, after prolonged birth pangs, from capitalist society. Right can never be higher than the economic structure of society and its cultural development conditioned thereby.

And so, in the first phase of communist society (usually called socialism) "bourgeois right" is *not* abolished in its entirety, but only in part, only in proportion to the economic revolution so far attained, i.e., only in respect of the means of production. "Bourgeois right" recognises them as the private property of individuals. Socialism converts them into *common* property. *To that extent*—and to that extent alone—"bourgeois right" disappears.

However, it persists as far as its other part is concerned; it persists in the capacity of regulator (determining factor) in the distribution of products and the allotment of labour among the members of society. The socialist principle, "He who does not work shall not eat," is *already* realised; the other socialist principle, "An equal amount of products for an equal amount of labour," is also *already* realised. But this is not yet communism, and it does not yet abolish "bourgeois right," which gives unequal individuals, in return for unequal (really unequal) amounts of labour, equal amounts of products.

This is a "defect," says Marx, but it is unavoidable in the first phase of communism; for if we are not to indulge in utopianism, we must not think that having overthrown capitalism people will at once learn to work for society *without any standard of right*. Besides, the abolition of capitalism *does not immediately create* the economic prerequisites for *such a* change.

Now, there is no other standard than that of "bourgeois right." To this extent, therefore, there still remains the need for a state, which, while safeguarding the common ownership of the means of production, would safeguard equality in labour and in the distribution of products.

The state withers away insofar as there are no longer any capitalists, any classes, and, consequently, no *class* can be *suppressed*.

But the state has not yet completely withered away, since there still remains the safeguarding of "bourgeois right," which sanctifies actual inequality. For the state to wither away completely, complete communism is necessary.

4 The Higher Phase of Communist Society Marx continues:

> ...In a higher phase of communist society, after the enslaving subordination of the individual to the division of labour and with it also the antithesis between mental and physical labour has vanished, after labour has become not only a livelihood but life's prime want, after the productive forces have increased with the all-round development of the individual, and all the springs of co-operative wealth flow more abundantly—only then can the narrow horizon of bourgeois right be crossed in its entirety and society inscribe on its banner: From each according to his ability, to each according to his needs!

Only now can we fully appreciate the correctness of Engels's remarks mercilessly ridiculing the absurdity of combining the words "freedom" and "state." So long as the state exists there is no freedom. When there is freedom, there will be no state.

The economic basis for the complete withering away of the state is such a high stage of development of communism at which the antithesis between mental and physical labour disappears, at which there consequently disappears one of the principal sources of modern *social* inequality—a source, moreover, which cannot on any account be removed immediately by the mere conversion of the means of production into public property, by the mere expropriation of the capitalists.

This expropriation will make it *possible* for the productive forces to develop to a tremendous extent. And when we see how incredibly capitalism is already *retarding* this development, when we see how much progress could be achieved on the basis of the level of technique already attained, we are entitled to say with the fullest confidence that the expropriation of the capitalists will inevitably result in an enormous development of the productive forces of human society. But how rapidly this development will proceed, how soon it will reach the point of breaking away from the division of labour, of doing away with the antithesis between mental and physical labour, of transforming labour into "life's prime want"—we do not and *cannot* know.

That is why we are entitled to speak only of the inevitable withering away of the state, emphasizing the protracted nature of this process and its dependence upon the rapidity of development of the *higher phase* of communism, and leaving the question of the time required for, or the concrete forms of, the withering away quite open, because there is *no* material for answering these questions.

The state will be able to wither away completely when society adopts the rule: "From each according to his ability, to each according to his needs," i.e., when people have become so accustomed to observing the fundamental rules of social intercourse and when their labour has become so productive that they will voluntarily work *according to their ability*. "The narrow horizon of bourgeois right," which compels one to calculate with the heartlessness of a Shylock whether one has not worked half an hour more than somebody else, whether one is not getting less pay than somebody else—this narrow horizon will then be crossed. There will then be no need for society, in distributing products, to regulate the quantity to be received by each; each will take freely "according to his needs."

From the bourgeois point of view, it is easy to declare that such a social order is "sheer utopia" and to sneer at the socialists for promising everyone the right to receive from society, without any control over the labour of the individual citizen, any quantity of truffles, cars, pianos, etc. Even to this day, most bourgeois "savants" [i.e., "wise men"] confine themselves to sneering in this way, thereby betraying both their ignorance and their selfish defence of capitalism.

Ignorance—for it has never entered the head of any socialist to "promise" that the higher phase of the development of communism will arrive; as for the great socialists' *forecast* that it will arrive, it presupposes not the present productivity of labour and *not the present* ordinary run of people, who, like the seminary students in [Nikolai] Pomyalovsky's stories, are capable of damaging the stocks of public wealth "just for fun," and of demanding the impossible. Until the "higher" phase of communism arrives, the socialists demand the *strictest* control by society *and by the state* over the measure of labour and the measure of consumption; but this control must *start* with the expropriation of the capitalists, with the establishment of workers' control over the capitalists, and must be exercised not by a state of bureaucrats, but by a state of *armed workers*.

...And this brings us to the question of the scientific distinction between socialism and communism....

[T]he scientific distinction between socialism and communism is clear. What is usually called socialism was termed by Marx the "first," or lower, phase of communist society. Insofar as the means of production become *common* property, the word "communism" is also applicable here, providing we do not forget that this is *not* complete communism. The great significance of Marx's explanations is that here, too, he consistently applies materialist dialectics, the theory of development, and regards communism as something which develops *out* of capitalism. Instead of scholastically invented, "concocted" definitions and fruitless disputes over words (What is socialism? What is communism?), Marx gives an analysis of what might be called the stages of the economic maturity of communism.

In its first phase, or first stage, communism *cannot* as yet be fully mature economically and entirely free from traditions or vestiges of capitalism. Hence the interesting phenomenon that communism in its first phase retains "the narrow horizon of *bourgeois* right." Of course, bourgeois right in regard to the distribution of *consumer* goods inevitably presupposes the existence of the *bourgeois state,* for right is nothing without an apparatus capable of *enforcing* the observance of the standards of right.

It follows that under communism there remains for a time not only bourgeois right, but even the bourgeois state, without the bourgeoisie!

This may sound like a paradox or simply a dialectical conundrum, of which Marxism is often accused by people who have not taken the slightest trouble to study its extraordinarily profound content.

But in fact, remnants of the old, surviving in the new, confront us in life at every step, both in nature and in society. And Marx did not arbitrarily insert a scrap of "bourgeois" right into communism, but indicated what is economically and politically inevitable in a society emerging *out of the womb* of capitalism.

Democracy is of enormous importance to the working class in its struggle against the capitalists for its emancipation. But democracy is by no means a boundary not to be overstepped; it is only one of the stages on the road from feudalism to capitalism, and from capitalism to communism.

Democracy means equality. The great significance of the proletariat's struggle for equality and of equality as a slogan will be clear if we correctly interpret it as meaning the abolition of *classes.* But democracy means only *formal* equality. And as soon as equality is achieved for all members of society in *relation* to ownership of the means of production, that is, equality of labour and wages, humanity will inevitably be confronted with the question of advancing farther, from formal equality to actual equality, i.e., to the operation of the rule "from each according to his ability, to each according to his needs." By what stages, by means of what practical measures humanity will proceed to this supreme aim we do not and cannot know. But it is important to realise how infinitely mendacious is the ordinary bourgeois conception of socialism as something lifeless, rigid, fixed once and for all, whereas in reality *only* socialism will be the beginning of a rapid, genuine, truly mass forward movement, embracing first the *majority* and then the whole of the population, in all spheres of public and private life.

Democracy is a form of the state, one of its varieties. Consequently, it, like every state, represents, on the one hand, the organised, systematic use of force against persons; but, on the other hand, it signifies the formal recognition of equality of citizens, the equal right of all to determine the structure of, and to administer, the state. This, in turn, results in the fact that, at a certain stage in the development of democracy, it first welds together the class that wages a revolutionary struggle against capitalism—the proletariat—and enables it to crush, smash to atoms, wipe off the face of the earth the bourgeois, even the republican-bourgeois, state machine, the standing army, the police and the bureaucracy and to substitute for them a *more* democratic state machine, but a state machine nevertheless, in the shape of armed workers who proceed to form a militia involving the entire population.

Here "quantity turns into quality": *such* a degree of democracy implies overstepping the boundaries of bourgeois society and beginning its socialist reorganisation. If really *all* take part in the administration of the state, capitalism cannot retain its hold. The development of capitalism, in turn, creates the *preconditions* that *enable* really "all" to take part in the administration of the state. Some of these preconditions are: universal literacy, which has already been achieved in a number of the most advanced capitalist countries, then the "training and disciplining" of millions of workers by the huge, complex, socialised apparatus of the postal service, railways, *big* factories, large-scale commerce, banking, etc.

Given these *economic* preconditions, it is quite possible, after the overthrow of the capitalists and the bureaucrats, to proceed immediately, overnight, to replace them in the *control* over production and distribution, in the work of *keeping account* of labour and products, by the armed workers, by the whole of the armed population. (The question of control and accounting should not be confused with the question of the scientifically trained staff of engineers, agronomists, and so on. These gentlemen are working today in obedience to the wishes of the capitalists, and will work even better tomorrow in obedience to the wishes of the armed workers.)

Accounting and control—that is *mainly* what is needed for the "smooth working," for the proper functioning, of the *first phase* of communist society. *All* citizens are transformed into hired employees of the state, which consists of the armed workers. *All* citizens become employees and workers of a *single* country-wide state "syndicate." All that is required is that they should work equally, do their proper share of work, and get equal pay. The accounting and control necessary for this have been *simplified* by capitalism to the utmost and reduced to the extraordinarily simple operations—which any literate person can perform—of supervising and recording, knowledge of the four rules of arithmetic, and issuing appropriate receipts.

When the *majority* of the people begin independently and everywhere to keep such accounts and exercise such control over the capitalists (now converted into employees) and over the intellectual gentry who preserve their capitalist habits, this control will really become universal, general and popular; and there will be no getting away from it, there will be "nowhere to go."

The whole of society will have become a single office and a single factory, with equality of labour and pay.

But this "factory" discipline, which the proletariat, after defeating the capitalists, after overthrowing the exploiters, will extend to the whole of society, is by no means our ideal, or our ultimate goal. It is only a necessary *step* for thoroughly cleansing society of all the infamies and abominations of capitalist exploitation, *and for further* progress.

From the moment all members of society, or at least the vast majority, have learned to administer the state *themselves,* have taken this work into their own hands, have organised control over the insignificant capitalist minority, over the gentry who wish to preserve their capitalist habits and over the workers who have been thoroughly corrupted by capitalism—from this moment the need for government of any kind begins to disappear altogether. The more complete the democracy, the nearer the moment when it becomes unnecessary. The more democratic the "state" which consists of the armed workers, and which is "no longer a state in the proper sense of the word," the more rapidly *every form* of state begins to wither away.

For when *all* have learned to administer and actually do independently administer social production, independently keep accounts and exercise control over the parasites, the sons of the wealthy, the swindlers and other "guardians of capitalist traditions," the escape from this popular accounting and control will inevitably become so incredibly difficult, such a rare exception, and will probably be accompanied by such swift and severe punishment (for the armed workers are practical men and not sentimental intellectuals, and they will scarcely allow anyone to trifle with them), that the *necessity* of observing the simple, fundamental rules of the community will very soon become a *habit.*

Then the door will be thrown wide open for the transition from the first phase of communist society to its higher phase, and with it to the complete withering away of the state.

39

The Permanent Revolution

LEON TROTSKY

Leon Trotsky was the revolutionary name of Lev Davidovich Bronstein (1879–1940), one of the leading theorists and strategists of the Russian Bolsheviks. In the years before the Bolsheviks (or the Communists) seized power in 1917, Trotsky developed the idea of "the permanent revolution" as a way of justifying a socialist regime in a nonindustrial country like Russia. After the Communists gained control and formed the Soviet Union, Trotsky fell out with Joseph Stalin, whose policy of "socialism in one country" was directly opposed to Trotsky's "permanent revolution." Trotsky went into exile in 1929—the year in which he wrote *The Permanent Revolution*—and was living in Mexico when he was murdered in 1940 by one of Stalin's secret agents.

Source: Leon Trotsky, *The Permanent Revolution* (New York: Pathfinder Press, 1969). Copyright © 1969 by Pathfinder Press. Reprinted by permission.

WHAT IS THE PERMANENT REVOLUTION?

Basic Postulates

I hope that the reader will not object if, to end this book, I attempt, without fear of repetition, to formulate succinctly my principal conclusions.

1. The theory of the permanent revolution now demands the greatest attention from every Marxist, for the course of the class and ideological struggle has fully and finally raised this question from the realm of reminiscences over old differences of opinion among Russian Marxists, and converted it into a question of the character, the inner connexions and methods of the international revolution in general.

2. With regard to countries with a belated bourgeois development, especially the colonial and semi-colonial countries, the theory of the permanent revolution signifies that the complete and genuine solution of their tasks of achieving *democracy and national emancipation* is conceivable only through the dictatorship of the proletariat as the leader of the subjugated nation, above all of its peasant masses.

3. Not only the agrarian, but also the national question assigns to the peasantry—the overwhelming majority of the population in backward countries—an exceptional place in the democratic revolution. Without an alliance of the proletariat with the peasantry the tasks of the democratic revolution cannot be solved, nor even seriously posed. But the alliance of these two classes can be realized in no other way than through an irreconcilable struggle against the influence of the national-liberal bourgeoisie.

4. No matter what the first episodic stages of the revolution may be in the individual countries, the realization of the revolutionary alliance between the proletariat and the peasantry is conceivable only under the political leadership of the proletarian vanguard, organized in the Communist Party. This in turn means that the victory of the democratic revolution is conceivable only through the dictatorship of the proletariat which bases itself upon the alliance with the peasantry and solves first of all the tasks of the democratic revolution.

5. Assessed historically, the old slogan of Bolshevism—"the democratic dictatorship of the proletariat and peasantry"—expressed precisely the above-characterized relationship of the proletariat, the peasantry and the liberal bourgeoisie. This has been confirmed by the experience of October [1917, when the Communists seized power in Russia]. But Lenin's old formula did not settle in advance the problem of what the reciprocal relations would be between the proletariat and the peasantry within the revolutionary bloc. In other words, the formula deliberately retained a certain algebraic quality, which had to make way for more precise arithmetical quantities in the process of historical experience. However, the latter showed, and under circumstances that exclude any kind of misinterpretation, that no matter how great the revolutionary role of the peasantry may be, it nevertheless cannot be an independent role and even less a leading one. The peasant follows either the worker or the bourgeois. This means that the "democratic dictatorship of the proletariat and peasantry" is only conceivable as a *dictatorship of the proletariat that leads the peasant masses behind it.*

6. A democratic dictatorship of the proletariat and peasantry, as a regime that is distinguished from the dictatorship of the proletariat by its class content, might be realized only in a case where an *independent revolutionary* party could be constituted, expressing the interests of the peasants and in general of petty-bourgeois democracy—a party capable of conquering power with this or that degree of aid from the proletariat, and of determining its revolutionary pro-

gramme. As all modern history attests—especially the Russian experience of the last twenty-five years—an insurmountable obstacle on the road to the creation of a peasants' party is the petty-bourgeoisie's lack of economic and political independence and its deep internal differentiation. By reason of this the upper sections of the petty-bourgeoisie (of the peasantry) go along with the big bourgeoisie in all decisive cases, especially in war and in revolution; the lower sections go along with the proletariat; the intermediate section being thus compelled to choose between the two extreme poles. Between Kerenskyism and the Bolshevik power, between the Kuomintang and the dictatorship of the proletariat, there is not and cannot be any intermediate stage, that is, no democratic dictatorship of the workers and peasants.[1]

7. The Comintern's [i.e., Communist International's] endeavour to foist upon the Eastern countries the slogan of the democratic dictatorship of the proletariat and peasantry, finally and long ago exhausted by history, can have only a reactionary effect. Insofar as this slogan is counterposed to the slogan of the dictatorship of the proletariat, it contributes politically to the dissolution of the proletariat in the petty-bourgeois masses and thus creates the most favourable conditions for the hegemony of the national bourgeoisie and consequently for the collapse of the democratic revolution. The introduction of this slogan into the programme of the Comintern is a direct betrayal of Marxism and of the October tradition of Bolshevism.

8. The dictatorship of the proletariat which has risen to power as the leader of the democratic revolution is inevitably and very quickly confronted with tasks, the fulfilment of which is bound up with deep inroads into the rights of bourgeois property. The democratic revolution grows over directly into the socialist revolution and thereby becomes a *permanent* revolution.

9. The conquest of power by the proletariat does not complete the revolution, but only opens it. Socialist construction is conceivable only on the foundation of the class struggle, on a national and international scale. This struggle, under the conditions of an overwhelming predominance of capitalist relationships on the world arena, must inevitably lead to explosions, that is, internally to civil wars and externally to revolutionary wars. Therein lies the permanent character of the socialist revolution as such, regardless of whether it is a backward country that is involved, which only yesterday accomplished its democratic revolution, or an old capitalist country which already has behind it a long epoch of democracy and parliamentarism.

10. The completion of the socialist revolution within national limits is unthinkable. One of the basic reasons for the crisis in bourgeois society is the fact that the productive forces created by it can no longer be reconciled with the framework of the national state. From this follow, on the one hand, imperialist wars, on the other, the utopia of a bourgeois United States of Europe. The socialist revolution begins on the national arena, it unfolds on the international arena, and is completed on the world arena. Thus, the socialist revolution becomes a permanent revolution in a newer and broader sense of the word; it attains completion only in the final victory of the new society on our entire planet.

11. The above-outlined sketch of the development of the world revolution eliminates the question of countries that are "mature" or "immature" for socialism in the spirit of that pedantic, lifeless classification given by the present programme of the Comintern. Insofar as capitalism has created a world market, a world division of labour and world productive forces, it has also prepared the world economy as a whole for socialist transformation.

Different countries will go through this process at different tempos. Backward countries may, under certain conditions, arrive at the dictatorship of the proletariat sooner than advanced countries, but they will come later than the latter to socialism.

A backward colonial or semi-colonial country, the proletariat of which is insufficiently prepared to unite the peasantry and take power, is thereby incapable of bringing the democratic revolution to its conclusion. Contrariwise, in a country where the proletariat has power in its hands as the result of the democratic revolution, the subsequent fate of the dictatorship and socialism depends in the last analysis not only and not so much upon the national productive forces as upon the development of the international socialist revolution.

12. The theory of socialism in one country, which rose on the yeast of the reaction against October, is the only theory that consistently and to the very end opposes the theory of the permanent revolution.

The attempt of the epigones, under the lash of our criticism, to confine the application of the theory of socialism in one country exclusively to Russia, because of its specific characteristics (its vastness and its natural resources), does not improve matters but only makes them worse. The break with the internationalist position always and invariably leads to national *messianism,* that is, to attributing special superiorities and qualities to one's own country, which allegedly permit it to play a role to which other countries cannot attain.

The world division of labour, the dependence of Soviet industry upon foreign technology, the dependence of the productive forces of the advanced countries of Europe upon Asiatic raw materials, etc., make the construction of an independent socialist society in any single country in the world impossible.

13. The theory of Stalin and [Nikolai] Bukharin, running counter to the entire experience of the Russian revolution, not only sets up the democratic revolution mechanically in contrast to the socialist revolution, but also makes a breach between the national revolution and the international revolution.

This theory imposes upon revolutions in backward countries the task of establishing an unrealizable regime of democratic dictatorship, which it counterposes to the dictatorship of the proletariat. Thereby this theory introduces illusions and fictions into politics, paralyses the struggle for power of the proletariat in the East, and hampers the victory of the colonial revolution.

The very seizure of power by the proletariat signifies, from the standpoint of the epigones' theory, the completion of the revolution ("to the extent of nine-tenths," according to Stalin's formula) and the opening of the epoch of national reforms. The theory of the *kulak* [farmer] growing into socialism and the theory of the "neutralization" of the world bourgeoisie are consequently inseparable from the theory of socialism in one country. They stand or fall together.

By the theory of national socialism, the Communist International is down-graded to an auxiliary weapon useful only for the struggle against military intervention. The present policy of the Comintern, its regime and the selection of its leading personnel correspond entirely to the demotion of the Communist International to the role of an auxiliary unit which is not destined to solve independent tasks.

14. The programme of the Comintern created by Bukharin is eclectic through and through. It makes the hopeless attempt to reconcile the theory of socialism in one country with Marxist internationalism, which is, however, inseparable from the permanent character of the world revolution. The struggle of the

Communist Left Opposition for a correct policy and a healthy regime in the Communist International is inseparably bound up with the struggle for the Marxist programme. The question of the programme is in turn inseparable from the question of the two mutually exclusive theories: the theory of permanent revolution and the theory of socialism in one country. The problem of the permanent revolution has long ago outgrown the episodic differences of opinion between Lenin and Trotsky, which were completely exhausted by history. The struggle is between the basic ideas of Marx and Lenin on the one side and the eclecticism of the centrists on the other.

NOTE

1. Alexander Kerensky (1881–1970) was a Russian socialist reformer and prime minister of the provisional government that the Bolsheviks overthrew in 1917; the Kuomintang was the Nationalist Party of China.—Eds.

40

On the People's Democratic Dictatorship

MAO ZEDONG

The Chinese Communist Revolution, led by Mao Zedong (1893–1976), routed the Kuomintang (Nationalist) forces of Chiang Kai-shek in 1949. In attempting to adapt Marxism-Leninism to Chinese conditions, Mao set even greater store by the peasantry than had Lenin. After the revolution the "people"—by which Mao meant mainly the peasantry, under the stern guidance of the Chinese Communist Party—were to rule. The "people's democratic dictatorship" meant rule not so much by as on behalf of the numerically largest class, namely, the peasantry. This interim "dictatorship" was to be a period of civic "education" for the peasantry and harsh "re-education" for others. Once in power, Mao—like Stalin in the Soviet Union—made himself an object of veneration and worship.

Source: Mao Zedong, "On the People's Democratic Dictatorship," *Selected Works* (Beijing: Foreign Languages Press, 1971), pp. 411–423.

ON THE PEOPLE'S DEMOCRATIC DICTATORSHIP

In Commemoration of the Twenty-Eighth Anniversary of the Communist Party of China

June 30, 1949 The first of July 1949 marks the fact that the Communist Party of China has already lived through twenty-eight years. Like a man, a political party has its childhood, youth, manhood and old age. The Communist Party of China is no longer a child or a lad in his teens but has become an adult. When a man reaches old age, he will die; the same is true of a party. When classes disappear, all instruments of class struggle—parties and the state machinery—will lose their function, cease to be necessary, therefore gradually wither away and end their historical mission; and human society will move to a higher stage. We are the opposite of the political parties of the bourgeoisie. They are afraid to speak of the extinction of classes, state power and parties. We, on the contrary, declare openly that we are striving hard to create the very conditions which will bring about their extinction. The leadership of the Communist Party and the state power of the people's dictatorship are such conditions. Anyone who does not recognize this truth is no communist. Young comrades who have not studied Marxism-Leninism and have only recently joined the Party may not yet understand this truth. They must understand it—only then can they have a correct world outlook. They must understand that the road to the abolition of classes, to the abolition of state power and to the abolition of parties is the road all mankind must take; it is only a question of time and conditions. Communists the world over are wiser than the bourgeoisie, they understand the laws governing the existence and development of things, they understand dialectics and they can see farther. The bourgeoisie does not welcome this truth because it does not want to be overthrown. To be overthrown is painful and is unbearable to contemplate for those overthrown, for example, for the Kuomintang [Nationalist] reactionaries whom we are now overthrowing and for Japanese imperialism which we together with other peoples overthrew some time ago. But for the working class, the labouring people and the Communist Party the question is not one of being overthrown, but of working hard to create the conditions in which classes, state power and political parties will die out very naturally and mankind will enter the realm of Great Harmony.[1] We have mentioned in passing the long-range perspective of human progress in order to explain clearly the problems we are about to discuss.

As everyone knows, our Party passed through these twenty-eight years not in peace but amid hardships, for we had to fight enemies, both foreign and domestic, both inside and outside the Party. We thank Marx, Engels, Lenin and Stalin for giving us a weapon. This weapon is not a machine-gun, but Marxism-Leninism.

In his book *"Left-Wing" Communism, an Infantile Disorder* written in 1920, Lenin described the quest of the Russians for revolutionary theory.[2] Only after several decades of hardship and suffering did the Russians find Marxism. Many things in China were the same as, or similar to, those in Russia before the October Revolution [of 1917]. There was the same feudal oppression. There was similar economic and cultural backwardness. Both countries were backward, China even more so. In both countries alike, for the sake of national regeneration progressives braved hard and bitter struggles in their quest for revolutionary truth.

From the time of China's defeat in the Opium War of 1840,[3] Chinese progressives went through untold hardships in their quest for truth from the Western countries. Hung Hsiu-chuan,[4] Kang Yu-wei,[5] Yen Fu[6] and Sun Yat-sen were representative of those who had looked to the West for truth before the Communist Party of China was born. Chinese who then sought progress would read any book containing the new knowledge from the West. The number of students sent to Japan, Britain, the United States, France and Germany was amazing. At home, the imperial examinations[7] were abolished and modern schools sprang up like bamboo shoots after a spring rain; every effort was made to learn from the West. In my youth, I too engaged in such studies. They represented the culture of Western bourgeois democracy, including the social theories and natural sciences of that period, and they were called "the new learning" in contrast to Chinese feudal culture, which was called "the old learning." For quite a long time, those who had acquired the new learning felt confident that it would save China, and very few of them had any doubts on this score, as the adherents of the old learning had. Only modernization could save China, only learning from foreign countries could modernize China. Among the foreign countries, only the Western capitalist countries were then progressive, as they had successfully built modern bourgeois states. The Japanese had been successful in learning from the West, and the Chinese also wished to learn from the Japanese. The Chinese in those days regarded Russia as backward, and few wanted to learn from her. That was how the Chinese tried to learn from foreign countries in the period from the 1840s to the beginning of the 20th century.

Imperialist aggression shattered the fond dreams of the Chinese about learning from the West. It was very odd—why were the teachers always committing aggression against their pupil? The Chinese learned a good deal from the West, but they could not make it work and were never able to realize their ideals. Their repeated struggles, including such a country-wide movement as the Revolution of 1911,[8] all ended in failure. Day by day, conditions in the country got worse, and life was made impossible. Doubts arose, increased and deepened. World War I shook the whole globe. The Russians made the October Revolution and created the world's first socialist state. Under the leadership of Lenin and Stalin, the revolutionary energy of the great proletariat and labouring people of Russia, hitherto latent and unseen by foreigners, suddenly erupted like a volcano, and the Chinese and all mankind began to see the Russians in a new light. Then, and only then, did the Chinese enter an entirely new era in their thinking and their life. They found Marxism-Leninism, the universally applicable truth, and the face of China began to change.

It was through the Russians that the Chinese found Marxism. Before the October Revolution, the Chinese were not only ignorant of Lenin and Stalin, they did not even know of Marx and Engels. The salvoes of the October Revolution brought us Marxism-Leninism. The October Revolution helped progressives in China, as throughout the world, to adopt the proletarian world outlook as the instrument for studying a nation's destiny and considering anew their own problems. Follow the path of the Russians—that was their conclusion. In 1919, the May 4th Movement took place in China. In 1921, the Communist Party of China was founded. Sun Yat-sen, in the depths of despair, came across the October Revolution and the Communist Party of China. He welcomed the October Revolution, welcomed Russian help to the Chinese and welcomed co-operation of the Communist Party of China. Then Sun Yat-sen died and Chiang Kai-shek rose to power. Over a long period of twenty-two years, Chiang Kai-shek dragged China into ever more hopeless straits. In this period, during the anti-fascist Second World War in which the Soviet Union was the main force, three big imperialist powers were knocked out, while two others were weakened. In the whole world only one big imperialist power, the United States of America, remained uninjured. But the United States faced a grave domestic crisis. It wanted to enslave the whole world; it supplied arms to help Chiang Kai-shek slaughter several million Chinese. Under the leadership of the Communist Party of China, the Chinese people, after driving out Japanese imperialism, waged the People's War of Liberation for three years and have basically won victory.

Thus Western bourgeois civilization, bourgeois democracy and the plan for a bourgeois republic have all gone bankrupt in the eyes of the Chinese people. Bourgeois democracy has given way to people's democracy under the leadership of the working class and the bourgeois republic to the people's republic. This has made it possible to achieve socialism and communism through the people's republic, to abolish classes and enter a world of Great Harmony. Kang Yu-wei wrote *Ta Tung Shu*, or the *Book of Great Harmony*, but he did not and could not find the way to achieve Great Harmony. There are bourgeois republics in foreign lands, but China cannot have a bourgeois republic because she is a country suffering under imperialist oppression. The only way is through a people's republic led by the working class.

All other ways have been tried and failed. Of the people who hankered after those ways, some have fallen, some have awakened and some are changing their ideas. Events are developing so swiftly that many feel the abruptness of the change and the need to learn anew. This state of mind is understandable and we welcome this worthy desire to learn anew.

The vanguard of the Chinese proletariat learned Marxism-Leninism after the October Revolution and founded the Communist Party of China. It entered at once into political struggles and only now, after a tortuous course of twenty-eight years, has it won basic victory. From our twenty-eight years' experience we have drawn a conclusion similar to the one Sun Yat-sen drew in his testament from his "experience of forty years"; that is, we are deeply convinced that to win victory, "we must arouse the masses of the people and unite in a common struggle with those nations of the world which treat us as equals." Sun Yat-sen had a world outlook different from ours and started from a different class standpoint in studying and tackling problems; yet, in the 1920s he reached a conclusion basically the same as ours on the question of how to struggle against imperialism.

Twenty-four years have passed since Sun Yat-sen's death, and the Chinese revolution, led by the Communist Party of China, has made tremendous advances both in theory and practice and has radically changed the face of China. Up to now the principal and fundamental experience the Chinese people have gained is two-fold:

1. Internally, arouse the masses of the people. That is, unite the working class, the peasantry, the urban petty bourgeoisie and the national bourgeoisie, form a domestic united front under the leadership of the working class, and advance from this to the establishment of a state which is a people's democratic dictatorship under the leadership of the working class and based on the alliance of workers and peasants.
2. Externally, unite in a common struggle with those nations of the world which treat us as equals and unite with the peoples of all countries. That is, ally ourselves with the Soviet Union, with the People's Democracies and with the proletariat and the broad masses of the people in all other countries, and form an international united front.

"You are leaning to one side." Exactly. The forty years' experience of Sun Yat-sen and the twenty-eight years' experience of the Communist Party have taught us to lean to one side, and we are firmly convinced that in order to win victory and consolidate it we must lean to one side. In the light of the experiences accumulated in these forty years and these twenty-eight years, all Chinese without exception must lean either to the side of imperialism or to the side of socialism. Sitting on the fence will not do, nor is there a third road. We oppose the Chiang Kai-shek reactionaries who lean to the side of imperialism, and we also oppose the illusions about a third road.

"You are too irritating." We are talking about how to deal with domestic and foreign reactionaries, the imperialists and their running dogs, not about how to deal with anyone else. With regard to such reactionaries, the question of irritating them or not does not arise. Irritated or not irritated, they will remain the same because they are reactionaries. Only if we draw a clear line between reactionaries and revolutionaries, expose the intrigues and plots of the reactionaries, arouse the vigilance and attention of the revolutionary ranks, heighten our will to fight and crush the enemy's arrogance can we isolate the reactionaries, vanquish them or supersede them. We must not show the slightest timidity before a wild beast. We must learn from Wu Sung[9] on the Chingyang Ridge. As Wu Sung saw it, the tiger on Chingyang Ridge was a man-eater, whether irritated or not. Either kill the tiger or be eaten by him—one or the other.

"We want to do business." Quite right, business will be done. We are against no one except the domestic and foreign reactionaries who hinder us from doing business. Everybody should know that it is none other than the imperialists and their running dogs, the Chiang Kai-shek reactionaries, who hinder us from doing business and also from establishing diplomatic relations with foreign countries. When we have beaten the internal and external reactionaries by uniting all domestic and international forces, we shall be able to do business and establish diplomatic relations with all foreign countries on the basis of equality, mutual benefit and mutual respect for territorial integrity and sovereignty.

"Victory is possible even without international help." This is a mistaken idea. In the epoch in which imperialism exists, it is impossible for a genuine people's revolution to win victory in any country without various forms of help from the international revolutionary forces, and even if victory were won, it could not be consolidated. This was the case with the victory and consolidation of the great October Revolution, as Lenin and Stalin told us long ago. This was also the case with the overthrow of the three imperialist powers in World War II and the establishment of the People's Democracies. And this is also the case with the present and the future of People's China. Just imagine! If the Soviet Union had not existed, if there had been no victory in the anti-fascist Second World War, if Japanese imperialism had not been defeated, if the People's Democracies had not come into being, if the oppressed nations of the East were not rising in struggle and if there were no struggle of the masses of the people against their reactionary rulers in the United States, Britain, France, Germany, Italy, Japan and other capitalist countries—if not for all these in combination, the international reactionary forces bearing down upon us would certainly be many times greater than now. In such circumstances, could we have won victory? Obviously not. And even with victory, there could be no consolidation. The Chinese people have had more than enough experience of this kind. This experience was reflected long ago in Sun Yat-sen's death-bed statement on the necessity of uniting with the international revolutionary forces.

"We need help from the British and U.S. governments." This, too, is a naïve idea in these times. Would the present rulers of Britain and the United States, who are imperialists, help a people's state? Why do these countries do business with us and, supposing they might be willing to lend us money on terms of mutual benefit in the future, why would they do so? Because their capitalists want to make money and their bankers want to earn interest to extricate themselves from their own crisis—it is not a matter of helping the Chinese people. The Communist Parties and progressive groups in these countries are urging their governments to establish trade and even diplomatic relations with us. This is good-will, this is help, this cannot be mentioned in the same breath with the conduct of the bourgeoisie in the same countries. Throughout his life, Sun Yat-sen appealed countless times to the capitalist countries for help and got nothing but heartless rebuffs. Only once in his whole life did Sun Yat-sen receive foreign help, and that was Soviet help. Let readers refer to Dr. Sun Yat-sen's testament; his earnest advice was not to look for help from the imperialist countries but to "unite with those nations of the world which treat us as equals." Dr. Sun had experience; he had suffered, he had been deceived. We should remember his words and not allow ourselves to be deceived again. Internationally, we belong to the side of the anti-imperialist front headed by the Soviet Union, and so we can turn only to this side for genuine and friendly help, not to the side of the imperialist front.

"You are dictatorial." My dear sirs, you are right, that is just what we are. All the experience the Chinese people have accumulated through several decades teaches us to enforce the people's democratic dictatorship, that is, to deprive the reactionaries of the right to speak and let the people alone have that right.

Who are the people? At the present stage in China, they are the working class, the peasantry, the urban petty bourgeoisie and the national bourgeoisie. These classes, led by the working class and the Communist Party, unite to form their own state and elect their own government; they enforce their dictatorship over the running dogs of imperialism—the landlord class and bureaucrat-bourgeoisie, as well as the representatives of those classes, the Kuomintang reactionaries and their accomplices—suppress them, allow them only to behave themselves and not to be unruly in word or deed. If they speak or act in an unruly way, they will be promptly stopped and punished. Democracy is practised within the ranks of the people, who enjoy the rights of freedom of speech, assembly, association and so on. The right to vote belongs only to the people, not to the reactionaries. The combination of these two aspects, democracy for the people and dictatorship over the reactionaries, is the people's democratic dictatorship.

Why must things be done this way? The reason is quite clear to everybody. If things were not done this way, the revolution would fail, the people would suffer, the country would be conquered.

"Don't you want to abolish state power?" Yes, we do, but not right now; we cannot do it yet. Why? Because imperialism still exists, because domestic reaction still exists, because classes still exist in our country. Our present task is to strengthen the people's state apparatus—mainly the people's army, the people's police and the people's courts—in order to consolidate national defence and protect the people's interests. Given this condition, China can develop steadily, under the leadership of the working class and the Communist Party, from an agricultural into an industrial country and from a new-democratic into a socialist and communist society, can abolish classes and realize the Great Harmony. The state apparatus, including the army, the police and the courts, is the instrument by which one class oppresses another. It is an instrument for the oppression of antagonistic classes; it is violence and not "benevolence." "You are not benevolent!" Quite so. We definitely do not apply a policy of benevolence to the reactionaries and towards the reactionary activities of the reactionary classes. Our policy of benevolence is applied only within the ranks of the people, not beyond them to the reactionaries or to the reactionary activities of reactionary classes.

The people's state protects the people. Only when the people have such a state can they educate and remould themselves by democratic methods on a country-wide scale, with everyone taking part, and shake off the influence of domestic and foreign reactionaries (which is still very strong, will survive for a long time and cannot be quickly destroyed), rid themselves of the bad habits and ideas acquired in the old society, not allow themselves to be led astray by the reactionaries, and continue to advance—to advance towards a socialist and communist society.

Here, the method we employ is democratic, the method of persuasion, not of compulsion. When anyone among the people breaks the law, he too should be punished, imprisoned or even sentenced to death; but this is a matter of a few individual cases, and it differs in principle from the dictatorship exercised over the reactionaries as a class.

As for the members of the reactionary classes and individual reactionaries, so long as they do not rebel, sabotage or create trouble after their political power has been overthrown, land and work will be given to them as well in order to allow them to live and remould themselves through labour into new people. If they are not willing to work, the people's state will compel them to work. Propaganda and educational work will be done among them too and will be done, moreover, with as much care and thoroughness as among the captured army officers in the past. This, too, may be called a "policy of benevolence" if you like, but it is imposed by us on the members of the enemy classes and cannot be mentioned in the same breath with the work of self-education which we carry on within the ranks of the revolutionary people.

Such remoulding of members of the reactionary classes can be accomplished only by a state of the people's democratic dictatorship under the leadership of the Communist Party. When it is well done, China's major exploiting classes, the landlord class and the bureaucrat-bourgeoisie (the monopoly capitalist class), will be eliminated for good. There remain the national bourgeoisie; at the present stage, we can already do a good deal of suitable educational work with many of them. When the time comes to realize socialism, that is, to nationalize private enterprise, we shall carry the work of educating and remoulding them a step further. The people have a powerful state apparatus in their hands—there is no need to fear rebellion by the national bourgeoisie.

The serious problem is the education of the peasantry. The peasant economy is scattered, and the socialization of agriculture, judging by the Soviet Union's experience, will require a long time and painstaking work. Without socialization of agriculture, there can be no complete, consolidated socialism. The steps to socialize agriculture must be co-ordinated with the development of a powerful industry having state enterprise as its backbone.[10] The state of the people's democratic dictatorship must systematically solve the problems of industrialization. Since it is not proposed to discuss economic problems in detail in this article, I shall not go into them further.

In 1924 a famous manifesto was adopted at the Kuomintang's First National Congress, which Sun Yat-sen himself led and in which Communists participated. The manifesto stated:

> The so-called democratic system in modern states is usually monopolized by the bourgeoisie and has become simply an instrument for oppressing the common people. On the other hand, the Kuomintang's Principle of Democracy means a democratic system shared by all the common people and not privately owned by the few.

Apart from the question of who leads whom, the Principle of Democracy stated above corresponds as a general political programme to what we call People's Democracy or New Democracy. A state system which is shared only by the common people and which the bourgeoisie is not allowed to own privately—add to this the leadership of the working class, and we have the state system of the people's democratic dictatorship.

Chiang Kai-shek betrayed Sun Yat-sen and used the dictatorship of the bureaucrat-bourgeoisie and the landlord class as an instrument for oppressing the common people of China. This counter-revolutionary dictatorship was enforced for twenty-two years and has only now been overthrown by the common people of China under our leadership.

The foreign reactionaries who accuse us of practising "dictatorship" or "totalitarianism" are the very persons who practise it. They practise the dictatorship or totalitarianism of one class, the bourgeoisie, over the proletariat and the rest of the people. They are the very persons Sun Yat-sen spoke of as the bourgeoisie of modern states who oppress the common people. And it is from these reactionary scoundrels that Chiang Kai-shek learned his counter-revolutionary dictatorship.

Chu Hsi, a philosopher of the Sung Dynasty, wrote many books and made many remarks which are now forgotten, but one remark is still remembered, "Deal with a man as he deals with you."[11] This is just what we do; we deal with the imperialists and their running dogs, the Chiang Kai-shek reactionaries, as they deal with us. That is all there is to it!

Revolutionary dictatorship and counterrevolutionary dictatorship are by nature opposites, but the former was learned from the latter. Such learning is very important. If the revolutionary people do not master this method of ruling over the counter-revolutionary classes, they will not be able to maintain their state power, domestic and foreign reaction will overthrow that power and restore its own rule over China, and disaster will befall the revolutionary people.

The people's democratic dictatorship is based on the alliance of the working class, the peasantry and the urban petty bourgeoisie, and mainly on the alliance of the workers and the peasants, because these two classes comprise 80 to 90 per cent of China's population. These two classes are the main force in overthrowing imperialism and the Kuomintang reactionaries. The transition from New Democracy to socialism also depends mainly upon their alliance.

The people's democratic dictatorship needs the leadership of the working class. For it is only the working class that is most farsighted, most selfless and most thoroughly revolutionary. The entire history of revolution proves that without the leadership of the working class revolution fails and that with the leadership of the working class revolution triumphs. In the epoch of imperialism, in no country can any other class lead any genuine revolution to victory. This is clearly proved by the fact that the many revolutions led by China's petty bourgeoisie and national bourgeoisie all failed.

The national bourgeoisie at the present stage is of great importance. Imperialism, a most ferocious enemy, is still standing alongside us. China's modern industry still forms a very small proportion of the national economy. No reliable statistics are available, but it is estimated, on the basis of certain data, that before the War of Resistance Against Japan the value of output of modern industry constituted only about 10 percent of the total value of output of the national economy. To counter imperialist oppression and to raise her backward economy to a higher level, China must utilize all the factors of urban and rural capitalism that are beneficial and not harmful to the national economy and the people's livelihood; and we must unite with the national bourgeoisie in common struggle. Our present policy is to regulate capitalism, not to destroy it. But the national bourgeoisie cannot be the leader of the revolution, nor should it have the chief role in state power. The reason it cannot be the leader of the revolution and should not have the chief role in state power is that the social and economic position of the national bourgeoisie determines its weakness; it lacks foresight and sufficient courage and many of its members are afraid of the masses.

Sun Yat-sen advocated "arousing the masses of the people" or "giving assistance to the peasants and workers." But who is to "arouse" them or "give assistance" to them? Sun Yat-sen had the petty bourgeoisie and the national bourgeoisie in mind. As a matter of fact, they cannot do so. Why did forty years of revolution under Sun Yat-sen end in failure? Because in the epoch of imperialism the petty bourgeoisie and the national bourgeoisie cannot lead any genuine revolution to victory.

Our twenty-eight years have been quite different. We have had much valuable experience. A well-disciplined Party armed with the theory of Marxism-Leninism, using the method of self-criticism and linked with the masses of the people; an army under the leadership of such a Party; a united front of all revolutionary classes and all revolutionary groups under the leadership of such a Party—these are the three main weapons with which we have defeated the enemy. They distinguish us from our predecessors. Relying on them, we have won basic victory. We have travelled a tortuous road. We have struggled against opportunist deviations in our Party, both Right and "Left." Whenever we made serious mistakes on these three matters, the revolution suffered setbacks. Taught by mistakes and setbacks, we have become wiser and handle our affairs better. It is hard for any political party or person to avoid mistakes, but we should make as few as possible. Once a mistake is made, we should correct it, and the more quickly and thoroughly the better.

To sum up our experience and concentrate it into one point, it is: the people's democratic dictatorship under the leadership of the working class (through the Communist Party) and based upon the alliance of workers and peasants. This dictatorship must unite as one with the international revolutionary forces. This is our formula, our principal experience, our main programme.

Twenty-eight years of our Party are a long period, in which we have accomplished only one thing—we have won basic victory in the revolutionary war. This calls for celebration, because it is the people's victory, because it is a victory in a country as large as China. But we still have much work to do; to use the analogy of a journey, our past work is only the first step in a long march of ten thousand *li*. Remnants of the enemy have yet to be wiped out. The serious task of economic construction lies before us. We shall soon put aside some of the things we know well and be compelled to do things we don't know well. This means difficulties. The imperialists reckon that we will not be able to manage our economy; they are standing by and looking on, awaiting our failure.

We must overcome difficulties, we must learn what we do not know. We must learn to do economic work from all who know how, no matter who they are. We must esteem them as teachers, learning from them respectfully and conscientiously. We must not pretend to know when we do not know. We must not put on bureaucratic airs. If we dig into a subject for several months, for a year or two, for three or five years, we shall eventually master it. At first some of the Soviet Communists also were not very good at handling economic matters and the imperialists awaited their failure too. But the Communist Party of the Soviet Union emerged victorious and, under the leadership of Lenin and Stalin, it learned not only how to make the revolution but also how to carry on construction. It has built a great and splendid socialist state. The Communist Party of the Soviet Union is our best teacher and we must learn from it. The situation both at home and abroad is in our favour, we can rely fully on the weapon of the people's democratic dictatorship, unite the people throughout the country, the reactionaries excepted, and advance steadily to our goal.

NOTES

1. Also known as the World of Great Harmony. It refers to a society based on public ownership, free from class exploitation and oppression—a lofty ideal long cherished by the Chinese people. Here the realm of Great Harmony means communist society.
2. See V. I. Lenin, *"Left-Wing" Communism, an Infantile Disorder*, Chapter 2. Lenin said: "For nearly half a century—approximately from the [1840s to 1890s]—advanced thinkers in Russia, under the oppression of an unparalleled savage and reactionary tsardom, eagerly sought for the correct revolutionary theory and followed each and every 'last word' in Europe and America in this sphere with astonishing diligence and thoroughness. Russia achieved Marxism, the only correct revolutionary theory, veritably through *suffering*, by half a century of unprecedented torment and sacrifice, of unprecedented revolutionary heroism, incredible energy, devoted searching, study, testing in practice, disappointment, verification and comparison with European experience."
3. Faced with the opposition of the Chinese people to her traffic in opium, Britain sent forces in 1840–1842 to invade Kwangtung and other coastal regions of China under the pretext of protecting trade. The troops in Kwangtung, led by Lin Tse-hau, fought a war of resistance.
4. Hung Hsiu-chuan (1814–1864), who was born in Kwangtung, was the leader of a peasant revolutionary war in the middle of the 19th century. In 1851 he led a mass uprising in Kwangsi and proclaimed the establishment of the Tsiping Heavenly Kingdom, which held many provinces and fought the Ching Dynasty for fourteen years. In 1864 this revolutionary war failed and Hung Hsiu-chuan committed suicide by poison.
5. Kang Yu-wei (1858–1927), of Nanhai County, Kwangtung Province. In 1895, after China had been defeated by Japanese imperialism in the previous year, he led thirteen hundred candidates for the third grade in the imperial examinations at Peking in submitting a "ten thousand word memorial" to Emperor Kuang Hsu, asking for "constitutional reform and modernization" and asking that the autocratic monarchy be changed into a constitutional monarchy. In 1898, in an attempt to introduce reforms, the emperor promoted Kang Yu-wei together with Tan Szetung, Liang Chi-chao and others to key posts in the government. Later, the Empress Dowager Tzu Hsi, representing the diehards, again took power and the reform movement failed. Kang Yu-wei and Liang Chi-chao fled abroad and formed the Protect-the-Emperor Party, which became a reactionary political faction in opposition to the bourgeois and petty bourgeois revolutionaries represented by Sun Yat-sen. Among Kang's works were *Forgeries in the Classics of the Confucian Canon, Confucius as a Reformer*, and *Ta Tung Shu* or the *Book of Great Harmony.*
6. Yen Fu (1853–1921), of Foochow, Fukien Province, studied at a naval academy in Britain. After the Sino-Japanese War of 1894, he advocated constitutional monarchy and reforms to modernize China. His translations of T. H. Hux-

ley's *Evolution and Ethics,* Adam Smith's *The Wealth of Nations,* J. S. Mill's *System of Logic,* Montesquieu's *L'Esprit des Lois,* and other works were vehicles for the spread of European bourgeois thought in China.

7. A system of examinations adopted by China's autocratic dynasties. It was a method used by the feudal ruling class for selecting personnel to govern the people and also for enticing the intellectuals. The system, dating from the 7th century, persisted into the early 20th century.

8. The Revolution of 1911 overthrew the autocratic regime of the Ching Dynasty. On October 10 of that year, a section of the New Army, at the urging of the revolutionary societies of the bourgeoisie and petty bourgeoisie, staged an uprising in Wu-chang. This was followed by uprisings in other provinces, and very soon the rule of the Ching Dynasty crumbled. On January 1, 1912, the Provisional Government of the Republic of China was set up in Nanking, and Sun Yat-sen was elected provisional president. The revolution achieved victory through the alliance of the bourgeoisie, peasants, workers, and urban petty bourgeoisie. But because the group which led the revolution was compromising in nature, failed to bring real benefits to the peasants, and yielded to the pressure of imperialism and the feudal forces, state power fell into the hands of the Northern warlord Yuan Shih-kai and the revolution failed.

9. A hero in the novel *Shui Hu Chuan* (*Heroes of the Marshes*), who killed a tiger with his bare hands on the Chingyang Ridge. This is one of the most popular episodes in that famous novel.

10. For the relation between the socialization of agriculture and the industrialization of the country, see *On the Question of Agricultural Co-operation* (Sections 7 and 8), a report made by Comrade Mao Zedong July 31, 1955 at the Conference of the Secretaries of the Provincial, Municipal and Autonomous Region Committees of the Chinese Communist Party. In this report Comrade Mao Zedong, on the basis of Soviet experience and our own country's [i.e., China's] practice, greatly developed the thesis that socialization of agriculture should proceed in step with socialist industrialization.

11. The quotation is from Chu Hsi's commentary on the *Confucian Doctrine of the Mean,* Chapter 13.

41

Anarcho-Communism vs. Marxism

MIKHAIL BAKUNIN

Among Marx's earliest critics were "anarcho-communists," including Mikhail Bakunin (1814–1876). A Russian anarchist (from the Greek *an archos,* meaning "no rule" or "no government"), Bakunin disputed Marx's claim that communism would lead to "the withering away of the state." Instead, Bakunin predicted, the supposedly temporary interim state that Marx called "the dictatorship of the proletariat" would prove to be a permanent dictatorship *over* the proletariat by state officials who would jealously guard their own power and privilege. Bakunin insisted that state power must be smashed once and for all by a proletarian revolution. Only in a voluntary anarchist society, he claimed, could people combine and associate as free and equal producers.

Source: Michel Bakounine [Mikhail Bakunin], "Lettre á *la Liberté,*" *Oeuvres* (Paris: P.-V. Stock, 1910), vol. 4, pp. 341–350, 378. Translated from the French by Terence Ball.

LETTER TO *LA LIBERTÉ* (BRUSSELS)

5 October 1872, Zurich

Gentlemen:

The victory of Mr. Karl Marx and his disciples is now complete.... The Marxists have now removed their masks and, as is all-too-typical of power-loving men, always in the name of that "sovereignty of the people" which from now on will be the platform from which all who aspire to control the masses will operate, they have boldly begun to enslave the people of the Socialist International.

If the International were less vital and vigorous—if it were based, as they believe, only on the organized command centers, rather than on the real solidarity of the objective interests and aims of the workers of every civilized country...—the declarations of that wretched Hague Congress, the ever-malleable representative of Marxist theory and practice, would have killed it....

A state, a government, a universal dictatorship! The dream of [such would-be despots as Pope] Gregory VIII, Pope Boniface, King Charles V or the Emperor Napoleon, now reproduced in a new form but still with the same aims, this time in the camp of the democratic socialists! Can one conceive of anything more ridiculous, or more revolting?

To pretend that a group of men—even the brightest and best-intentioned among them—could become the mind, soul, and shaping and unifying will of the revolutionary movement and economic organization of the proletariat of all countries is such a massive affront to common sense and historical experience that one is astonished that a brilliant man like Mr. Marx could have conceived of it.

At least the Popes could excuse themselves by resorting to the Absolute Truth which they claimed the Holy Spirit had given to them, and which they had no choice but to believe. Mr. Marx has no such excuse, and I shall not insult him by saying that he fancies himself to have scientifically discovered some sort of absolute truth. But accepting that the absolute does not exist, no infallible dogma is available to the International and thus no authoritative political or economic theory. Our assemblies and councils should never try to be like the ecumenical councils, decreeing compulsory principles for the faithful to believe.

Only one law unites all members, individuals, sections and federations of the International, and constitutes its only true foundation. That law is THE INTERNATIONAL SOLIDARITY OF ALL WORKERS IN ALL COUNTRIES IN THEIR ECONOMIC STRUGGLE AGAINST THE EXPLOITERS OF LABOR. The actual organization of that solidarity through the free action of the proletariat...constitutes the real and living unity of the International.

Who can doubt that from this ever broader organization of militant proletarian solidarity against bourgeois exploitation that the political struggle of the proletariat must intensify? We anarcho-communists agree with the Marxists about that. But we must now confront the question that separates us so profoundly from the Marxists.

We hold that the necessarily revolutionary policy of the proletariat must have as its one and only objective the smashing of the State. We cannot conceive of talking about international solidarity while, at the same time, attempting to preserve states—except perhaps in some dream about a universal state, i.e., universal slavery, as dreamed by powerful emperors and popes—because by its very nature the state subverts solidarity and is a permanent cause of war. We cannot conceive of talking about the liberty or the emancipation of the proletariat within or by means of the state. To speak of the state is to speak of domination. And all domination entails the subjugation of the people and thus their exploitation by some governing minority.

We do not accept, even in the course of revolutionary transition, either national conventions, or constituent assemblies, or "revolutionary dictatorships"; because we are convinced that a sincere, real and honest revolution can only be made by the masses. When [the revolution] is directed by a small number of ruling individuals it inevitably and immediately turns reactionary. Such is our belief, though this is not the time to explain it in detail.

The Marxists profess very different ideas. Like good Germans, they worship at the shrine of State power.... The only kind of emancipation the Marxists recognize is what comes out of their so-called "People's State" (*Volkstaat*). Far from being opponents of "patriotism," they all too often fly the flag of Pan-Germanism. There may well be a noticeable difference between German Chancellor Otto von Bismarck's policies and Marx's; but between the Marxists and ourselves there is a deep divide. They favor government, while we do not: we are anarchists.

These are the two political tendencies that today divide the International into two camps. On the one side is Germany, all but alone; on the other, to one or another degree, are Italy, Spain, the Swiss Jura, much of France, Belgium, Holland, and, shortly, the Slavs. These two tendencies locked horns at the Hague Congress and, thanks to the cleverness of Mr. Marx and the completely artificial organization of that Congress, the German tendency emerged victorious.

Was the crucial question then resolved? No. It was not even properly discussed. The majority voted like a well-trained regiment, trampling all discussion under its vote. The contradiction is thus more lively and more menacing than ever, and Mr. Marx himself, despite being drunk with victory, can hardly imagine otherwise. And even if he had for an instant held such a vain hope, the combined protest of the Swiss, Spanish, Belgian and Dutch delegations (not to mention Italy, which did not send delegates to such an obviously rigged Congress)—so moderate in form but all the more powerful for that—must soon have disabused him.

That protest, in itself, is merely a mild harbinger of the storm of opposition which will rage in every country penetrated by the principles and passion of social revolution. And the entire storm will have been stirred up by the Marxists' unhappy preoccupation with making the political question a basis and a binding principle of the International.

Between these two tendencies no conciliation or compromise is possible. Only the practice of social revolution, great new historical experiments, and the logic of events might one day direct them toward a shared solution. And, as we are persuaded of the worth of our own principle, we hope that the Germans themselves—the workers of Germany, that is, not their leaders—will finally join us in destroying those people's prisons which some call states, and to condemn politics, which is merely the art of dominating and deceiving the masses.

...I can see how despots, crowned or uncrowned, could have dreamed of ruling the world. But what can we say when a friend of the proletariat, a revolutionary who says he sincerely supports the emancipation of the masses, then sets himself up as director and ultimate judge of every revolutionary movement which might emerge in every country, and boldly dreams of subjecting them to a singular thought that he has hatched in his own head!

I think that Mr. Marx is a very serious if not always very honest revolutionary, and that he is truly in favor of the elevation of the masses; and so I marvel at how he manages to ignore the fact that the establishment of a universal dictatorship (whether individual or collective) which would require some sort of engineer-in-chief of world revolution, to rule and direct the insurrectionary movement of the masses throughout the world, in much the same way as a machine is operated—that the establishment of such a supreme dictatorship would be sufficient to stifle revolution and distort and paralyze all popular movements....

The political state in every country, he says, is always the product and faithful expression of its economic situation; in order to change the former it is necessary to change the latter. The entire secret of historical evolutions, according to Marx, is this. He pays no attention to other factors in history, such as the consequence (utterly clear though it is) of political, legal and religious institutions on the economic conditions. He says: "Misery produces political slavery, the state"; but he does not recognize the converse: "Political slavery, the state, reproduces and maintains misery, as a condition of its existence; thus in order to destroy misery, the state must be destroyed."

42

Anarchism: What It Really Stands For

EMMA GOLDMAN

In the late nineteenth and early twentieth centuries, Emma Goldman (1869–1940) was widely known as "Red Emma" because of her activity on behalf of radical causes. Born in Russia, she moved to the United States when she was seventeen and remained there for most of her life. Her outspoken advocacy of anarchism, socialism, and women's rights led to prison sentences for, among other things, openly promoting birth control and opposing the draft during World War I. She was deported to Russia in 1919, where she became an outspoken critic of the newly established communist regime. In the following essay, Goldman defends anarcho-communism by clarifying its aims and responding to common criticisms—and, in her view, misconceptions—of anarchism.

Source: Emma Goldman, *Anarchism and Other Essays* (New York: Mother Earth Association Publishers, 1910).

ANARCHISM: WHAT IT REALLY STANDS FOR

The history of human growth and development is at the same time the history of the terrible struggle of every new idea heralding the approach of a brighter dawn. In its tenacious hold on tradition, the Old has never hesitated to make use of the foulest and cruelest means to stay the advent of the New, in whatever form or period the latter may have asserted itself. Nor need we retrace our steps into the distant past to realize the enormity of opposition, difficulties, and hardships placed in the path of every progressive idea. The rack, the thumbscrew, and the knout are still with us; so are the convict's garb and the social wrath, all conspiring against the spirit that is serenely marching on.

Anarchism could not hope to escape the fate of all other ideas of innovation. Indeed, as the most revolutionary and uncompromising innovator, Anarchism must needs meet with the combined ignorance and venom of the world it aims to reconstruct.

To deal even remotely with all that is being said and done against Anarchism would necessitate the writing of a whole volume. I shall therefore meet only two of the principal objections. In so doing, I shall attempt to elucidate what Anarchism really stands for.

The strange phenomenon of the opposition to Anarchism is that it brings to light the relation between so-called intelligence and ignorance. And yet this is not so very strange when we consider the relativity of all things. The ignorant mass has in its favor that it makes no pretense of knowledge or tolerance. Acting, as it always does, by mere impulse, its reasons are like those of a child. "Why?" "Because." Yet the opposition of the uneducated to Anarchism deserves the same consideration as that of the intelligent man.

What, then, are the objections? First, Anarchism is impractical, though a beautiful ideal. Second, Anarchism stands for violence and destruction, hence it must be repudiated as vile and dangerous. Both the intelligent man and the ignorant mass judge not from a thorough knowledge of the subject, but either from hearsay or false interpretation.

A practical scheme, says Oscar Wilde,[1] is either one already in existence, or a scheme that could be carried out under the existing conditions; but it is exactly the existing conditions that one objects to, and any scheme that could accept these conditions is wrong and foolish. The true criterion of the practical, therefore, is not whether the latter can keep intact the wrong or foolish; rather is it whether the scheme has vitality enough to leave the stagnant waters of the old, and build, as well as sustain, new life. In the light of this conception, Anarchism is indeed practical. More than any other idea, it is helping to do away with the wrong and foolish; more than any other idea, it is building and sustaining new life.

The emotions of the ignorant man are continuously kept at a pitch by the most bloodcurdling stories about Anarchism. Not a thing is too outrageous to be employed against this philosophy and its exponents. Therefore Anarchism represents to the unthinking what the proverbial bad man does to the child—a black monster bent on swallowing everything; in short, destruction and violence.

Destruction and violence! How is the ordinary man to know that the most violent element in society is ignorance; that its power of destruction is the very thing Anarchism is combating? Nor is he aware that Anarchism, whose roots, as it were, are part of nature's forces, destroys, not healthful tissue, but parasitic growths that feed on the life's essence of society. It is merely clearing the soil from weeds and sagebrush, that it may eventually bear healthy fruit.

Someone has said that it requires less mental effort to condemn than to think. The widespread mental indolence, so prevalent in society, proves this to be only too true. Rather than to go to the bottom of any given idea, to examine into its origin and meaning, most people will either condemn it altogether, or rely on some superficial or prejudicial definition of non-essentials.

Anarchism urges man to think, to investigate, to analyze every proposition; but that the brain capacity of the average reader be not taxed too much, I also shall begin with a definition, and then elaborate on the latter.

> ANARCHISM:—The philosophy of a new social order based on liberty unrestricted by man-made law; the theory that all forms of government rest on violence, and are therefore wrong and harmful, as well as unnecessary.

The new social order rests, of course, on the materialistic basis of life; but while all Anarchists agree that the main evil today is an economic one, they maintain that the solution of that evil can be brought about only through the consideration of *every phase* of life—individual, as well as the collective; the internal, as well as the external phases.

A thorough perusal of the history of human development will disclose two elements in bitter conflict with each other; elements that are only now beginning to be understood, not as foreign to each other, but as closely related and truly harmonious, if only placed in proper environment: the individual and social instincts. The individual and society have waged a relentless and bloody battle for ages, each striving for supremacy, because each was blind to the value and importance of the other. The individual and social instincts—the one a most potent factor for individual endeavor, for growth, aspiration, self-realization; the other an equally potent factor for mutual helpfulness and social well-being.

The explanation of the storm raging within the individual, and between him and his surroundings, is not far to seek. The primitive man, unable to understand his being, much less the unity of all life, felt himself absolutely dependent on blind, hidden forces ever ready to mock and taunt him. Out of that attitude grew the religious concepts of man as a mere speck of dust dependent on superior powers on high, who can only be appeased by complete surrender. All the early sagas rest on that idea, which continues to be the *leit-motif* of the biblical tales dealing with the relation of man to God, to the State, to society. Again and again the same motif, *man is nothing, the powers are everything*. Thus Jehovah would only endure man on condition of complete surrender. Man can have all the glories of the earth, but he must not become conscious of himself. The State, society, and moral laws all sing the same refrain: Man can have all the glories of the earth, but he must not become conscious of himself.

Anarchism is the only philosophy which brings to man the consciousness of himself; which maintains that God, the State, and society are non-existent, that their promises are null and void, since they can be fulfilled only through man's subordination. Anarchism is therefore the teacher of the unity of life; not merely in nature, but in man. There is no conflict between the individual and the social instincts, any more than there is between the heart and the lungs: the one the receptacle of a precious life essence, the other the repository of the element that keeps the essence pure and strong. The individual is the heart of society, conserving the essence of social life; society is the lungs which are distributing the element to keep the life essence—that is, the individual—pure and strong.

"The one thing of value in the world," says Emerson,[2] "is the active soul; this every man contains within him. The active soul sees absolute truth and utters truth and creates." In other words, the individual instinct is the thing of value in the world. It is the true soul that sees and creates the truth alive, out of which is to come a still greater truth, the re-born social soul.

Anarchism is the great liberator of man from the phantoms that have held him captive; it is the arbiter and pacifier of the two forces for individual and social harmony. To accomplish that unity, Anarchism has declared war on the pernicious influences which have so far prevented the harmonious blending of individual and social instincts, the individual and society.

Religion, the dominion of the human mind; Property, the dominion of human needs; and Government, the dominion of human conduct, represent the stronghold of man's enslavement and all the horrors it entails. Religion! How it dominates man's mind, how it humiliates and degrades his soul. God is everything, man is nothing, says religion. But out of that nothing

God has created a kingdom so despotic, so tyrannical, so cruel, so terribly exacting that naught but gloom and tears and blood have ruled the world since gods began. Anarchism rouses man to rebellion against this black monster. Break your mental fetters, says Anarchism to man, for not until you think and judge for yourself will you get rid of the dominion of darkness, the greatest obstacle to all progress.

Property, the dominion of man's needs, the denial of the right to satisfy his needs. Time was when property claimed a divine right, when it came to man with the same refrain, even as religion, "Sacrifice! Abnegate! Submit!" The spirit of Anarchism has lifted man from his prostrate position. He now stands erect, with his face toward the light. He has learned to see the insatiable, devouring, devastating nature of property, and he is preparing to strike the monster dead.

"Property is robbery," said the great French Anarchist, Proudhon.[3] Yes, but without risk and danger to the robber. Monopolizing the accumulated efforts of man, property has robbed him of his birth-right, and has turned him loose a pauper and an outcast. Property has not even the time-worn excuse that man does not create enough to satisfy all needs. The A B C student of economics knows that the productivity of labor within the last few decades far exceeds normal demand a hundredfold. But what are normal demands to an abnormal institution? The only demand that property recognizes is its own gluttonous appetite for greater wealth, because wealth means power: the power to subdue, to crush, to exploit, the power to enslave, to outrage, to degrade. America is particularly boastful of her great power, her enormous national wealth. Poor America, of what avail is all her wealth, if the individuals comprising the nation are wretchedly poor? If they live in squalor, in filth, in crime, with hope and joy gone, a homeless, soilless army of human prey.

It is generally conceded that unless the returns of any business venture exceed the cost, bankruptcy is inevitable. But those engaged in the business of producing wealth have not yet learned even this simple lesson. Every year the cost of production in human life is growing larger (50,000 killed, 100,000 wounded in America last year); the returns to the masses, who help to create wealth, are ever getting smaller. Yet America continues to be blind to the inevitable bankruptcy of our business of production. Nor is this the only crime of the latter. Still more fatal is the crime of turning the producer into a mere particle of a machine, with less will and decision than his master of steel and iron. Man is being robbed not merely of the products of his labor, but of the power of free initiative, of originality, and the interest in, or desire for, the things he is making.

Real wealth consists in things of utility and beauty, in things that help to create strong, beautiful bodies and surroundings inspiring to live in. But if man is doomed to wind cotton around a spool, or dig coal, or build roads for thirty years of his life, there can be no talk of wealth. What he gives to the world is only gray and hideous things, reflecting a dull and hideous existence—too weak to live, too cowardly to die. Strange to say, there are people who extol this deadening method of centralized production as the proudest achievement of our age. They fail utterly to realize that if we are to continue in machine subserviency, our slavery is more complete than was our bondage to the King. They do not want to know that centralization is not only the death knell of liberty, but also of health and beauty, of art and science, all these being impossible in a clock-like, mechanical atmosphere.

Anarchism cannot but repudiate such a method of production: its goal is the freest possible expression of all the latent powers of the individual. Oscar Wilde defines a perfect personality as "one who develops under perfect conditions, who is not wounded, maimed, or in danger." A perfect personality, then, is only possible in a state of society where man is free to choose the mode of work, the conditions of work, and the freedom to work. One to whom the making of a table, the building of a house, or the tilling of the soil, is what the painting is to the artist and the discovery to the scientist—the result of inspiration, of intense longing, and deep interest in work as a creative force. That being the ideal of Anarchism, its economic arrangements must consist of voluntary productive and distributive associations, gradually developing into free communism, as the best means of producing with the least waste of human energy. Anarchism, however, also recognizes the right of the individual, or numbers of individuals, to arrange at all times for other forms of work, in harmony with their tastes and desires.

Such free display of human energy being possible only under complete individual and social freedom, Anarchism directs its forces against the third and greatest foe of all social equality; namely, the State, organized authority, or statutory law—the dominion of human conduct.

Just as religion has fettered the human mind, and as property, or the monopoly of things, has subdued and stifled man's needs, so has the State enslaved his spirit, dictating every phase of conduct. "All government in essence," says Emerson, "is tyranny." It matters not whether it is government by divine right or majority rule. In every instance its aim is the absolute subordination of the individual.

Referring to the American government, the greatest American Anarchist, David Thoreau,[4] said: "Government, what is it but a tradition, though a recent one, endeavoring to transmit itself unimpaired to posterity, but each instance losing its integrity; it has not the vitality and force of a single living man. Law never made man a whit more just; and by means of their respect for it, even the well disposed are daily made agents of injustice."

Indeed, the keynote of government is injustice. With the arrogance and self-sufficiency of the King who could do no wrong, governments ordain, judge, condemn, and punish the most insignificant offenses, while maintaining themselves by the greatest of all offenses, the annihilation of individual liberty. Thus Ouida[5] is right when she maintains that "the State only aims at instilling those qualities in its public by which its demands are obeyed, and its exchequer is filled. Its highest attainment is the reduction of mankind to clockwork. In its atmosphere all those finer and more delicate liberties, which require treatment and spacious expansion, inevitably dry up and perish. The State requires a taxpaying machine in which there is no hitch, an exchequer in which there is never a deficit, and a public, monotonous, obedient, colorless, spiritless, moving humbly like a flock of sheep along a straight high road between two walls."

Yet even a flock of sheep would resist the chicanery of the State, if it were not for the corruptive, tyrannical, and oppressive methods it employs to serve its purposes. Therefore Bakunin[6] repudiates the State as synonymous with the surrender of the liberty of the individual or small minorities—the destruction of social relationship, the curtailment, or complete denial even, of life itself, for its own aggrandizement. The State is the altar of political freedom and, like the religious altar, it is maintained for the purpose of human sacrifice.

In fact, there is hardly a modern thinker who does not agree that government, organized authority, or the State, is necessary *only* to maintain or protect property and monopoly. It has proven efficient in that function only.

Even George Bernard Shaw, who hopes for the miraculous from the State under Fabianism,[7] nevertheless admits that "it is at present a huge machine for robbing and slave-driving of the poor by brute force." This being the case, it is hard to see why the clever prefacer wishes to uphold the State after poverty shall have ceased to exist.

Unfortunately there are still a number of people who continue in the fatal belief that government rests on natural laws, that it maintains social order and harmony, that it diminishes crime, and that it prevents the lazy man from fleecing his fellows. I shall therefore examine these contentions.

A natural law is that factor in man which asserts itself freely and spontaneously without any external force, in harmony with the requirements of nature. For instance, the demand for nutrition, for sex gratification, for light, air, and exercise, is a natural law. But its expression needs not the machinery of government, needs not the club, the gun, the handcuff, or the prison. To obey such laws, if we may call it obedience, requires only spontaneity and free opportunity. That governments do not maintain themselves through such harmonious factors is proven by the terrible array of violence, force, and coercion all governments use in order to live. Thus Blackstone[8] is right when he says, "Human laws are invalid, because they are contrary to the laws of nature."

Unless it be the order of Warsaw after the slaughter of thousands of people, it is difficult to ascribe to governments any capacity for order or social harmony. Order derived through submission and maintained by terror is not much of a safe guaranty; yet that is the only "order" that governments have ever maintained. True social harmony grows naturally out of solidarity of interests. In a society where those who always work never have anything, while those who never work enjoy everything, solidarity of interests is non-existent; hence social harmony is but a myth. The only way organized authority meets this grave situation is by extending still greater privileges to those who have already monopolized the earth, and by still further enslaving the disinherited masses. Thus the entire arsenal of government—laws, police, soldiers, the courts, legislatures, prisons—is strenuously engaged in "harmonizing" the most antagonistic elements in society.

The most absurd apology for authority and law is that they serve to diminish crime. Aside from the fact that the State is itself the greatest criminal, breaking every written and natural law, stealing in the form of taxes, killing in the form of war and capital punishment, it has come to an absolute standstill in coping with crime. It has failed utterly to destroy or even minimize the horrible scourge of its own creation.

Crime is naught but misdirected energy. So long as every institution of today, economic, political, social, and moral, conspires to misdirect human energy into wrong channels; so long as most people are out of place doing the things they hate to do, living a life they loathe to live, crime will be inevitable, and all the laws on the statutes can only increase, but never do away with, crime. What does society, as it exists today, know of the process of despair, the poverty, the horrors, the fearful struggle the human soul must pass on its way to crime and degradation. Who that knows this terrible process can fail to see the truth in these words of Peter Kropotkin:[9]

"Those who will hold the balance between the benefits thus attributed to law and punishment and the degrading effect of the latter on humanity; those who will estimate the torrent of depravity poured abroad in human society by the informer, favored by the Judge even, and paid for in clinking cash by governments, under the pretext of aiding to unmask crime; those who will go within prison walls and there see what human beings become when deprived of liberty, when subjected to the care of brutal keepers, to coarse, cruel words, to a thousand stinging, piercing humiliations, will agree with us that the entire apparatus of prison and punishment is an abomination which ought to be brought to an end."

The deterrent influence of law on the lazy man is too absurd to merit consideration. If society were only relieved of the waste and expense of keeping a lazy class, and the equally great expense of the paraphernalia of protection this lazy class requires, the social tables would contain an abundance for all, including even the occasional lazy individual. Besides, it is well to consider that laziness results either from special privileges, or physical and mental abnormalities. Our present insane system of production fosters both, and the most astounding phenomenon is that people should want to work at all now. Anarchism aims to strip labor of its deadening, dulling aspect, of its gloom and compulsion. It aims to make work an instrument of joy, of strength, of color, of real harmony, so that the poorest sort of a man should find in work both recreation and hope.

To achieve such an arrangement of life, government, with its unjust, arbitrary, repressive measures, must be done away with. At best it has but imposed one single mode of life upon all, without regard to individual and social variations and needs. In destroying government and statutory laws, Anarchism proposes to rescue the self-respect and independence of the individual from all restraint and invasion by authority. Only in freedom can man grow to his full stature. Only in freedom will he learn to think and move, and give the very best in him. Only in freedom will he realize the true force of the social bonds which knit men together, and which are the true foundation of a normal social life.

But what about human nature? Can it be changed? And if not, will it endure under Anarchism?

Poor human nature, what horrible crimes have been committed in thy name! Every fool, from king to policeman, from the flatheaded parson to the visionless dabbler in science, presumes to speak authoritatively of human nature. The greater the mental charlatan, the more definite his insistence on the wickedness and weaknesses of human nature. Yet, how can any one speak of it today, with every soul in a prison, with every heart fettered, wounded, and maimed?

John Burroughs[10] has stated that experimental study of animals in captivity is absolutely useless. Their character, their habits, their appetites undergo a complete transformation when torn from their soil in field and forest. With human nature caged in a narrow space, whipped daily into submission, how can we speak of its potentialities?

Freedom, expansion, opportunity, and, above all, peace and repose, alone can teach us the real dominant factors of human nature and all its wonderful possibilities.

Anarchism, then, really stands for the liberation of the human mind from the dominion of religion; the liberation of the human body from the dominion of property; liberation from the shackles and restraint of government. Anarchism stands for a social order based on the free grouping of individuals for the purpose of producing real social wealth; an order that will guarantee to every human being free access to the earth and full enjoyment of the necessities of life, according to individual desires, tastes, and inclinations.

This is not a wild fancy or an aberration of the mind. It is the conclusion arrived at by hosts of intellectual men and women the world over; a conclusion resulting from the close and studious observation of the tendencies of modern society: individual liberty and economic equality, the twin forces for the birth of what is fine and true in man.

As to methods. Anarchism is not, as some may suppose, a theory of the future to be realized through divine inspiration. It is a living force in the affairs of our life, constantly creating new conditions. The methods of Anarchism therefore do not comprise an iron-clad program to be carried out under all circumstances. Methods must grow out of the economic needs of each place and clime, and of the intellectual and temperamental requirements of the individual. The serene, calm character of a Tolstoy[11] will wish different methods for social reconstruction than the intense, overflowing personality of a Michael Bakunin or a Peter Kropotkin. Equally so it must be apparent that the economic and political needs of Russia will dictate more drastic measures than would England or America. Anarchism does not stand for military drill and uniformity; it does, however, stand for the spirit of revolt, in whatever form, against everything that hinders human growth. All Anarchists agree in that, as they also agree in their opposition to the political machinery as a means of bringing about the great social change.

"All voting," says Thoreau, "is a sort of gaming, like checkers, or backgammon, a playing with right and wrong; its obligation never exceeds that of expediency. Even voting for the right thing is doing nothing for it. A wise man will not leave the right to the mercy of chance, nor wish it to prevail through the power of the majority." A close examination of the machinery of politics and its achievements will bear out the logic of Thoreau.

What does the history of parliamentarism show? Nothing but failure and defeat, not even a single reform to ameliorate the economic and social stress of the people. Laws have been passed and enactments made for the improvement and protection of labor. Thus it was proven only last year that Illinois, with the most rigid laws for mine protection, had the greatest mine disasters. In States where child labor laws prevail, child exploitation is at its highest, and though with us the workers enjoy full political opportunities, capitalism has reached the most brazen zenith.

Even were the workers able to have their own representatives, for which our good Socialist politicians are clamoring, what chances are there for their honesty and good faith? One has but to bear in mind the process of politics to realize that its path of good intentions is full of pitfalls: wire-pulling, intriguing, flattering, lying, cheating; in fact, chicanery of every description, whereby the political aspirant can achieve success. Added to that is a complete demoralization of character and conviction, until nothing is left that would make one hope for anything from such a human derelict. Time and time again the people were foolish enough to trust, believe, and support with their last farthing aspiring politicians, only to find themselves betrayed and cheated.

It may be claimed that men of integrity would not become corrupt in the political grinding mill. Perhaps not; but such men would be absolutely helpless to exert the slightest influence in behalf of labor, as indeed has been shown in numerous instances. The State is the economic master of its servants. Good men, if such there be, would either remain true to their political faith and lose their economic support, or they would cling to their economic master and be utterly unable to do the slightest good. The political arena leaves one no alternative, one must either be a dunce or a rogue.

The political superstition is still holding sway over the hearts and minds of the masses, but the true lovers of liberty will have no more to do with it. Instead, they believe with Stirner[12] that man has as much liberty as he is willing to take. Anarchism therefore stands for direct action, the open defiance of, and resistance to, all laws and restrictions, economic, social, and moral. But defiance and resistance are illegal. Therein lies the salvation of man. Everything illegal necessitates integrity, self-reliance, and courage. In short, it calls for free, independent spirits, for "men who are men, and who have a bone in their backs which you cannot pass your hand through."

Universal suffrage itself owes its existence to direct action. If not for the spirit of rebellion, of the defiance on the part of the American revolutionary fathers, their posterity would still wear the King's coat. If not for the direct action of a John Brown[13] and his comrades, America would still trade in the flesh of the black man. True, the trade in white flesh is still going on; but that, too, will have to be abolished by direct action. Trade unionism, the economic arena of the modern gladiator, owes its existence to direct action. It is but recently that law and government have attempted to crush the trade union movement, and condemned the exponents of man's right to organize to prison as conspirators. Had they sought to assert their cause through begging, pleading, and compromise, trade unionism would today be a negligible quantity. In France, in Spain, in Italy, in Russia, nay even in England (witness the growing rebellion of English labor unions) direct, revolutionary, economic action has become so strong a force in the battle for industrial liberty as to make the world realize the tremendous importance of labor's power. The General Strike, the supreme expression of the economic consciousness of the workers, was ridiculed in America but a short time ago. Today every great strike, in order to win, must realize the importance of the solidaric general protest.

Direct action, having proved effective along economic lines, is equally potent in the environment of the individual. There a hundred forces encroach upon his being, and only persistent resistance to them will finally set him free. Direct action against the authority in the shop, direct action against the authority of the law, direct action against the invasive, meddlesome authority of our moral code, is the logical, consistent method of Anarchism.

Will it not lead to a revolution? Indeed, it will. No real social change has ever come about without a revolution. People are either not familiar with their history, or they have not yet learned that revolution is but thought carried into action.

Anarchism, the great leaven of thought, is today permeating every phase of human endeavor. Science, art, literature, the drama, the effort for economic betterment, in fact every individual and social opposition to the existing disorder of things, is illumined by the spiritual light of Anarchism. It is the philosophy of the sovereignty of the individual. It is the theory of social harmony. It is the great, surging, living truth that is reconstructing the world, and that will usher in the Dawn.

NOTES

1. The Irish playwright Oscar Wilde (1854–1900). —Eds.
2. The American essayist Ralph Waldo Emerson (1803–1882).—Eds.
3. The French anarcho-socialist Pierre-Joseph Proudhon (1809–1865), who held that "[private] property is theft."—Eds.
4. The American author Henry David Thoreau (1817–1862). Here and elsewhere Goldman quotes from Thoreau's "Civil Disobedience" (1849). Her assertion that Thoreau was an anarchist, however, is open to doubt. In "Civil Disobedience" he writes that "unlike those who call themselves no-government men [i.e., anarchists], I ask for, not at once no government, but at once a better government." Far from wishing to smash the state, Thoreau concludes his famous essay by envisioning "a still more perfect and glorious State, which also I have imagined, but not yet anywhere seen."—Eds.
5. Ouida was the pseudonym of the English novelist Marie Louise de la Ramée (1839–1908).—Eds.
6. The Russian anarchist Mikhail Bakunin (1814–1876). See selection 41 in this volume.—Eds.
7. The Irish dramatist and essayist George Bernard Shaw (1856–1950), who was also a Fabian socialist.—Eds.
8. The English jurist Sir William Blackstone (1723–1780), author of *Commentaries on the Laws of England* (1769).—Eds.
9. The Russian anarchist and nobleman Peter Kropotkin (1842–1921).—Eds.
10. The American naturalist and author John Burroughs (1837–1921).—Eds.
11. Count Leo Tolstoy (1828–1910), Russian pacifist and author of *War and Peace* (1869) and *Anna Karenina* (1877).—Eds.
12. Max Stirner was the pseudonym of Johann Casper Schmidt (1806–1856), author of *The Ego and His Own* (1844).—Eds.
13. The American abolitionist John Brown (1800–1859), who led the ill-fated raid on the U.S. arsenal at Harpers Ferry in West Virginia.—Eds.

43

Looking Backward

EDWARD BELLAMY

Like Bernstein and some anarcho-communists, the American socialist Edward Bellamy (1850–1898) thought that the process of evolution was leading inevitably to a cooperative socialist society. Unlike the anarchists, however, Bellamy believed that the state would continue to have a role under socialism, albeit a very different one. Bellamy put these ideas into his best-selling novel *Looking Backward* (1888). There Bellamy's late nineteenth-century hero, Julian West, falls into a deep, trancelike sleep, awakening (or so it seems) in the year 2000 to find that a socialist evolution had occurred in the interim. In the following excerpts from *Looking Backward,* West's host, Dr. Leete, and the minister, Mr. Barton, lament the evils of the old capitalist system and explain the advantages of the new and more just socialist society.

Source: Edward Bellamy, *Looking Backward* (Boston: Ticknor, 1888).

LOOKING BACKWARD

By way of attempting to give the reader some general impression of the way people lived together in those days, and especially of the relations of the rich and poor to one another, perhaps I cannot do better than to compare society as it then was to a prodigious [stage-]coach which the masses of humanity were harnessed to and dragged toilsomely along a very hilly and sandy road. The driver was hunger, and permitted no lagging, though the pace was necessarily very slow. Despite the difficulty of drawing the coach at all along so hard a road, the top was covered with passengers who never got down, even at the steepest ascents. These seats on top were very breezy and comfortable. Well up out of the dust, their occupants could enjoy the scenery at their leisure, or critically discuss the merits of the straining team. Naturally such places were in great demand and the competition for them was keen, every one seeking as the first end in life to secure a seat on the coach for himself and to leave it to his child after him. By the rule of the coach a man could leave his seat to whom he wished, but on the other hand there were many accidents by which it might at any time be wholly lost. For all that they were so easy, the seats were very insecure, and at every sudden jolt of the coach persons were slipping out of them and falling to the ground, where they were instantly compelled to take hold of the rope and help to drag the coach on which they had before ridden so pleasantly. It was naturally regarded as a terrible misfortune to lose one's seat, and the apprehension that this might happen to them or their friends was a constant cloud upon the happiness of those who rode.

But did they think only of themselves? you ask. Was not their very luxury rendered intolerable to them by comparison with the lot of their brothers and sisters in the harness, and the knowledge that their own weight added to their toil? Had they no compassion for fellow beings from whom fortune only distinguished them? Oh, yes; commiseration was frequently expressed by those who rode for those who had to pull the coach, especially when the vehicle came to a bad place in the road, as it was constantly doing, or to a particular steep hill. At such times, the desperate straining of the team, their agonized leaping and plunging under the pitiless lashing of hunger, the many who fainted at the rope and were trampled in the mire, made a very distressing spectacle which often called forth highly creditable displays of feeling on the top of the coach. At such times the passengers would call down encouragingly to the toilers of the rope, exhorting them to patience, and holding out hopes of possible compensation in another world for the hardness of their lot, while others contributed to buy salves and liniments for the crippled and injured. It was agreed that it was a great pity that the coach should be so hard to pull, and there was a sense of general relief when the specially bad piece of road was gotten over. This relief was not, indeed, wholly on account of the team, for there was always some danger at these bad places of a general overturn in which all would lose their seats.

It must in truth be admitted that the main effect of the spectacle of the misery of the toilers at the rope was to enhance the passengers' sense of the value of their seats upon the coach, and to cause them to hold on to them more desperately than before. If the passengers could only have felt assured that neither they nor their friends would ever fall from the top, it is probable that, beyond contributing to the funds for liniments and bandages, they would have troubled themselves extremely little about those who dragged the coach.

I am well aware that this will appear to the men and women of the twentieth century as incredible inhumanity, but there are two facts, both very curious, which partly explain it. In the first place, it was firmly and sincerely believed that there was no other way in which Society could get along, except the many pulled at the rope and the few rode, and not only this, but that no very radical improvement even was possible, either in the harness, the coach, the roadway, or the distribution of the toil. It had always been as it was, and it always would be so. It was a pity, but it could not be helped, and philosophy forbade wasting compassion on what was beyond remedy.

The other fact is yet more curious, consisting in a singular hallucination which those on the top of the coach generally shared, that they were not exactly like their brothers and sisters who pulled at the rope, but of finer clay, in some way belonging to a higher order of beings who might justly expect to be drawn. This seems unaccountable, but, as I once rode on this very coach and shared that very hallucination, I ought to be believed. The strangest thing about the hallucination was that those who had but just climbed up from the ground, before they had outgrown the marks of the rope upon their hands, began to fall under its influence. As for those whose parents and grandparents before them had been so fortunate as to keep their seats on the top, the conviction they cherished of the essential difference between their sort of humanity and the common article was absolute....

Production and Distribution

[T]he warehouse...[provided a] remarkable illustration...of the prodigiously multiplied efficiency which perfect organization can give to labor. It is like a gigantic mill, into the hopper of which goods are being constantly poured by the train-load and ship-load, to issue at the other end in packages of pounds and ounces, yards and inches, pints and gallons, corresponding to the infinitely complex personal needs of half a million people. Dr. Leete, with the assistance of data furnished by me as to the way goods were sold in my day, figured out some astounding results in the way of the economies effected by the modern system.

As we set out homeward, I said: "After what I have seen today, together with what you have told me, and what I learned under Miss Leete's tutelage at the sample store, I have a tolerably clear idea of your system of distribution, and how it enables you to dispense with a circulating medium. But I should like very much to know something more about your system of production. You have told me in general how your industrial army is levied and organized, but who directs its efforts? What supreme authority determines what shall be done in every department, so that enough of everything is produced and yet no labor wasted? It seems to me that this must be a wonderfully complex and difficult function, requiring very unusual endowments."

"Does it indeed seem so to you?" responded Dr. Leete. "I assure you that it is nothing of the kind, but on the other hand so simple, and depending on principles so obvious and easily applied, that the functionaries at Washington to whom it is trusted require to be nothing more than men of fair abilities to discharge it to the entire satisfaction of the nation. The machine which they direct is indeed a vast one, but so logical in its principles and direct and simple in its workings, that it all but runs itself; and nobody but a fool could derange it, as I think you will agree after a few words of explanation. Since you already have a pretty good idea of the working of the distributive system, let us begin at that end. Even in your day statisticians were able to tell you the number of yards of cotton, velvet, woolen, the number of barrels of flour, potatoes, butter, number of pairs of shoes, hats, and umbrellas annually consumed by the nation. Owing to the fact that production was in private hands, and that there was no way of getting statistics of actual distribution, these figures were not exact, but they were nearly so. Now that every pin which is given out from a national warehouse is recorded, of course the figures of consumption for any week, month, or year, in the possession of the department of distribution at the end of that period, are precise. On these figures, allowing for tendencies to increase or decrease and for any special causes likely to affect demand, the estimates, say for a year ahead, are based. These estimates, with a proper margin for security, having been accepted by the general administration, the responsibility of the distributive department ceases until the goods are delivered to it. I speak of the estimates being furnished for an entire year ahead, but in reality they cover that much time only in case of the great staples for which the demand can be calculated on as steady. In the great majority of smaller industries for the product of which popular taste fluctuates, and novelty is frequently required, production is kept barely ahead of consumption, the distributive department furnishing frequent estimates based on the weekly state of demand.

"Now the entire field of productive and constructive industry is divided into ten great departments, each representing a group of allied industries, each particular industry being in turn represented by a subordinate bureau, which has a complete record of the plant and force under its control, of the present product, and means of increasing it. The estimates of the distributive department, after adoption by the administration, are sent as mandates to the ten great departments, which allot them to the subordinate bureaus representing the particular industries, and these set the men at work. Each bureau is responsible for the task given it, and this responsibility is enforced by departmental oversight and that of the administration; nor does the distributive department accept the product without its own inspection; while even if in the hands of the consumer an article turns out unfit, the system enables the fault to be traced back to the original work-man. The production of the commodities for actual public consumption does not, of course, require by any means all the national force of workers. After the necessary contingents have been detailed for the various industries, the amount of labor left for other employment is expended in creating fixed capital, such as buildings, machinery, engineering works, and so forth."

"One point occurs to me," I said, "on which I should think there might be dissatisfaction. Where there is no opportunity for private enterprise, how is there any assurance that the claims of small minorities of the people to have articles produced, for which there is no wide demand, will be respected? An official decree at any moment may deprive them of the means of gratifying some special taste, merely because the majority does not share it."

"That would be tyranny indeed," replied Dr. Leete, "and you may be very sure that it does not happen with us, to whom liberty is as dear as equality or fraternity. As you come to know our system better, you will see that our officials are in fact, and not merely in name, the agents and servants of the people. The administration has no power to stop the production of any commodity for which there continues to be a demand. Suppose the demand for any article declines to such a point that its production becomes very costly. The price has to be raised in proportion, of course, but as long as the consumer cares to pay it, the production goes on. Again, suppose an article not before produced is demanded. If the administration doubts the reality of the demand, a popular petition guaranteeing a certain basis of consumption compels it to produce the desired article. A government, or a majority, which should undertake to tell the people, or a minority, what they were to eat, drink, or wear, as I believe governments in America did in your day, would be regarded as a curious anachronism indeed. Possibly you had reasons for tolerating these infringements of personal independence, but we should not think them endurable. I am glad you raised this point, for it has given me a chance to show you how much more direct and efficient is the control over production exercised by the individual citizen now than it was in your day, when what you called private initiative prevailed, though it should have been called capitalist initiative, for the average private citizen had little enough share in it."

"You speak of raising the price of costly articles," I said, "How can prices be regulated in a country where there is no competition between buyers or sellers?"

"Just as they were with you," replied Dr. Leete. "You think that needs explaining," he added, as I looked incredulous, "but the explanation need not be long; the cost of the labor which produced it was recognized as the legitimate basis of the price of an article in your day, and so it is in ours. In your day, it was the difference in wages that made the difference in the cost of labor; now it is the relative number of hours constituting a day's work in different trades, the maintenance of the worker being equal in all cases. The cost of a man's work in a trade so difficult that in order to attract volunteers the hours have to be fixed at four a day is twice as great as that in a trade where the men work eight hours. The result as to the cost of labor, you see, is just the same as if the man working four hours were paid, under your system, twice the wages the other gets. This calculation applied to the labor employed in the various processes of a manufactured article gives its price relatively to other articles. Besides the cost of production and transportation, the factor of scarcity affects the prices of some commodities. As regards the great staples of life, of which an abundance can always be secured, scarcity is eliminated as a factor. There is always a large surplus kept on hand from which any fluctuations of demand or supply can be corrected, even in most cases of bad crops. The prices of the staples grow less year by year, but rarely, if ever, rise. There are, however, certain classes of articles permanently, and others temporarily, unequal to the demand, as, for example, fresh fish or dairy products in the latter category, and the products of high skill and rare materials in the other. All that can be done here is to equalize the inconvenience of the scarcity. This is done by temporarily raising the price if the scarcity be temporary, or fixing it high if it be permanent. High prices in your day meant restriction of the articles affected to the rich, but nowadays, when the means of all are the same, the effect is only that those to whom the articles seem most desirable are the ones who purchase them. Of course the nation, as any other caterer for the public needs must be, is frequently left with small lots of goods on its hands by changes in taste, unseasonable weather, and various other causes. These it has to dispose of at a sacrifice just as merchants often did in your day, charging up the loss to the expenses of the business. Owing, however, to the vast body of consumers to which such lots can be simultaneously offered, there is rarely any difficulty in getting rid of them at trifling loss. I have given you now some general notion of our system of production, as well as distribution. Do you find it as complex as you expected?"

I admitted that nothing could be much simpler.

"I am sure," said Dr. Leete, "that it is within the truth to say that the head of one of the myriad private businesses of your day, who had to maintain sleepless vigilance against the fluctuations of the market, the machinations of his rivals, and the failure of his debtors, had a far more trying task than the group of men at Washington who nowadays direct the industries of the entire nation. All this merely shows, my dear fellow, how much easier it is to do things the right way than the wrong. It is easier for a general up in a balloon, with perfect survey of the field, to manoeuvre a million men to victory than for a sergeant to manage a platoon in a thicket."

"The general of this army, including the flower of the manhood of the nation, must be the foremost man in the country, really greater even than the President of the United States," I said.

"He is the President of the United States," replied Dr. Leete, "or rather the most important function of the presidency is the headship of the industrial army."

"How is he chosen?" I asked.

"I explained to you before," replied Dr. Leete, "when I was describing the force of the motive of emulation among all grades of the industrial army, that the line of promotion for the meritorious lies through three grades to the officer's grade, and thence up through the lieutenancies to the captaincy or foremanship, and superintendency or colonel's rank. Next, with an intervening grade in some of the larger trades, come the general of the guild, under whose immediate control all the operations of the trade are conducted. This officer is at the head of the national bureau representing his trade, and is responsible for its work to the administration. The general of his guild holds a splendid position, and one which amply satisfies the ambition of most men, but above his rank, which may be compared—to follow the military analogies familiar to you—to that of a general of division or major-general, is that of the chiefs of the ten great departments, or groups of allied trades. The chiefs of these ten grand divisions of the industrial army may be compared to your commanders of army corps, or lieutenant-generals, each having from a dozen to a score of generals of separate guilds reporting to him. Above these ten great officers, who form his council, is the general-in-chief, who is the President of the United States.

"The general-in-chief of the industrial army must have passed through all the grades below him, from the common laborers up. Let us see how he rises. As I have told you, it is simply by the excellence of his record as a worker that one rises through the grades of the privates and becomes a candidate for a lieutenancy. Through the lieutenancies he rises to the colonelcy, or superintendent's position, by appointment from above, strictly limited to the candidates of the best records. The general of the guild appoints to the ranks under him, but he himself is not appointed, but chosen by suffrage."

"By suffrage!" I exclaimed. "Is not that ruinous to the discipline of the guild, by tempting the candidates to intrigue for the support of the workers under them?"

"So it would be, no doubt," replied Dr. Leete, "if the workers had any suffrage to exercise, or anything to say about the choice. But they have nothing. Just here comes in a peculiarity of our system. The general of the guild is chosen from among the superintendents by vote of the honorary members of the guild, that is, of those who have served their time in the guild and received their discharge. As you know, at the age of forty-five we are mustered out of the army of industry, and have the residue of life for the pursuit of our own improvement or recreation. Of course, however, the associations of our active lifetime retain a powerful hold on us. The companionships we formed then remain our companionships till the end of life. We always continue honorary members of our former guilds, and retain the keenest and most jealous interest in their welfare and repute in the hands of the following generation. In the clubs maintained by the honorary members of the several guilds, in which we meet socially, there are no topics of conversation so commonly as those which relate to these matters, and the young aspirants for guild leadership who can pass the criticism of us old fellows are likely to be pretty well equipped. Recognizing this fact, the nation entrusts to the honorary members of each guild the election of its general, and I venture to claim that no previous form of society could have developed a body of electors so ideally adapted to their office, as regards absolute impartiality, knowledge of the special qualifications and record of candidates, solicitude for the best result, and complete absence of self-interest.

"Each of the ten lieutenant-generals or heads of departments is himself elected from among the generals of the guilds grouped as a department, by vote of the honorary members of the guilds thus grouped. Of course there is a tendency on the part of each guild to vote for its own general, but no guild of any group has nearly enough votes to elect a man not supported by most of the others. I assure you that these elections are exceedingly lively."

"The President, I suppose, is selected from among the ten heads of the great departments," I suggested.

"Precisely, but the heads of departments are not eligible to the presidency till they have been a certain number of years out of office. It is rarely that a man passes through all the grades to the headship of a department much before he is forty, and at the end of a five years' term he is usually forty-five. If more, he still serves through his term, and if less, he is nevertheless discharged from the industrial army at its termination. It would not do for him to return to the ranks. The interval before he is a candidate for the presidency is intended to give time for him to recognize fully that he has returned into the general mass of the nation, and is identified with it rather than with the industrial army. Moreover, it is expected that he will employ this period in studying the general condition of the army, instead of that of the special group of guilds of which he was the head. From among the former heads of departments who may be eligible at the time, the President is elected by vote of all the men of the nation who are not connected with the industrial army."

"The army is not allowed to vote for President?"

"Certainly not. That would be perilous to its discipline, which it is the business of the President to maintain as the representative of the nation at large. His right hand for this purpose is the inspectorate, a highly important department of our system; to the inspectorate come all complaints or information as to defects in goods, insolence or inefficiency of officials, or dereliction of any sort in the public service. The inspectorate, however, does not wait for complaints. Not only is it on the alert to catch and sift every rumor of a fault in the service, but it is its business, by systematic and constant oversight and inspection of every branch of the army, to find out what is going wrong before anybody else does. The President is usually not far from fifty when elected, and serves five years, forming an honorable exception to the rule of retirement at forty-five. At the end of his term of office, a national Congress is called to receive his report and approve or condemn it. If it is approved, Congress usually elects him to represent the nation for five years more in the international council. Congress, I should also say, passes on the reports of the outgoing heads of departments, and a disapproval renders any one of them ineligible for President. But it is rare, indeed, that the nation has occasion for other sentiments than those of gratitude toward its high officers. As to their ability, to have risen from the ranks, by tests so various and severe, to their positions, is proof in itself of extraordinary qualities, while as to faithfulness, our social system leaves them absolutely without any other motive than that of winning the esteem of their fellow citizens. Corruption is impossible in a society where there is neither poverty to be bribed nor wealth to bribe, while as to demagoguery or intrigue for office, the conditions of promotion render them out of the question."

"One point I do not quite understand," I said. "Are the members of the liberal professions eligible to the presidency? and if so, how are they ranked with those who pursue the industries proper?"

"They have no ranking with them," replied Dr. Leete. "The members of the technical professions, such as engineers and architects, have a ranking with the constructive guilds; but the members of the liberal professions, the doctors and teachers, as well as the artists and men of letters who obtain remissions of industrial service, do not belong to the industrial army. On this ground they vote for the President, but are not eligible to his office. One of its main duties being the control and discipline of the industrial army, it is essential that the President should have passed through all its grades to understand his business."

"That is reasonable," I said; "but if the doctors and teachers do not know enough of industry to be President, neither, I should think, can the President know enough of medicine and education to control those departments."

"No more does he," was the reply. "Except in the general way that he is responsible for the enforcement of the laws as to all classes, the President has nothing to do with the faculties of medicine and education, which are controlled by boards of regents of their own, in which the President is ex-officio chairman, and has the casting vote. These regents, who, of course, are responsible to Congress, are chosen by the honorary members of the guilds of education and medicine, the retired teachers and doctors of the country."

"Do you know," I said, "the method of electing officials by votes of the retired members of the guilds is nothing more than the application on a national scale of the plan of government by alumni, which we used to a slight extent occasionally in the management of our higher educational institutions."

"Did you, indeed?" exclaimed Dr. Leete, with animation. "That is quite new to me, and I fancy will be to most of us, and of much interest as well. There has been great discussion as to the germ of the idea, and we fancied that there was for once something new under the sun. Well! well! In your higher educational institutions! that is interesting indeed. You must tell me more of that."

"Truly, there is very little more to tell than I have told already," I replied. "If we had the germ of your idea, it was but as a germ...."

[Later Julian West attends a church service and hears the following sermon.—Eds.]

Mr. Barton's Sermon

"We have had among us, during the past week, a critic from the nineteenth century, a living representative of the epoch of our great-grand-parents. It would be strange if a fact so extraordinary had not somewhat strongly affected our imaginations. Perhaps most of us have been stimulated to some effort to realize the society of a century ago, and figure to ourselves what it must have been like to live then. In inviting you now to consider certain reflections upon this subject which have occurred to me, I presume that I shall rather follow than divert the course of your own thoughts....

"Although the idea of the vital unity of the family of mankind, the reality of human brotherhood, was very far from being apprehended by them as the moral axiom it seems to us, yet it is a mistake to suppose that there was no feeling at all corresponding to it. I could read you passages of great beauty from some of their writers which show that the conception was clearly attained by a few, and no doubt vaguely by many more. Moreover, it must not be forgotten that the nineteenth century was in name Christian, and the fact that the entire commercial and industrial frame of society was the embodiment of the anti-Christian spirit must have had some weight, though I admit it was strangely little, with the nominal followers of Jesus Christ.

"When we inquire why it did not have more, why, in general, long after a vast majority of men had agreed as to the crying abuses of the existing social arrangement, they still tolerated it, or contented themselves with talking of petty reforms in it, we come upon an extraordinary fact. It was the sincere belief of even the best of men at that epoch that the only stable elements in human nature, on which a social system could be safely founded were its worst propensities. They had been taught and believed that greed and self-seeking were all that held mankind together, and that all human associations would fall to pieces if anything were done to blunt the edge of these motives or curb their operation. In a word, they believed—even those who longed to believe otherwise—the exact reverse of what seems to us self-evident; they believed, that is, that the anti-social qualities of men, and not their social qualities, were what furnished the cohesive force of society. It seemed reasonable to them that men lived together solely for the purpose of overreaching and oppressing one another, and of being overreached and oppressed, and that while a society that gave full scope to these propensities could stand, there would be little chance for one based on the idea of co-operation for the benefit of all. It seems absurd to expect any one to believe that convictions like these were ever seriously entertained by men; but that they were not only entertained by our great-grandfathers, but were responsible for the long delay in doing away with the ancient order, after a conviction of its intolerable abuses had become general, is as well established as any fact in history can be. Just here you will find the explanation of the profound pessimism of the literature of the last quarter of the nineteenth century, the note of melancholy in its poetry, and the cynicism of its humor.

"Feeling that the condition of the race was unendurable, they had no clear hope of anything better. They believed that the evolution of humanity had resulted in leading it into a *cul de sac*, and that there was no way of getting forward. The frame of men's minds at this time is strikingly illustrated by treatises which have come down to us, and may even now be consulted in our libraries by the curious, in which laborious arguments are pursued to prove that despite the evil plight of men, life was still, by some slight preponderance of considerations, probably better worth living than leaving. Despising themselves, they despised their Creator. There was a general decay of religious belief. Pale and watery gleams, from skies thickly veiled by doubt and dread, alone lighted up the chaos of earth. That men should doubt Him whose breath is in their nostrils, or dread the hands that moulded them, seems to us indeed a pitiable insanity; but we must remember that children who are brave by day have sometimes foolish fears at night. The dawn has come since then. It is very easy to believe in the fatherhood of God in the twentieth century....

"You know the story of that last, greatest, and most bloodless of revolutions. In the time of one generation men laid aside the social traditions and practices of barbarians, and assumed a social order worthy of rational and human beings. Ceasing to be predatory in their habits, they became co-workers, and found in fraternity, at once, the science of wealth and happiness. 'What shall I eat and drink, and wherewithal shall I be clothed?' stated as a problem beginning and ending in self, had been an anxious and an endless one. But when once it was conceived, not from the individual, but the fraternal standpoint, 'What shall we eat and drink, and wherewithal shall we be clothed?'—its difficulties vanished.

"Poverty with servitude had been the result, for the mass of humanity, of attempting to solve the problem of maintenance from the individual standpoint, but no sooner had the nation become the sole capitalist and employer than not alone did plenty replace poverty, but the last vestige of the serfdom of man to man disappeared from earth. Human slavery, so often vainly scotched, at last was killed. The means of subsistence no longer doled out by men to women, by employer to employed, by rich to poor, was distributed from a common stock as among children at the father's table. It was impossible for a man any longer to use his fellow-men as tools for his own profit. His esteem was the only sort of gain he could thenceforth make out of him. There was no more either arrogance or servility in the relations of human beings to one another. For the first time since the creation every man stood up straight before God. The fear of want and the lust of gain became extinct motives when abundance was assured to all and immoderate possessions were made impossible of attainment. There were no more beggars nor almoners. Equity left charity without an occupation. The ten commandments became well-nigh obsolete in a world where there was no temptation to theft, no occasion to lie either for fear or favor, no room for envy where all were equal, and little provocation to violence where men were disarmed of power to injure one another. Humanity's ancient dream of liberty, equality, fraternity, mocked by so many ages, at last was realized.

"As in the old society the generous, the just, the tender-hearted had been placed at a disadvantage by the possession of those qualities, so in the new society the cold-hearted, the greedy, and self-seeking found themselves out of joint with the world. Now that the conditions of life for the first time ceased to operate as a forcing process to develop the brutal qualities of human nature, and the premium which had heretofore encouraged selfishness was not only removed, but placed upon unselfishness, it was for the first time possible to see what unperverted human nature really was like. The depraved tendencies, which had previously overgrown and obscured the better to so large an extent, now withered like cellar fungi in the open air, and the nobler qualities showed a sudden luxuriance which turned cynics into panegyrists and for the first time in human history tempted mankind to fall in love with itself. Soon was fully revealed, what the divines and philosophers of the old world never would have believed, that human nature in its essential qualities is good, not bad, that men by their natural intention and structure are generous, not selfish, pitiful, not cruel, sympathetic, not arrogant, godlike in aspiration, instinct with divinest impulses of tenderness and self-sacrifice, images of God indeed, not the travesties upon Him they had seemed. The constant pressure, through numberless generations, of conditions of life which might have perverted angels, had not been able to essentially alter the natural nobility of the stock, and these conditions once removed, like a bent tree, it had sprung back to its normal uprightness....

"But how is it with us who stand on this height which they gazed up to? Already we have well-nigh forgotten, except when it is especially called to our minds by some occasion like the present, that it was not always with men as it is now. It is a strain on our imaginations to conceive the social arrangements of our immediate ancestors. We find them grotesque. The solution of the problem of physical maintenance so as to banish care and crime, so far from seeming to us an ultimate attainment, appears but as a preliminary to anything like real human progress. We have but relieved ourselves of an impertinent and needless harassment which hindered our ancestors from undertaking the real ends of existence. We are merely stripped for the race; no more. We are like a child which has just learned to stand upright and to walk. It is a great event, from the child's point of view, when he first walks. Perhaps he fancies that there can be little beyond that achievement, but a year later he has forgotten that he could not always walk. His horizon did but widen when he rose, and enlarge as he moved. A great event indeed, in one sense, was his first step, but only as a beginning, not as the end. His true career was but then first entered on. The enfranchisement of humanity in the last century, from mental and physical absorption in working and scheming for the mere bodily necessities, may be regarded as a species of second birth of the race, without which its first birth to an existence that was but a burden would forever have remained unjustified, but whereby it is now abundantly vindicated. Since then, humanity has entered on a new phase of spiritual development, an evolution of higher faculties, the very existence of which in human nature our ancestors scarcely suspected. In place of the dreary hopelessness of the nineteenth century, its profound pessimism as to the future of humanity, the animating idea of the present age is an enthusiastic conception of the opportunities of our earthly existence, and the unbounded possibilities of human nature. The betterment of mankind from generation to generation, physically, mentally, morally, is recognized as the one great object supremely worthy of effort and of sacrifice. We believe the race for the first time to have entered on the realization of God's ideal of it, and each generation must now be a step upward.

"Do you ask what we look for when unnumbered generations shall have passed away? I answer, the way stretches far before us, but the end is lost in light. For twofold is the return of man to God 'who is our home,' the return of the individual by the way of death, and the return of the race by the fulfilment of the evolution, when the divine secret hidden in the germ shall be perfectly unfolded. With a tear for the dark past, turn we then to the dazzling future, and, veiling our eyes, press forward. The long and weary winter of the race is ended. Its summer has begun. Humanity has burst the chrysalis. The heavens are before it."

44

Can the Working Class Change the World?

MICHAEL D. YATES

By the end of the twentieth century, it appeared to many people that Marxist socialism was as dead as Karl Marx himself. The Union of Soviet Socialist Republics had collapsed, and the People's Republic of China was clearly turning its economy in a capitalist direction. Nor was there much evidence that the industrial working class—Marx's "proletariat"—was eager to replace capitalism with socialism. Was this, then, the end of socialism, at least as Marx had conceived of it?

To Michael Yates, an American economist and associate editor of the Marxist journal *Monthly Review*, the answer is definitely not. Socialism remains the best hope for humanity, Yates argues in the following essay, and the working class remains the agent with the best chance of transforming capitalist economies into free and prosperous socialist societies. Moreover, he says, socialism provides the means for dealing with the pressing problems of environmental pollution (see the essays in Part Nine of this volume) and of globalization (see Part Eleven).

Source: Michael D. Yates, "Can the Working Class Change the World?" *Monthly Review* (March 2004): http://www.monthlyreview.org. Reprinted by permission.

CAN THE WORKING CLASS CHANGE THE WORLD?

Radicals of every stripe believe that capitalist economies are incompatible with human liberation. That is, while human beings have enormous capacities to think and to do, capitalism prevents the vast majority of people from developing these capacities. Therefore if we want a society in which the full flowering of human competencies can become a reality, we will have to bring capitalism to an end and replace it with something radically different.

Marx believed that the new society would have to be one in which the means of production were controlled democratically and collectively and in which the goal was to create a society in which labor was offered voluntarily for the good of the whole and in which society's outputs were distributed more or less equally. The primary agent of the transition from capitalism to this new society would be the class of wage laborers created by capitalism itself.

The question which immediately comes to mind is whether the working class is capable of fulfilling the role Marx sets for it. Today, the consensus among radicals is that it is probably not; it has had a lot of time to do so but so far has not. I disagree, and in this paper I attempt to say why.

Before doing so, some preliminary remarks are necessary, to put the question in its proper context. The first thing to note is that capitalism, like the class societies that preceded it, is an exploitive society. A class of property owners, capitalists, extracts a surplus from the non-owning or working class which actually does the work of producing society's output.

While the history of capitalism shows that the working class has often enough included slave and serf labor, the largest and, over time, increasingly dominant part of this class consists of wage laborers, workers formally free, in the double sense of being free to sell their ability to work to any employer and free from the nonhuman means of production.

Second, unlike slaves and serfs, wage laborers are exploited not by direct coercion (although direct coercion may be used either by the capitalists or by the capitalist state) but behind the veil of the market. Wage workers are not owned by the capitalists nor do they pay a part of the output they produce directly to them. However, they are exploited nonetheless, by virtue of their dependence as a class upon being hired by employers. Employers use their ownership of the nonhuman means of production to compel wage workers to work longer hours than those necessary for the workers to produce the output needed for their own subsistence. This extraction of surplus labor, which is the source of the capitalists' profits, is maintained in part by the creation of a reserve army of labor, brought about by the very nature of the system itself.

Third, capitalism, again by its nature, is an expansionary economic system. It pushes local markets into national markets and national markets into international markets. Since profits depend upon wage labor, the relentless accumulation of capital, the drive to maximize both profits and growth, which is the very heart of capitalism, tends to continuously enlarge the working class and more and more divide the world into two classes: capitalists and wage laborers.

Fourth, from the beginning, capital accumulation has been embedded inside strong states, and these have greatly aided the capitalists in their drive to accumulate capital, not least by suppressing the collective actions of workers. These states have shown no sign of collapsing or disappearing.

Fifth, the accumulation of capital requires the constant revolutionizing of the techniques of production, which in turn requires systematic thinking, that is, the development of science and engineering. Invention is, in effect, internalized, made a necessary part of the system.

Sixth, and of great importance, the constant development of the means of production, both human and nonhuman, opens up the possibility of abundance, that is, of a high level of material comfort for all, along with a reduction in the time each person must devote to work. The possibility, in other words, of the full flowering of human capacities. The possibility of an end to the base subsistence life of prior class society and a return to the egalitarian and integrated original economies of gatherers and hunters, but with a higher, conscious, level of development.

Is it possible that capitalism can fulfill the possibilities it creates? The answer must be no. This is because capitalism is a class system, and because of this, it presents insurmountable barriers to an abundant life. Let us look at these. We have seen that capital accumulation requires the exploitation of wage labor. This exploitation, in turn, requires things obviously detrimental to the good life, however defined. Exploitation demands a sharp separation between the conceptualization and execution of work. A few get to think and the many get to do. Exploitation demands a universally employed detailed division of labor which condemns the masses of people to boring and tedious labor. And exploitation demands a reserve army of labor. The ILO [International Labor Organization] estimates that there are some 160 million openly unemployed persons in the world and between 700 and 900 million underemployed persons. Not much abundance for them.

Capitalism also creates and continually reproduces an uneven development both within and among nations. This, in turn, implies that whatever inequality exists to start with will continue to exist as a result of the normal operation of market forces. As economist John Gurley put it, capitalism must and does "build on the best." To put this into the vernacular: "them that's got is them that gets." What abundance there is must be concentrated into a few nations and a few hands within each nation.

Capitalist economies inevitably pass through periodic crises, so just as some people are beginning to see light at the end of the tunnel, the lights go out. And if those at the bottom get too uppity, the state always stands ready to use its many repressive apparatuses to beat them back down again.

We are led inexorably to the conclusion that to bring about that which capitalism makes possible, capitalism must be superseded, abolished and replaced by an egalitarian mode of production, one in which whatever surplus is created by labor is controlled by labor. How might this happen?

We know that, given capitalism's great power and resilience, it will not likely collapse of its own weight. An agent (or agents) is needed to lead a struggle against capitalism. Our objective, then, is to identify the agents of change.

The capitalists themselves, even so-called "enlightened" capitalists like George Soros, will not be their own grave diggers. The most fundamental contradiction of capitalism, its inability to allow full human development, demands an end to the capitalist class.

This leaves the remaining classes. Let us look at each one in turn. In all capitalist societies there are independent proprietors, neither capitalists nor wage laborers. History tells us that most of those in family business, private practice, or cottage industry are looking to become capitalists, and it is unusual when these people oppose themselves to the capitalist system. Sometimes they ally themselves with mass progressive movements, but this cannot be assured. The system can, in the end, function without them.

Peasants comprise another class in nearly all capitalist societies. Peasants are capitalism's first victims; everywhere capitalism touches down, peasants find their ancient attachments to the land threatened by commodity-loving capital. Land cannot be used to produce food for subsistence. Instead it must be converted into private property for the production of profit-seeking commodities, including food for export—an element of capital accumulation. As Marx was coming to understand toward the end of his life, peasants can be a revolutionary, anti-capitalist force. They want land and will often fight for it. In addition, they have collective ways of doing things, and these make them amenable to the more collective organization of a post-capitalist society. Mao grasped this most deeply and built his Red army upon a peasant base. Today, the communists in Nepal are doing the same thing. Egyptian economist Samir Amin estimates that nearly half the world's population is still embedded in fundamentally peasant circumstances. Given this, we cannot ignore the radical potential of peasants nor refuse to ally ourselves with their existing progressive organizations, such as the Landless Peasants' Movement in Brazil.

But while peasants can be important elements in a revolutionary struggle, it is doubtful that they can be the primary agent of it. For one thing, in many places peasants are isolated and under such intense economic pressure that it would be miraculous if they could organize effectively enough to challenge capitalism on a global scale. They are being dispossessed en masse, and it is more likely that they will cause trouble as members of the urban reserve army of labor than as peasants. Second, in the rich capitalist countries, peasants are such a tiny minority that their possible political strength is minimal. In the end, peasants are not needed by capital; the system can survive and expand without them. This is not to say that it is progressive to applaud their disappearance. We should do what we can to stop or slow down this process. Society is confronted daily with the anti-human nature of large-scale capitalist farming, which pollutes the environment and poisons the food supply. We are going to have to find ways to produce our food differently, and peasants and their knowledge are invaluable resources for all of us. [I might note in passing the tremendous strides toward a more human-centered agriculture being made in Cuba, which is pioneering a pesticide-free and smaller-scale farming still capable of achieving national food self-sufficiency. I might also note in passing a certain anti-rural bias among some leftists. They are too much taken with Marx's famous comment about the "idiocy of rural life." But as the editors of *Monthly Review* pointed out recently (October 2003), "idiocy" is not the correct translation of Marx's German. A better word is "isolation." And it is this isolation which must be ended as we strive for a better integration of urban and rural life. In this connection, let me recommend a fine article by Jeremy Seabrook in the April/June 2002 issue of *Race & Class* titled "The Soul of Man Under Globalism."]

If neither small-scale proprietors nor peasants are likely agents of change, the default class, so to speak, the only one which has the possibility of leading the struggle against capitalism, is the working class. This class has many advantages in terms of its capacity to wage war against capital. First, it is the dominant class everywhere capitalism has had enough time to assert its rule. The overwhelming tendency of capitalism is to create wage workers, so while peasants and independent proprietors live with the possibility of extinction, wage workers are always expanding in numbers, foolish talk of a "jobless future" notwithstanding. Second, and in connection with the first, wage workers are absolutely essential for capital, the source of the surplus value which is in turn the source of the profits which fuel capital accumulation. If as Istvan Meszaros argues, capitalism is the perfection of class society, the wage workers it creates are the perfect class in terms of exploitation. They are exploited, so to speak, behind their backs, behind the veil of seemingly equal market relationships, and what is more, they are wholly responsible for their own reproduction.

Third, since workers are at the center of the system, inside the workplaces where the surplus value is taken from them, they are best situated to figure out what is going on, to grasp the nature of the system. This is not to say that most workers will be able to grasp the nature of the system on their own. But some will and they can teach others. Often skilled workers have done this. And there will be those outside the working class who will come into opposition to capitalism, and they can be teachers as well. [Let me note here that I have been a labor educator for twenty-five years, and I can say that almost without exception, working people react positively to the labor theory of value. It fits their experiences, and when someone explains it to them, eyes light up around the room. It is always an "aha!" moment.] Of course, once workers understand the nature of the system, they are bound to become more class conscious and may become willing to struggle against it.

Fourth, wage workers are more likely to be forward looking. Unlike peasants they have not lost anything to look backward toward. They are propertyless, with only their labor power to sell.

Skilled workers are sometimes backward looking, seeking a return to the time when their skills commanded status and respect. But capitalism wages war against skilled labor, so the homogenization of the masses of workers strengthens the forward-looking thinking of the working class.

Before examining the achievements and failures of the working class, that is, how it has changed the world and how it has failed to make a revolutionary change, I want to address an issue brought to the fore by [Michael] Hardt and [Antonio] Negri in their much-discussed book *Empire*. In this book, they argue against the collectively organized working class (organized nationally and internationally) as an agent of revolutionary change. They argue in favor of working people disengaging from the system, deserting it in favor of self-production. While a "do-it-yourself" movement has arisen and has managed to engage in some production independent of the market mechanism, it seems to me that a politics of desertion is bound to fail. Capitalism has created at least some large-scale production units which we will not want to abandon. Can we "do it yourself" and get steel produced or electricity produced and distributed? Some production will always have to be coordinated across large territories. How will this get done? And can it really be imagined that tens of millions of workers are going to desert work and do their own thing? Under what coordination and with what strategies against the states that will actively and viciously oppose them? No wonder Hardt and Negri think the state is now irrelevant. It is a very convenient argument.

In terms of the working class as the primary agent of opposition to capitalism, I agree with Ralph Milliband, who said,

> the "primacy" of organized labour in struggle arises from the fact that no other group, movement or force in capitalist society is remotely capable of mounting as effective and formidable a challenge to the existing structures of power and privilege as it is in the power of organized labour to mount. In no way is this to say that movements of women, blacks, peace activists, ecologists, gays, and others are not important, or cannot have effect, or that they ought to surrender separate identity. Not at all. It is only to say that the principal (not the only) "gravedigger" of capitalism remains the organized working class. Here is the necessary, indispensable "agency of historical change." And if, as one is constantly told is the case, the organized working class will refuse to do the job, then the job will not be done. (*New Left Review* 1 [15], 1985)

It is easy to get discouraged by focusing on the failings of the working class, but it is necessary to take a look at our achievements. The self-consciousness of the working class is not much more than 200 years old. Subject to the control devices implemented by employers, workers take advantage of the contradictions brought forth by these devices and begin to organize themselves into trade unions. For example, employers introduce factory production to enhance control, but workers find themselves more class conscious due to their proximity with one another. Workers employ the very language of the bourgeoisie and turn it to their own advantage. When the capitalists speak of freedom of contract, the workers talk of freedom of assembly.

The unions organized by workers serve not only as defensive organizations, winning for their members some protections against the insecurities inherent in a capitalist economy, but as educational enterprises, teaching workers the ABCs of the system in which they live and labor. The organization of the working class forces intellectuals to take notice of it, and some of these not only try to analyze the system but become active allies of the workers. From their workplaces, labor spreads its organization to the level of society as a whole, forming political organizations and parties, which both agitate for political reform and for direct control of the state itself. Workers also form self-help organizations, newspapers, music groups, theater; in a word, a working class culture forms alongside and in conjunction with unions and political parties.

It is difficult to think of a part of capitalist society that has not been transformed by the activities of the working class and its allies. It is not just that labor unions and labor-based political organizations have improved the material lives of workers, though they certainly have done that: higher wages, benefits of all sorts, an end to arbitrary boss rule of workplaces, protections against the insecurities of layoffs, injuries, sickness, and old age, the right to vote, freedom of speech and assembly, safer workplaces, the opening up of the schools to the masses of people, the overall enhancement of democracy, and much more. But it is also that the working class has forced itself upon bourgeois society and changed all of its culture: from literature (think of how common it is to believe that the class surroundings of a writer matter in terms of what is written or of how the working class becomes a subject of literature) to art (think of the murals of Diego Rivera), to films ([Sergei] Eisenstein and many others), even to music (folk music of course but sometimes classical music too). What is more, there have been times when the working class, often in alliance with and sometimes in subordination to peasants, has overthrown capitalism and attempted to establish a noncapitalist, socialist mode of production. Examples include the USSR, China, and Cuba.

But despite its many achievements, the working class has not made much of a dent in capitalism's hegemony. In fact, the Soviet Union, once the beacon of hope for working people around the world and even toward its end a counterbalance to the rule of capital, was ignominiously torn apart more than a decade ago, and since then the people in the former soviet republics have suffered the kind of degradation normally associated with the "primitive accumulation of capital." And China, which once fired the radical imagination, is rushing headlong toward capitalism and has seen what must surely be one of the most massive regressive shifts in the distribution of income in world history, complete with an enormous reserve army of labor, starvation wages, and sweatshop labor. Only tiny Cuba holds onto the socialist vision, the two-tiered economy created by tourism notwithstanding.

In the rich capitalist countries, capital unleashed a vicious attack on the working class in the early 1970s and over the next three decades dealt workers a seemingly unending string of defeats. There is no use to spell these out; I am sure that you are well aware of them. In the poor capitalist countries, economists speak of lost decades. Everywhere neoliberalism had descended, and everywhere it is still the order of the day. Despite the onslaught of capital, workers are, for the most part, far from taking to the barricades and trying to put an end to this oppressive system. It is no wonder that many people who concern themselves with such matters have concluded that the world's workers cannot and even if they could, will not lead the struggle for a better world.

What went wrong? Looking at the broad sweep of history, we can perhaps identify some of the forces at work and bad decisions taken. First, as Marx pointed out, capitalism creates workers in its own image. It is hard for workers to grasp the nature of their circumstances, to see that they create capital rather than the other way around. So even when organized, they strive for a "fairer" wage and better conditions rather than an end to the wage labor system that is the ultimate source of their circumstances. The system appears to them as inevitable and immutable, though they might win a better deal. Of course, this notion is reinforced by a vast propaganda machine, including the media and the schools.

Second, the accumulation process itself creates divisions among workers, and employers are quick to encourage these and to utilize those which predate capitalism. For example, capital accumulation inevitably creates a split between skilled and unskilled workers, a division often exacerbated by ethnic, gender, racial, and religious differences. In the United States, the most troublesome division has been that of race. The legacy of slavery has never been overcome and has poisoned the labor movement from its beginning. In addition, until recently the labor movement has been defined in gender terms, as a movement of men, and this too has sharply impeded the ability of the movement to both organize and unite the working class.

Capital accumulation also creates a reserve army of labor, and this mass of unemployed labor threatens those who are working. The circumstances of the unemployed make it hard for them to organize, and when they do they cannot be assured of support from the employed or even from the unions of the employed. The labor federations in Argentina were not in the forefront of support of the movement of Argentina's unemployed.

Once workers are at all successful in winning some of their demands, they inevitably develop a stake in the status quo. This may be true both of the relationship with employers and with the state. Successful negotiations with a particular employer can lead to a union embrace of labor-management cooperation, especially if this employer faces difficulties in the marketplace. This can lead to a situation in which the union members identify more with the employer than with workers at other facilities, even when these other workers are in the same union. This problem is exacerbated when the state uses its considerable power to coopt union leadership. When there was an opportunity for the new industrial unions of the United States to develop an independent politics in the 1930s, the Roosevelt administration was able to coopt certain CIO [Congress of Industrial Organizations] leaders, such as Sidney Hillman and Phillip Murray, and use them as a wedge against the more independent John L. Lewis. Even the Communists fell into this trap, the end result of which was the close and deadly alliance between organized labor and the increasingly anti-labor Democratic Party. In Europe, the threat of the Soviet Union and the strength of left-led labor organizations added urgency to the cooptation strategy. A full-fledged partnership among employers, unions, and the state was established, and while this "labor accord" proved beneficial to workers in that it led to the formation of the welfare state, it has proved labor's undoing in recent years when employers have abandoned the accord but unions have no alternative to it.

While seeking the protection of the state or even making alliances with employers can sometimes be useful tactics for labor, they cannot be labor's strategy. In the United States, the consequences of the "labor accord" have proved particularly disastrous. The most basic condition for the embrace of the accord by some employers and the state was the abandonment of labor's left-wing. The left-led unions were purged from the CIO, the very unions that not only embraced the struggle for civil rights and to a lesser extent gender equality, and the unions that upheld the tradition of international working class solidarity, but also the unions that won the best contracts and were often the most democratic. As a consequence of the CIO's embrace of a virulent anti-communism (joining the already rabidly anti-communist AFL [American Federation of Labor]), labor was left bereft of its best people and without any kind of working class ideology to guide working people as they tried to make sense of the world. Labor abandoned the growing civil rights movement and came to be dominated by white male bureaucrats, sometimes still dedicated to the members but often enough union careerists intent mainly on holding office and sometimes corrupt semi-mobsters. The president of the AFL-CIO, George Meany, actually bragged that he had never walked a picket line. Some of his minions worked for the CIA and helped overthrow democratic governments around the world. The post–World War Two economic boom and the initial unique power of the U.S. economy allowed the labor movement to claim a share of the booty for union members, but when the long expansion ended in the mid-1970s and employers went on the attack, labor's weaknesses were glaring and near-complete capitulation followed.

The power of the market mechanism along with the deal labor made with capital made what went on inside the workplace off-limits for organized labor. While some workers won high wages and good benefits, their employers were given free reign to strengthen managerial control of the labor process. Continued use of the detailed division of labor, mechanization, and Taylorism,[1] along with the many techniques developed first by Japanese auto companies and given the apt name of "management by stress," have allowed employers not only to rely less on union labor (by reducing the need for workers by mechanization, outsourcing, exporting jobs, etc.) but to make many modern workplaces into what Ben Hamper, in his book *Rivethead,* called modern gulags. With unions relinquishing the right to contest the nature of work, is it any wonder that so many workers buy into the various managerial schemes which claim to empower them?

Third, I think that the joint forces of nationalism and imperialism have seriously derailed the labor movements of the rich capitalist countries....

Of course, we no longer live in a world in which capital is bound inside a nation. Far from it. But the nationalism and the racism deriving from an earlier period linger on and make it difficult to do the things which must be done to forge an international labor movement. Even today, some years after the AFL-CIO's notorious International Affairs Department was abolished, the AFL-CIO's website has precious little news about workers in the rest of the world. When unemployed workers in Argentina were blockading highways and discharged workers were occupying factories, the AFL-CIO took little note. Today, the occupation of Iraq is providing cover for the oppression of Iraq's nascent labor movement, but you don't hear much about this from organized labor. On another level, labor organizations find it necessary to begin meetings with the national anthem or worse yet, a flag salute. Worst of all, working class parents countenance the enlistment of their children into the military and, with rare exceptions, hale them as heroes even if they get killed.

I suppose that it is fair to say that, given the array of forces set against them, it is amazing that workers have accomplished what they have.

Now it is time to return to our initial question: can labor change the world? Let me make two preliminary points. First, I want to reiterate what I said before. The world will not be changed permanently for the better unless the mass of workers do the changing. Wage workers are necessary for capitalism to reproduce itself, so it is clear that only labor can stop this reproduction and reorganize society's mode of production and distribution.

Second, we have seen that capitalism inevitably generates contradictions and these open up chances for workers and their allies to challenge the power of capital. However, capital always stands ready to learn from these challenges and blunt their impact or even turn them to its advantage. Capitalism is resilient and hegemonic in its development. This makes the task of its supersession a daunting one.

So, given this, what does the future hold? Even in the midst of what appears to be a desperate environment for the working class, there are many hopeful signs. I am sure readers are aware of most of these so I won't go into details, but merely mention the burgeoning global justice movement, the student-led anti-sweatshop movement, numerous successful living wage campaigns, all sorts of successful bridge-building by the labor movement (these along with innovative organizing campaigns, many led by women, minorities, and immigrants, are skillfully analyzed by Dan Clawson in his new book *The Next Upsurge: Labor and the New Social Movements*), the current debate within organized labor about how to increase union density, the anti-war movement, which now includes U.S. Labor Against the War, and many others. I have also discussed some of the new movements, here and in the rest of the world, in the last chapter of my book *Naming the System.*

However, no matter how you slice it, capitalism shows little sign of imminent collapse, and even its most virulent form, neoliberalism, shows few signs of waning in significance. So, what kinds of things might be done to really rejuvenate the labor movement, to at least make it ready to lead the "next upsurge"? I confine myself to the United States here, although some of my points are probably relevant to the rest of the world. And I suggest these things with the assumption that I am talking about what we on the left can do. We must try to build the left in everything we do. In my labor education I must stress the nature of capitalism first and foremost. In environmental work, we must argue that capitalism is the primary source of our alienation from the natural world. We must do what we can to make the anti-globalization movement an anti-capitalist movement. We must push a left perspective in our unions. We must never cease pointing out the essential sameness of the major political parties. We must be alert to show the connections between capitalism and patriarchy and race oppression. And all forms of oppression.

Specifically, here are some things to consider:

1. Organized labor (the AFL-CIO in particular) must confront its racist and anti-left past. We must continue to demand national meetings within organized labor on these issues, and we must bring them up whenever we can. We must proudly point out the tremendous achievements of the left-led unions, not just on nationally and internationally critical issues such as race and peace but in terms of collective bargaining agreements and union democracy.
2. We must promote a left ideology, a worker-friendly way of seeing the world. We must hammer home the same themes (right to a job, health care, right to organize, meaningful labor, community and worker control, a democratic state, a healthy environment, no to war, anti-imperialism, equality in all human relationships, etc.) over and over as the right did with its demands from the 1960s on. Workers have to know why they are organizing. Here we need to promote and develop a left culture—in all of the arts.
3. We must focus on democracy and equality. All forms of oppression must be fought together, not least of all in our unions. And we must insist on as much democracy as possible in all of our organizations. This is not to say that leaders shouldn't lead and be out front in terms of the demands made on employers and the state but only to say that change cannot come solely from the top down.
4. The working class needs to educate itself, and this means that there must be a lot more labor education. Working people need to embrace a working class way of looking at the world, an ideology which will give them direction and a way to judge what is going on in the world. What if the AFL-CIO and its affiliated unions spent some of the millions they now spend supporting Democratic Party politicians, with precious little in return, on labor education (classes for every new union member, full-time education directors, labor radio, etc.)?
5. International solidarity is a must. U.S. labor does a better job here than it used to do, but lots more could be done, including real support for all progressive activities by workers abroad and, most especially, opposition to U.S. foreign policy, which is invariably anti-worker in both intent and impact.
6. Building the left inside and outside the labor movement means building political independence. And this means keeping class foremost in mind (broadly construed) and trying to build a labor political presence.
7. The working class must, and soon, come to grips with the rapid despoliation of our natural environment. As labor productivity continues to rise, output must grow more and more rapidly to absorb a growing labor force. However, under capitalism, this can only mean more poisons in the water and air, more contaminated food, and more workplace sickness and injuries. What will be needed is more labor-intensive, smaller-scale, more localized, and energy-conserving production. Such a production regime could be combined with demands for universal health insurance, meaningful job training, generous leave programs, universal education, and reduced working hours—all things the working class should champion, with its leaders showing the way.

Let me conclude by saying that this is not the time to abandon the working class. Capital is conquering the world, making the earth a gigantic cesspool of exploitation. What is more, this is happening pretty much as Marx said it would. His analysis is as relevant today as it ever was.

And his singling out of the working class as the only viable agent of capital's demise is as correct now as it was when he wrote *Capital.* Workers are the necessary element of the system, and they are the only force capable of forcing this system into the dustbin of history. Those who write it off as reactionary or too nationalistic or racist or sexist or not attuned to the environment cannot offer us an agent to replace it. Of course, if we look to our history, we do see that workers have been all of those things.... But we also see that workers have done the most remarkable things too, and have shown the world what collective solidarity and the action based upon it can do. We must remember that the class struggle is a long hard slog. But one well-worth making and the only one capable of leading us toward a society that can even begin to realize the radical dream: from each according to ability, to each according to need.

NOTE

1. "Taylorism" is the system of industrial management developed in the late nineteenth century by Frederick W. Taylor (1856–1915), an American engineer who aimed to increase productivity through the more efficient use of labor—Eds.

PART SEVEN

Fascism

Fascism emerged after World War I as a reaction against the two leading ideologies of the time, liberalism and socialism. Fascists complained that liberalism and socialism divide the members of society against one another—liberals by emphasizing individualism, socialists by stressing the conflict between social classes. In contrast, fascism presents a picture of individuals and classes merely as cells in a larger, all-embracing organism—the society or state—which can be strong only when all the parts unite behind a single party and a supreme leader.

This was the core of the fascist ideology as it developed in Italy under Benito Mussolini (1883–1945) and in Germany under Adolf Hitler (1889–1945). Mussolini's Fascist Party took its name from the Italian word *fasciare,* "to fasten or bind," and its derivative *fasci,* meaning "group." Fascism was the force that would lead Italy to a new empire as glorious as the Roman Empire of ancient times. Everything and everyone would have to be dedicated to the service of the state, which was the legal and institutional embodiment of the power, unity, and majesty of the Italian people or nation. As Mussolini and his followers repeated over and over, "Everything in the state, nothing outside the state, nothing against the state."

As this slogan suggests, fascism in its pure form is a totalitarian ideology. In fact, the Italian fascists coined the word "totalitarian" to define their antidemocratic aims and to distinguish their ideology from liberalism and socialism, which they saw as advocating democracy. Democracy requires equality of some sort, whether it be in the liberals' insistence on equality before the law and equal opportunity for individuals or in the socialists' insistence on equal power for all in a classless society. But Mussolini and his followers had no use for either democracy or equality. Democracy is all talk and no action; equality merely restrains the strong in order to protect the weak. The fascists did appeal to the masses for support, to be sure, but in their view the common people were to exercise power not by thinking or speaking for themselves but by blindly following their leaders to victory. As another of Mussolini's many slogans proclaimed, "Believe, obey, fight!"

Hitler and his National Socialists (or "Nazis" for short) adopted a similar position in Germany in the 1920s and 1930s. With Hitler as supreme leader, the Nazi Party was to unify all German-speaking peoples into a single state that would go on to become a great new empire (or *Reich*). Hence the Nazi slogan, *Ein Volk, ein Reich, ein Führer*—"one people, one empire, one supreme leader."

The chief difference between German Nazism and Italian fascism was the racial element in Nazi theory. For Nazis, race is the fundamental fact of human life. There is no such thing as a single or universal human nature, for human beings belong to different races, and each race has its own unique characteristics and its own destiny. One race, the Aryan, is naturally stronger, more intelligent, and more creative than all of the others, and the destiny of this "master race" is to subjugate or eliminate all other races.

Aside from this important difference, fascism and Nazism are essentially similar. Both emerged from a combination of forces that developed during the nineteenth century—the Counter-Enlightenment, elitism, irrationalism, racism, and nationalism. The Counter-Enlightenment included a number of thinkers, such as Joseph de Maistre (see Part Four), who rejected the key elements of eighteenth-century Enlightenment thought (for a classic exposition of Enlightenment thought, see Immanuel Kant's essay "What is Enlightenment?" in Part Three). The Counter-Enlightenment thinkers denied that reason alone can bring about great progress and improvement in human life. Counter-Enlightenment theorists and various elitist theories of the late 1800s were also alike in denying that the common people are capable of ruling themselves. In this way both contributed to the antidemocratic character of fascism. This was also true of such "irrationalists" as Georges Sorel (1847–1922), who maintained that "myths" and emotions play a greater part than reason in motivating the masses.

Finally, and perhaps most significantly, fascists are intensely nationalistic. Nationalism is the belief that the world is naturally divided into distinct nations, or peoples, each of which ought to be united in its own political unit, or nation-state. Although nationalistic tendencies have been evident in many parts of the world throughout history, they became especially powerful in the latter half of the nineteenth century, particularly in Italy and Germany—two countries that were not forged into distinct nation-states until the 1860s and 1870s. The desire to preserve and strengthen this unity played a large part in the rise of Italian fascism and German Nazism.

Mussolini and Hitler both died in 1945, the former killed by antifascist Italian guerrillas, the latter a suicide in his Berlin bunker. Their defeat in World War II dealt a crushing, if not a fatal, blow to the fascists and Nazis. We should not forget that fascism was not confined to Italy and Germany, nor has it altogether disappeared—as the activities of various fascists and neo-Nazis in Europe, South Africa, the Middle East, and the Americas clearly remind us. The neo-Nazi elements of the "militia" movement in the United States have attracted Americans opposed to racial integration and the idea of a "color-blind" constitution. They hold that the "white" race should dominate blacks, Jews, and other "inferior" races. Their numbers may not be large, but they provide evidence that the legacy of Mussolini and Hitler is still a powerful political force.

45

Civilization and Race

JOSEPH-ARTHUR DE GOBINEAU

Why do great empires and civilizations rise to power and glory, only to decay and disappear? In the nineteenth century the French diplomat Joseph-Arthur de Gobineau (1816–1882) thought he had found a simple but compelling answer to this question: race. In his *Essay on the Inequality of Human Races* (1853–1855), from which the following selection is taken, Gobineau argued that the mingling of races led, and must continue to lead, to the downfall of great civilizations.

Source: Joseph-Arthur de Gobineau, *The Inequality of Human Races,* translated by Adrian Collins (New York: Howard Fertig, 1967; reprint of 1915 ed.), pp. 1–2, 25, 150–151, 154–155, 178–179, 205–211.

THE INEQUALITY OF HUMAN RACES: INTRODUCTION

...The racial question overshadows all other problems of history, it holds the key to them all, and the inequality of the races from whose fusion a people is formed is enough to explain the whole course of its destiny. Every one must have had some inkling of this colossal truth, for every one must have seen how certain agglomerations of men have descended on some country, and utterly transformed its way of life; how they have shown themselves able to strike out a new vein of activity where, before their coming, all had been sunk in torpor. Thus, to take an example, a new era of power was opened for Great Britain by the Anglo-Saxon invasion, thanks to a decree of Providence, which by sending to this island some of the peoples governed by the sword of your Majesty's illustrious ancestors, was to bring two branches of the same nation under the sceptre of a single house—a house that can trace its glorious title to the dim sources of the heroic nation itself.

Recognizing that both strong and weak races exist, I preferred to examine the former, to analyse their qualities, and especially to follow them back to their origins. By this method I convinced myself at last that everything great, noble, and fruitful in the works of man on this earth, in science, art, and civilization, derives from a single starting-point, is the development of a single germ and the result of a single thought; it belongs to one family alone, the different branches of which have reigned in all the civilized countries of the universe....

Chapter I: The Mortal Disease of Civilizations and Societies Proceeds from General Causes Common to Them All

The fall of civilizations is the most striking, and, at the same time, the most obscure, of all the phenomena of history. It is a calamity that strikes fear into the soul, and yet has always something so mysterious and so vast in reserve, that the thinker is never weary of looking at it, of studying it, of groping for its secrets. No doubt the birth and growth of peoples offer a very remarkable subject for the observer; the successive development of societies, their gains, their conquests, their triumphs, have something that vividly takes the imagination and holds it captive. But all these events, however great one may think them, seem to be easy of explanation; one accepts them as the mere outcome of the intellectual gifts of man. Once we recognize these gifts, we are not astonished at their results; they explain, by the bare fact of their existence, the great stream of being whose source they are. So, on this score, there need be no difficulty or hesitation. But when we see that after a time of strength and glory all human societies come to their decline and fall—all, I say, not this or that; when we see in what awful silence the earth shows us, scattered on its surface, the wrecks of the civilizations that have preceded our own—not merely the famous civilizations, but also many others, of which we know nothing but the names, and some, that lie as skeletons of stone, deep in world-old forests, and have not left us even this shadow of a memory; when the mind returns to our modern States, reflects on their extreme youth, and confesses that they are a growth of yesterday, and that some of them are already toppling to their fall: then at last we recognize, not without a certain philosophic shudder, that the words of the prophets on the instability of mortal things apply with the same rigour to civilizations as to peoples, to people as to States, to States as to individuals; and we are forced to affirm that every assemblage of men, however ingenious the network of social relations that protects it, acquires on the very day of its birth, hidden among the elements of its life, the seed of an inevitable death.

But what is this seed, this principle of death? Is it uniform, as its results are, and do all civilizations perish from the same cause?

At first sight we are tempted to answer in the negative; for we have seen the fall of many empires, Assyria, Egypt, Greece, Rome, amid the clash of events that had no likeness one to the other. Yet, if we pierce below the surface, we soon find that this very necessity of coming to an end, that weighs imperiously on all societies without exception, presupposes such a general cause, which, though hidden, cannot be explained away. When we start from this fixed principle of natural death—a principle unaffected by all the cases of violent death—we see that all civilizations, after they have lasted some time, betray to the observer some little symptoms of uneasiness, which are difficult to define, but not less difficult to deny; these are of a like nature in all times and all places. We may admit one obvious point of difference between the fall of States and that of civilizations, when we see the same kind of culture sometimes persisting in a country under foreign rule and weathering every storm of calamity, at other times being destroyed or changed by the slightest breath of a contrary wind; but we are, in the end, more and more driven to the idea that the principle of death which can be seen at the base of all societies is not only inherent in their life, but also uniform and the same for all.

...How and why is a nation's vigour lost? How does it degenerate? These are the questions which we must try to answer. Up to the present, men have been content with finding the word, without unveiling the reality that lies behind. This further step I shall now attempt to take.

The word *degenerate,* when applied to a people, means (as it ought to mean) that the people has no longer the same intrinsic value as it had before, because it has no longer the same blood in its veins, continual adulterations having gradually affected the quality of that blood. In other words, though the nation bears the name given by its founders, the name no longer connotes the same race; in fact, the man of a decadent time, the *degenerate* man properly so called, is a different being, from the racial point of view from the heroes of the great ages. I agree that he still keeps something of their essence; but the more he degenerates the more attenuated does this "something" become. The heterogeneous elements that henceforth prevail in him give him quite a different nationality—a very original one, no doubt, but such originality is not to be envied. He is only a very distant kinsman of those he still calls his ancestors. He, and his civilization with him, will certainly die on the day when the primordial race-unit is so broken up and swamped by the influx of foreign elements, that its effective qualities have no longer a sufficient freedom of action. It will not, of course, absolutely disappear, but it will in practice be so beaten down and enfeebled, that its power will be felt less and less as time goes on. It is at this point that all the results of degeneration will appear, and the process may be considered complete.

Chapter XIII: The Human Races Are Intellectually Unequal; Mankind Is Not Capable of Infinite Progress

In order to appreciate the intellectual differences between races, we ought first to ascertain the degree of stupidity to which mankind can descend. We know already the highest point that it can reach, namely civilization.

Most scientific observers up to now have been very prone to make out the lowest types as worse than they really are.

Nearly all the early accounts of a savage tribe paint it in hideous colours, far more hideous than the reality. They give it so little power of reason and understanding, that it seems to be on a level with the monkey and below the elephant. It is true that we find the contrary opinion. If a captain is well received in an island, if he meets, as he believes, with a kind and hospitable welcome, and succeeds in making a few natives do a small amount of work with his sailors, then praises are showered on the happy people. They are declared to be fit for anything and capable of everything; and sometimes the enthusiasm bursts all bounds, and swears it has found among them some higher intelligences.

We must appeal from both judgments—harsh and favourable alike. The fact that certain Tahitians have helped to repair a whaler does not make their nation capable of civilization. Because a man of Tonga-Tabu shows goodwill to strangers, he is not necessarily open to ideas of progress. Similarly, we are not entitled to degrade a native of a hitherto unknown coast to the level of the brute, just because he receives his first visitors with a flight of arrows, or because he is found eating raw lizards and mud pies. Such a banquet does not certainly connote a very high intelligence or very cultivated manners. But even in the most hideous cannibal there is a spark of the divine fire, and to some extent the flame of understanding can always be kindled in him. There are no tribes so low that they do not pass some judgments, true or false, just or unjust, on the things around them; the mere existence of such judgments is enough to show that in every branch of mankind some ray of intelligence is kept alive. It is this that makes the most degraded savages accessible to the teachings of religion and distinguishes them in a special manner, of which they are themselves conscious, from even the most intelligent beasts.

Are however these moral possibilities, which lie at the back of every man's consciousness, capable of infinite extension? Do all men possess in an equal degree an unlimited power of intellectual development? In other words, has every human race the capacity for becoming equal to every other? The question is ultimately concerned with the infinite capacity for improvement possessed by the species as a whole, and with the equality of races. I deny both points.

The idea of an infinite progress is very seductive to many modern philosophers, and they support it by declaring that our civilization has many merits and advantages which our differently trained ancestors did not possess. They bring forward all the phenomena that distinguished our modern societies. I have spoken of these already; but I am glad to be able to go through them again.

We are told that our scientific opinions are truer than they were; that our manners are, as a rule, kindly, and our morals better than those of the Greeks and Romans. Especially with regard to political liberty, they say, have we ideas and feelings, beliefs and tolerances, that prove our superiority. There are even some hopeful theorists who maintain that our institutions should lead us straight to that garden of the Hesperides which was sought so long, and with such ill-success, since the time when the ancient navigators reported that it was not in the Canaries....[1]

A little more serious consideration of history will show what truth there is in these high claims....

Chapter XVI: Recapitulation; the Respective Characteristics of the Three Great Races; the Superiority of the White Type, and, Within This Type, of the Aryan Family

I have shown the unique place in the organic world occupied by the human species, the profound physical, as well as moral, differences separating it from all other kinds of living creatures. Considering it by itself, I have been able to distinguish, on physiological grounds alone, three great and clearly marked types, the black, the yellow, and the white. However uncertain the aims of physiology may be, however meagre its resources, however defective its methods, it can proceed thus far with absolute certainty.

The negroid variety is the lowest, and stands at the foot of the ladder. The animal character, that appears in the shape of the pelvis, is stamped on the negro from birth, and foreshadows his destiny. His intellect will always move within a very narrow circle. He is not however a mere brute, for behind his low receding brow, in the middle of his skull, we can see signs of a powerful energy, however crude its objects. If his mental faculties are dull or even non-existent, he often has an intensity of desire, and so of will, which may be called terrible. Many of his senses, especially taste and smell, are developed to an extent unknown to the other two races.

The very strength of his sensations is the most striking proof of his inferiority. All food is good in his eyes, nothing disgusts or repels him. What he desires is to eat, to eat furiously, and to excess; no carrion is too revolting to be swallowed by him. It is the same with odours; his inordinate desires are satisfied with all, however coarse or even horrible. To these qualities may be added an instability and capriciousness of feeling, that cannot be tied down to any single object, and which, so far as he is concerned, do away with all distinctions of good and evil. We might even say that the violence with which he pursues the object that has aroused his senses and inflamed his desires is a guarantee of the desires being soon satisfied and the object forgotten. Finally, he is equally careless of his own life and that of others: he kills willingly, for the sake of killing; and this human machine, in whom it is so easy to arouse emotion, shows, in face of suffering, either a monstrous indifference or a cowardice that seeks a voluntary refuge in death.

The yellow race is the exact opposite of this type. The skull points forward, not backward. The forehead is wide and bony, often high and projecting. The shape of the face is triangular, the nose and chin showing none of the coarse protuberances that mark the negro. There is further a general proneness to obesity, which, though not confined to the yellow type, is found there more frequently than in the others. The yellow man has little physical energy, and is inclined to apathy; he commits none of the strange excesses so common among negroes. His desires are feeble, his will-power rather obstinate than violent; his longing for material pleasures, though constant, is kept within bounds. A rare glutton by nature, he shows far more discrimination in his choice of food. He tends to mediocrity in everything; he understands easily enough anything not too deep or sublime. He has a love of utility and a respect for order, and knows the value of a certain amount of freedom. He is practical, in the narrowest sense of the word. He does not dream or theorize; he invents little, but can appreciate and take over what is useful to him. His whole desire is to live in the easiest and most comfortable way possible. The yellow races are thus clearly superior to the black. Every founder of a civilization would wish the backbone of this society, his middle class, to consist of such men. But no civilized society could be created by them; they could not supply its nerve-force, or set in motion the springs of beauty and action.

We come now to the white peoples. These are gifted with reflective energy, or rather with an energetic intelligence. They have a feeling for utility, but in a sense far wider and higher, more courageous and ideal, than the yellow races; a perseverance that takes account of obstacles and ultimately finds a means of overcoming them; a greater physical power, an extraordinary instinct for order, not merely as a guarantee of peace and tranquility, but as an indispensable means of self-preservation. At the same time, they have a remarkable, and even extreme, love of liberty, and are openly hostile to the formalism under which the Chinese are glad to vegetate, as well as to the strict despotism which is the only way of governing the negro.

The white races are, further, distinguished by an extraordinary attachment to life. They know better how to use it, and so, as it would seem, set a greater price on it; both in their own persons and those of others, they are more sparing of life. When they are cruel, they are conscious of their cruelty; it is very doubtful whether such a consciousness exists in the negro. At the same time, they have discovered reasons why they should surrender this busy life of theirs, that is so precious to them. The principal motive is honour, which under various names has played an enormous part in the ideas of the race from the beginning. I need hardly add that the word honour, together with all the civilizing influences connoted by it, is unknown to both the yellow and the black man.

On the other hand, the immense superiority of the white peoples in the whole field of the intellect is balanced by an inferiority in the intensity of their sensations. In the world of the senses, the white man is far less gifted than the others, and so is less tempted and less absorbed by considerations of the body, although in physical structure he is far the most vigorous.

Such are the three constituent elements of the human race. I call them secondary types, as I think myself obliged to omit all discussion of the Adamite [i.e., original] man. From the combination, by intermarriage, of the varieties of these types come the tertiary groups. The quaternary formations are produced by the union of one of these tertiary types, or of a pure-blooded tribe, with another group taken from one of the two foreign species.

Below these categories others have appeared—and still appear. Some of these are very strongly characterized, and form new and distinct points of departure, coming as they do from races that have been completely fused. Others are incomplete, and ill-ordered, and, one might even say, anti-social, since their elements, being too numerous, too disparate, or too barbarous, have had neither the time nor the opportunity for combining to any fruitful purpose. No limits, except the horror excited by the possibility of infinite intermixture, can be assigned to the number of these hybrid and chequered races that make up the whole of mankind.

It would be unjust to assert that every mixture is bad and harmful. If the three great types had remained strictly separate, the supremacy would no doubt have always been in the hands of the finest of the white races, and the yellow and black varieties would have crawled forever at the feet of the lowest of the whites. Such a state is so far ideal, since it has never been beheld in history; and we can imagine it only by recognizing the undisputed superiority of those groups of the white races which have remained the purest.

It would not have been all gain. The superiority of the white race would have been clearly shown, but it would have been bought at the price of certain advantages which have followed the mixture of blood. Although these are far from counter-balancing the defects they have brought in their train, yet they are sometimes to be commended. Artistic genius, which is equally foreign to each of the three great types, arose only after the intermarriage of white and black. Again, in the Malayan variety, a human family was produced from the yellow and black races that had more intelligence than either of its ancestors. Finally, from the union of white and yellow, certain intermediary peoples have sprung, who are superior to the purely Finnish tribes as well as to the negroes.

I do not deny that these are good results. The world of art and great literature that comes from the mixture of blood, the improvement and ennoblement of inferior races—all these are wonders for which we must need be thankful. The small have been raised. Unfortunately, the great have been lowered by the same process; and this is an evil that nothing can balance or repair. Since I am putting together the advantages of racial mixtures, I will also add that to them is due the refinement of manners and beliefs, and especially the tempering of passion and desire. But these are merely transitory benefits, and if I recognize that the mulatto, who may become a lawyer, a doctor, or a businessman, is worth more than his negro grandfather, who was absolutely savage, and fit for nothing, I must also confess that the Brahmans of primitive India, the heroes of the Iliad and the Shahnameh, the warriors of Scandinavia—the glorious shades of noble races that have disappeared—give us a higher and more brilliant idea of humanity, and were more active, intelligent, and trusty instruments of civilization and grandeur than the peoples, hybrid a hundred times over, of the present day. And the blood even of these was no longer pure.

However it has come about, the human races, as we find them in history, are complex; and one of the chief consequences has been to throw into disorder most of the primitive characteristics of each type. The good as well as the bad qualities are seen to diminish in intensity with repeated intermixture of blood; but they also scatter and separate off from each other, and are often mutually opposed. The white race originally possessed the monopoly of beauty, intelligence, and strength. By its union with other varieties, hybrids were created, which were beautiful without strength, strong without intelligence, or, if intelligent, both weak and ugly. Further, when the quantity of white blood was increased to an indefinite amount of successive infusions, and not by a single admixture, it no longer carried with it its natural advantages, and often merely increased the confusion already existing in the racial elements. Its strength, in fact, seemed to be its only remaining quality, and even its strength served only to promote disorder. The apparent anomaly is easily explained. Each stage of a perfect mixture produces a new type from diverse elements, and develops special faculties. As soon as further elements are added, the vast difficulty of harmonizing the whole creates a state of anarchy. The more this increases, the more do even the best and richest of the new contributions diminish in value, and by their mere presence add fuel to an evil which they cannot abate. If mixtures of blood are, to a certain extent, beneficial to the mass of mankind, if they raise and ennoble it, this is merely at the expense of mankind itself, which is stunted, abased, enervated, and humiliated in the persons of its noblest sons. Even if we admit that it is better to turn a myriad of degraded beings into mediocre men than to preserve the race of princes whose blood is adulterated and impoverished by being made to suffer this dishonourable change, yet there is still the unfortunate fact that the change does not stop here; for when the mediocre men are once created at the expense of the greater, they combine with other mediocrities, and from such unions, which grow ever more and more degraded, is born a confusion which, like that of Babel, ends in utter impotence, and leads societies down to the abyss of nothingness whence no power on earth can rescue them.

Such is the lesson of history. It shows us that all civilizations derive from the white race, that none can exist without its help, and that a society is great and brilliant only so far as it preserves the blood of the noble group that created it, provided that this group itself belongs to the most illustrious branch of our species.

Of the multitude of peoples which live or have lived on the earth, ten alone have risen to the position of complete societies. The remainder have gravitated round these more or less independently, like planets round their suns. If there is any element of life in these ten civilizations that is not due to the impulse of the white races, any seed of death that does not come from the inferior stocks that mingled with them, then the whole theory on which this book rests is false. On the other hand, if the facts are as I say, then we have an irrefragable proof of the nobility of our own species. Only the actual details can set the final seal of truth on my system, and they alone can show with sufficient exactness the full implications of my main thesis, that peoples degenerate only in consequence of the various admixtures of blood which they undergo; that their degeneration corresponds exactly to the quantity and quality of the new blood, and that the rudest possible shock to the vitality of a civilization is given when the ruling elements in a society and those developed by racial change have become so numerous that they are clearly moving away from the homogeneity necessary to their life, and it therefore becomes impossible for them to be brought into harmony and so acquire the common instincts and interests, the common logic of existence, which is the sole justification for any social bond whatever. There is no greater curse than such disorder, for however bad it may have made the present state of things, it promises still worse for the future.

NOTE

1. In classical mythology the Hesperides were nymphs who guarded a garden where golden apples grew—a garden once thought to be in the Canary Islands off the northwest coast of Africa.—Eds.

46

The Doctrine of Fascism

BENITO MUSSOLINI

As founder and leader of the Fascist Party of Italy, Benito Mussolini (1883–1945) brought together the various elements that make fascism a distinctive ideology. As a young man Mussolini considered himself a Marxian socialist, but World War I convinced him that nations, not social classes, are the primary forces in history and politics. After seizing control of the Italian government in 1922, Mussolini set out to convert Italy into a modern industrial and military power in order to create a new Italian empire. The following article, published under Mussolini's name but written by scholars sympathetic to fascism, appeared in the *Enciclopedia Italiana* in 1932.

Source: The Social and Political Doctrines of Contemporary Europe, edited by Michael Oakeshott, pp. 164–179. Copyright © 1939, Cambridge University Press. Reprinted with the permission of Cambridge University Press.

FUNDAMENTAL IDEAS

1. Like every sound political conception, Fascism is both practice and thought; action in which a doctrine is immanent, and a doctrine which, arising out of a given system of historical forces, remains embedded in them and works there from within. Hence it has a form correlative to the contingencies of place and time, but it has also a content of thought which raises it to a formula of truth in the higher level of the history of thought. In the world one does not act spiritually as a human will dominating other wills without a conception of the transient and particular reality under which it is necessary to act, and of the permanent and universal reality in which the first has its being and its life. In order to know men it is necessary to know man; and in order to know man it is necessary to know reality and its laws. There is no concept of the State which is not fundamentally a concept of life: philosophy or intuition, a system of ideas which develops logically or is gathered up into a vision or into a faith, but which is always, at least virtually, an organic conception of the world.

2. Thus Fascism could not be understood in many of its practical manifestations as a party organization, as a system of education, as a discipline, if it were not always looked at in the light of its whole way of conceiving life, a spiritualized way. The world seen through Fascism is not this material world which appears on the surface, in which man is an individual separated from all others and standing by himself, and in which he is governed by a natural law that makes him instinctively live a life of selfish and momentary pleasure. The man of Fascism is an individual who is nation and fatherland, which is a moral law, binding together individuals and the generations into a tradition and a mission, suppressing the instinct for a life enclosed within the brief round of pleasure in order to restore within duty a higher life free from the limits of time and space: a life in which the individual, through the denial of himself, through the sacrifice of his own private interests, through death itself, realizes that completely spiritual existence in which his value as a man lies.

3. Therefore it is a spiritualized conception, itself the result of the general reaction of modern times against the flabby materialistic positivism of the nineteenth century. Antipositivistic, but positive: not sceptical, nor agnostic, nor pessimistic, nor passively optimistic, as are, in general, the doctrines (all negative) that put the centre of life outside man, who with his free will can and must create his own world. Fascism desires an active man, one engaged in activity with all his energies: it desires a man virilely conscious of the difficulties that exist in action and ready to face them. It conceives of life as a struggle, considering that it behooves man to conquer for himself that life truly worthy of him, creating first of all in himself the instrument (physical, moral, intellectual) in order to construct it. Thus for the single individual, thus for the nation, thus for humanity. Hence the high value of culture in all its forms (art, religion, science), and the enormous importance of education. Hence also the essential value of work, with which man conquers nature and creates the human world (economic, political, moral, intellectual).

4. This positive conception of life is clearly an ethical conception. It covers the whole of reality, not merely the human activity which controls it. No action can be divorced from moral judgement; there is nothing in the world which can be deprived of the value which belongs to everything in its relation to moral ends. Life, therefore, as conceived by the Fascist, is serious, austere, religious: the whole of it is poised in a world supported by

the moral and responsible forces of the spirit. The Fascist disdains the "comfortable" life.

5. Fascism is a religious conception in which man is seen in his immanent relationship with a superior law and with an objective Will that transcends the particular individual and raises him to conscious membership of a spiritual society. Whoever has seen in the religious politics of the Fascist regime nothing but mere opportunism has not understood that Fascism besides being a system of government is also, and above all, a system of thought.

6. Fascism is an historical conception, in which man is what he is only in so far as he works with the spiritual process in which he finds himself, in the family or social group, in the nation and in the history in which all nations collaborate. From this follows the great value of tradition, in memories, in language, in customs, in the standards of social life. Outside history man is nothing. Consequently Fascism is opposed to all the individualistic abstractions of a materialistic nature like those of the eighteenth century; and it is opposed to all Jacobin utopias and innovations.[1] It does not consider that "happiness" is possible upon earth, as it appeared to be in the desire of the economic literature of the eighteenth century, and hence it rejects all teleological theories according to which mankind would reach a definitive stabilized condition at a certain period in history. This implies putting oneself outside history and life, which is a continual change and coming to be. Politically, Fascism wishes to be a realistic doctrine; practically, it aspires to solve only the problems which arise historically of themselves and that of themselves find or suggest their own solution. To act among men, as to act in the natural world, it is necessary to enter into the process of reality and to master the already operating forces.

7. Against individualism, the Fascist conception is for the State; and it is for the individual in so far as he coincides with the State, which is the conscience and universal will of man in his historical existence. It is opposed to classical Liberalism, which arose from the necessity of reacting against absolutism, and which brought its historical purpose to an end when the State was transformed into the conscience and will of the people. Liberalism denied the State in the interests of the particular individual; Fascism reaffirms the State as the true reality of the individual. And if liberty is to be the attribute of the real man, and not of that abstract puppet envisaged by individualistic Liberalism, Fascism is for liberty. And for the only liberty which can be a real thing, the liberty of the State and of the individual within the State. Therefore, for the Fascist, everything is in the State, and nothing human or spiritual exists, much less has value, outside the State. In this sense Fascism is totalitarian, and the Fascist State, the synthesis and unity of all values, interprets, develops and gives strength to the whole life of the people.

8. Outside the State there can be neither individuals nor groups (political parties, associations, syndicates, classes). Therefore Fascism is opposed to Socialism, which confines the movement of history within the class struggle and ignores the unity of classes established in one economic and moral reality in the State; and analogously it is opposed to class syndicalism. Fascism recognizes the real exigencies for which the socialist and syndicalist movement arose, but while recognizing them wishes to bring them under the control of the State and give them a purpose within the corporative system of interests reconciled within the unity of the State.

9. Individuals form classes according to the similarity of their interests, they form syndicates according to differentiated economic activities within these interests; but they form first, and above all, the State, which is not to be thought of numerically as the sum-total of individuals forming the majority of a nation. And consequently Fascism is opposed to Democracy, which equates the nation to the majority, lowering it to the

level of that majority; nevertheless it is the purest form of democracy if the nation is conceived, as it should be, qualitatively and not quantitatively, as the most powerful idea (most powerful because most moral, most coherent, most true) which acts within the nation as the conscience and the will of a few, even of One, which ideal tends to become active within the conscience and the will of all—that is to say, of all those who rightly constitute a nation by reason of nature, history or race, and have set out upon the same line of development and spiritual formation as one conscience and one sole will. Not a race,[2] nor a geographically determined region, but as a community historically perpetuating itself, a multitude unified by a single idea, which is the will to existence and to power: consciousness of itself, personality.

10. This higher personality is truly the nation in so far as it is the State. It is not the nation that generates the State, as according to the old naturalistic concept which served as the basis of the political theories of the national States of the nineteenth century. Rather the nation is created by the State, which gives to the people, conscious of its own moral unity, a will and therefore an effective existence. The right of a nation to independence derives not from a literary and ideal consciousness of its own being, still less from a more or less unconscious and inert acceptance of a *de facto* situation, but from an active consciousness, from a political will in action and ready to demonstrate its own rights: that is to say, from a state already coming into being. The State, in fact, as the universal ethical will, is the creator of right.

11. The nation as the State is an ethical reality which exists and lives in so far as it develops. To arrest its development is to kill it. Therefore the State is not only the authority which governs and gives the form of laws and the value of spiritual life to the wills of individuals, but it is also a power that makes its will felt abroad, making it known and respected, in other words, demonstrating the fact of its universality in all the necessary directions of its development. It is consequently organization and expansion, at least virtually. Thus it can be likened to the human will which knows no limits to its development and realizes itself in testing its own limitlessness.

12. The Fascist State, the highest and most powerful form of personality, is a force, but a spiritual force, which takes over all the forms of the moral and intellectual life of man. It cannot therefore confine itself simply to the functions of order and supervision as Liberalism desired. It is not simply a mechanism which limits the sphere of the supposed liberties of the individual. It is the form, the inner standard and the discipline of the whole person; it saturates the will as well as the intelligence. Its principle, the central inspiration of the human personality living in the civil community, pierces into the depths and makes its home in the heart of the man of action as well as of the thinker, of the artist as well as of the scientist: it is the soul of the soul.

13. Fascism, in short, is not only the giver of laws and the founder of institutions, but the educator and promoter of spiritual life. It wants to remake, not the forms of human life, but its content, man, character, faith. And to this end it requires discipline and authority that can enter into the spirits of men and there govern unopposed. Its sign, therefore, is the Lictors' rods, the symbol of unity, of strength and justice....

POLITICAL AND SOCIAL DOCTRINE

3. Above all, Fascism, in so far as it considers and observes the future and the development of humanity quite apart from the political considerations of the moment, believes neither in the possibility nor in the utility of perpetual peace. It thus repudiates the

doctrine of Pacifism—born of a renunciation of the struggle and an act of cowardice in the face of sacrifice. War alone brings up to their highest tension all human energies and puts the stamp of nobility upon the peoples who have the courage to meet it. All other trials are substitutes, which never really put a man in front of himself in the alternative of life and death. A doctrine, therefore, which begins with a prejudice in favour of peace is foreign to Fascism; as are foreign to the spirit of Fascism, even though acceptable by reason of the utility which they might have in given political situations, all internationalistic and socialistic systems which, as history proves, can be blown to the winds when emotional, idealistic and practical movements storm the hearts of peoples. Fascism carries over this anti-pacifist spirit even into the lives of individuals. The proud motto of the *Squadrista,* "Me ne frego" ["I don't give a damn"], written on the bandages of a wound is an act of philosophy which is not only stoical, it is the epitome of a doctrine that is not only political: it is education for combat, the acceptance of the risks which it brings; it is a new way of life for Italy. Thus the Fascist accepts and loves life, he knows nothing of suicide and despises it; he looks on life as duty, ascent, conquest: life which must be noble and full: lived for oneself, but above all for those others near and far away, present and future.

4. The "demographic" policy of the regime follows from these premises. Even the Fascist does in fact love his neighbour, but this "neighbour" is not for him a vague and ill-defined concept; love for one's neighbour does not exclude necessary educational severities, and still less differentiations and distances. Fascism rejects universal concord, and, since it lives in the community of civilized peoples, it keeps them vigilantly and suspiciously before its eyes, it follows their states of mind and the changes in their interests and it does not let itself be deceived by temporary and fallacious appearances.

5. Such a conception of life makes Fascism the precise negation of that doctrine which formed the basis of the so-called Scientific or Marxian Socialism: the doctrine of historical Materialism, according to which the history of human civilizations can be explained only as the struggle of interest between the different social groups and as arising out of change in the means and instruments of production. That economic improvements—discoveries of raw materials, new methods of work, scientific inventions—should have an importance of their own, no one denies, but that they should suffice to explain human history to the exclusion of all other factors is absurd: Fascism believes, now and always, in holiness and in heroism, that is in acts in which no economic motive—remote or immediate—plays a part. With this negation of historical materialism, according to which men would be only by-products of history, who appear and disappear on the surface of the waves while in the depths the real directive forces are at work, there is also denied the immutable and irreparable "class struggle" which is the natural product of this economic conception of history, and above all it is denied that the class struggle can be the primary agent of social changes. Socialism, being thus wounded in these two primary tenets of its doctrine, nothing of it is left save the sentimental aspiration—old as humanity—towards a social order in which the sufferings and the pains of the humblest folk could be alleviated. But here Fascism rejects the concept of an economic "happiness" which would be realized socialistically and almost automatically at a given moment of economic evolution by assuring to all a maximum prosperity. Fascism denies the possibility of the materialistic conception of "happiness" and leaves it to the economists of the first half of the eighteenth century; it denies, that is, the equation of prosperity with happiness, which would transform men into animals with one sole preoccupation:

that of being well-fed and fat, degraded in consequence to a merely physical existence.

6. After Socialism, Fascism attacks the whole complex of democratic ideologies and rejects them both in their theoretical premises and in their applications or practical manifestations. Fascism denies that the majority, through the mere fact of being a majority, can rule human societies; it denies that this majority can govern by means of a periodical consultation; it affirms the irremediable, fruitful and beneficent inequality of men, who cannot be levelled by such a mechanical and extrinsic fact as universal suffrage. By democratic regimes we mean those in which from time to time the people is given the illusion of being sovereign, while true effective sovereignty lies in other, perhaps irresponsible and secret, forces. Democracy is a regime without a king, but with very many kings, perhaps more exclusive, tyrannical and violent than one king even though a tyrant....

7. ...Fascism rejects in democracy the absurd conventional lie of political equalitarianism clothed in the dress of collective irresponsibility and the myth of happiness and indefinite progress. But if democracy can be understood in other ways, that is, if democracy means not to relegate the people to the periphery of the State, then Fascism could be defined as an "organized, centralized, authoritarian democracy."

8. In face of Liberal doctrines, Fascism takes up an attitude of absolute opposition both in the field of politics and in that of economics. It is not necessary to exaggerate—merely for the purpose of present controversies—the importance of Liberalism in the past century, and to make of that which was one of the numerous doctrines sketched in that century a religion of humanity for all times, present and future.... The "Liberal" century, after having accumulated an infinity of Gordian knots,[3] tried to untie them by the hecatomb [i.e., mass slaughter] of the World War. Never before has any religion imposed such a cruel sacrifice. Were the gods of Liberalism thirsty for blood? Now Liberalism is about to close the doors of its deserted temples because the peoples feel that its agnosticism in economics, its indifferentism in politics and in morals, would lead, as they have led, the States to certain ruin. In this way one can understand why all the political experiences of the contemporary world are anti-Liberal, and it is supremely ridiculous to wish on that account to class them outside of history; as if history were a hunting ground reserved to Liberalism and its professors, as if Liberalism were the definitive and no longer surpassable message of civilization.

9. But the Fascist repudiations of Socialism, Democracy, Liberalism must not make one think that Fascism wishes to make the world return to what it was before 1789, the year which has been indicated as the year of the beginning of the liberal-democratic age. One does not go backwards. The Fascist doctrine has not chosen De Maistre as its prophet.[4] Monarchial absolutism is a thing of the past and so also is every theocracy. So also feudal privileges and division into impenetrable and isolated castes have had their day. The theory of Fascist authority has nothing to do with the police State. A party that governs a nation in a totalitarian way is a new fact in history. References and comparisons are not possible. Fascism takes over from the ruins of Liberal Socialistic democratic doctrines those elements which still have a living value. It preserves those that can be called the established facts of history, it rejects all the rest, that is to say the idea of a doctrine which holds good for all times and all peoples. If it is admitted that the nineteenth century has been the century of Socialism, Liberalism and Democracy, it does not follow that the twentieth must also be the century of Liberalism, Socialism and Democracy. Political doctrines pass; peoples remain. It is to be expected that this century may be that of authority, a century of the

"Right," a Fascist century. If the nineteenth was the century of the individual (Liberalism means individualism) it may be expected that this one may be the century of "collectivism" and therefore the century of the State. That a new doctrine should use the still vital elements of other doctrines is perfectly logical. No doctrine is born quite new, shining, never before seen. No doctrine can boast of an absolute "originality." It is bound, even if only historically, to other doctrines that have been, and to develop into other doctrines that will be. Thus the scientific socialism of Marx is bound to the Utopian Socialism of the Fouriers, the Owens and the Saint-Simons[5]; thus the Liberalism of the nineteenth century is connected with the whole "Enlightenment" of the eighteenth century. Thus the doctrines of democracy are bound to the *Encyclopédie*.[6] Every doctrine tends to direct the activity of men towards a determined objective; but the activity of man reacts upon the doctrine, transforms it, adapts it to new necessities or transcends it. The doctrine itself, therefore, must be, not words, but an act of life. Hence, the pragmatic veins in Fascism, its will to power, its will to be, its attitude in the face of the fact of "violence" and of its own courage.

10. The keystone of Fascist doctrine is the conception of the State, of its essence, of its tasks, of its ends. For Fascism the State is an absolute before which individuals and groups are relative. Individuals and groups are "thinkable" in so far as they are within the State. The Liberal State does not direct the interplay and the material and spiritual development of the groups, but limits itself to registering the results; the Fascist State has a consciousness of its own, a will of its own, on this account it is called an "ethical" State....

11. From 1929 up to the present day these doctrinal positions have been strengthened by the whole economico-political evolution of the world. It is the State alone that grows in size, in power. It is the State alone that can solve the dramatic contradictions of capitalism. What is called the crisis cannot be overcome except by the State, within the State.... But when one says liberalism, one says the individual; when one says Fascism, one says the State. But the Fascist State is unique; it is an original creation. It is not reactionary, but revolutionary in that it anticipates the solutions of certain universal problems. These problems are no longer seen in the same light: in the sphere of politics they are removed from party rivalries, from the supreme power of parliament, from the irresponsibility of assemblies; in the sphere of economics they are removed from the sphere of the syndicates' activities—activities that were ever widening their scope and increasing their power both on the workers' side and on the employers'—removed from their struggles and their designs; in the moral sphere they are divorced from ideas of the need for order, discipline and obedience, and lifted into the plane of the moral commandments of the fatherland. Fascism desires the State to be strong, organic and at the same time founded on a wide popular basis. The Fascist State has also claimed for itself the field of economics and, through the corporative, social and educational institutions which it has created, the meaning of the State reaches out to and includes the farthest offshoots; and within the State, framed in their respective organizations, there revolve all the political, economic and spiritual forces of the nation. A State founded on millions of individuals who recognize it, feel it, are ready to serve it, is not the tyrannical State of the medieval lord. It has nothing in common with the absolutist States that existed either before or after 1789. In the Fascist State the individual is not suppressed, but rather multiplied, just as in a regiment a soldier is not weakened but multiplied by the number of his comrades. The Fascist State organizes the nation, but it leaves sufficient scope to individuals; it has limited useless or harmful liberties and has preserved those that are

essential. It cannot be the individual who decides in this matter, but only the State.

12. The Fascist State does not remain indifferent to the fact of religion in general and to that particular positive religion which is Italian Catholicism. The State has no theology, but it has an ethic. In the Fascist State religion is looked upon as one of the deepest manifestations of the spirit; it is, therefore, not only respected, but defended and protected. The Fascist State does not create a "God" of its own, as Robespierre once, at the height of the Convention's foolishness, wished to do; nor does it vainly seek, like Bolshevism, to expel religion from the minds of men; Fascism respects the God of the ascetics, of the saints, of the heroes, and also God as seen and prayed to by the simple and primitive heart of the people.

13. The Fascist State is a will to power and to government. In it the tradition of Rome is an idea that has force. In the doctrine of Fascism Empire is not only a territorial, military or mercantile expression, but spiritual or moral. One can think of an empire, that is to say a nation that directly or indirectly leads other nations, without needing to conquer a single square kilometre of territory. For Fascism the tendency to Empire, that is to say, to the expansion of nations, is a manifestation of vitality; its opposite, staying at home, is a sign of decadence: peoples who rise or re-rise are imperialist, peoples who die are renunciatory. Fascism is the doctrine that is most fitted to represent the aims, the states of mind, of a people, like the Italian people, rising again after many centuries of abandonment or slavery to foreigners. But Empire calls for discipline, co-ordination of forces, duty and sacrifice; this explains many aspects of the practical working of the regime and the direction of many of the forces of the State and the necessary severity shown to those who would wish to oppose this spontaneous and destined impulse of the Italy of the twentieth century, to oppose it in the name of the superseded ideologies of the nineteenth, repudiated wherever great experiments of political and social transformation have been courageously attempted: especially where, as now, peoples thirst for authority, for leadership, for order. If every age has its own doctrine, it is apparent from a thousand signs that the doctrine of the present age is Fascism. That it is a doctrine of life is shown by the fact that it has resuscitated a faith. That this faith has conquered minds is proved by the fact that Fascism has had its dead and its martyrs.

Fascism henceforward has in the world the universality of all those doctrines which, by fulfilling themselves, have significance in the history of the human spirit.

NOTES

1. The Jacobins were a utopian-radical sect in the French Revolution.—Eds.
2. "Race; it is an emotion, not a reality; ninety-five percent of it is emotion."—Mussolini.
3. According to ancient legend, the knot tied by the peasant-turned-king Gordius was so complex that no one could untie it, although many had tried. The Gordian knot was finally "untied" by Alexander the Great, who cut it with his sword.—Eds.
4. The monarchist and reactionary critic of the French Revolution, Joseph de Maistre (1753–1821). See selection 26 in this volume.—Eds.
5. Charles Fourier (1772–1837), Robert Owen (1771–1858), and Count Claude-Henri de Saint-Simon (1760–1825) were early nineteenth-century socialists whom Marx and Engels scorned as "utopian" rather than "scientific" thinkers.—Eds.
6. The massive eighteenth-century French encyclopedia that attempted to classify and communicate all human knowledge in a comprehensive and systematic way. It was both an achievement and a symbol of the European Enlightenment.—Eds.

47

The Political Theory of Fascism

ALFREDO ROCCO

As the previous selection shows, the Italian fascists took pains to distinguish their political ideology from liberalism and socialism. By stressing their differences with liberalism and socialism—and by rejecting democracy—they tried to define a coherent and distinctive fascist ideology. This task fell to intellectuals such as Alfredo Rocco (1875–1935), the author of the following selection. Rocco was a professor of law and a theorist for the Italian National Association, which was a precursor of the Italian Fascist Party. He subsequently joined the fascists and served as minister of justice in Mussolini's government.

Source: Alfredo Rocco, *The Political Doctrine of Fascism,* translated by D. Bigongiari (Carnegie Endowment for International Peace, no. 223: 1926). © Carnegie Endowment for International Peace.

THE POLITICAL THEORY OF FASCISM

It is true that Fascism is, above all, action and sentiment and that such it must continue to be. Were it otherwise, it could not keep up that immense driving force, that renovating power which it now possesses and would merely be the solitary meditation of a chosen few. Only because it is feeling and sentiment, only because it is the unconscious reawakening of our profound racial instinct, has it the force to stir the soul of the people, and to set free an irresistible current of national will. Only because it is action, and as such actualizes itself in a vast organization and in a huge movement, has it the conditions for determining the historical course of contemporary Italy.

But Fascism is thought as well and it has a theory, which is an essential part of this historical phenomenon, and which is responsible in a great measure for the successes that have been achieved. To the existence of this ideal content of Fascism, to the truth of this Fascist logic we ascribe the fact that though we commit many errors of detail, we very seldom go astray on fundamentals, whereas all the parties of the opposition, deprived as they are of an informing, animating principle, of a unique directing concept, do very often wage their war faultlessly in minor tactics, better trained as they are in parliamentary and journalistic manoeuvres, but they constantly break down on the important issues. Fascism, moreover, considered as action, is a typically Italian phenomenon and acquires a universal validity because of the existence of this coherent and organic doctrine. The originality of Fascism is due in great part to the autonomy of its theoretical principles. For even when, in its external behavior and in its conclusions, it seems identical with other political creeds, in reality it possesses an inner originality due to the new spirit which animates it and to an entirely different theoretical approach.

Common Origins and Common Background of Modern Political Doctrines: From Liberalism to Socialism

Modern political thought remained, until recently, both in Italy and outside of Italy under the absolute control of those doctrines which, proceeding from the Protestant Reformation and developed by the adepts of natural law in the XVII and XVIII centuries, were firmly grounded in the institutions and customs of the English, of the American, and of the French Revolutions. Under different and sometimes clashing forms these doctrines have left a determining imprint upon all theories and actions both social and political, of the XIX and XX centuries down to the rise of Fascism. The common basis of all these doctrines…is a social and state concept which I shall call mechanical or atomistic.

Society according to this concept is merely a sum total of individuals, a plurality which breaks up into its single components. Therefore the ends of a society, so considered, are nothing more than the ends of the individuals which compose it and for whose sake it exists. An atomistic view of this kind is also necessarily anti-historical, inasmuch as it considers society in its spatial attributes and not in its temporal ones; and because it reduces social life to the existence of a single generation. Society becomes thus a sum of determined individuals, viz., the generation living at a given moment. This doctrine which I call atomistic and which appears to be anti-historical, reveals from under a concealing cloak a strongly materialistic nature. For in its endeavors to isolate the present from the past and the future, it rejects the spiritual inheritance of ideas and sentiments which each generation receives from those preceding and hands down to the following generation, thus destroying the unity and the spiritual life itself of human society.

This common basis shows the close logical connection existing between all political doctrines; the substantial solidarity, which unites all the political movements, from Liberalism to Socialism, that until recently have dominated Europe. For these political schools differ from one another in their methods, but all agree as to the ends to be achieved. All of them consider the welfare and happiness of individuals to be the goal of society, itself considered as composed of individuals of the present generation. All of them see in society and in its juridical organization, the state, the mere instrument and means whereby individuals can attain their ends. They differ only in that the methods pursued for the attainment of these ends vary considerably one from the other....

Thus Liberalism, Democracy, and Socialism, appear to be, as they are in reality, not only the offspring of one and the same theory of government, but also logical derivations one of the other. Logically developed, Liberalism leads to Democracy; the logical development of Democracy issues into Socialism. It is true that for many years, and with some justification, Socialism was looked upon as antithetical to Liberalism. But the antithesis is purely relative and breaks down as we approach the common origin and foundation of the two doctrines, for we find that the opposition is one of method, not of purpose. The end is the same for both, viz., the welfare of the individual members of society. The difference lies in the fact that Liberalism would be guided to its goal by liberty, whereas Socialism strives to attain it by the collective organization of production. There is therefore no antithesis nor even a divergence as to the nature and scope of the state and the relation of individuals to society. There is only a difference of evaluation of the means for bringing about these ends and establishing these relations, which difference depends entirely on the different economic conditions which prevailed at the time when the various doctrines were formulated. Liberalism arose and began to thrive in the period of small industry; Socialism grew with the rise of industrialism and of world-wide capitalism. The dissension therefore between these two points of view, or the antithesis, if we wish so to call it, is limited to the economic field. Socialism is at odds with Liberalism only on the question of the organization of production and of the division of wealth. In religious, intellectual, and moral matters it is liberal, as it is liberal and democratic in its politics. Even the anti-liberalism and anti-democracy of Bolshevism are in themselves purely contingent.[1] For Bolshevism is opposed to Liberalism only in so far as the former is revolutionary, not in its socialistic aspect. For if the opposition of the Bolsheviki to liberal and democratic doctrines were to continue, as now seems more and more probable, the result might be a complete break between Bolshevism and Socialism notwithstanding the fact that the ultimate aims of both are identical.

Fascism as an Integral Doctrine of Sociality Antithetical to the Atomism of Liberal, Democratic, and Socialistic Theories

The true antithesis, not to this or that manifestation of the liberal-democratic-socialistic conception of the state but to the concept itself, is to be found in the doctrine of Fascism. For while the disagreement between Liberalism and Democracy, and between Liberalism and Socialism lies in a difference of method, as we have said, the rift between Socialism, Democracy, and Liberalism on one side and Fascism on the other is caused by a difference in concept. As a matter of fact, Fascism never raises the question of methods, using in its political praxis now liberal ways, now democratic means and at times even socialistic devices. This indifference to method often exposes Fascism to the charge of incoherence on the part of superficial observers, who do not see that what counts with us is the end and that therefore even when we employ the same means we act with a radically different spiritual attitude and strive for entirely different results. The Fascist concept then of the nation, of the scope of the state, and of the relations obtaining between society and its individual components, rejects entirely the doctrine which I said proceeded from the theories of natural law developed in the course of the XVI, XVII, and XVIII centuries and which form the basis of the liberal, democratic, and socialistic ideology....

Fascism replaces therefore the old atomistic and mechanical state theory which was at the basis of the liberal and democratic doctrines with an organic and historic concept. When I say organic I do not wish to convey the impression that I consider society as an organism after the manner of the so-called "organic theories of the state"; but rather to indicate that the social groups as fractions of the species receive thereby a life and scope which transcend the scope and life of the individuals identifying themselves with the history and finalities of the uninterrupted series of generations. It is irrelevant in this connection to determine whether social groups, considered as fractions of the species, constitute organisms. The important thing is to ascertain that this organic concept of the state gives to society a continuous life over and beyond the existence of the several individuals.

The relations therefore between state and citizens are completely reversed by the Fascist doctrine. Instead of the liberal-democratic formula, "society for the individual," we have, "individuals for society," with this difference, however: that while the liberal doctrines eliminated society, Fascism does not submerge the individual in the social group. It subordinates him, but does not eliminate him; the individual as a part of his generation ever remaining an element of society however transient and insignificant he may be. Moreover the development of individuals in each generation, when coordinated and harmonized, conditions the development and prosperity of the entire social unit.

At this juncture the antithesis between the two theories must appear complete and absolute. Liberalism, Democracy, and Socialism look upon social groups as aggregates of living individuals; for Fascism they are the recapitulating unity of the indefinite series of generations. For Liberalism, society has no purposes other than those of the members living at a given moment. For Fascism, society has historical and immanent ends of preservation, expansion, improvement, quite distinct from those of the individuals which at a given moment compose it; so distinct in fact that they may even be in opposition. Hence the necessity, for which the older doctrines make little allowance, of sacrifice, even up to the total immolation of individuals, in behalf of society; hence the true explanation of war, eternal law of mankind, interpreted by the liberal-democratic doctrines as a degenerate absurdity or as a maddened monstrosity.

For Liberalism, society has no life distinct from the life of the individuals.... For Fascism, the life of society overlaps the existence of individuals and projects itself into the succeeding generations through centuries and millennia. Individuals come into being, grow, and die, followed by others, unceasingly; social unity remains always identical to itself. For Liberalism, the individual is the end and society the means; nor is it conceivable that the individual, considered in the dignity of an ultimate finality, be lowered to mere instrumentality. For Fascism, society is the end, individuals the means, and its whole life consists in using individuals as instruments for its social ends. The state therefore guards and protects the welfare and development of individuals not for their exclusive interest, but because of the identity of the needs of individuals with those of society as a whole. We can thus accept and explain institutions and practices, which like the death penalty, are condemned by Liberalism in the name of the preeminence of individualism.

The fundamental problem of society in the old doctrines is the question of the rights of individuals. It may be the right to freedom as the Liberals would have it; or the right to the government of the commonwealth as the Democrats claim it, or the right to economic justice as the Socialists contend; but in every case it is the right of individuals, or groups of individuals (classes). Fascism on the other hand faces squarely the problem of the right of the state and of the duty of individuals. Individual rights are only recognized in so far as they are implied in the rights of the state. In this preeminence of duty we find the highest ethical value of Fascism.

The Problems of Liberty, of Government, and of Social Justice in the Political Doctrine of Fascism

This, however, does not mean that the problems raised by the other schools are ignored by Fascism. It means simply that it faces them and solves them differently, as, for example, the problem of liberty.

There is a Liberal theory of freedom, and there is a Fascist concept of liberty. For we, too, maintain the necessity of safeguarding the conditions that make for the free development of the individual; we, too, believe that the oppression of individual personality can find no place in the modern state. We do not, however, accept a bill of rights which tends to make the individual superior to the state and to empower him to act in opposition to society. Our concept of liberty is that the individual must be allowed to develop his personality in behalf of the state, for these ephemeral and infinitesimal elements of the complex and permanent life of society determine by their normal growth the development of the state. But this individual growth must be normal. A huge and disproportionate development of the individual of classes, would prove as fatal to society as abnormal growths are to living organisms. Freedom therefore is due to the citizen and to classes on condition that they exercise it in the interest of society as a whole and within the limits set by social exigencies, liberty being, like any other individual right, a concession of the state. What I say concerning civil liberties applies to economic freedom as well. Fascism does not look upon the doctrine of economic liberty as an absolute dogma. It does not refer economic problems to individual needs, to individual interest, to individual solutions. On the contrary it considers the economic development, and especially the production of wealth, as an eminently social concern, wealth being for society an essential element of power and prosperity. But Fascism maintains that in the ordinary run of events economic liberty serves the social purposes best; that it is profitable to entrust to individual initiative the task of economic development both as to production and as to distribution; that in the economic world individual ambition is the most effective means for obtaining the best social results with the least effort. Therefore, on the question also of economic liberty the Fascists differ fundamentally from the Liberals; the latter see in liberty a principle, the Fascists accept it as a method. By the Liberals, freedom is recognized in the interest of the citizens; the Fascists grant it in the interest of society. In other terms, Fascists make of the individual an economic instrument for the advancement of society, an instrument which they use so long as it functions and which they subordinate when no longer serviceable. In this guise Fascism solves the eternal problem of economic freedom and of state interference, considering both as mere methods which may or may not be employed in accordance with the social needs of the moment.

What I have said concerning political and economic Liberalism applies also to Democracy. The latter envisages fundamentally the problem of sovereignty; Fascism does also, but in an entirely different manner. Democracy vests sovereignty in the people, that is to say, in the mass of human beings. Fascism discovers sovereignty to be inherent in society when it is juridically organized as a state. Democracy therefore turns over the government of the state to the multitude of living men that they may use it to further their own interests; Fascism insists that the government be entrusted to men capable of rising above their own private interests and of realizing the aspirations of the social collectivity, considered in its unity and in its relation to the past and future. Fascism therefore not only rejects the dogma of popular sovereignty and substitutes for it that of state sovereignty, but it also proclaims that the great mass of citizens is not a suitable advocate of social interests for the reason that the capacity to ignore individual private interests in favor of the higher demands of society and of history is a very rare gift and the privilege of the chosen few. Natural intelligence and cultural preparation are of great service in such tasks. Still more valuable perhaps is the intuitiveness of rare great minds, their traditionalism and their inherited qualities. This must not however be construed to mean that the masses are not to be allowed to exercise any influence on the life of the state. On the contrary, among peoples with a great history and with noble traditions, even the lowest elements of society possess an instinctive discernment of what is necessary for the welfare of the race, which in moments of great historical crises reveals itself to be almost infallible. It is therefore as wise to afford to this instinct the means of declaring itself as it is judicious to entrust the normal control of the commonwealth to a selected elite.

As for Socialism, the Fascist doctrine frankly recognizes that the problem raised by it as to the relations between capital and labor is a very serious one, perhaps the central one of modern life. What Fascism does not countenance is the collectivistic solution proposed by the Socialists. The chief defect of the socialistic method has been clearly demonstrated by the experience of the last few years. It does not take into account human nature, it is therefore outside of reality, in that it will not recognize that the most powerful spring of human activities lies in individual self-interest and that therefore the elimination from the economic field of this interest results in complete paralysis. The suppression of private ownership of capital carries with it the suppression of capital itself, for capital is formed by savings and no one will want to save, but will rather consume all he makes if he knows he cannot keep and hand down to his heirs the results of his labors. The dispersion of capital means the end of production since capital, no matter who owns it, is always an indispensable tool of production. Collective organization of production is followed therefore by the paralysis of production since, by eliminating from the productive mechanism the incentive of individual interest, the product becomes rarer and more costly. Socialism then, as experience has shown, leads to increase in consumption, to the dispersion of capital and therefore to poverty. Of what avail is it, then, to build a social machine which will more justly distribute wealth if this very wealth is destroyed by the construction of this machine? Socialism committed an irreparable error when it made of private property a matter of justice while in truth it is a problem of social utility. The recognition of individual property rights, then, is a part of the Fascist doctrine not because of its individual bearing but because of its social utility.

We must reject, therefore, the socialistic solution but we cannot allow the problem raised by the Socialists to remain unsolved, not only because justice demands a solution but also because the persistence of this problem in liberal and democratic regimes has been a menace to public order and to the authority of the state. Unlimited and unrestrained class self-defense, evinced by strikes and lockouts, by boycotts and sabotage, leads inevitably to anarchy. The Fascist doctrine, enacting justice among the classes in compliance with a fundamental necessity of modern life, does away with class self-defense, which, like individual self-defense in the days of barbarism, is a source of disorder and of civil war.

Having reduced the problem of these terms, only one solution is possible, the realization of justice among the classes by and through the state. Centuries ago the state, as the specific organ of justice, abolished personal self-defense in individual controversies and substituted for it state justice. The time has now come when class self-defense also must be replaced by state justice. To facilitate the change Fascism has created its own syndicalism.[2] The suppression of class self-defense does not mean the suppression of class defense which is an inalienable necessity of modern economic life. Class organization is a fact which cannot be ignored but it must be controlled, disciplined, and subordinated by the state. The syndicate, instead of being, as formerly, an organ of extra-legal defense, must be turned into an organ of legal defense which will become judicial defense as soon as labor conflicts become a matter of judicial settlement. Fascism therefore has transformed the syndicate, that old revolutionary instrument of syndicalistic socialists, into an instrument of legal defense of the classes both within and without the law courts. This solution may encounter obstacles in its development; the obstacles of malevolence, of suspicion of the untried, of erroneous calculation, etc., but it is destined to triumph even though it must advance through progressive stages.

NOTES

1. Bolshevism refers to the Bolshevik or Leninist variant of Marxist theory and practice.—Eds.
2. Syndicalism, from the French *syndicat* or trade union, was a socialist theory that called for direct action, such as workers' strikes, by trade unions and other working-class organizations.—Eds.

48

Nation and Race

ADOLF HITLER

Although Adolf Hitler (1889–1945) was neither an original nor a consistent thinker, his blend of fascism and racism proved to be one of the most potent ideological forces in history. The following selections are from Hitler's autobiography, *Mein Kampf,* which he wrote in 1924 while imprisoned for leading an attempt to overthrow the government of the German province of Bavaria. The selections reveal Hitler's racial ideas and anti-Semitism, his hatred of socialism and liberalism, and other ideas he and the Nazis put into practice once they gained power in Germany in 1933.

Source: Adolf Hitler, *Mein Kampf,* translated by Ralph Manheim. Copyright © 1943, renewed 1971 by Houghton Mifflin Co. Reprinted by permission of Houghton Mifflin Company. All rights reserved.

MEIN KAMPF

More than any theoretical literature, my daily reading of the Social Democratic press enabled me to study the inner nature of these thought-processes.

For what a difference between the glittering phrases about freedom, beauty, and dignity in the theoretical literature, the delusive welter of words seemingly expressing the most profound and laborious wisdom, the loathsome humanitarian morality—all this written with the incredible gall that comes with prophetic certainty—and the brutal daily press, shunning no villainy, employing every means of slander, lying with a virtuosity that would bend iron beams, all in the name of this gospel of a new humanity. The one is addressed to the simpletons of the middle, not to mention the upper, educated, "classes," the other to the masses.

For me immersion in the literature and press of this doctrine and organization meant finding my way back to my own people.

What had seemed to me an unbridgable gulf became the source of a greater love than ever before.

Only a fool can behold the work of this villainous poisoner and still condemn the victim. The more independent I made myself in the next few years, the clearer grew my perspective, hence my insight into the inner causes of the Social Democratic successes. I now understood the significance of the brutal demand that I read only Red papers, attend only Red meetings, read only Red books, etc. With plastic clarity I saw before my eyes the inevitable result of this doctrine of intolerance.

The psyche of the great masses is not receptive to anything that is half-hearted and weak.

Like the woman, whose psychic state is determined less by grounds of abstract reason than by an indefinable emotional longing for a force which will complement her nature, and who, consequently, would rather bow to a strong man than dominate a weakling, likewise the masses love a commander more than a petitioner and feel inwardly more satisfied by a doctrine, tolerating no other beside itself, than by the granting of liberalistic freedom with which, as a rule, they can do little, and are prone to feel that they have been abandoned. They are equally unaware of their shameless spiritual terrorization and the hideous abuse of their human freedom, for they absolutely fail to suspect the inner insanity of the whole doctrine. All they see is the ruthless force and brutality of its calculated manifestations, to which they always submit in the end.

If Social Democracy is opposed by a doctrine of greater truth, but equal brutality of methods, the latter will conquer, though this may require the bitterest struggle.

Before two years had passed, the theory as well as the technical methods of Social Democracy were clear to me.

I understood the infamous spiritual terror which this movement exerts, particularly on the bourgeoisie, which is neither morally nor mentally equal to such attacks; at a given sign it unleashes a veritable barrage of lies and slanders against whatever adversary seems most dangerous, until the nerves of the attacked persons break down and, just to have peace again, they sacrifice the hated individual.

However, the fools obtain no peace.

The game begins again and is repeated over and over until fear of the mad dog results in suggestive paralysis.

Since the Social Democrats best know the value of force from their own experience, they most violently attack those in whose nature they detect any of this substance which is so rare. Conversely, they praise every weakling on the opposing side, sometimes cautiously, sometimes loudly, depending on the real or supposed quality of his intelligence.

They fear an impotent, spineless genius less than a forceful nature of moderate intelligence.

But with the greatest enthusiasm they commend weaklings in both mind and force.

They know how to create the illusion that this is the only way of preserving the peace, and at the same time, stealthily but steadily, they conquer one position after another, sometimes by silent blackmail, sometimes by actual theft, at moments when the general attention is directed toward other matters, and either does not want to be disturbed or considers the matter too small to raise a stir about, thus again irritating the vicious antagonist.

This is a tactic based on precise calculation of all human weaknesses, and its result will lead to success with almost mathematical certainty unless the opposing side learns to combat poison gas with poison gas.

It is our duty to inform all weaklings that this is a question of to be or not to be.

I achieved an equal understanding of the importance of physical terror toward the individual and the masses.

Here, too, the psychological effect can be calculated with precision.

Terror at the place of employment, in the factory, in the meeting hall, and on the occasion of mass demonstrations will always be successful unless opposed by equal terror.

In this case, to be sure, the party will cry bloody murder; though it has long despised all state authority, it will set up a howling cry for that same authority and in most cases will actually attain its goal amid the general confusion: it will find some idiot of a higher official who, in the imbecilic hope of propitiating the feared adversary for later eventualities, will help this world plague to break its opponent.

The impression made by such a success on the minds of the great masses of supporters as well as opponents can only be measured by those who know the soul of a people, not from books, but from life. For while in the ranks of their supporters the victory achieved seems a triumph of the justice of their own cause, the defeated adversary in most cases despairs of the successes of any further resistance....

***

There are some truths which are so obvious that for this very reason they are not seen or at least not recognized by ordinary people. They sometimes pass by such truisms as though blind and are most astonished when someone suddenly discovers what everyone really ought to know. Columbus's eggs lie around by the hundreds of thousands, but Columbuses are met with less frequently.

Thus men without exception wander about in the garden of Nature; they imagine that they know practically everything and yet with few exceptions pass blindly by one of the most patent principles of Nature's rule: the inner segregation of the species of all living beings on this earth.

Even the most superficial observation shows that Nature's restricted form of propagation and increase is an almost rigid basic law of all the innumerable forms of expression of her vital urge. Every animal mates only with a member of the same species. The titmouse seeks the titmouse, the finch the finch, the stork the stork, the field mouse the field mouse, the dormouse the dormouse, the wolf the she-wolf, etc.

Only unusual circumstances can change this, primarily the compulsion of captivity or any other cause that makes it impossible to mate within the same species. But then Nature begins to resist this with all possible means, and her most visible protest consists either in refusing further capacity for propagation to bastards or in limiting the fertility of later offspring; in most cases, however, she takes away the power of resistance to disease or hostile attacks.

This is only too natural.

Any crossing of two beings not at exactly the same level produces a medium between the level of the two parents. This means: the offspring will probably stand higher than the racially lower parent, but not as high as the higher one. Consequently, it will later succumb in the struggle against the higher level. Such mating is contrary to the will of Nature for a higher breeding of all life. The precondition for this does not lie in associating superior and inferior, but in the total victory of the former. The stronger must dominate and not blend with the weaker, thus sacrificing his own greatness. Only the born weakling can view this as cruel, but he after all is only a weak and limited man; for if this law did not prevail, any conceivable higher development of organic living beings would be unthinkable.

The consequence of this racial purity, universally valid in Nature, is not only the sharp outward delimitation of the various races, but their uniform character in themselves. The fox is always a fox, the goose a goose, the tiger a tiger, etc., and the difference can lie at most in the varying measure of force, strength, intelligence, dexterity, endurance, etc., of the individual specimens. But you will never find a fox who in his inner attitude might, for example, show humanitarian tendencies toward geese, as similarly there is no cat with a friendly inclination toward mice.

Therefore, here, too, the struggle among themselves arises less from inner aversion than from hunger and love. In both cases, Nature looks on calmly, with satisfaction, in fact. In the struggle for daily bread all those who are weak and sickly or less determined succumb, while the struggle of the males for the female grants the right or opportunity to propagate only to the healthiest. And struggle is always a means for improving a species' health and power of resistance and, therefore, a cause of its higher development.

If the process were different, all further and higher development would cease and the opposite would occur. For, since the inferior always predominates numerically over the best, if both had the same possibility of preserving life and propagating, the inferior would multiply so much more rapidly that in the end the best would inevitably be driven into the background, unless a correction of this state of affairs were undertaken. Nature does just this by subjecting the weaker part to such severe living conditions that by them alone the number is limited, and by not permitting the remainder to increase promiscuously, but making a new and ruthless choice according to strength and health.

No more than Nature desires the mating of weaker with stronger individuals, even less does she desire the blending of a higher with a lower race, since, if she did, her whole work of higher breeding, over perhaps hundreds of thousands of years, might be ruined with one blow.

Historical experience offers countless proofs of this. It shows with terrifying clarity that in every mingling of Aryan blood with that of lower peoples the result was the end of the cultured people. North America, whose population consists in by far the largest part of Germanic elements who mixed but little with the lower colored peoples, shows a different humanity and culture from Central and South America, where the predominantly Latin immigrants often mixed with the aborigines on a large scale. By this one example, we can clearly and distinctly recognize the effect of racial mixture. The Germanic inhabitant of the American continent, who has remained racially pure and unmixed, rose to be master of the continent; he will remain the master as long as he does not fall a victim to defilement of the blood.

The result of all racial crossing is therefore in brief always the following:

a. Lowering of the level of the higher race;
b. Physical and intellectual regression and hence the beginning of a slowly but surely progressing sickness.

To bring about such a development is, then, nothing else but to sin against the will of the eternal creator.

And as a sin this act is rewarded.

When man attempts to rebel against the iron logic of Nature, he comes into struggle with the principles to which he himself owes his existence as a man. And this attack must lead to his own doom.

Here, of course, we encounter the objection of the modern pacifist, as truly Jewish in its effrontery as it is stupid! "Man's role is to overcome Nature!"

Millions thoughtlessly parrot this Jewish nonsense and end up by really imagining that they themselves represent a kind of conqueror of Nature; though in this they dispose of no other weapon than an idea, and at that such a miserable one, that if it were true no world at all would be conceivable.

But quite aside from the fact that man has never yet conquered Nature in anything, but at most has caught hold of and tried to lift one or another corner of her immense gigantic veil of eternal riddles and secrets, that in reality he invents nothing but only discovers everything, that he does not dominate Nature, but has only risen on the basis of his knowledge of various laws and secrets of Nature to be lord over those other living creatures who lack this knowledge—quite aside from all this, an idea cannot overcome the preconditions for the development of being of humanity, since the idea itself depends only on man. Without human beings there is no human idea in this world, therefore, the idea as such is always conditioned by the presence of human beings and hence of all the laws which created the precondition for their existence.

And not only that! Certain ideas are even tied up with certain men. This applies most of all to those ideas whose content originates, not in an exact scientific truth, but in the world of emotion, or, as it is so beautifully and clearly expressed today, reflects an "inner experience." All these ideas, which have nothing to do with cold logic as such, but represent only pure expressions of feeling, ethical conceptions, etc., are chained to the existence of men, to whose intellectual imagination and creative power they owe their existence. Precisely in this case the preservation of these definite races and men is the precondition for the existence of these ideas. Anyone, for example, who really desired the victory of the pacifistic idea in this world with all his heart would have to fight with all the means at his disposal for the conquest of the world by the Germans; for, if the opposite should occur, the last pacifist would die out with the last German, since the rest of the world has never fallen so deeply as our own people, unfortunately, has for this nonsense so contrary to Nature and reason. Then, if we were serious, whether we liked it or not, we would have to wage wars in order to arrive at pacifism. This and nothing else was what [U.S. President Woodrow] Wilson, the American world savior, intended, or so at least our German visionaries believed—and thereby his purpose was fulfilled.

In actual fact the pacifistic-humane idea is perfectly all right perhaps when the highest type of man has previously conquered and subjected the world to an extent that makes him the sole ruler of this earth. Then this idea lacks the power of producing evil effects in exact proportion as its practical application becomes rare and finally impossible. Therefore, first struggle and then we shall see what can be done. Otherwise mankind has passed the high point of its development and the end is not the domination of any ethical idea but barbarism and consequently chaos. At this point someone or other may laugh, but this planet once moved through the ether for millions of years without human beings and it can do so again some day if men forget that they owe their higher existence, not to the ideas of a few crazy ideologists, but to the knowledge and ruthless application of Nature's stern and rigid laws.

Everything we admire on this earth today—science and art, technology and inventions—is only the creative product of a few peoples and originally perhaps of *one* race. On them depends the existence of this whole culture. If they perish, the beauty of this earth will sink into the grave with them.

However much the soil, for example, can influence men, the result of the influence will always be different depending on the races in question. The low fertility of a living space may spur the one race to the highest achievements; in others it will only be the cause of bitterest poverty and final undernourishment with all its consequences. The inner nature of peoples is always determining for the manner in which outward influences will be effective. What leads the one to starvation trains the other to hard work.

All great cultures of the past perished only because the originally creative race died out from blood poisoning.

The ultimate cause of such a decline was their forgetting that all culture depends on men and not conversely; hence that to preserve a certain culture the man who creates it must be preserved. This preservation is bound up with the rigid law of necessity and the right to victory of the best and stronger in this world.

Those who want to live, let them fight, and those who do not want to fight in this world of eternal struggle do not deserve to live.

Even if this were hard—that is how it is! Assuredly, however, by far the harder fate is that which strikes the man who thinks he can overcome Nature, but in the last analysis only mocks her. Distress, misfortune, and diseases are her answer.

The man who misjudges and disregards the racial laws actually forfeits the happiness that seems destined to be his. He thwarts the triumphal march of the best race and hence also the precondition for all human progress, and remains, in consequence, burdened with all the sensibility of man, in the animal realm of helpless misery.

It is idle to argue which race or races were the original representatives of human culture and hence the real founders of all that we sum up under the word "humanity." It is simpler to raise this question with regard to the present, and here an easy, clear answer results. All the human culture, all the results of art, science, and technology that we see before us today, are almost exclusively the creative product of the Aryan. This very fact admits of the not unfounded inference that he alone was the founder of all higher humanity, therefore representing the prototype of all that we understand by the word "man." He is the Prometheus[1] of mankind from whose bright forehead the divine spark of genius has sprung at all times, forever kindling anew that fire of knowledge which illumined the night of silent mysteries and thus caused man to climb the path to mastery over the other beings of this earth. Exclude him—and perhaps after a few thousand years darkness will again descend on the earth, human culture will pass, and the world turn to a desert.

If we were to divide mankind into three groups, the founders of culture, the bearers of culture, the destroyers of culture, only the Aryan could be considered as the representative of the first group. From him originate the foundations and walls of all human creation, and only the outward form and color are determined by the changing traits of character of the various peoples. He provides the mightiest building stones and plans for all human progress and only the execution corresponds to the nature of the varying men and races. In a few decades, for example, the entire east of Asia will possess a culture whose ultimate foundation will be Hellenic [i.e., Greek] spirit and Germanic technology, just as much as in Europe. Only the *outward* form—in part at least—will bear the features of Asiatic character. It is not true, as some people think, that Japan adds European technology to its culture; no, European science and technology are trimmed with Japanese characteristics. The foundation of actual life is no longer the special Japanese culture, although it determines the color of life—because outwardly, in consequence of its inner difference, it is more conspicuous to the European—but the gigantic scientific-technical achievements of Europe and America; that is, of Aryan peoples. Only on the basis of these achievements can the Orient follow general human progress. They furnish the basis of the struggle for daily bread, create weapons and implements for it, and only the outward form is gradually adapted to Japanese character.

If beginning today all further Aryan influence on Japan should stop, assuming that Europe and America should perish, Japan's present rise in science and technology might continue for a short time; but even in a few years the well would dry up, the Japanese special character would gain, but the present culture would freeze and sink back into the slumber from which it was awakened seven decades ago by the wave of Aryan culture. Therefore, just as the present Japanese development owes its life to Aryan origin, long ago in the gray past foreign influence and foreign spirit awakened the Japanese culture of that time. The best proof of this is furnished by the fact of its subsequent sclerosis and total petrifaction. This can occur in a people only when the original creative racial nucleus has been lost, or if the external influence which furnished the impetus and the material for the first development in the cultural field was later lacking. But if it is established that a people receives the most essential basic materials of its culture from foreign races, that it assimilates and adapts them, and that then, if further external influence is lacking, it rigidifies again and again, such a race may be designated as *"culture-bearing,"* but never as *"culture-creating."* An examination of the various peoples from this standpoint points to the fact that practically none of them were originally *culture-founding,* but almost always *culture-bearing.*

Approximately the following picture of their development always results:

Aryan races—often absurdly small numerically—subject foreign peoples, and then, stimulated by the special living conditions of the new territory (fertility, climatic conditions, etc.) and assisted by the multitude of lower-type beings standing at their disposal as helpers, develop the intellectual and organizational capacities dormant within them. Often in a few millenniums or even centuries they create cultures which originally bear all the inner characteristics of their nature, adapted to the above-indicated special qualities of the soil and subjected beings. In the end, however, the conquerors transgress against the principle of blood purity, to which they had first adhered; they begin to mix with the subjugated inhabitants and thus end their own existence; for the fall of man in paradise has always been followed by his expulsion....

We see this most distinctly in connection with the race which has been and is the bearer of human cultural development—the Aryans. As soon as Fate leads them toward special conditions, their latent abilities begin to develop in a more and more rapid sequence and to mold themselves into tangible forms. The cultures which they found in such cases are nearly always decisively determined by the existing soil, the given climate, and—the subjected people. This last item, to be sure, is almost the most decisive. The more primitive the technical foundations for a cultural activity, the more necessary is the presence of human helpers who, organizationally assembled and employed, must replace the force of the machine. Without this possibility of using lower human beings, the Aryan would never have been able to take his first steps toward his future culture; just as without the help of various suitable beasts which he knew how to tame, he would not have arrived at a technology which is now gradually permitting him to do without these beasts. The saying, "The Moor has worked off his debt, the Moor can go," unfortunately has only too deep a meaning. For thousands of years the horse had to serve man and help him lay the foundations of a development which now, in consequence of the motor car, is making the horse superfluous. In a few years his activity will have ceased, but without his previous collaboration man might have had a hard time getting where he is today.

Thus, for the formation of higher cultures the existence of lower human types was one of the most essential preconditions, since they alone were able to compensate for the lack of technical aids without which a higher development is not conceivable. It is certain that the first culture of humanity was based less on the tamed animal than on the use of lower human beings.

Only after the enslavement of subjected races did the same fate strike beasts, and not the other way around, as some people would like to think. For first the conquered warrior drew the plow—and only after him the horse. Only pacifistic fools can regard this as a sign of human depravity, failing to realize that this development had to take place in order to reach the point where today these sky-pilots could force their drivel on the world.

The progress of humanity is like climbing an endless ladder; it is impossible to climb higher without first taking the lower steps. Thus, the Aryan had to take the road to which reality directed him and not the one that would appeal to the imagination of a modern pacifist. The road of reality is hard and difficult, but in the end it leads where our friend would like to bring humanity by dreaming, but unfortunately removes more than bringing it closer.

Hence it is no accident that the first cultures arose in places where the Aryan, in his encounters with lower peoples, subjugated them and bent them to his will. They then became the first technical instrument in the service of a developing culture.

Thus, the road which the Aryan had to take was clearly marked out. As a conqueror he subjected the lower beings and regulated their practical activity under his command, according to his will and for his aims. But in directing them to a useful, though arduous activity, he not only spared the life of those he subjected; perhaps he gave them a fate that was better than their previous so-called "freedom." As long as he ruthlessly upheld the master attitude, not only did he really remain master, but also the preserver and increaser of culture. For culture was based exclusively on his abilities and hence on his actual survival. As soon as the subjected people began to raise themselves up and probably approached the conqueror in language, the sharp dividing wall between master and servant fell. The Aryan gave up the purity of his blood and, therefore, lost his sojourn in the paradise which he had made for himself. He became submerged in the racial mixture, and gradually, more and more, lost his cultural capacity, until at last, not only mentally but also physically, he began to resemble the subjected aborigines more than his own ancestors. For a time he could live on the existing cultural benefits, but then petrifaction set in and he fell a prey to oblivion.

Thus cultures and empires collapsed to make place for new formations.

Blood mixture and the resultant drop in the racial level is the sole cause of the dying out of old cultures; for men do not perish as a result of lost wars, but by the loss of that force of resistance which is contained only in pure blood.

All who are not of good race in this world are chaff.

And all occurrences in world history are only the expression of the races' instinct of self-preservation, in the good or bad sense.

...The Aryan is not greatest in his mental qualities as such, but in the extent of his willingness to put all his abilities in the service of the community. In him the instinct of self-preservation has reached the noblest form, since he willingly subordinates his own ego to the life of the community and, if the hour demands, even sacrifices it.

Not in his intellectual gifts lies the source of the Aryan's capacity for creating and building culture. If he had just this alone, he could only act destructively, in no case could he organize; for the innermost essence of all organization requires that the individual renounce putting forward his personal opinion and interests and sacrifice both in favor of a larger group. Only by way of this general community does he again recover his share. Now, for example, he no longer works directly for himself, but with his activity articulates himself with the community, not only for his own advantage, but for the advantage of all. The most wonderful elucidation of this attitude is provided by his word "work," by which he does not mean an activity for maintaining life in itself, but exclusively a creative effort that does not conflict with the interests of the community. Otherwise he designates human activity, in so far as it serves the instinct of self-preservation without consideration for his fellow men, as theft, usury, robbery, burglary, etc.

This state of mind, which subordinates the interests of the ego to the conservation of the community, is really the first premise for every truly human culture. From it alone can arise all the great works of mankind, which bring the founder little reward, but the richest blessings to posterity. Yes, from it alone can we understand how so many are able to bear up faithfully under a scanty life which imposes on them nothing but poverty and frugality, but gives the community the foundations of its existence. Every worker, every peasant, every inventor, official, etc., who works without ever being able to achieve any happiness or prosperity for himself, is a representative of this lofty idea, even if the deeper meaning of his activity remains hidden in him.

What applies to work as the foundation of human sustenance and all human progress is true to an even greater degree for the defense of man and his culture. In giving one's own life for the existence of the community lies the crown of all sense of sacrifice. It is this alone that prevents what human hands have built from being overthrown by human hands or destroyed by Nature.

Our own German language possesses a word which magnificently designates this kind of activity: *Pflichterfüllung* (fulfillment of duty); it means not to be self-sufficient but to serve the community.

The basic attitude from which such activity arises, we call—to distinguish it from egoism and selfishness—idealism. By this we understand only the individual's capacity to make sacrifices for the community, for his fellow men.

How necessary it is to keep realizing that idealism does not represent a superfluous expression of emotion, but that in truth it has been, is, and will be, the premise for what we designate as human culture, yes, that it alone created the concept of "man"! It is to this inner attitude that the Aryan owes his position in this world, and to it the world owes man; for it alone formed from pure spirit the creative force which, by a unique pairing of the brutal fist and the intellectual genius, created the monuments of human culture.

Without his idealistic attitude all, even the most dazzling faculties of the intellect, would remain mere intellect as such—outward appearance without inner value, and never creative force.

But, since true idealism is nothing but the subordination of the interests and life of the individual to the community, and this in turn is the precondition for the creation of organizational forms of all kinds, it corresponds in its innermost depths to the ultimate will of Nature. It alone leads men to voluntary recognition of the privilege of force and strength, and thus makes them into a dust particle of that order which shapes and forms the whole universe....

The mightiest counterpart to the Aryan is represented by the Jew. In hardly any people in the world is the instinct of self-preservation developed more strongly than in the so-called "chosen." Of this, the mere fact of the survival of this race may be considered the best proof. Where is the people which in the last two thousand years has been exposed to so slight changes of inner disposition, character, etc., as the Jewish people? What people, finally, has gone through greater upheavals than this one—and nevertheless issued from the mightiest catastrophes of mankind unchanged? What an infinitely tough will to live and preserve the species speaks from these facts!

The mental qualities of the Jew have been schooled in the course of many centuries. Today he passes as "smart," and this in a certain sense he has been at all times. But his intelligence is not the result of his own development, but of visual instruction through foreigners. For the human mind cannot climb to the top without steps; for every step upward he needs the foundation of the past, and this in the comprehensive sense in which it can be revealed only in general culture. All thinking is based only in small part on man's own knowledge, and mostly on the experience of the time that has preceded. The general cultural level provides the individual man, without his noticing it as a rule, with such a profusion of preliminary knowledge that, thus armed, he can more easily take further steps of his own. The boy of today, for example, grows up among a truly vast number of technical acquisitions of the last centuries, so that he takes for granted and no longer pays attention to much that a hundred years ago was a riddle to even the greatest minds, although for following and understanding our progress in the field in question it is of decisive importance to him. If a very genius from the twenties of the past century should suddenly leave his grave today, it would be harder for him even intellectually to find his way in the present era than for an average boy of fifteen today. For he would lack all the infinite preliminary education which our present contemporary unconsciously, so to speak, assimilates while growing up amidst the manifestations of our present general civilization.

Since the Jew—for reasons which will at once become apparent—was never in possession of a culture of his own, the foundations of his intellectual work were always provided by others. His intellect at all times developed through the cultural world surrounding him.

The reverse process never took place.

For if the Jewish people's instinct of self-preservation is not smaller but larger than that of other peoples, if his intellectual faculties can easily arouse the impression that they are equal to the intellectual gifts of other races, he lacks completely the most essential requirement for a cultured people, the idealistic attitude.

In the Jewish people the will to self-sacrifice does not go beyond the individual's naked instinct of self-preservation. Their apparently great sense of solidarity is based on the very primitive herd instinct that is seen in many other living creatures in this world. It is a noteworthy fact that the herd instinct leads to mutual support only as long as a common danger makes this seem useful or inevitable. The same pack of wolves which has just fallen on its prey together disintegrates when hunger abates into its individual beasts. The same is true of horses which try to defend themselves against an assailant in a body, but scatter again as soon as the danger is past.

It is similar with the Jew. His sense of sacrifice is only apparent. It exists as long as the existence of the individual makes it absolutely necessary. However, as soon as the common enemy is conquered, the danger threatening all averted and the booty hidden, the apparent harmony of the Jews among themselves ceases, again making way for their old causal tendencies. The Jew is only united when a common danger forces him to be or a common booty entices him; if these two grounds are lacking, the qualities of the crassest egoism come into their own, and in the twinkling of an eye the united people turns into a horde of rats, fighting bloodily among themselves.

If the Jews were alone in this world, they would stifle in filth and offal; they would try to get ahead of one another in hate-filled struggle and exterminate one another, in so far as the absolute absence of all sense of self-sacrifice, expressing itself in their cowardice, did not turn battle into comedy here too.

So it is absolutely wrong to infer any ideal sense of sacrifice in the Jews from the fact that they stand together in struggle, or, better expressed, in the plundering of their fellow men.

Here again the Jew is led by nothing but the naked egoism of the individual.

That is why the Jewish state—which should be the living organism for preserving and increasing a race—is completely unlimited as to territory. For a state formation to have a definite spatial setting always presupposes an idealistic attitude on the part of the state-race, and especially a correct interpretation of the concept of work. In the exact measure in which this attitude is lacking, any attempt at forming, even of preserving, a spatially delimited state fails. And thus the basis on which alone culture can arise is lacking.

Hence the Jewish people, despite all apparent intellectual qualities, is without any true culture, and especially without any culture of its own. For what sham culture the Jew today possesses is the property of other peoples, and for the most part it is ruined in his hands.

In judging the Jewish people's attitude on the question of human culture, the most essential characteristic we must always bear in mind is that there has never been a Jewish art and accordingly there is none today either; that above all the two queens of all the arts, architecture and music, owe nothing original to the Jews. What they do accomplish in the field of art is either patchwork or intellectual theft. Thus, the Jew lacks those qualities which distinguish the races that are creative and hence culturally blessed.

To what an extent the Jew takes over foreign culture, imitating or rather ruining it, can be seen from the fact that he is mostly found in the art which seems to require least original invention, the art of acting. But even here, in reality, he is only a "juggler," or rather an ape; for even here he lacks the last touch that is required for real greatness; even here he is not the creative genius, but a superficial imitator, and all the twists and tricks that he uses are powerless to conceal the inner lifelessness of his creative gift. Here the Jewish press most lovingly helps him along by raising such a roar of hosannahs about even the most mediocre bungler, just so long as he is a Jew, that the rest of the world actually ends up by thinking that they have an artist before them, while in truth it is only a pitiful comedian.

No, the Jew possesses no culture-creating force of any sort, since the idealism, without which there is no true higher development of man, is not present in him and never was present. Hence his intellect will never have a constructive effect, but will be destructive, and in very rare cases perhaps will at most be stimulating, but then as the prototype of the "force which always wants evil and nevertheless creates good." Not through him does any progress of mankind occur, but in spite of him.

Since the Jew never possessed a state with definite territorial limits and therefore never called a culture his own, the conception arose that this was a people which should be reckoned among the ranks of the *nomads*. This is a fallacy as great as it is dangerous. The nomad does possess a definitely limited living space, only he does not cultivate it like a sedentary peasant, but lives from the yield of his herds with which he wanders about in his territory. The outward reason for this is to be found in the small fertility of a soil which simply does not permit of settlement. The deeper cause, however, lies in the disparity between the technical culture of an age or people and the natural poverty of a living space [*Lebensraum*]. There are territories in which even the Aryan is enabled only by his technology, developed in the course of more than a thousand years, to live in regular settlements, to master broad stretches of soil and obtain from it the requirements of life. If he did not possess this technology, either he would have to avoid these territories or likewise have to struggle along as a nomad in perpetual wandering, provided that his thousand-year-old education and habit of settled residence did not make this seem simply unbearable to him. We must bear in mind that in the time when the American continent was being opened up, numerous Aryans fought for their livelihood as trappers, hunters, etc., and often in larger troops with wife and children, always on the move, so that their existence was completely like that of the nomads. But as soon as their increasing number and better implements permitted them to clear the wild soil and make a stand against the natives, more and more settlements sprang up in the land.

Probably the Aryan was also first a nomad, settling in the course of time, but for that very reason he was never a Jew! No, the Jew is no nomad; for the nomad had also a definite attitude toward the concept of work which could serve as a basis for his later development in so far as the necessary intellectual premises were present. In him the basic idealistic view is present, even if in infinite dilution, hence in his whole being he may seem strange to the Aryan peoples, but not unattractive. In the Jew, however, this attitude is not at all present; for that reason he was never a nomad, but only and always a *parasite* in the body of other peoples. That he sometimes left his previous living space has nothing to do with his own purpose, but results from the fact that from time to time he was thrown out by the host nations he had misused. His spreading is a typical phenomenon for all parasites; he always seeks a new feeding ground for his race.

This, however, has nothing to do with nomadism, for the reason that a Jew never thinks of leaving a territory that he has occupied, but remains where he is, and he sits so fast that even by force it is very hard to drive him out. His extension to ever-new countries occurs only in the moment in which certain conditions for his existence are there present, without which—unlike the nomad—he would not change his residence. He is and remains the typical parasite, a sponger who like a noxious bacillus keeps spreading as soon as a favorable medium invites him. And the effect of his existence is also like that of spongers: wherever he appears, the host people dies out after a shorter or longer period.

Thus, the Jew of all times has lived in the states of other peoples, and there formed his own state, which, to be sure, habitually sailed under the disguise of "religious community" as long as outward circumstances made a complete revelation of his nature seem inadvisable. But as soon as he felt strong enough to do without the protective cloak, he always dropped the veil and suddenly became what so many of the others previously did not want to believe and see: the Jew.

The Jew's life as a parasite in the body of other nations and states explains a characteristic which once caused Schopenhauer to call him the "great master in lying."[2] Existence impels the Jew to lie, and to lie perpetually, just as it compels the inhabitants of the northern countries to wear warm clothing.

His life within other peoples can only endure for any length of time if he succeeds in arousing the opinion that he is not a people but a "religious community," though of a special sort.

And this is the first great lie.

In order to carry on his existence as a parasite on other peoples, he is forced to deny his inner nature. The more intelligent the individual Jew is, the more he will succeed in this deception. Indeed, things can go so far that large parts of the host people will end by seriously believing that the Jew is really a Frenchman or an Englishman, a German or an Italian, though of a special religious faith. Especially state authorities, which always seem animated by the historical fraction of wisdom, most easily fall a victim to this infinite deception. Independent thinking sometimes seems to these circles a true sin against holy advancement, so that we may not be surprised if even today a Bavarian state ministry, for example, still has not the faintest idea that the Jews are members of a *people* and not of a *"religion"* though a glance at the Jew's own newspapers should indicate this even to the most modest mind. The *Jewish Echo* is not yet an official organ, of course, and consequently is unauthoritative as far as the intelligence of one of these government potentates is concerned.

The Jew has always been a people with definite racial characteristics and never a religion; only in order to get ahead he early sought for a means which could distract unpleasant attention from his person. And what would have been more expedient and at the same time more innocent than the "embezzled" concept of a religious community? For here, too, everything is borrowed or rather stolen. Due to his own original special nature, the Jew cannot possess a religious institution, if for no other reason because he lacks idealism in any form, and hence belief in a hereafter is absolutely foreign to him. And a religion in the Aryan sense cannot be imagined which lacks the conviction of survival after death in some form. Indeed, the Talmud is not a book to prepare a man for the hereafter, but only for a practical and profitable life in this world.[3]

The Jewish religious doctrine consists primarily in prescriptions for keeping the blood of Jewry pure and for regulating the relation of Jews among themselves, but even more with the rest of the world; in other words, with non-Jews. But even here it is by no means ethical problems that are involved, but extremely modest economic ones. Concerning the moral value of Jewish religious instruction, there are today and have been at all times rather exhaustive studies (not by Jews; the drivel of the Jews themselves on the subject is, of course, adapted to its purpose) which make this kind of religion seem positively monstrous according to Aryan conceptions. The best characterization is provided by the product of this religious education, the Jew himself. His life is only of this world, and his spirit is inwardly as alien to true Christianity as his nature two thousand years previous was to the great founder of the new doctrine. Of course, the latter made no secret of his attitude toward the Jewish people, and when necessary he even took to the whip to drive from the temple of the Lord this adversary of all humanity, who then as always saw in religion nothing but an instrument for his business existence. In return, Christ was nailed to the cross, while our present-day party Christians debase themselves to begging for Jewish votes at elections and later try to arrange political swindles with atheistic Jewish parties—and this against their own nation.

On this first and greatest lie, that the Jews are not a race but a religion, more and more lies are based in necessary consequence. Among them is the lie with regard to the language of the Jew. For him it is not a means for expressing his thoughts, but a means for concealing them. When he speaks French, he thinks Jewish, and while he turns out German verses, in his life he only expresses the nature of his nationality. As long as the Jew has not become the master of the other peoples, he must speak their languages whether he likes it or not, but as soon as they became his slaves, they would all have to learn a universal language (Esperanto, for instance!), so that by this additional means the Jews could more easily dominate them!

To what an extent the whole existence of this people is based on a continuous lie is shown incomparably by the *Protocols of the Wise Men of Zion*, so infinitely hated by the Jews.[4] They are based on a forgery, the *Frankfurter Zeitung* moans and screams once every week: the best proof that they are authentic. What many Jews may do unconsciously is here consciously exposed. And that is what matters. It is completely indifferent from what Jewish brain these disclosures originate; the important thing is that with positively terrifying certainty they reveal the nature and activity of the Jewish people and expose their inner contexts as well as their ultimate final aims. The best criticism applied to them, however, is reality. Anyone who examines the historical development of the last hundred years from the standpoint of this book will at once understand the screaming of the Jewish press. For once this book has become the common property of a people, the Jewish menace may be considered as broken....

With satanic joy in his face, the black-haired Jewish youth lurks in wait for the unsuspecting girl whom he defiles with his blood, thus stealing her from her people. With every means he tries to destroy the racial foundations of the people he has set out to subjugate. Just as he himself systematically ruins women and girls, he does not shrink back from pulling down the blood barriers for others, even on a large scale. It was and it is Jews who bring the Negroes into the Rhineland, always with the same secret thought and clear aim of ruining the hated white race by the necessarily resulting bastardization, throwing it down from its cultural and political height, and himself rising to be its master.

For a racially pure people which is conscious of its blood can never be enslaved by the Jew. In this world he will forever be master over bastards and bastards alone.

And so he tries systematically to lower the racial level by a continuous poisoning of individuals.

And in politics he begins to replace the idea of democracy by the dictatorship of the proletariat.

In the organized mass of Marxism he has found the weapon which lets him dispense with democracy and in its stead allows him to subjugate and govern the peoples with a dictatorial and brutal fist.

He works systematically for revolutionization in a twofold sense: economic and political.

Around peoples who offer too violent a resistance to attack from within he weaves a net of enemies, thanks to his international influence, incites them to war, and finally, if necessary, plants the flag of revolution on the very battlefields.

In economics he undermines the states until the social enterprises which have become unprofitable are taken from the state and subjected to his financial control.

In the political field he refuses the state the means for its self-preservation, destroys the foundations of all national self-maintenance and defense, destroys faith in the leadership, scoffs at its history and past, and drags everything that is truly great into the gutter.

Culturally he contaminates art, literature, the theater, makes a mockery of natural feeling, overthrows all concepts of beauty and sublimity, of the noble and the good, and instead drags men down into the sphere of his own base nature.

Religion is ridiculed, ethics and morality represented as outmoded, until the last props of a nation in its struggle for existence in this world have fallen.

Now begins the great last revolution. In gaining political power the Jew casts off the few cloaks that he still wears. The democratic people's Jew becomes the blood-Jew and tyrant over peoples. In a few years he tries to exterminate the national intelligentsia and by robbing the peoples of their natural intellectual leadership makes them ripe for the slave's lot of permanent subjugation.

The most frightful example of this kind is offered by Russia, where he killed or starved about thirty million people with positively fanatical savagery, in part amid inhuman tortures, in order to give a gang of Jewish journalists and stock exchange bandits domination over a great people.

The end is not only the end of the freedom of the peoples oppressed by the Jew, but also the end of this parasite upon the nations. After the death of his victim, the vampire sooner or later dies too....

In the first volume [of *Mein Kampf*] I have dealt with the word "folkish" [*volkische*] in so far as I was forced to establish that this term seems inadequately defined to permit the formation of a solid fighting community. All sorts of people, with a yawning gulf between everything essential in their opinions, are running around today under the blanket term "folkish." Therefore, before I proceed to the tasks and aims of the National Socialist German Workers' Party, I should like to give a clarification of the concept "folkish," as well as its relation to the party movement.

The concept "folkish" seems as vaguely defined, open to as many interpretations and as unlimited in practical application as, for instance, the word "religious," and it is very hard to conceive of anything absolutely precise under this designation, either in the sense of intellectual comprehension or of practical effects. The designation "religious" only becomes tangibly conceivable in the moment when it becomes connected with a definitely outlined form of its practice. It is a very lovely statement and usually apt, to describe a man's nature as "profoundly religious." Perhaps there are a few people who feel satisfied by such a very general description, to whom it can even convey a definite, more or less sharp, picture of that soul-state. But, since the great masses consist neither of philosophers nor of saints, such a very general religious idea will as a rule mean to the individual only the liberation of his individual thought and action, without, however, leading to that efficacy which arises from religious inner longing in the moment when, from the purely metaphysical infinite world of ideas, a clearly delimited faith forms. Assuredly, this is not the end in itself, but only a means to the end; yet it is the indispensably necessary means which alone makes possible the achievement of the end. This end, however, is not only ideal, but in the last analysis also eminently practical. And in general we must clearly acknowledge the fact that the highest ideals always correspond to a deep vital necessity, just as the nobility of the most exalted beauty lies in the last analysis only in what is logically most expedient.

By helping to raise man above the level of bestial vegetation, faith contributes in reality to the securing and safeguarding of his existence. Take away from present-day mankind its education-based, religious-dogmatic principles—or, practically speaking, ethical-moral principles—by abolishing this religious education, but without replacing it by an equivalent, and the result will be a grave shock to the foundations of their existence. We may therefore state that not only does man live in order to serve higher ideals, but that, conversely, these higher ideals also provide the premise for his existence. Thus the circle closes.

Of course, even the general designation "religious" includes various basic ideas or convictions, for example, the indestructibility of the soul, the eternity of its existence, the existence of a higher being, etc. But all these ideas, regardless how convincing they may be for the individual, are submitted to the critical examination of this individual and hence to a fluctuating affirmation or negation until emotional divination or knowledge assumes the binding force of apodictic faith. This, above all, is the fighting factor which makes a breach and opens the way for the recognition of basic religious views.

Without clearly delimited faith, religiosity with its unclarity and multiplicity of form would not only be worthless for human life, but would probably contribute to general disintegration.

The situation with the term "folkish" is similar to that with the term "religious." In it, too, there lie various basic realizations. Though of eminent importance, they are, however, so unclearly defined in form that they rise above the value of a more or less acceptable opinion only if they are fitted into the framework of a political party as basic elements. *For the realization of philosophical ideals and of the demands derived from them no more occurs through men's pure feeling or inner will in themselves than the achievement of freedom through the general longing for it. No, only when the ideal urge for independence gets a fighting organization in the form of military instruments of power can the pressing desire of a people be transformed into glorious reality.*

Every philosophy of life, even if it is a thousand times correct and of highest benefit to humanity, will remain without significance for the practical shaping of a people's life, as long as its principles have not become the banner of a fighting movement which for its part in turn will be a party as long as its activity has not found completion in the victory of its ideas and its party dogmas have not become the new state principles of a people's community.

But if a spiritual conception of a general nature is to serve as a foundation for a future development, the first presupposition is to obtain unconditional clarity with regard to the nature, essence, and scope of this conception, since only on such a basis can a movement be formed which by the inner homogeneity of its convictions can develop the necessary force for struggle. From general ideas a political program must be stamped, from a general philosophy of life a definite political faith. The latter, since its goal must be practically attainable, will not only have to serve the idea in itself, but will also have to take into consideration the means of struggle which are available and must be used for the achievement of this idea. The abstractly correct spiritual conception, which the theoretician has to proclaim, must be coupled with the practical knowledge of the politician. And so an eternal ideal, serving as the guiding star of mankind, must unfortunately resign itself to taking the weaknesses of this mankind into consideration, if it wants to avoid shipwreck at the very outset on the shoals of general human inadequacy. To draw from the realm of the eternally true and ideal that which is humanly possible for small mortals, and make it take form, the search after truth must be coupled with knowledge of the people's psyche.

This transformation of a general, philosophical, ideal conception of the highest truth into a definitely delimited, tightly organized political community of faith and struggle, unified in spirit and will, is the most significant achievement, since on its happy solution alone the possibility of the victory of an idea depends. From the army of often millions of men, who as individuals more or less clearly and definitely sense these truths, and in part perhaps comprehend them, *one* man must step forward who with apodictic force will form granite principles from the wavering idea-world of the broad masses and take up the struggle for their sole correctness, until from the shifting waves of a free thought-world there will arise a brazen cliff of solid unity in faith and will.

The general right for such an activity is based on necessity, the personal right on success....

If from the word "folkish" we try to peel out the innermost kernel of meaning, we arrive at the following:

Our present political world view, current in Germany, is based in general on the idea that creative, culture-creating force must indeed be attributed to the state, but that it has nothing to do with racial considerations, but is rather a product of economic necessities, or, at best, the natural result of a political urge for power. This underlying view, if logically developed, leads not only to a mistaken conception of basic racial forces, but also to an underestimation of the individual. For a denial of the difference between the various races with regard to their general culture-creating forces must necessarily extend this greatest of all errors to the judgment of the individual. The assumption of the equality of the races then becomes a basis for a similar way of viewing peoples and finally individual men. And hence international Marxism itself is only the transference, by the Jew, Karl Marx, of a philosophical attitude and conception, which had actually long been in existence, into the form of a definite political creed. Without the subsoil of such generally existing poisoning, the amazing success of this doctrine would never have been possible. Actually Karl Marx was only the *one* among millions who, with the sure eye of the prophet, recognized in the morass of a slowly decomposing world the most essential poisons, extracted them, and, like a wizard, prepared them into a concentrated solution for the swifter annihilation of the independent existence of free nations of this earth. And all this in the service of his race.

His Marxist doctrine is a brief spiritual extract of the philosophy of life that is generally current today. And for this reason alone any struggle of our so-called bourgeois world against it is impossible, absurd in fact, since this bourgeois world is also essentially infected by these poisons, and worships a view of life which in general is distinguished from the Marxists only by degrees and personalities. The bourgeois world is Marxist, but believes in the possibility of the rule of certain groups of men (bourgeoisie), while Marxism itself systematically plans to hand the world over to the Jews.

In opposition to this, the folkish philosophy finds the importance of mankind in its basic racial elements. In the state it sees on principle only a means to an end and construes its end as the preservation of the racial existence of man. Thus, it by no means believes in an equality of the races, but along with their difference it recognizes their higher or lesser value and feels itself obligated, through this knowledge, to promote the victory of the better and stronger, and demand the subordination of the inferior and weaker in accordance with the eternal will that dominates this universe. Thus, in principle, it serves the basic aristocratic idea of Nature and believes in the validity of this law down to the last individual. It sees not only the different value of the races, but also the different value of individuals. From the mass it extracts the importance of the individual personality, and thus, in contrast to disorganizing Marxism, it has an organizing effect. It believes in the necessity of an idealization of humanity, in which alone it sees the premise for the existence of humanity. But it cannot grant the right to existence even to an ethical idea if this idea represents a danger for the racial life of the bearers of a higher ethics; for in a bastardized and niggerized world all the concepts of the humanly beautiful and sublime, as well as all ideas of an idealized future of our humanity, would be lost forever.

Human culture and civilization on this continent are inseparably bound up with the presence of the Aryan. If he dies out or declines, the dark veils of an age without culture will again descend on this globe.

The undermining of the existence of human culture by the destruction of its bearer seems in the eyes of a folkish philosophy the most execrable crime. Anyone who dares to lay hands on the highest image of the Lord commits sacrilege against the benevolent creator of this miracle and contributes to the expulsion from paradise.

And so the folkish philosophy of life corresponds to the innermost will of Nature, since it restores that free play of forces which must lead to a continuous mutual higher breeding, until at last the best of humanity, having achieved possession of this earth, will have a free path for activity in domains which will lie partly above it and partly outside it.

We all sense that in the distant future humanity must be faced by problems which only a highest race, become master people and supported by the means and possibilities of an entire globe, will be equipped to overcome....

It is self-evident that so general a statement of the meaningful content of a folkish philosophy can be interpreted in thousands of ways. And actually we find hardly a one of our newer political formations which does not base itself in one way or another on this world view. And, by its very existence in the face of the many others, it shows the difference of its conceptions. And so the Marxist world view, led by a unified top organization, is opposed by hodgepodge of views which even as ideas are not very impressive in the face of the solid, hostile front. Victories are not gained by such feeble weapons! Not until the international world view—politically led by organized Marxism—is confronted by a folkish world view, organized and led with equal unity, will success, supposing the fighting energy to be equal on both sides, fall to the side of eternal truth.

A philosophy can only be organizationally comprehended on the basis of a definite formulation of that philosophy, and what dogmas represent for religious faith, party principles are for a political party in the making.

Hence an instrument must be created for the folkish world view which enables it to fight, just as the Marxist party organization creates a free path for internationalism.

This is the goal pursued by the National Socialist German Workers' Party.

That such a party formulation of the folkish concept is the precondition for the victory of the folkish philosophy of life is proved most sharply by a fact which is admitted indirectly at least by the enemies of such a party tie. Those very people who never weary of emphasizing that the folkish philosophy is not the "hereditary estate" of an individual, but that it slumbers or "lives" in the hearts of God knows how many millions, thus demonstrate the fact that the general existence of such ideas was absolutely unable to prevent the victory of the hostile world view, classically represented by a political party. If this were not so, the German people by this time would have been bound to achieve a gigantic victory and not be standing at the edge of an abyss. What gave the international world view success was its representation by a political party organized into storm troops; what caused the defeat of the opposite world view was its lack up to now of a unified body to represent it. Not by unlimited freedom to interpret a general view, but only in the limited and hence integrating form of a political organization can a world view fight and conquer.

Therefore, I saw my own task especially in extracting those nuclear ideas from the extensive and unshaped substance of a general world view and remolding them into more or less dogmatic forms which in their clear delimitation are adapted for holding solidly together those men who swear allegiance to them. In other words: *From the basic ideas of a general folkish world conception the National Socialist German Workers' Party takes over the essential fundamental traits, and from them, with due consideration of practical reality, the times, and the available human material as well as its weaknesses, forms a political creed which, in turn, by the strict organizational integration of large human masses thus made possible, creates the precondition for the victorious struggle of this world view.*

NOTES

1. In Greek mythology Prometheus stole fire from the gods to give to mankind. For this transgression he was chained to a mountain peak and daily suffered the torture of having vultures tear open his skin and devour his liver, which grew back overnight.—Eds.
2. The German philosopher Arthur Schopenhauer (1788–1860), author of *The World as Will and Idea*.—Eds.
3. The Talmud is a collection of Jewish religious and civil laws as well as ethical instruction in the form of commentaries on and interpretations and applications of the Pentateuch (the first five books of the Old Testament).—Eds.
4. *The Protocols of the Learned Elders of Zion* was a nineteenth-century document purporting to lay out Jewish plans for world domination. Although shown to be a forgery, *The Protocols* continues to be a powerful propaganda weapon in the anti-Semitic arsenal. Hitler was merely one of the more prominent anti-Semites to make use of this forged document.—Eds.

PART EIGHT

Liberation Ideologies and the Politics of Identity

The latter half of the twentieth century witnessed the emergence of several "liberation" ideologies. These include women's liberation, black liberation, gay liberation, native people's (or aboriginal) liberation, liberation theology, and even animal liberation. In one respect, these are vastly different ideologies in that each addresses different groups—women, native and black people, gays, and others. But these groups need not be opposed or antithetical in their aims. Indeed, one liberation movement's membership may, and often does, overlap with another's. For that matter, there would be no contradiction in a gay, black, woman, liberation theologian dedicating herself to the defense of aboriginal rights. But by and large we can view these various liberation ideologies as separate members of a diverse and extended ideological family.

This family shares several common characteristics. First, each liberation ideology addresses itself to a particular group, sex, race, class, species, and so on. Second, this group is in some sense oppressed by another (blacks oppressed by whites, women by men, gays by "straights," indigenous people by colonizers, the poor by the rich, animals by humans). Third, the ideology aims to liberate the oppressed group from its oppressors not only by removing external obstacles (for example, laws that discriminate against Native Americans) but by exposing, criticizing, and overcoming *internal* barriers—or in the poet William Blake's phrase, the "mind-forged manacles"—to their self-emancipation. These internal obstacles might include, for example, self-loathing, low self-esteem, feelings of inferiority, incompetence, stupidity, and so on. A fourth feature common to all liberation ideologies is their attempt to "raise the consciousness" of the oppressed, thereby enabling them to free themselves from their own internalized fetters. (This feature, as we shall see, does not apply in the case of animal liberation.) Fifth and finally, liberation ideologies are also addressed to the oppressors, who, as the philosophers G. W. F. Hegel and Jean-Jacques Rousseau both noted, are enslaved by their own sense of superiority. "The one who thinks himself the master of others," Rousseau wrote in his *Social Contract* (1762), "is as much a slave as they."

The ideology of black liberation is addressed to people of African ancestry, particularly those whose feelings of inferiority have been intensified by their having accepted uncritically the dominant "white" standards of talent, intelligence, beauty, "normal" behavior, musical tastes, and so on. Black liberationists have tried to raise the consciousness of blacks by affirming the integrity and worth of African cultures, promoting black pride and identity through "black is beautiful" campaigns, and encouraging black history's recovery and remembrance of black people's contributions to Western history and culture. In these and many other ways, the ideology of black liberation helps blacks to discover, criticize, and break their own mind-forged manacles. But it also leads white people to examine their own deep-seated attitudes and prejudices as a prelude to overcoming them.

Much the same is true of the ideology of women's liberation, or feminism. That ideology is addressed to women of all races, on the assumption that women of every color and creed and class face problems that are unique to them as women. In addition to overt discrimination—legal and economic barriers and sexual harassment in the workplace and elsewhere—women face the covert or hidden obstacles of sexist attitudes and beliefs. Such attitudes include, for example, views about what is and is not "women's work," women as sex objects, and many others as well. The women's liberation movement has tried to raise women's consciousness by exposing and criticizing sexist attitudes in the classroom, the workplace, the family, the media—and in women's own minds as well. Many women have internalized and accepted sexist stereotypes about women's limitations and shortcomings. By exposing and criticizing these false beliefs, feminism helps women break down and overcome these internalized barriers. But the ideology of women's liberation is also addressed to men, encouraging them to examine their own hidden or half-conscious sexist stereotypes and attitudes toward women. Thus feminism attempts to liberate both women and men from the mutually stifling confines of sexual prejudice.

The ideology of gay liberation is of relatively recent vintage. Homosexual men and women face numerous obstacles, particularly if their sexual orientation is publicly known. Many gay men and lesbians prefer to keep their homosexuality a secret, fearing that they will lose their jobs, housing, health insurance, and other benefits that heterosexuals take for granted. In addition to such overt discrimination, many gays experience more subtle oppression, which comes from internalizing straight or homophobic beliefs about and attitudes toward so-called sexual deviants or perverts. Such people sometimes suffer from feelings of shame, worthlessness, and self-loathing. Some contemplate suicide; others engage in other kinds of self-destructive actions and practices. The ideology of the gay liberation movement attempts to counter these tendencies by exposing and criticizing homophobic beliefs and attitudes, by instilling a sense of gay pride and identity, and by encouraging gays to "come out of the closet" and openly proclaim their sexual orientation. This ideology is also addressed to straights, inviting them to examine and overcome their own homophobic beliefs and attitudes.

Similar concerns are at work in the native people's liberation movement. The ideology of this movement is addressed to aboriginal or indigenous people in several parts of the world, including Australia, New Zealand, and North America. It aims to reclaim and celebrate customs, traditions, and identities that were eclipsed by European settlers and missionaries. These newly arrived immigrants typically dismissed native beliefs and practices as primitive, savage, and uncivilized, and set out—sometimes by fraud and by force—to "civilize" the original inhabitants of the lands they were settling. Once proud peoples were made ashamed of their traditions and customs. Now the advocates of aboriginal liberation seek to restore this pride and revive the sense of their people's identity. This they do in various ways: by publicizing their people's history and accomplishments, by working for the recovery of tribal lands and self-government, and by restoring ancient customs, languages, and religious beliefs, among others. Like other liberation ideologies, however, the basic aim is to overcome demeaning stereotypes and prejudices, thereby freeing both oppressed and oppressor.

The primary audience of liberation theology is poor people, particularly peasants in Latin America and elsewhere, who not only face overt oppression from landlords and perhaps military death squads but have internalized the "culture of silence." This phrase refers to deep-seated beliefs about one's powerlessness and helplessness—the belief that one's views and voice will not and cannot make any difference in one's condition. One is, in short, doomed to suffer in silence, to accept one's unhappy lot in life as fate, the will of God, or of other forces beyond one's control. Liberation theology attempts to expose and criticize these attitudes in order to help poor peasants overcome them. It does so by offering a radical interpretation of the Bible that views Jesus as a liberator and a champion of the poor and downtrodden. Rightly understood, Jesus's teachings can help the poor find their voices and liberate themselves from the forces that oppress them. In addition to being addressed to the poor and oppressed, liberation theology also speaks to their affluent oppressors, inviting them to examine their own consciences and exercise their "preferential option for the poor" by supporting the peasants' struggles against poverty and oppression.

The ideology of animal liberation is likewise intended to liberate an oppressed group, in this case nonhuman animals, from their human oppressors. According to the proponents of animal liberation, many, perhaps most, humans harbor "speciesist" views about the innate inferiority of animals and the superiority of humans. We humans therefore feel free to confine them in tiny cages, to kill them and eat them or wear their fur, and to perform painful experiments on them. It is precisely this prejudice that the animal liberation movement aims to expose and overcome. One qualification is necessary, of course, in the case of animal liberation. Since one presumably cannot reason with or raise the consciousness of nonhuman animals, the addressee must therefore be their oppressors, namely, humans who participate in, or benefit from, the suffering and deaths of animals. The ideology of animal liberation thus aims to raise the consciousness of humans, thereby helping them to challenge their speciesist attitudes and alter their actions accordingly.

Different as they are, the various liberation ideologies constitute a continuing challenge to conventional beliefs and outlooks.

49

Letter from Birmingham Jail

MARTIN LUTHER KING JR.

Although American liberals in the 1960s advocated the extension of civil rights to African-Americans, many favored a gradualist strategy to achieve this goal and criticized the confrontational tactics—including the use of civil disobedience, sit-ins, and protest marches—favored by some black leaders. One of these leaders was the Reverend Dr. Martin Luther King, Jr., (1929–1968) who wrote the following essay while confined to a cell in the Birmingham, Alabama, jail for leading a march against segregation. The immediate provocation for the letter was a statement by several white clergymen, who complained that the demonstrations he led were "unwise," "untimely," and "extreme." To this, King responded that black people had already waited too long and too patiently to be "given" rights that were already theirs. The time for waiting was over, he said, and the time had come to act decisively, albeit nonviolently.

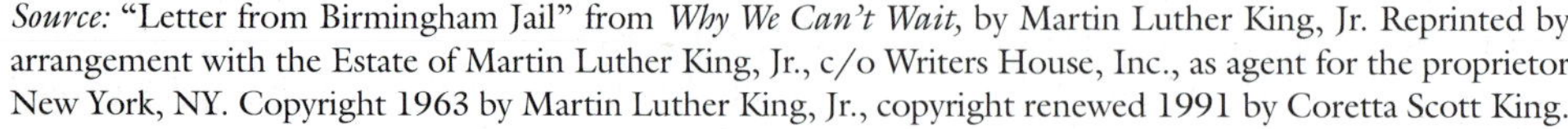

Source: "Letter from Birmingham Jail" from *Why We Can't Wait,* by Martin Luther King, Jr. Reprinted by arrangement with the Estate of Martin Luther King, Jr., c/o Writers House, Inc., as agent for the proprietor New York, NY. Copyright 1963 by Martin Luther King, Jr., copyright renewed 1991 by Coretta Scott King.

LETTER FROM BIRMINGHAM JAIL[1]

April 16, 1963

My Dear Fellow Clergymen:

While confined here in the Birmingham city jail, I came across your recent statement calling my present activities "unwise and untimely." Seldom do I pause to answer criticism of my work and ideas. If I sought to answer all criticisms that cross my desk, my secretaries would have little time for anything other than such correspondence in the course of the day, and I would have no time for constructive work. But since I feel that you are men of genuine good will and that your criticisms are sincerely set forth, I want to try to answer your statement in what I hope will be patient and reasonable terms.

I think I should indicate why I am here in Birmingham, since you have been influenced by the view which argues against "outsiders coming in." I have the honor of serving as president of the Southern Christian Leadership Conference, an organization operating in every southern state, with headquarters in Atlanta, Georgia. We have some eighty-five affiliated organizations across the South, and one of them is the Alabama Christian Movement for Human Rights. Frequently we share staff, educational and financial resources with our affiliates. Several months ago the affiliate here in Birmingham asked us to be on call to engage in a nonviolent direct-action program if such were deemed necessary. We readily consented, and when the hour came we lived up to our promise. So I, along with several members of my staff, am here because I was invited here. I am here because I have basic organizational ties here.

Beyond this, I am in Birmingham because injustice is here. Just as the prophets of the eighth century B.C. left their villages and carried their "thus saith the Lord" far beyond the boundaries of their home towns, and just as the Apostle Paul left his village of Tarsus and carried the gospel of Jesus Christ to the far corners of the Greco-Roman world, so am I compelled to carry the gospel of freedom beyond my own home town. Like Paul, I must constantly respond to the Macedonian call for aid.

Moreover, I am cognizant of the interrelatedness of all communities and states. I cannot sit idly by in Atlanta and not be concerned about what happens in Birmingham. Injustice anywhere is a threat to justice everywhere. We are caught in an inescapable network of mutuality, tied in a single garment of destiny. Whatever affects one directly, affects all indirectly. Never again can we afford to live with the narrow, provincial "outside agitator" idea. Anyone who lives inside the United States can never be considered an outsider anywhere within its bounds.

You deplore the demonstrations taking place in Birmingham. But your statement, I am sorry to say, fails to express a similar concern for the conditions that brought about the demonstrations. I am sure that none of you would want to rest content with the superficial kind of social analysis that deals merely with effects and does not grapple with underlying causes. It is unfortunate that demonstrations are taking place in Birmingham at this time, but I would say in even more emphatic terms that it is even more unfortunate that the city's white power structure left the Negro community with no alternative.

In any nonviolent campaign there are four basic steps: collection of the facts to determine whether injustices exist; negotiation; self-purification; and direct action. We have gone through all these steps in Birmingham. There can be no gainsaying the fact that racial injustice engulfs this community. Birmingham is probably the most thoroughly segregated city in the United States. Its ugly record of brutality is widely known. Negroes have experienced grossly unjust treatment in the courts. There have been more unsolved bombings of Negro homes and churches in Birmingham than in any other city in the nation. These are the hard, brutal facts of the case. On the basis of these conditions, Negro leaders sought to negotiate with the city fathers. But the latter consistently refused to engage in good-faith negotiation.

Then, last September, came the opportunity to talk with leaders of Birmingham's economic community. In the course of the negotiations, certain promises were made by the merchants—for example, to remove the stores' humiliating racial signs. On the basis of these promises, the Reverend Fred Shuttlesworth and the leaders of the Alabama Christian Movement for Human Rights agreed to a moratorium on all demonstrations. As the weeks and months went by, we realized that we were the victims of a broken promise. A few signs, briefly removed, returned; the others remained.

As in so many past experiences, our hopes had been blasted, and the shadow of deep disappointment settled upon us. We had no alternative except to prepare for direct action, whereby we would present our very bodies as a means of laying our case before the conscience of the local and the national community. Mindful of the difficulties involved, we decided to undertake a process of self-purification. We began a series of workshops on nonviolence, and we repeatedly asked ourselves: "Are you able to accept blows without retaliating?" "Are you able to endure the ordeal of jail?" We decided to schedule our direct-action program for the Easter season, realizing that except for Christmas, this is the main shopping period of the year. Knowing that a strong economic-withdrawal program would be the byproduct of direct action, we felt that this would be the best time to bring pressure to bear on the merchants for the needed change.

Then it occurred to us that Birmingham's mayoral election was coming up in March, and we speedily decided to postpone action until after election day. When we discovered that the Commissioner of Public Safety, Eugene "Bull" Connor, had piled up enough votes to be in the run-off, we decided again to postpone action until the day after the run-off so that the demonstrations could not be used to cloud the issues. Like many others, we waited to see Mr. Connor defeated, and to this end we endured postponement after postponement. Having aided in this community need, we felt that our direct-action program could be delayed no longer.

You may well ask: "Why direct action? Why sit-ins, marches and so forth? Isn't negotiation a better path?" You are quite right in calling for negotiation. Indeed, this is the very purpose of direct action. Nonviolent direct action seeks to create such a crisis and foster such a tension that a community which has constantly refused to negotiate is forced to confront the issue. It seeks so to dramatize the issue that it can no longer be ignored. My citing the creation of tension as part of the work of the nonviolent-resister may sound rather shocking. But I must confess that I am not afraid of the word "tension." I have earnestly opposed violent tension, but there is a type of constructive, nonviolent tension which is necessary for growth. Just as Socrates felt that it was necessary to create a tension in the mind so that individuals could rise from the bondage of myths and half-truths to the unfettered realm of creative analysis and objective appraisal, so must we see the need for nonviolent gadflies to create the kind of tension in society that will help men rise from the dark depths of prejudice and racism to the majestic heights of understanding and brotherhood.

The purpose of our direct-action program is to create a situation so crisis-packed that it will inevitably open the door to negotiation. I therefore concur with you in your call for negotiation. Too long has our beloved Southland been bogged down in a tragic effort to live in monologue rather than dialogue.

One of the basic points in your statement is that the action that I and my associates have taken in Birmingham is untimely. Some have asked: "Why didn't you give the new city administration time to act?" The only answer that I can give to this query is that the new Birmingham administration must be prodded about as much as the outgoing one, before it will act. We are sadly mistaken if we feel that the election of Albert Boutwell as mayor will bring the millennium to Birmingham. While Mr. Boutwell is a much more gentle person than Mr. Connor, they are both segregationists, dedicated to maintenance of the status quo. I have hope that Mr. Boutwell will be reasonable enough to see the futility of massive resistance to desegregation. But he will not see this without pressure from devotees of civil rights. My friends, I must say to you that we have not made a single gain in civil rights without determined legal and nonviolent pressure. Lamentably, it is an historical fact that privileged groups seldom give up their privileges voluntarily. Individuals may see the moral light and voluntarily give up their unjust posture; but, as Reinhold Niebuhr has reminded us, groups tend to be more immoral than individuals.

We know through painful experience that freedom is never voluntarily given by the oppressor; it must be demanded by the oppressed. Frankly, I have yet to engage in a direct-action campaign that was "well timed" in the view of those who have not suffered unduly from the disease of segregation. For years now I have heard the word "Wait!" It rings in the ear of every Negro with piercing familiarity. This "Wait" has almost always meant "Never." We must come to see, with one of our distinguished jurists, that "justice too long delayed is justice denied."

We have waited for more than 340 years for our constitutional and God-given rights. The nations of Asia and Africa are moving with jetlike speed toward gaining political independence, but we still creep at horse-and-buggy pace toward gaining a cup of coffee at a lunch counter. Perhaps it is easy for those who have never felt the stinging darts of segregation to say, "Wait." But when you have seen vicious mobs lynch your mothers and fathers at will and drown your sisters and brothers at whim; when you have seen hate-filled policemen curse, kick and even kill your black brothers and sisters; when you see the vast majority of your twenty million Negro brothers smothering in an airtight cage of poverty in the midst of an affluent society; when you suddenly find your tongue twisted and your speech stammering as you seek to explain to your six-year-old daughter why she can't go to the public amusement park that has just been advertised on television, and see tears welling up in her eyes when she is told that Funtown is closed to colored children, and see ominous clouds of inferiority beginning to form in her little mental sky, and see her beginning to distort her personality by developing an unconscious bitterness toward white people; when you have to concoct an answer for a five-year-old son who is asking: "Daddy, why do white people treat colored people so mean?"; when you take a cross-country drive and find it necessary to sleep night after night in the uncomfortable corners of your automobile because no motel will accept you; when you are humiliated day in and day out by nagging signs reading "white" and "colored"; when your first name becomes "nigger," your middle name becomes "boy" (however old you are) and your last name becomes "John," and your wife and mother are never given the respected title "Mrs."; when you are harried by day and haunted by night by the fact that you are a Negro, living constantly at tiptoe stance, never quite knowing what to expect next, and are plagued with inner fears and outer resentments; when you are forever fighting a degenerating sense of "nobodiness"—then you will understand why we find it difficult to wait. There comes a time when the cup of endurance runs over, and men are no longer willing to be plunged into the abyss of despair. I hope, sirs, you can understand our legitimate and unavoidable impatience.

You express a great deal of anxiety over our willingness to break laws. This is certainly a legitimate concern. Since we so diligently urge people to obey the Supreme Court's decision of 1954 [i.e., *Brown v. Board of Education*] outlawing segregation in the public schools, at first glance it may seem rather paradoxical for us consciously to break laws. One may well ask: "How can you advocate breaking some laws and obeying others?" The answer lies in the fact that there are two types of laws: just and unjust. I would be the first to advocate obeying just laws. One has not only a legal but a moral responsibility to obey just laws. Conversely, one has a moral responsibility to disobey unjust laws. I would agree with St. Augustine that "an unjust law is no law at all."

Now, what is the difference between the two? How does one determine whether a law is just or unjust? A just law is a man-made code that squares with the moral law or the law of God. An unjust law is a code that is out of harmony with the moral law. To put it in the terms of St. Thomas Aquinas:

An unjust law is a human law that is not rooted in eternal law and natural law. Any law that uplifts human personality is just. Any law that degrades human personality is unjust. All segregation statutes are unjust because segregation distorts the soul and damages the personality. It gives the segregator a false sense of superiority and the segregated a false sense of inferiority. Segregation, to use the terminology of the Jewish philosopher Martin Buber,[2] substitutes an "I-it" relationship for an "I-thou" relationship and ends up relegating persons to the status of things. Hence segregation is not only politically, economically and sociologically unsound, it is morally wrong and sinful. Paul Tillich has said that sin is separation.[3] Is not segregation an existential expression of man's tragic separation, his awful estrangement, his terrible sinfulness? Thus it is that I can urge men to obey the 1954 decision of the Supreme Court, for it is morally right; and I can urge them to disobey segregation ordinances, for they are morally wrong.

Let us consider a more concrete example of just and unjust laws. An unjust law is a code that a numerical or power majority group compels a minority group to obey but does not make binding on itself. This is *difference* made legal. By the same token, a just law is a code that a majority compels a minority to follow and that it is willing to follow itself. This is *sameness* made legal.

Let me give another explanation. A law is unjust if it is inflicted on a minority that, as a result of being denied the right to vote, had no part in enacting or devising the law. Who can say that the legislature of Alabama which set up that state's segregation laws was democratically elected? Throughout Alabama all sorts of devious methods are used to prevent Negroes from becoming registered voters, and there are some counties in which, even though Negroes constitute a majority of the population, not a single Negro is registered. Can any law enacted under such circumstances be considered democratically structured?

Sometimes a law is just on its face and unjust in its application. For instance, I have been arrested on a charge of parading without a permit. Now, there is nothing wrong in having an ordinance which requires a permit for a parade. But such an ordinance becomes unjust when it is used to maintain segregation and to deny citizens the First-Amendment privilege of peaceful assembly and protest.

I hope you are able to see the distinction I am trying to point out. In no sense do I advocate evading or defying the law, as would the rabid segregationist. That would lead to anarchy. One who breaks an unjust law must do so openly, lovingly, and with a willingness to accept the penalty. I submit that an individual who breaks a law that conscience tells him is unjust, and who willingly accepts the penalty of imprisonment in order to arouse the conscience of the community over its injustice, is in reality expressing the highest respect for law.

Of course, there is nothing new about this kind of civil disobedience. It was evidenced sublimely in the refusal of Shadrach, Meshach and Abednego to obey the laws of Nebuchadnezzar, on the ground that a higher moral law was at stake.[4] It was practiced superbly by the early Christians, who were willing to face hungry lions and the excruciating pain of chopping blocks rather than submit to certain unjust laws of the Roman Empire. To a degree, academic freedom is a reality today because Socrates practiced civil disobedience. In our own nation, the Boston Tea Party represented a massive act of civil disobedience.

We should never forget that everything Adolf Hitler did in Germany was "legal" and everything the Hungarian freedom fighters did in Hungary was "illegal." It was "illegal" to aid and comfort a Jew in Hitler's Germany. Even so, I am sure that, had I lived in Germany at the time, I would have aided and comforted my Jewish brothers. If today I lived in a Communist country where certain principles dear to the Christian faith are suppressed, I would openly advocate disobeying that country's antireligious laws.

I must make two honest confessions to you, my Christian and Jewish brothers. First, I must confess that over the past few years I have been gravely disappointed with the white moderate. I have almost reached the regrettable conclusion that the Negro's great stumbling block in his stride toward freedom is not the White Citizen's Counciler or the Ku Klux Klanner, but the white moderate, who is more devoted to "order" than to justice; who prefers a negative peace which is the absence of tension to a positive peace which is the presence of justice; who constantly says: "I agree with you in the goal you seek, but I cannot agree with your methods of direct action"; who paternalistically believes he can set the timetable for another man's freedom; who lives by a mythical concept of time and who constantly advises the Negro to wait for a "more convenient season." Shallow understanding from people of good will is more frustrating than absolute misunderstanding from people of ill will. Lukewarm acceptance is much more bewildering than outright rejection.

I had hoped that the white moderate would understand that law and order exist for the purpose of establishing justice and that when they fail in this purpose they become the dangerously structured dams that block the flow of social progress. I had hoped that the white moderate would understand that the present tension in the South is a necessary phase of the transition from an obnoxious negative peace, in which the Negro passively accepted his unjust plight, to a substantive and positive peace, in which all men will respect the dignity and worth of human personality. Actually, we who engage in nonviolent direct action are not the creators of tension. We merely bring to the surface the hidden tension that is already alive. We bring it out in the open, where it can be seen and dealt with. Like a boil that can never be cured so long as it is covered up but must be opened with all its ugliness to the natural medicines of air and light, injustice must be exposed, with all the tension its exposure creates, to the light of human conscience and the air of national opinion before it can be cured.

In your statement you assert that our actions, even though peaceful, must be condemned because they precipitate violence. But is this a logical assertion? Isn't this like condemning a robbed man because his possession of money precipitated the evil act of robbery? Isn't this like condemning Socrates because his unswerving commitment to truth and his philosophical inquiries precipitated the act by the misguided populace in which they made him drink hemlock? Isn't this like condemning Jesus because his unique God-consciousness and never-ceasing devotion to God's will precipitated the evil act of crucifixion? We must come to see that, as the federal courts have consistently affirmed, it is wrong to urge an individual to cease his efforts to gain his basic constitutional rights because the quest may precipitate violence. Society must protect the robbed and punish the robber.

I had also hoped that the white moderate would reject the myth concerning time in relation to the struggle for freedom. I have just received a letter from a white brother in Texas. He writes: "All Christians know that the colored people will receive equal rights eventually, but it is possible that you are in too great a religious hurry. It has taken Christianity almost two thousand years to accomplish what it has. The teachings of Christ take time to come to earth." Such an attitude stems from a tragic misconception of time, from the strangely irrational notion that there is something in the very flow of time that will inevitably cure all ills. Actually, time itself is neutral; it can be used either destructively or constructively. More and more I feel that the people of ill will have used time much more effectively than have the people of good will. We will have to repent in this generation not merely for the hateful words and actions of the bad people but for the appalling silence of the good people. Human progress never rolls in on wheels of inevitability; it comes through the tireless efforts of men willing to be co-workers with God, and without this hard work, time itself becomes an ally of the forces of social stagnation. We must use time creatively, in the knowledge that the time is always ripe to do right. Now is the time to make real the promise of democracy and transform our pending national elegy into a creative psalm of brotherhood. Now is the time to lift our national policy from the quicksand of racial injustice to the solid rock of human dignity.

You speak of our activity in Birmingham as extreme. At first I was rather disappointed that fellow clergymen would see my nonviolent efforts as those of an extremist. I began thinking about the fact that I stand in the middle of two opposing forces in the Negro community. One is a force of complacency, made up in part of Negroes who, as a result of long years of oppression, are so drained of self-respect and a sense of "somebodiness" that they have adjusted to segregation; and in part of a few middle-class Negroes who, because of a degree of academic and economic security and because in some ways they profit by segregation, have become insensitive to the problems of the masses. The other force is one of bitterness and hatred, and it comes perilously close to advocating violence. It is expressed in the various black nationalist groups that are springing up across the nation, the largest and best-known being Elijah Muhammad's Muslim movement. Nourished by the Negro's frustration over the continued existence of racial discrimination, this movement is made up of people who have lost faith in America, who have absolutely repudiated Christianity, and who have concluded that the white man is an incorrigible "devil."

I have tried to stand between these two forces, saying that we need emulate neither the "do-nothingism" of the complacent nor the hatred and despair of the black nationalist. For there is the more excellent way of love and nonviolent protest. I am grateful to God that, through the influence of the Negro church, the way of nonviolence became an integral part of our struggle.

If this philosophy had not emerged, by now many streets of the South would, I am convinced, be flowing with blood. And I am further convinced that if our white brothers dismiss as "rabble-rousers" and "outside agitators" those of us who employ nonviolent direct action, and if they refuse to support our nonviolent efforts, millions of Negroes will, out of frustration and despair, seek solace and security in black-nationalist ideologies—a development that would inevitably lead to a frightening racial nightmare.[5]

Oppressed people cannot remain oppressed forever. The yearning for freedom eventually manifests itself, and that is what has happened to the American Negro. Something within has reminded him of his birthright of freedom, and something without has reminded him that it can be gained. Consciously or unconsciously, he has been caught up by the *Zeitgeist* [i.e., the spirit of the times], and with his black brothers of Africa and his brown and yellow brothers of Asia, South America and the Caribbean, the United States Negro is moving with a sense of great urgency toward the promised land of racial justice. If one recognizes this vital urge that has engulfed the Negro community, one should readily understand why public demonstrations are taking place. The Negro has many pent-up resentments and latent frustrations, and he must release them. So let him march; let him make prayer pilgrimages to the city hall; let him go on freedom rides—and try to understand why he must do so. If his repressed emotions are not released in nonviolent ways, they will seek expression through violence; this is not a threat but a fact of history. So I have not said to my people: "Get rid of your discontent." Rather, I have tried to say that this normal and healthy discontent can be channeled into the creative outlet of nonviolent direct action. And now this approach is being termed extremist.

But though I was initially disappointed at being categorized as an extremist, as I continued to think about the matter I gradually gained a measure of satisfaction from the label. Was not Jesus an extremist for love: "Love your enemies, bless them that curse you, do good to them that hate you, and pray for them which despitefully use you, and persecute you." Was not Amos an extremist for justice: "Let justice roll down like waters and righteousness like an ever-flowing stream." Was not Paul an extremist for the Christian gospel: "I bear in my body the marks of the Lord Jesus." Was not Martin Luther an extremist: "Here I stand; I cannot do otherwise, so help me God." And John Bunyan: "I will stay in jail to the end of my days before I make a butchery of my conscience."[6] And Abraham Lincoln: "This nation cannot survive half slave and half free." And Thomas Jefferson: "We hold these truths to be self-evident, that all men are created equal...." So the question is not whether we will be extremists, but what kinds of extremists we will be. Will we be extremists for hate or for love? Will we be extremists for the preservation of injustice or for the extension of justice? In that dramatic scene on Calvary's hill three men were crucified. We must never forget that all three were crucified for the same crime—the crime of extremism. Two were extremists for immorality, and thus fell below their environment. The other, Jesus Christ, was an extremist for love, truth and goodness, and thereby rose above his environment. Perhaps the South, the nation and the world are in dire need of creative extremists.

I had hoped that the white moderate would see this need. Perhaps I was too optimistic; perhaps I expected too much. I suppose I should have realized that few members of the oppressor race can understand the deep groans and passionate yearnings of the oppressed race, and still fewer have the vision to see that injustice must be rooted out by strong, persistent and determined action. I am thankful, however, that some of our white brothers in the South have grasped the meaning of this social revolution and committed themselves to it. They are still all too few in quantity, but they are big in quality. Some...have written about our struggle in eloquent and prophetic terms. Others have marched with us down nameless streets of the South. They have languished in filthy, roach-infested jails, suffering the abuse and brutality of policemen who view them as "dirty nigger-lovers." Unlike so many of their moderate brothers and sisters, they have recognized the urgency of the moment and sensed the need for powerful "action" antidotes to combat the disease of segregation.

Let me take note of my other major disappointment. I have been so greatly disappointed with the white church and its leadership. Of course, there are some notable exceptions. I am not unmindful of the fact that each of you has taken some significant stands on this issue. I commend you, Reverend Stallings, for your Christian stand on this past Sunday, in welcoming Negroes to your worship service on a nonsegregated basis. I commend the Catholic leaders of this state for integrating Spring Hill College several years ago.

But despite these notable exceptions, I must honestly reiterate that I have been disappointed with the church. I do not say this as one of those negative critics who can always find something wrong with the church. I say this as a minister of the gospel, who loves the church; who was nurtured in its bosom; who has been sustained by its spiritual blessings and who will remain true to it as long as the cord of life shall lengthen.

When I was suddenly catapulted into the leadership of the bus protest in Montgomery, Alabama, a few years ago, I felt we would be supported by the white church. I felt that the white ministers, priests and rabbis of the South would be among our strongest allies. Instead, some have been outright opponents, refusing to understand the freedom movement and misrepresenting its leaders; all too many others have been more cautious than courageous and have remained silent behind the anesthetizing security of stained-glass windows.

In spite of my shattered dreams, I came to Birmingham with the hope that the white religious leadership of this community would see the justice of our cause and, with deep moral concern, would serve as the channel through which our just grievances could reach the power structure. I had hoped that each of you would understand. But again I have been disappointed.

I have heard numerous southern religious leaders admonish their worshipers to comply with a desegregation decision because it is the law, but I have longed to hear white ministers declare: "Follow this decree because integration is morally right and because the Negro is your brother." In the midst of blatant injustices inflicted upon the Negro, I have watched white churchmen stand on the sideline and mouth pious irrelevancies and sanctimonious trivialities. In the midst of a mighty struggle to rid our nation of racial and economic injustice, I have heard many ministers say: "Those are social issues, with which the gospel has no real concern." And I have watched many churches commit themselves to a completely otherworldly religion which makes a strange, un-Biblical distinction between body and soul, between the sacred and the secular.

I have traveled the length and breadth of Alabama, Mississippi and all the other southern states. On sweltering summer days and crisp autumn mornings I have looked at the South's beautiful churches with their lofty spires pointing heavenward. I have beheld the impressive outlines of her massive religious-education buildings. Over and over I have found myself asking: "What kind of people worship here? Who is their God? Where were their voices when the lips of Governor [Ross] Barnett [of Mississippi] dripped with words of interposition and nullification? Where were they when Governor [George] Wallace [of Alabama] gave a clarion call for defiance and hatred? Where were their voices of support when bruised and weary Negro men and women decided to rise from the dark dungeons of complacency to the bright hills of creative protest?"

Yes, these questions are still in my mind. In deep disappointment I have wept over the laxity of the church. But be assured that my tears have been tears of love. There can be no deep disappointment where there is not deep love. Yes, I love the church. How could I do otherwise? I am in the rather unique position of being the son, the grandson and the great-grandson of preachers. Yes, I see the church as the body of Christ. But, oh! How we have blemished and scarred that body through social neglect and through fear of being nonconformists.

There was a time when the church was very powerful—in the time when the early Christians rejoiced at being deemed worthy to suffer for what they believed. In those days the church was not merely a thermometer that recorded the ideas and principles of popular opinion; it was a thermostat that transformed the mores of society. Whenever the early Christians entered a town, the people in power became disturbed and immediately sought to convict the Christians for being "disturbers of the peace" and "outside agitators." But the Christians pressed on, in the conviction that they were "a colony of heaven," called to obey God rather than man. Small in number, they were big in commitment. They were too God-intoxicated to be "astronomically intimidated." By their effort and example they brought an end to such ancient evils as infanticide and gladiatorial contests.

Things are different now. So often the contemporary church is a weak, ineffectual voice with an uncertain sound. So often it is an archdefender of the status quo. Far from being disturbed by the presence of the church, the power structure of the average community is consoled by the church's silent—and often even vocal—sanction of things as they are.

But the judgment of God is upon the church as never before. If today's church does not recapture the sacrificial spirit of the early church, it will lose its authenticity, forfeit the loyalty of millions, and be dismissed as an irrelevant social club with no meaning for the twentieth century. Every day I meet young people whose disappointment with the church has turned into outright disgust.

Perhaps I have once again been too optimistic. Is organized religion too inextricably bound to the status quo to save our nation and the world? Perhaps I must turn my faith to the inner spiritual church, the church within the church, as the true *ekklesia* [congregation] and the hope of the world. But again I am thankful to God that some noble souls from the ranks of organized religion have broken loose from the paralyzing chains of conformity and joined us as active partners in the struggle for freedom. They have left their secure congregations and walked the streets of Albany, Georgia, with us. They have gone down the highways of the South on tortuous rides for freedom. Yes, they have gone to jail with us. Some have been dismissed from their churches, have lost the support of their bishops and fellow ministers. But they have acted in the faith that right defeated is stronger than evil triumphant. Their witness has been the spiritual salt that has preserved the true meaning of the gospel in these troubled times. They have carved a tunnel of hope through the dark mountain of disappointment.

I hope the church as a whole will meet the challenge of this decisive hour. But even if the church does not come to the aid of justice, I have no despair about the future. I have no fear about the outcome of our struggle in Birmingham, even if our motives are at present misunderstood.

We will reach the goal of freedom in Birmingham and all over the nation, because the goal of America is freedom. Abused and scorned though we may be, our destiny is tied up with America's destiny. Before the pilgrims landed at Plymouth, we were here. Before the pen of Jefferson etched the majestic words of the Declaration of Independence across the pages of history, we were here. For more than two centuries our forebears labored in this country without wages; they made cotton king; they built the homes of their masters while suffering gross injustice and shameful humiliation—and yet out of a bottomless vitality they continued to thrive and develop. If the inexpressible cruelties of slavery could not stop us, the opposition we now face will surely fail. We will win our freedom because the sacred heritage of our nation and the eternal will of God are embodied in our echoing demands.

Before closing I feel impelled to mention one other point in your statement that has troubled me profoundly. You warmly commended the Birmingham police force for keeping "order" and "preventing violence." I doubt that you would have so warmly commended the police force if you had seen its dogs sinking their teeth into unarmed, nonviolent Negroes. I doubt that you would so quickly commend the policemen if you were to observe their ugly and inhumane treatment of Negroes here in the city jail; if you were to watch them push and curse old Negro women and young Negro girls; if you were to see them slap and kick old Negro men and young boys; if you were to observe them, as they did on two occasions, refuse to give us food because we wanted to sing our grace together. I cannot join you in your praise of the Birmingham police department.

It is true that the police have exercised a degree of discipline in handling the demonstrators. In this sense they have conducted themselves rather "nonviolently" in public. But for what purpose? To preserve the evil system of segregation. Over the past few years I have consistently preached that nonviolence demands that the means we use must be as pure as the ends we seek. I have tried to make clear that it is wrong to use immoral means to attain moral ends. But now I must affirm that it is just as wrong, or perhaps even more so, to use moral means to preserve immoral ends. Perhaps Mr. Connor and his policemen have been rather nonviolent in public, as was Chief Pritchett in Albany, Georgia, but they have used the moral means of nonviolence to maintain the immoral end of racial injustice. As T. S. Eliot has said: "The last temptation is the greatest treason: To do the right deed for the wrong reason."[7]

I wish you had commended the Negro sit-inners and demonstrators of Birmingham for their sublime courage, their willingness to suffer and their amazing discipline in the midst of great provocation. One day the South will recognize its real heroes. They will be the James Merediths,[8] with the noble sense of purpose that enables them to face jeering and hostile mobs, and with the agonizing loneliness that characterizes the life of the pioneer. They will be old, oppressed, battered Negro women, symbolized in a seventy-two-year-old woman in Montgomery, Alabama, who rose up with a sense of dignity and with her people decided not to ride segregated buses, and who responded with ungrammatical profundity to one who inquired about her weariness: "My feets is tired, but my soul is at rest." They will be the young high school and college students, the young ministers of the gospel and a host of their elders, courageously and nonviolently sitting in at lunch counters and willingly going to jail for conscience's sake. One day the South will know that when these disinherited children of God sat down at lunch counters, they were in reality standing up for what is best in the American dream and for the most sacred values in our Judeo-Christian heritage, thereby bringing our nation back to those great wells of democracy which were dug deep by the founding fathers in their formulation of the Constitution and the Declaration of Independence.

Never before have I written so long a letter. I'm afraid it is much too long to take your precious time. I can assure you that it would have been much shorter if I had been writing from a comfortable desk, but what else can one do when he is alone in a narrow jail cell, other than write long letters, think long thoughts and pray long prayers?

If I have said anything in this letter that overstates the truth and indicates an unreasonable impatience, I beg you to forgive me. If I have said anything that understates the truth and indicates my having a patience that allows me to settle for anything less than brotherhood, I beg God to forgive me.

I hope this letter finds you strong in the faith. I also hope that circumstances will soon make it possible for me to meet each of you, not as an integrationist or a civil-rights leader but as a fellow clergyman and a Christian brother. Let us all hope that the dark clouds of racial prejudice will soon pass away and the deep fog of misunderstanding will be lifted from our fear-drenched communities, and in some not too distant tomorrow the radiant stars of love and brotherhood will shine over our great nation with all their scintillating beauty.

Yours for the cause of Peace and Brotherhood,

Martin Luther King, Jr.

NOTES

1. AUTHOR'S NOTE: This response to a published statement by eight fellow clergymen from Alabama (Bishop C. C. J. Carpenter, Bishop Joseph A. Durick, Rabbi Hilton L. Grafman, Bishop Paul Hardin, Bishop Holan B. Harmon, the Reverend George M. Murray, the Reverend Edward V. Ramage and the Reverend Earl Stallings) was composed under somewhat constricting circumstances. Begun on the margins of the newspaper in which the statement appeared while I was in jail, the letter was continued on scraps of writing paper supplied by a friendly Negro trusty, and concluded on a pad my attorneys were eventually permitted to leave me. Although the text remains in substance unaltered, I have indulged in the author's prerogative of polishing it for publication.
2. Martin Buber (1878–1965), author of *I and Thou* (1923).—Eds.
3. The German-born American theologian Paul Tillich (1886–1965), author of *Systematic Theology* (3 vols., 1951–1963) and other works.—Eds.
4. See the Book of Daniel, Chapter 3, in the Old Testament.—Eds.
5. Reverend King refers here, as he does two paragraphs above, to the Nation of Islam movement of Elijah Muhammad and, at the time, Malcolm X.—Eds.
6. John Bunyan (1628–1688), English Puritan preacher and author of *The Pilgrim's Progress* (1678).—Eds.
7. Thomas Stearns Eliot (1888–1965) was an American-born poet and critic who lived and worked mostly in England.—Eds.
8. James Meredith was the first African-American to enroll—in the face of violent opposition—at the University of Mississippi.—Eds.

50

Black Consciousness and the Quest for a True Humanity

STEVE BIKO

Steve Biko (1946–1977) was one of the leaders of the Black Consciousness Movement in South Africa during the era of apartheid. His outspoken opposition to the official policy of racial separation led the government to charge him with terrorism, although he was never convicted. In 1977, while detained for "questioning" by the security police, Biko was badly beaten and suffered brain damage. He died, at age thirty-one, for lack of medical attention. Biko wrote the following essay four years before his death.

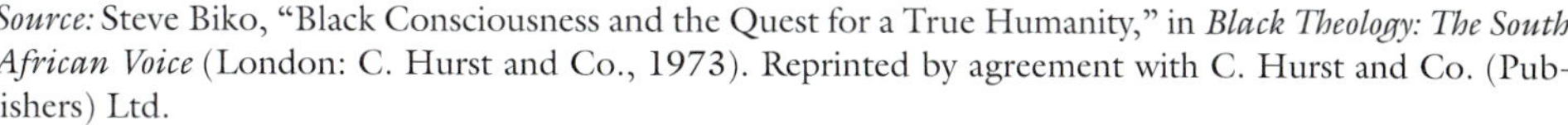

Source: Steve Biko, "Black Consciousness and the Quest for a True Humanity," in *Black Theology: The South African Voice* (London: C. Hurst and Co., 1973). Reprinted by agreement with C. Hurst and Co. (Publishers) Ltd.

BLACK CONSCIOUSNESS AND THE QUEST FOR A TRUE HUMANITY

We [black South Africans] must learn to accept that no group, however benevolent, can ever hand power to the vanquished on a plate. We must accept that the limits of tyrants are prescribed by the endurance of those whom they oppress. As long as we go to Whitey begging cap in hand for our own emancipation, we are giving him further sanction to continue with his racist and oppressive system. We must realise that our situation is not a mistake on the part of whites but a deliberate act, and that no amount of moral lecturing will persuade the white man to "correct" the situation. The system concedes nothing without demand, for it formulates its very method of operation on the basis that the ignorant will learn to know, the child will grow into an adult and therefore demands will begin to be made. It gears itself to resist demands in whatever way it sees fit. When you refuse to make these demands and choose to come to a round table to beg for your deliverance, you are asking for the contempt of those who have power over you. This is why we must reject the beggar tactics that are being forced on us by those who wish to appease our cruel masters. This is where the SASO [South African Student's Organization] message and cry *"Black man, you are on your own!"* becomes relevant.

The concept of integration, whose virtues are often extolled in white liberal circles, is full of unquestioned assumptions that embrace white values. It is a concept long defined by whites and never examined by blacks. It is based on the assumption that all is well with the system apart from some degree of mismanagement by irrational conservatives at the top. Even the people who argue for integration often forget to veil it in its supposedly beautiful covering. They tell each other that, were it not for job reservation, there would be a beautiful market to exploit. They forget they are talking about people. They see blacks as additional levers to some complicated industrial machines. This is white man's integration—an integration based on exploitative values. It is an integration in which black will compete with black, using each other as rungs up a step ladder leading them to white values. It is an integration in which the black man will have to prove himself in terms of these values before meriting acceptance and ultimate assimilation, and in which the poor will grow poorer and the rich richer in a country where the poor have always been black. We do not want to be reminded that it is we, the indigenous people, who are poor and exploited in the land of our birth. These are concepts which the Black Consciousness approach wishes to eradicate from the black man's mind before our society is driven to chaos by irresponsible people from Coca-Cola and hamburger cultural backgrounds.

Black Consciousness is an attitude of mind and a way of life, the most positive call to emanate from the black world for a long time. Its essence is the realisation by the black man of the need to rally together with his brothers around the cause of their oppression—the blackness of their skin—and to operate as a group to rid themselves of the shackles that bind them to perpetual servitude. It is based on a self-examination which has ultimately led them to believe that by seeking to run away from themselves and emulate the white man, they are insulting the intelligence of whoever created them black. The philosophy of Black Consciousness therefore expresses group pride and the determination of the black to rise and attain the envisaged self. Freedom is the ability to define oneself with one's possibilities held back not by the power of other people over one but only by one's relationship to God and to natural surroundings. On his own, therefore, the black man wishes to explore his surroundings and test his possibilities—in other words to make his freedom real by whatever means he deems fit. At the heart of this kind of thinking is the realisation by blacks that the most potent weapon in the hands of the oppressor is the mind of the oppressed. If one is free at heart, no manmade chains can bind one to servitude, but if one's mind is so manipulated and controlled by the oppressor as to make the oppressed believe that he is a liability to the white man, then there will be nothing the oppressed can do to scare his powerful masters. Hence thinking along lines of Black Consciousness makes the black man see himself as a being complete in himself. It makes him less dependent and more free to express his manhood. At the end of it all he cannot tolerate attempts by anybody to dwarf the significance of his manhood.

In order that Black Consciousness can be used to advantage as a philosophy to apply to people in a position like ours, a number of points have to be observed. As people existing in a continuous struggle for truth, we have to examine and question old concepts, values and systems. Having found the right answers we shall then work for consciousness among all people to make it possible for us to proceed towards putting these answers into effect. In this process, we have to evolve our own schemes, forms and strategies to suit the need and situation, always keeping in mind our fundamental beliefs and values.

In all aspects of the black-white relationship, now and in the past, we see a constant tendency by whites to depict blacks as of an inferior status. Our culture, our history and indeed all aspects of the black man's life have been battered nearly out of shape in the great collision between the indigenous values and the Anglo-Boer culture.

The first people to come and relate to blacks in a human way in South Africa were the missionaries. They were in the vanguard of the colonisation movement to "civilise and educate" the savages and introduce the Christian message to them. The religion they brought was quite foreign to the black indigenous people. African religion in its essence was not radically different from Christianity. We also believed in one God, we had our own community of saints through whom we related to our God, and we did not find it compatible with our way of life to worship God in isolation from the various aspects of our lives. Hence worship was not a specialised function that found expression once a week in a secluded building, but rather it featured in our wars, our beer-drinking, our dances and our customs in general. Whenever Africans drank they would first relate to God by giving a portion of their beer away as a token of thanks. When anything went wrong at home they would offer sacrifice to God to appease him and atone for their sins. There was no hell in our religion. We believed in the inherent goodness of man—hence we took it for granted that all people at death joined the community of saints and therefore merited our respect.

It was the missionaries who confused the people with their new religion. They scared our people with stories of hell. They painted their God as a demanding God who wanted worship "or else." People had to discard their clothes and their customs in order to be accepted in this new religion. Knowing how religious the African people were, the missionaries stepped up their terror campaign on the emotions of the people with their detailed accounts of eternal burning, tearing of hair and gnashing of teeth. By some strange and twisted logic, they argued that theirs was a scientific religion and ours a superstition—all this in spite of the biological discrepancy which is at the base of their religion. This cold and cruel religion was strange to the indigenous people and caused frequent strife between the converted and the "pagans," for the former, having imbibed the false values from white society, were taught to ridicule and despise those who defended the truth of their indigenous religion. With the ultimate acceptance of the western religion down went our cultural values!

While I do not wish to question the basic truth at the heart of the Christian message, there is a strong case for a re-examination of Christianity. It has proved a very adaptable religion which does not seek to supplement existing orders but—like any universal truth—to find application within a particular situation. More than anyone else, the missionaries knew that not all they did was essential to the spread of the message. But the basic intention went much further than merely spreading the word. Their arrogance and their monopoly on truth, beauty and moral judgment taught them to despise native customs and traditions and to seek to infuse their own new values into these societies.

Here then we have the case for Black Theology. While not wishing to discuss Black Theology at length, let it suffice to say that it seeks to relate God and Christ once more to the black man and his daily problems. It wants to describe Christ as a fighting God, not a passive God who allows a lie to rest unchallenged. It grapples with existential problems and does not claim to be a theology of absolutes. It seeks to bring back God to the black man and to the truth and reality of his situation. This is an important aspect of Black Consciousness, for quite a large proportion of black people in South Africa are Christians still swimming in a mire of confusion—the aftermath of the missionary approach. It is the duty therefore of all black priests and ministers of religion to save Christianity by adopting Black Theology's approach and thereby once more uniting the black man with his God.

A long look should also be taken at the educational system for blacks. The same tense situation was found as long ago as the arrival of the missionaries. Children were taught, under the pretext of hygiene, good manners and other such vague concepts, to despise their mode of upbringing at home and to question the values and customs of their society. The result was the expected one—children and parents saw life differently and the former lost respect for the latter. Now in African society it is a cardinal sin for a child to lose respect for his parent. Yet how can one prevent the loss of respect between child and parent when the child is taught by his know-all white tutors to disregard his family teachings? Who can resist losing respect for his tradition when in school his whole cultural background is summed up in one word—barbarism?

Thus we can immediately see the logic of placing the missionaries in the forefront of the colonisation process. A man who succeeds in making a group of people accept a foreign concept in which he is expert makes them perpetual students whose progress in the particular field can only be evaluated by him; the student must constantly turn to him for guidance and promotion. In being forced to accept the Anglo-Boer culture, the blacks have allowed themselves to be at the mercy of the white man and to have him as their eternal supervisor. Only he can tell us how good our performance is and instinctively each of us is at pains to please this powerful, all-knowing master. This is what Black Consciousness seeks to eradicate.

As one black writer says, colonialism is never satisfied with having the native in its grip but, by some strange logic, it must turn to his past and disfigure and distort it. Hence the history of the black man in this country is most disappointing to read. It is presented merely as a long succession of defeats. The Xhosas[1] were thieves who went to war for stolen property; the Boers[2] never provoked the Xhosas but merely went on "punitive expeditions" to teach the thieves a lesson. Heroes like Makana[3] who were essentially revolutionaries are painted as superstitious troublemakers who lied to the people about bullets turning into water. Great nation-builders like Shaka[4] are cruel tyrants who frequently attacked smaller tribes for no reason but for some sadistic purpose. Not only is there no objectivity in the history taught us but there is frequently an appalling misrepresentation of facts that sickens even the uninformed student.

Thus a lot of attention has to be paid to our history if we as blacks want to aid each other in our coming into consciousness. We have to rewrite our history and produce in it the heroes that formed the core of our resistance to the white invaders. More has to be revealed, and stress has to be laid on the successful nation-building attempts of men such as Shaka, Moshoeshoe and Hintsa.[5] These areas call for intense research to provide some sorely needed missing links. We would be too naive to expect our conquerors to write unbiased histories about us but we have to destroy the myth that our history starts in 1652, the year Van Riebeeck landed at the Cape.[6] Our culture must be defined in concrete terms. We must relate the past to the present and demonstrate a historical evolution of the modern black man. There is a tendency to think of our culture as a static culture that was arrested in 1652 and has never developed since. The "return to the bush" concept suggests that we have nothing to boast of except lions, sex and drink. We accept that when colonisation sets in it devours the indigenous culture and leaves behind a bastard culture that may thrive at the pace allowed it by the dominant culture. But we also have to realise that the basic tenets of our culture have largely succeeded in withstanding the process of bastardisation and that even at this moment we can still demonstrate that we appreciate a man for himself. Ours is a true man-centred society whose sacred tradition is that of sharing. We must reject, as we have been doing, the individualistic cold approach to life that is the cornerstone of the Anglo-Boer culture. We must seek to restore to the black man the great importance we used to give to human relations, the high regard for people and their property and for life in general; to reduce the triumph of technology over man and the materialistic element that is slowly creeping into our society.

These are essential features of our black culture to which we must cling. Black culture above all implies freedom on our part to innovate without recourse to white values. This innovation is part of the natural development of any culture. A culture is essentially the society's composite answer to the varied problems of life. We are experiencing new problems every day and whatever we do adds to the richness of our cultural heritage as long as it has man as its centre. The adoption of black theatre and drama is one such important innovation which we need to encourage and to develop. We know that our love of music and rhythm has relevance even in this day.

Being part of an exploitative society in which we are often the direct objects of exploitation, we need to evolve a strategy towards our economic situation. We are aware that the blacks are still colonised even within the borders of South Africa. Their cheap labour has helped to make South Africa what it is today. Our money from the townships takes a one-way journey to white shops and white banks, and all we do in our lives is pay the white man either with labour or in coin. Capitalistic exploitative tendencies, coupled with the overt arrogance of white racism, have conspired against us. Thus in South Africa now it is very expensive to be poor. It is the poor people who stay furthest from town and therefore have to spend more money on transport to come and work for white people; it is the poor people who use uneconomic and inconvenient fuel like paraffin and coal because of the refusal of the white man to install electricity in black areas; it is the poor people who are governed by many ill-defined restrictive laws and therefore have to spend money on fines for "technical" offences; it is the poor people who have no hospitals and are therefore exposed to exorbitant charges by private doctors; it is the poor people who use untarred roads, have to walk long distances, and therefore experience the greatest wear and tear on commodities like shoes; it is the poor people who have to pay for their children's books while whites get them free. It does not need to be said that it is the black people who are poor.

We therefore need to take another look at how best to use our economic power, little as it may seem to be. We must seriously examine the possibilities of establishing business co-operatives whose interests will be ploughed back into community development programmes. We should think along such lines as the "buy black" campaign once suggested in Johannesburg and establish our own banks for the benefit of the community. Organisational development amongst blacks has only been low because we have allowed it to be. Now that we know we are on our own, it is an absolute duty for us to fulfil these needs.

The last step in Black Consciousness is to broaden the base of our operation. One of the basic tenets of Black Consciousness is totality of involvement. This means that all blacks must sit as one big unit, and no fragmentation and distraction from the mainstream of events be allowed. Hence we must resist the attempts by protagonists of the bantustan theory to fragment our approach.[7] We are oppressed not as individuals, not as Zulus, Xhosas, Vendas or Indians. We are oppressed because we are black. We must use that very concept to unite ourselves and to respond as a cohesive group. We must cling to each other with a tenacity that will shock the perpetrators of evil.

Our preparedness to take upon ourselves the cudgels of the struggle will see us through. We must remove from our vocabulary completely the concept of fear. Truth must ultimately triumph over evil, and the white man has always nourished his greed on this basic fear that shows itself in the black community. Special Branch agents[8] will not turn the lie into truth, and one must ignore them. In a true bid for change we have to take off our coats, be prepared to lose our comfort and security, our jobs and positions of prestige, and our families, for just as it is true that "leadership and security are basically incompatible," a struggle without casualties is no struggle. We must realise that prophetic cry of black students: "Black man, you are on your own!"

Some will charge that we are racist, but these people are using exactly the values we reject. We do not have the power to subjugate anyone. We are merely responding to provocation in the most realistic possible way. Racism does not only imply exclusion of one race by another—it always presupposes that the exclusion is for the purposes of subjugation. Blacks have had enough experience as objects of racism not to wish to turn the tables. While it may be relevant now to talk about black in relation to white, we must not make this our preoccupation, for it can be a negative exercise. As we proceed further towards the achievement of our goals let us talk more about ourselves and our struggle and less about whites.

We have set out on a quest for true humanity, and somewhere on the distant horizon we can see the glittering prize. Let us march forth with courage and determination, drawing strength from our common plight and our brotherhood. In time we shall be in a position to bestow upon South Africa the greatest gift possible—a more human face.

NOTES

1. The Xhosa are a South African tribe residing mainly in the Transkei region.—Eds.
2. The Boers are white South Africans of Dutch descent.—Eds.
3. Early nineteenth-century Xhosa prophet, sentenced to life imprisonment on Robben Island and drowned while escaping in a boat. Refusal by blacks to accept the truth of his death led to the mythical hope of his eventual return.—Eds.
4. Shaka was the powerful nineteenth-century chieftain who united the Zulu tribe to fight against white settlers.—Eds.
5. Moshoeshoe and Hintsa were tribal chieftains opposed to white settlement of native lands.—Eds.
6. Jan Van Riebeeck led the first Dutch settlers in the mid-seventeenth century.—Eds.
7. The "bantustan theory" threatened to fragment the Black Consciousness Movement by encouraging the members of Bantu tribes, such as the Vendas, to set themselves apart from other black South Africans.—Eds.
8. The Special Branch was the internal security (secret police) force under the apartheid government. Steve Biko died of injuries resulting from a beating he suffered while in Special Branch custody.—Eds.

51

A Vindication of the Rights of Woman

MARY WOLLSTONECRAFT

Mary Wollstonecraft (1759–1797) was an English novelist and political writer. In *A Vindication of the Rights of Men* (1790) she defended the French Revolution against Edmund Burke's attack (see selection 25 for excerpts from Burke's *Reflections on the Revolution in France*). In her longer and more famous book, *A Vindication of the Rights of Woman* (1792), Wollstonecraft argued that "the rights of man" must extend to the other half of the human race, namely, women. In this second *Vindication,* from which the following selection is taken, Wollstonecraft places particular stress upon the importance of education. Education is vital to men and women alike, she believed, for it enables them to acquire knowledge and to develop reason and virtue. Indeed, her claim is that women, "in common with men, are placed on this earth to unfold their faculties."

Source: Mary Wollstonecraft, *A Vindication of the Rights of Woman* (Philadelphia: Matthew Carey, 1794), pp. 87–109.

OBSERVATIONS ON THE STATE OF DEGRADATION TO WHICH WOMAN IS REDUCED BY VARIOUS CAUSES

That woman is naturally weak, or degraded by a concurrence of circumstances, is, I think, clear. But this position I shall simply contrast with a conclusion, which I have frequently heard fall from sensible men in favour of an aristocracy; that the mass of mankind cannot be anything, or the obsequious slaves, who patiently allow themselves to be driven forward, would feel their own consequence, and spurn their chains. Men, they further observe, submit everywhere to oppression, when they have only to lift up their heads to throw off the yoke; yet, instead of asserting their birthright, they quietly lick the dust, and say, "Let us eat and drink, for tomorrow we die." Women, I argue from analogy, are degraded by the same propensity to enjoy the present moment, and at last despise the freedom which they have not sufficient virtue to struggle to attain. But I must be more explicit.

With respect to the culture of the heart, it is unanimously allowed that sex is out of the question; but the line of subordination in the mental powers is never to be passed over. Only "absolute in loveliness," the portion of rationality granted to woman is, indeed, very scanty; for denying her genius and judgment, it is scarcely possible to divine what remains to characterise intellect.

The stamen of immortality, if I may be allowed the phrase, is the perfectibility of human reason; for, were man created perfect, or did a flood of knowledge break upon him, when he arrived at maturity, that precluded error, I should doubt whether his existence would be continued after the dissolution of the body. But, in the present state of things, every difficulty in morals that escapes from human discussion, and equally baffles the investigation of profound thinking, and the lightning glance of genius, is an argument on which I build my belief of the immortality of the soul. Reason is, consequently, the simple power of improvement; or, more properly speaking, of discerning truth. Every individual is in this respect a world in itself. More or less may be conspicuous in one being than another; but the nature of reason must be the same in all, if it be an emanation of divinity, the tie that connects the creature with the Creator; for, can that soul be stamped with the heavenly image, that is not perfected by the exercise of its own reason? Yet outwardly ornamented with elaborate care, and so adorned to delight man, "that with honour he may love," the soul of woman is not allowed to have this distinction, and man, ever placed between her and reason, she is always represented as only created to see through a gross medium, and to take things on trust. But dismissing these fanciful theories, and considering woman as a whole, let it be what it will, instead of a part of man, the inquiry is whether she have reason or not. If she have,...she was not created merely to be the solace of man....

The power of generalising ideas, of drawing comprehensive conclusions from individual observations, is the only acquirement, for an immortal being, that really deserves the name of knowledge. Merely to observe, without endeavouring to account for anything, may (in a very incomplete manner) serve as the common sense of life; but where is the store laid up that is to clothe the soul when it leaves the body?

This power has not only been denied to women; but writers have insisted that it is inconsistent, with a few exceptions, with their sexual character. Let men prove this, and I shall grant that woman only exists for man. I must, however, previously remark, that the power of generalising ideas, to any great extent, is not very common amongst men or women. But this exercise is the true cultivation of the understanding; and everything conspires to render the cultivation of the understanding more difficult in the female than the male world.

I am naturally led by the assertion to the main subject of the present chapter, and shall now attempt to point out some of the causes that degrade the sex, and prevent women from generalising their observations.

I shall not go back to the remote annals of antiquity to trace the history of woman; it is sufficient to allow that she has always been either a slave or a despot, and to remark that each of these situations equally retards the progress of reason. The grand source of female folly and vice has ever appeared to me to arise from narrowness of mind; and the very constitution of civil governments has put almost insuperable obstacles in the way to prevent the cultivation of the female understanding; yet virtue can be built on no other foundation. The same obstacles are thrown in the way of the rich, and the same consequences ensue.

Necessity has been proverbially termed the mother of invention; the aphorism may be extended to virtue. It is an acquirement, and an acquirement to which pleasure must be sacrificed; and who sacrifices pleasure when it is within the grasp, whose mind has not been opened and strengthened by adversity, or the pursuit of knowledge goaded on by necessity? Happy is it when people have the cares of life to struggle with, for these struggles prevent their becoming a prey to enervating vices, merely from idleness. But if from their birth men and women be placed in a torrid zone, with the meridian sun of pleasure darting directly upon them, how can they sufficiently brace their minds to discharge the duties of life, or even to relish the affections that carry them out of themselves?

Pleasure is the business of woman's life, according to the present modification of society; and while it continues to be so, little can be expected from such weak beings. Inheriting in a lineal descent from the first fair defect in nature—the sovereignty of beauty—they have, to maintain their power, resigned the natural rights which the exercise of reason might have procured them, and chosen rather to be short-lived queens than labour to obtain the sober pleasures that arise from equality. Exalted by their inferiority (this sounds like a contradiction), they constantly demand homage as women, though experience should teach them that men who pride themselves upon paying this arbitrary insolent respect to the sex, with the most scrupulous exactness, are most inclined to tyrannise over, and despise the very weakness they cherish....

Ah! why do women—I write with affectionate solicitude—condescend to receive a degree of attention and respect from strangers different from that reciprocation of civility which the dictates of humanity and the politeness of civilisation authorise between man and man? And why do they not discover, when "in the noon of beauty's power," that they are treated like queens only to be deluded by hollow respect, till they are led to resign, or not assume, their natural prerogatives? Confined, then, in cages like the feathered race, they have nothing to do but to plume themselves, and stalk with mock majesty from perch to perch. It is true they are provided with food and raiment, for which they neither toil nor spin; but health, liberty, and virtue are given in exchange. But where, amongst mankind, has been found sufficient strength of mind to enable a being to resign these adventitious prerogatives—one who, rising with the calm dignity of reason above opinion, dared to be proud of the privileges inherent in man? And it is vain to expect it whilst hereditary power chokes the affections, and nips reason in the bud....

Mankind, including every description, wish to be loved and respected by *something,* and the common herd will always take the nearest road to the completion of their wishes. The respect paid to wealth and beauty is the most certain and unequivocal, and, of course, will always attract the vulgar eye of common minds. Abilities and virtues are absolutely necessary to raise men from the middle rank of life into notice, and the natural consequence is notorious—the middle rank contains most virtue and abilities. Men have thus, in one station at least, an opportunity of exerting themselves with dignity, and of rising by the exertions which really improve a rational creature; but the whole female sex are, till their character is formed, in the same condition as the rich, for they are born—I now speak of a state of civilisation—with certain sexual privileges; and whilst they are gratuitously granted them, few will ever think of works of supererogation to obtain the esteem of a small number of superior people.

When do we hear of women who, starting out of obscurity, boldly claim respect on account of their great abilities or daring virtues? Where are they to be found? "To be observed, to be attended to, to be taken notice of with sympathy, complacency, and approbation, are all the advantages which they seek." True! my male readers will probably exclaim; but let them, before they draw any conclusion, recollect that this was not written originally as descriptive of women, but of the rich. In Dr. [Adam] Smith's *Theory of Moral Sentiments* I have found a general character of people of rank and fortune, that, in my opinion, might with the greatest propriety be applied to the female sex. I refer the sagacious reader to the whole comparison, but must be allowed to quote a passage to enforce an argument that I mean to insist on, as the one most conclusive against a sexual character. For if, excepting warriors, no great men of any denomination have ever appeared amongst the nobility, may it not be fairly inferred that their local situation swallowed up the man, and produced a character similar to that of women, who are *localised*—if I may be allowed the word—by the rank they are placed in by *courtesy*? Women, commonly called ladies, are not to be contradicted in company, are not allowed to exert any manual strength; and from them the negative virtues only are expected, when any virtues are expected—patience, docility, good humour, and flexibility—virtues incompatible with any vigorous exertion of intellect. Besides, by living more with each other, and being seldom absolutely alone, they are more under the influence of sentiments than passions. Solitude and reflection are necessary to give to wishes the force of passions, and to enable the imagination to enlarge the object, and make it the most desirable. The same may be said of the ideas, collected by impassioned thinking or calm investigation, to acquire that strength of character on which great resolves are built....

In the middle rank of life, to continue the comparison, men, in their youth, are prepared for professions, and marriage is not considered as the grand feature in their lives; whilst women, on the contrary, have no other scheme to sharpen their faculties. It is not business, extensive plans, or any of the excursive flights of ambition, that engross their attention; no, their thoughts are not employed in rearing such noble structures. To rise in the world, and have the liberty of running from pleasure to pleasure, they must marry advantageously, and to this object their time is sacrificed, and their persons often legally prostituted. A man when he enters any profession has his eye steadily fixed on some future advantage (and the mind gains great strength by having all its efforts directed to one point), and, full of his business, pleasure is considered as mere relaxation; whilst women seek for pleasure as the main purpose of existence. In fact, from the education, which they receive from society, the love of pleasure may be said to govern them all; but does this prove that there is a sex in souls? It would be just as rational to declare that the courtiers in France, when a destructive system of despotism had formed their character, were not men, because liberty, virtue, and humanity, were sacrificed to pleasure and vanity. Fatal passions, which have ever domineered over the *whole* race!

The same love of pleasure, fostered by the whole tendency of their education, gives a trifling turn to the conduct of women in most circumstances; for instance, they are ever anxious about secondary things; and on the watch for adventures instead of being occupied by duties....

In short, women, in general, as well as the rich of both sexes have acquired all the follies and vices of civilisation, and missed the useful fruit. It is not necessary for me always to premise that I speak of the condition of the whole sex, leaving exceptions out of the question. Their senses are inflamed, and their understandings neglected, consequently they become the prey of their sense, delicately termed sensibility, and are blown about by every momentary gust of feeling. Civilised women are, therefore, so weakened by false refinement, that, respecting morals, their condition is much below what it would be were they left in a state nearer to nature. Ever restless and anxious, their over-exercised sensibility not only renders them uncomfortable themselves, but troublesome, to use a soft phrase, to others. All their thoughts turn on things calculated to excite emotion and feeling, when they should reason, their conduct is unstable, and their opinions are wavering—not the wavering produced by deliberation or progressive views, but by contradictory emotions. By fits and starts they are warm in many pursuits; yet this warmth, never concentrated into perseverance, soon exhausts itself; exhaled by its own heat, or meeting with some other fleeting passion, to which reason has never given any specific gravity, neutrality ensues. Miserable, indeed, must be that being whose cultivation of mind has only tended to inflame its passions! A distinction should be made between inflaming and strengthening them. The passions thus pampered, whilst the judgment is left unformed, what can be expected to ensue? Undoubtedly, a mixture of madness and folly!...

And will moralists pretend to assert that this is the condition in which one-half of the human race should be encouraged to remain with listless inactivity and stupid acquiescence? Kind instructors! what were we created for? To remain, it may be said, innocent; they mean in a state of childhood. We might as well never have been born, unless it were necessary that we should be created to enable man to acquire the noble privilege of reason, the power of discerning good from evil, whilst we lie down in the dust from whence we were taken, never to rise again....

I come round to my old argument; if woman be allowed to have an immortal soul, she must have, as the employment of life, an understanding to improve. And when, to render the present state more complete, though everything proves it to be but a fraction of a mighty sum, she is incited by present gratification to forget her grand destination, nature is counteracted, or she was born only to procreate and rot. Or, granting brutes of every description a soul, though not a reasonable one, the exercise of instinct and sensibility may be the step which they are to take, in this life, towards the attainment of reason in the next; so that through all eternity they will lag behind man, who, why we cannot tell, had the power given him of attaining reason in his first mode of existence.

When I treat of the peculiar duties of women, as I should treat of the peculiar duties of a citizen or father, it will be found that I do not mean to insinuate that they should be taken out of their families, speaking of the majority. "He that hath wife and children," says Lord [Francis] Bacon, "hath given hostages to fortune; for they are impediments to great enterprises, either of virtue or mischief. Certainly the best works, and of greatest merit for the public, have proceeded from the unmarried or childless men." I say the same of women. But the welfare of society is not built on extraordinary exertions; and were it more reasonably organised, there would be still less need of great abilities, or heroic virtues.

In the regulation of a family, in the education of children, understanding, in an unsophisticated sense, is particularly required—strength both of body and mind; yet the men who, by their writings, have most earnestly laboured to domesticate women, have endeavored, by arguments dictated by a gross appetite, which satiety had rendered fastidious, to weaken their bodies and cramp their minds. But, if even by these sinister methods they really *persuaded* women, by working on their feelings, to stay at home, and fulfill the duties of a mother and a mistress of a family, I should cautiously oppose opinions that led women to right conduct, by prevailing on them to make the discharge of such important duties the main business of life, though reason were insulted. Yet, and I appeal to experience, if by neglecting the understanding they be as much, nay, more detached from these domestic employments than they could by the most serious intellectual pursuit, though it may be observed, that the mass of mankind will never vigorously pursue an intellectual object, I may be allowed to infer that reason is absolutely necessary to enable a woman to perform any duty properly, and I must again repeat, that sensibility is not reason.

The comparison with the rich still occurs to me; for, when men neglect the duties of humanity, women will follow their example; a common stream hurries them both along with thoughtless celerity. Riches and honours prevent a man from enlarging his understanding, and enervate all his powers by reversing the order of nature, which has ever made true pleasure the reward of labor. Pleasure—enervating pleasure—is, likewise, within women's reach without earning it. But, till hereditary possessions are spread abroad, how can we expect men to be proud of virtue? And, till they are, women will govern them by the most direct means, neglecting their dull domestic duties to catch the pleasure that sits lightly on the wing of time.

52

Declaration of the Rights of Woman and the Female Citizen

OLYMPE DE GOUGES

Olympe de Gouges was the pen name of Marie Gouze (1748–1793), an early feminist, playwright, anti-slavery activist, and political pamphleteer during the French Revolution. She thought it outrageous and unjust that the 1789 Declaration of the Rights of Man and of Citizens (see selection 16) did not recognize women as citizens with political and civil rights. In 1791 de Gouges wrote the following counter-declaration, to which she appended a model marriage contract that took the form of an egalitarian "social contract" between a man and a woman. One of the noteworthy features of her Declaration is the way in which it connects political rights with responsibilities and legal liabilities, as when she proclaims: "Woman has the right to mount the gallows; she should equally have the right to mount the rostrum" to express her opinions publicly. Although her advocacy of sexual equality was considered radical at the time, de Gouges associated with the moderate Girondist faction during the French Revolution and opposed the execution of King Louis XVI. Her criticism of Robespierre and other radical revolutionaries during the Reign of Terror led to her arrest and execution in 1793.

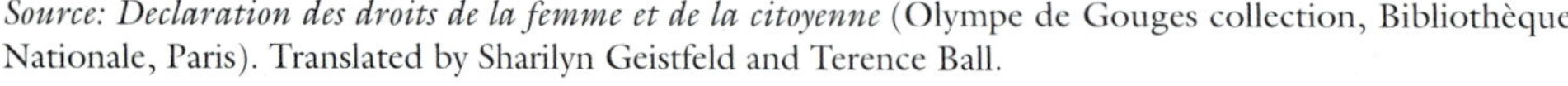
Source: Declaration des droits de la femme et de la citoyenne (Olympe de Gouges collection, Bibliothèque Nationale, Paris). Translated by Sharilyn Geistfeld and Terence Ball.

DECLARATION OF THE RIGHTS OF WOMAN

Preamble

Mothers, daughters, sisters—the female representatives of the nation—demand to be constituted as a national assembly. Considering that ignorance, neglect or scorn for the rights of woman are the sole cause of public miseries and governmental corruption, they have resolved to affirm in a solemn declaration the natural, unchangeable and sacred rights of woman. This declaration, being constantly present to all members of the social body, will always remind them of their rights and duties. It will enable women's acts of power, and those of powerful men, to be judged at all times against the aim of all political institutions and, accordingly, to gain greater respect. By being founded on simple and incontestable principles, female citizens' demands will henceforth tend always to maintain the constitution, good morals, and the happiness of all.

Consequently, the sex that is as superior in beauty as it is in courage during the ordeal of child-birth, recognizes and declares in the presence and under the auspices of the Supreme Being, the following Rights of Woman and of Female Citizens.

1. Woman is born free and remains equal to man in rights. Social distinctions may be based only on common utility.
2. The aim of all political associations is the preservation of the natural and imprescriptible rights of woman and man. These rights are liberty, property, security, and especially resistance to oppression.
3. The principle of all sovereignty resides essentially in the nation, which is nothing but the rejoining of woman and man. No body, nor any individual, may exercise authority which does not emanate expressly from the nation.
4. Liberty and justice consist of restoring all that belongs to others. Hence only man's perpetual tyranny imposes limits on the exercise of women's natural rights. These limits are to be lifted by the laws of nature and reason.
5. The laws of nature and reason forbid all acts that harm society. All acts which are not forbidden by these wise and divine laws may not be prevented, and no one can be forced to do what these laws do not require.
6. Law must be the expression of the general will. All male and female citizens must contribute to its formation either in person or through their representatives. The law should be the same for all: female and male citizens, being equal in the eyes of the law, must be equally eligible for all public honors, positions, and forms of employment according to their ability and without any distinctions other than their virtues and their talents.
7. No woman is exempted. She is to be accused, arrested and detained in cases determined by law. Women, like men, obey this rigorous law.
8. The law should establish only punishments that are strictly and evidently necessary, and no one can be punished except by means of a law established and publicized prior to commission of the crime, and legally applicable to women.
9. Once a woman is found guilty, the law is to be applied rigorously.
10. No one should be disturbed for expressing even his most basic opinions. Woman has the right to mount the gallows; she should equally have the right to mount the rostrum, if what she says does not disturb the public order as established by law.
11. The free communication of thoughts and opinions is one of the most precious rights of woman, since this liberty assures the legitimacy of children to their fathers. Every female citizen may thus say freely, I am the mother of a child who belongs to you, without being forced to conceal the truth due to a barbarous prejudice [against having a child out of wedlock], as long as responsibility is taken for any abuse of this liberty in cases determined by

law [i.e., women are not allowed to lie about the identity of the father].

12. Guaranteeing the rights of woman and citizen requires the guarantee's general utility. This guarantee should be instituted for the advantage of all and not for the particular benefit of individuals entrusted with it.

13. For the support of public authority and paying the expenses of administration, men and women should be taxed equally. Since woman must share all duties and other painful tasks, she should also share the benefits that come from holding offices, honors and jobs.

14. Female and male citizens have the right to verify, either personally or through their representatives, the necessity of public taxes. Female citizens can agree to pay taxes only if they receive an equal share, not only of wealth, but also of public administration, and have a hand in determining the apportionment, assessment, collection and duration of taxes.

15. The mass of women, joined together with men in having to pay taxes, has the right to demand an accounting for his administration from every public agent.

16. Any society in which the guarantee of rights is not assured, or the separation of powers is uncertain, has no constitution. The constitution is null if the majority of people comprising the nation have not cooperated in writing it.

17. Property belongs to both sexes whether united or separated. For each sex this is an inviolable and sacred right. No one can be deprived of property, since it is the true patrimony of nature, except when public necessity, legally certified, obviously requires it. Even then, owners of property confiscated for public purposes must be compensated in advance of its seizure.

53

Letters on the Equality of the Sexes

SARAH GRIMKÉ

Sarah Moore Grimké (1792–1873) and her sister Angelina were largely responsible for linking the campaign against slavery in the United States with the movement for women's rights. Born in Charleston, South Carolina, to a slave-owning family, Grimké knew slavery close up and was revolted by it. She moved north in 1821, where she soon became an active abolitionist. Her sister also joined the cause, and the two became the first women to lecture for the American Anti-Slavery Society. The connection that Grimké drew between slavery and the treatment of women is evident in the following excerpts from her *Letters on the Equality of the Sexes.*

Source: Sarah Grimké, *Letters on the Equality of the Sexes* (Boston: Isaac Knapp, 1838).

LETTER IV

Social Intercourse of the Sexes

Andover, 7th Mo. 27th, 1837

My Dear Friend,

Before I proceed with the account of that oppression which woman has suffered in every age and country from her *protector*, man, permit me to offer for your consideration, some views relative to the social intercourse of the sexes. Nearly the whole of this intercourse is, in my apprehension, derogatory to man and woman, as moral and intellectual beings. We approach each other, and mingle with each other, under the constant pressure of a feeling that we are of different sexes; and, instead of regarding each other only in the light of immortal creatures, the mind is fettered by the idea which is early and industriously infused into it, that we must never forget the distinction between male and female. Hence our intercourse, instead of being elevated and refined, is generally calculated to excite and keep alive the lowest propensities of our nature. Nothing, I believe, has tended more to destroy the true dignity of woman, than the fact that she is approached by man in the character of a female. The idea that she is sought as an intelligent and heaven-born creature, whose society will cheer, refine and elevate her companion, and that she will receive the same blessings she confers, is rarely held up to her view. On the contrary, man almost always addresses himself to the weakness of woman. By flattery, by an appeal to her passions, he seeks access to her heart; and when he has gained her affections, he uses her as the instrument of his pleasure—the minister of his temporal comfort. He furnishes himself with a housekeeper, whose chief business is in the kitchen, or the nursery. And whilst he goes abroad and enjoys the means of improvement afforded by collision of intellect with cultivated minds, his wife is condemned to draw nearly all her instruction from books, if she has time to peruse them; and if not, from her meditations, whilst engaged in those domestic duties which are necessary for the comfort of her lord and master....

LETTER VIII

On the Condition of Women in the United States

Brookline, 1837

My Dear Sister,

I have now taken a brief survey of the condition of woman in various parts of the world. I regret that my time has been so much occupied by other things, that I have been unable to bestow that attention upon the subject which it merits, and that my constant change of place has prevented me from having access to books, which might probably have assisted me in this part of my work. I hope that the principles I have asserted will claim the attention of some of my sex, who may be able to bring into view, more thoroughly than I have done, the situation and degradation of woman. I shall now proceed to make a few remarks on the condition of women in my own country.

During the early part of my life, my lot was cast among the butterflies of the *fashionable* world; and of this class of women, I am constrained to say, both from experience and observation, that their education is miserably deficient; that they are taught to regard marriage as the one thing needful, the only avenue to distinction; hence to attract the notice and win the attentions of men, by their external charms, is the chief business of fashionable girls. They seldom think that men will be allured by intellectual acquirements, because they find, that where any mental superiority exists, a woman is generally shunned and regarded as stepping out of her "appropriate sphere," which, in their view, is to dress, to dance, to set out to the best possible advantage her person, to read the novels which inundate the press, and which do more to destroy her character as a rational creature, than any thing else. Fashionable women regard themselves, and are regarded by men, as pretty toys or as mere instruments of pleasure; and the vacuity of mind, the heartlessness, the frivolity which is the necessary result of this false and debasing estimate of women, can only be fully understood by those who have mingled in the folly and wickedness of fashionable life; and who have been called from such pursuits by the voice of the Lord Jesus, inviting their weary and heavy laden souls to come unto Him and learn of Him, that they may find something worthy of their immortal spirit, and their intellectual powers; that they may learn the high and holy purposes of their creation, and consecrate themselves unto the service of God; and not, as is now the case, to the pleasure of man.

There is another and much more numerous class in this country, who are withdrawn by education or circumstances from the circle of fashionable amusements, but who are brought up with the dangerous and absurd idea, that *marriage* is a kind of preferment; and that to be able to keep their husband's house, and render his situation comfortable, is the end of her being. Much that she does and says and thinks is done in reference to this situation; and to be married is too often held up to the view of girls as the sine qua non [i.e., necessary condition] of human happiness and human existence. For this purpose more than for any other, I verily believe the majority of girls are trained. This is demonstrated by the imperfect education which is bestowed upon them, and the little pains taken to cultivate their minds, after they leave school, by the little time allowed them for reading, and by the idea being constantly inculcated, that although all household concerns should be attended to with scrupulous punctuality at particular seasons, the improvement of their intellectual capacities is only a secondary consideration, and may serve as an occupation to fill up the odds and ends of time. In most families, it is considered a matter of far more consequence to call a girl off from making a pie, or a pudding, than to interrupt her whilst engaged in her studies. This mode of training necessarily exalts, in their view, the animal above the intellectual and spiritual nature, and teaches women to regard themselves as a kind of machinery, necessary to keep the domestic engine in order, but of little value as the *intelligent* companions of men.

Let no one think, from these remarks, that I regard a knowledge of housewifery as beneath the acquisition of women. Far from it: I believe that a complete knowledge of household affairs is an indispensable requisite in a woman's education,—that by the mistress of a family, whether married or single, doing her duty thoroughly and *understandingly,* the happiness of the family is increased to an incalculable degree, as well as a vast amount of time and money saved. All I complain of is, that our education consists so almost exclusively in culinary and other manual operations. I do long to see the time, when it will no longer be necessary for women to expend so many precious hours in furnishing "a well spread table," but that their husbands will forgo some of their accustomed indulgences in this way, and encourage their wives to devote some portion of their time to mental cultivation, even at the expense of having to dine sometimes on baked potatoes, or bread and butter.

I believe the sentiment expressed by the author [Catherine Maria Sedgewick] of "Live and let Live," is true:

> Other things being equal, a woman of the highest mental endowments will always be the best housekeeper, for domestic economy, is a science that brings into action the qualities of the mind, as well as the graces of the heart. A quick perception, judgment, discrimination, decision and order are high attributes of mind, and are all in daily exercise in the well ordering of a family. If a sensible woman, an intellectual woman, a woman of genius, is not a good housewife, it is not because she is either, or all of those, but because there is some deficiency in her character, or some omission of duty which should make her very humble, instead of her indulging in any secret self-complacency on account of a certain superiority, which only aggravates her fault.

The influence of women over the minds and character of *children* of both sexes, is allowed to be far greater than that of men. This being the case by the very ordering of nature, women should be prepared by education for the performance of their sacred duties as mothers and as sisters. A late American writer [Grimké's older brother, Thomas S. Grimké] speaking on this subject, says in reference to an article in the *Westminster Review*:

> I agree entirely with the writer in the high estimate which he places on female education, and have long since been satisfied, that the subject not only merits, but *imperiously demands* a thorough reconsideration. The whole scheme must, in my opinion, be reconstructed. The great elements of usefulness and duty are too little attended to. Women ought, in my view of the subject, to approach to the best education now given to men (I except mathematics and the classics) far more I believe than has ever yet been attempted. Give me a host of educated, pious mothers and sisters, and I will do more to revolutionize a country, in moral and religious taste, in manners and in social virtues and intellectual cultivation, than I can possibly do in double or treble the time, with a similar host of educated men. I cannot but think that the miserable condition of the great body of the people in all ancient communities, is to be ascribed in a very great degree to the degradation of women.

There is another way in which the general opinion, that women are inferior to men, is manifested, that bears with tremendous effect on the laboring class, and indeed on almost all who are obliged to earn a subsistence, whether it be by mental or physical exertion—I allude to the disproportionate value set on the time and labor of men and of women. A man who is engaged in teaching, can always, I believe, command a higher price for tuition than a woman—even when he teaches the same branches, and is not in any respect superior to the woman. This I know is the case inboarding and other schools with which I have been acquainted, and it is so in every occupation in which the sexes engage indiscriminately. As for example, in tailoring, a man has twice, or three times as much for making a waistcoat or pantaloons as a woman, although the work done by each may be equally good. In those employments which are peculiar to women, their time is estimated at only half the value of that of men. A woman who goes out to wash, works as hard in proportion as a wood sawyer, or a coal heaver, but she is not generally able to make more than half as much by a day's work. The low remuneration which women receive for their work, has claimed the attention of a few philanthropists, and I hope it will continue to do so until some remedy is applied for this enormous evil. I have known a widow, left with four or five children, to provide for, unable to leave home because her helpless babes demand her attention, compelled to earn a scanty subsistence, by making coarse shirts at 12½ cents a piece, or by taking in washing, for which she was paid by some wealthy persons 12½ cents per dozen. All these things evince the low estimation in which woman is held. There is yet another and more disastrous consequence arising from this unscriptural notion—women being educated, from earliest childhood, to regard themselves as inferior creatures, have not that self-respect which conscious equality would engender, and hence when their virtue is assailed, they yield to temptation with facility, under the idea that it rather exalts than debases them, to be connected with a superior being.

There is another class of women in this country, to whom I cannot refer, without feelings of the deepest shame and sorrow. I allude to our female slaves. Our southern cities are whelmed beneath a tide of pollution; the virtue of female slaves is wholly at the mercy of irresponsible tyrants, and women are bought and sold in our slave markets, to gratify the brutal lust of those who bear the name of Christians. In our slave States, if amid all her degradation and ignorance, a woman desires to preserve her virtue unsullied, she is either bribed or whipped into compliance, or if she dares resist her seducer, her life by the laws of some of the slave States may be, and has actually been sacrificed to the fury of disappointed passion. Where such laws do not exist, the power which is necessarily vested in the master over his property, leaves the defenceless slave entirely at his mercy, and the sufferings of some females on this account, both physical and mental, are intense. Mr. Gholson, in the House of Delegates of Virginia, in 1832, said, "He really had been under the impression that he owned his slaves. He had lately purchased four women and ten children, in whom he thought he had obtained a great bargain; for he supposed they were his own property, *as were his brood mares.*" But even if any laws existed in the United States, as in Athens formerly, for the protection of female slaves, they would be null and void, because the evidence of a colored person is not admitted against a white, in any of our Courts of Justice in the slave States. "In Athens, if a female slave had cause to complain of any want of respect to the laws of modesty, she could seek the protection of the temple, and demand a change of owners; and such appeals were never discountenanced, or neglected by the magistrate." In Christian America, the slave has no refuge from unbridled cruelty and lust.

S. A. Forrall, speaking of the state of morals at the South, says, "Negresses when young and likely, are often employed by the planter, or his friends, to administer to their sensual desires. This frequently is a matter of speculation, for if the offspring, a mulatto, be a handsome female, 800 or 1000 dollars may be obtained for her in the New Orleans market. It is an occurrence of no uncommon nature to see a Christian father sell his own daughter, and the brother his own sister." The following is copied by the *N.Y. Evening Star* from the *Picayune,* a paper published in New Orleans. "A very beautiful girl, belonging to the estate of John French, a deceased gambler at New Orleans, was sold a few days since for the round sum of $7,000. An ugly-looking bachelor named Gouch, a member of the Council of one of the Principalities, was the purchaser. The girl is a brunette; remarkable for her beauty and intelligence, and there was considerable contention, who should be the purchaser. She was, however, persuaded to accept Gouch, he having made her princely promises." I will add but one more from the numerous testimonies respecting the degradation of female slaves, and the licentiousness of the South. It is from the Circular of the *Kentucky Union,* for the moral and religious improvement of the colored race. "To the female character among our black population, we cannot allude but with feelings of the bitterest shame. A similar condition of moral pollution and utter disregard of a pure and virtuous reputation, is to be found *only without the pale of Christendom.* That such a state of society should exist in a Christian nation, claiming to be the most enlightened upon earth, without calling forth any *particular attention* to its existence, though ever before our eyes and *in our* families, is a moral phenomenon at once unaccountable and disgraceful." Nor does the colored woman suffer alone: the moral purity of the white woman is deeply contaminated. In the daily habit of seeing the virtue of her enslaved sister sacrificed without hesitancy or remorse, she looks upon the crimes of seduction and illicit intercourse without horror, and although not personally involved in the guilt, she loses that value for innocence in her own, as well as the other sex, which is one of the strongest safeguards to virtue. She lives in habitual intercourse with men, whom she knows to be polluted by licentiousness, and often is she compelled to witness in her own domestic circle, those disgusting and heart-sickening jealousies and strifes which disgraced and distracted the family of Abraham. In addition to all this, the female slaves suffer every species of degradation and cruelty, which the most wanton barbarity can inflict; they are indecently divested of their clothing, sometimes tied up and severely whipped, sometimes prostrated on the earth, while their naked bodies are torn by the scorpion lash.

> The whip on WOMAN's shrinking flesh!
> Our soil yet reddening with the stains
> Caught from her scourging warm and
> fresh.

Can any American woman look at these scenes of shocking licentiousness and cruelty, and fold her hands in apathy and say, "I have nothing to do with slavery"? *She cannot and be guiltless.*

I cannot close this letter, without saying a few words on the benefits to be derived by men, as well as women, from the opinions I advocate relative to the equality of the sexes. Many women are now supported, in idleness and extravagance, by the industry of their husbands, fathers, or brothers, who are compelled to toil out their existence, at the counting house, or in the printing office, or some other laborious occupation, while the wife and daughters and sisters take no part in the support of the family, and appear to think that their sole business is to spend the hard bought earnings of their male friends. I deeply regret such a state of things, because I believe that if women felt their responsibility, for the support of themselves, or their families it would add strength and dignity to their characters, and teach them more true sympathy for their husbands, than is now generally manifested,—a sympathy which would be exhibited by actions as well as words. Our brethren may reject my doctrine, because it runs counter to common opinions, and because it wounds their pride; but I believe they would be "partakers of the benefit" resulting from the Equality of the Sexes, and would find that woman, as their equal, was unspeakably more valuable than woman as their inferior, both as a moral and an intellectual being.

LETTER XII

Legal Disabilities of Women

Concord, 9th Mo., 6th, 1837

My Dear Sister,

There are few things which present greater obstacles to the improvement and elevation of woman to her appropriate sphere of usefulness and duty, than the laws which have been enacted to destroy her independence, and crush her individuality; laws which, although they are framed for her government, she has had no voice in establishing, and which rob her of some of her *essential rights.* Woman has no political existence. With the single exception of presenting a petition to the legislative body, she is a cipher in the nation; or, if not actually so in representative governments, she is only counted, like the slaves of the South, to swell the number of law-makers who form decrees for her government, with little reference to her benefit, except so far as her good may promote their own.... I shall confine myself to the laws of our country. These laws bear with peculiar rigor on married women. [The English jurist Sir William] Blackstone, in the chapter entitled "Of husband and wife," says:—

> By marriage, the husband and wife are one person in law; that is, *the very being, or legal existence of the woman* is suspended during the marriage, or at least is incorporated and consolidated into that of the husband under whose wing, protection and cover she performs everything. For this reason, a man cannot grant anything to his wife, or enter into covenant with her; for the grant would be to suppose her separate existence, and to covenant with her would be to covenant with himself; and therefore it is also generally true, that all compacts made between husband and wife when single, are voided by the intermarriage. A woman indeed may be attorney for her husband, but that implies no separation from, but is rather a representation of, her love.

Here now, the very being of a woman, like that of a slave, is absorbed in her master. All contracts made with her, like those made with slaves by their owners, are a mere nullity. Our kind defenders have legislated away almost all our legal rights, and in the true spirit of such injustice and oppression, have kept us in ignorance of those very laws by which we are governed. They have persuaded us, that we have no right to investigate the laws, and that, if we did, we could not comprehend them; they alone are capable of understanding the mysteries of Blackstone, &c. But they are not backward to make us feel the practical operation of their power over our actions.

> The husband is bound to provide his wife with necessaries by law, as much as himself; and if she contracts debts for them, he is obliged to pay for them; but for anything besides necessaries, he is not chargeable.

Yet a man may spend the property he has acquired by marriage at the ale-house, the gambling table, or in any other way that he pleases. Many instances of this kind have come to my knowledge; and women, who have brought their husbands handsome fortunes, have been left, in consequence of the wasteful and dissolute habits of their husbands, in straitened circumstances, and compelled to toil for the support of their families.

> If the wife be indebted before marriage, the husband is bound afterwards to pay the debt; for he has adopted her and her circumstances together.

The wife's property is, I believe, equally liable for her husband's debts contracted before marriage.

> If the wife be injured in her person or property, she can bring no action for redress without her husband's concurrence, and his name as well as her own: neither can she be sued, without making her husband a defendant.

This law that "a wife can bring no action," [Blackstone] &c., is similar to the law respecting slaves. "A slave cannot bring a suit against his master, or any other person, for an injury—his master, must bring it." So if any damages are recovered for an injury committed on a wife, the husband pockets it; in the case of the slave, the master does the same.

> In criminal prosecutions, the wife may be indicted and punished separately, unless there be evidence of coercion from the fact that the offence was committed in the presence, or by the command of her husband. A wife is excused from punishment for theft committed in the presence, or by the command of her husband.

It would be difficult to frame a law better calculated to destroy the responsibility of woman as a moral being, or a free agent. Her husband is supposed to possess unlimited control over her; and if she can offer the flimsy excuse that he bade her steal, she may break the eighth commandment with impunity, as far as human laws are concerned.

> Our law, in general, considers man and wife as one person; yet there are some instances in which she is separately considered, as inferior to him and acting by his compulsion. Therefore, all deeds executed, and acts done by her during her coverture (i.e., marriage) are void, except it be a fine, or like matter of record, in which case she must be solely and secretly examined, to learn if her act be voluntary.

Such a law speaks volumes of the abuse of that power which men have vested in their own hands. Still the private examination of a wife, to know whether she accedes to the disposition of property made by her husband is, in most cases, a mere form; a wife dares not do what will be disagreeable to one who is, in his own estimation, her superior, and who makes her feel, in the privacy of domestic life, that she has thwarted him....

> The husband, by the old law, might give his wife moderate correction, as he is to answer for her misbehavior. The law thought it reasonable to entrust him with this power of restraining her by domestic chastisement. The courts of law will still permit a husband to restrain a wife of her liberty, in case of any gross misbehavior.

What a mortifying proof this law affords, of the estimation in which woman is held! She is placed completely in the hands of a being subject like herself to the outbursts of passion, and therefore unworthy to be trusted with power. Perhaps I may be told respecting this law, that it is a dead letter, as I am sometimes told about the slave laws; but this is not true in either case. The slaveholder does kill his slave by moderate correction, as the law allows; and many a husband, among the poor, exercises the right given him by the law, of degrading woman by personal chastisement. And among the higher ranks, if actual imprisonment is not resorted to, women are not unfrequently restrained of the liberty of going to places of worship by irreligious husbands, and of doing many other things about which, as moral and responsible beings, *they* should be the *sole* judges.

> A woman's personal property by marriage becomes absolutely her husband's, which, at his death, he may leave entirely away from her.

And further, all the avails of her labor are absolutely in the power of her husband. All that she acquires by her industry is his; so that she cannot, with her own honest earnings, become the legal purchaser of any property. If she expends her money for articles of furniture, to contribute to the comfort of her family, they are liable to be seized for her husband's debts: and I know an instance of a woman, who by labor and economy had scraped together a little maintenance for herself and a do-little husband, who was left, at his death, by virtue of his last will and testament, to be supported by charity....

That the laws which have generally been adopted in the United States, for the government of women, have been framed almost entirely for the exclusive benefit of men, and with a design to oppress women, by depriving them of all control over their property, is too manifest to be denied. Some liberal and enlightened men, I know, regret the existence of these laws; and I quote with pleasure an extract from Harriet Martineau's *Society in America* [1837] as a proof of the assertion. "A liberal minded lawyer of Boston, told me that his advice to testators always is to leave the largest possible amount to the widow, subject to the condition of her leaving it to the children; but that it is with shame that he reflects that any woman should owe that to his professional advice, which the law should have secured to her as a right." I have known a few instances where men have left their whole property to their wives, when they have died, leaving only minor children; but I have known more instances of "the friend and helper of many years, being portioned off like a salaried domestic," instead of having a comfortable independence secured to her, while the children were amply provided for.

As these abuses do exist, and women suffer intensely from them, our brethren are called upon in this enlightened age, by every sentiment of honor, religion and justice, to repeal these unjust and unequal laws, and restore to woman those rights which they have wrested from her. Such laws approximate too nearly to the laws enacted by slaveholders for the government of their slaves, and must tend to debase and depress the mind of that being, whom God created as a help meet for man, or "helper like unto himself," and designed to be his equal and his companion. Until such laws are annulled, woman never can occupy that exalted station for which she was intended by her Maker. And just in proportion as they are practically disregarded, which is the case to some extent, just so far is woman assuming that independence and nobility of character which she ought to exhibit.

The various laws which I have transcribed leave women very little more liberty, or power, in some respects, than the slave. "A slave," says the civil code of Louisiana, "is one who is in the power of a master, to whom he belongs. He can possess nothing, nor acquire anything, but what must belong to his master." I do not wish by any means to intimate that the condition of free women can be compared to that of slaves in suffering, or in degradation; still, I believe the laws which deprive married women of their rights and privileges, have a tendency to lessen them in their own estimation as moral and responsible beings, and that their being made by civil law inferior to their husbands, has a debasing and mischievous effect upon them, teaching them practically the fatal lesson to look unto man for protection and indulgence.

54

Seneca Falls Declaration of Sentiments and Resolutions

In 1840 a group of American women delegates were excluded from the World Anti-Slavery Convention in London because of their sex. One member of the delegation, Lucretia Mott (1793–1880), later joined Elizabeth Cady Stanton (1815–1902) in organizing the Seneca Falls (New York) Convention of 1848 to protest the various forms of discrimination to which women were subjected. The Convention adopted the following Declaration of Sentiments and Resolutions, with its intentionally ironic echoes of the U.S. Declaration of Independence.

Source: Elizabeth Cady Stanton, Susan B. Anthony, and Matilda Joslyn Gage, eds., *History of Woman Suffrage*, 2 vols. (New York, 1881), vol. 1, pp. 70–73.

1. DECLARATION OF SENTIMENTS

When, in the course of human events, it becomes necessary for one portion of the family of man to assume among the people of the earth a position different from that which they have hitherto occupied, but one to which the laws of nature and of nature's God entitle them, a decent respect to the opinions of mankind requires that they should declare the causes that impel them to such a course.

We hold these truths to be self-evident: that all men and women are created equal; that they are endowed by their Creator with certain inalienable rights; that among these are life, liberty, and the pursuit of happiness; that to secure these rights governments are instituted, deriving their just powers from the consent of the governed. Whenever any form of government becomes destructive of these ends, it is the right of those who suffer from it to refuse allegiance to it, and to insist upon the institution of a new government, laying its foundation on such principles, and organizing its powers in such form, as to them shall seem most likely to effect their safety and happiness. Prudence, indeed, will dictate that governments long established should not be changed for light and transient causes; and accordingly all experience hath shown that mankind are more disposed to suffer while evils are sufferable, than to right themselves by abolishing the forms to which they are accustomed. But when a long train of abuses and usurpations, pursuing invariably the same object, evinces a design to reduce them under absolute despotism, it is their duty to throw off such government, and to provide new guards for their future security. Such has been the patient sufferance of the women under this government, and such is now the necessity which constrains them to demand the equal station to which they are entitled.

The history of mankind is a history of repeated injuries and usurpations on the part of man toward woman, having in direct object the establishment of an absolute tyranny over her. To prove this, let facts be submitted to a candid world.

He has never permitted her to exercise her inalienable right to the elective franchise.

He has compelled her to submit to laws, in the formation of which she had no voice.

He has withheld from her rights which are given to the most ignorant and degraded men—both natives and foreigners.

Having deprived her of this first right of a citizen, the elective franchise, thereby leaving her without representation in the halls of legislation, he has oppressed her on all sides.

He has made her, if married, in the eye of the law, civilly dead.

He has taken from her all right in property, even to the wages she earns.

He has made her, morally, an irresponsible being, as she can commit many crimes with impunity, provided they be done in the presence of her husband. In the covenant of marriage, she is compelled to promise obedience to her husband, he becoming, to all intents and purposes, her master—the law giving him power to deprive her of her liberty, and to administer chastisement.

He has so framed the laws of divorce, as to what shall be the proper causes, and in case of separation, to whom the guardianship of the children shall be given, as to be wholly regardless of the happiness of women—the law, in all cases, going upon a false supposition of the supremacy of man, and giving all power into his hands.

After depriving her of all rights as a married woman, if single, and the owner of property, he has taxed her to support a government which recognizes her only when her property can be made profitable to it.

He has monopolized nearly all the profitable employments, and from those she is permitted to follow, she receives but a scanty remuneration. He closes against her all the avenues to wealth and distinction which he considers most honorable to himself. As a teacher of theology, medicine, or law, she is not known.

He has denied her the facilities for obtaining a thorough education, all colleges being closed against her.

He allows her in Church, as well as State, but a subordinate position, claiming Apostolic authority for her exclusion from the ministry, and, with some exceptions, from any public participation in the affairs of the Church.

He has created a false public sentiment by giving to the world a different code of morals for men and women, by which moral delinquencies which exclude women from society, are not only tolerated, but deemed of little account in man.

He has usurped the prerogative of Jehovah himself, claiming it as his right to assign for her a sphere of action, when that belongs to her conscience and to her God.

He has endeavored, in every way that he could, to destroy her confidence in her own powers, to lessen her self-respect and to make her willing to lead a dependent and abject life.

Now, in view of this entire disfranchisement of one-half the people of this country, their social and religious degradation—in view of the unjust laws above mentioned, and because women do feel themselves aggrieved, oppressed, and fraudulently deprived of their most sacred rights, we insist that they have immediate admission to all the rights and privileges which belong to them as citizens of the United States.

In entering upon the great work before us, we anticipate no small amount of misconception, misrepresentation, and ridicule; but we shall use every instrumentality within our power to effect our object. We shall employ agents, circulate tracts, petition the State and National legislatures, and endeavor to enlist the pulpit and the press in our behalf. We hope this Convention will be followed by a series of Conventions embracing every part of the country.

2. RESOLUTIONS

WHEREAS, The great precept of nature is conceded to be, that "man shall pursue his own true and substantial happiness." [The English jurist Sir William] Blackstone in his *Commentaries* remarks, that this law of Nature being coeval with mankind, and dictated by God himself, is of course superior in obligation to any other. It is binding over all the globe, in all countries and at all times; no human laws are of any validity if contrary to this, and such of them as are valid, derive all their force, and all their validity, and all their authority, mediately and immediately, from this original; therefore,

Resolved, That all laws which prevent woman from occupying such a station in society as her conscience shall dictate, or which place her in a position inferior to that of man, are contrary to the great precept of nature, and therefore of no force or authority.

Resolved, That woman is man's equal—was intended to be so by the Creator, and the highest good of the race demands that she should be recognized as such.

Resolved, That the women of this country ought to be enlightened in regard to the laws under which they live, that they may no longer publish their degradation by declaring themselves satisfied with their present position, nor their ignorance, by asserting that they have all the rights they want.

Resolved, That inasmuch as man, while claiming for himself intellectual superiority, does accord to woman moral superiority, it is pre-eminently his duty to encourage her to speak and teach, as she has an opportunity, in all religious assemblies.

Resolved, That the same amount of virtue, delicacy, and refinement of behavior that is required of woman in the social state, should also be required of man, and the same transgressions should be visited with equal severity on both man and woman.

Resolved, That the objection of indelicacy and impropriety, which is so often brought against woman when she addresses a public audience, comes with a very ill-grace from those who encourage, by their attendance, her appearance on the stage, in the concert, or in feats of the circus.

Resolved, That woman has too long rested satisfied in the circumscribed limits which corrupt customs and a perverted application of the Scriptures have marked out for her, and that it is time she should move in the enlarged sphere which her great Creator has assigned her.

Resolved, That it is the duty of the women of this country to secure to themselves their sacred right to the elective franchise.

Resolved, That the equality of human rights results necessarily from the fact of the identity of the race in capabilities and responsibilities.

Resolved, That the speedy success of our cause depends upon the zealous and untiring efforts of both men and women, for the overthrow of the monopoly of the pulpit, and for the securing to women an equal participation with men in the various trades, professions, and commerce.

Resolved, therefore, That, being invested by the Creator with the same capabilities, and the same consciousness of responsibility for their exercise, it is demonstrably the right and duty of woman, equally with man, to promote every righteous cause by every righteous means; and especially in regard to the great subjects of morals and religion, it is self-evidently her right to participate with her brother in teaching them, both in private and in public, by writing and by speaking, by any instrumentalities proper to be used, and in any assemblies proper to be held; and this being a self-evident truth growing out of the divinely implanted principles of human nature, any custom or authority adverse to it, whether modern or wearing the hoary sanction of antiquity, is to be regarded as a self-evident falsehood, and at war with mankind.

55

Oppression

MARILYN FRYE

Oppression takes many forms, including those subtle forms that are half-hidden in our language and habits of thought. So argues the feminist author and activist Marilyn Frye (1941–), who teaches philosophy at Michigan State University. Frye is the author of *The Politics of Reality,* from which the following essay is taken, and other essays in feminism and philosophy.

Source: Reprinted by permission from *The Politics of Reality* by Marilyn Frye. Copyright © 1983 by Marilyn Frye, published by The Crossing Press, a division of Ten Speed Press, Berkeley, CA. www.tenspeed.com.

OPPRESSION

It is a fundamental claim of feminism that women are oppressed. The word "oppression" is a strong word. It repels and attracts. It is dangerous and dangerously fashionable and endangered. It is much misused, and sometimes not innocently.

The statement that women are oppressed is frequently met with the claim that men are oppressed too. We hear that oppressing is oppressive to those who oppress as well as to those they oppress. Some men cite as evidence of their oppression their much-advertised inability to cry. It is tough, we are told, to be masculine. When the stresses and frustrations of being a man are cited as evidence that oppressors are oppressed by their oppressing, the word "oppression" is being stretched to meaninglessness; it is treated as though its scope includes any and all human experience of limitation of suffering no matter the cause, degree or consequence. Once such usage has been put over on us, then if ever we deny that any person or group is oppressed, we seem to imply that we think they never suffer and have no feelings. We are accused of insensitivity; even of bigotry. For women, such accusation is particularly intimidating, since sensitivity is one of the few virtues that has been assigned to us. If we are found insensitive, we may fear we have no redeeming traits at all and perhaps are not real women. Thus are we silenced before we begin: the name of our situation drained of meaning and our guilt mechanisms tripped.

But this is nonsense. Human beings can be miserable without being oppressed, and it is perfectly consistent to deny that a person or group is oppressed without denying that they have feelings or that they suffer.

We need to think clearly about oppression, and there is much that mitigates against this. I do not want to undertake to prove that women are oppressed (or that men are not), but I want to make clear what is being said when we say it. We need this word, this concept, and we need it to be sharp and sure.

I

The root of the word "oppression" is the element "press." *The press of the crowd; pressed into military service; to press a pair of pants; printing press; press the button.* Presses are used to mold things or flatten them or reduce them in bulk, sometimes to reduce them by squeezing out the gases or liquids in them. Something pressed is something caught between or among forces and barriers which are so related to each other that jointly they restrain, restrict or prevent the thing's motion or mobility. Mold. Immobilize. Reduce.

The mundane experience of the oppressed provides another clue. One of the most characteristic and ubiquitous features of the world as experienced by oppressed people is the double bind—situations in which options are reduced to a very few and all of them expose one to penalty, censure or deprivation. For example, it is often a requirement upon oppressed people that we smile and be cheerful. If we comply, we signal our docility and our acquiescence in our situation. We need not, then, be taken note of. We acquiesce in being made invisible, in our occupying no space. We participate in our own erasure. On the other hand, anything but the sunniest countenance exposes us to being perceived as mean, bitter, angry or dangerous. This means, at the least, that we may be found "difficult" or unpleasant to work with, which is enough to cost one one's livelihood; at worst, being seen as mean, bitter, angry or dangerous has been known to result in rape, arrest, beating and murder. One can only choose to risk one's preferred form and rate of annihilation.

Another example: It is common in the United States that women, especially younger women, are in a bind where neither sexual activity nor sexual inactivity is all right. If she is heterosexually active, a woman is open to censure and punishment for being loose, unprincipled or a whore. The "punishment" comes in the form of criticism, snide and embarrassing remarks, being treated as an easy lay by men, scorn from her more restrained female friends. She may have to lie and hide her behavior from her parents. She must juggle the risks of unwanted pregnancy and dangerous contraceptives. On the other hand, if she refrains from heterosexual activity, she is fairly constantly harassed by men who try to persuade her into it and pressure her to "relax" and "let her hair down"; she is threatened with labels like "frigid," "uptight," "manhater," "bitch" and "cocktease." The same parents who would be disapproving of her sexual activity may be worried by her inactivity because it suggests she is not or will not be popular, or is not sexually normal. She may be charged with lesbianism. If a woman is raped, then if she has been heterosexually active she is subject to the presumption that she liked it (since her activity is presumed to show that she likes sex), and if she has not been heterosexually active, she is subject to the presumption that she liked it (since she is supposedly "repressed and frustrated"). Both heterosexual activity and heterosexual nonactivity are likely to be taken as proof that you wanted to be raped, and hence, of course, weren't *really* raped at all. You can't win. You are caught in a bind, caught between systematically related pressures.

Women are caught like this, too, by networks of forces and barriers that expose one to penalty, loss or contempt whether one works outside the home or not, is on welfare or not, bears children or not, raises children or not, marries or not, stays married or not, is heterosexual, lesbian, both or neither. Economic necessity; confinement to racial and/or sexual job ghettos; sexual harassment; sex discrimination; pressures of competing expectations and judgments about *women, wives* and *mothers* (in the society at large, in racial and ethnic subcultures and in one's own mind); dependence (full or partial) on husbands, parents or the state; commitment to political ideas; loyalties to racial or ethnic or other "minority" groups; the demands of self-respect and responsibilities to others. Each of these factors exists in complex tension with every other, penalizing or prohibiting all of the apparently available options. And nipping at one's heels, always, is the endless pack of little things. If one dresses one way, one is subject to the assumption that one is advertising one's sexual availability; if one dresses another way, one appears to "not care about oneself" or to be "unfeminine." If one uses "strong language," one invites categorization as a whore or slut; if one does not, one invites categorization as a "lady"—one too delicately constituted to cope with robust speech or the realities to which it presumably refers.

The experience of oppressed people is that the living of one's life is confined and shaped by forces and barriers which are not accidental or occasional and hence avoidable, but are systematically related to each other in such a way as to catch one between and among them and restrict or penalize motion in any direction. It is the experience of being caged in: all avenues, in every direction, are blocked or booby trapped.

Cages. Consider a birdcage. If you look very closely at just one wire in the cage, you cannot see the other wires. If your conception of what is before you is determined by this myopic focus, you could look at that one wire, up and down the length of it, and be unable to see why a bird would not just fly around the wire any time it wanted to go somewhere. Furthermore, even if, one day at a time, you myopically inspected each wire, you still could not see why a bird would have trouble going past the wires to get anywhere. There is no physical property of any one wire, *nothing* that the closest scrutiny could discover, that will reveal how a bird could be inhibited or harmed by it except in the most accidental way. It is only when you step back, stop looking at the wires one by one, microscopically, and take a macroscopic view of the whole cage, that you can see why the bird does not go anywhere; and then you will see it in a moment. It will require no great subtlety of mental powers. It is perfectly *obvious* that the bird is surrounded by a network of systematically related barriers, no one of which would be the least hindrance to its flight, but which, by their relations to each other, are as confining as the solid walls of a dungeon.

It is now possible to grasp one of the reasons why oppression can be hard to see and recognize: one can study the elements of an oppressive structure with great care and some good will without seeing the structure as a whole, and hence without seeing or being able to understand that one is looking at a cage and that there are people there who are caged, whose motion and mobility are restricted, whose lives are shaped and reduced.

The arresting of vision at a microscopic level yields such common confusion as that about the male door-opening ritual. This ritual, which is remarkably widespread across classes and races, puzzles many people, some of whom do and some of whom do not find it offensive. Look at the scene of the two people approaching a door. The male steps slightly ahead and opens the door. The male holds the door open while the female glides through. Then the male goes through. The door closes after them. "Now how," one innocently asks, "can those crazy women's libbers say that is oppressive? The guy *removed* a barrier to the lady's smooth and unruffled progress." But each repetition of this ritual has a place in a pattern, in fact in several patterns. One has to shift the level of one's perception in order to see the whole picture.

The door-opening pretends to be a helpful service, but the helpfulness is false. This can be seen by noting that it will be done whether or not it makes any practical sense. Infirm men and men burdened with packages will open doors for able-bodied women who are free of physical burdens. Men will impose themselves awkwardly and jostle everyone in order to get to the door first. The act is not determined by convenience or grace. Furthermore, these very numerous acts of unneeded or even noisome "help" occur in counterpoint to a pattern of men not being helpful in many practical ways in which women might welcome help. What *women* experience is a world in which gallant princes charming commonly make a fuss about being helpful and providing small services when help and services are of little or no use, but in which there are rarely ingenious and adroit princes at hand when substantial assistance is really wanted either in mundane affairs or in situations of threat, assault or terror. There is no help with the (his) laundry; no help typing a report at 4:00 A.M.; no help in mediating disputes among relatives or children. There is nothing but advice that women should stay indoors after dark, be chaperoned by a man, or when it comes down to it, "lie back and enjoy it."

The gallant gestures have no practical meaning. Their meaning is symbolic. The door-opening and similar services provided are services which really are needed by people who are for one reason or another incapacitated—unwell, burdened with parcels, etc. So the message is that women are incapable. The detachment of the acts from the concrete realities of what women need and do not need is a vehicle for the message that women's actual needs and interests are unimportant or irrelevant. Finally, these gestures imitate the behavior of servants toward masters and thus mock women, who are in most respects the servants and caretakers of men. The message of the false helpfulness of male gallantry is female dependence, the invisibility or insignificance of women, and contempt for women.

One cannot see the meanings of these rituals if one's focus is riveted upon the individual event in all its particularity, including the particularity of the individual man's present conscious intentions and motives and the individual woman's conscious perception of the event in the moment. It seems sometimes that people take a deliberately myopic view and fill their eyes with things seen microscopically in order not to see macroscopically. At any rate, whether it is deliberate or not, people can and do fail to see the oppression of women because they fail to see macroscopically and hence fail to see the various elements of the situation as systematically related in larger schemes.

As the cageness of the birdcage is a macroscopic phenomenon, the oppressiveness of the situations in which women live our various and different lives is a macroscopic phenomenon. Neither can be *seen* from a microscopic perspective. But when you look macroscopically you can see it—a network of forces and barriers which are systematically related and which conspire to the immobilization, reduction and molding of women and the lives we live.

II

The image of the cage helps convey one aspect of the systematic nature of oppression. Another is the selection of occupants of the cages, and analysis of this aspect also helps account for the invisibility of the oppression of women.

It is as a woman (or as a Chicano or as a Black or Asian or lesbian) that one is entrapped.

> "Why can't I go to the park; you let Jimmy go!"
>
> "Because it's not safe for girls."
>
> "I want to be a secretary, not a seamstress; I don't want to learn to make dresses."
>
> "There's no work for negroes in that line; learn a skill where you can earn your living."

When you question why you are being blocked, why this barrier is in your path, the answer has not to do with individual talent or merit, handicap or failure; it has to do with your membership in some category understood as a "natural" or "physical" category. The "inhabitant" of the "cage" is not an individual but a group, all those of a certain category. If an individual is oppressed, it is in virtue of being a member of a group or category of people that is systematically reduced, molded, immobilized. Thus, to recognize a person as oppressed, one has to see that individual as belonging to a group of a certain sort.

There are many things which can encourage or inhibit perception of someone's membership in the sort of group or category in question here. In particular, it seems reasonable to suppose that if one of the devices of restriction and definition of the group is that of physical confinement or segregation, the confinement and separation would encourage recognition of the group as a group. This in turn would encourage the macroscopic focus which enables one to recognize oppression and encourages the individual's identification and solidarity with other individuals of the group or category. But physical confinement and segregation of the group is not common to all oppressive structures, and when an oppressed group is geographically and demographically dispersed the perception of it as a group is inhibited. There may be little or nothing in the situation of the individuals encouraging the macroscopic focus which would reveal the unity of the structure bearing down on all members of that group.

A great many people, female and male and of every race and class, simply do not believe that *woman* is a category of oppressed people, and I think that this is in part because they have been fooled by the dispersal and assimilation of women throughout and into the systems of the class and race which organize men. Our simply being dispersed makes it difficult for women to have knowledge of each other and hence difficult to recognize the shape of our common cage. The dispersal and assimilation of women throughout economic classes and races also divides us against each other practically and economically and thus attaches *interest* to the inability to see: for some, jealousy of their benefits, and for some, resentment of the others' advantages.

To get past this, it helps to notice that in fact women of all races and classes *are* together in a ghetto of sorts. There is a women's place, a sector, which is inhabited by women of all classes and races, and it is not defined by geographical boundaries but by function. The function is the service of men and men's interests as men define them, which includes the bearing and rearing of children. The details of the service and the working conditions vary by race and class, for men of different races and classes have different interests, perceive their interests differently, and express their needs and demands in different rhetorics, dialects and languages. But there are also some constants.

Whether in lower-, middle- or upper-class home or work situations, women's service always includes personal service (the work of maids, butlers, cooks, personal secretaries), sexual service (including provision for his genital sexual needs and bearing his children, but also including "being nice," "being attractive for him," etc.), and ego service (encouragement, support, praise, attention). Women's service work also is characterized everywhere by the fatal combination of responsibility and powerlessness: we are held responsible and we hold ourselves responsible for good outcomes for men and children in almost every respect though we have in almost no case power adequate to that project. The details of the subjective experience of this servitude are local. They vary with economic class and race and ethnic tradition as well as the personalities of the men in question. So also are the details of the forces which coerce our tolerance of this servitude particular to the different situations in which different women live and work.

All this is not to say that women do not have, assert and manage sometimes to satisfy our own interests, nor to deny that in some cases and in some respects women's independent interests do overlap with men's. But at every race/class level and even across race/class lines men do not serve women as women serve men. "Women's sphere" may be understood as the "service sector," taking the latter expression much more widely and deeply than is usual in discussions of the economy.

III

It seems to be the human condition that in one degree or another we all suffer frustration and limitation, all encounter unwelcome barriers, and all are damaged and hurt in various ways. Since we are a social species, almost all of our behavior and activities are structured by more than individual inclination and the conditions of the planet and its atmosphere. No human is free of social structures, nor (perhaps) would happiness consist in such freedom. Structure consists of boundaries, limits and barriers; in a structured whole, some motions and changes are possible, and others are not. If one is looking for an excuse to dilute the word "oppression," one can use the fact of social structure as an excuse and say that everyone is oppressed. But if one would rather get clear about what oppression is and is not, one needs to sort out the sufferings, harms and limitations and figure out which are elements of oppression and which are not.

From what I have already said here, it is clear that if one wants to determine whether a particular suffering, harm or limitation is part of someone's being oppressed, one has to look at it *in context* in order to tell whether it is an element in an oppressive structure: one has to see if it is part of an enclosing structure of forces and barriers which tends to the immobilization and reduction of a group or category of people. One has to look at how the barrier or force fits with others and to whose benefit or detriment it works. As soon as one looks at examples, it becomes obvious that not everything which frustrates or limits a person is oppressive, and not every harm or damage is due to or contributes to oppression.

If a rich white playboy who lives off income from his investments in South African diamond mines should break a leg in a skiing accident at Aspen and wait in pain in a blizzard for hours before he is rescued, we may assume that in that period he suffers. But the suffering comes to an end; his leg is repaired by the best surgeon money can buy and he is soon recuperating in a lavish suite, sipping Chivas Regal. Nothing in this picture suggests a structure of barriers and forces. He is a member of several oppressor groups and does not suddenly become oppressed because he is injured and in pain. Even if the accident was caused by someone's malicious negligence, and hence someone can be blamed for it and morally faulted, that person still has not been an agent of oppression.

Consider also the restriction of having to drive one's vehicle on a certain side of the road. There is no doubt that this restriction is almost unbearably frustrating at times, when one's lane is not moving and the other lane is clear. There are surely times, even, when abiding by this regulation would have harmful consequences. But the restriction is obviously wholesome for most of us most of the time. The restraint is imposed for our benefit, and does benefit us; its operation tends to encourage our *continued* motion, not to immobilize us. The limits imposed by traffic regulations are limits most of us would cheerfully impose on ourselves given that we knew others would follow them too. They are part of a structure which shapes our behavior, not to our reduction and immobilization, but rather to the protection of our continued ability to move and act as we will.

Another example: The boundaries of a racial ghetto in an American city serve to some extent to keep white people from going in, as well as to keep ghetto dwellers from going out. A particular white citizen may be frustrated or feel deprived because s/he cannot stroll around there and enjoy the "exotic" aura of a "foreign" culture, or shop for bargains in the ghetto swap shops. In fact, the existence of the ghetto, of racial segregation, does deprive the white person of knowledge and harm her/his character by nurturing unwarranted feelings of superiority. But this does not make the white person in this situation a member of an oppressed race or a person oppressed because of her/his race. One must look at the barrier. It limits the activities and the access of those on both sides of it (though to different degrees). But it is a product of the intention, planning and action of whites for the benefit of whites, to secure and maintain privileges that are available to whites generally, as members of the dominant and privileged group. Though the existence of the barrier has some bad consequences for whites, the barrier does not exist in a systematic relationship with other barriers and forces forming a structure oppressive to whites; quite the contrary. It is part of a structure which oppresses the ghetto dwellers and thereby (and by white intention) protects and furthers white interests as dominant white culture understands them. This barrier is not oppressive to whites, even though it is a barrier to whites.

Barriers have different meanings to those on opposite sides of them, even though they are barriers to both. The physical walls of a prison no more dissolve to let an outsider in than to let an insider out, but for the insider they are confining and limiting while to the outsider they may mean protection from what s/he takes to be threats posed by insiders—freedom from harm or anxiety. A set of social and economic barriers and forces separating two groups may be felt, even painfully, by members of both groups and yet may mean confinement to one and liberty and enlargement of opportunity to the other.

The service sector of the wives/mommas/assistants/girls is almost exclusively a woman-only sector; its boundaries not only enclose women but to a very great extent keep men out. Some men sometimes encounter this barrier and experience it as a restriction on this movement, their activities, their control of their choices of "lifestyle." Thinking they might like the simple nurturant life (which they may imagine to be quite free of stress, alienation and hard work), and feeling deprived since it seems closed to them, they thereupon announce the discovery that they are oppressed, too, by "sex roles." But that barrier is erected and maintained by men, for the benefit of men. It consists of cultural and economic forces and pressures in a culture and economy controlled by men in which, at every economic level and in all racial and ethnic subcultures, economy, tradition—and even ideologies of liberation—work to keep at least local culture and economy in male control.

The boundary that sets apart women's sphere is maintained and promoted by men generally for the benefit of men generally, and men do benefit from its existence, even the man who bumps into it and complains of the inconvenience. That barrier is protecting his classification and status as a male, as superior, as having a right to sexual access to a female or females. It protects a kind of citizenship which is superior to that of females of his class and race, his access to a wider range of better paying and higher status work, and his right to prefer unemployment to the degradation of doing lower status or "women's" work.

If a person's life or activity is affected by some force or barrier that person encounters, one may not conclude that the person is oppressed simply because the person encounters that barrier or force; not simply because the encounter is unpleasant, frustrating or painful to that person at that time; nor simply because the existence of the barrier or force, or the processes which maintain or apply it, serve to deprive that person of something of value. One must look at the barrier or force and answer certain questions about it. Who constructs and maintains it? Whose interests are served by its existence? Is it part of a structure which tends to confine, reduce, and immobilize some group? Is the individual a member of the confined group? Various forces, barriers and limitations a person may encounter or live with may be part of an oppressive structure or not, and if they are, that person may be on either the oppressed or the oppressor side of it. One cannot tell which by how loudly or how little the person complains.

IV

Many of the restrictions and limitations we live with are more or less internalized and self-monitored, and are part of our adaptations to the requirements and expectations imposed by the needs and tastes and tyrannies of others. I have in mind such things as women's cramped postures and attenuated strides and men's restraint of emotional self-expression (except for anger). Who gets what out of the practice of those disciplines, and who imposes what penalties for improper relaxations of them? What are the rewards of this self-discipline?

Can men cry? Yes, in the company of women. If a man cannot cry, it is in the company of men that he cannot cry. It is men, not women, who require this restraint; and men not only require it, they reward it. The man who maintains a steely or tough or laid-back demeanor (all are forms which suggest invulnerability) marks himself as a member of the male community and is esteemed by other men. Consequently, the maintenance of that demeanor contributes to the man's self-esteem. It is felt as good, and he can feel good about himself. The way this restriction fits into the structures of men's lives is as one of the socially required behaviors which, if carried off, contribute to their acceptance and respect by significant others and to their own self-esteem. It is to their benefit to practice this discipline.

Consider, by comparison, the discipline of women's cramped physical postures and attenuated stride. This discipline can be relaxed in the company of women; it generally is at its most strenuous in the company of men. Like men's emotional restraint, women's physical restraint is required by men. But unlike the case of men's emotional restraint, women's physical restraint is not rewarded. What do we get for it? Respect and esteem and acceptance? No. They mock us and parody our mincing steps. We look silly, incompetent, weak and generally contemptible. Our exercise of this discipline tends to low esteem and low self-esteem. It does not benefit us. It fits in a network of behaviors through which we constantly announce to others our membership in a lower caste and our unwillingness and/or inability to defend our bodily or moral integrity. It is degrading and part of a pattern of degradation.

Acceptable behavior for both groups, men and women, involves a required restraint that seems in itself silly and perhaps damaging. But the social effect is drastically different. The woman's restraint is part of a structure oppressive to women; the man's restraint is part of a structure oppressive to women.

V

One is marked for application of oppressive pressures by one's membership in some group or category. Much of one's suffering and frustration befalls one partly or largely because one is a member of that category. In the case at hand, it is the category, *woman*. Being a woman is a major factor in my not having a better job than I do; being a woman selects me as a likely victim of sexual assault or harassment; it is my being a woman that reduces the power of my anger to a proof of my insanity. If a woman has little or no economic or political power, or achieves little of what she wants to achieve, a major causal factor in this is that she is a woman. For any woman of any race or economic class, being a woman is significantly attached to whatever disadvantages and deprivations she suffers, be they great or small.

None of this is the case with respect to a person's being a man. Simply being a man is not what stands between him and a better job; whatever assaults and harassments he is subject to, being male is not what selects him for victimization; being male is not a factor which would make his anger impotent—quite the opposite. If a man has little or no material or political power, or achieves little of what he wants to achieve, his being male is no part of the explanation. Being male is something he has going *for* him, even if race or class or age or disability is going against him.

Women are oppressed, *as women*. Members of certain racial and/or economic groups and classes, both the males and the females, are oppressed *as* members of those races and/or classes. But men are not oppressed *as men*.

...and isn't it strange that any of us should have been confused and mystified about such a simple thing?

56

Homosexuality: The Nature and Harm Arguments

JOHN CORVINO

One of the aims of the Gay Liberation movement is to enable "gay" or homosexual men and women to be happy, healthy, contributing members of a society that recognizes and accepts differences in sexual orientation among its members. This requires educating or "raising the consciousness" not only of gay people but of their heterosexual or "straight" neighbors and co-workers as well. In the following essay, the philosopher John Corvino (1969–) confronts and criticizes two mainstays of anti-gay attitudes: the assertions that homosexuality is unnatural and harmful. Like other advocates of Gay Liberation, Corvino believes that confronting their own homophobia—that is, their fear of homosexuals and homosexuality—can lead "gays" and "straights" alike to overcome homophobia's stunting and stifling effects.

Source: John Corvino, "Homosexuality: The Nature and Harm Arguments," pp. 137–148 in *The Philosophy of Sex: Contemporary Readings,* ed. Alan Soble (Lanham, MD: Rowman & Littlefield, 1997). Reprinted by permission of the publisher.

HOMOSEXUALITY: THE NATURE AND HARM ARGUMENTS

Tommy and Jim are a homosexual couple I know. Tommy is an accountant; Jim is a botany professor. They are in their early forties and have been together fourteen years, the last five of which they've lived in a Victorian house that they've lovingly restored. Though their relationship has had its challenges, each has made sacrifices for the sake of the other's happiness and the relationship's long-term success.

I assume that Tommy and Jim have sex with each other (although I've never bothered to ask). Furthermore, I suspect that they probably *should* have sex with each other. For one thing, sex is pleasurable. But it is also much more than that: a sexual relationship can unite two people in a way that virtually nothing else can. It can be an avenue of growth, communication, and lasting interpersonal fulfillment. These are reasons most heterosexual couples have sex even if they don't want children, don't want children yet, or don't want additional children. And if these reasons are good enough for most heterosexual couples, then they should be good enough for Tommy and Jim.

Of course, having a reason to do something does not preclude there being an even better reason for not doing it. Tommy might have a good reason for drinking orange juice (it's tasty and nutritious) but an even better reason for not doing so (he's allergic). The point is that one would need a pretty good reason for denying a sexual relationship to Tommy and Jim, given the intense benefits widely associated with such relationships. The question I shall consider in this paper is thus quite simple: Why shouldn't Tommy and Jim have sex?[1]

I. Homosexuality is Unnatural

Many contend that homosexual sex is "unnatural." But what does that mean? Many things that people value—clothing, houses, medicine, and government, for example—are unnatural in some sense. On the other hand, many things that people detest—disease, suffering, and death, for example—are natural in some sense (after all, they occur "in nature"). If the unnaturalness charge is to be more than empty rhetorical flourish, those who levy it must specify what they mean. Borrowing from Burton Leiser, I will examine several possibilities.[2]

1. *What is unusual or abnormal is unnatural.* One meaning of "unnatural" refers to that which deviates from the norm, that is, from what most people do. Obviously, most people engage in heterosexual relationships. But does it follow that it is wrong to engage in homosexual relationships? Relatively few people read Sanskrit, pilot ships, play the mandolin, breed goats, or write with both hands, yet none of these activities is immoral simply because it is unusual. As the Ramsey Colloquium, a group of Jewish and Christian scholars who oppose homosexuality, write, "The statistical frequency of an act does not determine its moral status."[3] So while homosexuality might be "unnatural" in the sense of being unusual, that fact is morally irrelevant.

2. *What is not practiced by other animals is unnatural.* Some people argue, "Even animals know better than to behave homosexually; homosexuality must be wrong." This argument is doubly flawed. First, it rests on a false premise. Numerous studies—including Anne Perkins's study of "gay" sheep and George and Molly Hunt's study of "lesbian" seagulls—have shown that some animals do form homosexual pair-bonds.[4] Second, even if that premise were true, it would not prove that homosexuality is immoral. After all, animals don't cook their food, brush their teeth, attend college, or drive cars; human beings do all these things without moral censure. Indeed, the idea that animals could provide us with our standards, especially our sexual standards, is simply amusing.

3. *What does not proceed from innate desires is unnatural.* Recent studies suggesting a

biological basis for homosexuality have resulted in two popular positions. One side says, "Homosexual people are born that way; therefore it's natural (and thus good) for them to form homosexual relationships." The other side retorts, "No, homosexuality is a lifestyle choice, therefore it's unnatural (and thus wrong)." Both sides seem to assume a connection between the cause or origin of homosexual orientation, on the one hand, and the moral value of homosexual activity, on the other. And insofar as they share that assumption, both sides are wrong.

Consider first the pro-homosexual side: "They are born that way; therefore it's natural and good." This inference assumes that all innate desires are good ones (that is, that they should be acted upon). But that assumption is clearly false. Research suggests that some people are born with a predisposition towards violence, but such people have no more right to strangle their neighbors than anyone else. So while some people may be born with homosexual tendencies, it doesn't follow that they ought to act on them.

Nor does it follow that they ought *not* to act on them, even if the tendencies are not innate. I probably do not have any innate tendency to write with my left hand (since I, like everyone else in my family, have always been right-handed), but it doesn't follow that it would be immoral for me to do so. So simply asserting that homosexuality is a "lifestyle choice" will not show that it is an immoral lifestyle choice.

Do people "choose" to be homosexual? People certainly don't seem to choose their sexual *feelings,* at least not in any direct or obvious way. (Do you? Think about it.) Rather, they find certain people attractive and certain activities arousing, whether they "decide" to or not. Indeed, most people at some point in their lives wish that they could control their feelings more (for example, in situations of unrequited love) and find it frustrating that they cannot. What they *can* control to a considerable degree is how and when they act upon those feelings. In that sense, both homosexuality and heterosexuality involve "lifestyle choices." But in either case, determining the cause or origin of the feelings will not determine whether it is moral to act upon them.

4. *What violates an organ's principal purpose is unnatural.* Perhaps when people claim that homosexual sex is unnatural they mean that it cannot result in procreation. The idea behind the argument is that human organs have various "natural" purposes: eyes are for seeing, ears are for hearing, genitals are for procreating. According to this argument, it is immoral to use an organ in a way that violates its particular purpose.

Many of our organs, however, have multiple purposes. Tommy can use his mouth for talking, eating, breathing, licking stamps, chewing gum, kissing Jim, and it seems rather arbitrary to claim that all but the last use are "natural."[5] (And if we say that some of the other uses are "unnatural, but not immoral," we have failed to specify a morally relevant sense of the term "natural.")

Just because people can and do use their sexual organs to procreate, it does not follow that they should not use them for other purposes. Sexual organs seem very well suited for expressing love, for giving and receiving pleasure, and for celebrating, replenishing, and enhancing a relationship, even when procreation is not a factor. Unless opponents of homosexuality are prepared to condemn heterosexual couples who use contraception or individuals who masturbate, they must abandon this version of the unnaturalness argument. Indeed, even the Roman Catholic Church, which forbids contraception and masturbation, approves of sex for sterile couples and of sex during pregnancy, neither of which can lead to procreation. The Church concedes here that intimacy and pleasure are morally legitimate purposes for sex, even in cases where procreation is impossible. But since homosexual sex can achieve these purposes as well, it is inconsistent for the Church to condemn it on the grounds that it is not procreative.

One might object that sterile heterosexual couples do not *intentionally* turn away from procreation, whereas homosexual couples do. But this distinction doesn't hold. It is no more possible for Tommy to procreate with a woman whose uterus has been removed than it is for him to procreate with Jim. By having sex with either one, he is intentionally engaging in a nonprocreative sexual act.

Yet one might press the objection further: Tommy and the woman *could* produce children if the woman were fertile. Whereas homosexual relationships are essentially infertile, heterosexual relationships are only incidentally so. But what does that prove? Granted, it might require less of a miracle for a woman without a uterus to become pregnant than for Jim to become pregnant, but it would require a miracle nonetheless. Thus it seems that the real difference here is not that one couple is fertile and the other not, or that one couple "could" be fertile (with the help of a miracle) and the other not, but rather that one couple is male-female and the other male-male. In other words, sex between Tommy and Jim is wrong because it's male-male—that is, because it's homosexual. But that, of course, is no argument at all.[6]

5. *What is disgusting or offensive is unnatural.* It often seems that when people call homosexuality "unnatural" they really just mean that it's disgusting. But plenty of morally neutral activities—handling snakes, eating snails, performing autopsies, cleaning toilets, and so on—disgust people. Indeed, for centuries most people found interracial relationships disgusting, yet that feeling, which has by no means disappeared, hardly proves that such relationships are wrong. In sum, the charge that homosexuality is unnatural, at least in its most common forms, is longer on rhetorical flourish than on philosophical cogency.

II. Homosexuality is Harmful

One might argue, instead, that homosexuality is harmful. The Ramsey Colloquium, for instance, argues that homosexuality leads to the breakdown of the family and, ultimately, of human society, and points to the "alarming rates of sexual promiscuity, depression, and suicide and the ominous presence of AIDS within the homosexual subculture."[7] Thomas Schmidt marshals copious statistics to show that homosexual activity undermines physical and psychological health.[8] Such charges, if correct, would seem to provide strong evidence against homosexuality. But are the charges correct? And do they prove what they purport to prove?

One obvious (and obviously problematic) way to answer the first question is to ask people like Tommy and Jim. It would appear that no one is in a better position to judge the homosexual "lifestyle" than those who live it. Yet it is unlikely that critics would trust their testimony. Indeed, the more that homosexual people try to explain their lives, the more critics accuse them of deceitfully promoting an agenda. (It's like trying to prove that you're not crazy. The more you object, the more people think, "That's exactly what a crazy person would say.")

One might instead turn to statistics. An obvious problem with this tack is that both sides of the debate bring forth extensive statistics and "expert" testimony, leaving the average observer confused. There is a more subtle problem as well. Because of widespread antigay sentiment, many homosexual people will not acknowledge their feelings to themselves, much less to researchers.[9] I have known a number of gay men who did not "come out" until their 40s and 50s, and no amount of professional competence on the part of interviewers would have been likely to open their closets sooner. Such problems compound the usual difficulties of finding representative population samples for statistical study.

Yet even if the statistical claims of gay-rights opponents were true, would they prove what they purport to prove? I think not, for the following reasons. First, as any good statistician realizes, correlation does not equal cause. Even if homosexual people were more likely to commit suicide, be promiscuous, or contract AIDS than the general population, it would not follow that their homosexuality causes them to do these things. An alternative and very plausible explanation is that these phenomena, like the disproportionately high crime rates among blacks, are at least partly a function of society's treatment of the group in question. Suppose you were told from a very early age that the romantic feelings that you experienced were sick, unnatural, and disgusting. Suppose further that expressing these feelings put you at risk of social ostracism or, worse yet, physical violence. Is it not plausible that you would, for instance, be more inclined to depression than you would be without such obstacles? And that such depression could, in its extreme forms, lead to suicide or other self-destructive behaviors? (It is indeed remarkable that in the face of such obstacles couples like Tommy and Jim continue to flourish.)

A similar explanation can be given for the alleged promiscuity of homosexuals.[10] The denial of legal marriage, the pressure to remain in the closet, and the overt hostility toward homosexual relationships are all more conducive to transient, clandestine encounters than they are to long-term unions. As a result, that which is challenging enough for heterosexual couples—settling down and building a life together—becomes far more challenging for homosexual couples.

Indeed, there is an interesting tension in the critics' position here. Opponents of homosexuality commonly claim that "marriage and the family...are fragile institutions in need of careful and continuing support."[11] And they point to the increasing prevalence of divorce and premarital sex among heterosexuals as evidence that such support is declining. Yet they refuse to concede that the complete absence of similar support for homosexual relationships might explain many of the alleged problems of homosexuals. The critics can't have it both ways: If heterosexual marriages are in trouble despite the various social, economic, and legal incentives for keeping them together, society should be little surprised that homosexual relationships—which not only lack such supports but face overt attack—are difficult to maintain.

One might object that if social ostracism were the main cause of homosexual people's problems, then homosexual people in more "tolerant" cities like New York and San Francisco should exhibit fewer such problems than their small-town counterparts; yet statistics do not seem to bear this out. This objection underestimates the extent of anti-gay sentiments in our society. By the time many gay and lesbian people move to urban centers, much damage has already been done to their psyches. Moreover, the visibility of homosexuality in urban centers makes homosexual people there more vulnerable to attack (and thus more likely to exhibit certain difficulties). Finally, note that urbanites *in general* (not just homosexual urbanites) tend to exhibit higher rates of promiscuity, depression, and sexually transmitted disease than the rest of the population.

But what about AIDS? Opponents of homosexuality sometimes claim that even if homosexual sex is not, strictly speaking, immoral, it is still a bad idea, since it puts people at risk for AIDS and other sexually transmitted diseases. But that claim is misleading. Note that it is infinitely more risky for Tommy to have sex with a woman who is HIV-positive than with Jim, who is HIV-negative. The reason is simple: It's not homosexuality that's harmful, it's the virus, and the virus may be carried by both heterosexual and homosexual people.

Now it may be the case that in a given population a homosexual male is statistically more likely to carry the virus than a heterosexual female, and thus, from a purely statistical standpoint, male homosexual sex is more risky than heterosexual sex (in cases where the partner's HIV status is unknown). But surely opponents of homosexuality need something stronger than this statistical claim. For if it is wrong for men to have sex with men because their doing so puts them at a higher AIDS risk than heterosexual sex, then it is also wrong for women to have sex with men because their doing so puts them at a higher AIDS risk than homosexual sex (lesbians as a group have the lowest incidence of AIDS). Purely from the standpoint of AIDS risk, women ought to prefer lesbian sex.

If this response seems silly, it is because there is obviously more to choosing a romantic or sexual partner than determining AIDS risk. And a major part of the decision, one that opponents of homosexuality consistently overlook, is considering whether one can have a mutually fulfilling relationship with the partner. For many people like Tommy and Jim, such fulfillment, which most heterosexuals recognize to be an important component of human flourishing, is only possible with members of the same sex.

Of course, the foregoing argument hinges on the claim that homosexual sex can only cause harm indirectly. Some would object that there are certain activities (anal sex, for instance) that for anatomical reasons are intrinsically harmful. But an argument against anal intercourse is by no means tantamount to an argument against homosexuality: neither all nor only homosexuals engage in anal sex. There are plenty of other things for both gay men and lesbians to do in bed. Indeed, for women, it appears that the most common forms of homosexual activity may be *less* risky than penile-vaginal intercourse, since the latter has been linked to cervical cancer.[12]

In sum, there is nothing *inherently* risky about sex between persons of the same gender. It is only risky under certain conditions: for instance, if they exchange diseased bodily fluids or if they engage in certain "rough" forms of sex that could cause tearing of delicate tissue. Heterosexual sex is equally risky under such conditions. Thus, even if statistical claims like those of Schmidt and the Ramsey Colloquium were true, they would not prove that homosexuality is immoral. At best they would prove that homosexual people, like everyone else, ought to take great care when deciding to become sexually active.

Of course, there's more to a flourishing life than avoiding harm. One might argue that even if Tommy and Jim are not harming each other by their relationship, they are still failing to achieve the higher level of fulfillment possible in a heterosexual relationship, which is rooted in the complementarity of male and female. But this argument just ignores the facts. Tommy and Jim are homosexual *precisely because* they find relationships with men (and in particular, with each other) more fulfilling than relationships with women. Even evangelicals (who have long advocated "faith healing" for homosexuals) are beginning to acknowledge that the choice for most homosexual people is not between homosexual relationships and heterosexual relationships, but rather between homosexual relationships and celibacy.[13] What the critics need to show, therefore, is that no matter how loving, committed, mutual, generous, and fulfilling the relationship may be, Tommy and Jim would flourish more if they were celibate. This is a formidable (indeed, probably impossible) task.

Thus far I have focused on the allegation that homosexuality harms those who engage in it. But what about the allegation that homosexuality harms other, nonconsenting parties? Here I will briefly consider two claims: that homosexuality threatens children and that it threatens society.

Those who argue that homosexuality threatens children may mean one of two things. First, they may mean that homosexual people are child molesters. Statistically, the vast majority of reported cases of child sexual abuse involve young girls and their fathers, stepfathers, or other familiar (and presumably heterosexual) adult males.[14] But opponents of homosexuality argue that when one adjusts for relative percentages in the population, homosexual males appear more likely than heterosexual males to be child molesters. As I argued above, the problems with obtaining reliable statistics on homosexuality render such calculations difficult. Fortunately, they are also unnecessary.

Child abuse is a terrible thing. But when a heterosexual male molests a child (or rapes a woman, or commits assault), the act does not reflect upon all heterosexuals. Similarly, when a homosexual male molests a child, there is no reason why that act should reflect upon all homosexuals. Sex with adults of the same sex is one thing; sex with *children* of the same sex is quite another. Conflating the two not only slanders innocent people, it also misdirects resources intended to protect children. Furthermore, many men convicted of molesting young boys are sexually attracted to adult women and report no attraction to adult men.[15] To call such men "homosexual" or even "bisexual" is probably to stretch such terms too far.[16]

Alternatively, those who charge that homosexuality threatens children might mean that the increasing visibility of homosexual relationships makes children more likely to become homosexual. The argument for this view is patently circular. One cannot prove that doing *X* is bad by arguing that it causes people to do *X*, which is bad. One must first establish independently that *X* is bad. That said, there is not a shred of evidence to demonstrate that exposure to homosexuality leads children to become homosexual.

But doesn't homosexuality threaten society? A Roman Catholic priest once put the argument to me as follows: "Of course homosexuality is bad for society. If everyone were homosexual, there would be no society."

Perhaps it is true that if everyone were homosexual, there would be no society. But if everyone were a celibate priest, society would collapse just as surely, and my priest-friend didn't seem to think that he was doing anything wrong simply by failing to procreate. Jeremy Bentham made the point somewhat more acerbically roughly two hundred years ago: "If then merely out of regard to population it were right that [homosexuals] should be burnt alive, monks ought to be roasted alive by a slow fire."[17]

From the fact that the continuation of society requires procreation, it does not follow that *everyone* must procreate. Moreover, even if such an obligation existed, it would not preclude homosexuality. At best it would preclude *exclusive* homosexuality: Homosexual people who occasionally have heterosexual sex can procreate just fine. And given artificial insemination, even those who are exclusively homosexual can procreate. In short, the priest's claim—if everyone were homosexual, there would be no society—is false, and even if it were true, it would not establish that homosexuality is immoral.

The Ramsey Colloquium commits a similar fallacy.[18] Noting (correctly) that heterosexual marriage promotes the continuation of human life, they then infer that homosexuality is immoral because it fails to accomplish the same.[19] But from the fact that procreation is good it does not follow that childlessness is bad, a point that the members of the Colloquium, several of whom are Roman Catholic priests, should readily concede.

I have argued that Tommy and Jim's sexual relationship harms neither them nor society. On the contrary, it benefits both. It benefits them because it makes them happier, not merely in a short-term, hedonistic sense, but in a long-term, "big picture" sort of way. And in turn it benefits society, since it makes Tommy and Jim more stable, more productive, and more generous than they would otherwise be. In short, their relationship, including its sexual component, provides the same kinds of benefits that infertile, heterosexual relationships provide (and perhaps other benefits as well). Nor should we fear that accepting their relationship and others like it will cause people to flee in droves from the institution of heterosexual marriage. After all, as Thomas Williams points out, the usual response to a gay person is not "How come he gets to be gay and I don't?"[20]

Conclusion

As a last resort, opponents of homosexuality typically change the subject: "But what about incest, polygamy, and bestiality? If we accept Tommy and Jim's sexual relationship, why shouldn't we accept those as well?" Opponents of interracial marriage used a similar slippery-slope argument thirty years ago when the Supreme Court struck down antimiscegenation laws.[21] It was a bad argument then and it is a bad argument now.

Just because there are no good reasons to oppose interracial or homosexual relationships, it does not follow that there are no good reasons to oppose incestuous, polygamous, or bestial relationships. One might argue, for instance, that incestuous relationships threaten delicate familial bonds, that polygamous relationships result in unhealthy jealousies (and sexism), or that bestial relationships (do I need to say it?) aren't really "relationships" at all, at least not in the sense we've been discussing. Perhaps even better arguments could be offered (given much more space than I have here). The point is that there is no logical connection between homosexuality, on the one hand, and incest, polygamy, and bestiality, on the other.

Why, then, do critics continue to push this objection? Perhaps it's because accepting homosexuality requires them to give up one of their favorite arguments: "It's wrong because we've always been taught that it's wrong." This argument—call it the argument from tradition—has an obvious appeal: People reasonably favor "tried and true" ideas over unfamiliar ones, and they recognize the foolishness of trying to invent morality from scratch. But the argument from tradition is also a dangerous argument, as any honest look at history will reveal.

To recognize Tommy and Jim's relationship as good is to admit that our moral traditions are imperfect. Condemning people out of habit is easy. Overcoming deep-seated prejudice takes courage.[22]

NOTES

1. Although my central example in the paper is a gay male couple, much of what I say will apply *mutatis mutandis* to lesbians as well, since many of the same arguments are used against them. This is not to say that gay male sexuality and lesbian sexuality are largely similar or that discussions of the former will cover all that needs to be said about the latter. Furthermore, the fact that I focus on a long-term couple should not be taken to imply any judgment about homosexual activity outside of such unions. If the argument of this paper is successful, then the evaluation of homosexual activity outside of committed unions should be largely (if not entirely) similar to the evaluation of heterosexual activity outside of committed unions.
2. Burton, M. Leiser, *Liberty, Justice, and Morals: Contemporary Value Conflicts* (New York: Macmillan, 1986), pp. 51–57.
3. The Ramsey Colloquium, "The Homosexual Movement," *First Things,* March 1994, pp. 15–20.
4. For an overview of some of these studies, see Simon LeVay's *Queer Science* (Cambridge, Mass: M.I.T. Press, 1996), Chap. 10.
5. I have borrowed some items in this list from Richard Mohr's pioneering work, *Gays/Justice* (New York: Columbia University Press, 1988), p. 36.
6. For a fuller explanation of this type of natural law argument, see John Finnis, "Law, Morality, and 'Sexual Orientation,'" *Notre Dame Law Review* 69:5 (1994): 1049–76; revised, shortened, and reprinted in John Corvino, ed., *Same Sex: Debating the Ethics, Science, and Culture of Homosexuality* (Lanham, Md.: Rowman and Littlefield, 1997). For a cogent and well-developed response, see Andrew Koppleman, "A Reply to the New Natural Lawyers," in the same volume.
7. The Ramsey Colloquium, p. 19.
8. Thomas Schmidt, *Straight and Narrow? Compassion and Clarity in the Homosexuality Debate* (Downer's Grove, Ill.: InterVarsity Press, 1995), Chap. 6, "The Price of Love."
9. Both the American Psychological Association and the American Public Health Association have conceded this point. "Reliable data on the incidence of homosexual orientation are difficult to obtain due to the criminal penalties and social stigma attached to homosexual behavior and the consequent difficulty of obtaining representative samples of people to study." See *Amici Curiae* brief in *Bowers v. Hardwick*, Supreme Court No. 85–140 (October Term 1985).
10. It is worth noting that allegations of promiscuity are probably exaggerated. Note that the study most commonly cited to prove homosexual male promiscuity, the Bell and Weinberg study, took place in 1978, in an urban center (San Francisco), at the height of the sexual revolution—hardly a broad sample. (See Alan P. Bell and Martin S. Weinberg, *Homosexualities* [New York: Simon and Schuster, 1978].) The far more recent and extensive University of Chicago study agreed that homosexual and bisexual people "have higher average numbers of partners than the rest of the sexually active people in the study," but concluded that the differences in the mean number

of partners "do not appear very large" (Edward O. Laumann, et al., *The Social Organization of Sexuality: Sexual Practices in the United States* [Chicago: University of Chicago Press, 1994], pp. 314, 316). I am grateful to Andrew Koppelman for drawing my attention to the Chicago study.

11. The Ramsey Colloquium, p. 19.
12. See S. R. Johnson, E. M. Smith, and S. M. Guenther, "Comparison of Gynecological Health Care Problems Between Lesbian and Bisexual Women," *Journal of Reproductive Medicine* 32 (1987): 805–11.
13. See, for example, Stanton L. Jones, "The Loving Opposition," *Christianity Today*, 37:8 (July 19, 1993).
14. See Danya Glaser and Stephen Frosh, *Child Sexual Abuse*, 2nd ed. (Houndmills, Eng.: Macmillan, 1993), pp. 13–17, and Kathleen Coulbourn Faller, *Understanding Child Sexual Maltreatment* (Newbury Park, Calif.: Sage, 1990), pp. 16–20.
15. See Frank G. Bolton, Jr., Larry A. Morris, and Ann E. MacEachron, *Males at Risk: The Other Side of Child Sexual Abuse* (Newbury Park, Calif.: Sage, 1989), p. 61.
16. Part of the problem here arises from the grossly simplistic categorization of people into two or, at best, three sexual orientations: heterosexual, homosexual, and bisexual. Clearly, there is great variety within (and beyond) these categories. See Frederick Suppe, "Explaining Homosexuality: Philosophical Issues, and Who Cares Anyhow?" in Timothy F. Murphy, ed., *Gay Ethics: Controversies in Outing, Civil Rights, and Sexual Science* (New York: Haworth Press, 1994), especially pp. 234–38.
17. "An Essay on 'Paederasty,' " in Robert Baker and Frederick Elliston, eds., *The Philosophy of Sex* (Buffalo, N.Y.: Prometheus, 1984), pp. 360–61. Bentham uses the word "paederast" where we would use the term "homosexual"; the latter term was not coined until 1869, and the term "heterosexual" was coined a few years after that. Today, "pederasty" refers to sex between men and boys, a different phenomenon from the one Bentham was addressing.
18. The Ramsey Colloquium, pp. 17–18.
19. The argument is a classic example of the fallacy of denying the antecedent: If *X* promotes procreation, then *X* is good; *X* does not promote procreation; therefore, *X* is not good. Compare: If *X* is president, then *X* lives in the White House; Chelsea Clinton is not president; therefore Chelsea Clinton does not live in the White House.
20. Actually, Williams makes the point with regard to celibacy, while making an analogy between celibacy and homosexuality. See Thomas Williams, "A Reply to the Ramsey Colloquium," in *Same Sex*.
21. *Loving v. Virginia*, 1967.
22. This paper grew out of a lecture, "What's (Morally) Wrong with Homosexuality?" which I first delivered at the University of Texas in 1992 and have since delivered at numerous other universities around the country. I am grateful to countless audience members, students, colleagues, and friends for helpful dialogue over the years. I would especially like to thank the following individuals for detailed comments on recent drafts of the paper: Edwin B. Allaire, Daniel Bonevac, David Bradshaw, David Cleaves, Mary Beth Mader, Richard D. Mohr, Jonathan Rauch, Robert Schuessler, Alan Soble, James P. Sterba, and Thomas Williams. I dedicate this paper to my partner, Carlos Casillas.

57

I Am Indigenist

WARD CHURCHILL

Native or indigenous peoples have long had their religions, languages, and cultural traditions ridiculed or even suppressed by people of European descent. The aim of native people's liberation is to reclaim and restore a sense of pride, dignity, and cultural identity to indigenous peoples. These aims are manifest in the following essay by Ward Churchill (1947—), Professor of Ethnic Studies at the University of Colorado at Boulder. Churchill is an author, activist, and self-described "indigenist" who places the well-being of native people at the center of his political perspective. He became especially controversial in 2005 as a result of comments he made about the role of U.S. policy in bringing about the terrorist attacks of September 11, 2001. The following essay, however, is based on talks Churchill delivered at Alfred University, the University of Vermont, and California Polytechnic State University at San Luis Obispo in the early 1990s.

Source: Acts of Rebellion: The Ward Churchill Reader (London: Routledge, 2003). Reproduced by permission of Routledge/Taylor & Francis Books, Inc.

I AM INDIGENIST

Notes on the Ideology of the Fourth World

Very often in my writings and lectures, I have identified myself as being "indigenist" in outlook. By this, I mean that I am one who not only takes the rights of indigenous peoples as the highest priority of my political life, but who draws upon the traditions—the bodies of knowledge and corresponding codes of value—evolved over many thousands of years by native peoples the world over. This is the basis upon which I not only advance critiques of, but conceptualize alternatives to the present social, political, economic, and philosophical status quo. In turn, this gives shape not only to the sorts of goals and objectives I pursue, but the kinds of strategy and tactics I advocate, the variety of struggles I tend to support, the nature of the alliances I'm inclined to enter into, and so on.

Let me say, before I go any further, that I am hardly unique or alone in adopting this perspective. It is a complex of ideas, sentiments, and understandings which motivate the whole of the American Indian Movement, broadly defined, here in North America. This is true whether you call it AIM, or Indians of All Tribes (as was done during the 1969 occupation of Alcatraz), the Warriors Society (as was the case with the Mohawk rebellion at Oka in 1990), Women of All Red Nations, or whatever.[1] It is the spirit of resistance which shapes the struggles of traditional Indian people on the land, whether the struggle is down at Big Mountain, in the Black Hills, or up at James Bay, in the Nevada desert or out along the Columbia River in what is now called Washington State.[2] In the sense that I use the term, indigenism is also, I think, the outlook which guided our great leaders of the past: King Philip and Pontiac, Tecumseh and Creek Mary and Osceola, Black Hawk and Big Bear, Nancy Ward, and Satanta, Little Wolf and Red Cloud, Satank and Quannah Parker, Left Hand and Crazy Horse, Dull Knife and Chief Joseph, Sitting Bull, Roman Nose, and Captain Jack, Louis Ríel and Poundmaker and Geronimo, Cochise and Mangus, Victorio, Chief Seattle, and on and on.[3]

In my view, those—Indian and nonindian alike—who do not recognize these names and what they represent have no sense of the true history, the reality, of North America. They have no sense of where they've come from or where they are, and thus can have no genuine sense of who or what they are. By not looking at where they've come from, they cannot know where they're going, or where it is they should go. It follows that they cannot understand what it is they are to do, how to do it, or why.[4] In their confusion, they identify with the wrong people, the wrong things, the wrong traditions. They therefore inevitably pursue the wrong goals and objectives, putting last things first and often forgetting the first things altogether, perpetuating the very structures of oppression and degradation they think they oppose.[5] Obviously if things are to be changed for the better in this world, then this particular problem must itself be changed as a matter of first priority.

In any event, all this is not to say that I think I'm one of the people I have named, or the host of others, equally worthy, who've gone unnamed. I have no "New Age" conception of myself as the reincarnation of someone who has come before. But it *is* to say that I take these ancestors as my inspiration, as the only historical examples of proper attitude and comportment on this continent, this place, this land on which I live and of which I am a part. I embrace them as my heritage, my role models, the standard by which I must measure myself. I try always to be worthy of the battles they fought, the sacrifices they made. For the record, I've always found myself wanting in this regard, but I subscribe to the notion that one is obligated to speak the truth, even if one cannot live up to or fully practice it. As Chief Dan George once put it, I "endeavor to persevere,"[6] and I suppose this is a circumstance which is shared more or less equally by everyone presently involved in what I refer to as "indigenism."

Others whose writings and speeches and actions may be familiar, and who fit the definition of indigenist—or "Fourth Worlder," as we are sometimes called[7]—include Winona LaDuke and John Trudell, Simon Ortiz, Russell Means and Dennis Banks and Leonard Peltier, and Glenn Morris and Leslie Silko, Jimmie Durham, John Mohawk and Oren Lyons, Bob Robideau and Dino Butler, Vine Deloria, Ingrid Washinawatok and Dagmar Thorpe. There are scholars and attorneys like Don Grinde, Pam Colorado, Sharon Venne, George Tinker, Bob Thomas, Jack Forbes, Rob Williams, and Hank Adams. There are poets like Wendy Rose, Adrian Louis, Dian Million, Chrystos, Elizabeth Woody, and Barnie Bush. There are grassroots contemporary warriors, people like Bobby Castillo, Rob Chanate and Regina Brave, Chief Bernard Ominayak, Art Montour and Buddy Lamont, Madonna Thunderhawk, Anna Mae Aquash, Kenny Kane and Joe Stuntz, Minnie Garrow and Bobby Garcia, Dallas Thundershield, Phyllis Young, Andrea Smith and Richard Oaks, Margo Thunderbird, Tina Trudell, and Roque Duenas. And, of course, there are the elders, those who have given, and continue to give, continuity and direction to indigenist expression; I'm referring to people like Chief Fools Crow and Matthew King, Henry Crow Dog and Grampa David Sohappy, David Monongye and Janet McCloud and Thomas Banyacya, Roberta Black-goat and Katherine Smith and Pauline Whitesinger, Marie Leggo and Philip Deer and Ellen Moves Camp, Raymond Yowell, and Nellie Red Owl.[8]

Like the historical figures I mentioned earlier, these are names representing positions, struggles and aspirations which should be well known to every socially conscious person in North America. They embody the absolute antithesis of the order represented by the "Four Georges"—George Washington, George Custer, George Patton, and George Bush—emblemizing the sweep of "American" history as it is conventionally taught in that system of indoctrination the United States passes off as "education." They also stand as the negation of a long stream of "Vichy Indians" spawned and deemed "respectable" by the process of predation, colonialism, and genocide the Four Georges signify.[9]

The names I've named cannot be associated with the legacy of the "Hang Around the Forts," Indians broken, disempowered, and intimidated by their conquerors, the sellouts who undermined the integrity of their own cultures, appointed by the United States to sign away their peoples' homelands in exchange for trinkets, sugar, and alcohol.[10] They are not the figurative descendants of those who participated in the assassination of men like Crazy Horse and Sitting Bull, and who filled the ranks of the colonial police to enforce an illegitimate and alien order against their own.[11] They are not among those who have queued up to roster the régimes installed by the U.S. to administer Indian Country from the 1930s onward, the craven puppets who to this day cling to and promote the "lawful authority" of federal force as a means of protecting their positions of petty privilege, imagined prestige, and often their very identities as native people....[12]

Instead, indigenism offers an antidote to all that, a vision of how things might be which is based in how things have been since time immemorial, and how things must be once again if the human species, and perhaps the planet itself, is to survive much longer. Predicated in a synthesis of the wisdom attained over thousands of years by indigenous, landbased peoples around the globe—the Fourth World or, as Winona LaDuke puts it, "The Host World upon which the first, second and third worlds all sit at the present time"—indigenism stands in diametrical opposition to the totality of what might be termed "Eurocentric Business as usual."[13]

Indigenism

The manifestation of indigenism in North America has much in common with the articulation of what in Latin America is called *indigenismo*. One of the major proponents of this, the Mexican anthropologist/activist Guillermo Bonfil Batalla, has framed its precepts this way: "[I]n America there exists only one unitary Indian civilization. All the Indian peoples participate in this civilization. The diversity of cultures and languages is not an obstacle to affirmation of the unity of this civilization. It is a fact that all civilizations, including Western civilization, have these sorts of internal differences. But the level of unity—the civilization—is more profound than the level of specificity (the cultures, the languages, the communities). The civilizing dimension transcends the concrete diversity."[14]

> The differences between the diverse peoples (or ethnic groups) have been accentuated by the colonizers as part of the strategy of domination.... In contrast to this, the Indian thinking affirms the existence of one—a unique and different—Indian civilization, from which extend as particular expressions the cultures of diverse peoples. Thus, the identification and solidarity among Indians. Their "Indianness" is not a simple tactic postulated, but rather the necessary expression of an historical unity, based in common civilization, which the colonizer has wanted to hide. Their Indianness, furthermore, is reinforced by the common experience of almost five centuries of [Eurocentric] domination.[15]

"The past is also unifying," Bonfil Batalla continues. "The achievements of the classic Mayas, for instance, can be reclaimed as part of the Quechua foundation [in present-day Guatemala], much the same as the French affirm their Greek past. And even beyond the remote past which is shared, and beyond the colonial experience that makes all Indians similar, Indian peoples also have a common historic project for the future. The legitimacy of that project rests precisely in the existence of an Indian civilization, within which framework it could be realized, once the 'chapter of colonialism ends.' One's own civilization signifies the right and the possibility to create one's own future, a different future, not Western."[16]

As has been noted elsewhere, the "new" indigenous movement Bonfil describes equates "colonialism/imperialism with the West; in opposing the West, [indigenists] view themselves as anti-imperialist. Socialism, or Marxism, is viewed as just another Western manifestation."[17] A query is thus posed:

> What, then, distinguishes Indian from Western civilization? Fundamentally, the difference can be summed up in terms of [humanity's] relationship with the natural world. For the West...the concept of nature is that of an enemy to be overcome, with man as boss on a cosmic scale. Man in the West believes he must dominate everything, including other [people around him] and other peoples. The converse is true in Indian civilization, where [humans are] part of an indivisible cosmos and fully aware of [their] harmonious relationship with the universal order of nature. [S]he neither dominates nor tries to dominate. On the contrary, she exists within nature as a moment of it.... Traditionalism thus constitutes a potent weapon in the [indigenous] civilization's struggle for survival against colonial domination.[18]

Bonfil contends that the nature of the indigenist impulse is essentially socialist, insofar as socialism—or what Karl Marx described as "primitive communism"—was and remains the primary mode of indigenous social organization in the Americas.[19] Within this framework, he remarks that there are "six fundamental demands identified with the Indian movement," all of them associated with sociopolitical, cultural, and economic autonomy (or sovereignty) and self-determination:

> First there is land. There are demands for occupied ancestral territories...; demands for control of the use of the land and subsoil; and struggles against the invasion of...commercial interests. Defense of land held and recuperation of land lost are the central demands. Second, the demand for recognition of the ethnic and cultural specificity of the Indian is identified. All [indigenist] organizations reaffirm the right to be distinct in culture, language and institutions, and to increase the value of their own technological, social and ideological practices. Third is the demand for [parity] of political rights in relation to the state.... Fourth, there is a call for the end of repression and violence, particularly that against the leaders, activists and followers of the Indians' new political organizations. Fifth, Indians demand the end of family planning programmes which have brought widespread sterilization of Indian women and men. Finally, tourism and folklore are rejected, and there is a demand for

> true Indian cultural expression to be respected. The commercialization of Indian music and dance are often mentioned...and there is a particular dislike for the exploitation of those that have sacred content and purpose for Indians. An end to the exploitation of Indian culture in general is [demanded].[20]

In North America, these indigenista demands have been adopted virtually intact, and have been conceived as encompassing basic needs of native peoples wherever they have been subsumed by the sweep of Western expansionism. This is the idea of the Fourth World, explained by Cree author George Manuel, founding president of the World Council of Indigenous Peoples:

> The 4th World is the name given to indigenous peoples descended from a country's aboriginal population and who today are completely or partly deprived of their own territory and its riches. The peoples of the 4th World have only limited influence or none at all in the nation state [in which they are now encapsulated]. The peoples to whom we refer are the Indians of North and South America, the Inuit (Eskimos), the Sami people [of northern Scandinavia], the Australian aborigines, as well as the various indigenous populations of Africa, Asia and Oceana.[21]

Manuel might well have included segments of the European population itself, as evidenced by the ongoing struggles of the Irish, Welsh, Basques, and others to free themselves from the yoke of settler state oppression imposed upon them as long as 800 years ago.[22] In such areas of Europe, as well as in "the Americas and [large portions of] Africa, the goal is not the creation of a state, but the expulsion of alien rule and the reconstruction of societies."[23]

That such efforts are entirely serious is readily evidenced in the fact that, in a global survey conducted by University of California cultural geographer Bernard Neitschmann, it was discovered that of the more than one hundred armed conflicts then underway, some eighty-five percent were being waged by indigenous people against the state or states which had laid claim to and occupied their territories.[24] Theo van Boven, former director of the United Nations Division (now Center) for Human Rights, put it in 1981: the circumstances precipitating armed struggle "may be seen with particular poignancy in relation to the indigenous peoples of the world, who have been described somewhat imaginatively—and perhaps not without justification—as representing the fourth world: the world on the margin, on the periphery."[25]

The Issue of Land in North America

What must be understood about the context of the Americas north of the Río Grande is that neither of the states, the U.S. and Canada, which claim sovereignty over the territoriality involved has any legitimate basis at all in which to anchor its absorption of huge portions of that territory. I'm going to restrict my remarks in this connection mostly to the U.S., mainly because that's what I know best, but also because both the U.S. and Canada have evolved on the basis of the Anglo-Saxon common law tradition.[26] So, I think much of what can be said about the U.S. bears utility in terms of understanding the situation in Canada. Certain of the principles, of course, also extend to the situation in Latin America, but there you have an evolution of states based in the Spanish legal tradition, so a greater transposition in terms is required.[27] Let's just say that the shape of things down south was summarized eloquently enough by the Qechuan freedom fighter Hugo Blanco with his slogan, "Land or Death!"[28]

Anyway, during the first ninety-odd years of its existence, the United States entered into and ratified some 400 separate treaties with the peoples indigenous to the area now known as the 48 contiguous states.[29] There are a number of important dimensions to this, but two aspects will do for our purposes here. First, by customary international law and provision of the U.S. Constitution itself, each treaty ratification represented a formal recognition by the federal government that the other parties to the treaties—the native people(*s*) involved—were fully sovereign nations in our right.[30] Second, the purpose of the treaties, from the U.S. point of view, was to serve as real estate documents through which it acquired legal title to specified portions of North American geography from the indigenous nations it was thereby acknowledging already owned it. From the viewpoint of the indigenous nations, of course, the treaties served other purposes: the securing of permanently guaranteed borders to what remained of our national territories, assurance of the continuation of our ongoing self-governance, trade and military alliances, and so forth. The treaty relationships were invariably reciprocal in nature: Indians ceded certain portions of their land to the U.S., and the U.S. incurred certain obligations in exchange.[31]

Even at that, there were seldom any outright sales of land by Indian nations to the U.S. Rather, the federal obligations incurred were usually couched in terms of perpetuity. The arrangements were set up by the Indians so that, as long as the U.S. honored its end of the bargains struck, it would have the right to occupy and use defined portions of Indian land. In this sense, the treaties more resemble rental or leasing agreements than actual deeds. And you know what happens under Anglo-Saxon common law when a tenant violates the provisions of a rental agreement, eh?[32] The point here is that the U.S. has long since defaulted on its responsibilities under every single treaty obligation it ever incurred with regard to Indians.

There is really no dispute about this. In fact, there's even a Supreme Court opinion—the 1903 "*Lone Wolf*" case—in which the good "justices" held that the U.S. enjoyed a "right" to disregard any treaty obligation to Indians it found inconvenient, but that the remaining treaty provisions continued to be binding upon the Indians. This was, the high court said, because the U.S. was the stronger of the nations involved, and thus wielded "plenary" power—this simply means *full* power—over the affairs of the weaker indigenous nations. Therefore, the court felt itself free to unilaterally "interpret" each treaty as being a bill of sale rather than as a rental agreement.[33]

Stripped of its fancy legal language, the Supreme Court's position was (and remains) astonishingly crude. There's an old adage that "possession is nine-tenths of the law." Well, in this case the court went a bit further, arguing that possession was *all* of the law. Further, the highest court in the land went on record arguing bold-faced that, where Indian property rights are concerned, might, and might alone, makes right. The U.S. held the power to simply take Indian land, they said, and therefore it had the "right" to do so.[34] If you think about it, that's precisely what the nazis argued only thirty years later, while the United States displayed the unmitigated audacity to profess outrage and shock that Germany so blatantly transgressed elementary standards of international law and the most basic requirements of human decency.[35] It's not that the United States was wrong in its attitude towards the nazis, it's just that it was a clear case of the pot calling the kettle black.

An almost identical reasoning, that power equals rights, appears to have been at the heart of Sadam Hussein's decision to take Kuwait in 1990—actually, Iraq had a far stronger claim to rights over Kuwait than the U.S. has ever had with regard to Indian country—with the result that President George Bush the 41st immediately began babbling about being "legally required" to wage a "just war" for purposes of "roll[ing] back naked aggression wherever it occurs...freeing occupied territory [and] reinstating legitimate government[s]" that have been "usurped." If he was in any way sincere about *that* proposition, of course, he'd have had to call air strikes in on himself instead of ordering the bombing of Baghdad.[36] Any American Indian could tell you that much, obviously, and the double standard is once again glaring.

Be that as it may, there are a couple of other significant problems with the treaty constructions by which the U.S. allegedly assumed title over its landbase. On the one hand, a number of the ratified treaties can be shown to be fraudulent or coerced, and thus invalid. The nature of the coercion is fairly well known, so let's just say that perhaps a third of the ratified treaties involved direct coercion and shift over to the matter of fraud. This assumes the form of everything from the deliberate misinterpretation of proposed treaty provisions to Indian representatives during negotiations to the Senate's alteration of treaty language after the fact and without the knowledge of the Indian signatories. On a number of occasions, the U.S. appointed its own preferred Indian "leaders" to represent their nations in treaty negotiations.[37] In at least one instance—the 1861 Treaty of Fort Wise—U.S. negotiators appear to have forged the signatures of various Cheyenne and Arapaho leaders.[38] Additionally, there are about 400 treaties which were never ratified by the Senate, and were therefore never legally binding, but upon which the U.S. now asserts its claims concerning lawful use and occupancy rights to, and jurisdiction over, appreciable portions of North America.[39]

When all is said and done, however, even these extremely dubious bases for U.S. title are insufficient to cover the gross territoriality at issue. The federal government itself has tacitly admitted as much during the late 1970s, in the findings of the so-called Indian Claims Commission, an entity created in 1946 to "quiet" title to all illegally taken Indian land within the Lower 48.[40] What the commission did over the ensuing thirty-five years was in significant part to research the ostensible documentary basis for U.S. title to literally every square foot of its claimed territory. It found, among other things, that the U.S. had no legal basis whatsoever—no treaty, no agreement, not even an arbitrary act of Congress—to fully one-third of the area within its boundaries.[41] At the same time, the data revealed that the reserved areas still nominally possessed by Indians had been reduced to about 2.5 percent of the same area.[42]

What this means in plain English is that the United States cannot pretend to even a shred of legitimacy in its occupancy and control of upwards of thirty percent of its "home" territory. And, lest such matters be totally lost in the shuffle, I should note that it has even less legal basis for its claims to the land in Alaska and Hawai'i.[43] Beyond that, its "right"to assert dominion over Puerto Rico, the "U.S." Virgin Islands, "American" Samoa, Guam, and the Marshall Islands tends to speak for itself, don't you think?[44]...

Sharing the Land

There are several closely related matters which should be touched upon before wrapping this up. One has to do with the idea of self-determination. What is meant when indigenists demand an unrestricted exercise of self-determining rights by native peoples? Most nonindians, and even a lot of Indians, seem confused by this and want to know whether it's not the same as complete separation from the U.S., Canada, or whatever the colonizing power may be. The answer is, "not necessarily." The unqualified acknowledgement by the colonizer of the right of the colonized to total separation ("secession") is the necessary point of departure for any exercise of self-determination. Decolonization means the colonized exercise the right as we see fit, in accordance with our own customs, traditions, and appreciations of our needs. We decide for ourselves what degree of autonomy we wish to enjoy, and thus the nature of our political and economic relationship(s), not only with our former colonizers, but with all other nations as well.[45]

My own inclination, which is in some ways an emotional preference, tends to run toward complete sovereign independence, but that's not the point. I have no more right to impose my preferences on indigenous nations than do the colonizing powers; each indigenous nation will choose for itself the exact manner and extent to which it expresses its autonomy, its sovereignty.[46] To be honest, I suspect very few would be inclined to adopt my sort of "go it alone" approach (and, actually, I must admit that part of my own insistence upon it often has more to do with forcing concession of the right from those who seek to deny it than it does with putting it into practice). In the event, I expect you'd see the hammering out of a number of sets of international relations in the "free association" vein, a welter of variations of commonwealth and home rule governance.[47]

The intent here is not, no matter how much it may be deserved in an abstract sense, to visit some sort of retribution, real or symbolic, upon the colonizing or former colonizing powers. It is to arrive at new sets of relationships between peoples which effectively put an end to the era of international domination. The need is to gradually replace the existing world order with one which is predicated in collaboration and cooperation between nations.[48] The only way to ever really accomplish that is to physically disassemble the gigantic state structures which evolved from the imperialist era, structures which are literally predicated in systematic intergroup domination and cannot in any sense exist without it.[49] A concomitant of this disassembly is the inculcation of voluntary, consensual interdependence between formerly dominated and dominating nations, and a redefinition of the word "nation" itself to conform to its original meaning; bodies of people bound together by their bioregional and other natural cultural affinities.[50]

This last point is, it seems to me, crucially important. Partly, that's because of the persistent question of who it is who gets to remain in Indian Country once land restoration and consolidation has occurred. The answer, I think, is anyone who wants to, up to a point. By "anyone who wants to," I mean anyone who wishes to apply for formal citizenship within an indigenous nation, thereby accepting the idea that s/he is placing him/herself under unrestricted Indian jurisdiction and will thus be required to abide by native law.[51] Funny thing; I hear a lot of nonindians asserting that they reject nearly every aspect of U.S. law, but the idea of placing themselves under anyone else's jurisdiction seems to leave them pretty queasy. I have no idea how many nonindians might actually opt for citizenship in an indigenous nation when push comes to shove, but I expect there will be some. And I suspect some Indians have been so indoctrinated by the dominant society that they'll elect to remain within it rather than availing themselves of their own citizenship. So there'll be a bit of a trade-off in this respect.

Now, there's the matter of the process working only "up to a point." That point is very real. It is defined, not by political or racial considerations, but by the carrying capacity of the land. The population of indigenous nations everywhere has always been determined by the number of people who could be sustained in a given environment or bioregion without overpowering and thereby destroying that environment.[52] A very carefully calculated balance—one which was calibrated to the fact that in order to enjoy certain sorts of material comfort, human population had to be kept at some level below saturation—was always maintained between the number of humans and the rest of the habitat. In order to accomplish this, native peoples have always incorporated into the very core of our spiritual traditions the concept that all life forms and the earth itself possess rights equal to those enjoyed by humans.[53]

Rephrased, this means it would be a violation of a fundament of traditional indigenous law to supplant or eradicate another species, whether animal or plant, in order to make way for some greater number of humans, or to increase the level of material comfort available to those who already exist. Conversely, it is a fundamental requirement of traditional law that each human accept his or her primary responsibility, that of maintaining the balance and harmony of the natural order *as it is encountered*.[54] One is essentially free to do anything one wants in an indigenous society so long as this cardinal rule is adhered to. The bottom line with regard to the maximum population limit of Indian Country as it has been sketched in this presentation is some very finite number. My best guess is that five million people would be pushing things right to the limit.[55] Whatever. Citizens can be admitted until that point has been reached and no more. And the population cannot increase beyond that number over time, no matter at what rate. Carrying capacity is a fairly constant reality; it tends to change over thousands of years, when it changes at all.

Population and Environment

What I'm going to say next will probably startle a few people (as if what's been said already hasn't). I think this principle of population restraint is the single most important example Native North America can set for the rest of humanity. It is *the* thing which it is most crucial for others to emulate. Check it out. I recently heard that Japan, a small island nation which has so many people that they're literally tumbling into the sea, and which has exported about half again as many people as live on the home islands, is expressing "official concern" that its birth rate has declined very slightly over the last few years. The worry is that in thirty years there'll be fewer workers available to "produce," and thus to "consume" whatever it is that's produced.[56]

Ever ask yourself what it is that's used in "producing" something? Or what it is that's being "consumed"? Yeah. You got it. Nature is being consumed, and with it the ingredients which allow ongoing human existence. It's true that nature can replenish some of what's consumed, but only at a certain rate. That rate has been vastly exceeded, and the extent of excess is increasing by the moment. An overburgeoning humanity is killing the natural world, and thus itself. It's no more complicated than that.[57]

Here we are in the midst of a rapidly worsening environmental crisis of truly global proportions, every last bit of it attributable to a wildly accelerating human consumption of the planetary habitat, and you have one of the world's major offenders expressing grave concern that the rate at which it is able to consume might actually drop a notch or two. *Think* about it. I suggest that this attitude signifies nothing so much as stark, staring madness. It is insane: suicidally, homicidally, ecocidally, *omnicidally* insane. No, I'm not being rhetorical. I meant what I've just said in the most literal way possible,[58] but I don't want to convey the misimpression that I see the Japanese as being in this respect unique. Rather, I intend them to serve as merely an illustration of a far broader and quite virulent pathology called "industrialism"—or, lately, "postindustrialism"—a sickness centered in an utterly obsessive drive to dominate and destroy the natural order. (Words like "production," "consumption," "development," and "progress" are mere code words masking this reality.)[59]

It's not only the industrialized countries which are afflicted with this disease. One byproduct of the past five centuries of European expansionism and the resulting hegemony of eurocentric ideology is that the latter has been drummed into the consciousness of *most* peoples to the point where it is now subconsciously internalized. Everywhere, you find people thinking it "natural" to view themselves as the incarnation of God on earth—i.e., "created in the image of God"—and thus duty-bound to "exercise dominion over nature" in order that they can "multiply, grow plentiful, and populate the land" in ever increasing "abundance."[60]

NOTES

1. For what is probably the best available account of AIM, IAT, and WARN, see Paul Chaat Smith and Robert Allen Warrior, *Like a Hurricane: The American Indian Movement from Alcatraz to Wounded Knee* (New York: New Press, 1996). On Oka, see Gerald R. Alfred, *Heeding the Voices of Our Ancestors: Kahnewake Mohawk Politics and the Rise of Native Nationalism* (New York: Oxford University Press, 1995); Linda Pertusati, *In Defense of Mohawk Land: Ethnopolitical Conflict in Native North America* (Albany: State University of New York Press, 1997).
2. On James Bay, see Boyce Richardson's *Strangers Devour the Land* (Post Mills, VT: Chelsea Green, [2nd ed.] 1991). Also see the chapter entitled "Hydrological Rape in Northern Canada," in my *Struggle for the Land: Native North American Resistance to Genocide, Ecocide and Colonization* (Winnipeg: Arbeiter Ring, [2nd ed.] 1999), esp. pp. 298–309.
3. While it is hardly complete, a good point of departure for learning about many of the individuals named would be Alvin M. Josephy, Jr.'s *The Patriot Chiefs* (New York: Viking, 1961).
4. For implications, see Michel-Rolph Trouillot, *Silencing the Past: Power and the Production of History* (Boston: Beacon Press, 1995).

5. This problem is taken up in "Indians 'R' Us," herein. [Churchill refers here to another essay in his *Acts of Rebellion*—Eds.]
6. From a movie, *The Outlaw Josie Wales* (1976).
7. George Manuel and Michael Posluns, *The Fourth World: An Indian Reality* (New York: Free Press, 1974); Bernard Neitschmann, "The Fourth World: Nations versus States," in George J. Demko and William B. Wood, eds., *Reordering the World: Geopolitical Perspectives on the 21st Century* (Boulder, CO: Westview Press, 1994), pp. 225–42.
8. The bulk of those mentioned, and a number of others as well, appear in Roger Moody, ed., *The Indigenous Voice: Visions and Realities,* 2 vols. (London: Zed Books, 1988). Also see Alexander Ewen, ed., *Voice of Indigenous Peoples: Native People Address the United Nations* (Santa Fe, NM: Clear Light, 1994).
9. The term "Vichy Indians" comes from Russell Means, during a lecture at the University of Colorado/Denver in 1984.
10. For partial contextualization, see William E. Unrau, ed., *The White Man's Wicked Water: The Alcohol Trade and Prohibition in Indian Country, 1802–1892* (Lawrence: University Press of Kansas, 1996).
11. William Thomas Hagan, *Indian Police and Judges: Experiments in Acculturation and Control* (New Haven, CT: Yale University Press, 1966).
12. Kenneth R. Philp, ed., *Indian Self-Rule: First-Hand Accounts of Indian/White Relations from Roosevelt to Reagan* (Salt Lake City: Howe Bros., 1986).
13. See Winona LaDuke's "Natural to Synthetic and Back Again," the preface to my *Marxism and Native Americans* (Boston: South End Press 1983), pp. i–viii.
14. Guillermo Bonfil Batalla, *Utopía y Revolución: El Pensamiento Político Contemporáneo de los Indios en América Latina* (Mexico City: Editorial Nueva Imagen, 1981), p. 37; translation by Roxanne Dunbar Ortiz.
15. Ibid., pp. 37–38.
16. Ibid., p. 38.
17. Roxanne Dunbar Ortiz, *Indians of the Americas: Human Rights and Self-Determination* (London: Zed Books, 1984), p. 83.
18. Ibid., p. 84.
19. See Karl Marx, *Pre-Capitalist Economic Formation* (London: Lawrence and Wishart, 1964). Also see "False Promises," herein.
20. Dunbar Ortiz, *Indians of the Americas,* p. 85.
21. Manuel and Posluns, *Fourth World,* p. 1.
22. On the Irish and Welsh struggles, see Peter Berresford Ellis, *The Celtic Revolution: A Study in Anti-Imperialism* (Talybont, Wales: Y Lolfa, 1985). On the Basques, see Robert P. Clark, *Negotiating with ETA: Obstacles to Peace in the Basque Country, 1975–1988* (Reno: University of Nevada Press, 1990).
23. Dunbar Ortiz, *Indians of the Americas,* p. 89.
24. Bernard Neitschmann, "The Third World War: Militarism and Indigenous Peoples," *Cultural Survival Quarterly,* Vol. 11, No. 2, 1987. Also see his "Fourth World."
25. Geneva Offices of the United Nations, Press Release, Aug. 17, 1981 (Hr/1080).
26. See "The Law Stood Squarely on Its Head," herein.
27. On the Iberian legal tradition, see James Brown Scott, *The Spanish Origin of International Law* (Oxford, U.K.: Clarendon Press, 1934).
28. Hugo Blanco, *Land or Death: The Peasant Struggle in Peru* (New York: Pathfinder Press, 1972). Blanco was a marxist, and thus sought to pervert indigenous issues through rigid class analysis—defining Indians as "peasants" rather than by nationality—but his identification of land as the central issue was and is nonetheless valid.
29. The complete texts of 371 of these ratified treaties are compiled in Charles J. Kappler's *American Indian Treaties, 1778–1883* (New York: Interland, 1973). Additional treaty texts, plus a broad range of other relevant instruments, will be found in Vine Deloria, Jr., and Raymond J. DeMallie, *Documents of American Indian Diplomacy: Treaties, Agreements, and Conventions, 1775–1979,* 2 vols. (Norman: University of Oklahoma Press, 1999).
30. The constitutional provision comes at Article I, Section 10. Codification of customary international law in this connection is explained in Ian Sinclair's *The Vienna Convention on the Law of Treaties* (Manchester, U.K.: Manchester University Press, [2nd ed.] 1984).

31. See generally, Sidney L. Harring, *Crow Dog's Case: American Indian Sovereignty, Tribal Law, and United States Law in the Nineteenth Century* (Cambridge, U.K.: Cambridge University Press, 1994); David E. Wilkins, *American Indian Sovereignty and the U.S. Supreme Court* (Austin: University of Texas Press, 1997).
32. Anyone wishing to dig into this one is referred to Cornelius J. Moynihan's *Introduction to the Law of Real Property: An Historical Background of the Common Law of Real Property* (St. Paul, MN: West Legal Studies, 1987).
33. *"Lone Wolf" v. Hitchcock* (187 U.S. 553 [1903]). For analysis, see Blue Clark, *"Lone Wolf" v. Hitchcock: Treaty Rights and Indian Law at the End of the Nineteenth Century* (Lincoln: University of Nebraska Press, 1999).
34. An even more straightforward enunciation of this fetid doctrine was made by the Supreme Court in its *Tee-Hit-Ton* opinion (348 U.S. 272 [1955]). For analysis, see Wilkins, *American Indian Sovereignty*, pp. 166–85.
35. See Quincy Wright, "The Law of the Nuremberg Trials," *American Journal of International Law*, No. 41, Jan. 1947. Also see "Bringing the Law Home," herein.
36. A fuller articulation of this thesis may be found in my "On Gaining 'Moral High Ground': An Ode to George Bush and the 'New World Order,' " in Cynthia Peters, ed., *Collateral Damage: The "New World Order" at Home and Abroad* (Boston: South End Press, 1992), pp. 359–72.
37. For the origins of such practices, see Dorothy V. Jones, *License for Empire: Colonialism by Treaty in Early America* (Chicago: University of Chicago Press, 1982). For a good survey of U.S. adaptations, see Donald Worcester, ed., *Forked Tongues and Broken Treaties* (Caldwell, ID: Caxton, 1975).
38. The travesty at Fort Wise is adequately covered in Stan Hoig's *The Sand Creek Massacre* (Norman: University of Oklahoma Press, 1961), pp. 13–17.
39. Deloria and DeMallie, *Indian Diplomacy, Vol. 2*, pp. 1237–1473.
40. See my "Charades, Anyone? The Indian Claims Commission in Context," *American Indian Culture and Research Journal*, Vol. 24, No. 1, 2000.
41. See "The Earth Is Our Mother," herein.
42. The percentage is arrived at by juxtaposing the approximately fifty million acres within the current reservation landbase to the more than two *billion* acres of the lower 48 states. According to the Indian Claims Commission findings, Indians actually retain unfettered legal title to about 750 million acres of the continental U.S.; see Russel L. Barsh, "Indian Land Claims Policy in the United States," *North Dakota Law Review*, No. 58, 1982.
43. Concerning Alaska, see M. C. Berry, *The Alaska Pipeline: The Politics of Oil and Native Land Claims* (Bloomington: Indiana University Press, 1975). On Hawai'i, see Haunani-Kay Trask, *From a Native Daughter: Colonialism and Sovereignty in Hawai'i* (Honolulu: University of Hawai'i Press, [2nd ed.] 1999).
44. Those with questions should refer to Arnold Leibowitz, *Defining Status: A Comprehensive Analysis of U.S. Territorial Relations* (The Hague: Martinus Nijhoff, 1990).
45. For one of the best elaborations of these principles, see Ved Nanda, "Self-Determination in International Law: Validity of Claims to Secede," *Case Western Reserve Journal of International Law*, No. 13 1981. Also see Lee C. Buchheit, *Secession: The Legitimacy of Self-Determination* (New Haven, CT: Yale University Press, 1978).
46. A very clear delineation of the available options will be found in Hannum Hurst's *Autonomy, Sovereignty, and Self-Determination* (Philadelphia: University of Pennsylvania Press, 1990).
47. A prototype for this sort of arrangement exists between Greenland (populated mainly by Inuits) and Denmark. See Gudmundur Alfredson, "Greenland and the Law of Political Decolonization," *German Yearbook on International Law*, No. 25, 1982.
48. This is essentially the idea advanced by Richard Falk in an essay entitled "Anarchism and World Order," in his *End of World Order*. Also see Harvey Starr, *Anarchy, Order and Integration: How to Manage Interdependence* (Ann Arbor: University of Michigan Press, 1999).
49. A good argument as to why megastates will "inevitably fall apart" is made by Martin Van Creveld in his *The Rise and Decline of the State* (Cambridge, U.K.: Cambridge University Press, 1999). Also see Leopold Kohr, *The Breakdown of Nations* (New York: E. P. Dutton, 1975).

50. Barth, *Ethnic Boundaries;* Connor, *Ethnonationalism;* John Hutcheson, *The Dynamics of Cultural Nationalism* (New York: HarperCollins, [2nd ed.] 1994); Kirkpatrick Sale, *Dwellers in the Land: The Bioregional Vision* (Philadelphia: New Society, 1991).

51. This is the basic idea set forth in "TREATY." Also see Reinhard Bendix, *Nation-Building and Citizenship* (Berkeley: University of California Press, 1964).

52. The concepts at issue here are brought out very well in William R. Catton, Jr., *Overshoot: The Ecological Basis of Revolutionary Change* (Urbana: University of Illinois Press, 1982).

53. Such ideas have even caught on, at least as questions, among some Euroamerican legal practitioners; see Christopher D. Stone, *Should Trees Have Standing? Towards Legal Rights for Natural Objects* (Los Altos, CA: William Kaufman, 1972).

54. For further elaboration, see Vine Deloria, Jr., *God Is Red* (New York: Delta, 1973); "Native American Spirituality" in his *For This Land: Writings on Religion in America* (New York: Routledge, 1999), pp. 130–34. Also see "False Promises," herein.

55. I base my estimate in large part upon the regional preinvasion demographic estimates extrapolated by Henry F. Dobyns towards the end of his *Their Number Become Thinned.*

56. CNN "Dollars and Cents" reportage, May 27, 1992. Interestingly, the same sort of thinking has marked the analyses of marxists with regard to the "developmental problems" confronting Africa; see, e.g., Gérard Chaliand, *Revolution in the Third World: Myths and Prospects* (New York: Viking, 1977), p. 114.

57. The idea is developed in detail in Jeremy Rifkin's *Entropy: A New World View* (New York: Viking, 1980). It should be noted, however, that the worldview in question is hardly "new," since indigenous peoples have held it all along; see, e.g., Russell Means, "The Same Old Song," in my *Marxism and Native Americans* (Boston: South End Press, 1983), p. 22.

58. I am, however, borrowing the "controversial" definition of insanity offered by R. D. Laing in his *The Politics of Experience* (New York: Ballantine, 1967).

59. One good summary of this, utilizing extensive native sources—albeit many of them go unattributed—is Jerry Mander's *In the Absence of the Sacred: The Failure of Technology and the Survival of Indian Nations* (San Francisco: Sierra Club Books, 1991).

60. If this sounds a bit scriptural, it is meant to. A number of us see a direct line of continuity from the core imperatives of Judeochristian theology, through the capitalist secularization of church doctrine and its alleged marxian antithesis, right on through to the burgeoning technotopianism of today. This is a major conceptual cornerstone of what indigenists view as eurocentrism (a virulently anthropocentric outlook in its essence); see Vine Deloria, Jr., "Secularism, Civil Religion, and the Religious Freedom of American Indians," in his *For This Land,* pp. 218–28.

58

Liberation Theology

GUSTAVO GUTIERREZ

An influential movement within Christianity, especially the Roman Catholic Church, the "theology of liberation" views Jesus Christ as the champion and liberator of poor and oppressed people. Christ's teachings, as interpreted by liberation theologians such as Father Gustavo Gutierrez (1927–) of Peru, are aimed as much at social justice in this world as salvation in the next. Far from being "normal" or "natural" features of human life, poverty and oppression are the products of sin—of greed and lust for power—among the affluent. Liberation theology aims at raising the consciousness not only of the poor but also of affluent people, who are asked to confront and overcome their own sin by exercising the "option for the poor."

Source: A Theology of Liberation, 2nd ed., by Gustavo Gutierrez, translated by Sister Caridad Inda and John Eagleson. Copyright ©1988. Reprinted by permission of Orbis Books.

LIBERATION AND DEVELOPMENT

From the Critique of Developmentalism to Social Revolution

The term *development* has synthesized the aspirations of poor peoples during the last few decades. Recently, however, it has become the object of severe criticism due both to the deficiencies of the development policies proposed to the poor countries to lead them out of their underdevelopment and also to the lack of concrete achievements of the interested governments. This is the reason why *developmentalism (desarrollismo)*, a term derived from *development (desarrollo)*, is now used in a pejorative sense, especially in Latin America.

Much has been said in recent times about development. Poor countries competed for the help of the rich countries. There were even attempts to create a certain development mystique. Support for development was intense in Latin America in the '50s, producing high expectations. But since the supporters of development did not attack the roots of the evil, they failed and caused instead confusion and frustration.

One of the most important reasons for this turn of events is that development—approached from an economic and modernizing point of view—has been frequently promoted by international organizations closely linked to groups and governments which control the world economy. The changes encouraged were to be achieved within the formal structure of the existing institutions without challenging them. Great care was exercised, therefore, not to attack the interests of large international economic powers nor those of their natural allies, the ruling domestic interest groups. Furthermore, the so-called changes were often nothing more than new and underhanded ways of increasing the power of strong economic groups.

Developmentalism thus came to be synonymous with *reformism* and modernization, that is to say, synonymous with timid measures, really ineffective in the long run and counterproductive to achieving a real transformation. The poor countries are becoming ever more clearly aware that their underdevelopment is only the by-product of the development of other countries, because of the kind of relationship which exists between the rich and the poor countries. Moreover, they are realizing that their own development will come about only with a struggle to break the domination of the rich countries.

This perception sees the conflict implicit in the process. Development must attack the root causes of the problems and among them the deepest is economic, social, political and cultural dependence of some countries upon others—an expression of the domination of some social classes over others. Attempts to bring about changes within the existing order have proven futile. This analysis of the situation is at the level of scientific rationality. Only a radical break from the status quo, that is, a profound transformation of the private property system, access to power of the exploited class, and a social revolution that would break this dependence would allow for the change to a new society, a socialist society—or at least allow that such a society might be possible.

In this light, to speak about the process of *liberation* begins to appear more appropriate and richer in human content. Liberation in fact expresses the inescapable moment of radical change which is foreign to the ordinary use of the term *development*. Only in the context of such a process can a policy of development be effectively implemented, have any real meaning, and avoid misleading formulations.

Man, the Master of His Own Destiny

To characterize the situation of the poor countries as dominated and oppressed leads one to speak of economic, social, and political liberation. But we are dealing here with a much more integral and profound understanding of human existence and its historical future.

A broad and deep aspiration for liberation inflames the history of mankind in our day, liberation from all that limits or keeps man from self-fulfillment, liberation from all impediments to the exercise of his freedom. Proof of this is the awareness of new and subtle forms of oppression in the heart of advanced industrial societies, which often offer themselves as models to the underdeveloped countries. In them subversion does not appear as a protest against poverty, but rather against wealth. The context in the rich countries, however, is quite different from that of the poor countries: we must beware of all kinds of imitations as well as new forms of imperialism—revolutionary this time—of the rich countries, which consider themselves central to the history of mankind. Such mimicry would only lead the revolutionary groups of the Third World to a new deception regarding their own reality. They would be led to fight against windmills.

But, having acknowledged this danger, it is important to remember also that the poor countries would err in not following these events closely, since their future depends at least partially upon what happens on the domestic scene in the dominant countries. Their own efforts at liberation cannot be indifferent to that proclaimed by growing minorities in rich nations. There are, moreover, valuable lessons to be learned by the revolutionaries of the countries on the periphery, who could in turn use them as corrective measures in the difficult task of building a new society.

What is at stake in the South as well as in the North, in the West as well as the East, on the periphery and in the center is the possibility of enjoying a truly human existence, a free life, a dynamic liberty which is related to history as a conquest. We have today an ever-clearer vision of this dynamism and this conquest, but their roots stretch into the past....

[The German philosopher G. W. F.] Hegel followed this approach, introducing with vitality and urgency the theme of history. To a great extent his philosophy is a reflection on the French Revolution. This historical event had vast repercussions, for it proclaimed the right of every man to participate in the direction of the society to which he belongs. For Hegel man is aware of himself "only by being acknowledged or 'recognized'" by another consciousness. But this being recognized by another presupposes an initial conflict, "a life-and-death struggle," because it is "solely by risking life that freedom is obtained."[1]

Through the lord-bondsman dialectic (resulting from this original confrontation), the historical process will then appear as the genesis of consciousness and therefore of the gradual liberation of man. Through the dialectical process man constructs himself and attains a real awareness of his own being; he liberates himself in the acquisition of genuine freedom which through work transforms the world and educates man. For Hegel "world history is the progression of the awareness of freedom." Moreover, the driving force of history is the difficult conquest of freedom, hardly perceptible in its initial stages. It is the passage from awareness of freedom to real freedom. "It is Freedom in itself that comprises within itself the infinite necessity of bringing itself to consciousness and thereby, since knowledge about itself is its very nature, to reality." Thus man gradually takes hold of the reins of his own destiny. He looks ahead and turns towards a society in which he will be free of all alienation and servitude. This focus will initiate a new dimension in philosophy: social criticism.

[Karl] Marx deepened and renewed this line of thought in his unique way.... The new attitude was expressed clearly in the famous *Theses on Feuerbach*, in which Marx presented concisely but penetratingly the essential elements of his approach. In them, especially in the First Thesis, Marx situated himself equidistant between the old materialism and idealism; more precisely, he presented his position as the dialectical transcendence of both. Of the first he retained the affirmation of the objectivity of the external world; of the second he kept man's transforming capacity. For Marx, to know was something indissolubly linked to the transformation of the world through work. Basing his thought on these first intuitions, he went on to construct a scientific understanding of historical reality. He analyzed capitalistic society, in which were found concrete instances of the exploitation of man by his fellows and of one social class by another. Pointing the way towards an era in history when man can live humanly, Marx created categories which allowed for the elaboration of a science of history.

The door was opened for science to help man take one more step on the road to critical thinking.

It made him more aware of the socio-economic determinants of his ideological creations and therefore freer and more lucid in relation to them. But at the same time these new insights enabled man to have greater control and rational grasp of his historical initiatives. (This interpretation is valid unless of course one holds a dogmatic and mechanistic interpretation of history.) These initiatives ought to assure the change from the capitalistic mode of production to the socialistic mode, that is to say, to one oriented towards a society in which man can begin to live freely and humanly. He will have controlled nature, created the conditions for a socialized production of wealth, done away with private acquisition of excessive wealth, and established socialism.

But modern man's aspirations include not only liberation from *exterior* pressures which prevent his fulfillment as a member of a certain social class, country, or society. He seeks likewise an *interior* liberation, in an individual and intimate dimension; he seeks liberation not only on a social plane but also on a psychological. He seeks an interior freedom understood however not as an ideological evasion from social confrontation or as the internalization of a situation of dependency. Rather it must be in relation to the real world of the human psyche as understood since [Sigmund] Freud.

A new frontier was in effect opened up when Freud highlighted the unconscious determinants of human behavior, with repression as the central element of man's psychic makeup. Repression is the result of the conflict between instinctive drives and the cultural and ethical demands of the social environment. For Freud, unconscious motivations exercise a tyrannical power and can produce aberrant behavior. This behavior is controllable only if the subject becomes aware of these motivations through an accurate reading of the new language of meanings created by the unconscious. Since Hegel we have seen *conflict* used as a germinal explanatory category and *awareness* as a step in the conquest of freedom. In Freud however they appear in a psychological process which ought also to lead to a fuller liberation of man.

The scope of liberation on the collective and historical level does not always and satisfactorily include psychological liberation. Psychological liberation includes dimensions which do not exist in or are not sufficiently integrated with collective, historical liberation. We are not speaking here, however, of facilely separating them or putting them in opposition to another....

[A]lienation and exploitation as well as the very struggle for liberation from them have ramifications on the personal and psychological planes which it would be dangerous to overlook in the process of constructing a new society and a new man. These personal aspects—considered not as excessively privatized, but rather as encompassing all human dimensions—are also under consideration in the contemporary debate concerning greater participation of all in political activity. This is so even in a socialist society....

To conceive of history as a process of the liberation of man is to consider freedom as a historical conquest; it is to understand that the step from an abstract to a real freedom is not taken without a struggle against all the forces that oppress man, a struggle full of pitfalls, detours, and temptations to run away. The goal is not only better living conditions, a radical change of structures, a social revolution; it is much more: the continuous creation, never ending, of a new way to be a man, a *permanent cultural revolution*.

In other words, what is at stake above all is a dynamic and historical conception of man, oriented definitively and creatively toward his future, acting in the present for the sake of tomorrow. Teilhard de Chardin has remarked that man has taken hold of the reins of evolution.[2] History, contrary to essentialist and static thinking, is not the development of potentialities preexistent in man; it is rather the conquest of new, qualitatively different ways of being a man in order to achieve an ever more total and complete fulfillment of the individual in solidarity with all mankind.

The Concept of Liberation Theologically Considered

Although we will consider liberation from a theological perspective more extensively later, it is important at this time to attempt an initial treatment in the light of what we have just discussed.

The term *development* is relatively new in the texts of the ecclesiastical magisterium. Except for a brief reference by Pius XII, the subject is broached for the first time by John XXIII in the encyclical letter *Mater et Magistra*.[3] *Pacem in terris*[4] gives the term special attention. *Gaudium et spes*[5] dedicates a whole section to it, though the treatment is not original. All these documents stress the urgency of eliminating the existing injustices and the need for an economic development geared to the service of man. Finally, *Populorum progressio*[6] discusses development as its central theme. Here the language and ideas are clearer; the adjective *integral* is added to development, putting things in a different context and opening new perspectives....

The theme of liberation appears more completely discussed in the message from eighteen bishops of the Third World, published as a specific response to the call made by *Populorum progressio*. It is also treated frequently—almost to the point of being a synthesis of its message—in the conclusions of the Second General Conference of Latin American Bishops held in Medellín, Colombia, in 1968, which have more doctrinal authority than the eighteen bishops' message. In both these documents the focus has changed. The situation is not judged from the point of view of the countries at the center, but rather of those on the periphery, providing insiders' experience of their anguish and aspirations.

The product of a profound historical movement, this aspiration to liberation is beginning to be accepted by the Christian community as a sign of the times, as a call to commitment and interpretation. The Biblical message, which presents the work of Christ as a liberation, provides the framework for this interpretation. Theology seems to have avoided for a long time reflecting on the conflictual character of human history, the confrontations among men, social classes, and countries. St. Paul continuously reminds us, however, of the paschal core of Christian existence and of all of human life: the passage from the old man to the new, from sin to grace, from slavery to freedom.

"For freedom Christ has set us free" (Gal. 5:1), St. Paul tells us. He refers here to liberation from sin insofar as it represents a selfish turning in upon oneself. To sin is to refuse to love one's neighbors and, therefore, the Lord himself. Sin—a breach of friendship with God and others—is according to the Bible the ultimate cause of poverty, injustice, and the oppression in which men live. In describing sin as the ultimate cause we do not in any way negate the structural reasons and the objective determinants leading to these situations. It does, however, emphasize the fact that things do not happen by chance and that behind an unjust structure there is a personal or collective will responsible—a willingness to reject God and neighbor. It suggests, likewise, that a social transformation, no matter how radical it may be, does not automatically achieve the suppression of all evils.

But St. Paul asserts not only that Christ liberated us; he also tells us that he did it in order that we might be free. Free for what? Free to love. "In the language of the Bible," writes [German theologian Dietrich] Bonhoeffer, "freedom is not something man has for himself but something he has for others.... It is not a possession, a presence, an object...but a relationship and nothing else. In truth, freedom is a relationship between two persons. Being free means 'being free for the other,' because the other has bound me to him. Only in relationship with the other am I free."[7] The freedom to which we are called presupposes the going out of oneself, the breaking down of our selfishness and of all the structures that support our selfishness; the foundation of this freedom is openness to others. The fullness of liberation—a free gift from Christ—is communion with God and with other men.

Conclusion

Summarizing what has been said above, we can distinguish three reciprocally interpenetrating levels of meaning of the term *liberation*, or in other words, three approaches to the process of liberation.

In the first place, *liberation* expresses the aspirations of oppressed peoples and social classes, emphasizing the conflictual aspect of the economic, social, and political process which puts them at odds with wealthy nations and oppressive classes. In contrast, the word *development,* and above all the policies characterized as developmentalist [*desarrollista*], appear somewhat aseptic, giving a false picture of a tragic and conflictual reality. The issue of development does in fact find its true place in the more universal, profound, and radical perspective of liberation. It is only within this framework that *development* finds its true meaning and possibilities of accomplishing something worthwhile.

At a deeper level, *liberation* can be applied to an understanding of history. Man is seen as assuming conscious responsibility for his own destiny. This understanding provides a dynamic context and broadens the horizons of the desired social changes. In this perspective the unfolding of all the man's dimensions is demanded—a man who makes himself throughout his life and throughout history. The gradual conquest of true freedom leads to the creation of a new man and a qualitatively different society. This vision provides, therefore, a better understanding of what in fact is at stake in our times.

Finally, the word *development* to a certain extent limits and obscures the theological problems implied in the process designated by this term. On the contrary the word *liberation* allows for another approach leading to the Biblical sources which inspire the presence and action of man in history. In the Bible, Christ is presented as the one who brings us liberation. Christ the Savior liberates man from sin, which is the ultimate root of all disruption of friendship and of all injustice and oppression. Christ makes man truly free, that is to say, he enables man to live in communion with him; and this is the basis for all human brotherhood.

NOTES

1. *The Phenomenology of Mind,* trans. J. B. Baillie (New York: Humanities Press, Inc., 1964), pp. 229, 232–233.
2. Pierre Teilhard de Chardin (1881–1955), French Catholic priest and theologian.—Eds.
3. *Mother and Teacher;* English title, *Christianity and Social Progress.*
4. *Peace on Earth.*
5. *Joy and Hope;* English title, *The Church and the Modern World.*
6. *Development of Peoples.*
7. *Creation and Fall, Temptation* (New York: Macmillan Company, 1966), p. 37.

59

All Animals Are Equal

PETER SINGER

Just as oppressed people suffer from discriminatory beliefs and attitudes—women from sexism, people of color from racism, gays from homophobia—so too, says the Australian philosopher Peter Singer (1946–), do animals suffer from "speciesism." Speciesism is the belief that one particular animal species—the human species—is innately superior to all others. This supposed superiority leads humans to engage in the morally unjustifiable oppression, exploitation, and slaughter of other species. According to Singer, the aim of the animal liberation movement is to expose, criticize, and overcome these widely shared speciesist attitudes.

Source: Philosophic Exchange 1, Summer 1974. Reprinted by permission of Peter Singer. © Peter Singer 1974.

ALL AMINALS ARE EQUAL

In recent years a number of oppressed groups have campaigned vigorously for equality. The classic instance is the Black Liberation movement, which demands an end to the prejudice and discrimination that has made blacks second-class citizens. The immediate appeal of the black liberation movement and its initial, if limited, success made it a model for other oppressed groups to follow. We became familiar with liberation movements for Spanish-Americans, gay people, and a variety of other minorities. When a majority group—women—began their campaign, some thought we had come to the end of the road. Discrimination on the basis of sex, it has been said, is the last universally accepted form of discrimination, practiced without secrecy or pretense even in those liberal circles that have long prided themselves on their freedom from prejudice against racial minorities.

One should always be wary of talking of "the last remaining form of discrimination." If we have learnt anything from liberation movements, we should have learnt how difficult it is to be aware of latent prejudice in our attitudes to particular groups until this prejudice is forcefully pointed out.

A liberation movement demands an expansion of our moral horizons and an extension or reinterpretation of the basic moral principle of equality. Practices that were previously regarded as natural and inevitable come to be seen as the result of an unjustifiable prejudice. Who can say with confidence that all his or her attitudes and practices are beyond criticism? If we wish to avoid being numbered amongst the oppressors, we must be prepared to re-think even our most fundamental attitudes. We need to consider them from the point of view of those most disadvantaged by our attitudes, and the practices that follow from these attitudes. If we can make this unaccustomed mental switch we may discover a pattern in our attitudes and practices that consistently operates so as to benefit one group—usually the one to which we ourselves belong—at the expense of another. In this way we may come to see that there is a case for a new liberation movement. My aim is to advocate that we make this mental switch in respect of our attitudes and practices towards a very large group of beings: members of species other than our own—or, as we popularly though misleadingly call them, animals. In other words, I am urging that we extend to other species the basic principle of equality that most of us recognize should be extended to all members of our own species.

All this may sound a little far-fetched, more like a parody of other liberation movements than a serious objective. In fact, in the past the idea of "The Rights of Animals" really has been used to parody the case for women's rights. When Mary Wollstonecraft, a forerunner of later feminists, published her *Vindication of the Rights of Woman* in 1792, her ideas were widely regarded as absurd, and they were satirized in an anonymous publication entitled *A Vindication of the Rights of Brutes.* The author of this satire (actually Thomas Taylor, a distinguished Cambridge philosopher) tried to refute Wollstonecraft's reasonings by showing that they could be carried one stage further. If sound when applied to women, why should the arguments not be applied to dogs, cats, and horses? They seemed to hold equally well for these "brutes"; yet to hold that brutes had rights was manifestly absurd; therefore the reasoning by which this conclusion had been reached must be unsound, and if unsound when applied to brutes, it must also be unsound when applied to women, since the very same arguments had been used in each case.

One way in which we might reply to this argument is by saying that the case for equality between men and women cannot validly be extended to nonhuman animals. Women have a right to vote, for instance, because they are just as capable of making rational decisions as men are; dogs, on the other hand, are incapable of understanding the significance of voting, so they cannot have the right to vote. There are many other obvious ways in which men and women resemble each other closely, while humans and other animals differ greatly. So, it might be said, men and women are similar beings, and should have equal rights, while humans and nonhumans are different and should not have equal rights.

The thought behind this reply to Taylor's analogy is correct up to a point, but it does not go far enough. There *are* important differences between humans and other animals, and these differences must give rise to *some* differences in the rights that each have. Recognizing this obvious fact, however, is no barrier to the case for extending the basic principle of equality to nonhuman animals. The differences that exist between men and women are equally undeniable, and the supporters of Women's Liberation are aware that these differences may give rise to different rights. Many feminists hold that women have the right to an abortion on request. It does not follow that since these same people are campaigning for equality between men and women they must support the right of men to have abortions too. Since a man cannot have an abortion, it is meaningless to talk of his right to have one. Since a pig can't vote, it is meaningless to talk of his right to vote. There is no reason why either Women's Liberation or Animal Liberation should get involved in such nonsense. The extension of the basic principle of equality from one group to another does not imply that we must treat both groups in exactly the same way, or grant exactly the same rights to both groups. Whether we should do so will depend on the nature of the members of the two groups. The basic principle of equality, I shall argue, is equality of consideration; and equal consideration for different beings may lead to different treatment and different rights.

So there is a different way of replying to Taylor's attempt to parody Wollstonecraft's arguments, a way which does not deny the differences between humans and nonhumans, but goes more deeply into the question of equality, and concludes by finding nothing absurd in the idea that the basic principle of equality applies to so-called "brutes." I believe that we reach this conclusion if we examine the basis on which our opposition to discrimination on grounds of race or sex ultimately rests. We will then see that we would be on shaky ground if we were to demand equality for blacks, women, and other groups of oppressed humans while denying equal consideration to nonhumans.

When we say that all human beings, whatever their race, creed or sex, are equal, what is it that we are asserting? Those who wish to defend a hierarchical, inegalitarian society have often pointed out that by whatever test we choose, it simply is not true that all humans are equal. Like it or not, we must face the fact that humans come in different shapes and sizes; they come with differing moral capacities, differing intellectual abilities, differing amounts of benevolent feeling and sensitivity to the needs of others, differing abilities to communicate effectively, and differing capacities to experience pleasure and pain. In short, if the demand for equality were based on the actual equality of all human beings, we would have to stop demanding equality. It would be an unjustifiable demand.

Still, one might cling to the view that the demand for equality among human beings is based on the actual equality of the different races and sexes. Although humans differ as individuals in various ways, there are no differences between the races and sexes *as such*. From the mere fact that a person is black, or a woman, we cannot infer anything else about that person. This, it may be said, is what is wrong with racism and sexism. The white racist claims that whites are superior to blacks, but this is false—although there are differences between individuals, some blacks are superior to some whites in all of the capacities and abilities that could conceivably be relevant. The opponent of sexism would say the same: a person's sex is no guide to his or her abilities, and this is why it is unjustifiable to discriminate on the basis of sex.

This is a possible line of objection to racial and sexual discrimination. It is not, however, the way that someone really concerned about equality would choose, because taking this line could, in some circumstances, force one to accept a most inegalitarian society. The fact that humans differ as individuals, rather than as races or sexes, is a valid reply to someone who defends a hierarchical society like, say, South Africa, in which all whites are superior in status to all blacks. The existence of individual variations that cut across the lines of race or sex, however, provides us with no defence at all against a more sophisticated opponent of equality, one who proposes that, say, the interests of those with I.Q. ratings above 100 be preferred to the interests of those with I.Q.s below 100. Would a hierarchical society of this sort really be so much better than one based on race or sex? I think not. But if we tie the moral principle of equality to the factual equality of the different races or sexes, taken as a whole, our opposition to racism and sexism does not provide us with any basis for objecting to this kind of inegalitarianism.

There is a second important reason why we ought not to base our opposition to racism and sexism on any kind of factual equality, even the limited kind which asserts that variations in capacities and abilities are spread evenly between the different races and sexes: we can have no absolute guarantee that these abilities and capacities really are distributed evenly, without regard to race or sex, among human beings. So far as actual abilities are concerned, there do seem to be certain measurable differences between both races and sexes. These differences do not, of course, appear in each case, but only when averages are taken. More important still, we do not yet know how much of these differences is really due to the different genetic endowments of the various races and sexes, and how much is due to environmental differences that are the result of past and continuing discrimination. Perhaps all of the important differences will eventually prove to be environmental rather than genetic. Anyone opposed to racism and sexism will certainly hope that this will be so, for it will make the task of ending discrimination a lot easier; nevertheless it would be dangerous to rest the case against racism and sexism on the belief that all significant differences are environmental in origin. The opponent of, say, racism who takes this line will be unable to avoid conceding that if differences in ability did after all prove to have some genetic connection with race, racism would in some way be defensible.

It would be folly for the opponent of racism to stake his whole case on a dogmatic commitment to one particular outcome of a difficult scientific issue which is still a long way from being settled. While attempts to prove that differences in certain selected abilities between races and sexes are primarily genetic in origin have certainly not been conclusive, the same must be said of attempts to prove that these differences are largely the result of environment. At this stage of the investigation we cannot be certain which view is correct, however much we may hope it is the latter.

Fortunately, there is no need to pin the case for equality to one particular outcome of this scientific investigation. The appropriate response to those who claim to have found evidence of genetically-based differences in ability between the races or sexes is not to stick to the belief that the genetic explanation must be wrong, whatever evidence to the contrary may turn up: instead we should make it quite clear that the claim to equality does not depend on intelligence, moral capacity, physical strength, or similar matters of fact. Equality is a moral ideal, not a simple assertion of fact. There is no logically compelling reason for assuming that a factual difference in ability between two people justifies any difference in the amount of consideration we give to satisfying their needs and interests. The principle of the equality of human beings is not a description of an alleged actual equality among humans: it is a prescription of how we should treat humans.

Jeremy Bentham incorporated the essential basis of moral equality into his utilitarian system of ethics in the formula: "Each to count for one and none for more than one." In other words, the interests of every being affected by an action are to be taken into account and given the same weight as the like interests of any other being. A later utilitarian, Henry Sidgwick, put the point in this way: "The good of any one individual is of no more importance, from the point of view (if I may say so) of the Universe, than the good of any other."[1] More recently, the leading figures in contemporary moral philosophy have shown a great deal of agreement in specifying as a fundamental presupposition of their moral theories some similar requirement which operates so as to give everyone's interests equal consideration—

although they cannot agree on how this requirement is best formulated.[2]

It is an implication of this principle of equality that our concern for others ought not to depend on what they are like, or what abilities they possess—although precisely what this concern requires us to do may vary according to the characteristics of those affected by what we do. It is on this basis that the case against racism and the case against sexism must both ultimately rest; and it is in accordance with this principle that speciesism is also to be condemned. If possessing a higher degree of intelligence does not entitle one human to use another for his own ends, how can it entitle humans to exploit nonhumans?

Many philosophers have proposed the principle of equal consideration of interests, in some form or other, as a basic moral principle; but, as we shall see in more detail shortly, not many of them have recognised that this principle applies to members of other species as well as to our own. Bentham was one of the few who did realize this. In a forward-looking passage, written at a time when black slaves in the British dominions were still being treated much as we now treat nonhuman animals, Bentham wrote:

> The day *may* come when the rest of the animal creation may acquire those rights which never could have been witholden from them but by the hand of tyranny. The French have already discovered that the blackness of the skin is no reason why a human being should be abandoned without redress to the caprice of a tormentor. It may one day come to be recognized that the number of the legs, the villosity of the skin, or the termination of the *os sacrum,* are reasons equally insufficient for abandoning a sensitive being to the same fate. What else is it that should trace the insuperable line? Is it the faculty of reason, or perhaps the faculty of discourse? But a full-grown horse or dog is beyond comparison a more rational, as well as a more conversable animal, than an infant of a day, or a week, or even a month, old. But suppose they were otherwise, what would it avail? The question is not, Can they reason? nor Can they *talk?* but, *Can they suffer?*[3]

In this passage Bentham points to the capacity for suffering as the vital characteristic that gives a being the right to equal consideration. The capacity for suffering—or more strictly, for suffering and/or enjoyment or happiness—is not just another characteristic like the capacity for language, or for higher mathematics. Bentham is not saying that those who try to mark "the insuperable line" that determines whether the interests of a being should be considered happen to have selected the wrong characteristic. The capacity for suffering and enjoying things is a prerequisite for having interests at all, a condition that must be satisfied before we can speak of interests in any meaningful way. It would be nonsense to say that it was not in the interests of a stone to be kicked along the road by a schoolboy. A stone does not have interests because it cannot suffer. Nothing that we can do to it could possibly make any difference to its welfare. A mouse, on the other hand, does have an interest in not being tormented, because it will suffer if it is.

If a being suffers, there can be no moral justification for refusing to take that suffering into consideration. No matter what the nature of the being, the principle of equality requires that its suffering be counted equally with the like suffering—insofar as rough comparisons can be made—of any other being. If a being is not capable of suffering, or of experiencing enjoyment or happiness, there is nothing to be taken into account. This is why the limit of sentience (using the term as a convenient, if not strictly accurate, shorthand for the capacity to suffer or experience enjoyment or happiness) is the only defensible boundary of concern for the interests of others. To mark this boundary by some characteristic like intelligence or rationality would be to mark it in an arbitrary way. Why not choose some other characteristic, like skin color?

The racist violates the principle of equality by giving greater weight to the interests of members of his own race, when there is a clash between their interests and the interests of those of another race. Similarly the speciesist allows the interests of his own species to override the greater interests of members of other species.[4] The pattern is the same in each case. Most human beings are speciesists. I shall now very briefly describe some of the practices that show this.

For the great majority of human beings, especially in urban, industrialized societies, the most direct form of contact with members of other species is at meal times: we eat them. In doing so we treat them purely as means to our ends. We regard their life and well-being as subordinate to our taste for a particular kind of dish. I say "taste" deliberately; this is purely a matter of pleasing our palate. There can be no defence of eating flesh in terms of satisfying nutritional needs, since it has been established beyond doubt that we could satisfy our need for protein and other essential nutrients far more efficiently with a diet that replaced animal flesh by soy beans, or products derived from soy beans, and other high-protein vegetable products.[5]

It is not merely the act of killing that indicates what we are ready to do to other species in order to gratify our tastes. The suffering we inflict on the animals while they are alive is perhaps an even clearer indication of our speciesism than the fact that we are prepared to kill them.[6] In order to have meat on the table at a price that people can afford, our society tolerates methods of meat production that confine sentient animals in cramped, unsuitable conditions for the entire durations of their lives. Animals are treated like machines that convert fodder into flesh, and any innovation that results in a higher "conversion ratio" is liable to be adopted. As one authority on the subject has said, "cruelty is acknowledged only when profitability ceases...."[7]

Since, as I have said, none of these practices cater for anything more than our pleasures of taste, our practice of rearing and killing other animals in order to eat them is a clear instance of the sacrifice of the most important interests of other beings in order to satisfy trivial interests of our own. To avoid speciesism we must stop this practice, and each of us has a moral obligation to cease supporting the practice. Our custom is all the support that the meat industry needs. The decision to cease giving it that support may be difficult, but it is no more difficult than it would have been for a white Southerner to go against the traditions of his society and free his slaves: if we do not change our dietary habits, how can we censure those slaveholders who would not change their own way of living?

The same form of discrimination may be observed in the widespread practice of experimenting on other species in order to see if certain substances are safe for human beings, or to test some psychological theory about the effect of severe punishment on learning, or to try out various new compounds just in case something turns up....

In the past, argument about vivisection has often missed this point, because it has been put in absolutist terms: Would the abolitionist be prepared to let thousands die if they could be saved by experimenting on a single animal? The way to reply to this purely hypothetical question is to pose another: Would the experimenter be prepared to perform his experiment on an orphaned human infant, if that were the only way to save many lives? (I say "orphan" to avoid the complication of parental feelings, although in doing so I am being overfair to the experimenter, since the nonhuman subjects of experiments are not orphans.) If the experimenter is not prepared to use an orphaned human infant, then his readiness to use nonhumans is simple discrimination, since adult apes, cats, mice and other mammals are more aware of what is happening to them, more self-directing and, so far as we can tell, at least as sensitive to pain, as any human infant. There seems to be no relevant characteristic that human infants possess that adult mammals do not have to the same or a higher degree. (Someone might try to argue that what makes it wrong to experiment on a human infant is that the infant will, in time and if left alone, develop into more than the nonhuman, but one would then, to be consistent, have to oppose abortion, since the fetus has the same potential as the infant—indeed, even contraception and abstinence might be wrong on this ground, since the egg and sperm, considered jointly, also have the same potential. In any case, this argument still gives us no reason for selecting a nonhuman, rather than a human with severe and irreversible brain damage, as the subject for our experiments.)

The experimenter, then, shows a bias in favor of his own species whenever he carries out an experiment on a nonhuman for a purpose that he would not think justified him in using a human being at an equal or lower level of sentience, awareness, ability to be self-directing, etc. No one familiar with the kinds of results yielded by most experiments on animals can have the slightest doubt that if this bias were eliminated the number of experiments performed would be a minute fraction of the number performed today.

Experimenting on animals, and eating their flesh, are perhaps the two major forms of speciesism in our society. By comparison, the third and last form of speciesism is so minor as to be insignificant, but it is perhaps of some special interest to those for whom this article was written. I am referring to speciesism in contemporary philosophy.

Philosophy ought to question the basic assumptions of the age. Thinking through, critically and carefully, what most people take for granted is, I believe, the chief task of philosophy, and it is this task that makes philosophy a worthwhile activity. Regrettably, philosophy does not always live up to its historic role. Philosophers are human beings and they are subject to all the preconceptions of the society to which they belong. Sometimes they succeed in breaking free of the prevailing ideology: more often they become its most sophisticated defenders. So, in this case, philosophy as practiced in the universities today does not challenge anyone's preconceptions about our relations with other species. By their writings, those philosophers who tackle problems that touch upon the issue reveal that they make the same unquestioned assumptions as most other humans, and what they say tends to confirm the reader in his or her comfortable speciesist habits.

I could illustrate this claim by referring to the writings of philosophers in various fields—for instance, the attempts that have been made by those interested in rights to draw the boundary of the sphere of rights so that it runs parallel to the biological boundaries of the species *homo sapiens,* including infants and even mental defectives, but excluding those other beings of equal or greater capacity who are so useful to us at mealtimes and in our laboratories. I think it would be a more appropriate conclusion to this article, however, if I concentrated on the problem with which we have been centrally concerned, the problem of equality.

It is significant that the problem of equality, in moral and political philosophy, is invariably formulated in terms of human equality. The effect of this is that the question of the equality of other animals does not confront the philosopher, or student, as an issue itself—and this is already an indication of the failure of philosophy to challenge accepted beliefs. Still, philosophers have found it difficult to discuss the issue of human equality without raising, in a paragraph or two, the question of the status of other animals. The reason for this, which should be apparent from what I have said already, is that if humans are to be regarded as equal to one another, we need some sense of "equal" that does not require any actual, descriptive equality of capacities, talents or other qualities. If equality is to be related to any actual characteristics of humans, these characteristics must be some lowest common denominator, pitched so low that no human lacks them—but then the philosopher comes up against the catch that any such set of characteristics which covers *all* humans will not be possessed *only by humans.* In other words, it turns out that in the only sense in which we can truly say, as an assertion of fact, that all humans are equal, at least some members of other species are also equal—equal, that is, to each other and to humans. If, on the other hand, we regard the statement "All humans are equal" in some non-factual way, perhaps as a prescription, then, as I have already argued, it is even more difficult to exclude nonhumans from the sphere of equality.

This result is not what the egalitarian philosopher originally intended to assert. Instead of accepting the radical outcome to which their own reasonings naturally point, however, most philosophers try to reconcile their beliefs in human equality and animal inequality by arguments that can only be described as devious.

As a first example, I take William Frankena's well-known article "The Concept of Social Justice." Frankena opposes the idea of basing justice on merit, because he sees that this could lead to highly inegalitarian results. Instead he proposes the principle that

> all men are to be treated as equals, not because they are equal, in any respect, but simply because they are human. They are human because they have emotions and desires, and are able to think, and hence are capable of enjoying a good life in a sense in which other animals are not.[8]

But what is this capacity to enjoy the good life which all humans have, but no other animals? Other animals have emotions and desires, and appear to be capable of enjoying a good life. We may doubt that they can think—although the behavior of some apes, dolphins and even dogs suggests that some of them can—but what is the relevance of thinking? Frankena goes on to admit that by "the good life" he means "not so much the morally good life as the happy or satisfactory life," so thought would appear to be unnecessary for enjoying the good life; in fact to emphasize the need for thought would make difficulties for the egalitarian since only some people are capable of leading intellectually satisfying lives, or morally good lives. This makes it difficult to see what Frankena's principle of equality has to do with simply being *human*. Surely every sentient being is capable of leading a life that is happier or less miserable than some alternative life, and hence has a claim to be taken into account. In this respect the distinction between humans and nonhumans is not a sharp division, but rather a continuum along which we move gradually, and with overlaps between the species, from simple capacities for enjoyment and satisfaction, or pain and suffering, to more complex ones.

Faced with a situation in which they see a need for some basis for the moral gulf that is commonly thought to separate humans and animals but can find no concrete difference that will do the job without undermining the equality of humans, philosophers tend to waffle. They resort to high-sounding phrases like "the intrinsic dignity of the human individual."[9] They talk of the "intrinsic worth of all men" as if men (humans?) had some worth that other beings did not.[10] Or they say that humans, and only humans, are "ends in themselves," while "everything other than a person can only have value for a person."[11]

This idea of a distinctive human dignity and worth has a long history; it can be traced back directly to the Renaissance humanists, for instance, to Pico della Mirandola's *Oration on the Dignity of Man*. Pico and other humanists based their estimate of human dignity on the idea that man possessed the central, pivotal position in the "Great Chain of Being" that led from the lowliest forms of matter to God himself; this view of the universe, in turn, goes back to both classical and Judeo-Christian doctrines. Contemporary philosophers have cast off these metaphysical and religious shackles and freely invoke the dignity of mankind without needing to justify the idea at all. Why should we not attribute "intrinsic dignity" or "intrinsic worth" to ourselves? Fellow humans are unlikely to reject the accolades we so generously bestow on them, and those to whom we deny the honor are unable to object. Indeed, when one thinks only of humans, it can be very liberal, very progressive, to talk of the dignity of all human beings. In so doing, we implicitly condemn slavery, racism, and other violations of human rights. We admit that we ourselves are in some fundamental sense on a par with the poorest, most ignorant members of our own species. It is only when we think of humans as no more than a small subgroup of all the beings that inhabit our planet that we may realize that in elevating our own species we are at the same time lowering the relative status of all other species.

The truth is that the appeal to the intrinsic dignity of human beings appears to solve the egalitarian's problems only as long as it goes unchallenged. Once we ask *why* it should be that all humans—including infants, mental defectives, psychopaths, Hitler, Stalin and the rest—have some kind of dignity or worth that no elephant, pig, or chimpanzee can ever achieve, we see that this question is as difficult to answer as our original request for some relevant fact that justifies the inequality of humans and other animals. In fact, these two questions are really one: talk of intrinsic dignity or moral worth only takes the problem back one step, because any satisfactory defence of the claim that all and only humans have intrinsic dignity would need to refer to some relevant capacities or characteristics that all and only humans possess. Philosophers frequently introduce ideas of dignity, respect and worth at the point at which other reasons appear to be lacking, but this is hardly good enough. Fine phrases are the last resource of those who have run out of arguments.

In case there are those who still think it may be possible to find some relevant characteristic that distinguishes all humans from all members of other species, I shall refer again, before I conclude, to the existence of some humans who quite clearly are below the level of awareness, self-consciousness, intelligence, and sentience, of many nonhumans. I am thinking of humans with severe and irreparable brain damage, and also of infant humans. To avoid the complication of the relevance of a being's potential, however, I shall henceforth concentrate on permanently retarded humans.

Philosophers who set out to find a characteristic that will distinguish humans from other animals rarely take the course of abandoning these groups of humans by lumping them in and with the other animals. It is easy to see why they do not. To take this line without rethinking our attitudes to other animals would entail that we have the right to perform painful experiments on retarded humans for trivial reasons; similarly it would follow that we had the right to rear and kill these humans for food. To most philosophers these consequences are as unacceptable as the view that we should stop treating nonhumans in this way.

Of course, when discussing the problem of equality it is possible to ignore the problem of mental defectives, or brush it aside as if somehow insignificant.[12] This is the easiest way out. What else remains? My final example of speciesism in contemporary philosophy has been selected to show what happens when a writer is prepared to face the question of human equality and animal inequality without ignoring the existence of mental defectives, and without resorting to obscurantist mumbo jumbo. Stanley Benn's clear and honest article "Egalitarianism and Equal Consideration of Interests"[13] fits this description.

Benn, after noting the usual "evident human inequalities" argues, correctly I think, for equality of consideration as the only possible basis for egalitarianism. Yet Benn, like other writers, is thinking only of "equal consideration of human interests." Benn is quite open in his defence of this restriction of equal consideration:

> not to possess human shape is a disqualifying condition. However faithful or intelligent a dog may be, it would be a monstrous sentimentality to attribute to him interests that could be weighed in an equal balance with those of human beings...if, for instance, one had to decide between feeding a hungry baby or a hungry dog, anyone who chose the dog would generally be reckoned morally defective, unable to recognize a fundamental inequality of claims.
>
> This is what distinguishes our attitude to animals from our attitude to imbeciles. It would be odd to say that we ought to respect equally the dignity or personality of the imbecile and of the rational man...but there is nothing odd about saying that we should respect their interests equally, that is, that we should give to the interests of each the same serious consideration as claims to considerations necessary for some standard of well-being that we can recognize and endorse.

Benn's statement of the basis of the consideration we should have for imbeciles seems to me correct, but why should there be any fundamental inequality of claims between a dog and a human imbecile? Benn sees that if equal consideration depended on rationality, no reason could be given against using imbeciles for research purposes, as we now use dogs and guinea pigs. This will not do: "But of course we do distinguish imbeciles from animals in this regard," he says. That the common distinction is justifiable is something Benn does not question; his problem is how it is to be justified. The answer he gives is this:

> we respect the interests of men and give them priority over dogs not *insofar* as they are rational, but because rationality is the human norm. We say it is *unfair* to exploit the deficiencies of the imbecile who falls short of the norm, just as it would be unfair, and not just ordinarily dishonest, to steal from a blind man. If we do not think in this way about dogs, it is because we do not see the irrationality of the dog as a deficiency or a handicap, but as normal for the species. The characteristics, therefore, that distinguish the normal man from the normal dog make it intelligible for us to talk of other men having interests and capacities, and therefore claims, of precisely the same kind as we make on our own behalf. But although these characteristics may provide the point of the distinction between men and other species, they are not in fact the qualifying conditions for membership, or the distinguishing criteria of the class of morally considerable persons; and this is precisely because a man does not become a member of a different species, with its own standards of normality, by reason of not possessing these characteristics.

The final sentence of this passage gives the argument away. An imbecile, Benn concedes, may have no characteristics superior to those of a dog; nevertheless this does not make the imbecile a member of "a different species" as the dog is. *Therefore* it would be "unfair" to use the imbecile for medical research as we use the dog. But why? That the imbecile is not rational is just the way things have worked out, and the same is true of the dog—neither is any more responsible for their mental level. If it is unfair to take advantage of an isolated defect, why is it fair to take advantage of a more general limitation? I find it hard to see anything in this argument except a defence of preferring the interests of members of our own species because they are members of our own species. To those who think there might be more to it, I suggest the following mental exercise. Assume that it has been proven that there is a difference in the average, or normal, intelligence quotient for two different races, say whites and blacks. Then substitute the term "white" for every occurrence of "men" and "black" for every occurrence of "dog" in the passage quoted; and substitute "high I.Q." for "rationality" and when Benn talks of "imbeciles" replace this term by "dumb whites"—that is, whites who fall well below the normal white I.Q. score. Finally, change "species" to "race." Now reread the passage. It has become a defence of a rigid, no-exceptions division between whites and blacks, based on I.Q. scores, *notwithstanding an admitted overlap* between whites and blacks in this respect. The revised passage is, of course, outrageous, and this is not only because we have made fictitious assumptions in our substitutions. The point is that in the original passage Benn was defending a rigid division in the amount of consideration due to members of different species, despite admitted cases of overlap. If the original did not, at first reading, strike us as being as outrageous as the revised version does, this is largely because although we are not racists ourselves, most of us are speciesists. Like the other articles, Benn's stands as a warning of the ease with which the best minds can fall victim to a prevailing ideology.

NOTES

1. *The Methods of Ethics* (7th ed.), p. 382.
2. For example, R. M. Hare, *Freedom and Reason* (Oxford, 1963) and J. Rawls, *A Theory of Justice* (Harvard, 1972); for a brief account of the essential agreement on this issue between these and other positions, see R. M. Hare, "Rules of War and Moral Reasoning," *Philosophy and Public Affairs,* vol. 1, no. 2 (1972).
3. *Introduction to the Principles of Morals and Legislation,* chap. 17.
4. I owe the term "speciesism" to Richard Ryder.
5. In order to produce 1 lb. of protein in the form of beef or veal, we must feed 21 lbs. of protein to the animal. Other forms of livestock are slightly less inefficient, but the average ratio in the U.S. is still 1:8. It has been estimated that the amount of protein lost to humans in this way is equivalent to 90% of the annual world protein deficit. For a brief account, see Frances Moore Lappé, *Diet for*

a Small Planet (Friends of the Earth/Ballantine, New York, 1971), pp. 4–11.

6. Although one might think that killing a being is obviously the ultimate wrong one can do, I think that the infliction of suffering is a clearer indication of speciesism because it might be argued that at least part of what is wrong with killing a human is that most humans are conscious of their existence over time, and have desires and purposes that extend into the future—see, for instance, M. Tooley, "Abortion and Infanticide," *Philosophy and Public Affairs,* vol. 2, no. 1 (1972). Of course, if one took this view one would have to hold—as Tooley does—that killing a human infant or mental defective is not in itself wrong, and is less serious than killing certain higher mammals that probably do have a sense of their own existence over time.
7. Ruth Harrison, *Animal Machines* (Stuart, London, 1964).
8. In R. Brandt (ed.), *Social Justice* (Prentice Hall, Englewood Cliffs, 1962), p. 19.
9. Frankena, *op. cit.,* p. 23.
10. H. A. Bedau, "Egalitarianism and the Idea of Equality," in *Nomos IX: Equality,* ed. J. R. Pennock and J. W. Chapman, New York, 1967.
11. G. Vlastos, "Justice and Equality," in Brandt, *Social Justice,* p. 48.
12. For example, Bernard Williams, "The Idea of Equality," in *Philosophy, Politics and Society* (second series), ed. P. Laslett and W. Runciman (Blackwell, Oxford, 1962), p. 118; J. Rawls, *A Theory of Justice,* pp. 509–510.
13. *Nomos IX: Equality;* the passages quoted are on pp. 62ff.

PART NINE

Green Politics: Ecology as Ideology

A few years ago, the world entered the third millennium A.D. At first sight, the time scale—some 3,000 years of "civilization"—seems so vast as to defy comprehension. And yet such measures of human time are minuscule when compared to biological and geological time scales, in which 3,000 years is but the blink of an eye.

We live, Greens say, at a pivotal time, not only in human history but in the biological history of the earth's myriad species and the ecosystems that sustain them. What we human beings do—how we think and therefore act—will, for better or worse, affect future humans and animals and other forms of life for many generations. We are at a crisis point and a watershed. We need to learn to think in the longer term, and with a wider vision. And such thinking begins with a clear recognition and account of the crisis that we humans have helped to bring about.

There is by now little doubt that the world of the early twenty-first century is beset by an ecological crisis of unprecedented proportions. The killing of forests and lakes by acid rain; the depletion of the earth's protective ozone layer; the pollution of our air and water; radioactive waste from nuclear power plants; the destruction of tropical rain forests; the death of birds, fish, and mammals from oil spills and pesticides; the rapid extinction of hundreds of species—these and many other events are all part of the interconnected series of crises that is often spoken of as a single environmental crisis. This crisis can be traced, in large part, to the population explosion and the rise and rapid proliferation of particular technologies such as the internal combustion engine and the nuclear reactor. But the environmental crisis can also be traced to *ideologies*—that is, to widely shared and still prevalent ideas, beliefs, and attitudes about our relation to nature and to other species.

The ecological or green movement is a relatively recent arrival on the political scene. And, like other political movements, it has its own ideology—or, as many Greens prefer to say, an "ethic." Although not yet fully formed, this ideology or ethic is critical of other mainstream ideologies, right, left, and center. Liberalism, Marxism, and modern conservatism are alike, the Greens say, in picturing human beings as "masters" or "conquerors" of nature, which is viewed in turn as being without intrinsic value or worth. An alternative Green ideology invites us to see ourselves as members of a species that exists in and because of nature. Nature nurtures us and all our fellow species. We are all part of a marvelously intricate and complex web of life. To the degree that we are greedy and selfish, to the extent that we are ignorant and heedless of our proper place in nature, we endanger this delicate web. Yet this is precisely what we humans have done. And, unless we change our ways—and some of our basic beliefs—very soon, we and our children and grandchildren will pay a heavy price.

Clearly the green movement and its ideology raise deep and difficult questions about what it means to be a human being and how humans are related to nature, to other species, and to future generations. Difficult as they are, however, we will have to attempt to answer them aright if our species and others are to survive and flourish. But where might the answers be found? Some Greens say that the answers are to be found in the life sciences, such as biology and ecology. Others say that the answers are in philosophy or religion—in the meditations of Dr. Albert Schweitzer and Mahatma Gandhi, for example—or perhaps in the ideas and practices of supposedly primitive peoples such as Native Americans and Australian Aborigines. Still others claim that we must invent an entirely new religion or perhaps a "planetary ethic" with a respect for the earth and all life at its core. But whatever the source, say the Greens, the answers cannot be found in older ideologies, for they do not even pose the right questions in the first place. Hence, the need for an alternative ideology or ethic.

Exactly what such an ideology or ethic might look like remains a matter of dispute. There are at present two rival visions. One is the "garden" vision, which sees humans as caretakers and cultivators of the earth. According to this view, humans are to be responsible managers and conscientious stewards of the natural environment and not its exploiters or conquerors. Human beings are part of nature, but not reducible to it, and are responsible for its care and cultivation. Its model is the fertile and well-tended garden.

The alternative, or "wilderness" vision, sees human beings as a danger to themselves and especially to other species and their natural habitat. The human desire to dominate nature, to "develop" various natural resources for human enjoyment or benefit, is itself the problem to be overcome. Humans should resist the temptation to dominate, develop, and cultivate nature and learn to love wilderness and wild creatures by leaving them alone. Its model is an untamed and uncultivated wilderness.

These two visions or models are, of course, ideal types—simplified sketches of the complex relationship among human beings and other species, and of the ecosystems that sustain all life on earth. And yet each captures some sense of the difference between two fundamentally different, but recognizably green, outlooks. The thinking of most Greens incorporates elements of both the garden and wilderness visions. Each will no doubt figure, in some form or other, into a more fully worked-out environmental or green ideology.

Although it is too early to say precisely what form such a green ideology would take, several fundamental features are already quite clear. First and most important is the view that all things are connected. Every species, including our own, lives in interdependent relations with other species and with the environment that sustains all creatures. From this a second feature follows: all life, and the environment that sustains it, is intrinsically valuable and therefore deserves recognition, respect, and protection. A third feature is the recognition that all human actions, however small or seemingly insignificant, have consequences for the biosphere. Fourth, these consequences can and typically do stretch into the indefinite future, affecting human beings, animals, and ecosystems for generations to come. We must therefore extend our time horizon to take into account the health and well-being of future generations. A fifth feature of the emerging green ideology is its emphasis on individual or personal, as well as political or collective, responsibility. The slogan "Think globally, act locally" succinctly summarizes this view. From this follows a sixth feature—a green conception of democracy as a decentralized, grassroots form of self-rule that maximizes the opportunity for individual participation and personal responsibility at the local level.

Most Greens would probably agree that these six features form the core of their environmental ethic or ideology. But, despite a fairly widespread agreement about fundamental principles and ends, Greens disagree among themselves about the best means for achieving these ends. Some say that the green movement should act as an interest group within the present political system; others say that the system is in need of a fundamental transformation. Some Greens favor low-key, subtle strategies for educating and informing the public; others opt for highly visible campaigns of protest and acts of civil disobedience; and some radical environmentalists favor acts of "ecoterrorism" or "monkey wrenching" to deter polluters, developers, dumpers of toxic wastes, and others from despoiling the environment.

But whatever their differences regarding strategy and tactics, most Greens are in broad agreement regarding ends. Theirs is a voice that we shall hear more often and more loudly, as the new century unfolds.

60

The Land Ethic

ALDO LEOPOLD

The ecologist Aldo Leopold (1886–1948), one of the fathers of the modern environmental movement, brought a broad scientific training to his inquiries into our attitudes toward nature and its myriad creatures. His *A Sand County Almanac* (1949) combines observations on wildlife and human life and the way in which the two are irrevocably intertwined. If humans and other species are to survive and flourish, he believed, we will have to develop a more acute awareness of our interdependence with other species and the habitats that sustain us all. This heightened awareness and attitude of reverence he called "the land ethic."

Source: From *A Sand County Almanac and Sketches Here and There* by Aldo Leopod, copyright 1949, 1953, 1966, renewed 1977, 1981 by Oxford University Press, Inc. Used by permission of Oxford University Press, Inc.

THE LAND ETHIC

When god-like Odysseus returned from the wars in Troy, he hanged all on one rope a dozen slave-girls of his household whom he suspected of misbehavior during his absence.

This hanging involved no question of propriety. The girls were property. The disposal of property was then, as now, a matter of expediency, not of right and wrong.

Concepts of right and wrong were not lacking from Odysseus's Greece: witness the fidelity of his wife through the long years before at last his black-prowed galleys clove the wine-dark seas for home. The ethical structure of that day covered wives, but had not yet been extended to human chattels. During the three thousand years which have since elapsed, ethical criteria have been extended to many fields of conduct, with corresponding shrinkages in those judged by expediency only.

The Ethical Sequence

This extension of ethics, so far studied only by philosophers, is actually a process in ecological evolution. Its sequences may be described in ecological as well as in philosophical terms. An ethic, ecologically, is a limitation on freedom of action in the struggle for existence. An ethic, philosophically, is a differentiation of social from anti-social conduct. These are two definitions of one thing. The thing has its origin in the tendency of interdependent individuals or groups to evolve modes of co-operation. The ecologist calls these symbioses. Politics and economics are advanced symbioses in which the original free-for-all competition has been replaced, in part, by co-operative mechanisms with an ethical content.

The complexity of co-operative mechanisms has increased with population density, and with the efficiency of tools. It was simpler, for example, to define the anti-social uses of sticks and stones in the days of the mastodons than of bullets and billboards in the age of motors.

The first ethics dealt with the relation between individuals; the Mosaic Decalogue [i.e., the Ten Commandments] is an example. Later accretions dealt with the relation between the individual and society. The Golden Rule tries to integrate the individual to society; democracy to integrate social organization to the individual.

There is as yet no ethic dealing with man's relation to land and to the animals and plants which grow upon it. Land, like Odysseus' slave-girls, is still property. The land-relation is still strictly economic, entailing privileges but not obligations.

The extension of ethics to this third element in human environment is, if I read the evidence correctly, an evolutionary possibility and an ecological necessity. It is the third step in a sequence. The first two have already been taken. Individual thinkers since the days of Ezekiel and Isaiah have asserted that the despoliation of land is not only inexpedient but wrong. Society, however, has not yet affirmed their belief. I regard the present conservation movement as the embryo of such an affirmation.

An ethic may be regarded as a mode of guidance for meeting ecological situations so new or intricate, or involving such deferred reactions, that the path of social expediency is not discernible to the average individual. Animal instincts are modes of guidance for the individual in meeting such situations. Ethics are possibly a kind of community instinct in-the-making.

The Community Concept

All ethics so far evolved rest upon a single premise: that the individual is a member of a community of interdependent parts. His instincts prompt him to compete for his place in that community, but his ethics prompt him also to co-operate (perhaps in order that there may be a place to compete for).

The land ethic simply enlarges the boundaries of the community to include soils, waters, plants, and animals, or collectively, the land.

This sounds simple: do we not already sing our love for and obligation to the land of the free and the home of the brave? Yes, but just what and whom do we love? Certainly not the soil, which we are sending helter-skelter downriver. Certainly not the waters, which we assume have no function except to turn turbines, float barges, and carry off sewage. Certainly not the plants, of which we exterminate whole communities without batting an eye. Certainly not the animals, of which we have already extirpated many of the largest and most beautiful species. A land ethic of course cannot prevent the alteration, management, and use of these "resources," but it does affirm their right to continued existence, and, at least in spots, their continued existence in a natural state.

In short, a land ethic changes the role of *Homo sapiens* from conqueror of the land-community to plain member and citizen of it. It implies respect for his fellow-members, and also respect for the community as such.

In human history, we have learned (I hope) that the conqueror role is eventually self-defeating. Why? Because it is implicit in such a role that the conqueror knows, *ex cathedra,* just what makes the community clock tick, and just what and who is valuable, and what and who is worthless, in community life. It always turns out that he knows neither, and this is why his conquests eventually defeat themselves.

In the biotic community, a parallel situation exists. Abraham knew exactly what the land was for: it was to drip milk and honey into Abraham's mouth. At the present moment, the assurance with which we regard this assumption is inverse to the degree of our education.

The ordinary citizen today assumes that science knows what makes the community clock tick; the scientist is equally sure that he does not. He knows that the biotic mechanism is so complex that its workings may never be fully understood.

That man is, in fact, only a member of a biotic team is shown by an ecological interpretation of history. Many historical events, hitherto explained solely in terms of human enterprise, were actually biotic interactions between people and land. The characteristics of the land determined the fact quite as potently as the characteristics of men who lived on it.

Consider, for example, the settlement of the Mississippi valley. In the years following the [American] Revolution, three groups were contending for its control: the native Indian, the French and English traders, and the American settlers. Historians wonder what would have happened if the English at Detroit had thrown a little more weight into the Indian side of those tipsy scales which decided the outcome of the colonial migration into the cane-lands of Kentucky. It is time now to ponder the fact that the cane-lands, when subjected to the particular mixture of forces represented by the cow, plow, fire, and axe of the pioneer, became bluegrass. What if the plant succession inherent in this dark and bloody ground had, under the impact of these forces, given us some worthless sedge, shrub, or weed? Would Boone and Kenton have held out? Would there have been any overflow into Ohio, Indiana, Illinois, and Missouri? Any Louisiana Purchase? Any transcontinental union of new states? Any Civil War?

Kentucky was one sentence in the drama of history. We are commonly told what the human actors in this drama tried to do, but we are seldom told that their success, or the lack of it, hung in large degree on the reaction of particular soils to the impact of the particular forces exerted by their occupancy. In the case of Kentucky, we do not even know where the bluegrass came from—whether it is a native species, or a stowaway from Europe.

Contrast the cane-lands with what hindsight tells us about the Southwest, where the pioneers were equally brave, resourceful, and persevering. The impact of occupancy here brought no bluegrass, or other plant fitted to withstand the bumps and buffetings of hard use. This region, when grazed by livestock, reverted through a series of more and more worthless grasses, shrubs, and weeds to a condition of unstable equilibrium. Each recession of plant types bred erosion; each increment to erosion bred a further recession of plants. The result today is a progressive and mutual deterioration, not only of plants and soils, but of the animal community subsisting thereon. The early settlers did not expect this:

on the ciénegas of New Mexico some even cut ditches to hasten it. So subtle has been its progress that few residents of the region are aware of it. It is quite invisible to the tourist who finds this wrecked landscape colorful and charming (as indeed it is, but it bears scant resemblance to what it was in 1848).

This same landscape was "developed" once before, but with quite different results. The Pueblo Indians settled the Southwest in pre-Columbian times, but they happened *not* to be equipped with range livestock. Their civilization expired, but not because their land expired.

In India, regions devoid of any sod-forming grass have been settled, apparently without wrecking the land, by the simple expedient of carrying the grass to the cow, rather than vice versa. (Was this the result of some deep wisdom, or was it just good luck? I do not know.)

In short, the plant succession steered the course of history; the pioneer simply demonstrated, for good or ill, what successions inhered in the land. Is history taught in this spirit? It will be, once the concept of land as a community really penetrates our intellectual life.

The Ecological Conscience

Conservation is a state of harmony between men and land. Despite nearly a century of propaganda, conservation still proceeds at a snail's pace; progress still consists largely of letterhead pieties and convention oratory. On the back forty we still slip two steps backward for each forward stride.

The usual answer to this dilemma is "more conservation education." No one will debate this, but is it certain that only the *volume* of education needs stepping up? Is something lacking in the *content* as well?

It is difficult to give a fair summary of its content in brief form, but, as I understand it, the content is substantially this: obey the law, vote right, join some organization, and practice what conservation is profitable on your own land; the government will do the rest.

Is not this formula too easy to accomplish anything worthwhile? It defines no right or wrong, assigns no obligation, calls for no sacrifice, implies no change in the current philosophy of values. In respect to land-use, it urges only enlightened self-interest. Just how far will such education take us? An example will perhaps yield a partial answer.

By 1930 it had become clear to all except the ecologically blind that southwestern Wisconsin's topsoil was slipping seaward. In 1933 the farmers were told that if they would adopt certain remedial practices for five years, the public would donate CCC [Civilian Conservation Corps] labor to install them, plus the necessary machinery and materials. The offer was widely accepted, but the practices were widely forgotten when the five-year contract period was up. The farmers continued only those practices that yielded an immediate and visible economic gain for themselves.

This led to the idea that maybe farmers would learn more quickly if they themselves wrote the rules. Accordingly the Wisconsin Legislature in 1937 passed the Soil Conservation District Law. This said to farmers, in effect: *We, the public, will furnish you free technical service and loan you specialized machinery, if you will write your own rules for land-use. Each county may write its own rules, and these will have the force of law.* Nearly all the counties promptly organized to accept the proffered help, but after a decade of operation, *no county has yet written a single rule.* There has been visible progress in such practices as strip-cropping, pasture renovation, and soil liming, but none in fencing woodlots against grazing, and none in excluding plow and cow from steep slopes. The farmers, in short, have selected those remedial practices which were profitable anyhow, and ignored those which were profitable to the community, but not clearly profitable to themselves.

When one asks why no rules have been written, one is told that the community is not yet ready to support them; education must precede rules. But the education actually in progress makes no mention of obligations to land over and above those dictated by self-interest. The net result is that we have more education but less soil, fewer healthy woods, and as many floods as in 1937.

The puzzling aspect of such situations is that the existence of obligations over and above self-interest is taken for granted in such rural community enterprises as the betterment of roads, schools, churches, and baseball teams. Their existence is not taken for granted, nor as yet seriously discussed, in bettering the behavior of the water that falls on the land, or in the preserving of the beauty or diversity of the farm landscape. Land-use ethics are still governed wholly by economic self-interest, just as social ethics were a century ago.

To sum up: we asked the farmer to do what he conveniently could to save his soil, and he has done just that, and only that. The farmer who clears the woods off a 75 per-cent slope, turns his cows into the clearing, and dumps its rainfall, rocks, and soil into the community creek, is still (if otherwise decent) a respected member of society. If he puts lime on his fields and plants his crops on contour, he is still entitled to all the privileges and emoluments of his Soil Conservation District. The District is a beautiful piece of social machinery, but it is coughing along on two cylinders because we have been too timid, and too anxious for quick success, to tell the farmer the true magnitude of his obligations. Obligations have no meaning without conscience, and the problem we face is the extension of the social conscience from people to land.

No important change in ethics was ever accomplished without an internal change in our intellectual emphasis, loyalties, affections, and convictions. The proof that conservation has not yet touched these foundations of conduct lies in the fact that philosophy and religion have not yet heard of it. In our attempt to make conservation easy, we have made it trivial.

Substitutes for a Land Ethic

When the logic of history hungers for bread and we hand out a stone, we are at pains to explain how much the stone resembles bread. I now describe some of the stones which serve in lieu of a land ethic.

One basic weakness in a conservation system based wholly on economic motives is that most members of the land community have no economic value. Wildflowers and songbirds are examples. Of the 22,000 higher plants and animals native to Wisconsin, it is doubtful whether more than 5 per-cent can be sold, fed, eaten, or otherwise put to economic use. Yet these creatures are members of the biotic community, and if (as I believe) its stability depends on its integrity, they are entitled to continuance.

When one of these non-economic categories is threatened, and if we happen to love it, we invent subterfuges to give it economic importance. At the beginning of the century songbirds were supposed to be disappearing. Ornithologists jumped to the rescue with some distinctly shaky evidence to the effect that insects would eat us up if birds failed to control them. The evidence had to be economic in order to be valid.

It is painful to read these circumlocutions today. We have no land ethic yet, but we have at least drawn nearer the point of admitting that birds should continue as a matter of biotic right, regardless of the presence or absence of economic advantage to us.

A parallel situation exists in respect of predatory mammals, raptorial birds, and fish-eating birds. Time was when biologists somewhat overworked the evidence that these creatures preserve the health of game by killing weaklings, or that they control rodents for the farmer, or that they prey only on "worthless" species. Here again, the evidence had to be economic in order to be valid. It is only in recent years that we hear the more honest argument that predators are members of the community, and that no special interest has the right to exterminate them for the sake of a benefit, real or fancied, to itself. Unfortunately this enlightened view is still in the talk stage. In the field the extermination of predators goes merrily on: witness the impending erasure of the timber wolf by fiat of Congress, the Conservation Bureaus, and many state legislatures.

Some species of trees have been "read out of the party" by economics-minded foresters because they grow too slowly, or have too low a sale value to pay as timber crops; white cedar, tamarack, cypress, beech, and hemlock are examples. In Europe, where forestry is ecologically more advanced, the non-commercial tree species are recognized as members of the native forest community, to be preserved as such, within reason. Moreover, some (like beech) have been found to have a valuable function in building up soil fertility. The interdependence of the forest and its constituent tree species, ground flora, and fauna is taken for granted.

Lack of economic value is sometimes a character not only of species or groups, but of entire biotic communities: marshes, bogs, dunes, and "deserts" are examples. Our formula in such cases is to relegate their conservation to government as refuges, monuments, or parks. The difficulty is that these communities are usually interspersed with more valuable private lands; the government cannot possibly own or control such scattered parcels. The net effect is that we have relegated some of them to ultimate extinction over large areas. If the private owner were ecologically minded, he would be proud to be the custodian of a reasonable proportion of such areas, which add diversity and beauty to his farm and to his community.

In some instances, the assumed lack of profit in these "waste" areas has proved to be wrong, but only after most of them had been done away with. The present scramble to reflood muskrat marshes is a case in point.

There is a clear tendency in American conservation to relegate to government all necessary jobs that private landowners fail to perform. Government ownership, operation, subsidy, or regulation is now widely prevalent in forestry, range management, soil and watershed management, park and wilderness conservation, fisheries management, and migratory bird management, with more to come. Most of this growth in governmental conservation is proper and logical, some of it is inevitable. That I imply no disapproval of it is implicit in the fact that I have spent most of my life working for it. Nevertheless the question arises: What is the ultimate magnitude of the enterprise? Will the tax base carry its eventual ramifications? At what point will governmental conservation, like the mastodon, become handicapped by its own dimensions? The answer, if there is any, seems to be in a land ethic, or some other force which assigns more obligation to the private landowner.

Industrial landowners and users, especially lumbermen and stockmen, are inclined to wail long and loudly about the extension of government ownership and regulation to land, but (with notable exceptions) they show little disposition to develop the only visible alternative: the voluntary practice of conservation on their own lands.

When the private landowner is asked to perform some unprofitable act for the good of the community, he today assents only with outstretched palm. If the act costs him cash this is fair and proper, but when it costs only forethought, open-mindedness, or time, the issue is at least debatable. The overwhelming growth of land-use subsidies in recent years must be ascribed, in large part, to the government's own agencies for conservation education: the land bureaus, the agricultural colleges, and the extension services. As far as I can detect, no ethical obligation toward land is taught in these institutions.

To sum up: a system of conservation based solely on economic self-interest is hopelessly lopsided. It tends to ignore, and thus eventually to eliminate, many elements in the land community that lack commercial value, but that are (as far as we know) essential to its healthy functioning. It assumes, falsely, I think, that the economic parts of the biotic clock will function without the uneconomic parts. It ends to relegate to government many functions eventually too large, too complex, or too widely dispersed to be performed by government.

An ethical obligation on the part of the private owner is the only visible remedy for these situations.

The Land Pyramid

An ethic to supplement and guide the economic relation to land presupposed the existence of some mental image of land as a biotic mechanism. We can be ethical only in relation to something we can see, feel, understand, love, or otherwise have faith in.

The image commonly employed in conservation education is "the balance of nature." For reasons too lengthy to detail here, this figure of speech fails to describe accurately what little we know about the land mechanism. A much truer image is the one employed in ecology: the biotic pyramid. I shall first sketch the pyramid as a symbol of land, and later develop some of its implications in terms of land-use.

Plants absorb energy from the sun. This energy flows through a circuit called the biota, which may be represented by a pyramid consisting of layers. The bottom layer is the soil. A plant layer rests on the soil, an insect layer on the plants, a bird and rodent layer on the insects, and so on up through various animal groups to the apex layer, which consists of the larger carnivores.

The species of a layer are alike not in where they came from, or in what they look like, but rather in what they eat. Each successive layer depends on those below it for food and often for other services, and each in turn furnishes food and services to those above. Proceeding upward, each successive layer decreases in numerical abundance. Thus, for every carnivore there are hundreds of his prey, thousands of their prey, millions of insects, uncountable plants. The pyramidal form of the system reflects this numerical progression from apex to base. Man shares an intermediate layer with the bears, raccoons, and squirrels which eat both meat and vegetables.

The lines of dependency for food and other services are called food chains. Thus soil-oak-deer-Indian is a chain that has now been largely converted to soil-corn-cow-farmer. Each species, including ourselves, is a link in many chains. The deer eats a hundred plants other than oak, and the cow a hundred plants other than corn. Both, then, are links in a hundred chains. The pyramid is a tangle of chains so complex as to seem disorderly, yet the stability of the system proves it to be a highly organized structure. Its functioning depends on the co-operation and competition of its diverse parts.

In the beginning, the pyramid of life was low and squat, the food chains short and simple. Evolution has added layer after layer, link after link. Man is one of thousands of accretions to the height and complexity of the pyramid. Science has given us many doubts, but it has given us at least one certainty: the trend of evolution is to elaborate and diversify the biota.

Land, then, is not merely soil; it is a fountain of energy flowing through a circuit of soils, plants, and animals. Food chains are t he living channels which conduct energy upward; death and decay return it to the soil. The circuit is not closed; some energy is dissipated in decay, some is added by absorption from the air, some is stored in soils, peats, and long-lived forests; but it is a sustained circuit, like a slowly augmented revolving fund of life. There is always a net loss by downhill wash, but this is normally small and offset by the decay of rocks. It is deposited in the ocean and, in the course of geological time, raised to form new lands and new pyramids.

The velocity and character of the upward flow of energy depend on the complex structure of the plant and animal community, much as the upward flow of sap in a tree depends on its complex cellular organization. Without this complexity, normal circulation would presumably not occur. Structure means the characteristic numbers, as well as the characteristic kinds and functions, of the component species. This interdependence between the complex structure of the land and its smooth functioning as an energy unit is one of its basic attributes.

When a change occurs in one part of the circuit, many other parts must adjust themselves to it. Change does not necessarily obstruct or divert the flow of energy; evolution is a long series of self-induced changes, the net result of which has been to elaborate the flow mechanism and to lengthen the circuit. Evolutionary changes, however, are usually slow and local. Man's invention of tools has enabled him to make changes of unprecedented violence, rapidity, and scope.

One change is in the composition of floras and faunas. The larger predators are lopped off the apex of the pyramid; food chains, for the first time in history, become shorter rather than longer. Domesticated species from other lands are substituted for wild ones, and wild ones are moved to new habitats. In this world-wide pooling of faunas and floras, some species get out of bounds as pests and diseases; others are extinguished. Such effects are seldom intended or foreseen; they represent unpredicted and often untraceable readjustments in the structure. Agricultural science is largely a race between the emergence of new pests and the emergence of new techniques for their control.

Another change touches the flow of energy through plants and animals and its return to the soil. Fertility is the ability of soil to receive, store, and release energy. Agriculture, by overdrafts on the soil, or by too radical a substitution of domestic for native species in the superstructure, may derange the channels of flow or deplete storage. Soils depleted of their storage, or of the organic matter which anchors it, wash away faster than they form. This is erosion.

Waters, like soil, are part of the energy circuit. Industry, by polluting waters or obstructing them with dams, may exclude the plants and animals necessary to keep energy in circulation.

Transportation brings another basic change: the plants or animals grown in one region are now consumed and returned to the soil in another. Transportation taps the energy stored in rocks, and in the air, and uses it elsewhere; thus we fertilize the garden with nitrogen gleaned by the guano birds from the fishes of seas on the other side of the Equator. Thus the formerly localized and self-contained circuits are pooled on a world-wide scale.

The process of altering the pyramid for human occupation releases stored energy, and this often gives rise, during the pioneering period, to a deceptive exuberance of plant and animal life, both wild and tame. These releases of biotic capital tend to becloud or postpone the penalties of violence.

This thumbnail sketch of land as an energy circuit conveys three basic ideas:

1. That land is not merely soil.
2. That the native plants and animals kept the energy circuit open; others may or may not.
3. That man-made changes are of a different order than evolutionary changes, and have effects more comprehensive than is intended or foreseen.

These ideas, collectively, raise two basic issues: Can the land adjust itself to the new order? Can the desired alterations be accomplished with less violence?

Biotas seem to differ in their capacity to sustain violent conversion. Western Europe, for example, carries a far different pyramid than Caesar found there. Some large animals are lost; swampy forests have become meadows or plowland; many new plants and animals are introduced, some of which escape as pests; the remaining natives are greatly changed in distribution and abundance. Yet the soil is still there and, with the help of imported nutrients, still fertile; the waters flow normally; the new structure seems to function and to persist. There is no visible stoppage or derangement of the circuit.

Western Europe, then, has a resistant biota. Its inner processes are tough, elastic, resistant to strain. No matter how violent the alterations, the pyramid, so far, has developed some new *modus vivendi* [i.e., way of living together] which preserves its habitability for man, and for most of the other natives.

Japan seems to present another instance of radical conversion without disorganization.

Most other civilized regions, and some as yet barely touched by civilization, display various stages of disorganization, varying from initial symptoms to advanced wastage. In Asia Minor and North Africa diagnosis is confused by climatic changes, which may have been either the cause or the effect of advanced wastage. In the United States the degree of disorganization varies locally; it is worst in the Southwest, the Ozarks, and parts of the South, and least in New England and the Northwest. Better land-uses may still arrest it in the less advanced regions. In parts of Mexico, South America, South Africa, and Australia a violent and accelerating wastage is in progress, but I cannot assess the prospects.

This almost world-wide display of disorganization in the land seems to be similar to disease in an animal, except that it never culminates in complete disorganization or death. The land recovers, but at some reduced level of complexity, and with a reduced carrying capacity for people, plants, and animals. Many biotas currently regarded as "lands of opportunity" are in fact already subsisting on exploitative agriculture, i.e., they have already exceeded their sustained carrying capacity. Most of South America is overpopulated in this sense.

In arid regions we attempt to offset the process of wastage by reclamation, but it is only too evident that the prospective longevity of reclamation projects is often short. In our own West, the best of them may not last a century.

The combined evidence of history and ecology seem to support one general deduction: the less violent the man-made changes, the greater the probability of successful readjustment in the pyramid. Violence, in turn, varies with human population density; a dense population requires a more violent conversion. In this respect, North America has a better chance for permanence than Europe, if she can contrive to limit her density.

This deduction runs counter to our current philosophy, which assumes that because a small increase in density enriched human life, an indefinite increase will enrich it indefinitely. Ecology knows of no density relationship that holds for indefinitely wide limits. All gains from density are subject to a law of diminishing returns.

Whatever may be the equation for men and land, it is improbable that we as yet know all its terms. Recent discoveries in mineral and vitamin nutrition reveal unsuspected dependencies in the up-circuit: incredibly minute quantities of certain substances determine the value of soils to plants, of plants to animals. What of the down-circuit? What of the vanishing species, the preservation of which we now regard as an esthetic luxury? They helped build the soil; in what unsuspected ways may they be essential to its maintenance? Professor Weaver proposes that we use prairie flowers to reflocculate the wasting soils of the dust bowl; who knows for what purpose cranes and condors, otters and grizzlies may some day be used?

Land Health and the A-B Cleavage

A land ethic, then, reflects the existence of an ecological conscience, and this in turn reflects a conviction of individual responsibility for the health of the land. Health is the capacity of the land for self-renewal. Conservation is our effort to understand and preserve this capacity.

Conservationists are notorious for their dissensions. Superficially these seem to add up to mere confusion, but a more careful scrutiny reveals a single plane of cleavage common to many specialized fields. In each field one group (A) regards the land as soil, and its function as commodity-production; another group (B) regards the land as a biota, and its function as something broader. How much broader is admittedly in a state of doubt and confusion.

In my own field, forestry, Group A is quite content to grow trees like cabbages, with cellulose as the basic forest commodity. It feels no inhibition against violence; its ideology is agronomic. Group B, on the other hand, sees forestry as fundamentally different from agronomy because it employs natural species, and manages a natural environment rather than creating an artificial one. Group B prefers natural reproduction on principle. It worries on biotic as well as economic grounds about the loss of species like chestnut, and the threatened loss of the white pines. It worries about a whole series of secondary forest functions: wildlife, recreation, watersheds, wilderness areas. To my mind, Group B feels the stirrings of an ecological conscience.

In the wildlife field, a parallel cleavage exists. For Group A the basic commodities are sport and meat; the yardsticks of production are ciphers of take in pheasants and trout. Artificial propagation is acceptable as a permanent as well as a temporary recourse—if its unit costs permit. Group B, on the other hand, worries about a whole series of biotic side issues. What is the cost in predators of producing a game crop? Should we have further recourse to exotics? How can management restore the shrinking species, like prairie grouse, already hopeless as shootable game? How can management restore the threatened rarities, like trumpeter swan and whooping crane? Can management principles be extended to wildflowers? Here again it is clear to me that we have the same A-B cleavage as in forestry.

In the larger field of agriculture I am less competent to speak, but there seem to be somewhat parallel cleavages. Scientific agriculture was actively developing before ecology was born; hence a slower penetration of ecological concepts might be expected. Moreover the farmer, by the very nature of his techniques, must modify the biota more radically than the forester or the wildlife manager. Nevertheless, there are many discontents in agriculture which seem to add up to a new vision of "biotic farming."

Perhaps the most important of these is the new evidence that poundage or tonnage is no measure of the food-value of farm crops; the products of fertile soil may be qualitatively as well as quantitatively superior. We can bolster poundage from depleted soils by pouring on imported fertility, but we are not necessarily bolstering food-value. The possible ultimate ramifications of this idea are so immense that I must leave their exposition to abler pens.

The discontent that labels itself "organic farming," while bearing some of the earmarks of a cult, is nevertheless biotic in its direction, particularly in its insistence on the importance of soil flora and fauna.

The ecological fundamentals of agriculture are just as poorly known to the public as in other fields of land-use. For example, few educated people realize that the marvelous advances in technique made during recent decades are improvements in the pump, rather than the well. Acre for acre, they have barely sufficed to offset the sinking level of fertility.

In all of these cleavages, we see repeated the same basic paradoxes: man the conqueror *versus* man the biotic citizen; science the sharpener of his sword *versus* science the searchlight on his universe; land the slave and servant *versus* land the collective organism. Robinson's injunction to Tristram [in E. A. Robinson's poem *Tristram* (1927)] may well be applied, at this juncture, to *Homo sapiens* as a species in geological time:

> Whether you will or not
> You are a King, Tristram, for you are one
> Of the time-tested few that leave the world,
> When they are gone, not the same place it
>   was.
> Mark what you leave.

The Outlook

It is inconceivable to me that an ethical relation to land can exist without love, respect, and admiration for land, and a high regard for its value. By value, I of course mean something far broader than mere economic value; I mean value in the philosophical sense.

Perhaps the most serious obstacle impeding the evolution of a land ethic is the fact that our educational and economic system is headed away from, rather than toward, an intense consciousness of land. Your true modern is separated from the land by many middlemen, and by innumerable physical gadgets. He has no vital relation to it; to him it is the space between cities on which crops grow. Turn him loose for a day on the land, and if the spot does not happen to be a golf links or a "scenic" area, he is bored stiff. If crops could be raised by hydroponics instead of farming, it would suit him very well. Synthetic substitutes for wood, leather, wool, and other natural land products suit him better than the originals. In short, land is something he has "outgrown."

Almost equally serious as an obstacle to a land ethic is the attitude of the farmer for whom the land is still an adversary, or a taskmaster that keeps him in slavery. Theoretically, the mechanization of farming ought to cut the farmer's chains, but whether it really does is debatable.

One of the requisites for an ecological comprehension of land is an understanding of ecology, and this is by no means co-extensive with "education"; in fact, much higher education seems deliberately to avoid ecological concepts. An understanding of ecology does not necessarily originate in courses bearing ecological labels;

it is quite as likely to be labeled geography, botany, agronomy, history, or economics. This is as it should be, but whatever the label, ecological training is scarce.

The case for a land ethic would appear hopeless but for the minority which is in obvious revolt against these "modern" trends.

The "key-log" which must be moved to release the evolutionary process for an ethic is simply this: quit thinking about decent land-use as solely an economic problem. Examine each question in terms of what is ethically and esthetically right, as well as what is economically expedient. A thing is right when it tends to preserve the integrity, stability, and beauty of the biotic community. It is wrong when it tends otherwise.

It of course goes without saying that economic feasibility limits the tether of what can or cannot be done for land. It always has and it always will. The fallacy the economic determinists have tied around our collective neck, and which we now need to cast off, is the belief that economics determines *all* land-use. This is simply not true. An innumerable host of actions and attitudes, comprising perhaps the bulk of all land relations, is determined by the land-users' tastes and predilections, rather than by his purse. The bulk of all land relations hinges on investments of time, forethought, skill, and faith rather than on investments of cash. As a land-user thinketh, so is he.

I have purposely presented the land ethic as a product of social evolution because nothing so important as an ethic is ever "written." Only the most superficial student of history supposes that Moses "wrote" the Decalogue; it evolved in the minds of a thinking community, and Moses wrote a tentative summary of it for a "seminar." I say tentative because evolution never stops.

The evolution of a land ethic is an intellectual as well as emotional process. Conservation is paved with good intentions which prove to be futile, or even dangerous, because they are devoid of critical understanding either of the land, or of economic land-use. I think it is a truism that as the ethical frontier advances from the individual to the community, its intellectual content increases.

The mechanism of operation is the same for any ethic: social approbation for right actions; social disapproval for wrong actions.

By and large, our present problem is one of attitudes and implements. We are remodeling the Alhambra with a steam-shovel, and we are proud of our yardage. We shall hardly relinquish the shovel, which after all has many good points, but we are in need of gentler and more objective criteria for its successful use.

61

Getting Along with Nature

WENDELL BERRY

Wendell Berry (1934–) is a Kentucky farmer, poet, novelist, essayist, and conservationist. A longtime champion of the family farm and sustainable agriculture, Berry offers an eloquent defense of the "garden" view against advocates of the "wilderness" vision. Human beings are not a species set apart from nature and from nonhuman animals. They are natural creatures whose "nature" is to cultivate the earth. Such intervention does, of course, affect nature, but it need not always or necessarily do so for the worse. To cultivate the earth in ways that respect and protect its fertility and diversity is not contrary to nature but is to "get along with nature."

Source: "Getting Along with Nature" from *Home Economics* by Wendell Berry. Copyright © 1987 by Wendell Berry. Reprinted by permission of North Point Press, a division of Farrar, Straus and Giroux, LLC.

GETTING ALONG WITH NATURE

The defenders of nature and wilderness—like their enemies the defenders of the industrial economy—sometimes sound as if the natural and the human were two separate estates, radically different and radically divided. The defenders of nature and wilderness sometimes seem to feel that they must oppose any human encroachment whatsoever, just as the industrialists often apparently feel that they must make the human encroachment absolute or, as they say, "complete the conquest of nature." But there is danger in this opposition, and it can be best dealt with by realizing that these pure and separate categories are pure ideas and do not otherwise exist.

Pure nature, anyhow, is not good for humans to live in, and humans do not want to live in it—or not for very long. Any exposure to the elements that lasts more than a few hours will remind us of the desirability of the basic human amenities: clothing, shelter, cooked food, the company of kinfolk and friends—perhaps even of hot baths and music and books.

It is equally true that a condition that is *purely* human is not good for people to live in, and people do not want to live for very long in it. Obviously, the more artificial a human environment becomes, the more the word "natural" becomes a term of value. It can be argued, indeed, that the conservation movement, as we know it today, is largely a product of the industrial revolution. The people who want clean air, clear streams, and wild forests, prairies, and deserts are the people who no longer have them.

People cannot live apart from nature; that is the first principle of the conservationists. And yet, people cannot live in nature without changing it. But this is true of *all* creatures; they depend upon nature, and they change it. What we call nature is, in a sense, the sum of the changes made by the various creatures and natural forces in their intricate actions and influences upon each other and upon their places. Because of the woodpeckers, nature is different from what it would be without them. It is different also because of the borers and ants that live in tree trunks, and because of the bacteria that live in the soil under the trees. The making of these differences is the making of the world.

Some of the changes made by wild creatures we would call beneficent: beavers are famous for making ponds that turn into fertile meadows; trees and prairie grasses build soil. But sometimes, too, we would call natural changes destructive. According to early witnesses, for instance, large areas around Kentucky salt licks were severely trampled and eroded by the great herds of hoofed animals that gathered there. The buffalo "streets" through hilly country were so hollowed out by hoof-wear and erosion that they remain visible almost two centuries after the disappearance of the buffalo. And so it can hardly be expected that humans would not change nature. Humans, like all other creatures, must make a difference; otherwise, they cannot live. But unlike other creatures, humans must make a choice as to the kind and scale of the difference they make. If they choose to make too small a difference, they diminish their humanity. If they choose to make too great a difference, they diminish nature, and narrow their subsequent choices; ultimately, they diminish or destroy themselves. Nature, then, is not only our source but also our limit and measure. Or, as the poet Edmund Spenser put it almost four hundred years ago, Nature, who is the "greatest goddesse," acts as a sort of earthly lieutenant of God, and Spenser represents her as both a mother and judge. Her jurisdiction is over the relations between the creatures; she deals "Right to all...indifferently," for she is "the equall mother" of all "[a]nd knittest each to each, as brother unto brother." Thus, in Spenser, the natural principles of fecundity and order are pointedly linked with the principle of justice, which we may be a little surprised to see that he attributes also to nature. And yet in his insistence on an "indifferent" natural justice, resting on the "brotherhood" of *all* creatures, not just of humans, Spenser would now be said to be on sound ecological footing.

In nature we know that wild creatures sometimes exhaust their vital sources and suffer the natural remedy: drastic population reductions. If lynxes eat too many snowshoe rabbits—which they are said to do repeatedly—then the lynxes starve down to the carrying capacity of their habitat. It is the carrying capacity of the lynx's habitat, not the carrying capacity of the lynx's stomach, that determines the prosperity of lynxes. Similarly, if humans use up too much soil—which they have often done and are doing—then they will starve down to the carrying capacity of *their* habitat. This is nature's "indifferent" justice. As Spenser saw in the sixteenth century, and as we must learn to see now, there is no appeal from this justice. In the hereafter, the Lord may forgive our wrongs against nature, but on earth, so far as we know, He does not overturn her decisions.

One of the differences between humans and lynxes is that humans can see that the principle of balance operates between lynxes and snowshoe rabbits, as between humans and topsoil; another difference, we hope, is that humans have the sense to act on their understanding. We can see, too, that a stable balance is preferable to a balance that tilts back and forth like a seesaw, dumping a surplus of creatures alternately from either end. To say this is to renew the question of whether or not the human relationship with nature is necessarily an adversary relationship, and it is to suggest that the answer is not simple.

But in dealing with this question and in trying to do justice to the presumed complexity of the answer, we are up against an American convention of simple opposition to nature that is deeply established both in our minds and in our ways. We have opposed the primeval forests of the East and the primeval prairies and deserts of the West, we have opposed man-eating beasts and crop-eating insects, sheep-eating coyotes, and chicken-eating hawks. In our lawns and gardens and fields, we oppose what we call weeds. And yet more and more of us are beginning to see that this opposition is ultimately destructive even of ourselves, that it does not explain many things that need explaining—in short, that it is untrue.

If our proper relation to nature is not opposition, then what is it? This question becomes complicated and difficult for us because none of us, as I have said, wants to live in a "pure" primeval forest or in a "pure" primeval prairie; we do not want to be eaten by grizzly bears; if we are gardeners, we have a legitimate quarrel with weeds; if, in Kentucky, we are trying to improve our pastures, we are likely to be enemies of the nodding thistle. But, do what we will, we remain under the spell of the primeval forests and prairies that we have cut down and broken; we turn repeatedly and with love to the thought of them and to their surviving remnants. We find ourselves attracted to the grizzly bears, too, and know that they and other great, dangerous animals remain alive in our imaginations as they have been all through human time. Though we cut down the nodding thistles, we acknowledge their beauty and are glad to think that there must be some place where they belong. (They may, in fact, not always be out of place in pastures; if, as seems evident, overgrazing makes an ideal seedbed for these plants, then we must understand them as a part of nature's strategy to protect the ground against abuse by animals.) Even the ugliest garden weeds earn affection from us when we consider how faithfully they perform an indispensable duty in covering the bare ground and in building humus. The weeds, too, are involved in the business of fertility.

We know, then, that the conflict between the human and the natural estates really exists and that it is to some extent necessary. But we are learning, or relearning, something else, too, that frightens us: namely, that this conflict often occurs at the expense of *both* estates. It is not only possible but altogether probable that by diminishing nature we diminish ourselves, and vice versa.

The conflict comes to light most suggestively, perhaps, when advocates for the two sides throw themselves into absolute conflict where no absolute difference can exist. An example of this is the battle between defenders of coyotes and defenders of sheep, in which the coyote-defenders may find it easy to forget that the sheep ranchers are human beings with some authentic complaints against coyotes, and the sheep-defenders find it easy to sound as if they advocate the total eradication of both coyotes and conservationists. Such conflicts—like the old one between hawk-defenders and chicken-defenders—tend to occur between people who use nature indirectly and people who use it directly. It is a dangerous mistake, I think, for either side to pursue such a quarrel on the assumption that victory would be a desirable result.

The fact is that people need both coyotes and sheep, need a world in which both kinds of life are possible. Outside the heat of conflict, conservationists probably know that a sheep is one of the best devices for making coarse foliage humanly edible and that wool is ecologically better than the synthetic fibers, just as most shepherds will be aware that wild nature is of value to them and not lacking in interest and pleasure.

The usefulness of coyotes is, of course, much harder to define than the usefulness of sheep. Coyote fur is not a likely substitute for wool, and, except as a last resort, most people don't want to eat coyotes. The difficulty lies in the difference between what is ours and what is nature's: What is ours is ours because it is directly useful. Coyotes are useful *indirectly*, as part of the health of nature, from which we and our sheep alike must live and take our health. The fact, moreover, may be that sheep and coyotes need each other, at least in the sense that neither would prosper in a place totally unfit for the other.

This sort of conflict, then, does not suggest the possibility of victory so much as it suggests the possibility of a compromise—some kind of peace, even an alliance, between the domestic and the wild. We know that such an alliance is necessary. Most conservationists now take for granted that humans thrive best in ecological health and that the test or sign of this health is the survival of a diversity of wild creatures. We know, too, that we cannot imagine ourselves apart from those necessary survivals of our own wildness that we call our instincts. And we know that we cannot have a healthy agriculture apart from the teeming wilderness in the topsoil, in which worms, bacteria, and other wild creatures are carrying on the fundamental work of decomposition, humus making, water storage, and drainage. "In wildness is the preservation of the world," as Thoreau said, may be a spiritual truth, but it is also a practical fact.

On the other hand, we must not fail to consider the opposite proposition—that, so long at least as humans are in the world, in human culture is the preservation of wildness—which is equally, and more demandingly, true. If wildness is to survive, then *we* must preserve it. We must preserve it by public act, by law, by institutionalizing wildernesses in some places. But such preservation is probably not enough. I have heard Wes Jackson of the Land Institute say, rightly I think, that if we cannot preserve our farmland, we cannot preserve the wilderness. That said, it becomes obvious that if we cannot preserve our cities, we cannot preserve the wilderness. This can be demonstrated practically by saying that the same attitudes that destroy wildness in the topsoil will finally destroy it everywhere; or by saying that if *everyone* has to go to a designated public wilderness for the necessary contact with wildness, then our parks will be no more natural than our cities.

But I am trying to say something more fundamental than that. What I am aiming at—because a lot of evidence seems to point this way—is the probability that nature and human culture, wildness and domesticity, are not opposed but are interdependent. Authentic experience of either will reveal the need of one for the other. In fact, examples from both past and present prove that a human economy and wildness can exist together not only in compatibility but to their mutual benefit.

One of the best examples I have come upon recently is the story of two Sonora Desert oases in Gary Nabhan's book, *The Desert Smells Like Rain*. The first of these oases, A'al Waipia, in Arizona, is dying because the park service, intending to preserve the natural integrity of the place as a bird sanctuary for tourists, removed the Papago Indians who had lived and farmed there. The place was naturally purer after the Indians were gone, but the oasis also began to shrink as the irrigation ditches silted up. As Mr. Nabhan puts it, "an odd thing is happening to their 'natural' bird sanctuary. They are losing the heterogeneity of the habitat, and with it, the birds. The old trees are dying.... These riparian trees are essential for the breeding habitat of certain birds. Summer annual seed plants are conspicuously absent.... Without the soil disturbance associated with plowing and flood irrigation, these natural foods for birds and rodents no longer germinate."

The other oasis, Ki:towak, in old Mexico, still thrives because a Papago village is still there, still farming. The village's oldest man, Luis Nolia, is the caretaker of the oasis, cleaning the springs and ditches, farming, planting trees: "Luis...blesses the oasis," Mr. Nabhan says, "for his work keeps it healthy." An ornithologist who accompanied Mr. Nabhan found twice as many species of birds at the farmed oasis as he found at the bird sanctuary, a fact that Mr. Nabhan's Papago friend, Remedio, explained in this way: "That's because those birds, they come where the people are. When the people live and work in a place, and plant their seeds and water their trees, the birds go live with them. They like those places, there's plenty to eat and that's when we are friends to them."

Another example, from my own experience, is suggestive in a somewhat different way. At the end of July 1981, while I was using a team of horses to mow a small triangular hillside pasture that is bordered on two sides by trees, I was suddenly aware of wings close below me. It was a young red-tailed hawk, who flew up into a walnut tree. I mowed on to the turn and stopped the team. The hawk then glided to the ground not twenty feet away. I got off the mower, stood and watched, even spoke, and the hawk showed no fear. I could see every feather distinctly, claw and beak and eye, the creamy down of the breast. Only when I took a step toward him, separating myself from the team and mower, did he fly. While I mowed three or four rounds, he stayed near, perched in trees or standing erect and watchful on the ground. Once, when I stopped to watch him, he was clearly watching me, stooping to see under the leaves that screened me from him. Again, when I could not find him, I stooped, saying to myself, "This is what he did to look at me," and as I did so I saw him looking at me.

Why had he come? To catch mice? Had he seen me scare one out of the grass? Or was it curiosity?

A human, of course, cannot speak with authority of the motives of hawks. I am aware of the possibility of explaining the episode merely by the hawk's youth and inexperience. And yet it does not happen often or dependably that one is approached so closely by a hawk of any age. I feel safe in making a couple of assumptions. The first is that the hawk came because of the conjunction of the small pasture and its wooded borders, of open hunting ground and the security of trees. This is the phenomenon of edge or margin that we know to be one of the powerful attractions of a diversified landscape, both to wildlife and to humans. The human eye itself seems drawn to such margins, hungering for the difference made in the countryside by a hedgy fencerow, a stream, or a grove of trees. And we know that these margins are biologically rich, the meeting of two kinds of habitat. But another difference also is important here: the difference between a large pasture and a small one, or, to use Wes Jackson's terms, the difference between a field and a patch. The pasture I was mowing was a patch—small, intimate, nowhere distant from its edges.

My second assumption is that the hawk was emboldened to come so near because, though he obviously recognized me as a man, I was there with the team of horses, with whom he familiarly and confidently shared the world.

I am saying, in other words, that this little visit between the hawk and me happened because the kind and scale of my farm, my way of farming, and my technology *allowed* it to happen. If I had been driving a tractor in a hundred-acre cornfield, it would not have happened.

In some circles I would certainly be asked if one can or should be serious about such an encounter, if it has any value. And though I cannot produce any hard evidence, I would unhesitatingly answer yes. Such encounters involve another margin—the one between domesticity and wildness—that attracts us irresistibly; they are among the best rewards of outdoor work and among the reasons for loving to farm. When the scale of farming grows so great and obtrusive as to forbid them, the *life* of farming is impoverished.

But perhaps we do find hard evidence of a sort when we consider that *all* of us—the hawk, the horses, and I—were there for our benefit and, to some extent, for our *mutual* benefit: The horses live from the pasture and maintain it with their work, grazing, and manure; the team and I together furnish hunting ground to the hawk; the hawk serves us by controlling the field mouse population.

These meetings of the human and the natural estates, the domestic and the wild, occur invisibly, of course, in any well-farmed field. The wilderness of a healthy soil, too complex for human comprehension, can yet be husbanded, can benefit from human care, and can deliver incalculable benefits in return. Mutuality of interest and reward is a possibility that can reach to any city backyard, garden, and park, but in any place under human dominance—which is, now, virtually everyplace—it is a possibility that is *both* natural and cultural. If humans want wildness to be possible, then they have to make it possible. If balance is the ruling principle and a stable balance the goal, then, for humans, attaining this goal requires a consciously chosen and deliberately made partnership with nature.

In other words, we can be true to nature only by being true to human nature—to our animal nature as well as to cultural patterns and restraints that keep us from acting like animals. When humans act like animals, they become the most dangerous of animals to themselves and other humans, and this is because of another critical difference between humans and animals: Whereas animals are usually restrained by the limits of physical appetites, humans have mental appetites that can be far more gross and capacious than physical ones. Only humans squander and hoard, murder and pillage because of notions.

The work by which good human and natural possibilities are preserved is complex and difficult, and it probably cannot be accomplished by raw intelligence and information. It requires knowledge, skills, and restraints, some of which must come from our past. In the hurry of technological progress, we have replaced some tools and methods that worked with some that do not work. But we also need culture-borne instructions about who or what humans are and how and on what assumptions they should act. The Chain of Being, for instance—which gave humans a place between animals and angels in the order of Creation—is an old idea that has not been replaced by any adequate new one. It was simply rejected, and the lack of it leaves us without a definition.

Lacking the ancient definition, or any such definition, we do not know at what point to restrain or deny ourselves. We do not know how ambitious to be, what or how much we may safely desire, when or where to stop. I knew a barber once who refused to give a discount to a bald client, explaining that his artistry consisted, not in the cutting off, but in the knowing when to stop. He spoke, I think, as a true artist and a true human. The lack of such knowledge is extremely dangerous in and to an individual. But ignorance of when to stop is a modern epidemic; it is the basis of "industrial progress" and "economic growth." The most obvious practical result of this ignorance is a critical disproportion of scale between the scale of human enterprises and their sources in nature.

The scale of the energy industry, for example, is too big, as is the scale of the transportation industry. The scale of agriculture, from a technological or economic point of view, is too big, but from a demographic point of view, the scale is too small. When there are enough people on the land to use it but not enough to husband it, then the wildness of the soil that we call fertility begins to diminish, and the soil itself begins to flee from us in water and wind.

If the human economy is to be fitted into the natural economy in such a way that both may thrive, the human economy must be built to proper scale. It is possible to talk at great length about the difference between proper and improper scale. It may be enough to say here that that difference is *suggested* by the difference between amplified and unamplified music in the countryside, or the difference between the sound of a motorboat and the sound of oarlocks. A proper human sound, we may say, is one that allows other sounds to be heard. A properly scaled human economy or technology allows a diversity of other creatures to thrive.

"The proper scale," a friend wrote to me, "confers freedom and simplicity...and doubtless leads to long life and health." I think that it also confers joy. The renewal of our partnership with nature, the rejoining of our works to their proper places in the natural order, reshaped to their proper scale, implies the reenjoyment both of nature and of human domesticity. Though our task will be difficult, we will greatly mistake its nature if we see it as grim, or if we suppose that it must always be necessary to suffer at work in order to enjoy ourselves in places specializing in "recreation."

Once we grant the possibility of a proper human scale, we see that we have made a radical change of assumptions and values. We realize that we are less interested in technological "breakthroughs" than in technological elegance. Of a new tool or method we will no longer ask: Is it fast? Is it powerful? Is it a labor saver? How many workers will it replace? We will ask instead: Can we (and our children) afford it? Is it fitting to our real needs? Is it becoming to us? Is it unhealthy or ugly? And though we may keep a certain interest in innovation and in what we may become, we will renew our interest in what we have been, realizing that conservationists must necessarily conserve *both* inheritances, the natural and the cultural.

To argue the necessity of wildness to, and in, the human economy is by no means to argue against the necessity of wilderness. The survival of wilderness—of places that we do not change, where we allow the existence even of creatures we perceive as dangerous—is necessary. Our sanity probably requires it. Whether we go to those places or not, we need to know that they exist. And I would argue that we do not need just the great public wildernesses, but millions of small private or semiprivate ones. Every farm should have one; wildernesses can occupy corners of factory grounds and city lots—places where nature is given a free hand, where no human work is done, where people go only as guests. These places function, I think, whether we intend them to or not, as sacred groves—places we respect and leave alone, not because we understand well what goes on there, but because we do not.

We go to wilderness places to be restored, to be instructed in the natural economies of fertility and healing, to admire what we cannot make. Sometimes, as we find to our surprise, we go to be chastened or corrected. And we go in order to return with renewed knowledge by which to judge the health of our human economy and our dwelling places. As we return from our visits to the wilderness, it is sometimes possible to imagine a series of fitting and decent transitions from wild nature to the human community and its supports: from forest to woodlot to the "two-story agriculture" of tree crops and pasture to orchard to meadow to grain field to garden to household to neighborhood to village to city—so that even when we reached the city we would not be entirely beyond the influence of the nature of that place.

What I have been implying is that I think there is a bad reason to go to the wilderness. We must not go there to escape the ugliness and the dangers of the present human economy. We must not let ourselves feel that to go there is to escape. In the first place, such an escape is now illusory. In the second place, if, even as conservationists, we see the human and the natural economies as necessarily opposite or opposed, we subscribe to the very opposition that threatens to destroy them both. The wild and the domestic now often seem isolated values, estranged from one another. And yet these are not exclusive polarities like good and evil. There can be continuity between them, and there must be.

What we find, if we weight the balance too much in favor of the domestic, is that we involve ourselves in dangers both personal and public. Not the least of these dangers is dependence on distant sources of money and materials. Farmers are in deep trouble now because they have become too dependent on corporations and banks. They have been using methods and species that enforce this dependence. But such a dependence is not safe, either for farmers or for agriculture. It is not safe for urban consumers. Ultimately, as we are beginning to see, it is not safe for banks and corporations—which, though they have evidently not thought so, are dependent upon farmers. Our farms are endangered because—like the interstate highways or modern hospitals or modern universities—they cannot be inexpensively used. To be usable at all they require great expense.

When the human estate becomes so precarious, our only recourse is to move it back toward the estate of nature. We undoubtedly need better plant and animal species than nature provided us. But we are beginning to see that they can be too much better—too dependent on us and on "the economy," too expensive. In farm animals, for instance, we want good commercial quality, but we can see that the ability to produce meat or milk can actually be a threat to the farmer and to the animal if not accompanied by qualities we would call natural: thriftiness, hardiness, physical vigor, resistance to disease and parasites, ability to breed and give birth without assistance, strong mothering instincts. These natural qualities decrease care, work, and worry; they also decrease the cost of production. They save feed and time; they make diseases and cures exceptional rather than routine.

We need crop and forage species of high productive ability also, but we do not need species that will not produce at all without expensive fertilizers and chemicals. Contrary to the premise of agribusiness advertisements and of most expert advice, farmers do not thrive by production or by "skimming" a large "cash flow." They cannot solve their problems merely by increasing production or income. They thrive, like all other creatures, according to the difference between their income and their expenses.

One of the strangest characteristics of the industrial economy is the ability to increase production again and again without ever noticing—or without acknowledging—the *costs* of production. That one Holstein cow should produce 50,000 pounds of milk in a year may appear to be marvelous—a miracle of modern science. But what if her productivity is dependent upon the consumption of a huge amount of grain (about a bushel a day), and therefore upon the availability of cheap petroleum? What if she is too valuable (and too delicate) to be allowed outdoors in the rain? What if the proliferation of her kind will again drastically reduce the number of dairy farms and farmers? Or, to use a more obvious example, can we afford a bushel of grain at a cost of five to twenty bushels of topsoil lost to erosion?

"It is good to have Nature working for you," said Henry Besuden, the dean of American Southdown breeders. "She works for a minimum wage." That is true. She works at times for almost nothing, requiring only that we respect her work and give her a chance, as when she maintains—indeed, improves—the fertility and productivity of a pasture by the natural succession of clover and grass or when she improves a clay soil for us by means of the roots of a grass sod. She works for us by preserving health or wholeness, which for all our ingenuity we cannot make. If we fail to respect her health, she deals out her justice by withdrawing her protection against disease—which we *can* make, and do.

To make this continuity between the natural and the human, we have only two sources of instruction: nature herself and our cultural tradition. If we listen only to the apologists for the industrial economy, who respect neither nature nor culture, we get the idea that it is somehow our goodness that makes us so destructive: The air is unfit to breathe, the water is unfit to drink, the soil is washing away, the cities are violent and the countryside neglected, all because we are intelligent, enterprising, industrious, and generous, concerned only to feed the hungry and to "make a better future for our children." Respect for nature causes us to doubt this, and our cultural tradition confirms and illuminates our doubt: No good thing is destroyed by goodness; good things are destroyed by wickedness. We may identify that insight as Biblical, but it is taken for granted by both the Greek and the Biblical lineages of our culture, from Homer and Moses to William Blake. Since the start of the industrial revolution, there have been voices urging that this inheritance may be safely replaced by intelligence, information, energy, and money. No idea, I believe, could be more dangerous.

62

Putting the Earth First

DAVE FOREMAN

Dave Foreman (1946–) is a self-described radical environmentalist, a cofounder of Earth First!, and an articulate advocate of the "wilderness" vision. Unspoiled wilderness—what Foreman calls "the Big Outside"—is fast disappearing in the name of development and progress, and mainstream environmental groups have not done nearly enough to halt or reverse this trend. Here Foreman defends an uncompromising wilderness vision against advocates of compromise and conciliation, and makes the case for "putting the earth first."

Source: From *Confessions of an Eco-Warrior* by Dave Foreman, copyright © 1991 by Dave Foreman. Used by permission of Harmony Books, a division of Random House, Inc.

PUTTING THE EARTH FIRST

> These are the times that try men's souls; the summer soldier and the sunshine patriot will, in this crisis, shrink from the service of his country, but he that stands it now, deserves the love and thanks of man and woman.
>
> —Thomas Paine

In July 1987, seven years after the campfire gathering that spawned Earth First!, I rose among the Ponderosa Pines and scattered shafts of sunlight on the North Rim of the Grand Canyon and mounted a stage festooned with Earth First! banners and American flags. Before me sat several hundred people: hippies in tie-dyed shirts and Birkenstocks, rednecks for wilderness in cowboy boots and hats, middle-class hikers in waffle stompers, graybeards and children. The diversity was impressive. The energy was overpowering. Never in my wildest dreams had I imagined the Earth First! movement would attract so many. Never had I hoped that we would have begun to pack such a punch. We were attracting national attention; we were changing the parameters of the debate about ecological issues; we had become a legend in conservation lore.

Yet, after seven years, I was concerned we were losing some of our clarity of purpose, and blurring our focus. In launching Earth First!, I had said, "Let our actions set the finer points of our philosophy." But now I was concerned that the *what* of our actions might be overwhelming the *why*. For some of those newly attracted to Earth First!, action seemed to be its own justification. I felt a need to return to wilderness fundamentalism, to articulate what I thought were the principles that defined the Earth First! movement, that gave it a specific identity. The response to the principles I offered that day was so overwhelmingly positive that I elaborated on them in the *Earth First! Journal* later that fall. Here they are.

A placing of earth first! in all decisions, even ahead of human welfare if necessary. Our movement is called "Earth First!" not "People First!" Sometimes what appears to be in the short-term interest of human beings as a whole, a select group of human beings, or individual human beings is detrimental to the short-term or long-term health of the biosphere (and to the actual long-term welfare of human beings). Earth First! does not argue that native diversity should be preserved if it can be done without negatively impacting the material "standard of living" of a group of human beings. We simply state that native diversity should be preserved, that natural diversity a-building for three and a half billion years should be left unfettered. Human beings must adjust to the planet; it is supreme arrogance to expect the planet and all it contains to adjust to the demands of humans. In everything human society does, the primary consideration should be for the long-term health and biological diversity of Earth. After that, we can consider the welfare of humans. We should be kind, compassionate, and caring with other people, but Earth comes first.

A refusal to use human beings as the measure by which to value others. An individual human life has no more intrinsic value than does an individual grizzly bear life. Human suffering resulting from drought and famine in Ethiopia is tragic, yes, but the destruction there of other creatures and habitat is even more tragic. This leads quickly into the next point:

An enthusiastic embracing of the philosophy of deep ecology or biocentrism. This philosophy states simply and essentially that all living creatures and communities possess intrinsic value, inherent worth. Natural things live for their own sake, which is another way of saying they have value. Other beings (both animal and plant) and even so-called "inanimate" objects such as rivers and mountains are not placed here for the convenience of human beings. Our biocentric world-view denies the modern concept of "resources." The dominant philosophy of our time (which contains Judeo-Christianity, Islam, capitalism, Marxism, scientism, and secular humanism) is anthropocentrism. It places human beings at the center of the universe, separates them from nature, and endows them with unique value. EF!ers are in direct opposition to that philosophy. Ours is an ecological perspective that views Earth as a community and recognizes such apparent enemies as "disease" (e.g., malaria) and "pests" (e.g., mosquitoes) not as manifestations of evil to be overcome but rather as vital and necessary components of a complex and vibrant biosphere.

A realization that wilderness is the real world. The preservation of wilderness is the fundamental issue. Wilderness does not merely mean backpacking parks or scenery. It is the natural world, the arena for evolution, the cauldron from which humans emerged, the home of the others with whom we share this planet. Wilderness is the real world; our cities, our computers, our airplanes, our global business civilization all are but artificial and transient phenomena. It is important to remember that only a tiny portion of the history of the human species has occurred outside of wilderness. The preservation of wildness and native diversity is the most important issue. Issues directly affecting only humans pale in comparison. Of course, ecology teaches us that all things are connected, and in this regard all other matters become subsets of wilderness preservation—the prevention of nuclear war, for example—but the most important campaigns being waged today are those directly on behalf of wilderness.

A recognition that there are far too many human beings on earth. There are too many of us everywhere—in the United States, in Nigeria; in cities, in rural areas; with digging hoes, with tractors. Although there is obviously an unconscionable maldistribution of wealth and the basic necessities of life among humans, this fact should not be used—as some leftists are wont to do—to argue that overpopulation is not the problem. It is a large part of the problem; there are far too many of us already—and our numbers continue to grow astronomically. Even if inequitable distribution could be solved, six billion human beings converting the natural world to material goods and human food would devastate natural diversity.

This basic recognition of the overpopulation problem does not mean that we should ignore the economic and social causes of overpopulation, and shouldn't criticize the accumulation of wealth in fewer and fewer hands, the maldistribution of "resources," and the venality of multinational corporations and Third World juntas alike, but simply that we must understand that great blue whales, jaguars, black rhinoceroses, and rain forests are not compatible with an exploding human population.[1]

A deep questioning of, and even an antipathy to, "progress" and "technology." In looking at human history, we can see that we have lost more in our "rise" to civilization than we have gained. We can see that life in a hunter-gatherer society was on the whole healthier, happier, and more secure than our lives today as peasants, industrial workers, or business executives. For every material "achievement" of progress, there are a dozen losses of things of profound and ineffable value. We can accept the pejoratives of "Luddite" and "Neanderthal" with pride. (This does not mean that we must immediately eschew all the facets of technological civilization. We are of it, and use it; this does not mean that we can't critique it.)

A refusal to accept rationality as the only way of thinking. There is room for great diversity within Earth First! on matters spiritual, and nowhere is tolerance for diversity more necessary. But we can all recognize that linear, rational, logical left-brain thinking represents only part of our brain and consciousness. Rationality is a fine and useful tool, but it is just that—a tool, one way of analyzing matters. Equally valid, perhaps more so, is intuitive, instinctive awareness. We can become more cognizant of ultimate truths by sitting quietly in the wild than by studying in a library. Reading books, engaging in logical discourse, and compiling facts and figures are necessary in the modern context, but they are not the only ways to comprehend the world and our lives. Often our gut instincts enable us to act more effectively in a crisis than does careful rational analysis. An example would be a patient bleeding to death in a hospital emergency room—you can't wait for all the tests to be completed. Your gut says, "Act!" So it is with Earth First!'s actions in Earth's current emergency.

A lack of desire to gain credibility or "legitimacy" with the gang of thugs running human civilization. It is basic human nature to want to be accepted by the social milieu in which you find yourself. It hurts to be dismissed by the arbiters of opinion as "nuts," "terrorists," "wackos," or "extremists." But we are not crazy; we happen to be sane humans in an insane human society in a sane natural world. We do not have "credibility" with Senator Mark Hatfield or with Maxxam chairman Charles Hurwitz—but they do not have credibility with us! (We do have their attention, however.) They are madmen destroying the pure and beautiful. Why should we "reason" with them? We do not share the same worldview or values. There is, however, a dangerous pitfall here that some alternative groups fall into. That is that we gain little by being consciously offensive, by trying to alienate others. We can be strong and unyielding without being obnoxious.

The American system is very effective at coopting and moderating dissidents by giving them attention and then encouraging them to be "reasonable" so their ideas will be taken seriously. Putting a critic on the evening news, on the front page of the newspaper, in a national magazine—all of these are methods the establishment uses to entice one to share their worldview and to enter the negotiating room to compromise. The actions of Earth First!—both the bold and the comic—have gained attention. If they are to have results, we must resist the siren's offer of credibility, legitimacy, and a share in the decision making. We are thwarting the system, not reforming it. While we are therefore not concerned with political credibility, it must be remembered that the arguments and actions of Earth First! are based on the understandings of ecology. It is vitally important that we have biological credibility.

An effort to go beyond the tired, worn-out dogmas of left, right, and middle-of-the-road. These doctrines, whether blaming capitalism, communism, or the devil for all the problems in the world, merely represent internecine squabbles between different factions of humanism. Yes, multinational corporations commit great evil (the Soviet Union was essentially a state-run multinational corporation); there is a great injustice in the world; the rich are getting richer and the poor poorer—but all problems cannot be simplistically laid at the feet of evil capitalists in the United States, Europe, and Japan. Earth First! is not left or right; we are not even in front. Earth First! should not be in the political struggle between humanist sects at all. We're in a wholly different game.

An unwillingness to set any ethnic, class, or political group of humans on a pedestal and make them immune from questioning. It's easy, of course, to recognize that white males from North America and Europe (as well as Japanese males) hold a disproportionate share of responsibility for the mess we're in; that upper- and middle-class consumers from the First World take an excessive portion of the world's "resources" and therefore cause greater per capita destruction than do other peoples. But it does not follow that everyone else is blameless.

The Earth First! movement has great affinity with aboriginal groups throughout the world. They are clearly in the most direct and respectful relationship with the natural world. Earth First! should back such tribes in the common struggle whenever possible without compromising our ideals. For example, we are supportive of the Dine (Navajo) of Big Mountain against relocation, but this does not mean we overlook the severe overgrazing by domestic sheep on the Navajo Reservation. We may be supportive of subsistence lifestyles by natives in Alaska, but we should not be silent about clearcutting old-growth forest in southeast Alaska by native corporations, or about the Eskimo Doyon Corporation's push for oil exploration and development in the Arctic National Wildlife Refuge. It is racist either to condemn or to pardon someone based on their ethnic background.

Similarly, we are inconsistent when we castigate Charles Hurwitz for destroying the last wilderness redwood forest, yet feel sympathy for the loggers working for him. Industrial workers, by and large, share the blame for the destruction of the natural world. They may be yoked by the big-money boys, but they are generally willing servants who share the world-view of their bosses that Earth is a smorgasbord of resources for the taking. Sometimes, in fact, it is the sturdy yeoman from the bumpkin proletariat who holds the most violent and destructive attitudes toward the natural world (and toward those who would defend it).[2] Workers are victims of an unjust economic system, but that does not absolve them of what they do. This is not to deny that some woods workers oppose the destruction of ancient forests, that some may even be Earth First!ers, but merely that it is inappropriate to overlook abuse of the natural world simply because of the rung the perpetrators occupy on the economic ladder.

Some argue that workers are merely struggling to feed their families and are not delighting in destroying the natural world. They say that unless you deal with the needs of loggers to make a living, you can't save the forest. They also claim that loggers are manipulated by their bosses to express anti-wilderness viewpoints. I find this argument to be patronizing to loggers and other workers. When I read comments from timber fellers expressing hatred toward pristine forests and toward conservationists, it is obvious that they willingly buy into the worldview of the lumber barons. San Francisco's *Image Magazine* reports on a letter to the editor written by one logger: "Working people trying to feed their families have little time to be out in the woods acting like children and making things hard for other working people.... Anyone out there have a recipe for spotted owl? Food stamps won't go far, I'm afraid. And since they're always being shoved down my throat, I thought I'd like mine fried."[3] Bumper stickers proclaiming "Kill an owl. Save a logger" are rife in the Northwest. I at least respect the logger who glories in felling a giant tree and who hunts spotted owls enough to grant him the mental ability to have his own opinions instead of pretending he is a stupid oaf, manipulated by his bosses and unable to think for himself.

Of course the big timber companies do manipulate their workers with scare tactics about mill closings and wilderness lockups, but many loggers (or cat-skinners, oilfield workers, miners, and the like) simply hate the wild and delight in "civilizing" it. Even educating workers about ecological principles will not necessarily change the attitudes of many; there are basic differences of opinion and values. Conservationists should try to find common ground with loggers and other workers whenever possible, but the sooner we get rid of Marxist views about the noble proletariat, the better.

A willingness to let our actions set the finer points of our philosophy and a recognition that we must act. It is possible to debate endlessly the finer points of dogma, to feel that every nuance of something must be explored before one can act. Too often, political movements become mere debating societies where the participants engage in philosophical masturbation and never get down to the vital business at hand. Others argue that you have no right to argue for environmental preservation until you are living a pure, non-impacting life-style. We will never figure it all out, we will never be able to plan any campaign in complete detail, none of us will ever entirely transcend a polluting life-style—but we can act. We can act with courage, with determination, with love for things wild and free. We can't be perfect, but we can act. We are warriors. Earth First! is a warrior society. We have a job to do.

An acknowledgment that we must change our personal life-styles to make them more harmonious with natural diversity. We must eschew surplusage. Although to varying degrees we are all captives of our economic system and cannot break entirely free, we must practice what we preach to the best of our ability. Arne Naess, the Norwegian philosopher and originator of the term "Deep Ecology," points out that we are not able to achieve a true "Deep Ecology" life-style, but it is the responsibility of each of us to move in that direction. Most of us still need to make a living that involves some level of participation in "the system." Even for activists, there are trade-offs—flying in a jetliner to help hang a banner on the World Bank in Washington, D.C., in order to bring international attention to the plight of tropical rain forests; using a computer to write a book printed on tree pulp that will catalyze people to take action;

driving a pickup truck down a forest road to gain access to a proposed timber sale for preventive maintenance. We need to be aware of these tradeoffs, and to do our utmost to limit our impact.

A commitment to maintaining a sense of humor, and a joy in living. Most radicals are a dour, holier-than-thou, humorless lot. Earth First!ers strive to be different. We aren't rebelling against the system because we're losing in it. We're fighting for beauty, for life, for joy. We kick up our heels in delight in the wilderness, we smile at a flower and a hummingbird. We laugh. We laugh at our opponents—and, more important, we laugh at ourselves.

An awareness that we are animals. Human beings are primates, mammals, vertebrates. EF!ers recognize their animalness; we reject the New Age eco-la-la that says we must transcend our base animal nature and take charge of our evolution in order to become higher, moral beings. We believe we must return to being animal, to glorying in our sweat, hormones, tears, and blood. We struggle against the modern compulsion to become dull, passionless androids. We do not live sanitary, logical lives; we smell, taste, see, hear, and feel Earth; we live with gusto. We are Animal.

An acceptance of monkeywrenching as a legitimate tool for the preservation of natural diversity. Not all Earth First!ers monkeywrench, perhaps not even the majority, but we generally accept the idea and practice of monkeywrenching. Look at an EF! T-shirt. The monkeywrench on it is a symbol of resistance, an heir of the sabot—the wooden shoe dropped in the gears to stop the machine, from whence comes the word sabotage. The mystique and lore of "night work" pervades our tribe, and with it a general acceptance that strategic monkeywrenching is a legitimate tool for defense of the wild.

And finally: Earth First! is a warrior society. In addition to our absolute commitment to and love for this living planet, we are characterized by our willingness to defend Earth's abundance and diversity of life, even if that defense requires sacrifices of comfort, freedom, safety, or, ultimately, our lives. A warrior recognizes that her life is not the most important thing in her life. A warrior recognizes that there is a greater reality outside her life that must be defended. For us in Earth First!, that reality is Earth, the evolutionary process, the millions of other species with which we share this bright sphere in the void of space.

Not everyone can afford to make the commitment of being a warrior. There are many other roles that can—and must—be played in defense of Earth. One may not constantly be able to carry the burden of being a warrior; it may be only a brief period in one's life. There are risks and pitfalls in being a warrior. There may not be applause, there may not be honors and awards from human society. But there is no finer applause for the warrior of the Earth than the call of the loon at dusk or the sigh of wind in the pines.

***

Later that evening as I looked out over the darkening Grand Canyon, I knew that whatever hardships the future might bring, there was nothing better and more important for me to do than to take an intransigent stand in defense of life, to not compromise, to continue to be a warrior for the Earth. To be a warrior for the Earth regardless of the consequences.

NOTES

1. Two excellent books on the population issue that are also sensitive to social and economic issues are William R. Catton, Jr.'s *Overshoot: The Ecological Basis of Revolutionary Change* (Urbana, Ill., and Chicago: University of Illinois Press, 1982), and *The Population Explosion,* by Paul and Anne Ehrlich (New York: Simon and Schuster, 1990). No one concerned with the preservation of biological diversity should be without these.
2. A case in point involves the Spotted Owl, a threatened species dependent on ancient forests. These little owls are easily attracted by playing tapes of their call. Loggers in the Northwest are going into old-growth forests with tape recorders and shotguns to exterminate Spotted Owls. They feel that if they do so, they will eliminate a major reason to stop the logging of these pristine forests.
3. Jane Kay, "Tree Wars," *San Francisco Examiner Image Magazine* (December 17, 1989).

63

Women in Nature

VANDANA SHIVA

Vandana Shiva (1952—) of India is a prolific author and environmental activist who describes herself as an "ecofeminist." Shiva, who holds a Ph.D. in physics, is director of the Research Foundation for Science, Technology, and Natural Resource Policy, which supports research on Third World development and sustainable agriculture. In the following selection, and elsewhere, Shiva argues that economic "development" in the Third World comes at a high human and environmental price, doing more harm than good for those whom it purports to help. This is true especially of women, who are intimately linked to nature: "The women's and ecology movements are therefore one, and are primarily counter-trends to a patriarchal maldevelopment."

Source: Vandana Shiva, Staying Alive: Women, Ecology, and Development (London: Zed Books, 1988). Reprinted by permission of Zed Books.

WOMEN IN NATURE

With the violation of nature is linked the violation and marginalisation of women, especially in the Third World. Women produce and reproduce life not merely biologically, but also through their social role in providing sustenance. All ecological societies of forest dwellers and peasants, whose life is organised on the principle of sustainability and the reproduction of life in all its richness, also embody the feminine principle. Historically, however, when such societies have been colonised and broken up the men have usually started to participate in life-destroying activities or have had to migrate; the women meanwhile usually continue to be linked to life and nature through their role as providers of sustenance, food and water. The privileged access of women to the sustaining principle thus has a historical and cultural, and not merely biological, basis. The principle of creating and conserving life is lost to the ecologically alienated, consumerist elite women of the Third World and the over-consuming west, just as much as it is conserved in the lifestyle of the male and female forest-dwellers and peasants in small pockets of the Third World.

Maria Mies has called women's work in producing sustenance the *production of life* and views it as a truly productive relationship to nature, because women not only collected and consumed what grew in nature but they *made things grow*.[1] This organic process of growth in which women and nature work in partnership with each other has created a special relationship of women with nature, which, following Mies, can be summarised as follows:

a. Their interaction with nature, with their own nature as well as the external environment, was a reciprocal process. They conceived of their own bodies as being productive in the same way as they conceived of external nature being so.
b. Although they appropriate nature, their appropriation does not constitute a relationship of dominance or a property relation. Women are not owners of their own bodies or of the earth, but they co-operate with their bodies and with the earth in order "to let grow and to make grow."
c. As producers of new life they also became the first subsistence producers and the inventors of the first productive economy, implying from the beginning social production and the creation of social relations, i.e. of society and history.

Productivity, viewed from the perspective of survival, differs sharply from the dominant view of the productivity of labour as defined for processes of capital accumulation. "Productive" man, producing commodities, using some of nature's wealth and women's work as raw material and dispensing with the rest as waste, becomes the only legitimate category of work, wealth and production. Nature and women working to produce and reproduce life are declared "unproductive."

With Adam Smith, the wealth created by nature and women's work was turned invisible. Labour, and especially male labour, became the fund which originally supplies it with all the necessities and conveniences of life. As this assumption spread to all human communities, it introduced dualities within society, and between nature and man. No more was nature a source of wealth and sustenance; no more was women's work in sustenance "productive" work; no more were peasant and tribal societies creative and productive. They were all marginal to the framework of the industrial society, except as resources and inputs. The transforming, productive power was associated only with male western labour and economic development became a design of remodelling the world on that assumption. The devaluation and de-recognition of nature's work and productivity has led to the ecological crises; the devaluation and de-recognition of women's work has created sexism and inequality between men and women. The devaluation of subsistence, or rather sustenance economies, based on harmony between nature's work, women's work and man's work has created the various forms of ethnic and cultural crises that plague our world today.

The crisis of survival and the threat to sustenance arises from ecological disruption that is rooted in the arrogance of the west and those that ape it. This arrogance is grounded in a blindness towards the quiet work and the invisible wealth created by nature and women and those who produce sustenance. Such work and wealth are "invisible" because they are decentred, local and in harmony with local ecosystems and needs: The more effectively the cycles of life, as essential ecological processes, are maintained, the more invisible they become. Disruption is violent and visible; balance and harmony are experienced, not seen. The premium on visibility placed by patriarchal maldevelopment forces the destruction of invisible energies and the work of women and nature, and the creation of spectacular, centralised work and wealth. Such centralisation and the uniformity associated with it works further against the diversity and plurality of life. Work and wealth in accordance with the feminine principle are significant precisely because they are rooted in stability and sustainability. Decentred diversity is the source of nature's work and women's productivity; it is the work of "insignificant" plants in creating significant changes which shift the ecological equilibrium in life's favour. It is the energy of all living things, in all their diversity, and together, the diversity of lives wields tremendous energy. Women's work is similarly invisible in providing sustenance and creating wealth for basic needs. Their work in the forest, the field and the river creates sustenance in quiet but essential ways. Every woman in every house in every village of rural India works invisibly to provide the stuff of life to nature and people. It is this invisible work that is linked to nature and needs, which conserves nature through maintaining ecological cycles, and conserves human life through satisfying the basic needs of food, nutrition and water. It is this essential work that is destroyed and dispensed with by maldevelopment: the maintenance of ecological cycles has no place in a political economy of commodity and cash flows.

The existence of the feminine principle is linked with diversity and sharing. Its destruction through homogenisation and privatisation leads to the destruction of diversity and of the commons. The sustenance economy is based on a creative and organic nature, on local knowledge, on locally recycled inputs that maintain the integrity of nature, on local consumption for local needs, and on the marketing of surplus beyond the imperatives of equity and ecology. The commodity and cash economy destroys natural cycles and reduces nature to raw materials and commodities. It creates the need for purchase and sale to centralised inputs and commodity markets. When production is specialised and for export, surplus becomes a myth. There is only indebtedness, of peoples and nations. The debt trap is part of global commodity production and sale which destroys nurturing nature and nurturing economies in the name of development.

Sustenance, in the final analysis, is built on the continued capacity of nature to renew its forests, fields and rivers. These resource systems are intrinsically linked in life-producing and life-conserving cultures, and it is in managing the integrity of ecological cycles in forestry and agriculture that women's productivity has been most developed and evolved. Women transfer fertility from the forests to the field and to animals. They transfer animal waste as fertilizer for crops and crop by-products to animals as fodder. They work with the forest to bring water to their fields and families. This partnership between women's and nature's work ensures the sustainability of sustenance, and it is this critical partnership that is torn asunder when the project of "development" becomes a patriarchal project, threatening both nature and women. The forest is separated from the river, the field is separated from the forest, the animals are separated from the crops. Each is then separately developed, and the delicate balance which ensures sustainability and equity is destroyed. The visibility of dramatic breaks and ruptures is posited as "progress." Marginalised women are either dispensed with or colonised. Needs go unfulfilled, nature is crippled. The drama of violence and fragmentation cannot be sustained and the recovery of the feminine principle thus becomes essential for liberating not only women and nature, but also the patriarchal reductionist categories which give rise to maldevelopment.

The revolutionary and liberational potential of the recovery of the feminine principle consists in its challenging the concepts, categories and processes which have created the threat to life, and in providing oppositional categories that create and enlarge the spaces for maintaining and enriching all life in nature and society. The radical shift induced by a focus on the feminine principle is the recognition of maldevelopment as a culture of destruction. The feminine principle becomes a category of challenge which locates nature and women as the source of life and wealth, and as such, active subjects, maintaining and creating life-processes.

There are two implications that arise from the recognition of nature and women as producers of life. First, that what goes by the name of development is a maldevelopment process, a source of violence to women and nature throughout the world. This violence does not arise from the misapplication of an otherwise benign and gender-neutral model, but is rooted in the patriarchal assumptions of homogeneity, domination and centralisation that underlie dominant models of thought and development strategies. Second, that the crises that the maldevelopment model has given rise to cannot be solved within the paradigm of the crisis mind. Their solution lies in the categories of thought, perception and action that are life-giving and life-maintaining. In contemporary times, Third World women, whose minds have not yet been dispossessed or colonised, are in a privileged position to make visible the invisible oppositional categories that they are the custodians of. It is not only as victims, but also as leaders in creating new intellectual ecological paradigms, that women are central to arresting and overcoming ecological crises. Just as ecological recovery begins from centres of natural diversity which are gene pools, Third World women, and those tribals and peasants who have been left out of the processes of maldevelopment, are today acting as the intellectual gene pools of ecological categories of thought and action. Marginalisation has thus become a source for healing the diseased mainstream of patriarchal development. Those facing the biggest threat offer the best promise for survival because they have two kinds of knowledge that are not accessible to dominant and privileged groups. First, they have the knowledge of what it means to be the victims of progress, to be the ones who bear the costs and burdens. Second, they have the holistic and ecological knowledge of what the production and protection of life is about. They retain the ability to see nature's life as a *precondition* for human survival and the integrity of inter-connectedness in nature as a precondition for life. Women of the Third World have been dispossessed of their base for sustenance, but not of their minds, and in their uncolonised minds are conserved the oppositional categories that make the sustenance of life possible for all. The producers of life alone can be its real protectors. Women embedded in nature, producing life with nature, are therefore taking the initiative in the recovery of nature.

To say that women and nature are intimately associated is not to say anything revolutionary. After all, it was precisely just such an assumption that allowed the domination of both women and nature. The new insight provided by rural women in the Third World is that women and nature are associated *not in passivity but in creativity and in the maintenance of life.*

This analysis differs from most conventional analyses of environmentalists and feminists. Most work on women and environment in the Third World has focussed on women as special victims of environmental degradation. Yet the women who participate in and lead ecology movements in countries like India are not speaking merely as victims. Their voices are the voices of liberation and transformation which provide new categories of thought and new exploratory directions. In this sense, this study is a postvictimology study. It is an articulation of the categories of challenge that women in ecology movements are creating in the Third World. The women and environment issue can be approached either from these categories of challenge that have been thrown up by women in the struggle for life, or it can be approached through an extension of conventional categories of patriarchy and reductionism. In the perspective of women engaged in survival struggles which are, simultaneously, struggles for the protection of nature, women and nature are intimately related, and their domination and liberation similarly linked. The women's and ecology movements are therefore one, and are primarily counter-trends to a patriarchal maldevelopment. Our experience shows that ecology and feminism can combine in the recovery of the feminine principle, and through this recovery, can intellectually and politically restructure and transform maldevelopment.

Maldevelopment is seen here as a process by which human society marginalises the play of the feminine principle in nature and in society. Ecological breakdown and social inequality are intrinsically related to the dominant development paradigm which puts man against and above nature and women. The underlying assumptions of dialectical unity and cyclical recovery shared by the common concern for the liberation of nature and of women, contrast deeply with the dominant western patriarchal assumptions of duality in existence and linearity in process. Within the western paradigm, the environmental movement is separate from the women's movement. As long as this paradigm with its assumptions of linear progress prevails, "environmentalism" and "feminism" independently ask only for concessions *within* maldevelopment, because in the absence of oppositional categories, that is the only "development" that is conceivable. Environmentalism then becomes a new patriarchal project of technological fixes and political oppression. It generates a new subjugation of ecological movements and fails to make any progress towards sustainability and equity. While including a few women as tokens in "women and environment," it excludes the feminine visions of survival that women have conserved. Fragmented feminism, in a similar way, finds itself trapped in a gender-based ideology of liberation—taking off from either the "catching-up-with-men" syndrome (on the grounds that the masculine is superior and developed), or receding into a narrow biologism which accepts the feminine as gendered, and excludes the possibility of the recovery of the feminine principle in nature and women, *as well as* men....

The recovery of the feminine principle is a response to multiple dominations and deprivations not just of women, but also of nature and non-western cultures. It stands for ecological recovery and nature's liberation, for women's liberation and for the liberation of men who, in dominating nature and women, have sacrificed their own human-ness. Ashis Nandy says, one must choose the slave's standpoint not only because the slave is oppressed but also because he represents a higher-order cognition which perforce includes the master as a human, whereas the master's cognition has to exclude the slave except as a "thing."[2] Liberation must therefore begin from the colonised and end with the coloniser. As Gandhi was to so clearly formulate through his own life, freedom is indivisible, not only in the popular sense that the oppressed of the world are one, but also in the unpopular sense that the oppressor, too, is caught in the culture of oppression.

The recovery of the feminine principle is based on inclusiveness. It is a recovery in nature, woman and man of creative forms of being and perceiving. In nature it implies seeing nature as a live organism. In woman it implies seeing women as productive and active. Finally, in men the recovery of the feminine principle implies a relocation of action and activity to create life-enhancing, not life-reducing and life-threatening societies.

The death of the feminine principle in women and nature takes place through the association of the category of passivity with the feminine. The death of the feminine principle in men takes place by a shift in the concept of activity from creation to destruction, and the concept of power from empowerment to domination. Self-generated, non-violent, creative activity as the feminine principle dies simultaneously in women, men and nature when violence and aggression become the masculine model of activity, and women and nature are turned into passive objects of violence. The problem with a gender-based response to a gender-based ideology is that it treats ideologically constructed gender categorisation as given by nature. It treats passive non-violence as biological givens in women, and violence as a biological given in men, when both non-violence and violence are socially constructed and need have no gender association. Gandhi, the modern world's leading practitioner and preacher of non-violence was, after all, a man. The historical creation of a gender divide by a gender ideology cannot be the basis of gender liberation. And a gender-based ideology remains totally inadequate in either responding to the ecological crisis created by patriarchal and violent modes of relating to nature, or in understanding how Third World women are leading ecological struggles based on values of conservation which are immediately generalised as the concern for entire communities and regions, and even humanity as a whole.

NOTES

1. Maria Mies, *Patriarchy and Accumulation on a World Scale* (London: Zed Books, 1986), pp. 16–17, 55.
2. Ashis Nandy, *The Intimate Enemy* (Delhi: Oxford University Press, 1986), p. xv.

PART TEN

Islam and Radical Islam

In 1993 terrorists tried to destroy the World Trade Center in New York; in 2001, using hijacked airplanes rather than bombs, they succeeded. These and other horrific events have awakened people in the Western world to a new threat to their peace and security. This threat takes the form of an ideology that is variously called political Islam, radical Islam, Islamic fundamentalism, or simply Islamism. As all of its various names indicate, this new ideology is an outgrowth and an extreme form of the Islamic religion.

Islam takes its name from the Arabic word *islam,* which means "submission." It is not submission in general that Islam requires, however, but submission to Allah, or God. For it is only through submission to God's will that the individual can find peace in this life and paradise in the next. That is the central belief of Muslims, people of the Islamic faith. Muslims are of many different nationalities and inhabit almost every part of the globe, but their numbers are concentrated in North Africa, the Middle and Near East, and Indonesia. Islam has dominated most of this territory virtually since the religion began around 620 A.D., when the prophet Mohammed announced in Arabia that he had received a revelation from the angel Gabriel. The report of this and subsequent revelations make up the *Qur'an* (Koran), the holy book of Islam that Muslims take to be the divine word of Allah, or God. Together with Mohammed's own words and deeds (or Sunna), which Muslims are supposed to emulate, the *Qur'an* forms the basis of the Islamic faith–a monotheistic faith, like Judaism and Christianity, that worships one all-knowing, all-powerful, and merciful God.

Muslims in the Middle East and North Africa have long felt themselves and their faith threatened by external enemies. Radical Islam differs from mainstream Islam largely because the radicals see the threat as greater and the danger more imminent. To put the point simply, these threats have come in four waves. The first wave comprised the Christian Crusades (roughly 1100–1300 A.D.), or military expeditions to retake the Holy Land for Christendom, to convert or kill "infidels" (that is, non-Christians), and, not least, to gain territory and wealth for Europeans. A second threatening wave came with European imperial expansion into North Africa and the Middle East in the nineteenth and early twentieth centuries. France governed much of North Africa and Britain controlled most of the territory from Egypt through India, including Palestine, Arabia, and Persia (now Iran). The British were also instrumental in paving the way for what many Muslims saw as a third threat; the establishment of the state of Israel in Palestine after World War II. To them, a Jewish state in a predominantly Muslim region was both injury and insult. More recently, a fourth wave of threat has appeared in the form of influential Western ideas–liberalism, secularism, materialism, religious toleration, and sexual equality, for example–that fall under the general heading of "modernity" or "modernism." These "modern" ideas can be deeply disturbing to conservative Muslim sensibilities, especially as they are often communicated through satellite television, the Internet, videotapes, and other media that depict a world in which women are on socially equal terms with men and almost everyone is more concerned with sex and wealth than with God and religion.

Many Muslims also complain that the United States has added military insult to moral injury by using covert operations and military force to topple regimes believed to be unfriendly to American political and business interests. The United States has also supported pro-Western but undemocratic governments headed by hereditary monarchs in Saudi Arabia, Kuwait, and elsewhere. The monarchs have returned the favor by keeping the oil flowing to the United States and other nations. Following the Persian Gulf War of 1991, moreover, Saudi rulers allowed the United States to station troops inside Saudi Arabia, the home of Mecca and Medina, the two most sacred sites in Islam. To many Muslims, including a Saudi named Osama bin Laden, this was tantamount to an American invasion and occupation of Muslim holy lands, and thus a grave threat to Islam itself. Many Muslims have also been alarmed by the United States' strong and long-standing support of Israel, which in their view illegally occupies the land of Palestine and threatens its Arab neighbors.

What is to be done in response to this situation, or to the general threat posed to Islam by the West or by modernity? On these points there is much disagreement among Muslims. To the radical Islamist, however, there is a one-word response: *jihad*.

The Islamic faith calls all Muslims to *jihad*, which is the Arabic word for "struggle." To many Muslims–perhaps most of them–this means primarily that they are called to struggle against their own selfish and evil tendencies. The radical Islamists, however, take *jihad* to be first and foremost an outward struggle against the enemies of Islam; that is to say, against those who espouse any and all ideas that are inimical to or threaten the beliefs of Islam, such as liberalism and secularism. To protect the Islamic religion and way of life is a sacred duty. To that end radical Islamists believe that any means are permissible, including violence. Terrorism is a weapon of the weak against the strong. To those so-called moderate Muslims who say that the *Qur'an* forbids suicide and the shedding of innocent blood, radical Islamists say that they are following the *Qur'an* in giving like for like: Israelis have shed the blood of innocent Palestinian women and children; the Palestinian "martyrs" are therefore justified in shedding their own and the blood of supposedly "innocent" Israeli women and children. And, as in Israel, so too elsewhere: whoever threatens Muslims and their Islamic faith should be opposed by any means possible. In a sacred struggle to defend the faith, any means are morally permissible. Moreover, *jihad* is to be waged not only against the West—against the United States and its European and Israeli allies—but against corrupt and secular governments or regimes in supposedly Muslim countries. This view was put into practice in Egypt when the Muslim Brotherhood assassinated President Anwar Sadat, who had repressed radical Islamists and made peace with Israel. It also explains the hostility of al-Qaeda and other radical Islamists to the royal family of Saudi Arabia, which in their view rules ruthlessly and corruptly, and which for a time even allowed American bases and troops on the sacred soil of Islam. Before Iraq was invaded by the United States and its allies in 2003, moreover, radical Islamists were at odds with Saddam Hussein, who paid only lip service to Islam while ruling a secular state that allowed a measure of religious toleration, sexual equality, the selling of alcohol, and other abominations.

In short, radical Islam lives and flourishes in a world filled with real or imagined threats, of conspiracies and cabals, against Islam and its faithful adherents. It is a response to a real or perceived crisis—the crisis brought about by the clash of West and (Middle) East, of secular modernity and religious tradition. Radical Islam is thus a *reactionary* ideology, inasmuch as it represents a reaction against the threats posed by the pressures of modernization and secularization.

64

The Necessity for Islamic Government

RUHOLLAH KHOMEINI

The following selection consists of excerpts from the writings of Ruhollah Khomeini, a Shi'ite Muslim who was often called *imam* ("leader" or "pattern") and *ayatollah* (major religious leader). Khomeini was born in Iran at the beginning of the twentieth century—some sources say in 1900, others 1902—and by the early 1960s he was acclaimed the "grand *ayatollah.*" His opposition to the pro-Western government of the shah of Iran, Reza Pahlavi, led to Khomeini's forcible exile in 1964. Khomeini settled in neighboring Iraq, where he continued to denounce the shah's regime as ruthless, corrupt, and contrary to the true teachings of Islam. In 1978 the new leader of Iraq, Saddam Hussein, forced Khomeini into exile again. This time he settled in a suburb of Paris. From this location Khomeini continued his campaign against the shah's government until massive street demonstrations in Iran's capital persuaded the shah to flee to the United States. Khomeini returned to Iran in triumph in February 1979. That December a referendum declared Iran to be an Islamic republic with Khomeini as its political and religious leader for life—a position he held until his death in 1989. The following selection, written before the revolution that brought Khomeini to power, gives a clear indication both of his objection to "corrupt" regimes, such as that of the shah, and of what he thought an Islamic government should do. The explanatory notes were written by the translator, Hamid Algar.

Source: Islam and Revolution: Writings and Declarations of Imam Khomeini, translated by Hamid Algar (Berkeley, CA: Mizan Press, 1981). Reprinted by permission of Hamid Algar.

THE NECESSITY FOR ISLAMIC GOVERNMENT

A body of laws alone is not sufficient for a society to be reformed. In order for law to ensure the reform and happiness of man, there must be an executive power and an executor. For this reason, God Almighty, in addition to revealing a body of law (i.e., the ordinances of the *shari'a*), has laid down a particular form of government together with executive and administrative institutions.

The Most Noble Messenger [Mohammed] (peace and blessings be upon him) headed the executive and administrative institutions of Muslim society. In addition to conveying the revelation and expounding and interpreting the articles of faith and the ordinances and institutions of Islam, he undertook the implementation of law and the establishment of the ordinances of Islam, thereby bringing into being the Islamic state. He did not content himself with the promulgation of law; rather, he implemented it at the same time, cutting off hands and administering lashings and stonings. After the Most Noble Messenger, his successor had the same duty and function. When the Prophet appointed a successor, it was not for the purpose of expounding articles of faith and law; it was for the implementation of law and the execution of God's ordinances. It was this function—the execution of law and the establishment of Islamic institutions—that made the appointment of a successor such an important matter that the Prophet would have failed to fulfill his mission if he had neglected it. For after the Prophet, the Muslims still needed someone to execute laws and establish the institutions of Islam in society, so that they might attain happiness in this world and the hereafter....

It is self-evident that the necessity for enactment of the law, which necessitated the formation of a government by the Prophet (upon whom be peace), was not confined or restricted to his time, but continues after his departure from this world. According to one of the noble verses of the Qur'an, the ordinances of Islam are not limited with respect to time or place; they are permanent and must be enacted until the end of time. They were not revealed merely for the time of the Prophet, only to be abandoned thereafter, with retribution and the penal code of Islam no longer to be enacted, or the taxes prescribed by Islam no longer collected, and the defense of the lands and people of Islam suspended. The claim that the laws of Islam may remain in abeyance or are restricted to a particular time or place is contrary to the essential credal bases of Islam. Since the enactment of laws, then, is necessary after the departure of the Prophet from this world, and indeed, will remain so until the end of time, the formation of a government and the establishment of executive and administrative organs are also necessary. Without the formation of a government and the establishment of such organs to ensure that through enactment of the law, all activities of the individual take place in the framework of a just system, chaos and anarchy will prevail and social, intellectual, and moral corruption will arise. The only way to prevent the emergence of anarchy and disorder and to protect society from corruption is to form a government and thus impart order to all the affairs of the country....

The nature and character of Islamic law and the divine ordinances of the *shari'a* furnish additional proof of the necessity for establishing government, for they indicate that the laws were laid down for the purpose of creating a state and administering the political, economic, and cultural affairs of society.

First, the laws of the *shari'a* embrace a diverse body of laws and regulations, which amounts to a complete social system. In this system of laws, all the needs of man have been met: his dealings with his neighbors, fellow citizens, and clan, as well as children and relatives; the concerns of private and marital life; regulations concerning war and peace and intercourse with other nations; penal and commercial law; and regulations pertaining to trade and agriculture. Islamic law contains provisions relating to the preliminaries of marriage and the form in which it should be contracted, and others relating to the development of the embryo in the womb and what food the parents should eat at the time of conception. It further stipulates the duties that are incumbent upon them while the infant is being suckled, and specifies how the child should be reared, and how the husband and the wife should relate to each other and to their children. Islam provides laws and instructions for all of these matters, aiming, as it does, to produce integrated and virtuous human beings who are walking embodiments of the law, or to put it differently, the law's voluntary and instinctive executors. It is obvious, then, how much care Islam devotes to government and the political and economic relations of society, with the goal of creating conditions conducive to the production of morally upright and virtuous human beings.

The Glorious Qur'an and the Sunna [teachings of Mohammed] contain all the laws and ordinances man needs in order to attain happiness and the perfection of his state....

Second, if we examine closely the nature and character of the provisions of the law, we realize that their execution and implementation depend upon the formation of a government, and that it is impossible to fulfill the duty of executing God's commands without there being established properly comprehensive administrative and executive organs. Let us now mention certain types of provision in order to illustrate this point; the others you can examine yourselves.

The taxes Islam levies and the form of budget it has established are not merely for the sake of providing subsistence to the poor or feeding the indigent among the descendants of the Prophet (peace and blessings be upon him); they are also intended to make possible the establishment of a great government and to assure its essential expenditures.

For example, *khums* is a huge source of income that accrues to the treasury and represents one item in the budget. According to our Shi'i school of thought, *khums* is to be levied in an equitable manner on all agricultural and commercial profits and all natural resources whether above or below the ground—in short, on all forms of wealth and income. It applies equally to the greengrocer with his stall outside this mosque and to the shipping or mining magnate. They must all pay one-fifth of their surplus income, after customary expenses are deducted, to the Islamic ruler so that it enters the treasury. It is obvious that such a huge income serves the purpose of administering the Islamic state and meeting all its financial needs. If we were to calculate one-fifth of the surplus income of all the Muslim countries (or of the whole world, should it enter the fold of Islam), it would become fully apparent that the purpose for the imposition of such a tax is not merely the upkeep of the *sayyids*[1] or the religious scholars, but on the contrary, something far more significant—namely, meeting the financial needs of the great organs and institutions of government....

How could the *sayyids* ever need so vast a budget? The *khums* of the bazaar of Baghdad would be enough for the needs of the *sayyids* and the upkeep of the religious teaching institution, as well as all the poor of the Islamic world, quite apart from the *khums* of the bazaars of Tehran, Istanbul, Cairo, and other cities. The provision of such a huge budget must obviously be for the purpose of forming a government and administering the Islamic lands. It was established with the aim of providing for the needs of the people, for public services relating to health, education, defense, and economic development. Further, in accordance with the procedures laid down by Islam for the collection, preservation, and expenditure of this income, all forms of usurpation and embezzlement of public wealth have been forbidden, so that the head of state and all those entrusted with responsibility for conducting public affairs (i.e., members of the government) have no privileges over the ordinary citizen in benefiting from the public income and wealth; all have an equal share....

Thus, you see that the fiscal provisions of Islam also point to the necessity for establishing a government, for they cannot be fulfilled without the establishment of the appropriate Islamic institutions.

The ordinances pertaining to preservation of the Islamic order and defense of the territorial integrity and the independence of the Islamic *umma*[2] also demanded the formation of a government. An example is the command: "Prepare against them whatever force you can muster and horses tethered" (Qur'an, 8:60), which enjoins the preparation of as much armed defensive force as possible and orders the Muslims to be always on the alert and at the ready, even in time of peace.

If the Muslims had acted in accordance with this command and, after forming a government, made the necessary extensive preparations to be in a state of full readiness for war, a handful of Jews would never have dared to occupy our lands, and to burn and destroy the Masjid al-Aqsa[3] without the people's being capable of making an immediate response. All this has resulted from the failure of the Muslims to fulfill their duty of executing God's law and setting up a righteous and respectable government. If the rulers of the Muslim countries truly represented the believers and enacted God's ordinances, they would set aside their petty differences, abandon their subversive and divisive activities, and join together like the fingers of one hand. Then a handful of wretched Jews (the agents of America, Britain, and other foreign powers) would never have been able to accomplish what they have, no matter how much support they enjoyed from America and Britain. All this has happened because of the incompetence of those who rule over the Muslims.

The verse: "Prepare against them whatever force you can muster" commands you to be as strong and well-prepared as possible, so that your enemies will be unable to oppress you and transgress against you. It is because we have been lacking in unity, strength, and preparedness that we suffer oppression and are at the mercy of foreign aggressors.

There are numerous provisions of the law that cannot be implemented without the establishment of a governmental apparatus; for example, blood money, which must be exacted and delivered to those deserving it, or the corporeal penalties imposed by the law, which must be carried out under the supervision of the Islamic ruler. All of these laws refer back to the institutions of government, for it is governmental power alone that is capable of fulfilling this function.

After the death of the Most Noble Messenger (peace and blessings be upon him), the obstinate enemies of the faith, the Umayyads[4] (God's curses be upon them) did not permit the Islamic state to attain stability with the rule of 'Ali ibn Abi Talib (upon whom be peace). They did not allow a form of government to exist that was pleasing to God, Exalted and Almighty, and to his Most Noble Messenger. They transformed the entire basis of government, and their policies were, for the most part, contradictory to Islam. The form of government of the Umayyads and the Abbasids,[5] and the political and administrative policies they pursued, were anti-Islamic. The form of government was thoroughly perverted by being transformed into a monarchy, like those of the kings of Iran, the emperors of Rome, and the pharaohs of Egypt. For the most part, this non-Islamic form of government has persisted to the present day, as we can see.

Both law and reason require that we not permit governments to retain this non-Islamic or anti-Islamic character. The proofs are clear. First, the existence of a non-Islamic political order necessarily results in the non-implementation of the Islamic political order. Then, all non-Islamic systems of government are the systems of *kufr*,[6] since the ruler in each case is an instance of *taghut*,[7] and it is our duty to remove from the life of Muslim society all traces of *kufr* and destroy them. It is also our duty to create a favorable social environment for the education of believing and virtuous individuals, an environment that is in total contradiction with that produced by the rule of *taghut* and illegitimate power. The social environment created by *taghut* and *shirk*[8] invariably brings about corruption such as you can now observe in Iran, the corruption termed "corruption on earth."[9] This corruption must be swept away, and its instigators punished for their deeds. It is the same corruption that the Pharaoh generated in Egypt with his policies, so that the Qur'an says of him, "Truly he was among the corruptors" (28:4). A believing, pious, just individual cannot possibly exist in a socio-political environment of this nature and still maintain his faith and righteous conduct. He is faced with two choices: either he commits acts that amount to *kufr* and contradict righteousness, or in order not to commit such acts and not to submit to the orders and commands of the *taghut*, the just individual opposes him and struggles against him in order to destroy the environment of corruption. We have in reality, then, no choice but to destroy those systems of government that are corrupt in themselves and also entail the corruption of others, and to overthrow all treacherous, corrupt, oppressive, and criminal regimes.

This is a duty that all Muslims must fulfill, in every one of the Muslim countries, in order to achieve the triumphant political revolution of Islam.

We see, too, that together, the imperialists and the tyrannical self-seeking rulers have divided the Islamic homeland. They have separated the various segments of the Islamic *umma* from each other and artificially created separate nations. There once existed the great Ottoman State, and that, too, the imperialists divided. Russia, Britain, Austria, and other imperialist powers united, and through wars against the Ottomans, each came to occupy or absorb into its sphere of influence part of the Ottoman realm. It is true that most of the Ottoman rulers were incompetent, that some of them were corrupt, and that they followed a monarchical system. Nonetheless, the existence of the Ottoman State represented a threat to the imperialists. It was always possible that righteous individuals might rise up among the people and, with their assistance, seize control of the state, thus putting an end to imperialism by mobilizing the unified resources of the nation. Therefore, after numerous prior wars, the imperialists at the end of World War I divided the Ottoman State, creating in its territories about ten or fifteen petty states.[10] Then each of these was entrusted to one of their servants or a group of their servants, although certain countries were later able to escape the grasp of the agents of imperialism.

In order to assure the unity of the Islamic *umma,* in order to liberate the Islamic homeland from occupation and penetration by the imperialists and their puppet governments, it is imperative that we establish a government. In order to attain the unity and freedom of the Muslim peoples, we must overthrow the oppressive governments installed by the imperialists and bring into existence an Islamic government of justice that will be in the service of the people. The formation of such a government will serve to preserve the disciplined unity of the Muslims; just as Fatimat az-Zahra[11] (upon whom be peace) said in her address: "The Imamate exists for the sake of preserving order among the Muslims and replacing their disunity with unity."

Through the political agents they have placed in power over the people, the imperialists have also imposed on us an unjust economic order, and thereby divided our people into two groups: oppressors and oppressed. Hundreds of millions of Muslims are hungry and deprived of all forms of health care and education, while minorities comprised of the wealthy and powerful live a life of indulgence, licentiousness, and corruption. The hungry and deprived have constantly struggled to free themselves from the oppression of their plundering overlords, and their struggle continues to this day. But their way is blocked by the ruling minorities and the oppressive governmental structures they head. It is our duty to save the oppressed and deprived. It is our duty to be a helper to the oppressed and an enemy to the oppressor....

How can we stay silent and idle today when we see that a band of traitors and usurpers, the agents of foreign powers, have appropriated the wealth and the fruits of labor of hundreds of millions of Muslims—thanks to the support of their masters and through the power of the bayonet—granting the Muslims not the least right to prosperity? It is the duty of Islamic scholars and all Muslims to put an end to this system of oppression and, for the sake of the well-being of hundreds of millions of human beings, to overthrow these oppressive governments and form an Islamic government....

If someone should ask you, "Why has God, the All-Wise, appointed holders of authority and commanded you to obey them?" you should answer him as follows: "He has done so for various causes and reasons. One is that men have been set upon a certain well-defined path and commanded not to stray from it, not to transgress against the established limits and norms, for if they were to stray, they would fall prey to corruption.

Now men would not be able to keep to their ordained path and to enact God's laws unless a trustworthy and protective individual (or power) were appointed over them with responsibility for this matter, to prevent them from stepping outside the sphere of the licit and transgressing against the rights of others. If no such restraining individual or power were appointed, nobody would voluntarily abandon any pleasure or interest of his own that might result in harm or corruption to others; everybody would engage in oppressing and harming others for the sake of their own pleasures and interests.

"Another reason and cause is this: we do not see a single group, nation, or religious community that has ever been able to exist without an individual entrusted with the maintenance of its laws and institutions—in short, a head or a leader; for such a person is essential for fulfilling the affairs of religion and the world. It is not permissible, therefore, according to divine wisdom, that God should leave men, His creatures, without a leader and guide, for He knows well that they depend on the existence of such a person for their own survival and perpetuation. It is under his leadership that they fight against their enemies, divide the public income among themselves, perform Friday and congregational prayer, and foreshorten the arms of the transgressors who would encroach on the rights of the oppressed.

"Another proof and cause is this: were God not to appoint an Imam over men to maintain law and order, to serve the people faithfully as a vigilant trustee, religion would fall victim to obsolescence and decay. Its rites and institutions would vanish; the customs and ordinances of Islam would be transformed or even deformed. Heretical innovators would add things to religion and atheists and unbelievers would subtract things from it, presenting it to the Muslims in an inaccurate manner. For we see that men are prey to defects; they are not perfect and must needs strive after perfection. Moreover, they disagree with each other, having varying inclinations and discordant states. If God, therefore, had not appointed over men one who would maintain order and law and protect the revelation brought by the Prophet, in the manner we have described, men would fall prey to corruption; the institutions, laws, customs, and ordinances of Islam would be transformed; and faith and its content would be completely changed, resulting in the corruption of all humanity."

As you can deduce...there are numerous proofs and causes that necessitate formation of a government and establishment of an authority. These proofs, causes, and arguments are not temporary in their validity or limited to a particular time, and the necessity for the formation of a government, therefore, is perpetual. For example, it will always happen that men overstep the limits laid down by Islam and transgress against the rights of others for the sake of their personal pleasure and benefit.... The wisdom of the Creator has decreed that men should live in accordance with justice and act within the limits set by divine law. This wisdom is eternal and immutable, and constitutes one of the norms of God Almighty. Today and always, therefore, the existence of a holder of authority, a ruler who acts as trustee and maintains the institutions and laws of Islam, is a necessity—a ruler who prevents cruelty, oppression, and violation of the rights of others; who is a trustworthy and vigilant guardian of God's creatures; who guides men to the teachings, doctrines, laws, and institutions of Islam; and who prevents the undesirable changes that atheists and the enemies of religion wish to introduce in the laws and institutions of Islam....

If the ordinances of Islam are to remain in effect, then, if encroachment by oppressive ruling classes on the rights of the weak is to be prevented, if ruling minorities are not to be permitted to plunder and corrupt the people for the sake of pleasure and material interest, if the Islamic order is to be preserved and all individuals are to pursue the just path of Islam without any deviation, if innovation and the approval of anti-Islamic laws by sham parliaments[12] are to be prevented, if the influence of foreign powers in the Islamic lands is to be destroyed—government is necessary. None of these aims can be achieved without government and the organs of the state. It is a righteous government, of course, that is needed, one presided over by a ruler who will be a trustworthy and righteous trustee. Those who presently govern us are of no use at all for they are tyrannical, corrupt, and highly incompetent.

In the past we did not act in concert and unanimity in order to establish proper government and overthrow treacherous and corrupt rulers. Some people were apathetic and reluctant even to discuss the theory of Islamic government, and some went so far as to praise oppressive rulers. It is for this reason that we find ourselves in the present state. The influence and sovereignty of Islam in society have declined; the nation of Islam has fallen victim to division and weakness; the laws of Islam have remained in abeyance and been subjected to change and modification; and the imperialists have propagated foreign laws and alien culture among the Muslims through their agents for the sake of their evil purposes, causing people to be infatuated with the West. It was our lack of a leader, a guardian, and our lack of institutions of leadership that made all this possible. We need righteous and proper organs of government; that much is self-evident.

NOTES

1. *Sayyids:* the descendants of the Prophet through his daughter Fatima and son-in-law ʻAli, the first of the Twelve Imams.
2. *Umma:* the entire Islamic community, without territorial or ethnic distinction.
3. Masjid al-Aqsa: the site in Jerusalem where the Prophet ascended to heaven in the eleventh year of his mission (Qur'an, 17:1), also the complex of mosques and buildings erected on the site. The chief of these was extensively damaged by arson in 1969, two years after the Zionist usurpation of Jerusalem.
4. Umayyads: members of the dynasty that ruled at Damascus from 41/682 until 132/750 and transformed the caliphate into a hereditary institution. Muʻawiya, frequently mentioned in these pages, was the first of the Umayyad line.
5. Abbasids: the dynasty that replaced the Umayyads and established a new caliphal capital in Baghdad. With the rise of various local rulers, generally of military origin, the power of the Abbasids began to decline from the fourth/tenth century and it was brought to an end by the Mongol conquest in 656/1258.
6. *Kufr:* the rejection of divine guidance; the antithesis of Islam.
7. *Taghut:* one who surpasses all bounds in his despotism and tyranny and claims the prerogatives of divinity for himself, whether explicitly or implicitly.
8. *Shirk:* the assignment of partners to God, either by believing in a multiplicity of gods, or by assigning divine attributes and prerogatives to other-than-God.
9. "Corruption on earth": a broad term including not only moral corruption, but also subversion of the public good, embezzlement and usurpation of public wealth, conspiring with the enemies of the community against its security, and working in general for the overthrow of the Islamic order. See the commentary on Qur'an, 5:33 in Tabataba'i, *al-Mizan,* V, 330–332.
10. It may be apposite to quote here the following passage from a secret report drawn up in January 1916 by T. E. Lawrence, the British organizer of the so-called Arab revolt led by Sharif Husayn of Mecca: "Husayn's activity seems beneficial to us, because it matches with our immediate aims, the breakup of the Islamic bloc and the defeat and disruption of the Ottoman Empire....The Arabs are even less stable than the Turks. If properly handled they would remain in a state of political mosaic, a tissue of small jealous principalities incapable of political cohesion." See Philip Knightley and Colin Simpson, *The Secret Lives of Lawrence of Arabia* (New York, 1971), p. 55.
11. Fatimat az-Zahra: Fatima, the daughter of the Prophet and wife of Imam ʻAli.
12. Here the allusion may be in particular to the so-called Family Protection Law of 1967, which Imam Khomeini denounced as contrary to Islam in an important ruling. See Imam Khomeini, *Tauzih al-Masa'il,* n.p., n.d., pp. 462–463, par. 2836, and p. 441.

65

The Neglected Duty

ABD AL-SALAM FARAJ

The following pages are taken from a pamphlet by Abd al-Salam Faraj (1954–1982), an Egyptian Muslim who was executed in 1982 for his part in the assassination of Egyptian President Anwar Sadat on October 6, 1981. Faraj was also in contact with Sheikh Omar Abdel Rahman, who was later tried and imprisoned in the United States for his part in the 1993 bombing of the World Trade Center. Ayman al-Zawahiri, an Egyptian surgeon who later became one of Osama bin Laden's key advisors, was also actively involved in a group that participated in Sadat's assassination. There is, then, at least an indirect connection between the author of this pamphlet and al-Qaeda. The pamphlet itself provides a clear example of "political" or "radical" Islam, which understands the Muslim's duty of *jihad* not so much as the internal struggle to be righteous as the external struggle against forces believed to be hostile to the Islamic faith. The pamphlet was translated into English in 1986 by Johannes J. G. Jansen. Words enclosed in parentheses are the translator's interpolations.

Source: From *The Neglected Duty: The Creed of Sadat's Assassins and the Emergence of Islamic Militance in the Middle East,* by Johannes J.G. Jansen, Macmillan Reference USA, ©1986, Macmillan Reference USA. Reprinted by permission of The Gale Group.

THE NEGLECTED DUTY

(2) Glory to God. We praise Him, we ask for His help, we ask Him to forgive us, we ask Him to give us guidance. We seek protection with God against the wickedness of our souls and against the evilness of our acts. If God sends someone on the right path, no one can send him astray. If God sends someone astray, no one can guide him. I acknowledge that there is no god but God alone, He has no associate, and I acknowledge that Muhammad is His servant and His Apostle.

The most reliable Speech is the Book of God, and the best guidance is the guidance of Muhammad, may God's peace be upon him. The worst of all things are novelties, since every novelty is an innovation...and every innovation is a deviation, and all deviation is in Hell.

(3) *Jihad* (struggle) for God's cause, in spite of its extreme importance and its great significance for the future of this religion, has been neglected by the '*ulama*' (leading Muslim scholars) of this age. They have feigned ignorance of it, but they know that it is the only way to the return and the establishment of the glory of Islam anew. Every Muslim preferred his own favorite ideas and philosophies above the Best Road, which God—Praised and Exalted He is—drew Himself (a road that leads back) to (a state of) Honor for His Servants.

(4) There is no doubt that the idols of this world can only be made to disappear through the power of the sword. It is therefore that (the Apostle Muhammad)—God's peace be upon him— said: "I have been sent with the Sword at this Hour, so that God alone is worshiped, without associate to Him, He put my daily bread under the shadow of my lance, He brings lowness and smallness to those who disagree with what I command. Whosoever resembles a certain group of people will be counted as a member of that group." (This Tradition is) reported by Imam Ahmad (ibn Hanbal) on the authority of Ibn Umar....

...

(15) God gave a promise to a group of believers in His—Glorious and Majestic He is—word: "God has promised to those of you who have believed and wrought the works of righteousness, that He will surely make them successors (to power) in the land as He made those before them successors, and he will surely establish for them their religion which He has approved for them, and after their fear will give them in exchange security; 'They shall serve Me not associating anything with Me.'" (This Qur'an quotation) is taken from verse 55 of Surah 24. God does not break His promises. We ask Him—Majestic and Supreme He is—that He make us one of them (who are mentioned in the beginning of this Qur'an quotation).

(16) This is a duty which is rejected by some Muslims and neglected by others although the proof for the obligatory character of the establishment of a state is clear, and made obvious by the (text of the) Book of God—Blessed and Supreme He is,—for God—Glory to Him—says: "and that you must rule between them according to what God sent down," and He says: "Whosoever does not rule by what God sent down, those, they are the unbelievers." He says—Glorious and Majestic He is—in (the first verse of) Surah 24 (of which we quoted verse 55 in the previous paragraph), about the obligatory character of the prescripts of Islam: "a Surah which we sent down and which we made obligatory." From this (verse) (it follows) that the establishment of the Rule of God over this earth (mentioned in verse 55 of this Surah) must be considered to be obligatory for the Muslims. God's prescripts are an obligation for the Muslims. Hence, the establishment of an Islamic State is an obligation for the Muslims, for something without which something which is obligatory cannot be carried out becomes (itself) obligatory. If, moreover, (such a) state cannot be established without war, then this war is an obligation as well.

(17) Muslims are agreed on the obligatory character of the establishment of an Islamic Caliphate. To announce a Caliphate must be based on the existence of a (territorial) nucleus

(from which it can grow). This (nucleus) is the Islamic State. "Whosoever dies without having taken upon himself (the obligation of) a pledge of allegiance does not die as a Muslim." So, it is obligatory for every Muslim to seriously strive for the return of the Caliphate in order not to fall into the category of people (mentioned in the) Tradition (quoted in this paragraph). By "pledge of allegiance" (the text of the Tradition) means "allegiance to the Caliphate."

(18) Here a question appears: Do we live in an Islamic State? One of the characteristics of such a state is that it is ruled by the laws of Islam. The Imam Abu Hanifah gave us his opinion that the House of Islam changes into the House of Unbelief if three conditions are fulfilled simultaneously: 1. if it is ruled by other laws than those of Islam, 2. the disappearance of safety for the Muslim inhabitants, 3. its being adjacent or close...and this (means) that the House (of Islam) is close to the house of Unbelief to such an extent that this is a source of danger to the Muslims and a cause for the disappearance of their safety.

(19) The Imam Muhammad and the Imam Abu Yusuf, both (jurists) from the school of Abu Hanifah, gave as their opinion that a House must be categorized according to the laws by which it is ruled. If (a House) is ruled by the laws of Islam, then it is the House of Islam. If (a House) is ruled by the laws of Unbelief, it is the House of Unbelief....

(20) The *Shayk al-Islam* Ibn Taymiyah, in his Fatwa collection, vol. 4, the book on *jihad:* "When he was asked about a town called Mardin, which had been ruled by the Rule of Islam, but in which the situation had then changed and people had established the rule of Unbelief, whether (such a town) constitutes a House of War or House of Peace, he answered that these two concepts had become combined in it, and hence it could neither be categorized as a House of Peace which is ruled by the Laws of Islam nor as a House of War the inhabitants of which are infidels. It had become, however, a third category: a Muslim in it should be treated according to what is due to him, and someone who has rebelled against the Law of Islam should (in his turn) be treated according to what is due to him...."

As a matter of fact, we do not find (any) contradiction between the opinions of these Imams, because Abu Hanifah and the two (jurists) from his school did not mention that its inhabitants were infidels....So, peace to whom peace is due, and war to whom war is due.... The State (of Egypt in which we live today) is ruled by the Laws of Unbelief although the majority of its inhabitants are Muslims.

(21) The laws by which the Muslims are ruled today are the laws of Unbelief, they are actually codes of law that were made by infidels who then subjected the Muslims to these (codes) although God—Praised and Exalted He is—says in Surah 5 (of the Qur'an): "Whosoever does not rule...by what God sent down, those are the Unbelievers...." (This quotation is taken from Qur'an) 5.44. After the disappearance of the Caliphate definitively in the year 1924, and (after) the removal of the laws of Islam in their entirety, and (after) their substitution by laws that were imposed by infidels, the situation (of the Muslims) became identical to the situation of the Mongols, as the Qur'an commentary of Ibn Kathir corroborates (in its comment on) Qur'an 5.50: "Do they then desire the (mode) of judgment of the un-Islamic World...? But who is better than God (Himself) in Judgment, to a people who are convinced?"...

...

(25) The rulers of this age are in apostasy from Islam. They were raised at the tables of imperialism, be it Crusaderism, or Communism, or Zionism. They carry nothing from Islam but their names, even though they pray and fast and claim...to be Muslim. (")It is a well-established rule of Islamic Law that the punishment of an apostate will be heavier than the punishment of someone who is by origin an infidel (and has never been a Muslim), and this in many respects. For instance, an apostate has to be killed even if he is unable to (carry arms and) go to war. Someone, however, who is by origin an infidel and who is unable to (carry arms and) go to war (against the Muslims) should not be killed,

according to leading Muslim scholars like Abu Hanifah and Malik and Ahmad (ibn Hanbal). Hence, it is the view of the majority (of the jurists) that an apostate has to be killed, and this is in accordance with (the opinions held in) the schools of Malik, Al-Shafici, and Ahmad (ibn Hanbal). (Other examples of this difference are) that an apostate cannot inherit, cannot conclude a legally valid marriage, and to eat from the meat of animals which he slaughtered is forbidden. No such rules exist concerning someone who is an infidel (and has never been a Muslim). When apostasy from a religion is worse than always having been an infidel, then apostasy from the prescripts (of a religion) is (also) worse than having always been an infidel. So, apostasy is worse than rebellion against the prescripts of a religion which comes from someone who has always been outside (this religion).(")...

...

(47) In the Islamic world there are several ideas about the elimination of these Rulers and the establishment of the Rule of God—Exalted and Majestic He is—. To what extent are these ideas correct?

(48) There are those who say that we should establish societies that are subject to the State and urge people to perform their prayers and to pay their *zakat* tax and do (other) good works. Prayer, *zakat* and good works are (all equally) commands of God—Exalted and Majestic He is—which we should not at all neglect. However, when we ask ourselves: "Do these works, and acts of devotion, bring about the establishment of an Islamic State?"—then the immediate answer without any further consideration must be "No." Moreover, these societies would in principle be subject to the State, be registered in its files, and they would have to follow (the State's) instructions.

(49) There are those who say that we should occupy ourselves with Obedience to God, with educating the Muslims, and with exerting ourselves in acts of devotion, because the backwardness in which we live overpowered us on account of our sins and our (own) works. They sometimes prove this with a maxim which says on the authority of Malik Ibn Dinar: God—Exalted and Majestic He is—says: "I am God, the King of Kings; the hearts of the Kings are in My hand; When someone obeys Me, I make (the Kings) (My instrument of) mercy towards him; When someone disobeys Me, I make (the Kings) (My instrument of) revenge towards him. Do not occupy yourselves with kings, but turn in repentance to the Most Compassionate King you have."

(52) There are those who say: "We must establish an Islamic political party (and add this party) to the list of extant political parties." It is true that this is better than benevolent societies, because a party at least talks about politics. However, the purpose of the foundation (of such a party) is the destruction of the infidel State (and to replace it by an Islamic theocracy). To work through a political party will, however, have the opposite effect, since it means building the pagan State and collaborating with it.... (Moreover, such an Islamic political party) will participate in the membership of legislative councils that enact laws without consideration for God's Laws.

(53) There are those who say that the Muslims should do their best in order to obtain (socially) important positions. Only when all important centers are filled with Muslim doctors and Muslim engineers, will the existing pagan order perish automatically and the Muslim Ruler...establish himself.... Someone who hears this argument for the first time will think it is a fantasy or a joke, but there are, as a matter of fact, people in the Muslim world who embrace such philosophies and arguments, although there is nothing in the Book (of God) or the Example (of the Prophet) which supports or proves the(se arguments). Moreover, reality prevents (such aspirations) from ever coming true.... No matter how many Muslim doctors and Muslim engineers there are, they too will help to build the (pagan) State. Moreover, things will never go so far as to permit a Muslim personality to reach a ministerial post when he is not a 100 percent supporter of the existing order.

(54) Some of them say the right road to the establishment of an (Islamic) State is (nonviolent) propaganda...only, and the creation of a broad

base. This, however, does not bring about the foundation of an (Islamic) State. Nevertheless, some people make this point the basis for their withdrawal from (true) *jihad*. The truth is that an (Islamic) State can only be founded by a believing minority.... Those who follow the straight path that is in accordance with the Command of God and the Example of the Apostle of God—May God's Peace be upon Him—are always a minority. Scriptural proof of this is found in the Word of God—Exalted and Majestic He is—: "Few among my servants are thankful" (Qur'an 34.12) and in His Word—He be Praised—: "If thou obey the majority of those who are in the land they will lead thee astray from the Way of God" (Qur'an 6.116). This is the Custom of God...with regard to His World.... From where will we get this hoped-for majority? (Did not God) also say: "Most of the people, even though thou shouldst be zealous, are not believers"? (Qur'an 12.103).

(55) Islam does not triumph by (attracting the support of) the majority. Did not God—Praised and exalted He is—say: "How many a small band has, by the permission of God, conquered a numerous band?" (Qur'an 2.249)? And also: "(God has already helped you on many fields) and on the Day of Hunayn when ye prided yourselves on your numbers but they did not benefit you at all, and the land, wide as it was, became too narrow for you" (Qur'an 9.25)....

...

(57) But then, how can (nonviolent) propaganda be widely successful when all means of (mass) communication today are under the control of the pagan and wicked (State) and (under the control) of those who are at war with God's religion? The (only) really effective method could be to liberate the media from the control of these people. It is well known that compliance will only come about through a convincing victory. Does not God—Praised and Exalted He is—say: "When comes the victory of God, and the Conquest, thou seest the people entering into the religion of God in crowds" (Qur'an 110.1–2)....

...

(59) Some people have misunderstood what I say and have taken it to mean that we should refrain from (nonviolent) propaganda altogether. "Propaganda" here means "Calling upon people to be Muslims." Here it is basic to take Islam as a whole. This, however, is the refutation of those who see it as their aim to create a broad base and (in doing so) forget about (true) *jihad*, or even hinder or obstruct (true *jihad*) in order to realize this (peaceful aim of theirs)....

...

(63) There are some who say that at present the true road is the quest for knowledge. "How can we fight when we have no knowledge (of Islam and its prescripts)? The quest for knowledge is an obligation..., too." But we shall not heed the words of someone who permits the neglect of a religious command or one of the duties of Islam for the sake of (the quest for religious) knowledge, certainly not if this duty is the duty of *jihad*. How could we possibly neglect a personal individual duty (like *jihad*) for the sake of a collective duty (like the quest for knowledge)?

How can it have come about that we got to know the smallest (details of the Islamic doctrine of duties like) recommendable and desirable acts, and call upon people to perform these acts, but at the same time neglect a duty which the Apostle—May God's Peace be upon Him—glorified?

How can someone who has specialized in (Islamic) religious studies and who really knows all about small and great sins not have noticed the great importance of *jihad*, and the punishment for postponing or neglecting it?

Someone who says that (the quest for) knowledge (also) is (a form of) *jihad* has to understand that the duty (which is indicated by the Arabic word *jihad*) entails the obligation of fighting, for God—Praised and Exalted He is—says: "Prescribed for you is fighting" (Qur'an 2.216)....

...

(65) God—Exalted He is—made it clear that this Community differs from the other (religious) Communities as far as Fighting is concerned. In the case of earlier communities God—Praised and Exalted He is—made His punishment come down upon the infidels and

the enemies of His religion by means of natural phenomena like eclipses (of the moon), floods, shouts and storms.... With regard to the Community of Muhammad—God's Peace be upon Him—this differs, for God—Praised and Exalted He is—addressed them saying: "Fight them and God will punish them at your hands, will humiliate them and aid you against them, and will bring healing to the breasts of people who are believers" (Qur'an 9.14).

This means that a Muslim has first of all the duty to execute the command to fight with his hands. (Once he has done so) God—Praised and Exalted He is—will then intervene (and change) the laws of nature. In this way victory will be achieved through the hands of the believers by means of God's—Praised and Exalted He is—(intervention)....

...

(68) It is said that the battlefield of *jihad* today is the liberation of Jerusalem since it is (part of) the Holy Land. It is true that the liberation of the Holy Land is a religious command, obligatory for all Muslims, but the Apostle of God—May God's Peace be upon Him—described the believer as "sagacious and prudent"..., and this means that a Muslim knows what is useful and what is harmful, and gives priority to radical definitive solutions. This is a point that makes the explanation of the following necessary:

(69) First: To fight an enemy who is near is more important than to fight an enemy who is far.

Second: Muslim blood will be shed in order to realize this victory. Now it must be asked whether this victory will benefit the interests of an Islamic State? Or will this victory benefit the interests of Infidel Rule? It will mean the strengthening of a State which rebels against the Laws of God.... These rulers will take advantage of the nationalist ideas of these Muslims in order to realize their un-Islamic aims, even though at the surface (these aims) look Islamic. Fighting has to be done (only) under the Banner of Islam and under Islamic Leadership. About this there is no difference of opinion.

(70) Third: The basis of the existence of Imperialism in the Lands of Islam are (precisely) these Rulers. To begin by putting an end to imperialism is not a laudatory and not a useful act. It is only a waste of time. We must concentrate on our own Islamic situation: we have to establish the Rule of God's Religion in our own country first, and to make the Word of God supreme.... There is no doubt that the first battlefield for *jihad* is the extermination of these infidel leaders and to replace them by a complete Islamic Order. From here we should start.

(71) Concerning this question it is proper that we should refute those who say that *jihad* in Islam is defensive, and that Islam was not spread by the sword. This is a false view, which is (nevertheless) repeated by a great number of those who are prominent in the field of Islamic missionary activities. The right answer comes from the Apostle of God—God's peace be upon Him—when he was asked: "What is *jihad* for God's cause?" He then said: "Whosoever fights in order to make the Word of God supreme is someone who (really) fights for God's cause." To fight is, in Islam, to make supreme the Word of God in this world, whether it be by attacking or by defending....

...

(84) When God—Praised and Exalted He is—made fasting obligatory, he said (Qur'an 2.183): "Fasting is prescribed for you." In regard to fighting He said (Qur'an 2.216): "Fighting is prescribed for you." This refutes the view of whoever says that *jihad* is indeed a duty and then goes on by saying: "When I have fulfilled the duty of engaging in missionary activities for Islam..., then I have fulfilled the duty (of *jihad*, because (engagement in missionary activities for Islam) is *jihad* too." However, the (real character of this) duty is clearly spelled out in the text of Qur'an: It is fighting, which means confrontation and blood.

The question now is: when is *jihad* an individual duty? *Jihad* becomes an individual duty in three situations:

(85) First, when two armies meet and their ranks are facing each other, it is forbidden to

those who are present to leave, and it becomes an individual duty to remain standing, because God—Exalted He is—says: "O ye who have believed, when ye meet a hostile party, stand firm, and call God frequently to mind" (Qur'an 8.45) and also: "O ye who have believed, when ye meet those who have disbelieved moving into battle, turn them not your backs" (Qur'an 8.15).

Second, when the infidels descend upon a country, it becomes an individual duty for its people to fight them and drive them away.

Third, when the Imam calls upon a people to fight, they must depart into battle, for God—Exalted He is—says (Qur'an 9.38–39): "O ye who have believed, what is the matter with you? When one says to you: 'March out in the way of God,' ye are weighed down to the ground; are you so satisfied with this nearer life as to neglect the Hereafter? The enjoyment of this nearer life is in comparison with the Hereafter only a little thing. If ye do not march out He will inflict upon you a painful punishment, and will substitute (for you) another people; ye will not injure Him at all; God over everything has power." The Apostle—God's Peace be upon Him—says: "When you are called upon to fight, then hasten."

(86) With regard to the lands of Islam, the enemy lives right in the middle of them. The enemy even has got hold of the reins of power, for the enemy is (none other than) these rulers who have (illegally) seized the Leadership of the Muslims. Therefore, waging *jihad* against them is an individual duty, in addition to the fact that Islamic *jihad* today requires a drop of sweat from every Muslim.

(87) Know that when *jihad* is an individual duty, there is no (need to) ask permission of (your) parents to leave to wage *jihad*, as the jurists have said; it is thus similar to prayer and fasting....

...

(91) It is said that we fear to establish the State (because) after one or two days a reaction will occur that will put to an end everything we have accomplished.

The refutation of this (view) is that the establishment of an Islamic State is the execution of a divine Command. We are not responsible for its results. Someone who is so stupid as to hold this view—which has no use except to hinder Muslims from the execution of their religious duty by establishing the Rule of God—forgets that when the rule of the Infidel has fallen everything will be in the hands of the Muslims, whereupon...the downfall of the Islamic State will become inconceivable. Furthermore, the Laws of Islam are not too weak to be able to subject everyone who spreads corruption in the land and rebels against the Commands of God. Moreover, the Laws of God are all justice and will be welcomed by everyone, even by people who do not know Islam....

...

(94) ....So now there can be no valid excuse for any Muslim for neglecting the duty of *jihad* which has been thrown upon his shoulder. We must seriously begin to organize *jihad* activities to return Islam to this nation and to establish an Islamic State, and to exterminate the idols who are only human and who have not (yet) found in front of them anyone who has subdued them with the Command of God—Praised and Exalted He is....

...

(98) A Muslim has the duty to prepare himself for *jihad* for God's cause only, for the Apostle of God—God's Peace be upon Him—says: "God turns towards whomever goes out for His cause. He will not send someone out but to wage *jihad* for His cause and for belief in Him and for accepting the truthfulness of His Apostle. He guarantees that He will (either) make him enter Paradise or will make him come back to his home from which he went out with whatever reward or booty he obtained." There is no disagreement (on the reliability of this Tradition)....

...

(100) Neglecting *jihad* is the cause of the lowness, humiliation, division and fragmentation in which the Muslims live today....

...

(106) With the advance of time and the development of mankind emerges a question we must ask ourselves. There is no doubt that the

modern methods of fighting differ to a certain extent from the methods of fighting in the time of the Prophet—God's Peace be upon Him—. What is the Muslim's method of fighting in this day and age? Can he use his own intellect and his own individual judgment?

(107) (The Apostle) says: "War is deceit," and Al-Nawawi remarks in his commentary on this Tradition: "Scholars are agreed on the permissibility of deceiving the infidels in war however possible, except when this would imply a breach of a treaty or of a promise of safety (from attack), for then it is not allowed (to deceive them)." It is, however, a fact that there is no treaty between us and them since they wage war against the religion of God—Praised and Exalted He is—and (therefore) Muslims are free to choose the most suitable method of fighting so that deception, which is victory with the fewest losses and by the easiest means possible, is realized.

66

Jihad Against Jews and Crusaders

World Islamic Front Statement

OSAMA BIN LADEN AND OTHERS

In February of 1998—three years before the terrorist attacks of September 11, 2001, and five years before the U.S. invasion of Iraq—Osama bin Laden (or Usamah Bin-Ladin) and four other radical Islamist leaders issued the statement reprinted on the following pages. This statement purports to be a *fatwa*, a pronouncement of Islamic law by Islamic scholars, that makes the killing of "Americans and their allies—civilians and military—[a] duty for every Muslim who can do it in any country in which it is possible to do it...." As the two preceding selections indicate, the roots of radical Islam are quite deep. In this *fatwa*, however, bin-Ladin and the other leaders of the "World Islamic Front" concentrate on more immediate grievances that stemmed from the Persian Gulf War of 1991.

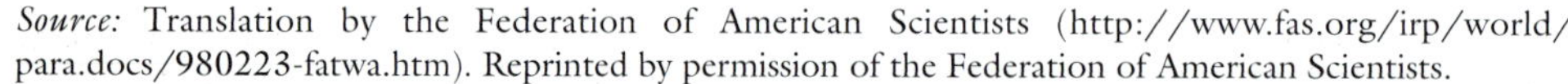

Source: Translation by the Federation of American Scientists (http://www.fas.org/irp/world/para.docs/980223-fatwa.htm). Reprinted by permission of the Federation of American Scientists.

JIHAD AGAINST JEWS AND CRUSADERS

23 February 1998

...

Shaykh Usamah Bin-Muhammad Bin-Ladin

Ayman al-Zawahiri, amir of the Jihad Group in Egypt

Abu-Yasir Rifa'i Ahmad Taha, Egyptian Islamic Group

Shaykh Mir Hamzah, secretary of the Jamiat-ul-Ulema-e-Pakistan

Fazlur Rahman, amir of the Jihad Movement in Bangladesh

Praise be to Allah, who revealed the Book [*Qur'an*], controls the clouds, defeats factionalism, and says in His Book: "But when the forbidden months are past, then fight and slay the pagans wherever ye find them, seize them, beleaguer them, and lie in wait for them in every stratagem (of war)"; and peace be upon our Prophet, Muhammad Bin-'Abdallah, who said: I have been sent with the sword between my hands to ensure that no one but Allah is worshipped, Allah who put my livelihood under the shadow of my spear and who inflicts humiliation and scorn on those who disobey my orders.

The Arabian Peninsula has never—since Allah made it flat, created its desert, and encircled it with seas—been stormed by any forces like the crusader armies spreading in it like locusts, eating its riches and wiping out its plantations. All this is happening at a time in which nations are attacking Muslims like people fighting over a plate of food. In the light of the grave situation and the lack of support, we and you are obliged to discuss current events, and we should all agree on how to settle the matter.

No one argues today about three facts that are known to everyone; we will list them, in order to remind everyone:

First, for over seven years the United States has been occupying the lands of Islam in the holiest of places, the Arabian Peninsula, plundering its riches, dictating to its rulers, humiliating its people, terrorizing its neighbors, and turning its bases in the Peninsula into a spearhead through which to fight the neighboring Muslim peoples.

If some people have in the past argued about the fact of the occupation, all the people of the Peninsula have now acknowledged it. The best proof of this is the Americans' continuing aggression against the Iraqi people, using the Peninsula as a staging post, even though all its rulers are against their territories being used to that end, but they are helpless.

Second, despite the great devastation inflicted on the Iraqi people by the crusader-Zionist alliance, and despite the huge number of those killed, which has exceeded 1 million...despite all this, the Americans are once again trying to repeat the horrific massacres, as though they are not content with the protracted blockade imposed after the ferocious war or the fragmentation and devastation.

So here they come to annihilate what is left of this people and to humiliate their Muslim neighbors.

Third, if the Americans' aims behind these wars are religious and economic, the aim is also to serve the Jews' petty state [Israel] and divert attention from its occupation of Jerusalem and murder of Muslims there. The best proof of this is their eagerness to destroy Iraq, the strongest neighboring Arab state, and their endeavor to fragment all the states of the region such as Iraq, Saudi Arabia, Egypt, and Sudan into paper statelets and through their disunion and weakness to guarantee Israel's survival and the continuation of the brutal crusade occupation of the Peninsula.

All these crimes and sins committed by the Americans are a clear declaration of war on Allah, his messenger, and Muslims. And ulema [Muslim scholars] have throughout Islamic history unanimously agreed that the jihad is an individual duty if the enemy destroys the Muslim countries. This was revealed by Imam Bin-Qadamah in "Al-Mughni," Imam al-Kisa'i in "Al-Bada'i," al-Qurtubi in his interpretation, and the shaykh of al-Islam in his books, where he said: "As for the fighting to repulse [an enemy], it is aimed at defending sanctity and religion, and it is a duty as agreed [by the ulema]. Nothing is more sacred than belief except repulsing an enemy who is attacking religion and life."

On that basis, and in compliance with Allah's order, we issue the following fatwa to all Muslims:

The ruling to kill the Americans and their allies—civilians and military—is an individual duty for every Muslim who can do it in any country in which it is possible to do it, in order to liberate the al-Aqsa Mosque in Jerusalem and the holy mosque [Mecca] from their grip, and in order for their armies to move out of all the lands of Islam, defeated and unable to threaten any Muslim. This is in accordance with the words of Almighty Allah, "and fight the pagans all together as they fight you all together," and "fight them until there is no more tumult or oppression, and there prevail justice and faith in Allah."

This is in addition to the words of Almighty Allah: "And why should ye not fight in the cause of Allah and of those who, being weak, are ill-treated (and oppressed)?—women and children, whose cry is: 'Our Lord, rescue us from this town, whose people are oppressors; and raise for us from thee one who will help!'"

We—with Allah's help—call on every Muslim who believes in Allah and wishes to be rewarded to comply with Allah's order to kill the Americans and plunder their money wherever and whenever they find it. We also call on Muslim ulema, leaders, youths, and soldiers to launch the raid on Satan's U.S. troops and the devil's supporters allying with them, and to displace those who are behind them so that they may learn a lesson.

Almighty Allah said: "O ye who believe, give your response to Allah and His Apostle, when He calleth you to that which will give you life. And know that Allah cometh between a man and his heart, and that it is He to whom ye shall all be gathered."

Almighty Allah also says: "O ye who believe, what is the matter with you, that when ye are asked to go forth in the cause of Allah, ye cling so heavily to the earth! Do ye prefer the life of this world to the hereafter? But little is the comfort of this life, as compared with the hereafter. Unless ye go forth, He will punish you with a grievous penalty, and put others in your place; but Him ye would not harm in the least. For Allah hath power over all things."

Almighty Allah also says: "So lose no heart, nor fall into despair. For ye must gain mastery if ye are true in faith."

PART ELEVEN

Globalization and the Future of Ideology

Anyone wishing to lead a quiet life," wrote the Russian revolutionary Leon Trotsky, "has done badly to be born in the twentieth century." It was a century of wars and revolutions, of concentration camps and gulags, of the Holocaust and hydrogen bombs. The ferocity of these conflicts was increased in part by new developments in technology, and particularly in the creation of newer and ever more murderous weapons of war. But political ideologies have also inspired and intensified these conflicts. The Russian Revolution of 1917, the rise of Mussolini, Hitler, and Stalin, of Mao and Pol Pot, and the systematic murder of millions of people—all of these and many more are traceable to political ideologies of one kind or another. Whatever else it may have been, the twentieth century was quite clearly an age of ideology.

Toward the end of the century, however, some people began to claim that the age of ideology was coming to an end. After all, they said, communism had crumbled in Eastern Europe and the Soviet Union. Democracies had replaced dictatorships. Everywhere people were demanding the right to shape their own destinies. In short, they claimed, ideology no longer seems to divide the world as it once did. An awareness of common hopes—the hope for peace, for prosperity, for a world fit for habitation by our children and grandchildren—is replacing the fear and hostility motivated and made worse by ideological differences. There may still be reasons for concern about the future, they admitted. There is reason to fear that the awesome weapons of war might be unleashed, as President John F. Kennedy once said, through madness or miscalculation. We also have reason to fear that the planet may be destroyed more slowly but no less surely by a series of interconnected environmental catastrophes. But these very real concerns also give us reason to believe that we can no longer afford (if ever we could) the luxury of ideological differences and disagreements. We can and we must now put aside our differences and work together for the good of all.

This "end of ideology" thesis, as advanced by Daniel Bell and others, offers an appealing vision of present possibilities and future prospects.[1] But is it true? Can ideology end? Our own view is that this is highly unlikely, if only because—as we noted in the Introduction—ideologies perform four important functions for those who subscribe to them. First, they help to *explain* political phenomena that would otherwise remain puzzling or mysterious. Second, they supply standards for *evaluating* political situations and developments. Third, ideologies provide their adherents with a means of *orienting* themselves in the complicated and changing political world. And fourth, ideologies provide *programs* of political action. It is unlikely that reasonably intelligent citizens could make their way in the world without some sort of ideology to perform these four important—and possibly indispensable—functions.

Although ideology per se is unlikely to end, it can and will be profoundly transformed. And that, we believe, is precisely what is happening in the twenty-first century. Some ideologies, such as the Marxist-Leninist version of socialism, appear to be dying, whereas others—such as the much newer ecological or green ideology—are emerging and gaining influence and importance. Meanwhile an older ideology, liberalism, is experiencing a revival. Indeed, Francis Fukuyama contends that liberalism—understood as the defense of individual rights and private property against state encroachment—has defeated its ideological rivals and emerged as *the* dominant ideology of our time. The older history of ideological conflict has come to an end with a single ideology triumphant. We have reached, Fukuyama says, "the end of history."[2]

One major trend that seems to support this conclusion is globalization. In the broad sense of the word, "globalization" refers to the cultural and technological changes that draw the peoples of the world more closely together. CNN and the Internet seem to be everywhere, as do the images of various pop stars and athletes. "Globalization" also has a narrow sense, however, which refers to the spread of free trade around the world—a process that is also known as "liberalization" and often linked to "neoliberalism." Through GATT (the General Agreement on Tariffs and Trade), NAFTA (North American Free Trade Agreement), and other free-trade treaties, the United States and other countries have committed themselves to eliminate or at least reduce restrictions to the free movement of goods across national borders. Countries that do not cooperate may find themselves under pressure from the World Trade Organization (WTO), which oversees the international terms of trade, and from the World Bank and the International Monetary Fund (IMF), two institutions created near the end of World War II to promote a stable, depression-free global economy. Following Adam Smith and the early liberals, advocates of globalization argue that free trade promotes efficiency, rewards producers who manufacture and sell goods at the lowest possible price, and benefits consumers, who can afford to buy more and better goods as international competition drives prices down and quality up. In fact, its proponents say, globalization is responsible for significant gains in health and prosperity in many parts of the world in recent years.

Globalization, however, also has its critics, and they are an ideologically diverse lot. Perhaps foremost among them are members of labor unions and environmental groups, who contend that global free trade means that workers in Third World countries will be overworked and underpaid, that workers in the industrial countries will lose jobs through "outsourcing," and that laws protecting the environment will be repealed or weakened in the name of higher productivity. Other critics include anarchists, who have attracted much attention with their attempts, such as the "battle of Seattle" in 1999, to close down meetings of the WTO and other free-trade organizations. Still other critics are Marxists who see globalization as a higher phase of imperialism—and thus of the capitalist exploitation of the working class throughout the world. There are conservative opponents of globalization, too, such as Patrick Buchanan, a traditional conservative who complains that free trade threatens national sovereignty by making national laws subject to international agreements.

None of these critics doubts that something like globalization is occurring, but they do deny that it is either good or inevitable. To them, globalization is not so much "the end of history" in the triumph of liberalism as it is the occasion for yet another ideological conflict.

On that point, at least, we believe that the critics are right. Predictions of "the end of ideology" (Bell) and "the end of history" (Hegel, Marx) have been made before, and they have never been borne out by events. We suspect that history—to turn Hegel's own phrase against him—is too cunning for humans, however clever, to predict its future course with any accuracy. Moreover, as Benjamin Barber has pointed out, nationalistic and religious sentiments have a way of frustrating the cosmopolitan or internationalist aspirations of political ideologies.[3] The rise of "radical" or "political" Islam bears out this point, as the essays in the previous section attest. If these sentiments persist—and the activities of al-Qaeda and related groups suggest that they will—then perhaps we should never expect ideological conflict to end with the triumph of any one ideology. Perhaps, instead, we should expect new crises to give rise to new and as yet unforeseen ideologies.

NOTES

1. Daniel Bell, *The End of Ideology* (New York: Free Press, 1960). Bell reiterated and updated the argument in his two-part essay "The End of Ideology—Revisited," *Government and Opposition* 23 (1988).
2. Francis Fukuyama, *The End of History and the Last Man* (New York: Free Press, 1992).
3. Benjamin Barber, *Jihad versus McWorld* (New York: Ballantine Books, 1996).

67

The Hidden Promise of Globalization: Liberty Renewed

JOHN MICKLETHWAIT AND ADRIAN WOOLDRIDGE

Globalization is one of the most important developments of the late twentieth and early twenty-first centuries. On that point almost everyone agrees. But is globalization a good or a bad development? On that point there is much disagreement, as the last two entries in this book indicate. The following essay by two members of the editorial staff of *The Economist*, an international journal, is the concluding chapter of their book *A Future Perfect*, which provides what the authors call "a measured defense of globalization." This defense rests in large part on the connection they draw between globalization and the classical liberal ideal of individual liberty. Indeed, the reader will find traces here of many writers already encountered in the pages of this book: of John Locke and Adam Smith, of Thomas Paine and Thomas Jefferson, of Alexis de Tocqueville and John Stuart Mill. Most conspicuous of all, however, is Karl Marx, the revolutionary socialist who was, the authors maintain, both right and wrong about globalization.

Source: John Micklethwait and Adrian Wooldridge, *A Future Perfect: The Challenge and Hidden Promise of Globalization* (London: Heinemann, 2000). © 2000 by Adrian Wooldridge and John Micklethwait, reprinted with the permission of the Wylie Agency Inc.

THE HIDDEN PROMISE OF GLOBALIZATION: LIBERTY RENEWED

Karl Marx's tomb in Highgate Cemetery is a sorry place. The sculpture of his great bearded head is sometimes soiled with pigeon droppings; the army of celebrated intellectuals and communist dignitaries that used to come to pay its respects to the master has dwindled into a tiny band of eccentrics. In one way, this is a pity. As a prophet of socialism, Marx may be kaput; but as a prophet of "the universal interdependence of nations," as he called globalization, he can still seem startlingly relevant.

For all his hatred of the Victorian bourgeoisie, Marx could not conceal his admiration for its ability to turn the world into a single marketplace. Some of this admiration was mere schadenfreude, to be sure, born of his belief that in creating a global working class the bourgeoisie was also creating its very own grave diggers; but a surprising amount of this respect was genuine, like a prizefighter's respect for his muscle-bound opponent. In less than a hundred years, Marx argued, the bourgeoisie had "accomplished wonders far surpassing Egyptian pyramids, Roman aqueducts and Gothic cathedrals"; had conducted "expeditions that put in the shade all former exoduses of nations and crusades"; and had "created more massive and more colossal productive forces" than all preceding generations put together. In achieving all this, it had begun to transform an agglomeration of warring nations and petty principalities into a global marketplace.[1]

Marx was at his most expansive on globalization in *The Communist Manifesto,* which he cowrote with Friedrich Engels, a factory owner turned revolutionary, and published in 1848, a year in which ancien régimes were tottering throughout Europe.

> The need of a constantly expanding market for its products chases the bourgeoisie over the entire surface of the globe. It must nestle everywhere, settle everywhere, establish connections everywhere.
>
> The bourgeoisie has through its exploitation of the world market given a cosmopolitan character to production and consumption in every country.... In place of the old wants, satisfied by the production of the country, we find new wants, requiring for their satisfaction the products of distant land and climes. In place of the old local and national seclusion and self-sufficiency, we have intercourse in every direction, universal interdependence of nations.[2]

Even Marx's final resting place is, to some extent, a vindication of this great insight. Opposite him in Highgate lies William Nassar Kennedy, a colonel of the Winnipeg Rifles who was "called home" in 1885 while returning to Canada from Egypt, where he was in command of the Nile Voyageurs. A little further down there is John MacKinlay and his wife, Caroline Louisa, "late of Bombay." Highgate Cemetery is strewn with the graves of Victorian soldiers, bureaucrats, and merchants who devoted their lives to turning the world into a single market.

What would Marx make of the world today? Imagine for a moment that the prayers of the faithful were answered and the great man awoke from his slumber.... There would, of course, be the shock of discovering that, on all the big issues, he had been proved hopelessly wrong. It was communism that succumbed to its own internal contradictions and capitalism that swept all before it. But he might at least console himself with the thought that his description of globalization remains as sharp today as it was 150 years ago.

Wandering down Highgate Hill, Marx would discover the Bank of Cyprus (which services the three hundred thousand Cypriots that live in London), several curry houses (now England's most popular sort of eatery), and a Restaurante do Brazil. He might be less surprised to find a large Irish community. But the sign inviting him to watch "Irish Sports Live," thanks to a pub's satellite-television linkup, might intrigue him. On the skyline, he would soon spot the twin towers of Canary Wharf, built by Canadian developers with money borrowed from Japanese banks and now occupied mostly by American investment banks.

Marx would hear Asian voices and see white schoolchildren proudly wearing T-shirts with pictures of black English soccer stars. Multicultural London (which is now home to thirty-three ethnic communities, each with a population of more than ten thousand) might well exhilarate a man who was called "the Moor" by his own children because of his dark complexion. He could stop at almost any newsstand and pick up a copy of the *Frankfurter Allgemeine Zeitung* that would be no more than a day old. Nearly swept off his feet by a passing Rolls-Royce, he might be more surprised to discover that the vehicle, like the rest of Britain's car industry, was now owned by a German company.

If Marx were to venture back to his old haunts in Soho, he would find a cluster of video-production companies and advertising agencies that sells its services to the world. If he climbed up to Hampstead Heath, the Marx family's favorite picnic spot, he might be surprised to discover that the neighborhood's most expensive house is now owned by an Indian, Lakshmi Mittal, who has built up one of the world's biggest steel companies. London is home to around a quarter of Europe's five hundred biggest companies. Its financial-services industry alone employs directly or indirectly 850,000 people, more than the population of the city of Frankfurt.[3]

Yet even as Marx marveled at these new creations of the bourgeoisie and perhaps applauded its meritocratic dynamism, it is hard to believe that some of the old revolutionary fires would not burn anew. Poverty of the grinding sort that inspired Engels to write *The Condition of the Working Class in England* (1845) might have disappeared; the rigid class system of the Victorians might have evaporated; Marx might even have been slightly shocked by the absence of domestic servants. But the founder of communism would have no trouble tracking down inequality and sensing that it was on the increase.

Barely ten miles separate elegant Chelsea (where ironically enough the Marx family lived when they first came to London, before being evicted for not paying the rent) from the crumbling wasteland of Newnham, but they seem like two different countries. In one, you might be forgiven for thinking that the biggest problem is the availability of residential parking permits; in the other, two thirds of the sixteen-year-olds fail their basic high-school exams, and the mortality rate for people under twenty-five is 50 percent above the national average.[4] As he studied the newspaper and looked at the pictures on the flashing television screens of, say, Somalia or even parts of Los Angeles, Marx might well see globalization as a process that is only just beginning—a job half done. Once again, he might consider, the world is hurtling toward a "crisis of capitalism"—not unlike the last one that his own theories did so much to make ruinous.

The Priority of Liberty

This, then, is the beginning of the future, perfect or not, that we have tried to describe in this book. The fact that it has much in common with the world of yesterday (and especially the world of a century ago) is not surprising. History condemns us to repeat ourselves, though not necessarily to repeat all our mistakes.

Throughout this book, we have tried to build a measured defense of globalization. Yes, it does increase inequality, but it does not create a winner-take-all society, and the winners hugely outnumber the losers. Yes, it leaves some people behind, but it helps millions more to leap ahead. Yes, it can make bad government worse, but the onus should be on crafting better government, not blaming globalization. Yes, it curtails some of the power of nation-states, but they remain the fundamental unit of modern politics. Globalization is not destroying geography, merely enhancing it.

In most cases, the bulwarks of our defense have been economic. The simple fact is that globalization makes us richer—or makes enough of us richer to make the whole process worthwhile. Globalization clearly benefits producers by giving them greater choice over their raw materials, production techniques, and human talent, not to mention over the markets where they sell their goods. Equally clearly, globalization benefits consumers by providing them with better goods at better prices. Globalization increases efficiency and thus prosperity.

These economic arguments need to be made, and with far more eloquence, by our leaders. Too many politicians take the Clintonesque tack of defending the easy bits of globalization—typically, the successes of their own country's exports—and shying away from talking about the benefits that flow, say, from imports or foreign takeovers of "their" companies. This is not only economically illiterate but dangerous, because it allows myths to emerge, such as the idea that globalization is a zero-sum game. But there is also a broader need to wrench globalization from all the dry talk of markets penetrated, currencies depreciated, and GDPs accelerated and to place the process in its proper political context: as an extension of the idea of liberty and as a chance to renew the fundamental rights of the individual.

Nowadays, "liberalism" has become just another political slogan. In the United States, Ronald Reagan made it into something of a swear-word for Republicans, and Democrats still use it gingerly. Around the world, liberal parties stand for everything from conservatism (Canada), fascism (Russia), and people with beards who want to legalize cannabis (Britain). Yet most of the tenets of modern democracy actually stem from the classical liberalism of a group of writers and thinkers who, from the seventeenth century onward, argued that society should be based on the rights of individuals rather than on the hierarchy of a "great chain of being," stretching from God downward, with everyone assigned a fixed place.

This belief in individualism, which was at the heart of both the Enlightenment and the American Revolution, was actually a fairly global movement itself. Its foundations were laid in Britain by groups such as the Levelers (whose belief that "the poorest he in England has a life to live as much as the richest he" so unsettled their rulers) and thinkers such as John Locke, who argued that individuals had a right to break their contracts with their sovereigns if he or she trampled on their rights. Later British theorists such as Adam Smith and John Stuart Mill refined and expanded the creed, turning it into the foundation of a new academic discipline (economics) and a new branch of philosophy (utilitarianism). But by then it had been carried around the world—and adapted to local conditions—by everybody from Thomas Paine (who announced the birth of the "rights of man") to Thomas Jefferson, Voltaire, and Alexis de Tocqueville. As we have already seen, both John Maynard Keynes and Friedrich von Hayek claimed allegiance to it (though Marx, of course, despised it).

In the process, liberalism has become something of a broad church, yet it always returns to two fundamental principles and one fundamental prejudice. The first principle is that rights belong to individuals rather than to governments or to social groups. The second is that the essence of freedom lies in individual choice. The ideal society allows individuals to make as many decisions as possible without reference to some external authority. The fundamental prejudice is skepticism and an abhorrence of certainty. One reason why liberals are drawn to free markets is because they distrust the power of bureaucrats. Absolutist creeds, whether those of the seventeenth-century papacy or of Marxism, are to be distrusted. And, crucially, liberalism—unlike its bastard child, libertarianism—is also distrustful of itself: it may be predisposed against governments interfering in peoples' lives, but it is quick to admit that there are times when this makes sense—for instance, in order to tax them so that it can provide education and health care.

The twentieth century was an awkward century for liberalism. The creed managed to see off the horrors of totalitarianism, yet by the end of the century the state was enormously more powerful than it had been at the beginning. The Fabian presumption that "the gentleman in Whitehall" or Washington knows "better what is good for people than the people know themselves" lingers not only in the nannyish environmentalism of Al Gore but in the preachy moralism of many Republicans. (In Britain, Blairism has even managed to combine both.) As for technology, for much of the twentieth century it only strengthened John Stuart Mill's lament that "the tendency of all the changes taking place in the world is to strengthen society and diminish the power of the individual." Mass production reduced workers to cogs in an infernal machine. Computers gathered information on us all.

The Open Society

Globalization redresses this balance in two ways. The most obvious is that it puts limits on the power of government. This advantage is most obvious in commerce. Free trade makes it easier for businesspeople to escape from interfering officials by moving their money and operations abroad. As we have pointed out, companies seldom want to flee, but the very fact that they might acts as a brake on those officials. The sullen fury of a Bangalore bureaucrat staring at the satellite dishes that allow "his" software companies to export their products without his grasping fingers interfering would delight Mill (even though he worked for the often more extortionate East India Company). More important still, free trade allows ordinary people to buy products from companies who make the best of their kind rather than from those that enjoy cozy relationships with governments. Similarly, they can put their retirement money in pension funds that are not tied to schemes of national aggrandizement.

Governments are not retreating from this easily. They can still slap controls on the flow of capital (as Malaysia did in the wake of the Asian crisis) or even on the flow of information. (Singapore employs a staff of censors whose job is to surf the Internet ceaselessly looking for objectionable information to block.) But the world is nevertheless a lot freer today than it was just a few decades ago, before globalization got into high gear. In 1966, for example, the British Labour government imposed a travel allowance that virtually confined Britons to their own country except for two weeks' worth of penny-pinching foreign vacation. Today, any politician who suggested such a restriction would be carted off to an asylum.

Indeed, the recent history of globalization can be written as a story, albeit an uneven story, of spreading a political culture that is based on individual liberty to areas that have been longing to embrace it for years. The last dozen years of the twentieth century saw not only the spectacular death of the biggest alternative to liberal democracy, totalitarian communism, but also the slow death of other collectivist models. Around the world, countries have abandoned attempts to plan their way to prosperity. Even the Asian crisis, in its own awful way, has made it more difficult for the continent's authoritarians to boast that they had discovered a nondemocratic way to generate growth.

Many on the left would argue that globalization has merely involved a change of master. Globalization may have liberated us from the onus of having to get our television programs—or our health care and pensions—from our governments, but it has forced us to get the same things from giant companies that are just as remote and even less accountable. The gentleman in Whitehall has been replaced by the knucklehead in the boardroom or, if you work in the Académie Française, by the illiterate in Hollywood.

This suspicion is healthy and should be encouraged. But so far the evidence is that it is misplaced. Of course, businesses will try to control markets, but that does not mean that they will be able to. As we have seen, one of the wonders of global capitalism is its capacity to hurl challenges at incumbent champions. Most of the forces of globalization—particularly the availability of capital and technology—favor small companies. In parts of Europe and Asia, commercial oligarchies are clinging to power, but only because governments collude with them. There is nothing global about, say, the importance of *guanxi* [personal relationships or networks] in Asia—quite the opposite. By the same token, the Department of Justice campaign to restrain Microsoft's power, no matter how misguided, has a legitimately global aim of trying to open up a market.

In fact, many of the most vengeful howls directed at globalization come from self-interested business elites who are being forced to surrender to consumer choice. Globalization does not mean homogenization. People want to consume books, movies, even potato chips, that reflect their own identities, and those identities remain primarily national. When politicians complain that globalization is changing society, they are correct, but they seldom bother to ask whose society it is. When society is defined by a fairly compact national economy, an elite has a chance of co-opting it. But when society is an open-ended international system, it becomes increasingly difficult for any elite to identify their values with the common good.

The Individual's Prayer

Restricting overmighty states and elites is all very well, but globalization increases the basic freedom of individuals as well. We have already talked about the tyranny of place: Most people's lots in life are determined by where they were born, something illiberal regimes everywhere have done their best to reinforce. As Leszek Kolakowski, a Polish intellectual, points out, one of the defining features of communist regimes is their refusal to allow people to move from city to city without official permission; they even made short journeys difficult, providing few road signs or decent street maps. Even today, the lives of half the world's population are bounded by local villages, and local markets.

Travel and migration have long provided a fraction of the world's population with freedom from the tyranny of place. The printing press and the television have allowed others a more imaginary form of escape. Globalization is now making these freedoms more pervasive. The impact of the Internet, particularly as it goes wireless, will also be dramatic. The World Wide Web allows people to gain access to information anywhere at any time. And it allows them to do so in a way that undermines local elites and expensive middlemen. People will never escape the pull of geography entirely, as the tendency of business to cluster in particular places shows. But those clusters only survive if they work with the grain of globalization. And the penalty for being born a long way from those clusters is diminishing. Remember the Bangladeshi farmers using their cell phones to check the proper prices for their produce rather than having to accept the diktats of local grain merchants.

The more these ties weaken, the more people can exercise what used to be called God-given talents. Again, businesspeople are the most obvious beneficiaries: If you have a good idea and the entrepreneurial vim to pursue it, you can take it anywhere you want. If, like Michael Skok of AlphaBlox, you think that your business belongs in Silicon Valley, not the Thames valley, you can take it there. But, there are also more spiritual, artistic reasons to believe that globalization is a good thing. The thousands of Miltons who remain "mute and inglorious" in their villages often begin to sing only after they move to the "mansion houses of liberty" that are the world's great cities. Bustling centers of trade from fifteenth-century Venice to twentieth-century New York have usually been centers of creativity, too. Even if your God-given talents are more prosaic, it is becoming ever easier to study abroad, and, thanks again to the Internet, you will soon be able to do so (more or less) without leaving home.

Somewhere behind the freedom to exercise our talents lies the most fundamental freedom of all: the freedom to define our own identities. This can sound like the moan of a petulant teenager, but it is at the heart of what is becoming one of the main debates of our time, between liberals and the growing band of communitarians. (To the extent that "the third way" means anything at all, its adherents are probably on the side of the communitarians.) Communitarians, as their name suggests, worry about the effect of things like globalization on communities. John Gray, one of globalization's most searching critics, has argued that human beings' "deepest need is a home, a network of common practices and inherited traditions that confers on them the blessings of a settled identity."

There can be no doubt that people need a home and a network. But does this home have to be the one they were born in? And does this network have to be the one provided by their ancestors? People also have a drive to better themselves, to extend their identities, to cross traditional boundaries, and to try out new experiences. John Gray himself happily abandoned the Newcastle working class into which he was born for the metropolitan intelligentsia. One of the many benefits of globalization is that it increases the number of people who can exercise Gray's privilege of fashioning his own identity.

This is not to say that conservative and communitarian worries about individualism run wild are empty. In the same breath that he praised America's faith in individualism, Tocqueville warned of the danger that each man may be "shut up in the solitude of his own heart."[5] One of the great risks of globalization is that it fosters anomie—the normlessness that comes from having your ties with the rest of society weakened. Anybody who spends long periods of time on business trips knows the loneliness of the long-distance traveler. Ex-pats [expatriates] complain that their children grow up not knowing their grandparents. The most common complaint among Internet addicts is that they end up feeling (rather like the compulsive masturbators of Victorian medical treatises) isolated, lonely, and depressed.

All too true. Yet the issue that separates liberals from communitarians is not the desirability of human ties but the question of coercion. For liberals, the best communities are the spontaneous creations of free individuals rather than the products of bossy politicians, and one of the many cases for globalization is that it lets a million of these spontaneous communities bloom. The smaller the world becomes, the more communities are defined by common interests and outlooks rather than by the mere accident of physical proximity.

The idea of spontaneous communities will hardly placate globalization's harshest critics. For some people, the idea that individuals take precedence over society is nothing more than Western cultural imperialism. Wee Kim Wee, the former president of Singapore, argues that "placing society above the self" is one of his country's "core values." It is all very well for the egomaniacs of Manhattan and Los Angeles to abandon their gods in pursuit of self-fulfillment. But everybody else knows that such selfishness leads inexorably to the wasteland.

Yet the yearning for freedom is no more peculiar to the West than the yearning for prosperity. Other parts of the world have been quieter on the subject not because their peoples are wedded to collectivism but because their rulers have been less fussy about the methods they have used to hold onto power. Singaporeans bitterly resent the fact that their government gives them a superb education but then proceeds to treat them like children. The students who were brutally crushed at Tiananmen Square constructed replicas of the Statue of Liberty.

An Empire Without End

Look around the world, and it is not hard to find examples of people for whom this message may seem a little empty. What does Reginaldo Gobetti care about the freedom to create his own identity; he just wants a job. Our argument is not that globalization is delivering the liberal dream, with billions of people gradually becoming the wired (or wireless) equivalent of Jefferson's yeoman farmers. Our argument is merely that globalization is delivering enough of that dream to make it worth pressing forward and to make it worth defending on more than just narrow economic grounds.

In fact, the two arguments should run in tandem. Globalization is helping to give birth to an economy that is closer to the classic theoretical model of capitalism, under which rational individuals pursue their interests in the light of perfect information, relatively free from government and geographical obstacles. It is also helping to create a society that is closer to the model that liberal political theorists once imagined, in which power lies increasingly in the hands of individuals rather than governments, and in which people are free, within reasonable bounds, to pursue the good life wherever they find it.

It would be nice if we could end on that optimistic, perhaps even slightly utopian, note. Yet we have also stressed the importance of vigilance and the need for not just politicians but also those who have prospered from globalization—particularly the cosmocrats—to help those who have done less well.

The trouble is that the devil has all the best tunes. One reason why globalization's enemies are so much more persuasive than its friends is that they are more visible: The victims are usually concentrated in particular places, whereas its beneficiaries are spread out all over the place. But supporters have also done a lousy job of making their case. We have already lamented the shortage of Peels and Rockefellers. But consider once again whether any modern leader would stand up and argue that "by encouraging freedom of intercourse between the nations of the world we are promoting the separate welfare of each and are fulfilling the beneficent designs of an all-seeing Creator" or invite his audience to celebrate "commerce, the happy instrument of promoting civilization, of abating national jealousies and prejudices and of encouraging the maintenance of general peace by every consideration as well as every obligation of Christian duty."

It is not just the passion that sets Sir Robert Peel apart from his modern peers. It is the fact that he bothered to make the case in what then amounted to the language of the streets—and made it, moreover, to the people rather than just to a group of bigwigs. When Peel died [in 1850], tens of thousands of people contributed their pennies to construct memorials to the man who had masterminded the repeal of the corn laws. Naturally, it would be nice if, say, the IMF [International Monetary Fund] made more of an effort to explain its ways; but you need only spend half an hour with any of its denizens to realize that you are more likely to get Ciceronian oratory from your typewriter. Kofi Annan has tried to make his voice heard, but his need to please all the UN's members has simultaneously blunted his message. The proper place for the trumpets of globalization to sound is from national political figures. George Bush the elder ushered in his new world order. Bill Clinton, a far more agile communicator, has failed to come up with one memorable phrase on the subject.

The time when such leadership will be needed could be close at hand. At the time of writing, support for free trade in America is nothing more than lukewarm, even though the economy is doing better than it has for decades: another recession, let alone another Wall Street crash, could turn protectionism into a powerful cause. American foreign policy, a phrase that Bill Clinton's meandering mind has reduced to an oxymoron, could lurch in any number of directions. Meanwhile, despite the terrible evidence of the Asian contagion, there are still plenty of countries around the world that are continuing to try to have it both ways, sucking in Western capital while refusing to open their economies. Given its penchant for funneling money into favored firms and concealing corporate and government activities from the prying eyes of outsiders, China could yet produce a disaster that would make the Asian crisis look like a tea party.

Highgate Man

Which brings us back to Highgate. It might seem perverse to end a book on globalization by returning to a hypothetically reincarnated German—particularly given that Karl Marx was a sworn enemy of the liberalism that we admire. Yet one of the things that Marx would recognize immediately about this particular global era is a paradox that he spotted in the last one: The more successful globalization becomes, the more it seems to whip up its own backlash. The process is not unlike waves sweeping up on a shore: Each one that rushes forward also creates its undertow.

The undoing of globalization, in Marx's view, would come not just from losers resenting the success of the winners but also from the winners themselves losing their appetite for the battle. Globalization's power, and much of its efficiency, is founded on its ability to keep on exposing weaknesses and imperfections. This is good for us all in the long run, but it makes it difficult for even the winners to enjoy the quiet life. The more relentless economic integration seems, the greater the short-term appeal of politicians who seek to resist it.

There is even a suspicion that globalization's psychic energy—the uncertainty that it creates which forces companies, governments, and people to perform better—may have a natural stall point, a moment when people can take no more. As Marx put it in *The Communist Manifesto:*

> Uninterrupted disturbance of all social conditions, everlasting uncertainty and agitation distinguish the bourgeois epoch from all earlier ones.... All that is solid melts into air, all that is holy is profaned, and man is at last compelled to face with sober senses his real conditions of life and his relations with his kind.[6]

Overcoming this paradox—the seeming invincibility of globalization and its underlying fragility—is the central challenge of the new century.

NOTES

1. Karl Marx and Friedrich Engels, *The Communist Manifesto* (London: Penguin Classics, 1985), pp. 83–84. [See selection 35 of *Ideals and Ideologies*—Eds.]
2. Ibid, p. 83.
3. "A Capital of Haves and Have Nots," *International Herald Tribune,* May 7, 1998.
4. Ibid.
5. Alexis de Tocqueville, *Democracy in America* (1835–1840), vol. 2, p. 99.
6. Marx and Engels, *The Communist Manifesto,* p. 83.

68

Globalization as Economic Treason

PATRICK J. BUCHANAN

The critics of globalization are a highly diverse group of people who give new meaning to the old expression "politics makes for strange bedfellows." Labor unionists and environmentalists have been among the most prominent of these critics, despite their disagreements on other matters, and they have been joined in their antiglobalization efforts by various anarchists, Marxists, and even conservatives. One of these conservative critics is the author of the following essay, Patrick J. Buchanan (1938—). Buchanan is an American author and political activist who calls himself a traditional conservative. He has served as a senior advisor to three presidents—Richard Nixon, Gerald Ford, and Ronald Reagan—and in 1992 and 1996 campaigned for the Republican presidential nomination. In 2000 he was the presidential candidate of the Reform Party. In all of these campaigns, as in the following excerpt from his book *Where the Right Went Wrong*, Buchanan has argued that globalization is a threat to both the sovereignty and the prosperity of the United States.

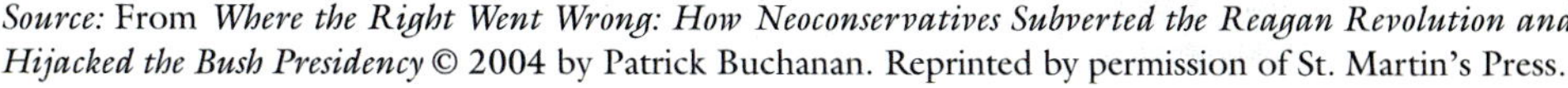

Source: From *Where the Right Went Wrong: How Neoconservatives Subverted the Reagan Revolution and Hijacked the Bush Presidency* © 2004 by Patrick Buchanan. Reprinted by permission of St. Martin's Press.

GLOBALIZATION AS ECONOMIC TREASON

In the title of a 1921 biography by Arthur Vandenberg, he was the Greatest American.

Born illegitimate, "the bastard son of a Scotch peddler" in [John] Adams's insult, he came to America from the West Indies as a boy and began to agitate for independence. When war came, he enlisted and fought at Trenton. Pleading for his own command, he was given the honor of leading the bayonet charge at Yorktown. After victory, when the thirteen independent states went their separate and quarrelsome ways, he plotted with Madison and Washington to hold a constitutional convention. He coauthored the Federalist Papers to explain the new nation he helped create. Washington named him secretary of the treasury. In that capacity, he wrote *The Report on Manufactures,* laying out the blueprints by which the American economy would be constructed and operate.

He was Alexander Hamilton, master architect of the United States. His vision had been forged in the fire of revolution and the furnace of war. The deprivations of the British blockade and winters at Valley Forge and Morristown had taught him the price of dependency. Without French muskets and French ships, the revolution would not have survived. Reflecting on how close his country had come to losing its liberty, Hamilton wrote:

> Not only the wealth, but the independence and security of a country, appear to be materially connected with the prosperity of manufactures. Every nation...ought to endeavor to possess within itself all the essentials of a national supply. These comprise the means of *subsistence, habitation, clothing and defense.*

America's political independence, Hamilton was saying, could not survive without economic independence. The guidelines he laid down, and nationalists from Washington to Madison to Lincoln to Theodore Roosevelt followed, were these:

- America must not be thirteen separate markets but a single free market. All state tariffs that impede domestic commerce are to be abolished. Free trade among the thirteen states is embedded in the Constitution.
- To ensure free trade among the states, a new national government has been created. How is it to be financed? With tariffs on imports from abroad, imposed at customs houses at the port of entry. All exports and all income of U.S. citizens are to be exempt from taxation. This prohibition was to be written into the Constitution.
- The tariff revenue extracted from foreign merchants will be used to build a new capital, create an army and navy to defend us from imperial predators, and construct the roads, harbors, and canals that will bind us together as a people.

From Hamilton's mind and pen had come the greatest free market in history. But as Hamilton was, like Washington, an American nationalist, it was a *national* free-trade zone he had created. All Americans participated in that free market as their birthright, but British merchants, who had held life-and-death power over the colonies, would pay a price of admission—a tariff. That tariff would finance a small but strong central government. And by raising the price of foreign goods, tariffs would stimulate our own people into building factories here in the United States. Strategic goal: Cut the ties of dependency to Europe and create bonds of commerce among Americans. The U.S. economy was designed to weld us into one nation and one people, dependent upon one another. What was best for America, and for our people as a whole, was the basis of Hamilton's great idea.

Washington and Hamilton wanted to wean the republic off a reliance on foreign trade so Americans would never again be drawn into the wars of the old continent. They wanted to cut the umbilical cord to Europe and set out over the mountains for the West. They were statesmen, visionaries, and patriots....

The Fruits of Globalism

At the end of World War II, with most of Europe and East Asia devastated, the United States undertook to open her markets to goods made in the countries that had suffered in the war. It was a necessary and selfless sacrifice of domestic industry to enable allies to get back on their feet to be able to contribute to the defense of the West.

This Eisenhower policy of opening America's markets to the world was continued by [Presidents] Kennedy, Johnson, and Nixon, despite a rising clamor at home that Europe and Japan had recovered and America should look again to the protection of her home industries and manufacturing base.

But Republican presidents of the postwar era had abandoned tradition. They were now all converts to the free-trade faith preached by the party of [Woodrow] Wilson and FDR [Franklin Delano Roosevelt]. Eisenhower and Nixon openly embraced what Theodore Roosevelt called the "pernicious" doctrine. "I thank God I am not a free trader," TR had once written to Henry Cabot Lodge.

Ronald Reagan championed free trade with Canada, a nation with first-world wages and environmental and labor standards. But it was the son and the grandson of Prescott Bush—who, with Barry Goldwater and Strom Thurmond, was among only eight U.S. senators to oppose JFK's Trade Expansion Act—who finally and forever renounced the America First economic patriotism of the Grand Old Party.

A third of a century has elapsed since completion of the Kennedy round of trade negotiations that inaugurated our free-trade era. Time to measure the promise against the performance.

In one generation, the house Hamilton built has collapsed. The most awesome industrial machine the world had ever seen has been gutted. The U.S. manufacturing base has been hollowed out. For seven decades, until 1970, Americans produced 96 percent of all they consumed. Now, a fourth of our steel is foreign-made, a third of our cars, half our machine tools, two-thirds of the clothes we wear, and almost all our shoes, radios, telephones, TVs, cameras, VCRs, and bicycles.

We have witnessed the fall of the American dollar, the end of our economic independence, the deindustrialization of our country and the abandonment of our working men and women to Darwinian competition with foreign labor forced to work for a fifth or a tenth of U.S. wages.

In 2002, the United States ran a merchandise trade deficit of $484 billion. In 2003, it hit $550 billion. Every month of the first thirty-eight of George W. Bush's presidency, manufacturing jobs disappeared. One in six have vanished since he took his oath, 2.6 million in all.

In 1950, a third of our labor force was in manufacturing, and ours was the most self-sufficient republic the world had ever seen. Now only 11 percent of U.S. workers are in manufacturing, which is in a death spiral, and it is not a natural death. It is premeditated murder. Globalists and corporatists plotted the evisceration of American manufacturing with the collusion of free-trade fundamentalists who cannot see that the theories they were fed by economics professors in college are killing the country they profess to love. Or they do not care.

In spring 2004, after mass at St. Mary's, a retired FBI agent who had worked as a boy in the giant steel plant in Weirton, West Virginia, and whose father had died in an accident at the mill, handed me the *Weirton Daily Times*. "Where Do We Go From Here?" read the May 20 banner. The front page was devoted to the bankruptcy filing of Weirton Steel, which had once employed fourteen thousand workers in a town of twenty-three thousand.

Mark Glyptis, president of the Independent Steelworkers Union, said it didn't have to happen. It was a poignant story. When I had begun my campaign of 2000 at the Weirton mill, Mark and his ISU had endorsed me.

That same week, a friend e-mailed me. Timco Lumber, where we spent the last day of the New Hampshire campaign of 1996, had shut down. As Weirton Steel had been hammered by subsidized steel dumped into the

U.S. market from overseas, Timco had to compete with subsidized lumber from Canada.

Across America, the story is the same. Steel and lumber mills going bankrupt, textile plants moving out to the Caribbean, Mexico, Central America, the Far East. Auto plants closing and opening overseas, mines being sealed in the Southwest, farms being sold off.

Michael Boskin, chairman of the Council of Economic Advisers under Bush I, flippantly remarked, "It does not make any difference whether a country makes computer chips or potato chips." Former Bush budget director Richard Darman said of U.S. makers of computer chips: "If our guys can't hack it, let 'em go."

Why does it matter where our goods are produced? As I wrote six years ago in *The Great Betrayal: How American Sovereignty and Social Justice Are Being Sacrificed to the Gods of the Global Economy*,

> Manufacturing is the key to national power. Not only does it pay more than service industries, the rates of productivity growth are higher and the potential of new industry arising is far greater. From radio came television, VCRs and flat-panel screens. From adding machines came calculators and computers. From the electric typewriter came the word processor. Research and development follows manufacturing.

Manufacturing is the muscle of a modern nation. In the eternal struggle of nations, the industrial powers have always risen to the top. When the Industrial Revolution began in England, Britain vaulted to the forefront. The Acts of Navigation kept her there. British statesmen knew it. [William] Pitt, architect of victory in the Seven Years' War that drove France out of North America, knew it. He supported the American colonies in their demand—"No taxation without representation!" But Pitt warned that if ever he caught Americans engaged in manufacturing—exclusive province of the Mother Country—he would send his ships into their harbors and blow their factories off the map.

Manufacturing power and the economic independence it gave Great Britain enabled her to adopt a policy of "splendid isolation" from the quarrels and wars of the continent, as she ruled her empire. But when Germany, united in 1871, began to eclipse Britain as first industrial power in Europe, Britain felt forced to enter the alliances that dragged her into the greatest war in history. Only U.S. industrial power, greater than that of Britain, France, and Germany combined, turned the tide in that war. And America, self-sufficient as she was by World War I, did not need allies and could stay out of the war as long as she wished. No more.

Since 1971, the trade deficits run by the United States add up to $4 trillion. The annual trade deficit in goods is now running at $600 billion. These dollars, shipped abroad to buy the products of foreign factories, are now being used by foreigners to buy up our stocks, bonds, companies, and real estate. By 2002, foreigners owned U.S. assets equal to 78 percent of our GDP [gross domestic product]. They owned 13 percent of our equity market, 22 percent of our corporations, 24 percent of our corporate bonds, 48 percent of the U.S. treasury market. Like Esau, we are selling our birthright. As Lou Dobbs declaims nightly on CNN, we are "exporting America."

"[F]oreigners are using our $1 billion per day trade deficit to buy up American firms," writes columnist Paul Craig Roberts, who helped craft the Reagan fiscal policy. "In 2000," he reports, "97% of direct investment by foreigners went for the purchase of existing U.S. assets. We are not only losing industrial jobs, we are losing ownership of our companies."

Year by year, the deindustrialization of America proceeds, step by step, with the de-Americanization of our greatest companies, as we become an ever more dependent nation and people. We work for others. We depend on others for the necessities of our national life. And when others tire of taking our dollars for their goods, the value of those dollars will fall. The decline of the dollar has already begun. One day, all those "cheap foreign goods" will not be cheap anymore.

America's New Dependency

Consider the depth of our dependency. Imports, 4 percent of GNP [gross national product] from 1900 to 1970, are now 14 percent, and a third of all manufactures we consume. From 1900 to 1970, America ran trade surpluses every year. We have now run thirty-three straight trade deficits, with the merchandise trade deficit now at $600 billion, or almost 6 percent of GDP. No great power has sustained trade deficits like these for decades without a collapse of its currency and the end of its supremacy.

Pat Choate, author of *Agents of Influence*, gives the following levels of U.S. dependency on foreign suppliers for critical goods.

Medicines and pharmaceuticals	72%
Metalworking machinery	51%
Engines and power equipment	56%
Computer equipment	70%
Communications equipment	67%
Semiconductors and electronics	64%

Dell Computers of Austin has 4,500 suppliers. It has an inventory of four days and a just-in-time supply line that stretches across the Atlantic and Pacific. A dock strike on either coast, writes Choate, and Dell begins to close down after ninety-six hours.

In 2003, Pentagon officials who buy for the U.S. armed forces and U.S. defense industries spoke out in opposition to a law that would require a 65 percent American content in U.S. weapons. Our missile defense system and Joint Strike Fighter would be imperiled, the Pentagon said, if two-thirds of their components had to be made in the USA.

NAFTA: The Big Sting

In 1993, the NAFTA debate gripped the country and Congress. In promoting his trade pact with Mexico, President Clinton had the backing of the Council on Foreign Relations and U.S. Chamber of Commerce, the *Wall Street Journal* and *Washington Post*, Heritage Foundation and the Brookings Institution, the *New Republic* and *National Review*. Ross Perot, Ralph Nader, this writer, and the AFL-CIO opposed it, as did the American people. It did not matter. Before the vote, the bazaar opened, and members of Congress began selling their votes to the White House. NAFTA won. Ten years later, the returns are in.

A year after NAFTA passed, Mexico devalued the peso, and the United States began running an unbroken string of rising trade deficits with Mexico that now runs over $40 billion a year. Drug cartels shifted operations from South America to the U.S. border. Mexico has became the primary source of the marijuana and heroin pouring in and poisoning the minds and souls of American children.

As the narcotics came north, U.S. companies began laying off $10- and $20-an-hour U.S. workers and moving south in search of labor willing to work for $2 an hour. By 2000, more than a million Mexicans were at work in *maquiladora* plants at jobs once held by Americans. In 2002, over 21 percent of the entire GDP of Mexico was shipped north. This is not trade in the traditional sense. It represents the transfer from the United States to Mexico of a large slice of U.S. production in pursuit of cheaper wages and tax avoidance. The "creative destruction" of globalization has now hit Mexico. Factories there are shutting down and moving to China, where wages are even lower.

Americans were told during the NAFTA debate that the only jobs we would lose were the "dead-end" jobs our high-tech labor force should no longer be doing. We would be creating the jobs at which Americans excel, like building commercial jetliners.

Since 1994, America has lost 689,000 jobs in apparel and textiles, "dead-end jobs" to pundits and think tank scribblers but the best jobs they ever had to the folks who lost them. For those apparel jobs paid 23 percent more, and the textile jobs 59 percent more, than the retail sales jobs they and their wives now probably have.

After the textile industry went, the auto industry followed, though the jobs of U.S. autoworkers are among the highest-paid factory jobs on earth. Mexico now exports 90 percent more cars to the United States than we do to the world. In 2003, the United States had a trade deficit in automobiles, trucks, and auto parts of $122 billion.

Now comes the turn of aerospace, the crown jewel of American manufacturing. It, too, is heading south. "Like the automakers that turned the cities of Tolucca, Hermosillo, and Sautillo into Little Detroit in the 1990s," writes Joel Millman of the *Wall Street Journal,* "Boeing Corp., General Dynamics Co., Honeywell International Inc., and General Electric Co.'s GE Aircraft Engines are beginning to make Mexico a base for both parts manufacture and assembly."

What is the attraction?

"You can only cut costs so much with new machinery," says John Monarch, president of GE supplier Smith West. "Pretty soon you need to lower labor costs, too." Driessen Aircraft Interior Systems pays Mexican workers $20 a day, which breaks down to $2.50 an hour, less than half the U.S. minimum wage.

If aircraft parts can be made by Mexican workers for $20 a day and computers can be made by Chinese workers for $10 a day, what is there left that cannot be manufactured more cheaply abroad? Almost nothing.

And the Mexican people? Half of the 100 million are still mired in poverty. Tens of millions are unemployed or underemployed. Because of devaluations, real wages are below what they were in 1993. Thus the great migration north continues. Some 1.5 million are apprehended every year on our southern border breaking into the United States. Of the perhaps 500,000 who make it, one-third head for Mexifornia where their claims on Medicaid, schools, courts, prisons, and welfare have tipped the Golden State toward bankruptcy and induced millions of native-born Americans to flee in the great exodus to Nevada, Idaho, Arizona, and Colorado.

Ten years after NAFTA, Mexico's leading export to America is still—Mexicans. America is becoming Mexamerica.

China: Factory Floor to the World

The abolition of tariffs between the United States and Mexico sent hundreds of thousands of jobs south in search of lower wages and weaker health, safety, and environmental laws. But the annual granting of Most Favored Nation trade status to China, followed by President Bush's grant of Permanent Normal Trade Relations—and the admission of China to the World Trade Organization—has sent millions of jobs to China.

China's boom began after Beijing devalued in 1994 to give herself a competitive advantage over the "Asian Tigers"—South Korea, Taiwan, Singapore, and Malaysia. With unrestricted access to the U.S. market, Beijing began to invite Western companies into China to build factories there, to tap her inexhaustible pool of low-wage labor and to produce for export to America. As the price of access to her own market, Beijing demanded that the companies transfer technology to their Chinese partners. If the companies balked, the Chinese extorted or pirated the technology.

By offering workers at $2 a day, guaranteeing no unions, allowing levels of pollution no Western nation would tolerate, China has converted herself into the factory floor of the world. In 2003, China surpassed the United States as the world's largest recipient of direct foreign investment. Once home to tough "Yankee traders," America has supinely accepted what analyst Charles McMillion calls "The World's Most Unequal Trading Relationship."

In 2002, the U.S. trade deficit with China was $103 billion. In 2003, it hit $124 billion, the largest trade deficit between two nations in history. By mid-2004, that deficit was approaching $150 billion a year. It is false to say President Bush presided over a "jobless recovery." His trade deficits have created many millions of jobs in China.

The relationship between America and China cannot be called a true trade partnership. For what is taking place is the systematic transfer, factory by factory, of our manufacturing base to China. America is being looted of her manufacturing patrimony by her own corporate class in a way that calls to mind the looting of Germany by Red Army scavengers after World War II. Beijing understands what economic nationalist Friedrich List wrote: "The power of producing wealth is infinitely more important than the wealth itself." China sacrifices the present for the future, while America sacrifices her future to the present.

China has now amassed close to $500 billion in reserves from her trade surpluses. Much of that vast hoard is invested in U.S. Treasury bonds, earning Beijing billions in annual interest from U.S. taxpayers. America may be the most advanced nation on earth and China a developing country, but you cannot tell that by studying the trade statistics.

In 2002, Americans purchased 10 percent of China's entire GDP, while China purchased one-fifth of 1 percent of ours. We bought 40 percent of China's exports. China bought 3 percent of ours. China ran up her largest trade surpluses with us in computers, electrical machinery, toys, games, footwear, furniture, clothing, plastics, articles of iron and steel, vehicles, optical and photographic equipment, and other manufactures.

Among the twenty-three items in which America had a trade surplus with China were soybeans, corn, wheat, animal feeds, meat, cotton, metal ores, scrap, hides and skins, pulp, waste paper, cigarettes, gold, coal, mineral fuels, rice, tobacco, fertilizers, glass. "It comes as something of a shock," writes Paul Craig Roberts, "to discover that the U.S.…has the export profile of a 19th century third world colony."

One who has studied the behavior of capitalists courting China is columnist Terry Jeffrey. Inspecting the Web site of Motorola, Jeffrey found this description of how this American company sees its future:

> Motorola is moving toward…taking China as its home and development base. Motorola Chinese Electronics…has increased its investment several times in China without taking away a single dollar. The company reinvested all the profits in China….
>
> Since the very beginning Motorola has brought forward the idea of trying to be a good citizen of China, taking China as its home and thriving with the Chinese people.… The development goal is to become a true Chinese company.

Motorola's kowtow reveals a hidden cost of globalization. When U.S. companies go global, they shed their loyalty to America. Boeing, last surviving U.S. manufacturer of commercial aircraft, threatened now by the European cartel Airbus, has apparently gone beyond making vertical fins and horizontal stabilizers for its fleet in China. On January 1, 2003, this item ran in the *New York Times:*

> The State Department has accused two leading American companies of 123 violations of export laws in connection with the transfer of rocket and satellite data to China during the 1990s. The Boeing company and Hughes Electronics Corporation, a unit of General Motors, were notified of the accusations last week.

The economic nationalists who directed America's destiny in the nineteenth century would instantly recognize China's policy for what it is and act to counter it. But America's free traders are clueless, or do not care.

The most puzzling are the neoconservatives who talk of an American empire of "pith helmets and jodhpurs." Do they not understand that trade is a means to, and a measure of, national power? Free trade is not free. There are costs, both visible and hidden, in those mammoth trade deficits we are running. What are they? What has a third of a century of free trade wrought?

- *The deindustrialization of America.* Factories and plants everywhere are closing as America becomes a service economy.
- *An end to national self-sufficiency* and growing dependence upon foreign sources for the necessities of our national life and the weapons of our national defense.
- *A loss of national sovereignty* as WTO bureaucrats force U.S. laws to be rewritten to conform to global trade rules.
- *A falling dollar* that robs Americans of their wealth.
- *Shattered lives* as company towns become ghost towns in the "creative destruction" that deracinated economists celebrate from the security of tenured chairs.

- *A crisis in Social Security and Medicare* as Americans move out of high-paying manufacturing jobs into lower-paying service jobs, and thus contribute less in payroll taxes.
- *Growing public pressure for federalized health insurance* as manufacturing jobs are replaced by service ones that carry no health insurance.
- *A deepening farm crisis* as traditional U.S. markets here and abroad are captured by countries like Brazil and Argentina, whose lower labor costs have attracted Western capital. The scores of billions of dollars in subsidies taxpayers will give farmers in future years is to make up for what the farmers lost from globalization.

Why did the Republican Party convert to an ideology that produced this? First, in the colleges and universities of the postwar, protectionism became a dirty word, as it is today. The conservative Republicans of the pre–New Deal era—Presidents Harding and Coolidge and Treasury Secretary Mellon, who raised tariffs and cut income taxes—were demonized. [President Herbert] Hoover and [the] Smoot-Hawley [tariff] were damned for the Great Depression. New Deal spending, not the war, was credited with its cure.

As important, the Fortune 500 concluded that protection of the home market was less critical to the bottom line than being able to move production out of the United States, thereby cutting the cost of taxes and regulations, and ridding their payrolls of highly compensated American workers, their own countrymen.

Finally, in the 1980s and 1990s, China abandoned Maoist isolation, India opened up, and the Soviet bloc overthrew Communism and broke free. These historic events, in a few short years, put literally hundreds of millions of workers into the world labor market, where they were willing and soon able to compete with American workers, whose wages were five, ten, and twenty times their own. For global corporations seeking lower taxes, lax regulation, and low-wage, high-productivity labor, it has become a buyer's market unlike any they have ever known.

Conservatives, said Ronald Reagan, believe in the values of "work, family, faith, community, and country." But free trade puts the demands of consumers ahead of the duties of citizens, the unbridled freedom of the individual in the marketplace ahead of all claims of family, community, and country. Free trade says what is best for me, now, at the cheapest price, is what is best for America. That is not conservatism.

Free trade does to a nation what alcohol does to a man. Saps him first of his vitality and energy, then of his independence, then of his life. America today exhibits the symptoms of a nation passing into late middle age. We spend more than we earn. We consume more than we produce. The evangelists of globalism who once promised us our trade deficits would disappear now assure us that trade deficits do not matter.

The truth: Free trade is the serial killer of American manufacturing and the Trojan Horse of world government. It is the primrose path to the loss of economic independence and national sovereignty. Free trade is a bright, shining lie.

Why Exports Are Better

According to former GM executive Gus Stelzer, 50 percent of the sticker price of a new Cadillac goes to pay taxes—Social Security, Medicare, state and federal income taxes withheld from the wages and salaries of GM workers and executives, GM's corporate tax, the property taxes on factories, offices, and dealerships, and state sales taxes.

When we buy cars made in the USA, we contribute to Social Security, Medicare, and the national defense. When we buy an American-made car, we help pay for our roads, schools, teachers, and cops. When foreigners buy goods made in the USA, they, too, underwrite the cost of government in America. But when we buy foreign goods, we pay taxes to the governments of the nations where those goods are produced. When we buy goods made in China, we subsidize the regime in Beijing.

Free trade, adds Stelzer, "is the only competitive activity in which the rules are not the same for every competitor.... No other competitive activity would tolerate such immoral and unconstitutional double-dealing."

Under WTO rules, 14th Amendment protections no longer apply. U.S. manufacturers in America must obey minimum-wage laws, health-and-safety laws, environmental laws, civil rights laws, and tax laws, from which U.S. manufacturers in China are exempt. Equal protection of the law is made a mockery of in a free-trade world.

But tariffs are taxes, comes the retort of Libertarians. Tariffs raise the prices of goods. True. But all taxes—tariffs, income taxes, sales taxes, property taxes—are factored into the final price of the goods we buy. When a nation puts a tariff on foreign goods coming into the country, it is able to cut taxes on goods produced inside the country. This is the way to give U.S. manufacturers and workers a "home-field advantage." This was Hamilton's way and we have now abandoned it. And for what?

The Myth of the "Level Playing Field"

What is President Bush's answer to the hemorrhaging of U.S. factory jobs? At a rally in Ohio, which had lost 160,000 manufacturing jobs since mid-2000, the president declared:

> We've lost thousands of manufacturing jobs because production moved overseas.... America must send a message overseas—say, look, we expect there to be a fair playing field when it comes to trade.... See, we in America believe we can compete with anybody, just so long as the rules are fair, and we intend to keep the rules fair.

But how do we maintain a level playing field when the United States imposes minimum-wage laws, environmental laws, health and safety laws, and antidiscrimination laws on manufacturers in America, from which U.S. manufacturers in China are exempt? When a U.S. factory worker earns $53,000 a year, while a Chinese worker can be hired for $2,000 a year, how does one keep the playing field level?

When President Bush speaks of keeping "the rules fair," does he mean China must start paying skilled workers $25 an hour and subject Chinese factories to the same wage-and-hour laws, OSHA [Occupational Safety and Health Administration] inspections, and environmental rules as U.S. factories? That is impossible. Cheap labor in China and the lack of protections for Chinese workers are the "comparative advantage" that enables Beijing to lure away America's industrial base. Why should China, which is winning its trade war against America, adopt the policy of the United States, which is losing that war?

President Bush and trade czar Robert Zoellick celebrated their free-trade agreement with Chile as a triumph. But Chile has a GDP of $70 billion, not even 1 percent of ours. Her per capita GDP of $4,400 is one-eighth of ours. With a free-trade deal with Chile we gain access to a tiny market whose consumers cannot afford high-quality U.S. goods, while manufacturers who move production to Chile get free access to an $11 trillion U.S. market where consumers have a per capita GDP of $37,000. Bush and Zoellick traded Seabiscuit for a rabbit.

Democrats like Richard Gephardt argue that other nations should have to adopt U.S. standards in how they treat and reward workers. But the Third World will never have the same standards we do, and Democrats only delude themselves or deceive us when they threaten to cut off trade with these nations. It will not happen. Why? Because the hidden agenda of the global economy is global socialism, the steady transfer of the wealth of the West to the less fortunate of the earth. Equality is the end of socialism. For it to be attained on a global scale, the pay of Third World workers must rise and that of First World workers must be arrested or fall. That is what globalization is doing and is intended to do to U.S. workers—and that is the economic treason that dare not speak its name.

Is our condition irreversible? Is the death of manufacturing an inevitability? The answer is no. There is nothing irretrievable about the loss of America's industrial base. It is a consequence of failed policies rooted in quasi-religious faith in a free-trade ideology that has failed every great nation that ever indulged: Holland, Spain and Great

Britain. It is the result of a bipartisan betrayal of our citizens by their political elites. But if we are to restore America's self-sufficiency, we must act soon.

Restoration of American independence requires only that we put the national interest ahead of any globalist agenda, that we have the courage to throw over a failed policy of free trade and walk out of the WTO, that we revisit the wisdom of Hamilton and the Founding Fathers, that we be willing to accept temporary sacrifice for long-term security, that we put America and Americans first again. It can be done.